EXPLORE CANADA

Explore Canada

AN ILLUSTRATED GUIDE

PUBLISHED BY THE CANADIAN AUTOMOBILE ASSOCIATION, IN CONJUNCTION WITH THE READER'S DIGEST ASSOCIATION (CANADA) LTD.

Acknowledgments The publisher acknowledges with thanks the major contributions of photographers Paul Baich, John de Visser, Pierre Gaudard, Freeman Patterson and Richard Vroom, and of John A. Elson (*The Shaping of Canada*), Kildare Dobbs (*The Heritage of Canada*) and Barbara A. Humphreys, B. Arch., M.R.A.I.C., and Meredith Sykes, M.A. (*The Buildings of Canada*).

Thanks is expressed also to the Department of Energy, Mines and Resources and the Department of Indian and Northern Affairs (especially the national parks branch, the national historic parks and sites branch and the Office of the Public Information Adviser); and to the Canadian Government Travel Bureau and the Library of Parliament;

To provincial archives and tourist bureaus, provincial information services, provincial parks and highways departments, chambers of commerce, regional tourist associations, museums and historical societies, municipal clerks and parish priests, and the following individuals, organizations and associations:

Arctic Institute of North America
   Library
B.C. Hydro
Canadian National
Canadian Pacific
Canadian Permanent Committee
   on Geographical Names
Canadian Wildlife Service
Mrs. Avis L. Choate
Communications-Québec
Selwyn Dewdney
A.L. Featherstone
Geological Survey of Canada
Heritage Canada
Hudson's Bay Company
Hydro Quebec
McCord Museum
McLennan Library (McGill
   University)
Manitoba Hydro

Mining Association of Canada
Montreal Museum of Fine Arts
Musée du Québec
National Gallery of Canada
National Harbors Board
National Museum of Man
Nova Scotia Museum
Office de la Langue Française
   (Province of Quebec)
Ontario Hydro
Public Archives of Canada
Royal Ontario Museum
St. Lawrence Seaway Authority
Service de Pastorale Liturgique
   (Montreal)
La Société Historique de la
   Gaspésie
Statistics Canada
Mrs. Roy Summers

The publisher expresses sincere appreciation also to the many private citizens who provided information for *Explore Canada*.

EDITOR: George Ronald
ART EDITOR: Louis Hamel
DESIGNER: Lucie Martineau
EDITORIAL ASSOCIATES: Paul Minvielle, Don McNaughton
EDITORIAL ASSISTANTS: Patrick Brown, Angel Castillo, John P. Hardy,
   Kathleen Keating, Carl E. Law, Douglas R. Long, Ann Pinkerton,
   Charles W. Smith, James Stewart
EDITORIAL RESEARCHERS: Julia Findlay (chief), Janet Holmes (assistant),
   Myra Clément, John R. Fitzgerald, Jeannette Gibbs, Elinor
   Griffith, Frances Lavendel, Natalie Macario, Eileen McKee,
   Catharine McKenty, Eileen Shea, Joan Voukides, Theresa Wilson
ART RESEARCHERS: Denise Hyde-Clarke (chief), Michèle Bordeleau
   (assistant), Lynne Abell, Andrea Facci
ARTISTS: Michael Middleton (*The Buildings of Canada*), Serge Roy
   (city maps), André L'Archevêque (*The Shaping of Canada*)
CARTOGRAPHER: Richard Hansen
INDEXER: Carolyn McConnell
PRODUCTION: Mark Recher

EDITOR, BOOK DIVISION: Fred Kerner

Second edition: ISBN 0-88850-070-X
(First edition: ISBN 0-88850-041-6)
Printed in Canada 78 79 80/5 4 3 2 1

Foreword

By John W. Fisher

I have spent most of my life on a fascinating voyage of discovery—up and down, back and forth across my country. The spread of Canada has at times overpowered me. Its diversity has ensnared me. The pulse of Canada I have felt in the speechless beauty of its face and in the promise of the people who inhabit it.

Too many Canadians wander to other countries without ever experiencing their own. They are losers. But Canada loses too, because the unity we seek can be woven only from the knowing, feeling and caring of all Canadians. How can we express our Canadianism without understanding compatriots in other regions and being aware of their contributions to our rich mosaic of cultures and lifestyles? When will we terminate the tedious debate about Canada's identity?

I am delighted that *Explore Canada* has been published because it should stir Canadians' curiosity to be contemporary voyageurs. I am amazed at how much of Canada's exciting geography and of Canadian social customs, history and man-made treasures have been collected in this one volume. The hundreds of excellent photographs, the dozens of maps and the historical detail will appeal to armchair voyageurs as well as to Canadians planning their own explorations in other parts of their country.

Canada needs *Explore Canada*: a unique, readable volume that reflects the uniqueness of this land. In helping us know Canada better, it makes Canada stronger.

John W. Fisher

(Centennial Commissioner, 1967)

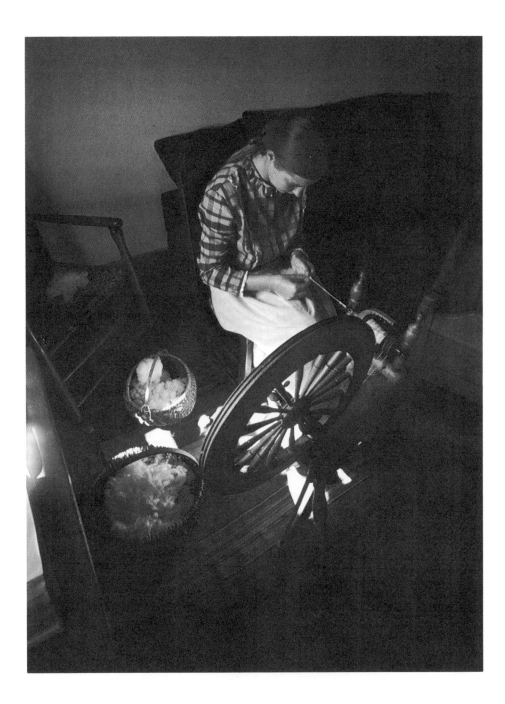

Contents

The Shaping of Canada
How Nature contoured a land of staggering variety and beauty

Few countries match Canada's variety of natural beauty. The landscape ranges from near-desert and rich rain forest to rolling prairie and tundra, from mountains and glaciers to meteorite craters and craggy seacoast. Dotting the face of the land are lakes that hold one-half of the world's fresh water.

The shaping of Canada was started some 2½ billion years ago. Signs of this endless sculpting of the land are everywhere—in the stubs of ancient peaks in the Atlantic provinces, in the young Rocky Mountains (a mere 50 million years old), in the eroded hills of the Red Deer Badlands, on western plains etched by an ice sheet that disappeared 10,000 years ago.

Scientists believe there once was only one continent, a huge mass surrounded by a single ocean. They call it Pangaea. Early in the earth's history Pangaea split into two land masses—Gondwana to the south, Laurasia to the north. These also split—many times—and the continents began to assume their present shapes. Scientists conclude from continental outlines and from rock samples that the Americas, Africa and Europe were one until the first rift developed about 440 million years ago. Then the sea flooded into a gap that was the forerunner of the Atlantic Ocean. The gap closed, reopened, closed again. About 250 million years ago it opened once more and the Americas were launched westward. Since then, at about an inch a year, North America has moved some 3,000 miles from Europe and Africa. It was during this movement of the continents that Canada was shaped.

The earth's surface is a crust, chemically and physically different from the solid material underneath. The crust and the solid material together form an outer shell of rock that is up to 95 miles thick in the continents, 45 miles thick under the oceans. Just under the shell is a hot, viscous substance that constantly reshapes itself.

The outer shell is actually a mosaic of a dozen "plates." They float on the viscous material and move as much as five inches a year. Where two plates pull apart, as is happening under the Atlantic Ocean, lava moves up through the rift to form undersea mountains. As the plates continue to separate, more lava moves up, more mountains are formed.

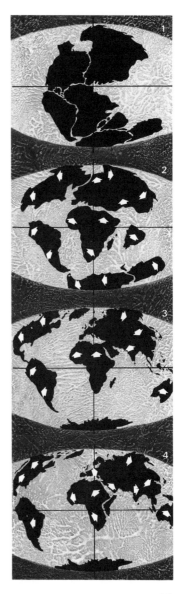

Pangaea (1) splits, continents start to form; 65 million years ago (2) India is an island, Australia is not. Continents drift today (3), will still be drifting 50 million years hence (4).

The world from 250,000 miles in space, as photographed by Apollo 10 astronauts.

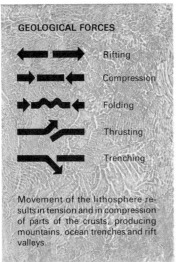

GEOLOGICAL FORCES

Rifting

Compression

Folding

Thrusting

Trenching

Movement of the lithosphere results in tension and in compression of parts of the crusts, producing mountains, ocean trenches and rift valleys.

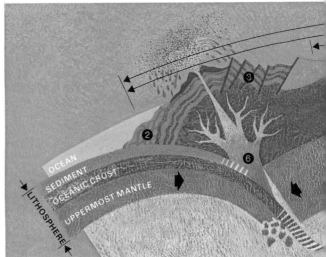

OCEAN
SEDIMENT
OCEANIC CRUST
UPPERMOST MANTLE
LITHOSPHERE

An ocean plate is extended by fresh lava on its trailing edge. It is often simultaneously destroyed where its leading edge collides with a continental plate. This is happening to the Pacific plate: the North American plate overrides it like a bulldozer.

About 50 million years ago western Canada had much the same pattern as now. Its broad mountainous plateau (perhaps less rugged than the present mountains) shed silt and clay east onto the plains and west into the ocean deeps, just as it does now.

For millions of years the North American plate moved westward. The Pacific plate, pushing northwest (as it still does), was overtaken by the overriding continental plate, which grew as new mountains were added to its leading edge. Western mountains were steadily worn down and rivers spread eroded material in an apron 1,000 miles wide. As weather-

The surface of the earth is made up of moving plates. Their edges are marked by ocean ridges, trenches and mountain chains, usually capped by volcanoes.

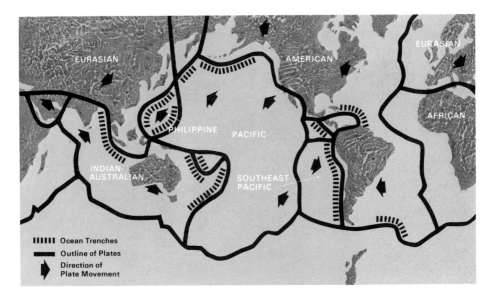

EURASIAN
AMERICAN
EURASIAN
PHILIPPINE
PACIFIC
AFRICAN
INDIAN-AUSTRALIAN
SOUTHEAST PACIFIC

||||| Ocean Trenches
▬▬ Outline of Plates
➤ Direction of Plate Movement

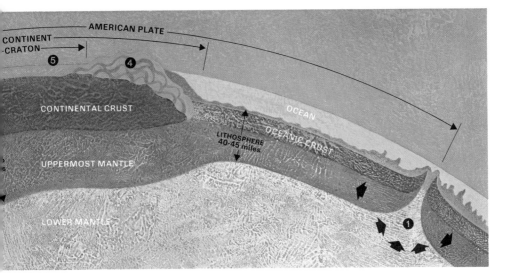

ing and erosion continued in other parts of the continent, the eastern continental shelf continued to expand. Winters were mild, summers moderate, extremes rare. The plains were covered with grass; mountain belts were thick with temperate forests but mountain-building activity was low. Now mammals began to evolve, especially grazing animals. Central North America is thought to have resembled the African veldt of today.

About 15 million years ago the western mountains began to rise higher, interfering more and more with the circulation of the atmosphere. Cool climates began to prevail at higher altitudes. The mountains, and possibly large quantities of dust from volcanic eruptions that blocked some of the sun's heat, started to change a universally mild climate to one of differing regional climates—some cool, some warm, some humid, some dry. But for millions of years it was cooling that dominated. Finally the stage was set for the Ice Age. A third of the world was plunged into a deep freeze that lasted a million years.

The eastern continental ice sheet was probably born in northern Quebec when snow lasted through a cool, short summer. More snow accumulated in succeeding years. It thickened and the bottom layers were compressed into ice. As the pressure increased, ice started to flow outward in all directions; soon all of Canada except for the northwest Yukon was covered. Some ice was more than a mile thick and its weight caused the earth's crust to sink.

The massive sheets formed and disappeared at least four times during the Ice Age. (There were many lesser advances and retreats along the margins each time.) Each sheet destroyed most of the evidence of its predecessor, so only the last one is well represented in Canada. The ice created no new major features but modified the existing landscape. It scraped away soil and the debris of weathered rock. The bedrock itself was abraded and a mixture of

1 Mid-ocean rift Hot material from the lower mantle rises through the crust and forms undersea volcanic mountains. As the mountains move away from the rift they subside and may be buried by sediment.

2 Trough The interaction of a continental plate overriding an ocean plate forms a trough. Sediment collects and is converted into rock, then compressed into folded mountains (which eventually rise from the ocean). The folding is like that of a cloth laid flat on water: as the edges are pressed toward the center, it buckles; part of it rises but most sinks.

3 Zone of compression This is where older rocks are thrust over younger rocks, as on the east side of the Rocky Mountains.

4 Old mountains Folded mountains are like floating ice: only a small portion shows and the mass floats higher as erosion (or melting) lightens the top. With this lightening, the roots withdraw from the hot zone. As new mountains are added to the leading edge of a continental plate, old mountains are worn down.

5 The Shield The broad roots of old, worn-down mountains become a platform (craton) in the central part of the continent. Some ancient mountains have floated so high that the rocks of their roots are exposed. The Precambrian shield is an example.

6 Melting zone Sedimentary rock from the trough and the ocean floor melts as it moves down into the hot zone. The melted rock then rises, some erupting as volcanoes.

clay, silt, sand and stones (called till) was deposited. Another result of the Ice Age was the depression of the earth's crust by the enormous load of ice. When a glacier melted, the crust rose an amount equal to one-third of the glacier's original thickness. The shorelines of glacial lakes that extended from an ice sheet are not horizontal; in central Canada they rise (at 1-3 feet a mile) toward Hudson Bay, where the crust rebounded faster than elsewhere. The land still rises slightly every century.

The snow that started and nurtured the ice sheets originated as evaporation from the oceans. As the ice formed, the sea level was lowered 350-400 feet and much of the continental shelf off the Maritimes was exposed. (Plants, freshwater peat and the teeth and bones of mammoths are occasionally dredged up by fishermen there.) When the sea level rose again with the melting of the glaciers, many river valleys were flooded. This created drowned estuaries such as the Richibucto River Valley in New Brunswick and Cascumpeque Bay and Tracadie Bay in Prince Edward Island. The sea reached its present level about 5,000 years ago and is still rising slowly.

In other parts of Canada there has been a contest between the rebound of the earth's crust and the rise of the sea level. The St. Lawrence lowland from Quebec to Arnprior and Brockville, Ont., was invaded about 12,000 years ago by an arm of the ocean called the Champlain Sea. Silt and clay from the Laurentian ice sheet blanketed the bottom of this sea (now important agricultural land). About 10,000 years ago the land rose out of the sea and a freshwater lake

Roches moutonnées (rocks that have been smoothed by ice) and huge glacial valleys are remnants of the Ice Age. The rocks above are in Black Bay on Lake Athabasca in Saskatchewan. Coronation Glacier (right) drains the Penny Ice Cap on Baffin Island in the Northwest Territories. Moraines (earth and stone carried by the glacier) are well developed here—both marginal moraines (those at the edges) and medial moraines (in the center).

Shale beds at Port au Port on Newfoundland's west coast are thought to have been contorted by folding of the earth's crust some 450,000,000 years ago.

existed briefly. For a time the rapidly rising sea encroached on the slowly rising land and the St. Lawrence River became a brackish estuary. As the land continued to rise—and the rise of the sea level slowed—the St. Lawrence again became fresh.

The story of the land is being written even today, as North America glides imperceptibly westward. The story continues on the surface of the land, as wind and waves and rain and rivers destroy and reshape seemingly impregnable mountains and rocky coasts. Icefields and glaciers reminiscent of the Ice Age still scour mountain valleys, feed streams with their meltwaters and deposit till in their tracks.

The land, with its mineral riches and fertile soils, has shaped Canada's past and has given the country an enviable present and a promising future.

The Heritage of Canada
How wave on wave of immigration
created the Canadian mosaic

An Indian fort perhaps not unlike the *kanata* that Jacques Cartier visited in 1535: an illustration from a map of French North America published in 1720.

When Jacques Cartier labeled the vast unknown land on his charts, he called it Canada. Cartier, from the Breton port of Saint-Malo, had sailed into the Gulf of St. Lawrence in 1534 in search of a passage to the Orient. The following year he went up the St. Lawrence to the site of the present city of Quebec. When an Indian spoke to him of *kanata* (meaning a village or a group of huts), the man from Saint-Malo concluded that was the name of the country.

Jacques Cartier was a latecomer. Men had imprinted the landscape of Canada for upward of 15,000 years. The first of them, we believe, came across the Bering Strait from Siberia, hunters who became the inadvertent colonizers of the New World. Their kill sites, marked by animal bones and projectile points, are remarkable for the wide area over which they have been discovered. Man was on the high plains of the American west by 12,000 years ago and had even reached the tip of South America by 9,000 years ago. The spread eastward was slower. It eventually gave rise to the Archaic culture of the eastern woodlands. Farther north a new wave of immigrants, not related to the American Indians, gave rise to the Paleo-Eskimo populations of the Canadian Arctic.

The northern cultures were highly sophisticated systems of supplying support for man in a hostile environment. But few substantial landscape features were built; very few survive. The traveler in northern Canada sees relatively little evidence of early human occupation: chiefly the remains of semi-subterranean winter dwellings and circles of stones called "tent rings." To the south in the sub-Arctic area a thinly spread population of Indian hunters and gatherers exploited the resources of the boreal forest. They too had a minimal effect on their area and left little record of their existence.

Farther south were concentrations of Indian peoples, notably in Huronia, between Lake Simcoe and Georgian Bay in what now is Ontario. Here lived perhaps 30,000 persons. The density of habitation reflected the fact that they were farmers, sedentary and therefore making a more concentrated and permanent impact on their surroundings. The cedar longhouse of Huronia and the St. Lawrence Valley was surrounded by a palisade, also of wood. One such village, apparently, was Cartier's *kanata*.

Cartier and the fishermen of France, Portugal and England were not the first Europeans to visit Canadian shores. About 1000 A.D. Norsemen found their way to regions they called Helluland, Markland and Vinland. Scholarship has identified Helluland as Baffin Island and Markland as Labrador; traces of their short-lived Vinland colony have been found at L'Anse aux Meadows in Newfoundland.

Cod first drew Europeans to the Grand Banks. Sometimes they camped ashore to dry or smoke their catch. But it was the abundance of beaver that led them to stay, together with the persistent dream of finding a northwest passage to the silks and spices of Cathay and the East Indies. The quest for furs drew white men ever deeper into the interior—once they had mastered Indian techniques of travel and survival: the birch-bark canoe, snowshoe and dogsled, skin clothing and native remedies for scurvy.

Although the first successful French settlement was in 1605 on the shore of the Annapolis Basin in Nova Scotia—then called Acadia—settlements along the St. Lawrence became the nucleus of New France. Most of the French chose the simple life of the farmer. Others sought fortune in the fur trade as coureurs de bois, traveling with Indians into the fastness of the Precambrian shield country. Two of these adventurers, Pierre-Esprit Radisson and Médard Chouart des Groseilliers, frustrated by taxes and other obstacles put in their way by the officials of New France, defected to the English, promoting a scheme to outflank the St. Lawrence by trading with London direct from Hudson Bay. London set up the Hudson's Bay Company, an enterprise that combined

Pierre-Esprit Radisson, fur trader and explorer, is one of the most colorful figures in Canadian history. He and his brother-in-law Médard Chouart des Groseilliers, irked by their treatment at the hands of French officials, joined the English in the struggle for control of the fur trade. They organized the expedition to Hudson Bay that led in 1670 to the establishment of the Hudson's Bay Company.

The Hudson's Bay Company coat of arms, apparently dating from the chartering of the company in 1670, has a Latin motto roughly translated as "We risk our skins to get furs." Less colorful translations include "Skin for skin" and "Skin for the sake of the fleece." The coat of arms contains the Cross of St. George, four beavers, a fox sitting on an ermine hat, and two moose as supporters.

Lord Durham's *Report on the Affairs of British North America* (1839) led to the union of Upper and Lower Canada in 1841 and to the introduction of responsible government and of municipal government. This photograph is from an oil painting by Sir Thomas Lawrence.

the advantages of British seapower, French enterprise and Indian know-how.

As part of the worldwide conflict between British and French, traders from New France and the HBC (mostly Scots and Orkneymen) were rivals in the thrust to the west. After 1763, when British seapower compelled the French to give up their North American empire, new competition developed between the HBC and the Scots who had taken over the French trade routes. Patterns of compromise and cooperation born of these rivalries have shaped Canada ever since.

Scots, French Canadians, Indians, English and Métis learned to work together in the school of the fur trade.

Canadians have won freedom and independence by constitutional means: the nation has had no birth in blood. Canadians have fought wars only in defense of Canadian territory (as when they repelled American invaders in the War of 1812) or in the service of Empire, Commonwealth or allies, as in the South African War, two world wars and the Korean War.

But if violence is rare here, conflict is not.

Canada's 23,000,000 people are divided by region, by ethnic origin, by language, by culture, by generation: every Canadian sometimes seems a separatist of some kind. Certainly every Canadian is a member of some ethnic minority, since no group enjoys absolute superiority of numbers. About 45 percent of the population is of British origin, about 29 percent is French. Some 20 percent claims other European origin and about five percent has roots in Africa, Asia and other parts of the world. There are some 280,000 native Canadian Indians and about 18,000 Eskimos.

Visiting Canada in 1838, Lord Durham found "two nations warring in the bosom of a single state." He would find a lot more today. The official languages are only two (English and French) but ethnic identities are legion.

Consider what happened a few years ago—more than 100 years after Confederation—on July 1, the official national holiday. . . .

Was it Dominion Day, as some English-language newspapers said? Was it Canada's National Day, as the Vancouver *Chinatown News* preferred to call it? Was it Confederation Day? Canada Day? Everyone had his opinion. On that day (whatever it was) the Prime Minister and his cabinet colleagues helped celebrate Manitoba's centennial with the first federal cabinet meeting ever held outside Ottawa. In Montreal the Canada Committee called on the federal government to prove Confederation worthwhile for all Canadians. But the French-speaking majority in Quebec had already celebrated their own national day on June 24, the feast of Saint Jean-Baptiste. Newfoundlanders that July 1 were commemorating a battle in World War I. And good Canadians of

Scottish origin were mumbling into their Scotch: "Here's tae us!" . . .

And so it went. Few other nations celebrate their existence with such apparent lack of enthusiasm. July 1 seems to be a great Ukrainian day for Ukrainians, a great Italian holiday for Italians, a great Irish day for the Irish. . . .

Canada is a pluralistic society which strives to keep ethnic and national identity, like religious affiliation, out of politics. Multiculturalism means cultural freedom. The nation is committed to the ideal of a cultural mosaic, a free association of free and equal citizens freely choosing their values and ways of living together.

"The co-existence of several nations under the same state is a test as well as the best security of its freedom," Lord Acton wrote in 1862. The great British thinker continued: "We must conclude that those states are substantially the most perfect which . . . include various distinct nationalities without oppressing them." Canadian historian J.M.S. Careless wrote more recently: "We are a highly pluralistic society in a bi-national union. That is our problem, our weakness, our distinction and reason to exist."

Canada has been a refuge for the poor and the oppressed. Dispossessed Scottish Highlanders came here after the disastrous Rebellion of 1745. United Empire Loyalists fled to Canada from political persecution in the newly-formed United States. Starving Irish peasants who survived the potato famine

This silk banner of Loyalists who settled in Nova Scotia after the American Revolution is in the Public Archives of Canada, in Ottawa. The 30-by-24-inch banner proclaims Loyalists' hopes for a new life in Canada (*Resurgam*: I shall rise up again).

19

A Doukhobor immigrant's house at Veregin, Sask.

of the 1840s and the cholera hell of the transport ships found new lives in Canada. Runaway slaves from the American south made their way to southwestern Ontario by the Underground Railroad. The great Count Tolstoy assisted the migration of Doukhobors oppressed by Tsarist Russia. Tens of thousands of "displaced persons" came to Canada from Europe after the convulsions of World War II. Victims of pogroms and purges . . . Jews, Hungarians, Poles, East African Asians . . . even, once more, American dissenters . . . have started life anew in the shelter of the Canadian peace. Everywhere in Canada distinct groups live by their own traditions: Germans in Lunenburg and Kitchener, Mennonites, Hutterites and Ukrainians on the prairies, Sikhs and Doukhobors in British Columbia.

But Canada does have a dominant culture, a way of life to which all minorities are slowly adapting. It is like the accents of English-language radio and television announcers: general North American. Only the peoples of Quebec and Newfoundland are nations in the Old World sense. Other Canadians tend to become general North Americans, all but indistinguishable from U.S. citizens in most aspects of material culture, in the way they speak, dress, eat and live—above all in how they buy and sell.

Though most of the time Canadians get along by agreeing to differ, they form a genuine national community. They think and act as such at moments of stress or crisis, when the national peace is threatened, or the vast territory they possess in common, the second largest in the world. Developing this territory has been a heroic achievement, awe-inspiring in scale and enterprise. Yet Canadians have no common view of their past, few shared myths, and no heroes who are not also villains to some of them. Regional identities, always more important than national ones, seem strongest in areas that have been settled for a long time. Men and women of European origin have lived for centuries in the Atlantic provinces and Quebec. Each group has developed a clear sense of identity, a distinct style in life and manners, and accents that are their own. Even so, none is uniform in character. There's more than one Newfoundland dialect, just as there are more ways than one to make a long splice. There are some Newfoundlanders whose first language is French.

□ Nova Scotia is as plural as Canada itself. Nova Scotians speak not only English and French but Gaelic too. Blacks and Micks and Macs and Micmacs are still learning to live together. New Brunswick is bilingual. Even Prince Edward Island has its clans and cliques—Scottish, Irish, Acadian, Dutch. Still, Maritimers do have many attitudes and traits in common. The past is near to them, and they have not forgotten who "invented" responsible government—a Nova Scotia newspaperman and politician, Joseph Howe.

□ The French Canadians of Quebec are an overwhelming majority in their own province but have not forgotten that they are a minority in North America. They have the tough character and the tragic sense of survivors. But they face a crisis of identity, at once Canadian and French-Canadian. They are citizens of Quebec first and foremost. For them the Canadian reality is conflict, a dialectic between themselves and English-speaking Canada.

□ Ontario people have no trouble identifying with Canada. But they sometimes worry: they can't believe that there's much distinctive about them or, by extension, about Canadians generally. In their view Canadians are just people. For Ontario is as much a mosaic as any other province, as much an achievement of give-and-take. Most immigrants to Canada come here. More than a third of the exploding population of Toronto is immigrants. Many pass on to their children the languages and traditions of old lands.

□ Prairie people think of themselves as Westerners. Something of the harshness of their winters, of the loneliness of their vast landscapes, has entered their character. The cowboy cult of manliness—borrowed from American plainsmen, and by them taken from Spanish caballeros—is found here in a Canadian mutation, losing violence and arrogance in the change. Appetites are hearty, voices cheerfully loud, handshakes crushing—under an immensity of prairie skies that makes it easy to feel the littleness of man. Westerners are not one people but many: Indians, Métis, French Canadians, Ontarians, Irish, British, Hutterites, Ukrainians, Americans, Russian Jews, Dutchmen, Chinese.

□ British Columbians too are Westerners—but with a difference. On the Pacific coast, a region of temperate rain forests, everything grows in lux-

SRAÍD NAH-EAGLAISE
CHURCH STREET

Canadian bilingualism: street signs are in Gaelic and English in the Nova Scotia town of Pugwash.

Journalist, orator and politician, Joseph Howe was a Nova Scotian whose trial for criminal libel in 1835 established the freedom of the press. A decade later he won a long struggle for responsible government in Nova Scotia.

uriance, including varieties of human character. Pleasure-loving, enterprising, extremist, British Columbians are more everything than anyone else: more British, more American; more conformist, more eccentric; more capitalist, more socialist; more uptight, more loose-and-easy; hairier, more crewcut; richer, poorer. Everyone is passionately committed to the region and its natural beauty.

□ And there is the true north of the Yukon and the Northwest Territories. What unites Canadians of the north is the sense of being part of a frontier community. Few in number and scattered over unimaginable distances, they feel close to the essential Canada. The rest of the world is Outside. There's a powerful mystique of the north, a compound of tall tales, rough jokes and hard living. This "true North strong and free" has caught the imagination of all Canadians but native-born citizens have never fought one another for seats on Arctic-bound planes—one reason so many Northerners are people who began their lives in other countries.

Traditional identities are changing as more and more Canadians crowd into cities. They are becoming nomads, drawn in ever larger numbers into new urban constellations. Each big city has become a kind of nation with its own special interests, its own

values and priorities, its own galaxy of celebrities.

But, for all their differences, Canada's people have always tended to approach life with a unique style. Its most striking aspect—and perhaps its most engaging—is modesty. It has been well said that Canadians are willing to concede the immense importance of the rest of the world. This attitude results in realism and tolerance; it grows out of past provincialism. There was a time when Canadians were too modest, when they felt, dimly, that history had neglected them, that great passions, great actions and great destinies were not for them. Rumors of far-off splendors reached them from outside, like music heard at a distance. Canadians sensed that the action was somewhere else. But the feeling of missing out on life has gone now. Few Canadians think they have to emigrate in order to live. With something like surprise they have come to see that here in Canada, as in the faraway places Canadians used to envy, there is beauty and dignity for all men to share.

Tolerance, readiness to compromise, a stunning lack of excitement about heroes and ideologies and flag-waving . . . all these are part of the Canadian style. Canada continues to be a haven for fugitives from injustice. It opens its frontiers to all men. These are the frontiers of a state based on the absolute value of every human person.

The dance, at Montreal's Man and His World, long-running successor to Expo 67, is Slavic . . . the faces, from lower left, are Japanese, Polish, Irish (with wool under the shamrocks for warmth on a cold St. Patrick's Day), Punjabi, Chinese, Eskimo . . . all part of the face of Canada.

The Places of Canada
A gazetteer of 1,200 cities, towns, villages and national parks

This 384-page gazetteer contains a remarkable collection of information about Canada. Here are scenic wonders and works of art, venerable houses, old forts and the excitement of great modern buildings. Here are cliff paintings by Indian artists lost in the mists of prehistory. Here are the relics of wars and the rubble of dreams, the monuments Canadians have raised to their heroes, the reconstructions with which they seek to recapture the Canada of Champlain and the Conquest and the Cariboo.

In *The Places of Canada*—almost 1,200 cities, towns, villages and national parks—is a fascinating variety ranging from the Columbia Icefield to the National Gallery, from the Cypress Hills and the Plains of Abraham to Signal Hill and Hell's Gate, from Toronto's huge Royal Ontario Museum to the Loyalist collection in Old St. Edward's on the Hill in Clementsport, N.S. Scattered through the gazetteer are some 50 features on subjects as varied as Sir Sam Steele, the Acadians, Crowfoot, Stefansson and the Calgary Stampede . . . and such distinctively Canadian things as wild rice, totem poles and the world's only wooden lacrosse stick factory.

Complementing the gazetteer text are more than 600 color photographs, most by photographers commissioned for this book: Paul Baich, John de Visser, Pierre Gaudard, Freeman Patterson and Richard Vroom.

Opposite the name of virtually every entry are coordinates locating that place on one or more of the 23 maps in the atlas (*The Faces of Canada*, p.433). The few entries with no coordinates are places beyond the area covered by the maps. Accompanying the entries on 27 major cities are maps locating the main attractions of those communities.

The names used in all gazetteer entries are as determined by government departments and shown in provincial gazetteers. Thus, for instance: Saint-François-du-Lac, Que., but St. François Xavier, Man.; Sault Ste. Marie, Ont., but Sainte-Marie-Beauce, Que. But on the maps, for space reasons, the abbreviations St and Ste are used in all such cases.

A

Abbotsford B.C.   2CZ/12FX

Rebuilt relics of war and the sky-high offices of space-age executives are among the aircraft at the annual Abbotsford International Air Show, a three-day event in August. It is North America's biggest public air show and aviation trade fair. Featured are a Canadian Armed Forces show, military aircraft from other countries, aerobatics, mock aerial dogfights, gliders, crop sprayers and water bombers.

□ Northwest of Abbotsford is Bradner, center of the flower bulb industry on the B.C. mainland. An April flower show has 200 acres of blooms.

□ A Sikh temple, built in 1920 for Sikhs who came from India to work for a logging company, is near here.

□ The Fraser Valley trout hatchery is one of three run by the B.C. Fish and Wildlife Branch.

Aberfoyle Ont.   7BY/17BY

A flea market is open the second and fourth Sundays of each month from May to September, outside a mill built about 1859. The mill houses a collection of Canadiana.

Adolphustown Ont.   7DY/18BZ

United Empire Loyalists who flocked to Ontario after the American Revolution named their new settlements for George III and his children—Kingston, Ernestown, Fredericksburgh, Adolphustown, Marysburgh, Ameliasburgh and Sophiasburgh. The towns were often referred to by their order of settlement: Adolphustown was "Fourth Town."

A plaque that records the landing of one

Abernethy Sask.—The William Richard Motherwell homestead near here is one of the few remaining cut-stone buildings on the prairies. Born in Perth, Ont., Motherwell went west in 1882 (by train to the end of rail, then by Red River cart). He helped launch what became the Saskatchewan Grain Growers and served as agriculture minister in Mackenzie King's government from 1921 to 1930. His 10-room house, built in 1897, has been restored to show how it looked in the 1920s. (4EY)

---

small group of Loyalists on the shores of Adolphus Reach in 1784 bears these words from Exodus 3:5—"Put off thy shoes from off thy feet for the place whereon thou standest is holy ground." In a nearby cemetery many Loyalists lie in graves now unmarked. A stone wall, with many of the original headstones embedded in it, and an obelisk were erected in memory of the settlers.

The first church in Adolphustown, built by Quakers, became an Anglican church. In 1884, on the 100th anniversary of the settlement, an enterprising minister sold memorial porcelain plaques to pay for a new church, St. Alban the Martyr. They hang on the church walls.

Descendants of Loyalists say only those on a list compiled by Lord Dorchester, governor-general of British North America, were privileged to use "U.E." after their names, as recognition of their commitment to the "unity of the Empire." Lord Simcoe, lieutenant governor of Upper Canada, added names to complete the "old U.E. list"; settlers arriving after that were "late Loyalists."

The United Empire Loyalist Museum in an 1877 house here contains maps tracing the development of the U.E.L. settlements; *The Compass*, a small navigation book; and pioneer documents, tools, utensils and furnishings.

At St. Paul's Anglican Church in nearby Sandhurst a plaque commemorates Lt. Col. James Rogers, who commanded the 2nd Battalion King's Rangers during the revolution. He forfeited 50,000 acres in New York because of his loyalty to the king.

Agassiz B.C.   2CZ/12FX

The Seabird Island band of Salish Indians, the group chiefly responsible for making Salishan weaving famous, lives near here. One of the best-known Salishan works hangs in the lobby of the Hotel Bonaventure in Montreal.

□ Five miles south, overlooking the Fraser River, a marker tells that the old rock floor of the valley is about a mile beneath the riverbed. The valley's rich soil was deposited over 50,000,000 years.

Agawa Ont.

On a cliff face at Agawa Bay, more than two centuries ago, an Ojibway chief painted a man on horseback, a horned panther and a crested serpent. But until recently there were few visitors to ponder the meaning of the mystical figures.

They were first recorded by Henry Schoolcraft, an Indian agent at Sault Ste. Marie, Mich. He was told how a great chief led a war party across Lake Superior and celebrated his victory with a rock painting. Schoolcraft was given a birch-bark reproduction. The centerpiece, he wrote, "was the Misshibezhieu, or fabulous panther. The drawing shows a human head crowned with horns, the usual symbol of power, with the body and claws of a panther, and a mane." Schoolcraft also described a "kind of fabulous serpent resembling a saurian [a prehistoric sea serpent], having two feet and armed with horns. . . . It is Misshikinabik, or Great Serpent." Despite his careful description of the paintings, Schoolcraft neglected to say where they were.

An avid reader of his work was Henry Wadsworth Longfellow, who used it as background for his epic poem *Hiawatha*. In a section on "picture-writing," Longfellow told of

> *The Great Serpent, the Kenabeek,*
> *With his bloody crest erected,*
> *Creeping, looking into heaven.*

The name was altered, but Misshikinabik is easily recognized.

Recorded by Schoolcraft in 1851, immortalized by Longfellow in 1855, the rock paintings went undiscovered for another century. In 1958 a Canadian museum art researcher, Selwyn Dewdney, determined to find them. After 14 months of tracking down clues, he paddled into Agawa Bay, in Lake Superior, clambered over the rocky shore—and suddenly his search was ended. In front of him was Misshibezhieu, the fabulous panther, exactly as Schoolcraft described it, although he had never seen it.

□ Agawa Canyon, 17 miles south of Agawa, is best reached in the comfort of the Algoma Central Railway's daily excursion train from Sault Ste. Marie (May to mid-October). En route it crosses the Montreal River on a 130-foot-high trestle and snakes around cliffs 1,500 feet above sea level. After a four-hour trip, the excursion cars are uncoupled. Passengers have two hours to explore the canyon, to fish, picnic and enjoy the patterns of Bridal Veil Falls. The southbound train from Hearst takes them back to the Soo.

Ainsworth B.C. 2EZ

Discovered in the 1880s by Henry Cody, a prospector searching the Kootenays for gold, the Cody Cave near Ainsworth received little publicity until 1966, when it was designated a provincial park. The first room of the system is about 140 by 400 feet and 30 feet high—and 20 feet below the surface. In the next room are "soda straws"—thin

Agawa rock paintings have withstood two centuries of wind, rain and snow. Top: a galloping horse and rider. Below: Misshibezhieu the fabulous panther and Misshikinabik the serpent.

limestone rods—and a thin layer of water that gives the floor an ice-covered look. There is an echo room, a stalagmite room, and—most impressive—the throne room. Here are stalactites hanging from the ceiling, stalagmites growing from the floor, more soda straws, layered formations called bacon strips and, where stalactite has met stalagmite, two-foot-thick columns. The walls and ceiling are of calcite ripple formation and the thin layer of water on the floor reflects the colors and shapes above. The more adventuresome explore a room where an underground creek drops 35 feet over upper and lower Cody Falls.

Aiyansh B.C.

Great jagged rocks strewn across 15 square miles of the Tseax River valley near here are a litter of lava from a volcano that erupted twice apparently about three centuries ago.

Kwakiutl Big House at Alert Bay is a community center for ceremonial dances and lectures on Kwakiutl culture. Craftsmen make totems and masks. Alert Bay has the world's tallest totem pole, a 173-footer that tells Kwakiutl history.

One Indian legend says that dancing children made headdresses of dried *oolichans*, smelt-like fish sacred to the Indians. Because the elders did not stop the children from misusing the *oolichans*, "the fire came out of the mountain and drove the people away from their homes."

The first eruption of the now-dormant volcano formed a crater 1,200 feet across; the second, inside the first, shaped a cone 300 feet high and 250 feet wide, with a crater 75 feet deep. Lava spilled into a valley three miles to the west, blocked the Tseax River and formed Lava Lake.

The Mad Trapper

Carved in a tree stump on the main street of Aklavik are the initials A.J., marking the grave of Albert Johnson, central figure in probably Canada's most famous manhunt. He became known as the Mad Trapper of Rat River but to a Mountie he was "an extremely shrewd and resolute man." Mounties first tried to question this mysterious drifter "with cold blue eyes" about interference with an Indian's traps in the winter of 1931-32. They had to retreat with a wounded officer. Then, from a pit in his log cabin, Johnson beat off a 15-hour siege by nine men, and escaped when they withdrew. For weeks he outwitted a posse in bitter weather, traveling on snowshoes, creating zigzag tracks so devious that two trackers once met head-on, killing one Mountie, finally achieving a feat Indians called impossible: he clawed over the imposing Richardson Mountains—in a blizzard. The Mounties followed with dog-teams and a spotting plane flown by the celebrated W.R. "Wop" May. Finally eight men outflanked and killed Johnson in a fire-fight. His body bore nine wounds and on his face, said war veteran May, was "the most awful grimace of hate I'd ever seen."

Aklavik N.W.T.   3GV

This community started as a Hudson's Bay Company post on the west channel of the Mackenzie River in 1912 and became the administrative center for the western Arctic. But silt and permafrost prevented the building of roads and a permanent airstrip, and the lack of sewers created a health hazard. The federal government chose a townsite (Inuvik) on the east channel and in 1961 many persons moved to Inuvik (*see entry*). Some 700 stayed here.

Alberni B.C. *see* Port Alberni

Alberton P.E.I.   9DX/23BV

Rooms furnished in the styles of middle-class Islanders of the 18th and 19th centuries are featured at the Alberton Museum.

Alert N.W.T.

The world's most northerly settlement, a weather and signals station only 427 miles from the Pole, was established in 1950 by the Canadian government. It is east of Halifax and closer to Moscow than to Toronto or Montreal. From a 1,250-foot hill near the station, Alert's handful of servicemen can see the mountains of Greenland, the icy wastes of the polar cap and mountains on Ellesmere Island.

Alert Bay B.C.   2BX

The Indians of Cormorant Island off Vancouver Island's northeast coast have kept their crafts and culture alive and their buildings reflect the best in coast Indian architecture.

The cemetery contains some of the finest totems on the west coast, including a memorial pole for Kwakiutl chief Mungo Martin, who kept the art of totem carving alive among his people. He restored totems on the University of British Columbia campus at Vancouver and in Thunderbird Park in Victoria. Martin taught the art to his son-in-law and grandson, Henry and Tony Hunt, and it was they who created Mungo's totem.

Alexandra Bridge B.C.   2DZ/12GW
Three bridges have spanned the Fraser River here, at a site chosen by a Royal Engineers sergeant in 1861. The first was built in 1863 by John W. Trutch, a contractor who became lieutenant governor of British Columbia. He used wooden towers and wire woven at the site—so well woven that not one thread snapped. It was named for Alexandra, Princess of Wales and later Edward VII's queen. The second bridge, of similar design and in the same place, still exists—upstream from a $14,000,000 Trans-Canada Highway bridge erected in 1962. On this latest bridge a cairn commemorates the work of the Royal Engineers.

Alexandria B.C.   1AZ/2DX
A forlorn little building at the side of the road here was a stopping place known as the McInnis house during the Cariboo gold rush.

Alliston Ont.   7CY/17BW
A high school here is named for Sir Frederick Banting, an Alliston native who, with Dr. Charles H. Best, discovered insulin in 1922 at the University of Toronto. A cairn outside the school commemorates Banting's role in finding this means of controlling diabetes. "He lives on," says the inscription on the cairn, "in the hearts of diabetics and in the minds of scientists the world over."

Banting attended school in Alliston—a class photograph is displayed in the South Simcoe Pioneer Museum—and served overseas as a medical corps captain in World War I.

Lac Saint-Jean racers start at Chambord and go 70 miles the first day to Roberval where there is a 20-mile closed circuit race. The second day they head for Dolbeau, 50 miles away, and a 35-mile closed circuit. From Dolbeau on the final day the racers cover 50 miles before a last 40-mile circuit in Alma.

He practised in London, Ont., before starting diabetes research at Toronto. Later, with Dr. W.R. Frank, he built the Allies' first centrifuge for testing the effects of gravity forces on pilots, and the two men developed the world's first G-suit. Banting was killed in a plane crash in Newfoundland in 1941.

□ The spectacle of trout struggling upstream to spawn is repeated every spring at the Nicolston dam, east of Alliston on the Nottawasaga River. The fish try to leap the six-foot dam several times before finding a fish ladder. There they are trapped, checked for length and sex, tagged, then released above the dam.

Alma Que.   9AW/21BW
The final 40 miles of the 265-mile, three-day Lac Saint-Jean bicycle race is on a closed circuit here. Six-man teams compete for cash and gifts in this late summer race sponsored by the Fédération Cyclisme du Québec.

An art center and an artists' lane where painters work in public are other summer attractions in this busy town. Sculptures by Quebec artists are displayed in the municipal park and the city hall gardens. The traditional architecture of Saint-Joseph Church is in interesting contrast to the daring style of Saint-Pierre Church.

The Aluminum Company of Canada plant on Isle Maligne and the Price paper mill offer tours. The companies established here after a 540,000-horsepower hydroelectric plant was built on the Grande Décharge River.

Almonte Ont.   7DY/18CX
A boy who played in the ruins of an Almonte gristmill in the years after Confederation was destined to return and give it immortality. He was Robert Tait McKenzie, and the Mill of Kintail is his memorial, a place whose timeless beauty is augmented by sculptures that brought him world acclaim.

McKenzie was McGill University's first medical director of physical education. During World War I he became famous for methods of rehabilitative medicine that he developed as a British Army medical officer. After the war he joined the medical staff of the University of Pennsylvania but frequently visited Almonte. He bought and restored the mill of his boyhood, renaming it the Mill of Kintail, for the McKenzie stronghold in the Scottish Highlands.

His fame as a sculptor competed with his renown as a surgeon and educator. His first sculptures, the four *Masks of Expression* depicting an athlete undergoing violent effort, breathlessness, fatigue and exhaustion, were completed while he was teaching anatomy at McGill. He produced hundreds of portrait plaques, monumental works, medals, athletic studies and war memorials.

The Mill of Kintail Museum (the Tait McKenzie Memorial) has more than 70 of his works and a large collection of Canadiana.

□ One mile west of Almonte is the Auld Kirk, a stone church built in 1835-36. Three

The Sprinter, by surgeon-sculptor Robert Tait McKenzie, is in the Mill of Kintail Museum, superbly set on the Indian River near Almonte.

miles north is a plaque honoring Dr. James Naismith, the inventor of basketball, who was born in Ramsey Township.

Altona Man.   6BZ/15CZ

Wareneki, schmoor kohl and *schmauntsuup* (cottage cheese dumplings, stewed cabbage with fruit and cucumber salad) are among Mennonite dishes served at the Manitoba Sunflower Festival at the end of July. Sunflowers, a source of vegetable oil, are a major crop here. The festival features agricultural and ethnic exhibits and displays of log sawing, hog butchering and soap- and sausage-making. Dramas are presented in the Low German dialect that is spoken by Mennonites in this area.

Amherst N.S.   9DY/23BX

The Tantramar marshes, 80 square miles of fertile land protected from the sea by old Acadian dikes, are known as the world's biggest hayfield. Tantramar is believed a corruption of the French *tintamarre* (loud noise), referring to the sound of the tides or the cacophony of birds in the marshes.

Near Amherst, toward the Bay of Fundy, are traces of the Chignecto Ship Railway that was to have carried 5,000-ton ships from Cumberland Basin to Northumberland Strait to avoid the long trip around Nova Scotia. The project employed 4,000 men for five years. Track was laid in 1890 and hoisting machinery installed at the Cumberland end but the project was stopped when money ran out.

A plaque marks the site of Fort Lawrence, built in 1751-52 by Lt. Col. Charles Lawrence for defense of the Chignecto Isthmus. It was abandoned after the British captured Fort Beauséjour in 1755. Lawrence became lieutenant governor of Nova Scotia; his clerk of stores, Sir Brook Watson, later became lord mayor of London.

The Confederation Memorial Building in Amherst is dedicated to four fathers of Confederation. Sir Charles Tupper was born in the town and it was home to Jonathan McCully, Edward Barron Chandler and Robert Barry Dickey.

□ Cumberland County is the blueberry center of Nova Scotia, and the importance of the multimillion-dollar industry is marked here by a three-day Blueberry Harvest Festival in early September. Events include selection of a queen, pancake breakfasts, pie-eating contests, street dancing, an old-time fiddlers' contest, an air show, a golf tournament, track-and-field events, a parade and a harvest ball.

Amherstburg Ont.   7AZ/16AZ

Few military sites in Canada have been as strategically important as Fort Malden, now a national historic park. Built at Amherstburg by the British in 1796, with outer blockhouses on Bois Blanc (now Bob-Lo) Island in the Detroit River, the fort was an important base in the War of 1812. Here Gen. Isaac Brock and the Indian chief Tecumseh planned their capture of Detroit. Little now remains at the site but the boulder on which Tecumseh stood to exhort his warriors is still there. When the Americans won the Battle of Lake Erie in 1813 the British pulled out of Fort Malden. The Americans occupied it until 1815, when the Treaty of Ghent ended the War of 1812.

Supporters of William Lyon Mackenzie attacked Fort Malden during the Rebellion of 1837-38 but were repelled by British regulars and Canadian militia. The schooner *Anne,* manned by Mackenzie sympathizers, ran aground after bombarding Amherstburg and was captured.

Indian, military and pioneer exhibits are housed in two museums at the fort. On Bob-Lo, now a park accessible by ferry, one of three original blockhouses is preserved.

Old buildings in Amherstburg include Christ Church, built in 1818, and Bellevue, the Georgian home of Robert Reynolds, who supplied the Fort Malden garrison. His sister Catherine lived at Bellevue and was one of Ontario's first artists.

Amherst Island Ont.   18BZ

When Daniel Fowler left England in 1843 he abandoned his trade as watercolorist and lithographer and took up farming on Amherst Island. But his interest in painting was rekindled on a visit to England 14 years later and he was soon back in Canada developing a strong style in watercolors. One watercolor,

Hollyhocks, won a medal at the 1876 Philadelphia Centennial Exhibition and, with other Fowler works, is in the National Gallery in Ottawa. A plaque honoring Fowler is on the grounds of his Amherst Island home.

Amherstview Ont.   18BZ
The Fairfield White House (picture, p. 48) is an excellent example of the homes of well-to-do Loyalists. It was built by William Fairfield, Sr., in 1793 and five generations later is still in the Fairfield family. Few houses of the same era are as well preserved. (Fairfield's son, William, Jr., built a house in Bath, six miles west, in 1796.)
□ The first woman landowner in what is now Ontario is honored by a plaque at Parrot's Bay, a mile west of the White House. Madeleine de Roybon d'Allonne was granted land here in 1683 by her friend René-Robert Cavelier de La Salle. She cleared it, built a house and barn and raised crops. Indians raided the farm in August 1687 and took Mlle d'Allonne and her escort of three soldiers to an Iroquois village on the south side of Lake Ontario. The English governor at Albany arranged her release after about a year. But warring Indians controlled the area around her farm and she was never able to return. She died penniless in Montreal in 1718.

Amos Que.   7DV
A Byzantine-style church and a bishop's palace are two attractions of this town in the heart of the mineral-rich Abitibi region. Founded in 1914, when a railway opened up the area, Amos became the center of gold-mining activity.

Anahim Lake B.C.   2CW
Special qualities mark the Anahim Lake Stampede as a rugged child of the Chilcotin River country. Purses are small and riders must arrange their own insurance, so professional rodeo cowboys pretty well ignore Anahim's festivities (held the second weekend of July). Whoever comes in from the outside world travels a dusty 200 miles of gravel from Williams Lake—a road "damn hard on cattle and worse on trucks." But everything from covered wagons and ponies to chrome campers and luxury cars uses the road. Cabin accommodation in the settlement is booked long before the stampede, but camping under the stars is part of the Anahim Lake lure. Rodeo seating is on corral fences or hillside bleachers.

Ancaster Ont.   7BZ/17BY
Whole grain flour is still stone-ground at the Ancaster Mountain Mills, built in 1790 on Beasley (or Ancaster) Creek and rebuilt in 1863. Originally powered by two overshot waterwheels, both 20 feet in diameter, the millstones are now turned by a water-powered turbine. An elevator of tin cups attached to an endless leather belt transfers the grain to bins on the second floor. The grain is

then gravity-fed to a ground-floor hopper. The corrugated "damsel" of the shaft that turns the upper stone vibrates against a wooden chute, feeding a stream of grain through the "eye" of the upper stone. It grinds the grain against the stationary bottom stone. A "warbler," a brass bell on a leather thong, is held away from the damsel by the flow of grain. When the grain stops, the warbler falls against the damsel and the ringing bell tells the miller to refill the hopper.
□ Beneath the floor of the mill is a stone chamber where men accused of treason during the War of 1812 were held prisoner. After a long trial eight persons were hanged despite impassioned pleas by friends and relatives. The trial became known as "The Bloody Assize." A plaque at Ancaster Memorial School tells the story.

Ancienne-Lorette Que. *see* Quebec

Annapolis Royal N.S.   9DY/22CW
Stately town houses and the silent cannon of Fort Anne National Historic Park recall the proud, violent past of this oldest and most fought over place in Canada. Its tortured history echoes in each heavy swing of the fort's powder magazine door: one hinge is French, the other English.
Annapolis Royal was a pawn in the struggle between France and England for New World supremacy in the 17th and 18th centuries. The first French settlement, the Port Royal of Champlain and de Monts in 1605, was on the north shore of the Annapolis Basin. Capt. Samuel Argall, the Virginia raider,

Annapolis Valley, now peaceful farmland, saw little peace for most of two centuries.

Hinges of history on a powder magazine at Annapolis Royal's Fort Anne: the top hinge is French, the other is English. Near the main building, a reproduction of British officers' quarters, is a cemetery in which are stones dating from 1720.

destroyed it in 1613. Scots led by Sir William Alexander had barely settled on the site when England's Charles I bartered Port Royal back to the French. In the 1630s a new French fort was built on the south shore of the basin, where Fort Anne stands.

In 1654 Port Royal was captured by the British; in 1670 it was given by treaty to the French; pirates burned the church and 28 houses in 1690, and later that year the British again captured the fort—only to have it returned to the French by another treaty seven years later. The French rebuilt it in 1702 and repelled several attacks. In 1710, after privateers preying on Boston ships took refuge here, New Englanders captured Port Royal in eight days. They renamed the town and fort Annapolis Royal and Fort Anne in honor of Queen Anne. From then until the founding of Halifax in 1749 Annapolis Royal was the capital of Nova Scotia.

The British enlarged and altered the fort. Commanded by Paul Mascarene, a French Huguenot in the British Army, it held out against several French and Indian attacks and two sieges. The last assault was in 1746. After a pirate raid in 1781 peace came to Annapolis Royal for good.

□ The 30-acre national historic park was established in 1917. Its rebuilt fort has one of the original French bastions, earthworks in excellent condition, and a museum and historical library in a concrete and steel reproduction of the old wooden British officers' quarters. The museum contains a handwritten daybook of Stephen Rodda, an Englishman, who started it in 1743 and continued writing until his death in 1770 in Annapolis Royal. The powder magazine, built in 1708, is the oldest building in Canada outside Quebec.

There are ramparts, moats, embrasures—and the Black Hole, built as a magazine but converted into a dungeon when found to be too damp to keep gunpowder dry.

A stone marks the grave of one of Annapolis Royal's most colorful figures, Spanish-born Gregoria Norman, whose husband James

served under Wellington in the Peninsular wars. They were married at Gibraltar in 1813 and—as favorites of Wellington, it was said—were sent to live in the peace of far-off Canada. She drew many an envious (if critical) stare for the bright colors and turban she wore and the four white French poodles she kept. Norman was Fort Anne's last ordnance keeper.

□ St. George Street in Annapolis Royal is lined with buildings that reveal glimpses of the town's past. Two that have been restored are the McNamara house—it was a school in the 1790s—and the O'Dell Inn and Tavern, a stagecoach stop in the mid-1800s. It is now a museum.

□ The Banks residence, said to be more than 250 years old, has two roofs, one 18 inches above the other. The space is filled with clay as insulation.

□ Old French dikes hold back Bay of Fundy tides that rise by 21-30 feet along the Annapolis Basin shore. The reversing action of the tides, which leaves extensive mud flats, can be seen at the floodgates of a dam at the east end of the basin.

□ A road of about 67 miles between Annapolis Royal and Blomidon forms part of the Fundy Trail, which eventually will extend 550 miles from Yarmouth, N.S., to St. Stephen, N.B. The Annapolis-Blomidon section runs through such picturesque places as Parker Cove, Hampton, Margaretville, Morden, Harbourville and Halls Harbour.

Anse-aux-Gascons Que.   9DW

Islands off this farming and fishing village on the north shore of Chaleur Bay are a nesting ground for thousands of cormorants from April to November. The village, in one of the loveliest parts of Gaspésie, owes its name to a shipwrecked Gascon sailor who settled here.

Lequille Mill First

The first grain-grinding mill in North America was built at Lequille, near Annapolis Royal, in 1605 after (so it is recorded) six men died from the exertion of grinding corn by hand. A replica disguises a hydroelectric power plant with the greatest harnessed drop of water in Nova Scotia (465 feet through pipelines).

Ansnorveldt Ont. 17CW

This thriving community was settled in 1931 by patient Dutch families who laboriously reclaimed a swampy wasteland and created the rich Holland Marsh market gardens, since grown to 5,000 acres. Vegetables in thousands of precise rows cover the great flats that John Galt in 1825 called "a mere ditch swarming with bullfrogs and snakes." A Christian Reformed church built in 1943 rises red and impressive from the marsh's black soil. (*See* Bradford)

Antigonish N.S. 9EY/23EY

Settled almost two centuries ago by Gaelic-speaking Scots, Antigonish is the home of St. Francis Xavier University and its world-famous Antigonish Movement—and of Canada's oldest Highland games.

Kilted clansmen from many parts of North America gather here in mid-July and for five days the town thrills to the skirl of massed pipes, the ruffle of drums and the roar of applause for mighty deeds done with caber and hammer and shot. The Antigonish Highland Society first staged the games in 1863. Although broadened to include a track-and-field meet, they retain a fundamental Scottish flavor and are recognized as "Canada's Braemar," after the Highland games in the Royal Braemar in Scotland.

The university was founded in 1853. In its Angus L. Macdonald Library, named for a beloved son (and premier) of Nova Scotia, is the Hall of Clans, its walls adorned with Scottish crests. When Mount St. Bernard College affiliated in 1894, "St. FX" became

---

Gaelic words *Tigh Dhe* above the sanctuary of St. Ninian's Cathedral in Antigonish mean House of God. Begun in 1868, completed seven years later, St. Ninian's was built of local blue limestone in Roman basilica style.

the first coeducational Roman Catholic college in North America. In 1951 Xavier College in Sydney, N.S., became a St. FX constituent. Self-help principles and techniques which originated at the university are now widely applied as extensions of the Antigonish Movement: adult education using an economic approach through group action.

The town has many other links with the past. A plaque at the federal building commemorates William Alexander Henry, an Antigonish native who was one of the Fathers of Confederation and helped write the first draft of the British North America Act. The

pillared white courthouse on the main business street also dates from the 1850s. The wheel and bell of the World War II frigate HMCS *Antigonish* are in the Royal Canadian Legion Hall.

□ Riverside Speedway, with a one-third-mile track and 18-degree banks, is one of the fastest stock car ovals in Canada. It was patterned after the Bristol International Speedway in Tennessee.

□ The 40-mile North Shore Drive, along St. George's Bay and over the point of Cape George, is a miniature Cabot Trail.

Oldest continuing weekly in the Maritimes, *The Casket* of Antigonish was named when the popular definition of the word was "a small chest for jewels or other valuables." It used to print some news in Gaelic.

Ardrossan Alta.   4AW/14FW

North America's only Chinese water deer and rare purebred vicunas (from Chile) are among the more than 4,000 mammals at the Alberta Game Farm. Some others are snow leopards, a pair of Przewalski's horses (the only true wild horse, once thought extinct), a herd of Tibetan yaks and some of the few hundred Père David's deer left in the world. The 1,400-acre farm has an estimated 4,000 birds of 90-odd species—peafowl and teal, flamingo, hawk, crane, falcon....

Zoologist Al Oeming started the farm in 1957. It has rolling meadows, bush, muskeg, ponds and 1½-mile-long Lost Lake (in which cavort freshwater seals from Russia's Lake Baikal). The farm was planned, and continues, to be a sanctuary for wild animals, particularly those threatened in their native habitats, in whatever parts of the world. Now the Arabian camel, the Sahara Desert addax and waterbuck from an African swamp winter on the same snowblanketed Canadian farm as grizzly bears, musk-oxen, caribou and Arctic fox. Animal shelters are insulated.

Arichat N.S.   9FY/23FY

When Thomas LeNoir came from the Magdalen Islands in the early 1800s, Arichat was a prosperous shipbuilding town, the main community on Isle Madame in Chedabucto Bay. The forge that his family built here served the builders and trained new craftsmen; eventually the LeNoirs established Nova Scotia's first blacksmith apprentice school. When shipbuilding declined, so did the forge. But it was restored in 1967 as a mu-

seum with exhibits of ship chandlery and anchor-making. Logs used in launchings at the LeNoir shipyard, just west, can be seen at low tide.

Isle Madame, settled by Acadians after the fall of Louisbourg in 1758, is ringed by picturesque fishing villages. A highway bridge across Lennox Passage links the island with the Cape Breton mainland. Arichat's twin-towered, wooden L'Assomption Church, built in 1838, was a cathedral until 1886 when the diocesan seat was moved to Antigonish. The original bishop's palace is now a hospital.

Armstrong B.C.   2EY

Near this proudly western town at the north end of Okanagan Lake is an historic ranch where Cornelius O'Keefe built a cattle empire a century ago. He came north from Oregon in 1867. The next year he homesteaded 162 acres and eventually his cattle grazed more than 15,000 acres. The ranch had its own post office (1872), general store and blacksmith shop—and little St. Ann's, the oldest Roman Catholic church in the B.C. interior. These buildings and the mansion that O'Keefe built toward the end of the century have been turned into a museum settlement by his son Tierney. St. Ann's stands apart, linked with the other buildings by a wooden walk and a parade of 10 antique street gas lamps from Scotland. Among the treasures in the mansion are 115 pieces of rare Meissen china (c. 1750).

Armstrong, center of the municipality of

Alberta Game Farm at Ardrossan provides plenty of space for the animals. Actual "farming"— breeding under close-to-natural conditions—is emphasized.

Spallumcheen, is famous for cheddar cheese. Three miles south is the Fort Spallumcheen Wildlife Museum.

Arnes Man.   6BX/15DV
A sculpture by Walter Yarwood in Vilhjalmur Stefansson Memorial Park commemorates the internationally renowned Arctic explorer, writer and lecturer, who was born here in 1879. He was the son of Icelandic immigrant parents.

Arnprior Ont.   18CW
The colorful story of a township that was ruled by a Scottish laird, then became an important lumbering center, is told in displays at the Arnprior & District Museum.

One features "the McNab era" of the early 1800s. Archibald McNab, 13th chief of Clan McNab, was in charge of a settlement of Scottish farmers but, letting on that he *owned* McNab Township, he ran a kind of backwoods feudal empire. When "the McNab's" deception was exposed, the settlement languished. But lumberman Daniel McLachlin bought land at deserted Arnprior in 1851, laid out a town, built sawmills and started big-scale lumbering on the Madawaska River. Arnprior revived to play a major role in the great days of timber rafting.

The museum records not only the McNab era and Arnprior's life "on the river" but also the early days of Indians and fur traders. Temporary displays range from the elegance of Arnprior homes in the Victorian era to

"I Know What I Have Experienced . . ."

The Vilhjalmur Stefansson sculpture at Arnes is composed of a three-foot-high bronze of Stefansson and a 10-foot representation of the Inukshuk (an Eskimo landmark built of rocks in the form of a man). A quotation from Stefansson's autobiography, *Discovery*, is inscribed on the Inukshuk in Icelandic, English and French: "I know what I have experienced, and I know what it has meant to me." The first of Stefansson's three famous expeditions to the Arctic was in the Mackenzie Delta in 1906-7. In 1908-12 he made an ethnological survey of the central Arctic coast. In 1913-18 he commanded a Canadian expedition which mapped large areas of the archipelago, using dogsleds after the loss in 1914 of his flagship *Karluk*. Stefansson demonstrated that men could live in the Arctic—on ice floes if necessary—with no supply of food from outside.

the rusticity of the country store. The museum building is a massive red stone former post office with an unusual clock tower.

□ The Canadian Civil Defense College is at Arnprior.

Arthabaska Que. 9AX/20AY

The homes of Wilfrid Laurier, who practised law and entered politics here, and painter-sculptor Marc-Aurèle de Foy Suzor-Coté, Arthabaska's most famous native son, are open to the public in this chief town of the Bois-Francs region.

Suzor-Coté was born in Arthabaska in 1869—three years after Laurier went there. He helped painter Maxime Rousseau to make church decorations, went to Paris in 1890 and studied at the Ecole des Beaux-Arts. He opened a studio in Montreal in 1908 and spent the summers painting at Arthabaska. One of the seven Suzor-Coté paintings in the National Gallery of Canada is the landscape *Coin de Mon Village, Arthabaska*. Best known of his sculptures is a 17¼-inch-high bronze, *Indiennes de Caughnawaga*, also in the National Gallery.

Arundel Que. 7EX/18EV

Under the trees beside Lake McDonald whole families practise with violins and recorders at a six-week music camp here. The program includes instruction from members of Canadian Amateur Musicians, a Montreal organization.

Aluminum smelter potline is where huge amounts of electricity are passed through aluminum oxide, producing molten metal. Arvida's smelter is the largest in the western world.

Wilfrid Laurier's house in Arthabaska is a museum, furnished as in his day.

Arvida Que. 9AW/21CW

This "city of aluminum," founded in 1927, imports bauxite from Guyana, Jamaica and parts of West Africa for a smelter with a daily capacity of 2,400,000 pounds. It is the largest planned city in Canada, named for ARthur VIning DAvis, at one time president of the Aluminum Company of America. The Alcan plants, 1½ miles long by three-quarters wide, are open for tours, as is the Shipshaw powerhouse, one of the world's biggest hydroelectric stations. An all-aluminum highway bridge spans the Saguenay River here. The

Manoir du Saguenay hotel is built of field-stone and has sloping roofs and dormer windows reminiscent of old Quebec farmhouses. A conservatory exhibits plants from countries that produce bauxite.

Asbestos Que. 9AY/20AY

Operations in one of the world's largest asbestos mines can be observed from a lookout near a huge open pit in this Eastern Townships town. It is one of 10 Townships mines that produce more than 85 percent of Canadian asbestos, a mineral that can be woven into insulation, cut into shingles, made into packing. These and other products are made at the Canadian Johns-Manville Company plant here.

Ashcroft B.C. 2DY

Freight wagons reminiscent of Ashcroft's link with pioneer days are to be seen at the Ashcroft Museum, along with archives, pioneer clothing and Indian artifacts. With completion of the CPR, Ashcroft took over from Yale as "the gateway to the Cariboo."

Ashcroft Manor B.C. 2DY

Two Cambridge-educated brothers who set up as cattlemen here in 1862 lived pioneer life like the gentlemen they were, sipping ritualistic tea in the afternoon wilderness and riding to the hounds through sagebrush and scrub—in pursuit of a coyote.

The house that Clement and Henry Cornwall built, naming it Ashcroft after their family home in Gloucestershire, became a famous stop on the Cariboo Wagon Road. The name was later changed to Ashcroft Manor. Here were a smithy, a sawmill, a

A **famous stopping house** on the Cariboo Wagon Road, Ashcroft Manor also served as a courthouse (Clement Cornwall, co-owner, presiding) beginning in 1867.

gristmill, a bar and race meets at which up to $2,000 a day was bet on the horses.

The Cornwalls' log church, with steeple and eight hand-hewn pews, still exists on what is now an Indian reserve. The stopping house remains in the family but is no longer in use.

Atikokan Ont. 6EY

Quetico Provincial Park, a 1,750-square-mile wilderness between Atikokan and the U.S. border, has changed little since La Vérendrye traded there in the mid-1700s and Fraser, Mackenzie and Thompson paddled its lakes and rivers en route to the Pacific. Quetico has known humans for 9,000 years—since the Stone Age ancestors of the Ojibway and Cree Indians—but the Stone Age was only yesterday in Quetico. Its youngest rocks have been there 2,500,000,000 years, its oldest 3,000,000,000.

About 1,500,000,000 years ago a sea covered Quetico. The land underwent volcanic action and violent earthquakes, then calm and another flood. Mountains were formed and eroded. During the Ice Age, glaciers gouged huge depressions and meltwater formed a tortured network of lakes and rivers amid harsh and awesome landscapes. One granite cliff rises 250 feet above Angus Lake and plunges 280 feet to the lake bottom.

On cliffs at 28 places in the park are primitive Indian paintings of animals and warriors. They are 8-12 inches high and most are about five feet above the waterline, as if the painters had stood in canoes. Most paintings are reddish; the Indians used hematite (from iron ore), probably mixed with fish oil.

Dams, locks and wagon roads along the park's Dawson Trail, surveyed by Simon J. Dawson in 1857, were completed in 1870 and used by troops sent to quell the Riel Rebellion in Manitoba. Settlers trekking west used the trail until the CPR was completed in 1885.

□ Four miles north of Atikokan are iron mines in what was the bed of Steep Rock Lake. It was drained during World War II to provide access to the rich ore deposits. Now the open-pit mining operation is a tourist attraction.

Atlin B.C. 1AW

Sixty miles south of Jake's Corner, Y.T. (Mile 868 on the Alaska Highway), is Atlin, a hamlet that once was a gold-rush boomtown of 5,000. It was born and thrived at the time of the Klondike gold strike 446 miles north at Dawson.

In the Atlin cemetery are the graves of Fritz Miller, a German American, and Kenneth McLaren, a Canadian (from Blue Mountain, N.S.), who discovered Atlin's wealth in 1898—along Pine Creek on the eastern shore of Atlin Lake. Three thousand persons flocked to Atlin that year and in 1899 the population was 5,000. Then, after the most accessible gold had been taken and with the introduction of hydraulic mining,

Prairie pioneers, the steam giants that helped break sod and power harvest operations, parade at a threshermen's reunion at Austin.

it began to decline—to 2,000 in 1901, to 1,500 by 1904. Gold production dropped from a record 40,000 ounces ($800,000) in 1899 to a 1900-7 average of 21,000 ounces. Total production from 1898 to 1949 was valued at more than $22,500,000.

A one-room museum behind the Discovery Shop, a handicraft store, displays mementoes of the gold rush and early days of the town. One relic remains where it has always stood: the ornate clock of "Jules Eggert, Jeweler" on a 10-foot pillar alongside the main street. The town's first fire wagon stands near the firehall, a sign recording that "this gem was once the pride" of the Portland, Ore., and Vancouver fire departments—before Atlin acquired it in 1901.

One of the steamers that connected Atlin with Carcross (and the White Pass and Yukon Route railway), the screwdriven *Tarahne,*

Ruins at Aulac are part of Fort Beauséjour National Historic Park. Cairns mark the site of Tonge's Island, once capital of Acadia, and commemorate Yorkshire settlers of 1772.

sits beached at the Atlin waterfront. *Duchess,* the engine on a 2¼-mile railroad between Atlin Lake and Taku, has been preserved in Carcross. A one-way ticket on the *Duchess* cost $2 and passengers had to sit on their baggage.

Auburn N.S. 22DV

Plaster on the walls of St. Mary's Anglican Church was made from the shells of mussels that Acadian refugees ate while in hiding during the winter of 1756. Loyalist settlers who built St. Mary's in 1790 powdered the piles of shells they found. Window frames and glass were brought from Halifax on horses; handmade nails were carried by soldiers who walked the 100 miles. One of three gilt balls on the spire fell in 1898 and was found to contain a record of the building of the church, from the names of the workmen to the number of nails used. The record was copied and replaced and the ball put back on the spire.

□ A plaque in St. Mary's is dedicated to the Rt. Rev. Charles Inglis, first bishop of Nova Scotia (1787). About 1½ miles west of Auburn is another plaque, on a well at the site of Clermont, for many years the bishop's home. While in the Annapolis Valley apple country, Bishop Charles Inglis propagated the "Bishop's Pippin" variety.

Aulac N.B. 9DY/23AX

Fort Beauséjour, one of the few forts in Canada to see any fighting, was built by the French in 1750-55 to counter the English at Fort Lawrence (just across what now is the New Brunswick-Nova Scotia border, near Amherst, N.S.).

At first, the opposing garrisons lived in harmony. Goods were smuggled back and forth, and officers mingled freely at an eating house in the no-man's-land between the forts. But in June 1755, some 2,000 New England volunteers and 250 regulars of the Fort Lawrence garrison, all led by Lt. Col. Robert Monckton, attacked Beauséjour. After three days of bombardment, the defenders—150 French soldiers and 200 reluctant Acadian settlers—surrendered.

Renamed Fort Cumberland, the post was besieged briefly during the American Revolution by Yankees who had settled in the area. It underwent repairs at the start of the War of 1812 but saw none of that conflict. When the garrison was withdrawn in 1833 the fort was abandoned and quickly fell into ruins. The site was designated a national historic park in 1926 and the old name Beauséjour was reinstated. The pentagonal shape of the fort can be seen, and one of the stone casemates built after the siege of 1755 has been restored.

Austin Man.   6AY/15AX
Steam and gas tractors, binders, threshing machines and an 1835 McCormick reaper are enshrined at the Manitoba Agricultural Museum, and the hardiest among them are revived each summer for the museum's Manitoba Threshermen's Reunion and Stampede. The clanking, snorting monsters bear such names as Case, Marshall, Sawyer, Abell, Hart-Parr, Nichols and Shepard—nostalgic echoes of the prairie pioneers. Also in the museum are buggies, a surrey, a democrat wagon and automobiles that include an 1895 Stanley Steamer, 1905 Cadillac, 1915 Buick and 1916 Saxon. Pioneer relics, from mustache cups and a sausage grinder to a 1771 cookbook and an 1850 sewing machine, are displayed in the museum. An 1890 one-room schoolhouse is on the grounds.

Auyuittuq *see* Baffin Island

Aylmer Ont.   7BZ/16DY
The Ontario Police College, where policemen from all parts of Ontario study everything from recruit training to criminal investigation and crowd control, is housed in one-time RCAF buildings near here. During tours (for groups only) the public is given descriptions of the training courses and sees fingerprint and weapons displays.

B

Baddeck N.S.   9FX/23GX
The centerpiece of 25-acre Alexander Graham Bell National Historic Park is a museum which mirrors the genius of the Scottish-born inventor of the telephone—whose research led to important contributions also in medicine, aeronautics, marine engineering, genetics and eugenics.

A monument commemorates the first airplane flight in the Commonwealth, by Bell's associate J.A.D. McCurdy in the *Silver Dart* on Feb. 23, 1909, above the ice of Baddeck Bay. Bell, McCurdy, F.W. "Casey" Baldwin and two Americans, Glenn H. Curtiss and Thomas E. Selfridge, had formed the Aerial Experiment Association in 1907. (Near Hammondsport, N.Y., on March 12, 1908, Baldwin became the first British subject and the seventh person in the world to fly.)

Bell first visited Baddeck in 1885. Seven years later he established his summer home *Beinn Bhreagh* (Gaelic for beautiful mountain) on a headland overlooking Baddeck Bay. There he did much of his research. He died

Hydrofoil model and a photograph of a "talking glove" for teaching the deaf are among Alexander Graham Bell memorabilia in a Baddeck museum. Its shape is the tetrahedron Bell used in testing the principles of flight.

A Lake Like a Scottish Loch

Bras d'Or Lake, a 400-square-mile inland sea, almost splits Cape Breton Island. To the north the Atlantic comes and goes on both sides of Boularderie Island, through Great Bras d'Or and Little Bras d'Or. To the south a strip of land less than a quarter-mile wide separates Bras d'Or from the sea. (But St. Peters Canal enables boats to move easily between the two.) Low mountains rise behind the channels, bays and harbors of Bras d'Or and it resembles a Scottish loch. The huge lake, virtually tideless, has excellent fishing and boating, scores of fine beaches and pine-clad islands. Baddeck, on the north shore, was a thriving shipbuilding center in the wooden ship era. Yachts and small boats are still built there.

In the Atlantic off Great Bras d'Or are the Bird Islands, where seabirds nest in huge numbers in June and July.

at Beinn Bhreagh in 1922 and was buried on the summit of his beautiful mountain amid scenery that had reminded him of Scotland. The Bell estate is private.

Bell's research was in fields as varied as education of the deaf and development of the hydrofoil boat. He produced a surgical probe, saw the possibility of artificial respiration by means of a "vacuum jacket" (today's iron lung), and suggested how radium could be used in the treatment of cancer.

Baden Ont.   7BY/17AY
Sir Adam Beck, "Father of Ontario Hydro," was born in 1857 in this Waterloo County town that his father, an immigrant from the grand duchy of Baden, had founded the year before. Beck was a cigar box manufacturer, mayor of London, Ont., and a member of the Ontario legislature when he espoused the cause of public power in 1903. He was chairman of the Hydro-Electric Power Commission of Ontario from its formation in 1906 until his death in 1925. He is commemorated here by a memorial park and a plaque.

□ Baden is noted for cheeses, especially Limburger, and its antique shops. The Livingston house is a good example of mid-19th-century Ontario architecture.

Baffin Island N.W.T.
Long narrow fjords, glacier-filled mountain valleys and a massive ice cap make 8,300-square-mile Auyuittuq National Park one of Canada's most spectacular. Cliffs tower 3,000 feet above the sea. Dominating the highlands, where mountains reach 7,000 feet, is the Penny Ice Cap. Largest of the glaciers extending from the 2,200-square-mile cap is Coronation Glacier, 20 miles long and two miles wide. There is one campground.

Whale, narwhal, seal and walrus are found in the fjords; land mammals include the polar bear, Arctic fox and caribou. The Canada goose and snowy owl are among 38 species of birds in the park; so are the rare gyrfalcon and whistling swan.

Baffin Island was a site of the Thule Eskimo culture 1,000 years ago and archaeologists have found the ruins of several communities in the Cumberland Sound area.

Bagotville Que.   9AW/21CX
The first stone construction in this part of the Saguenay country was Saint-Alphonse Church (1857), built 18 years after the town's founding. Another Bagotville church, Saint-Marc, with its multiple-peaked white roof,

is a newer landmark in this community at the head of the Baie-des-Ha! Ha! It was the first of many ultramodern churches for which the Lac Saint-Jean area has become famous since World War II.

Bagotville is a commercial and agricultural center, a rail terminal and deepwater port, long the terminus of the Saguenay boat tours from Montreal. McLean Park, in Florentine style, is on high land from which 30 miles of the majestic Saguenay fjord can be seen.

Baie-Comeau Que.   9BV
The remarkable development of Quebec's once isolated North Shore had its beginnings here in 1936 when publisher Robert R. McCormick built a pulp-and-newsprint mill to feed his newspapers in Chicago and New York. The town of Baie-Comeau took shape and was soon linked by road with towns up the St. Lawrence River. Development boomed in the 1950s and 1960s: an aluminum refinery and grain elevators were built here and the Manicouagan River and the Rivière aux Outardes were harnessed to produce a vast hydroelectric complex.

□ Hydro-Quebec's showpiece on the two rivers is the Daniel Johnson (Manic 5) Dam, 135 miles north of Baie-Comeau on the Manicouagan. It is the world's biggest multiple-arch dam—4,310 feet long with a central arch 703 feet high. The lake it created covers 750 square miles. The hydro complex may be visited during the summer.

□ Sainte-Amélie Church, built in 1940 in Dom Bellot style, with stained glass windows by Guido Nincheri, is named in honor of McCormick's wife Amelia.

□ The town has a gun from the brigantine *Mary,* part of the force that Sir William Phips

U.S. newspaper publisher Robert R. McCormick is memorialized by a statue at Baie-Comeau.

led against Port Royal and Quebec in 1690. The ship was lost off Anticosti Island.

□ In the North Shore Historical Society museum are such works as the 73-volume Twaites edition (French and English) of the Jesuit *Relations;* the 1720 edition of Adm. Hovenden Walker's journal about his disastrous expedition to Quebec in 1711; four volumes of Champlain's journeys, and a catechism in Montagnais Indian.

Baie-Sainte-Catherine Que.   9BW/21EX
The base of the parish church altar is made of a gilded cedar stump with intertwining roots.

Baie-Saint-Paul Que.   20CV
A superb setting between two promontories at the mouth of the Rivière du Gouffre and opposite Ile aux Coudres has made the Baie-Saint-Paul landscape a favorite of Canadian artists, including some of the best known. Among Quebec places, only Montreal and

Pangnirtung Fjord lends awesome splendor to Baffin Island National Park, the first national park above the Arctic Circle. It is 180 air miles from Frobisher Bay, 1,500 from Montreal.

First miller at Balmoral Mills was Alex MacKay, called "Lower Sandy" to distinguish him from "Upper Sandy" MacKay, a miller upstream.

Quebec City appear oftener than Baie-Saint-Paul in paintings in the National Gallery of Canada. Every year hundreds of visitors paint and photograph the fertile fields, the bold hills, two French regime gristmills (still in use), old farm buildings and picturesque town houses. Not far inland are the highest of the Laurentians (about 4,000 feet).

Here, in 1663, a massive earthquake toppled a low mountain into the St. Lawrence River, and destroyed one of the earliest saltpeter mines in Quebec.

Balmoral Mills N.S.   9EY/23CY
The 1½-ton stones of a gristmill built in 1830 still grind wheat, oats, barley and buckwheat—but at a pace befitting their age and the mill's new status as a museum. Tourists see the grinding one hour at a time, twice a day, from mid-May to mid-October.

Bancroft Ont.   7DY
A five-day Rockhound Gemboree attracts hundreds of collectors—and thousands of tourists—to this Madawaska Valley village every August. The Chamber of Commerce and the Bancroft Mineral Society started the event in 1963. Soon Bancroft was as well known for its gemboree as it had been for uranium before a world oversupply forced the closing of mines here.

□ Pioneer artifacts are displayed in the Bancroft Historical Museum, a log house built in 1857 by a lumber company operating in the Madawaska.

Banff National Park (Alta.)   2FY/13BV
Canada's oldest national park contains two of the country's finest resorts—Banff and Lake Louise—amid a Rocky Mountain wonderland of snowcapped peaks and deep valleys, awesome glaciers and icy crystal-clear lakes. The 2,564-square-mile park offers facilities for trail riders, hikers and mountain climbers. It has youth hostels, campgrounds and the world-famous Banff Springs Hotel and Château Lake Louise. There are nature trails, hoodoos, hot mineral spring pools (one open all year) and some of the world's finest skiing.

The park stretches for 150 miles along the eastern slope of the Great Divide. Its eastern gateway is only 75 miles from Calgary; on the west it is flanked by Yoho and Kootenay national parks (both in British Columbia); to the north the vast Columbia Icefield links it with Jasper National Park. (Banff, Jasper, Yoho and Kootenay parks together cover 7,814 square miles.)

Banff National Park (originally a 10-square-mile preserve known as Rocky Mountain Park) was established in 1887, not long after discovery of a cave in which was a steaming pool fed by sulphur springs. The park's alpine setting and dry climate, and the hot springs, quickly won it renown as a health and vacation resort. The Banff School of Fine Arts has made it an arts center too.

Among the park's highest peaks (from 9,800 to 11,870 feet) are Assiniboine, Cascade, Chephren, Eisenhower, Forbes, Hector, Lefroy and Rundle. It has scores of beautiful lakes —Lake Louise, Mirror Lake, Lake Agnes, and perhaps none lovelier than Moraine Lake, nestled in the superb Valley of the Ten Peaks.

The townsite of Banff is the park's business center. Here too are the park's administration buildings and Cascade Gardens, at the opposite end of the main street from Cascade Mountain. Among the attractions in or close to the townsite are the glacial-green Bow River, Bow Falls, Sundance Canyon, Lake Minnewanka, Johnston Canyon, the three Vermilion Lakes, Tunnel Mountain, a natural amphitheater on Cascade Mountain, buffalo paddocks and the Hoodoos nature trail.

□ Long a popular summer resort, Banff National Park blossomed anew in the 1960s as a winter sports center. It has some of the world's best ski slopes, plus skating, curling, sleighing, tobogganing—and outdoor swimming in the hot sulphur pools. Mount Norquay (8,275 feet), at Banff's doorstep, boasts an Olympic-standard ski jump and a downhill course with a 2,000-foot drop. Major ski meets are held at Norquay, Mount Temple (11,626 feet) and Mount Whitehorn (both near Lake Louise) and Sunshine Village (altitude 7,200 feet), 14 miles southwest of Banff.

ARCHIVES OF THE CANADIAN ROCKIES A community library, an art gallery with a permanent collection of paintings of mountain areas, and a research center for western Canadian mountaineering and mountain history.

World-famous Château Lake Louise, at the head of a lovely lake that springs from Victoria Glacier, is among Banff National Park's attractions. The park is a place of contrasts: animals roam wild close to sculptors at the Banff School of Fine Arts. Castle Mountain, here reflected in the Bow River, was renamed in 1946 for Gen. Dwight D. Eisenhower. A diorama by C.A. Beil at Banff's Luxton Museum, of buffalo being driven over a cliff, is based on a kill site at Jumping Pound, west of Calgary.

ATHABASCA GLACIER *see* Jasper National Park

BANFF FESTIVAL OF THE ARTS *see under* The Banff Center

BANFF INDIAN DAYS Parades and ceremonial dances highlight this three-day annual get-together of the Stony and other Alberta tribes.

BANFF NATURAL HISTORY MUSEUM Specimens of most birds and animals indigenous to the national park.

BANFF SCHOOL OF FINE ARTS *see under* The Banff Center

BANFF SPRINGS HOTEL One of the biggest (550 rooms) and loveliest of Canada's château hotels, the Banff Springs is in a magnificent setting overloooking the Bow Valley.

CAVE AND BASIN The cave encloses one of the springs whose discovery in 1885 triggered development of the park. (Since then, 27 other national parks have been created.) Sulphur springs, flowing at 575,000 gallons a day, feed a natural sulphur water pool (88 degrees) and a freshwater pool (80 degrees).

CHÂTEAU LAKE LOUISE This huge resort hotel looks across Lake Louise. Like the Banff Springs, it is a jewel among Canadian château hotels.

COLUMBIA ICEFIELD *see* Jasper National Park

ICEFIELDS PARKWAY All 142 miles of this great highroad (74 miles are in Banff National Park, the rest in Jasper National Park) command breathtaking scenery. It runs from Lake Louise to Jasper townsite, following in turn the Bow, Mistaya, North Saskatchewan, Sunwapta and Athabasca rivers, crossing the Bow and Sunwapta passes and presenting an endless but ever-changing panorama of peaks and glaciers, waterfalls and canyons.

LAKE LOUISE Icy, blue-green Lake Louise, in a hanging valley at an altitude of 5,680 feet, is about 1½ miles long, three-quarters of a mile wide, 225 feet deep. The lake was discovered in 1882 and named for Princess Louise, daughter of Queen Victoria.

The town of Lake Louise, once called Laggan, is near Kicking Horse Pass and some of the most magnificent scenery in the park —at Moraine Lake in the Valley of the Ten Peaks, Lake Agnes, Mirror Lake, the Plain of the Six Glaciers, Paradise Valley and 7,440-foot Big Beehive, towering above Lake Agnes.

LAKE MINNEWANKA Sightseeing launches ply this 12-mile-long lake near Banff, the only lake in the park on which motors are permitted.

LAKES-IN-THE-CLOUDS A three-mile nature trail leads from Lake Louise to Mirror Lake and Lake Agnes (and its teahouse). Another trail skirts Lake Agnes and climbs Big Beehive into the Plain of the Six Glaciers.

LUXTON MUSEUM Indian ceremonies, dances, hunting and daily life are shown in dioramas at this museum, a subsidiary of the Glenbow-Alberta Institute of Calgary. One major attraction is a diorama of a Sun Dance lodge in which a Plains Indian tortures himself as fellow warriors watch.

MOUNT ASSINIBOINE *see* Kootenay National Park

MOUNT EISENHOWER Indian legend says this majestic 9,076-foot mountain is the home of the chinook, a warm dry wind that sweeps out of the Rockies to melt snow in the foothills and on the prairies

MOUNT NORQUAY From Mount Norquay Lodge, a five-mile drive from Banff, a chair lift rises 1,300 feet in 10 minutes—to the 7,000-foot level.

MOUNT RUNDLE This 9,838-foot peak dominates the green valley of the Bow River at the Banff townsite. Mount Rundle's sequence of rocks, varying in hardness and resistance to erosion, is characteristic of many mountains in the front ranges of the eastern Rockies.

PEYTO LAKE Near the Bow Pass is Peyto Viewpoint, with its magnificent views of Peyto Glacier, Peyto Lake and falls and ranges to the north.

SULPHUR MOUNTAIN One of Banff's most popular attractions is the Sulphur Mountain lift. Four-passenger gondolas rise 2,300 feet in eight minutes, to the top of 7,495-foot

Cariboo Treasure

The Cariboo gold that lured men from around the world in the 1860s is gone. But another treasure, the Cariboo itself—30,000 square miles of mountains, pristine lakes and vast cattle ranches—is being discovered every year by growing numbers of tourists.

The real Cariboo came into its own after the gold rush, when most treasure-seekers had left for faraway homes or new goldfields. Some stayed, newly addicted to the Cariboo's clear blue skies and its relaxed pace. Their only link with the outside world was the 385-mile Cariboo Road, built between Yale and Barkerville during the gold rush and an engineering marvel of the day. Cattle thrived on the slopes of the Fraser Plateau and the great Cariboo ranches were started.

The boundaries of the Cariboo are inexact. Some say the Cariboo is all of the British Columbia interior north of Cache Creek. Perhaps it is best defined as an irregular circle of prime vacationland within a 100-mile radius of Williams Lake, the "cowboy capital" of B.C.

The Cariboo Road has been replaced by the 275-mile Cariboo Highway from Cache Creek to Prince George. Bustling cities and towns hum where gold-seekers camped. But the Cariboo is essentially unchanged. If there's not much gold left, the treasure of the Cariboo's great outdoors is there for the taking.

Sulphur Mountain, where there is an unrestricted view of the Banff ranges and valleys.

THE BANFF CENTER This institution, affiliated with the University of Calgary, includes the Banff School of Fine Arts, a School of Management Studies and a Conference Division, and houses the Banff School of Advanced Management.

The School of Fine Arts, founded in 1933, is one of North America's foremost schools of theater arts, musical theater, opera and ballet. Also taught are photography, figure skating, French, writing and crafts.

The School of Management Studies offers courses in business, government and allied fields, teaching management skills to executives. The Banff School of Advanced Management is sponsored by the Universities of Alberta, Manitoba and Saskatchewan.

Concerts, drama and ballet are year-round features at The Banff Center. The week-long Banff Festival of the Arts is held at the close of summer sessions at the School of Fine Arts. Performances are in the center's two theaters.

THE HOODOOS These light-colored natural pillars are made of glacial till (clay, sand, gravel and boulders). Tightly cemented by lime in the glacial water, the till has resisted erosion and the hoodoos have taken shape. Hoodoos are seen on a trail 2½ miles east of the Banff townsite.

UPPER HOT SPRINGS An outdoor swimming pool with a water temperature of 100 degrees is open year-round on the slopes of Sulphur Mountain.

Barkerville B.C. 1AZ/2DW

This gold-rush "capital" of the Cariboo (biggest town west of Chicago and north of San Francisco, people boasted in the 1860s) has been restored as a living museum. In Barkerville Historical Park are such buildings as the Wake-Up Jake Saloon, the gold commissioner's office, St. Saviour's Anglican Church with its "Cariboo gothic" arches of native

Barnard's Express stagecoach at Barkerville resembles wagons that thundered up from Yale in gold-rush days. One of the biggest buildings, the Barkerville Hotel (now a root beer saloon), flies the Union Jack. At the end of the main street is St. Saviour's Anglican Church, built of whipsawn timber and square nails, and with window glass freighted in from Victoria (for six times the price of the glass itself).

timber, and Billy Barker's mine shaft, where it all started one August day in 1862.

Barker, a Cornish seaman, made his strike four years after the first wave of fortune-seekers reached British Columbia. But early discoveries in the sandbars of the Fraser and Thompson rivers and the creeks of the Quesnel River simply set the stage for Barker's fabulous strike on Williams Creek. Almost overnight a town erupted around his claim—a confusion of false-front firetraps glowering across a narrow, muddy main street. They called it Barkerville. It was a place where a "hurdy-gurdy" girl collected $10 for dancing a few minutes with a lonesome miner whose boots had cost him $50. But if the cost of living and living it up was high, some men's Cariboo reward was phenomenal. Williams Creek alone surrendered gold worth $50,000,000. Billy Barker's take was some $600,000.

Fire all but destroyed the town in 1868. A new Barkerville rose from the ashes but never reached the size of the original. Then, inevitably, the gold began to peter out. By 1894 when Barker died in poverty in Victoria, the town named for him was dying too.

BOWRON LAKE PARK This 475 square miles of wilderness is framed by a rectangular chain of six major lakes. The park entrance is 10 miles north and east of here.

CARIBOO CAMERON'S GRAVE John A. "Cariboo" Cameron from Glengarry County in Ontario was another big winner on Williams Creek. He lost everything in a gold-mining gamble in Nova Scotia, returned to the Cariboo and, like Barker, died penniless.

RICHFIELD COURTHOUSE A 30-minute walk from Barkerville is Richfield where, in a restored courthouse, a bearded and bewigged actor plays Judge Matthew Baillie Begbie, who did much to preserve law and order during the gold rush. A stern but just man, he did not deserve his ugly sobriquet, "Hanging Judge." He became chief justice of British Columbia in 1870 and was knighted in 1875.

ST. SAVIOUR'S CHURCH Designed and built by the Rev. James Reynard, it replaced a church destroyed in the 1868 fire.

THEATER ROYAL Melodrama and music of the gold-rush days are revived by professional actors in a 1½-hour show such as the miners used to see.

THE CARIBOO SENTINEL The editor and proprietor of the Barkerville newspaper, Joshua Spencer Thompson, pretty well ran the town during the gold rush. He is believed to have been largely responsible for the Cariboo flag: a beaver surrounded by a wreath of maple leaves on a white ground in the center of the Union Jack.

WAKE-UP JAKE "Bakery, Coffee Saloon and Lunch House," it was called. Nothing stronger than coffee was ever served.

Barlochan Ont.   7CY
Appropriately for a museum in the Muskoka lake country, Woodwinds Historical Museum

Milady bathes in water that she heats with a tiny stove in the foot of her tub. Other pioneer devices at the Simcoe County Museum near Barrie include the huge wheeled stone picker (opposite). It dates from about 1860.

at Barlochan (Walker's Point) can be reached by boat. It is made up of a log church, a log house and a museum building containing such Muskoka relics as a much-mended copper kettle that Indian women used for maple sugaring and a pair of fitted leather logging boots with spikes.

Barrhead Alta.   4AW/14EV
The centennial museum in this northern Alberta town contains articles on loan from local residents. Among them are a pair of piano vases believed 300 years old, a settler's home gristmill and imitation fireplace, a hand-powered vacuum cleaner (c.1909) and a century-old wedding dress.

Barrie Ont.   7CY/17BW
A marker in Memorial Square indicates the east end of Nine Mile Portage, which led to Willow Creek Depot, an important supply base during and after the War of 1812. Its palisade and log buildings were roughly midway between York (Toronto) and the British posts on the upper Great Lakes. Supplies were carried over the Toronto portage to the southern tip of Lake Simcoe, then shipped to the head of Kempenfeldt Bay (now the site of Barrie). Nine Mile Portage led from here to Willow Creek, a tributary of the Nottawasaga River, which flows into Georgian Bay. The storage depot, also called Fort Willow, was on high ground about a mile from the creek landing. The North West Company's David Thompson walked Nine

Mile Portage; so did Sir John Franklin, in 1825, on his way to Penetanguishene, his jump-off for the Arctic.

□ The Barrie Winter Carnival, usually in February, has an air show, parachute drops and dogsled races. An estimated 5,000 fish huts dot Lake Simcoe in winter at Barrie, Keswick, Lefroy, Jacksons Point and Sutton.

□ Five miles north of Barrie are the Simcoe County Museum and Archives. An Indian wing tells the story of man in this part of the world from about 10,000 B.C. to the downfall of Huronia in 1650. Other exhibits include Indian handicrafts, a display about the War of 1812 and pioneer section.

Behind the museum is a log house built in 1834 and furnished in the style of the pioneers. Barns contain pioneer tools, blacksmith and cooper displays and a collection of sleighs, democrats and buggies. On the grounds is one of Ontario's few remaining wooden windmills.

□ Near town is Molson Park, a 70-acre recreation and conservation area with year-round activities including picnics, a Grass Roots music concert, an antique car show, dog shows, and cross-country skiing.

Barriefield Ont.   7DY/18CZ
In this town, east across the Cataraqui River from Kingston, are Vimy and McNaughton Barracks (where the 1st Canadian Signals Regiment is based), the Canadian Forces School of Communications and Electrical Engineers and a Canadian Forces hospital.

St. Mark's Anglican Church was built in 1843.

Barrington N.S.   9DZ/22BY
The oldest nonconformist house of worship left in Canada is Barrington's Old Meeting

House, run by the Cape Sable Historical Society for the Nova Scotia Museum. It was built in 1765 by New England Nonconformists (a strict fundamentalist sect). The first group came from Cape Cod in 1760, the second from Nantucket the following year.

The Old Meeting House, by New England custom, served as town hall as well as church until, around 1838, some of the congregation insisted it be a house of worship only. The minutes of an 1838 meeting record that "the Town meeting was held on the earth by the side of the Old Meeting House (the doors of which having been shut against the town)." Many meetings were held "outside" or "near" the Old Meeting House until a town hall (now the courthouse) was built in 1843.

A wall pulpit (c.1790) is reached by narrow steps and has a buttoned door. Ceiling beams are braced by "ship's knees," common when

Eastern Canada's last water-operated woolen mill, built in the 1880s, is now a Barrington museum. Like the town's Old Meeting House, it is run by the Cape Sable Historical Society.

most carpenters were shipbuilders. There was no stove until 1841, when finally it was conceded that a man needed more than the fire of his religion (and perhaps a foot-warmer) to keep warm through a three-hour gospel service. A wood and tin chandelier also dates from about 1841.

The oldest stones in the adjacent graveyard are head-and-foot slabs to Letitia Doane, who died in childbirth and was buried "with her Cheild in her Armes, July 26th, 1766." A plaque on a boulder in the graveyard honors Edmund Doane, an early settler, and his wife Elizabeth Osborn Myrick Paine, maternal grandmother of John Howard Paine, author of *Home, Sweet Home.*

Barrington Passage N.S.   9CZ/22BY
A 4,000-foot causeway connects the mainland with Cape Sable Island, Nova Scotia's most southerly point.

Bath Ont.   7DY/18BZ
A house that Loyalist Jeptha Hawley built here in the 1780s is one of the oldest in Ontario. Almost as old is Fairfield Place, built by William Fairfield, Jr., in 1796. (A house that Fairfield's father built at Amherstview in 1793 is another example of the homes of well-to-do Loyalists. It is extremely well preserved. See picture, this page.)

Bath was the seat of Upper Canada's first court and had its first sawmill, brewery, distillery and steamship-building yard. A cairn marks where the first Canadian steamship on the Great Lakes was launched Sept. 8, 1816. The 170-foot, 700-ton *Frontenac* was completed in May the next year but missed being the first steamship on the Great Lakes. The smaller American steamer *Ontario* sailed a few days before her.

□ Two miles west is Willowbank Forge, where 2,700 historic iron pieces are displayed. In owner Tom Riedel's house (c.1850) is a huge cooking fireplace (c.1770) typical of New France.

Bathurst N.B.   9DW
A cairn honors Nicolas Denys, French "Governor of the coasts and islands of the St. Lawrence" and author of one of the first books about the area. Published in Paris in 1672, it describes Acadia and the manners and customs of the Indians. Denys started several lumber and fishing operations in Acadia and was Canada's first lumber exporter. His last venture was in Bathurst (then Nepisiguit).

Until a base metals mining boom in 1953 the major industry here was boxboard and pulp. Groups may tour the plant of the Brunswick Mining and Smelting Corp.—Mining Division on request.

Sacré-Coeur Cathedral and the Collège de Bathurst (an affiliate of the Université de Moncton) are here.

□ Upstream on the Nepisiguit River is Grand Falls, a series of cataracts where the river drops 140 feet.

The Fairfield White House (above) at Amherstview, Ont., and the manor at Batiscan present an interesting contrast in early Canadian styles.

□ Tetagouche Falls on the Tetagouche River is the focal point of a day-use provincial park. The falls drop about 30 feet through a deep, narrow gorge.

Batiscan Que.   20AX
A handsome 17th-century fieldstone house —the rectory and manor house of Jesuit priests who were Batiscan's first seigneurs—is preserved in a small provincial park.

Batoche Sask.   4DX
Here in 1885 the Métis made a final futile bid to keep alive their fledgling independent prairie state. The remains of the Métis nation's "capital" include the tiny Church of Saint-Antoine-de-Padoue (1884), a nearby rectory still bearing the scars of battle, and a cemetery. Batoche Letendre's store and the houses that made up the rest of Batoche have disappeared, victims of war and weather. The rectory, which contains a small museum, and trenches, which survived years of plowing, are a national historic site.

Cemetery at Batoche, where Métis dreams died as the Northwest Rebellion was crushed in 1885.

□ The first seeds of the 1885 rebellion in Saskatchewan were sown in Manitoba's Red River Valley in 1812. With the arrival of Lord Selkirk's Scots, the Métis—offspring of Indian mothers and white fathers—learned that land did not necessarily belong to men who were born and lived on it. More and more settlers arrived and in 1869, when the Hudson's Bay Company sold the west to the Canadian government, surveyors ran lines across the Métis strip farms, each with its river frontage that guaranteed access for irrigation and transportation. The Métis rebelled and formed a provisional government under Louis Riel. The Canadian government moved quickly. Manitoba was made a province and 1,400,000 acres were set aside for Métis settlement. But Riel was exiled and when the government offered scrip, entitling each holder to 240 acres, the leaderless Métis did not understand its value. Many did not collect it, others sold it for a fraction of its worth. Further demoralized by the loss of freighting jobs when steamboats started operating, the Métis headed for the valley of the South Saskatchewan River.

For almost 15 years they survived on marginal farmland and Batoche became their unofficial capital. In 1884, after the government ignored petitions to grant them land rights, the Métis sent for Riel, then in Montana. His moderate program of reform gained no sympathy in Ottawa.

Riel knew of an impending solar eclipse. He told the Métis and Indians that if God were on their side He would blot out the sun on March 16, 1885. The "prophecy" came true and three days later Riel formed a provisional government, with Gabriel Dumont as his commander-in-chief. Within a week a Métis-Indian band crushed a force of 100 police and volunteers at Duck Lake. Militia units were organized in Ontario and Quebec and 850 men led by Maj. Gen. Frederick Middleton went west by CPR. After several brilliant Métis-Indian victories, Dumont wanted to harass Middleton's troops as they moved north. But Riel forced him into a static defense at Batoche. With about 160 men Dumont built an elaborate system of trenches and rifle pits.

Middleton and his main force of about 700 men arrived at Batoche May 8. For three days the Métis held, but on the fourth day two of Middleton's battalions launched a full-scale attack, using the new multibarreled Gatling gun which fired up to 500 rounds a minute. The Métis were reduced to charging their muzzle-loaders with nails and gravel. In two hours Batoche was taken.

Riel escaped, surrendered a few days later, was tried for treason and hanged at Regina. Dumont fled to the United States and joined William "Buffalo Bill" Cody's Wild West Show. As "Prince of the Plains," he entertained around the world with his sharpshooting and riding skill. Granted amnesty, he returned to Batoche; there he died in 1906. A large stone marks his grave.

□ The rectory museum displays facsimiles of letters written by Riel, his prayer book, brass pen case and inkwell; the diary of Peter Hourie, one of the men to whom Riel surrendered, and Dumont's revolver and braided bridle.

Battleford Sask. *see* North Battleford

Bay Bulls Nfld. 11DZ
A hint of this fishing community's stormy history is in the four old cannon used as gateposts at the Roman Catholic church.

Saints Patrick, Paul, Joseph and Theresa stand atop upright cannon at a church in Bay Bulls.

Bear River N.S.—This Annapolis Valley town is noted for its cherry trees and for a cherry festival usually held in July. (9DZ/22BW)

Settled in the early 16th century, Bay Bulls, one of Newfoundland's oldest settlements, was repeatedly attacked by the French and Dutch.

Bay Fortune P.E.I.　　　　　　9EX/23DW
The regard of a great playwright and a famous actress for a little-known character actor is perpetuated in this community where American theater people used to summer. A sundial on private property on Abell's Cape, sometimes called Flockton's Cape, was erected in memory of Charles Flockton by David Belasco and Mrs. Leslie Carter. The English-born Flockton had a summer home in Bay Fortune and when he died in 1904 his ashes were brought here. Belasco at one time managed Mrs. Carter, who starred in his play *Du Barry*. Her most famous role was in *The Heart of Maryland* (1895-98).

Bear Island Ont. *see* Temagami

Beauceville Que.　　　　　　9AX/20CX
Saint-François-d'Assise-de-Beauce Church contains many outstanding examples of religious art, including paintings by Antoine Plamondon and Alphonse Ferland and an ornate wooden pulpit by Ferdinand Villeneuve. Much ornamental sculpture and the two side altars were done by Adolphe Dion in 1815. That same year François Baillargé, probably assisted by his son Thomas, decorated the symbolic tomb of Christ in the high altar. Bronze cherubs hold a medallion which pictures the Madonna and Child. Many sculptures are covered with gold leaf.
　□ In Beauceville-Est a plaque marks the house where poet William Chapman was born in 1850. He was a leading French writer of the Quebec patriotic school and three volumes of his poetry were awarded prizes by the Académie française.

Beauharnois Que.　　　　　　7FY/19BY
A highway runs under one of two St. Lawrence Seaway locks here. They and a canal connect Lac Saint-Louis and, 78 feet higher, Lake St. Francis. Both lakes are widenings of the St. Lawrence River. The canal takes ships around the Beauharnois dam and a big hydroelectric power plant.
　Beauharnois was part of a seigniory granted in 1729 to the Marquis de Beauharnois, governor of New France for 21 years. A stone house on Richardson Street, the oldest house in the city, was Canadian headquarters during the Battle of Châteauguay in 1813.
　□ At the Domtar Limited plant visitors see paper being made.

Beaumont Que.　　　　　　20CW
On the door of Saint-Etienne de Beaumont Church, then only 26 years old, British troops in 1759 posted Wolfe's proclamation demanding surrender of the Canadians. When villagers tore down the proclamation, soldiers set fire to the church. But only the door was

Johnny Belinda

Playwright Elmer Harris, once a summer resident of Bay Fortune, based his drama *Johnny Belinda* on events in the nearby community of Dingwell's Mills. A Hollywood movie version of the story about a deaf-mute girl relocated the story in Nova Scotia's Cape Breton Island.

burned. The damage has long since been repaired. The church, built in 1733, and a nearby presbytery (1722), are among Quebec's oldest buildings. Two procession chapels are in the style of the church.

Beauport Que.   9AX/20BW
This is one of Canada's oldest communities (1634), the first settled parish on the Beaupré coast. Part of the Aimé Marcoux house was built in 1655, and the Cléophas Girardin house is about 300 years old. A plaque marks another house as the birthplace of Charles-Michel de Salaberry, whose victory as Canadian commander in the 1813 Battle of Châteauguay, near Montreal, averted an American invasion of Canada.

Beausejour Man.   6BY/15EX
A Farewell to Winter is Beausejour's annual carnival capitalization on a climate described as "10 months of winter and two months of tough sledding." The festivities each February feature the Canadian Power Toboggan Championships.

Beauvoir Hill Que. *see* Sherbrooke

Beaverdams Ont. *see* Thorold

Beaverlodge Alta.   1BZ/3EV
One of the first homesteaders in this part of northern Alberta was an Ontario Agricultural College graduate on whose farm was established what is now the Beaverlodge Research Station. W. D. Albright came west in 1913, before the railroad. Two years later, with Albright as superintendent, experimental work started on land leased from him. The federal government bought 314 acres in 1940.

□ A rough 80-mile road into British Columbia leads to the South Pine River and spectacular Kinuseo Falls, 300 feet wide and 200 feet high.

□ Near Beaverlodge is one of the few nesting areas of the rare trumpeter swan.

Beeton Ont.   7CY/17BW
This village was named Clarksville (for the first settler), then Tecumseth (for the township it's in), then, in 1878, to honor postmaster David Allanson Jones . . . not Jonesville but Beeton. He had imported queen bees from Europe in 1867, starting Canada's commercial honey industry and making Clarksville/Tecumseth North America's "bee town." Jones is commemorated by a plaque in Beeton Community Park.

Belfast P.E.I.   9EX/23DX
Stones at the base of a monument to Belfast's first Scottish settlers were ballast in *Polly*, one of three ships that landed them in 1803. The 20-foot granite shaft is outside St. John's Presbyterian Church (1823), whose 16-foot steeple resembles the style of Sir Christopher Wren. The church archives contain the original deed for the land that Lord Selkirk, founder of the settlement, donated for a church and cemetery. Outside the church is a monument to Lord Selkirk's daughter Mary Douglas, whom he brought to Belfast as a child and who died here in 1859, at the age of 60.

Beaupré Que.—Four-passenger gondolas on a 7,700-foot-long main lift carry skiers to Mont-Sainte-Anne's 2,625-foot summit in 13 minutes. The mountain's upper reaches have snow until well into spring. Mont-Sainte-Anne Park was developed by the town of Beaupré. (20CW)

Belfountain Ont.　　　　　　　　7CY/17BX

A church built in 1837 by Scottish immigrants, most from the Hebridean islands of Islay and Mull, is preserved by the Credit Valley Conservation Authority. A stone in the church cemetery marks the grave of two men named Duncan McNabb, uncle and nephew, aged 85 and 78, killed by a falling tree while clearing land.

Bella Coola B.C.　　　　　　　　2BW

Alexander Mackenzie, from Canada, by land, the twenty-second of July, one thousand seven hundred and ninety-three.

Painted on a rock in Dean Channel near here, with a mixture of vermilion and grease, these words recorded the first crossing of the continent—north of Mexico—by a white man.

Weather soon erased the inscription but the famous words have been embedded with red cement in what is believed to be Mackenzie's Rock, the focal point of Sir Alexander Mackenzie Provincial Park.

□ The Bella Coola Indians once numbered 5,000 in villages along the Bella Coola River. Disease all but destroyed the tribe and there are now only about 600, all in Bella Coola. Many buildings and sidewalks in the village are built of hewn planks. There are several fine totems.

□ The highway to Williams Lake, almost 300 miles inland, starts through the Bella Coola River valley, a lush rain forest of huge evergreens, moss and vines. The road then heads across the Fraser Plateau, cutting through the southern part of Tweedsmuir Provincial Park (*see* Burns Lake).

Belleville Ont.　　　　　　　　7DY/18AZ

Lighting devices that range from boat, buggy and bicycle lamps to a candle holder meant to clip onto a Bible are displayed at the Hastings County Museum. The more than 300 devices, collected by Dr. and Mrs. William Paul, include torches, two saucer lamps from Palestine (c.600 B.C.) and candles from ancient Rome (twisted fibers of papyrus dipped in sulphur and coated with wax). There are examples of containers for the flint and steel used before matches: a "gentle-

Bobcaygeon Ont.   7CY/17DV

Most of this resort village is on an island between Pigeon and Sturgeon lakes. A monument commemorates the construction of a lock to connect the two lakes, part of the Trent Canal System, in 1839.

Boischatel Que.   20CW

New earthworks have been built on the site of a redoubt used by British troops prior to the Battle of Montmorency on July 31, 1759. They are near a house said to have been Wolfe's headquarters for three days. In the house, whose stone walls are 3-4 feet thick, is a small museum with exhibits telling of Montcalm's victory over Wolfe at Montmorency. The house and the redoubt are in Montmorency Park. Nearby are two similar houses built about 1661 by a family called Vézina and, more than three centuries later, still occupied by Vézinas. The houses are not open to the public.

◻ De Charleville manor was built in 1677 in *pavillon français* style: the steep roof has four sides. The house is furnished with antiques, many dating to the 1700s. It may be toured only by special permission.

Boissevain Man.   6AZ

Sixteen miles from the Canada-U.S. border, Boissevain is the nearest Canadian town to the International Peace Garden (*see entry*). The Beckoning Hills Museum displays household and field relics of the prairie pioneers.

Bonaventure Que.   9DW

An historical museum here is in a 200-year-old building that was among the first built by the community's Acadian settlers. It contains Acadian cradles, spinning wheels, looms and tools and a collection of fossils estimated to be 400,000,000 years old.

The Festival of Saint Bonaventure (early summer) includes a 23-mile boat race across

Minas Basin shore near Blomidon is studded with unusual rock formations. Nova Scotia amethyst (lower photo) is from the same region.

Chaleur Bay from Petit Rocher, N.B., to Bonaventure. The best five-man crews make the crossing in 22-foot boats in about 3½ hours. Other festival features are a concert, a parade, horse races and exhibitions of Gaspé crafts, paintings and photographs.

Bonavista Nfld.   11DY

When it began operating in 1842, the Cape Bonavista lighthouse had a light from the Bell Rock (or Inchcape Rock) lighthouse in the North Sea off Arbroath, Scotland. That light was replaced by the present one, which is dated 1816 and probably came from the lighthouse at Harbour Grace, Nfld. The original Inchcape light has disappeared. The lighthouse, gallery and apparatus are open to visitors during the summer.

A statue of John Cabot stands on Cape Bonavista, which may have been the explorer's landfall in 1497.

Bonavista, one of Newfoundland's oldest communities, has a population of 4,200 and has been called the largest all-fishing town

Fish houses at Blue Rocks are built on stilts and reached by dory. Fishermen use the 12-by-14-foot "posts" to clean catches.

in the province. Its important cod industry has grown with the establishment of an artificial drying plant and cold-storage facilities. Deep-sea fishermen take tuna, swordfish, porpoise and dolphins in Bonavista Bay.

At Spillers Cove, near the cape, sea action has formed a double grotto in the rock.

Bond Head Ont. 17BW
Historic plaques commemorate two men born in this village 25 miles north of Toronto: Sir William Osler (1849-1919), one of the world's great doctors, and Sir William Mulock (1843-1944), postmaster general and minister of labor under Laurier, later chancellor of the University of Toronto and chief justice of Ontario. A special service for physicians and surgeons is held annually at Trinity Anglican Church (1845) to honor "the father of clinical medicine." This is "The Doctors' Church," where Osler's father was rector.

Bon Echo Ont. 7DY/18AX
A mile-long wall of granite known as Canada's Gibraltar thrusts some 375-400 feet straight up from the dark waters on the east side of Mazinaw Lake in Bon Echo Provincial Park. Just above the water are undeciphered Indian paintings done in red ocher and adhered to the rock with bear grease or fish eggs. Also on the rock is a memorial inscribed in 1919 and dedicated to the democratic ideals of the American poet Walt Whitman.

The 135 Bon Echo rock paintings are more numerous but less clearly defined than those on the north shore of Lake Superior (*see* Agawa). Their age, origin and meaning have not been determined.

Rabbit Man on a cliff face at Bon Echo may be Ojibway in origin, could represent a legendary hero and demigod who was traditionally a hare.

Mason Steamer at Bonshaw is steered by tiller, has maple paneling and one-candlepower lamps.

The Whitman memorial, dedicated by Flora Macdonald Denison (her family then owned the rock) and Horace Traubel, Whitman's friend and biographer, is on a part of the rock called Old Walt. The inscription includes these words by Whitman:

> My foothold is tenon'd and mortis'd
> in granite,
> I laugh at what you call dissolution,
> And I know the amplitude of time.

Author Merrill Denison, son of Flora, gave his property to the Ontario government in 1957 as a memorial to his mother and for conservation, recreation and education. With Crown land added, it was opened as a provincial park.

Bonshaw P.E.I. 9EX/23CX
A two-cylinder, five-horsepower car that runs on naphtha and has a boiler the size of a kettle—an 1898 Mason Steamer—is a prize exhibit in the Car Life Museum. Other exhibits are a 1914 Massey-Harris tractor, a 1918 Ford truck, a 1920 McLaughlin Buick, a 1925 Model T Ford touring car, a 1931 Willys sedan.

Strathgartney Homestead, built in 1846-47, is a big house overlooking Northumberland Strait and richly furnished in the Victorian style of pioneer Prince Edward Island. There are a century-old walnut table, a Franklin stove with the Last Supper depicted on the fireguard, a colonial fireplace and interesting tapestries, candle molds, china and pottery.

Borden Ont. 7CY/17BW
Fighting vehicles ranging from a World War I Whippet tank to a flail tank that beat through German minefields in Normandy in 1944 are on public display at CFB Borden. They are in Worthington Park, an outdoor museum named for Maj. Gen. F.F. Worthington, "father of the Armored Corps." Some other vehicles on display are the Churchill tank (first used at Dieppe in 1942), the Ram (which, with turret removed, became the Kangaroo personnel carrier of World War II), several versions of the Sherman tank, and the Staghound armored car.

The Worthington Museum, a building

near the outdoor display, has been expanded to incorporate several Borden museums. Among its highlights: a Canadian medical officer's field operating kit used in the South African War; German medical instruments (c.1937); uniforms of the Canadian Corps of Guides, forerunner of the Intelligence Corps; Canadian and enemy weapons, including a German curved 9-millimeter barrel that was attached to a rifle or machine gun for street fighting; Canadian and U.S. equipment for detecting radiation and fallout.

□ CFB Borden was established (as Camp Borden) during World War I and was Canada's biggest military camp until Camp Gagetown (N.B.) was opened in 1958. Borden special events open to the public include Canadian Forces Day in June and the November 11 Armistice Day parade.

Borden P.E.I.   9EX/23BW
Northumberland Strait car ferries link Borden with Cape Tormentine, N.B. One, the *Abegweit,* carries up to 16 railway boxcars as well as automobiles. She and the *John Hamilton Gray* were built as icebreakers and make the nine-mile trip in winter when other ferries are tied up.

Boston Bar B.C.   2DY/12GW
An electrically powered aerial ferry linking Boston Bar and North Bend takes 40 persons (or one three-ton vehicle) across the Fraser River canyon in 3½ minutes. The ferry car, suspended from 1,208 feet of 1¾-inch cables, is 90 feet above the turbulent Fraser at low water; 30 feet at high water.

Boucherville Que.   7FY/19BX
Sainte-Famille Church, built in 1801 and decorated in the style of the Opéra at Versailles, contains an important collection of religious art and has been designated an historic monument. Among many wood sculptures is a tabernacle probably designed by the Rev. Augustin Quintal, a Recollet priest, and carved about 1745 by Gilles Bolvin. *The Good Shepherd* (c.1745) is also by Bolvin; side altars and tabernacles (1807-8) are by Louis Quevillon, and baptismal fonts (c.1880) by Nicolas Manny. Among many paintings

La Chaumière, the oldest house in Boucherville, dates from about 1741.

High altar in Sainte-Famille Church at Boucherville. Above the tomb (foreground) is the tabernacle. The center stool is the celebrant's.

are three by Jean-Baptiste Roy-Audy. Exquisite gold and silver pieces include a censer, incense box and sanctuary lamp created by Michel Arnoldi about 1790. In the parish archives is the baptismal certificate of an Indian child, dated May 20, 1668, and signed by the Rev. Jacques Marquette, a Jesuit missionary who was interpreter to Louis Jolliet on his 1673 voyage of discovery down the Mississippi River.

Bowmanville Ont.   7CY/17DX
In an 1861 Ontario classic house, now the Bowmanville Museum, are an "old-time store" with boots, bitters and hog cure on its shelves, and exhibits of clothing and furniture from pioneer days to the early 1900s. There are collections of dolls and toys, and of pianos and organs made locally.

Bracebridge Ont.   7CY
This one-time lumber town in the heart of Muskoka is a year-round resort center. Its annual events are an international curling bonspiel in February and the Muskoka Arts and Crafts Festival in July. The Muskoka Winter Carnival is held in Bracebridge, Huntsville and Gravenhurst in late January and early February.

□ Near Bracebridge is St. Peter's on the Rock, a church constructed of hewn timber.

□ At Santa's Village, 3½ miles west, children meet Santa Claus, visit toy workshops, see storybook characters and ride a miniature train and a paddle-wheeler.

□ Dinosaur Park, 10 miles north, has a replica of a prehistoric village and life-size dinosaur models.

□ The 1,600-square-mile Muskoka District contains numerous lakes, more than 300 islands, beaches, waterfalls, rapids and vast forests. Hay fever sufferers find relief in the pine-scented air of an area that is ideal for boating, canoeing and other water sports. One of many lodges is Windermere House, opened in 1869 by a Shetland Islander, Thomas Aitken, and now run by his grand-daughter. Main lakes in the region are Muskoka, Rosseau and Joseph.

Brackley P.E.I.—Broad sand beaches are part of Prince Edward Island National Park. Opened in 1860, Brackley was the island province's first tourist area. Some dunes here are 60 feet high. (9EX/23CW)

Bradford Ont. 7CY/17CW
Mossy headstones at the Auld Kirk near here mark the graves of Scottish settlers who fled east in the early 1800s to escape the troubles of Lord Selkirk's Red River Colony. Plagued by crop failures and harassed by the North West Company, the first of about 140 arrived in this area in 1819. They held their first Presbyterian service, in Gaelic, in 1823. A frame church built in 1827 was replaced by the brick kirk in 1869. It is no longer used for services. Two graves in the churchyard are those of John Diefenbaker's maternal grandparents, George and Christina Bannerman.
  □ Prof. William Henry Day, who saw the market-garden possibilities of the Holland River valley when it was a swampy wasteland, is honored by a plaque and cairn at the Bradford town hall. Day came here from Guelph, Ont., in 1924 and harvested the first Holland Marsh crop in 1928. (*See* Ansnorveldt)

Bralorne B.C. 2CY
This former gold-mining town is in Bridge River country, where steep mountains rise from the riverbed to jagged peaks 4,000-5,000 feet above sea level. Mountains and waterways teem with game and fish.
  Rock blasted from mountains around Bralorne yielded gold worth more than $145,000,000 in 40 years. The last mine was shut down in 1971.

Brampton Ont. 7CY/17BX
Canada's most extensive greenhouses cover a total area almost as big as two dozen football fields. The major grower in "Flower Town" produces roses, chrysanthemums and potted plants under some 1,500,000 square feet of glass.
  □ Exhibits in the County of Peel Museum and Art Gallery trace the development of agriculture, industry and transportation in this area.
  □ North of Brampton are the Caledon Hills, where the Credit River winds through pleasant valleys and deep gorges. Two of Ontario's prominent geological features meet here: the Niagara Escarpment and the Oak Ridges moraine, a range of high hills created by retreating glaciers.

Brandon Man. 6AY
A log fort built in Churchill Park in 1967 is representative of eight trading posts that existed at various times in this part of southern Manitoba. A collection of pioneer artifacts is displayed in a log building inside the palisade.
  □ Brandon University was started as Brandon College in 1899. As a Baptist Church institution it was affiliated with the University of Manitoba until 1911, then with McMaster University in Hamilton, Ont., until 1938. At that time it became a nondenominational college and reassumed its U of M affiliation. In 1967 it became Brandon University. The university houses the B.J. Hales Museum of Natural History, a collection of mounted birds and animals, and Indian artifacts and items of pioneer agricultural settlement.
  □ The Manitoba Provincial Exhibition and Western Canada Trade Fair, in August, has livestock and horticultural exhibits; 4-H Club, handicraft and home-cooking competitions; parades, a midway and a grandstand show. In April, the Royal Manitoba Winter Fair features livestock exhibitions, trade displays and horse competitions.
  □ Eight miles northwest is Mount Glenorchy, a ski resort on the slopes of the Assiniboine Valley.
  □ Just east of Brandon is a cairn on the site of Grand Valley, a terminus for boats that steamed the Assiniboine River from 1879 to 1885. They carried cargo and passengers 200 miles downstream to Winnipeg and another 200 miles to Fort Pelly, Sask. The settlement disappeared soon after the CPR established Brandon as a divisional point.

Brantford Ont. 7BZ/17BY
A Mohawk chief gave Brantford its name and much of its rich heritage, and a Scottish-born inventor brought it world attention as

the birthplace of the telephone. Joseph Brant led the Six Nations here in 1784 when allegiance to the British Crown cost them their lands in New York's Mohawk Valley. Less than 100 years later, at a homestead a few miles downriver from Brant's Ford, Alexander Graham Bell proved his conviction that he could transmit the human voice by wire.

The city boasts of other famous persons, among them novelists Sara Jeannette Duncan and Thomas B. Costain, and other firsts: the world's first railway "sleeper" car was built here and in 1945 Brantford became the first Canadian city to fluoridate its water.

BELL HOMESTEAD (1) Here Alexander Graham Bell lived when he came to Canada from Scotland at 23 and later, on a visit from Boston, visualized the telephone. Said Bell: "The conception of the telephone took place during the summer visit to my father's residence in Brantford in 1874 and the apparatus was just as it was subsequently made, a one-membrane telephone on either end. The experiment of Aug. 10, 1876, made from Brantford to Paris [Ont.] was the first transmission, the first clear, intelligible [long-distance] transmission of speech . . . that had ever been made." The Bell house, on Tutela Heights Road, is a national historic site run by a local committee. It contains many of the Bell family's original furnishings.

BELL MEMORIAL (2) Bell himself, on Oct. 24, 1917, attended the unveiling of this im-

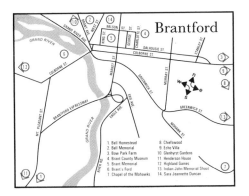

The Bell Homestead at Brantford was where Alexander Graham Bell conceived the telephone.

pressive monument to the invention of the telephone.

BOW PARK FARM (3) George Brown, founder of *The Globe* in Toronto and one of the principal architects of Confederation, owned this farm estate at Cainsville, just east of Brantford.

BRANT COUNTY MUSEUM (4) The museum has an extensive collection of pioneer and Indian artifacts, old firefighting equipment, an armory of antique weapons, rooms of period furniture, and displays honoring Bell, Brant, Costain, Indian poetess E. Pauline Johnson, and Ontario's fourth premier, Arthur Sturgis Hardy.

BRANT MEMORIAL (5) The Joseph Brant of this bronze and granite monument in Victoria Park is nine feet tall. Below him are the Six Nations, which sculptor Percy Wood represented with six life-size Indian figures in two groups. On two other sides of the pedestal, against backgrounds of snowshoes, tomahawks, war clubs, peace pipes and arrows, are inscribed the names of the Six Nations—Mohawks, Cayugas, Senecas, Onondagas, Oneidas, Tuscaroras—and Brant's Indian name, Thayendanegea. Bas-reliefs on the base of the monument represent a war dance, a council, a bear and a wolf.

BRANT'S FORD (6) An inscribed sundial in Lorne Park is at a Grand River bend where the Six Nations took up land given them by George III for their support during the American Revolution.

CHAPEL OF THE MOHAWKS (7) St. Paul's, Her Majesty's Chapel of the Mohawks, the first Protestant church in what is now Ontario, was built in 1785 with the aid of a grant from George III. From the Queen Anne Chapel at Fort Hunter, N.Y., the Indians brought a Bible and silver Communion vessels given them by Queen Anne more than 70 years before. In the churchyard are the tombs of Brant and his son John, who fought for the English in the War of 1812.

CHIEFSWOOD (8) Erected in 1853 by Chief G. H. M. Johnson of the Six Nations, this mansion was the birthplace of poet E. Pauline Johnson, the voice of Canadian Indians.

ECHO VILLA (9) The Rev. Peter Jones, Methodist missionary and preacher, built this house. He was the son of a pioneer land surveyor, Augustus Jones, and a Mississauga

Belts of wampum are presented to Queen Anne by Six Nations Indians who went to London in 1710. The window is in St. Paul's, Her Majesty's Chapel of the Mohawks, in Brantford.

chief's daughter. Jones converted many Indians and translated the Gospels and some hymns into Ojibwa.

GLENHYRST GARDENS (10) In this 11-room mansion, bequeathed to Brantford by E. L. Cockshutt, is The Glenhyrst Arts Council, backed by 16 community organizations. An antiques show is held every May.

HENDERSON HOUSE (11) Canada's first telephone business office was in the Rev. Thomas Henderson's house in downtown Brantford. The house, moved to the Bell homestead grounds in 1968, contains a typical early telephone exchange with a 50-line switchboard, the first to be designed specifically for telephone use.

HIGHLAND GAMES (12) Pipe bands, Scottish dancing and caber tossing feature Highland games held at Brant Park in July.

INDIAN JOHN MEMORIAL SHOOT (13) This first-rank North American competition is named for the Cayuga chief John Van Every, born on the Six Nations Reserve and widely known as a guide, woodsman and archery expert. About 125 archers compete each June.

SARA JEANNETTE DUNCAN (14) One of her 19 books, *The Imperialist*, deals with life in Brantford at the turn of the century. There is a plaque in front of her childhood home.

Bridgetown N.S. 9DY/22CV

This small community of fine old houses nestles near the head of navigation on the Annapolis River, in an area settled by Acadians in the 1650s, later by New Englanders and, after 1776, United Empire Loyalists. Two ambushes, in 1711 and 1757, in which French and Indians killed a total of 54 soldiers from

Annapolis Royal, are commemorated by a cairn at nearby Bloody Creek.

□ Mountain Park, between Bridgetown and Hampton, on the brow of North Mountain, gives a 50-mile view of the Annapolis Valley, from Greenwood air station to CFB Cornwallis.

Bridgetown P.E.I. 9EX/23DW

Wave action on rocks at the west end of Boughton Island have created a "natural armchair."

Bridgewater N.S. 9DZ/22DW

Situated on wooded hills overlooking the La Have River, one of Nova Scotia's better salmon streams, Bridgewater is the biggest town in Lunenburg County.

In the Des Brisay Museum the story of Lunenburg County is told with artifacts collected by Judge Mather Byles Des Brisay. They are of Micmac, French, English and German origin. Some German Bibles date from 1669.

The museum is in a 25-acre town park which includes a quarter-mile-long pond, a bird sanctuary and nature trails.

The International Ox-Pulling Championships are held in early August at the South Shore Exhibition.

Brighton Ont. 7DY/17EW

Presqu'ile Provincial Park, a curved spit of land jutting into Lake Ontario, provides a natural harbor for Brighton and a 2,000-acre expanse of marshes, forests, meadows and beaches. Presqu'ile Point lighthouse is no longer in service but the lightkeeper's house has been converted into a museum explaining the history and ecology of the region. Gravel "fingers" extending into the marshes support tree cover typical of forests 200 miles to the north. Offshore islands (which are inaccessible to the public) are breeding grounds for gulls and terns.

Brigus Nfld. 11DZ

Wooden houses in this town at the head of Conception Bay date from Brigus' great days as a codfishing and sealing center. Two thousand men in 66 vessels went sealing from Brigus in 1847; today fewer than two dozen fishermen go out from the town.

◻ Brigus was the birthplace of Capt. Robert Abram "Bob" Bartlett, the Arctic explorer. The son and grandson of men who navigated sailing ships in Arctic waters, Bartlett was first officer in Lt. Robert Edwin Peary's *Windward* in 1897 and commanded the *Roosevelt* on Peary's Arctic voyages in 1905-6 and 1908-9. In Vilhjalmur Stefansson's expedition in 1914 he led the crew of the whaling ship *Karluk* to safety five months after they had been feared lost. From 1926 to 1941 he made annual Arctic cruises.

Brilliant B.C. *see* Castlegar

Brockville Ont. 7EY/18CY

At the lower end of the Thousand Islands, Brockville is almost midway between the St. Lawrence River bridges at Ivy Lea and Johnstown. It was one of the first Loyalist settlements in Upper Canada and was named for Maj. Gen. Sir Isaac Brock, the War of 1812 hero.

BLOCKHOUSE ISLAND It got its name from a blockhouse built during the Rebellion of 1837-38 when "patriot" sympathizers threat-

The Bridge at Ivy Lea, between Brockville and Gananoque, soars across the Thousand Islands to Clayton and Alexandria Bay, N.Y.

Birch-bark cradle ornamented with dyed woven porcupine quills is probably the best-known example of Micmac Indian quill work. It was made in 1841 and is in the Des Brisay Museum in Bridgewater.

ened the Brockville area. Plague sheds had been constructed on the island during a cholera epidemic in 1832.

COURTHOUSE Built in 1842, the third courthouse on the site, this stone structure is one of Ontario's oldest public buildings.

HISTORIC PLAQUES Plaques commemorate R. Ogle Gowan (1796-1876), newspaperman, politician and soldier, who founded the

Grand Orange Lodge of British America; and George Chaffey (1848-1932), engineer and inventor, one of the great pioneers in irrigation. Chaffey established Australia's irrigated fruit-growing industry.

RAILWAY TUNNEL Massive oak doors stand at the entrance to a railway tunnel, Canada's oldest, built in 1854-60 to enable trains of the Brockville and Ottawa Railway to reach the riverfront here. The tunnel was used until 1954.

RECORDER AND TIMES Brockville's daily newspaper has been published since 1821, longer than any other paper in Ontario.

Bromont Que.   19DY
With 10 mountain peaks, two lakes and a superhighway at hand, Bromont was founded in 1964 by an Eastern Townships construction family with a vision of a "leisure city." The nine Desourdy brothers chose a site close enough to Montreal for commuting (45 minutes by autoroute) but too far ever to be incorporated into the metropolis. Planning and an airfield helped attract industry. As Bromont quickly became popular for skiing, and for golf, swimming and riding in summer, the town's population jumped from 200 to 2,000. In 1976, the Bromont Equestrian Center was the site of the Olympic riding events.

Brooklyn N.S.   9DZ/22DX
The Bowaters Mersey Paper Co. plant produces 180,000 tons of newsprint a year. Almost half is used by *The Washington Post.* There are tours during the summer months.

Dinosaur fossils preserved in rock are displayed in a provincial park near Brooks. Scores of skeletons from this area, part of the badlands along the Red Deer River, are in museums in Canada and the United States.

Brooks Alta.   4BY
Dinosaur Provincial Park, 30 miles northeast of Brooks, is the world's richest burial ground of prehistoric creatures. Skeletons of 70,000,000-year-old dinosaurs, relics of a time when Alberta was a tropical swamp, are dis-

played where they were found—but protected by stone shelters (*see* Drumheller).

In Dinosaur Park is the cabin of John Ware, who had been a slave in South Carolina. He became a cowboy and established one of Alberta's first ranches in the late 1800s.

□ A two-mile-long aqueduct near Brooks irrigates 50,000 acres of farmland. An inverted siphon carries the water under the CP mainline tracks.

□ Also near Brooks are the provincial pheasant farm, a 500-acre horticultural station that once was a CP demonstration farm, and Kinbrook Provincial Park on Lake Newell, Alberta's biggest artificial lake.

Brougham Ont.   17CX
A sturdy brick schoolhouse built in 1859—with high arched windows and a platform for the teacher's desk—is the main building of the Pickering Township Museum. It contains pioneer and Victorian furniture, clothing, toys and machines, and one of Ontario's best collections of pioneer tools. A two-story blacksmith shop in the museum complex (it was also a woodworking and paint shop) dates from 1856. Parts of an 1858 house have been left unrestored to show that all walls are formed by boards laid one atop another.

Among several barns is a relic of the days before refrigeration—a beef ring barn. Farmers in turn brought beasts to be slaughtered. Each carcass was divided among members of the beef ring, with no exchange of money.

Brownsburg Que.   7EX/19AX
Canada's biggest sporting ammunition and detonator factory is the Canadian Industries Limited plant in this Ottawa Valley village. It employs 950.

One old Brownsburg house was built by Arthur L. "Gatling Gun" Howard, founder (in 1886) of the Dominion Cartridge Company,

'Nuisance' Indians Were Wiped Out

The Beothuck Indians, a tribe of nomadic hunters and fishermen who wintered near present-day Buchans, were exterminated by Newfoundland settlers who considered them a nuisance. When Beothucks borrowed fishing gear they thought was public property, English and French killed to recover their goods. It was not a crime to murder a Beothuck until 1769—but the killing went on. It became popular to hunt such intelligent quarry and profitable to wipe out entire villages and take valuable furs and caribou hides. The last Beothuck, a girl named Shanawdithit, died in 1829. A doeskin coat she made is in the Newfoundland Museum at St. John's. So is the skeleton of a six-foot Beothuck man.

predecessor of CIL's ammunition division. Howard came from the United States during the Northwest Rebellion of 1885 as an observer and as demonstrator of the Gatling machine gun. He was killed in action with the Canadians in the South African War.

Bruce Mines Ont.   7AW
Exhibits in a turn-of-the-century church building which is now the Bruce Mines Museum reflect the heritage of the town's early settlers, many of whom were Cornish miners. They came here about 1850 to work Canada's first commercially successful copper mines.

In the Bruce Mines United Church is a framed Lord's Prayer, each letter hand-carved in wood and mounted on black velvet. It was a father's wedding gift to his daughter in 1898.

Brudenell Point P.E.I. *see* Georgetown

Buchans Nfld.   11BY
One of the few settlements in Newfoundland's forbidding interior, Buchans began to grow when the mining of rich lead-zinc-copper deposits was started in 1927. To the south is Red Indian Lake, once the main winter home of the Beothuck Indians, now extinct.

Buctouche N.B.   9DX/23AW
Wild and beautiful beaches, warm sands and the temperate water of huge Buctouche harbor make this east coast New Brunswick fishing village a tourist favorite.

Bulyea Sask.   4EY
One of North America's oldest bird sanctuaries is a 2,500-acre preserve established in 1887 at the north end of Last Mountain Lake. It is famous as a migratory stopover for sandhill cranes and for the rare whooping cranes that sometimes fly with them.

Rowan's Ravine Provincial Park (660 acres) is 14 miles west of Bulyea along a sandy shoreline of the narrow, 55-mile-long lake.

South of the town is Last Mountain House Historical Park, the site of a Hudson's Bay Company post established in 1869 when buffalo roamed the prairie here. Within three years the herds had retreated so far to the west that the post was closed.

Lakeside Museum near Bulyea displays dinosaur bones, Indian beadwork and relics of the South African War and the world wars.

Burlington Ont.   7CZ/17BY
A silver gorget—George III's "gift of a friend" to Joseph Brant—is displayed in the Brant Museum, a replica of a cedar house that the great Mohawk chief built about 1800. Brant (Thayendanegea) was granted 3,560 acres here in 1798 for his military services during the American Revolution. He lived here until his death in 1807.

The museum exhibits a collection of spear and arrow points, wampum, French and

Poet Robert Burns' birthplace in Alloway, Scotland; York Minster Cathedral and Shakespeare's birthplace in Stratford-on-Avon are among the Woodleigh Replicas at Burlington, P.E.I.

British trade axes, a copy of Brant's will, a letter in his hand, a musket Brant used, dishes from the original house and Brant's Masonic apron.

□ Part of the Royal Botanical Gardens (*see* Hamilton) is in Burlington.

Burlington P.E.I.   9EX/23BW

The Woodleigh Replicas are large-scale stone-and-concrete models (some big enough to enter) of British churches, castles and other landmarks. Among them are York Minster (26 feet long, 10 feet high; 145 windows, chimes); St. Giles's Church in Stoke Poges, believed the church of Thomas Gray's *Elegy*; the mill of George Eliot's *The Mill on the Floss*; Macbeth's Glamis Castle; Shakespeare's birthplace; the 14-room Anne Hathaway cottage, with picket fence and flower garden; the Tower of London; 60-foot-long Dunvegan Castle (one-third as big as the Skye original) with antique furnishings, Scottish artwork and a dungeon.

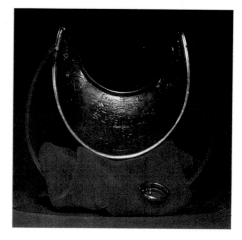

Silver gorget that George III gave to Joseph Brant and a gold ring that the Indian leader bought in England in 1776 are in the Brant Museum at Burlington, Ont.

Burns Lake B.C.   2CV

This town lies in the heart of a vast lake district and is a main gateway to the 2,424,400-acre wilderness of Tweedsmuir Provincial Park. Among the lakes in a 50-mile radius of the town are Babine (110 miles long), Tchesinkut (with water so clear that trout can be seen 20 feet down) and Ootsa, which feeds the Aluminum Company of Canada generators at Kemano and is the park's northern boundary.

□ Near Burns Lake on the road to Endako a white picket fence surrounds the grave of "Bulldog" Kelly, shot and killed in a poker game argument about 1913. The grave is all that remains of Freeport, a town that lived briefly during construction of the Grand Trunk Pacific Railway.

□ Three miles east of Burns Lake is a marker commemorating Perry Collins and his dream of a telegraph line from the United States to Asia via British Columbia, Alaska and Siberia. Eight hundred miles of the route north from New Westminster had been built when the success of the transatlantic cable in 1866 eliminated the need for the overland line.

TWEEDSMUIR PROVINCIAL PARK Most of this immense area is as unspoiled as when Alexander Mackenzie crossed on his way to the Pacific near Bella Coola in 1793. One road (a stretch of the Bella Coola/Williams Lake road) gives access to the southern part of the park. Tweedsmuir can be approached also along a 61-mile road from Vanderhoof to the Kenney Dam (although the road is passable only to four-wheel-drive vehicles). The most popular entry is by road and ferry from Burns Lake to François Lake to Ootsa Lake.

Peaks in the northern part include Tweedsmuir (7,160 feet), Michel (7,396) and Eutsuk (6,279). The Rainbow and Cariboo mountain areas in the south are separated by the Bella Coola River. Trails in the Cariboos lead to Turner Lake and 1,150-foot Hunlen Falls (picture, p. 52). Monarch Mountain (which is 11,590 feet) and its glacier are in the southernmost part of the park.

C

Cabri Sask.   4CY

The Saskatchewan towns of Antelope and Cabri (Indian for antelope) are named for the chunky, long-legged pronghorn that once roamed the prairies in the millions.

The little animal (100-125 pounds, about three feet high at the shoulder) is now found only in the sagebrush country of extreme southern Saskatchewan and Alberta. Before the white man settled on the prairie, the pronghorn may have been more numerous even than the buffalo. The fastest mammal in North America, it can reach 40 miles an hour over short distances and run at 30 miles an hour for several miles.

Mule deer and sharp-tailed grouse also are common in the hills south and west of Cabri.

□ The Cabri Museum displays rifle, pistol and shotgun ammunition; guns, knives, swords and bayonets.

Cache Creek B.C.   2DY

Once a gold-rush crossroads, Cache Creek now is at the junction of the east-west Trans-Canada Highway and the Cariboo Highway to the north. The town is in semi-desert country north of the big bend of the Thompson River. From Cache Creek in the 1860s trails led east to the Big Bend goldfields above present-day Revelstoke and north to Quesnel and Barkerville. The old Cariboo Road can be traced, often by two rows of snake fences that lined the right-of-way. Hat

Flat and fertile, checkerboard farmland stretches north from Cabri to the South Saskatchewan River.

Creek House, one of the oldest Cariboo Road stopping places, is 7½ miles north of here.

Cahiagué Ont. *see* Warminster

Indian church on a reserve at Cache Creek was built in 1894 near the old Cariboo Road.

Calgary Lives It Up
For 10 Days in July

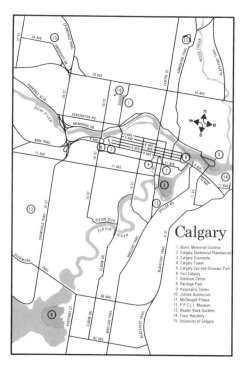

Dancing in the streets, Indians in colorful regalia, the thunder of hooves, the creak of harness and chuck wagon . . . for 10 days in July it's the Calgary Stampede, one of the biggest and most famous shows in the world. There's saddle and bareback bronc busting, Brahma bull and buffalo riding, a wild-horse race, calf wrestling and wild-cow milking as cowboys scramble for more than $200,000 in prizes. The most hair-raising event was invented in Alberta—races in which four chuck wagons, 20 riders and 32 horses eventually all dash for a single point on the track. There are fireworks, grandstand shows, a midway, a frontier casino, livestock exhibits, thoroughbred horse racing and a village with Sarcee, Stony, Peigan, Blood and Blackfoot tepees. The fun includes a parade of cowboys and Indians, Mounties and pretty girls—and flapjacks at curbside.

Calgary Alta.   4AY/13DW

The snowcapped Rockies, 40 miles to the west, are the stunning backdrop for this highest (3,439 feet) of Canada's big cities—a young city renowned for the dry, westerly chinook, low humidity, bright sunshine and the Calgary Stampede. Nestled in the valleys of the Bow and Elbow rivers where the plains meet the foothills, Calgary is an important oil, transportation and meat-packing center. It has some 10,000 acres of parkland, much of it on the two rivers, with miles of hiking, cycling and skiing trails, picnic sites, fishing, swimming, tennis and golf.

It started as Fort Calgary, a North West Mounted Police post built in 1875 to deter whiskey traders who were demoralizing the Indians of southern Alberta. The town that grew around the fort became a trading center and with the arrival of the Canadian Pacific Railway in 1883 came the first of a flood of homesteaders.

Oil was discovered in 1914, almost at the city limits. Now more than 400 companies in Calgary are directly involved in the oil industry and 28 major oil companies have head offices here. The population is more than 470,000.

BURNS MEMORIAL GARDENS (1) Sandstone

Calgary

1 Burns Memorial Gardens
2 Calgary Centennial Planetarium
3 Calgary Stampede
4 Calgary Tower
5 Calgary Zoo and Dinosaur Park
6 Fort Calgary
7 Glenbow Center
8 Heritage Park
9 Hospitality Center
10 Jubilee Auditorium
11 McDougall Plaque
12 P.P.C.L.I. Museum
13 Reader Rock Gardens
14 Trout Hatchery
15 University of Calgary

from the dismantled home of pioneer cattleman Senator Patrick Burns is used in the walls and walkways of this hillside beauty spot.

CALGARY CENTENNIAL PLANETARIUM (2) The stars and more. In the 255-seat Planetarium Chamber, images of planets and stars are projected onto a domed screen 65 feet in diameter. The 265-seat Pleiades Theater hosts stage plays, concerts, films and lectures. There are courses in mirror and telescope making, and carvings, sculptures and art works enrich the general effect. A museum stresses the technology of air transportation and has displays of aircraft and aircraft engines. Nearby there is a steam locomotive.

CALGARY TOWER (4) Soaring 626 feet above street level, it dominates the Calgary skyline. The top levels include an observation deck and a revolving restaurant with a panorama of prairie, foothills and mountains.

CALGARY ZOO AND DINOSAUR PARK (5) On St. George's Island, the zoo has 400 species of mammals, birds and reptiles, including a snow leopard from the Himalayas and Canada's only breeding pair of spectacled bears from South America. There are, as well, 46 reproductions of dinosaurs and a tropical aviary.

FORT CALGARY (6) At the junction of the Bow and Elbow rivers is the site of the 1875 North West Mounted Police post that soon became Fort Calgary. An interpretive center in today's 40-acre park displays items excavated there, all dating from the late 1800s and including a shaving brush with a carved bone

Family of Man by Mario Armengol, seen at Expo 67, is at Calgary's Education Center Building, which houses the public school board.

Range Burial, a 44-inch-long bronze by Harry Jackson, a toy touring car (c.1910) and objects from western Indian reserves are in the Glenbow Center at Calgary. A turn-of-the-century Prairie town is re-created in Heritage Park. A flag sewn by Princess Patricia is in a regimental museum in Calgary.

handle, an 1853 coin and tonic bottles. There are audio-visual and photo displays. Nearby is Calgary's oldest building on its original site, a shingled one-room log cabin built a century ago by the Hudson's Bay Company as a home for its interpreter.

GLENBOW CENTER (7) Oil millionaire-philanthropist Eric Harvie, in the 1950s, started a hobby of conserving western Canada's heritage. In 1976 the hobby flowered into this elaborate eight-story complex. A library and archives contain documents, diaries, movies, 100,000 photos, 30,000 books and pamphlets, and a map collection. A museum features Eskimo and Indian art and culture, and western history from exploration to oil. Included are a larger-than-life Indian teepée, Louis Riel letters, the medals and saddle of Col. Garnet Wolseley who suppressed Riel's 1870 Red River Rebellion, a two-wheeled cart taken into the Arctic by the 1851 McClintock expedition, and farm machinery and pioneer artifacts. There are Métis and ethnic exhibits.

Other features include replicas of the British Crown jewels, weapons and armor from the Middle Ages to World War II, and displays of minerals and coins, with North America's largest collection of Royal Maundy money from Britain. An art gallery contains works of historic importance to the west, some by local and native artists. The building's stairwell has a four-story-high sculpture, *Aurora Borealis,* by James Houston; hundreds of crystal-like acrylic forms are complemented by colored lights and mirrors. And in the main foyer stands a bust of the late Eric Harvie.

HERITAGE PARK (8) Sixty acres dedicated to portraying a Prairie Canadian town prior to World War I. It has a grain elevator, an opera house built of pine logs in 1896, a general store (c.1905) that sells penny candy, a 200-passenger stern wheeler, livery stable, a hotel with a two-story outhouse, and a combined North West Mounted Police depot and jail. Visitors can circle the park in a 1905 colonist car or other coaches behind a steam locomotive; a restored 1910 CPR depot was imported from Midnapore, eight miles south of Calgary.

HOSPITALITY CENTER (9) No. 5934, one of the 5900 series of steam locomotives, is in Mewata Park. Between 1929 and the early 1950s the CPR used 35 of these giants, known as the Selkirks, on its main line between Calgary and Revelstoke, B.C.

Rainbow over the plains, near Calgary.

JUBILEE AUDITORIUM (10) The 2,750-seat Southern Alberta Jubilee Auditorium is a twin of an auditorium in Edmonton. Both were built in 1955 to commemorate Alberta's 50th anniversary as a province.

McDOUGALL PLAQUE (11) Four miles north is a plaque where the pioneer missionary, the Rev. George McDougall, died.

P.P.C.L.I. MUSEUM (12) The original flag of the Princess Patricia's Canadian Light Infantry is in the regiment's museum. Designed and sewn by Princess Patricia of Connaught (later Lady Patricia Ramsay), it was carried into battle in World War I.

READER ROCK GARDENS (13) More than 2,000 varieties of plants, trees and shrubs.

TROUT HATCHERY (14) More than 6,000,000 trout fingerlings are hatched annually.

UNIVERSITY OF CALGARY (15) Once the University of Alberta at Calgary, it was granted autonomy in 1964 and renamed in 1966. It has an art gallery and herbarium.

Callander Ont. *see* North Bay

Cambridge Ont. 7BY/17BY
This new city, created Jan. 1, 1973, from the city of Galt and the towns of Hespeler and Preston, gets its name from Cambridge Mills, an early 19th-century settlement on the Speed River. (Cambridge Mills became Preston.)

Kirkmichael, a stone cottage built in 1832 by the son of Galt's founder, William Dickson, still stands on Byng Avenue. The first settlement in Galt was Shade's Mills, named after Dickson's superintendent Absalom Shade. Later Dickson renamed it for his friend John Galt of the Canada Company.

East of Cambridge is Shade's Mills Con-

Cape Mudge on Quadra Island, near Campbell River, has more Indian rock carvings than any other petroglyph site on the Pacific coast. Carvings on 26 boulders include mask faces and spirit beings. All are covered at high tide.

servation Area. Its 365 acres include a 96-acre reservoir behind a flood control dam 640 feet long and 36 feet high.

□ Southwest is the F.W.R. Dickson Wilderness Area of hardwood forest, tamarack swamp, marsh and meadows. A nature trail passes through them all (on an elevated boardwalk through the swamp and close to fox dens in the forest).

□ Ellis Chapel (Methodist), built in 1861, a fine example of rural architecture of the period, is northeast of the city.

Campbellford Ont. 7DY/17EW
Canal locks on the Trent waterway near here were set in tandem because the lifts involved (54 feet at Heeley Falls, 48 at Renney Falls) were thought too great for single locks. (In fact they are not. Similar "flight locks" at Burleigh Falls and Fenelon Falls have been replaced by single locks.) Operation is simple: the first lock lifts (or lowers) a boat about half the distance; the middle gate opens and

Discovery Islands are at the north end of the Strait of Georgia. This is Rebecca Spit on Quadra Island, reached from Campbell River.

the boat floats to the second chamber and is lifted (or lowered) the rest of the way.

Campbell River B.C.   2BY/12BV
One of the world's sport fishing capitals, famous for the fighting tyee salmon of Discovery Passage, Campbell River is headquarters for the Tyee Club. Membership is awarded to anyone who, using regulation tackle, takes a tyee of 30 pounds or more from these waters on the Strait of Georgia.

It is also a lumber and commercial fishing center. A pulp and paper mill three miles north at Duncan Bay conducts tours.

CAMPBELL RIVER CENTENNIAL MUSEUM Outside is an 18-foot bear totem pole, in the rotunda a huge thunderbird. The museum's Indian artifacts are principally Kwakiutl and Nootka; a few are Salishan.

ELK FALLS PROVINCIAL PARK The Campbell River tumbles a spectacular 90 feet into a deep and rocky canyon at Elk Falls.

JOHN HART DAM A power development west of Campbell River is named for a former B.C. premier, the man who started the province's publicly-owned hydro system.

QUADRA ISLAND Thirty minutes by ferry from Campbell River, Quadra has an Indian village and authentic old totem poles.

RIPPLE ROCK LOOKOUT Ripple Rock was the nemesis of ships using the Seymour Narrows near Campbell River until it was destroyed in 1958 in Canada's biggest controlled explosion up to that time.

STRATHCONA PROVINCIAL PARK A 60-mile road west from Campbell River to Gold River cuts through the northern part of 561,381-acre Strathcona Provincial Park, British Columbia's oldest (1911). Della Falls (1,443 feet) in the southern part of the park is the highest waterfall in Canada. Mount Golden Hind (7,219 feet), the highest mountain on Vancouver Island, is in the park.

Campbellton N.B.   9CW
Sugarloaf, a mass of volcanic rock 1,000 feet high and three miles in circumference at the base, is the nucleus of a provincial park and year-round recreation area near here.

Campbellton, on the south side of the Restigouche River estuary, opposite Cross Point, Que., is New Brunswick's third largest seaport and the commercial center of the province's north shore. A cairn in Riverside Park commemorates the 1760 Battle of the Restigouche, last naval encounter of the Seven Years' War (see Restigouche).

□ Salmon fishing is excellent in the Restigouche and Upsalquitch rivers. Campbellton holds an annual salmon festival, usually in early July.

Campobello Island N.B.   9CY
President Franklin D. Roosevelt's 32-room "summer cottage"—a red-shingled, green-roofed mansion—is the centerpiece of 2,600-acre Roosevelt Campobello International Park on this island near the entrance to Passamaquoddy Bay. Campobello is reached from Lubec, Me., by the Franklin D. Roosevelt Bridge.

The island belonged for more than a century (1767-1881) to Welshman William Owen and his family. Portraits and other mementoes of the Owens are displayed at Welshpool in the Campobello Library museum, where a Roosevelt collection has also been started. (Roosevelt, vice-president of the library in 1914, remained a board member until his death in 1945.)

The 1835 home of Adm. William Fitz-William Owen, who so loved the sea that he built a quarterdeck to pace, still stands at Deer Point.

□ James Roosevelt went to Campobello in 1883, when his son Franklin was one year

Dutch colonial summer home of U.S. President Franklin D. Roosevelt is in an "international domain" on Campobello Island.

old. From then until 1921, when he was stricken with polio, FDR spent most of his summers on the island. The big house that the public now visits was a wedding gift to FDR from his mother. He made only three visits to Campobello after the polio attack, all following his election as president, in 1933, 1936 and 1939.

In the study is a leather chair FDR used at his first cabinet meetings in Washington. A breakfront from the Roosevelt home at Hyde Park, N.Y., contains volumes from his collection of miniature books and personal china from the White House. On one wall is a set of four watercolors on rice paper, presented to Mrs. Eleanor Roosevelt by Mme Chiang Kai-shek. Among the other public rooms is the master bedroom where FDR lay after being felled by polio.

At the park reception center, a building opened in 1967, is a plaque that originally was at the Welshpool library. It was the first FDR memorial outside the United States. "In happy memory of Franklin Delano Roosevelt," it reads, "who . . . found in this tranquil island, rest, refreshment and freedom from care. To him it was always the 'Beloved Island.'"

On FDR's pew at the back of St. Anne's Anglican Church near Welshpool is a bronze plaque in his memory as "honorary vestryman."

Camrose Alta. 4BX/14GX
One of Canada's first ski clubs was formed here in 1911 by Norwegian immigrants. Many Canadians training for international competition have used the club's ski jump and the rolling parkland around Camrose.

It is land now dotted with hundreds of oil and gas wells—two are inside the city limits. There is a coal mine to the east.

Camrose Lutheran College, the Canadian Lutheran Bible Institute and the Alberta Bible Institute are located here.

Miquelon Lake Provincial Park, 17 miles north, has excellent beaches. Near Round Hill, 10 miles northeast, is a bird refuge.

Pioneer history is recounted in the Camrose and District Museum.

During a two-day Jaywalkers Jamboree each June the main street of Camrose is off limits to wheeled vehicles.

Canal Flats B.C. 2FZ/13AX
The remains of a canal that in effect linked the Kootenay and Columbia rivers can be seen near this settlement. Built in 1889 to reclaim flood lands, it crossed the narrow strip of flat land between the Kootenay and Lake Columbia, the source of the mighty Columbia. Because of regulations aimed at preventing·Columbia River flooding, the one-lock canal was used by only two steamboats—one in 1894, another in 1902. It fell into disuse soon after.

Cannington Ont. 7CY/17CW
A plaque commemorates Robert Holmes (1861-1930), who painted more than 100 varieties of wildflowers and is represented in the National Gallery of Canada by watercolors of moccasin flowers and geraniums.

Cannington Manor Sask. *see* Manor

Cap-Chat Que. 9CW/10GZ
The town overlooks the St. Lawrence from a cape whose profile, seen from the river, resembles a cat sitting on its haunches. Hence the name "Cape Cat."

Cap-de-la-Madeleine Que. 7FX/19DW
Since 1888, when three witnesses said they saw her eyes become momentarily animated, a Madonna in the Shrine of Our Lady of the Cape has been considered miraculous. The little stone chapel, built in 1714, became a national place of pilgrimage in 1909 and is Canada's national shrine to Mary.

BASILICA The octagonal Basilica of Our Lady of the Cape, begun in 1955 and inaugurated in 1964, seats 2,000.

BRIDGE OF THE ROSARIES This bridge over a stream in the shrine grounds commemorates a St. Lawrence River ice bridge across which parishioners carried stones to build the parish church in 1879.

SHRINE OF OUR LADY At the river end of Rue du Sanctuaire, the shrine is visited yearly by thousands of pilgrims. In 1659 a wooden chapel was built on this site and in 1694 the Confraternity of the Holy Rosary was established. The belfries of the stone chapel are believed the oldest in Canada.

Candlelight processions are held nightly from mid-May to mid-October at the basilica in Cap-de-la-Madeleine. A Madonna in a shrine there was crowned in 1904 and 1954 in the names of Popes Pius X and Pius XII.

Cap-des-Rosiers Que. 9DW/10HZ
The highest lighthouse in the Gaspé crowns a cape splashed with wild roses—where in 1759 the French first sighted the British fleet bound for Quebec.

Off the cape, where the St. Lawrence River (46 miles wide) becomes the Gulf of St. Lawrence, many shipwrecks have occurred. Near the village is a monument to 187 persons lost in the sinking of the Irish ship *Garrick* in 1847.

Cap-Rouge Que. 20BW
Somewhere near the red-rock cape are the lost graves of 50 Frenchmen who died of scurvy in the winter of 1542-43, hastening the tragic end of the first attempt at settlement in Canada. Not far away Jacques Cartier dug for treasure that proved worthless and spawned the bitter French saying *faux comme les diamants du Canada* (as phony as diamonds from Canada).

Cartier landed here in August 1541 with seamen, craftsmen, plowmen and soldiers, and supplies for three years, and called the place Charlesbourg-Royal. He discovered what he took to be gold (it was iron pyrites) and diamonds (this was quartz, as he found after taking ·10 barrels to France). Roberval brought more men in 1542 and renamed the settlement France-Roy. For the first time, wheat and European vegetables were grown on Canadian soil. But weather and sickness decimated the 200-man settlement; as more and more died, it died too. (A settlement on Sainte-Croix Island in the Bay of Fundy in 1604 was moved to Port Royal in 1605.)

□ Near Cap-Rouge is a 3,334-foot railway trestle, the longest in North America, which at low tide stands 185 feet above the Cap-Rouge River.

Cap-Saint-Ignace Que.   20CW
The stone tower of a communal mill built
in 1675—it was part of a manor-bakeshop-
windmill complex—stands at nearby L'Anse-
à-Gilles. It is 24 feet in diameter.

In Cap-Saint-Ignace, after Lauzon the oldest community on the south shore of the
St. Lawrence, is Gamache manor, a 1½-story
fieldstone house built about 1744.

Cap-Santé Que.   20AW
The site of historic Fort Jacques-Cartier, the
last place in New France to capitulate in
1760, is marked by a stone at the head of
a private road three miles east of the village.
The remnants of Montcalm's army withdrew
to Fort Jacques-Cartier after the Battle of
the Plains of Abraham at Quebec in September 1759. So did the Chevalier de Lévis
in April 1760. After defeating the English
at Sainte-Foy in a bid to retake Quebec,
Lévis had to retreat when English ships suddenly appeared. The fort, commanded by
the Marquis d'Albergatti-Vezza, held out
until Sept. 13, 1760, five days after Montreal
capitulated.

Cap-Santé's church was built in 1755. A
house on the Morisset farm, at the village's
western outskirts, dates from 1696.

Cap-Tourmente Que.   9AX/20CV
An estimated 100,000 greater snow geese
settle on the St. Lawrence River here for
about six weeks each fall and spring. It is
a stop on their long flights between nesting
grounds on Baffin Island and wintering places
along the U.S. east coast.

Cap Trinité Que. *see* Rivière-Eternité

Cape Breton Highlands National Park (N.S.)
                                     9FX/23GV
Most of northernmost Cape Breton Island is
national park—367 square miles of tableland
rising wild and high above the rugged shores
of the Atlantic and the Gulf of St. Lawrence.
The 184-mile Cabot Trail follows the park's
west, north and east boundaries. (Places
within an easy drive of the park boundaries
but listed separately in this gazetteer are Baddeck, Chéticamp and Cape North.)

In the remote center of the park—the Ever-
lasting Barren—are White Hill (at 1,747 feet
the highest point in Nova Scotia), Center
Barren (1,625) and Mica Hill (1,545). Mountains whose summits the Cabot Trail approaches are French (1,300 feet), Mackenzie
(1,200), North (1,500) and South (1,500).

Lookoffs include Cap Rouge, French
Mountain, Mackenzie Mountain and—just
outside the park—Big Intervale and Sunrise
Lookout. There are seven campgrounds; activities include golf, tennis, hiking and fishing.
BEULACH BAN FALLS Two miles southwest
of Big Intervale warden station, the falls can
be reached by road from the Cabot Trail.

INGONISH BEACH The park headquarters
are here, in the shadow of massive Cape
Smoky, a 1,200-foot headland often wreathed

in mist. A magnificent sand beach, about
800 feet, stretches between Middle Head and
Ingonish harbor; between the beach and the
mainland is Freshwater Lake. The Highlands
Golf Links skirts the seashore, crosses several
inland water hazards and winds through
wooded hills.

MARY ANN FALLS A secondary road leads
from the Cabot Trail to this picturesque spot
between Ingonish and Neil Harbour.

MIDDLE HEAD On this promontory a mile
north of Ingonish Beach is Keltic Lodge,
a resort owned by the Nova Scotia government. The head is a two-mile series of
rounded, forested hills and valleys and it
offers a magnificent view of Cape Smoky.
From the Middle Head nature trail are seen
colonies of common terns and great black-
backed gulls.

PLEASANT BAY The village lies just outside
the northwest boundary of the park. Until
1927 it could be reached only by water or
by a path over the mountains. About four
miles east, on the Cabot Trail, is the Lone
Shieling, a replica in stone of the huts used
by crofters when tending sheep and cattle
in the hills of Scotland. On a plaque are
these words from the "Canadian Boat Song":

From the lone shieling of the misty island
Mountains divide us, and the waste of seas—
Yet still the blood is strong, the heart
is highland,
And we in dreams behold the Hebrides.

Wooded highlands rise steeply behind a broad
beach at Ingonish, headquarters of Cape Breton
Highlands National Park. A 2½-mile hiking trail
leads up 1,405-foot Franey Peak from Ingonish
Centre.

A Great Road and the Beauty of Cape Breton

The Cabot Trail is a modern two-lane highway that soars and dips along 184 magnificent miles of northern Cape Breton. It challenges mountains, threads lush glens where salmon leap, skirts sandy beaches and rocky coves wet with Atlantic spindrift. Seldom far from the sea, always breath-takingly lovely, it is one of Canada's most exciting highways. Seventy miles of it is through Cape Breton Highlands National Park.

The trail is named for John Cabot, who apparently sighted the northern extremity of Cape Breton Island in 1497. At Cabot's Landing, near Cape North, are a cairn and a bust of Cabot (above). A wooded trail leads to the summit of Sugar Loaf (1,350 feet), which may have been Cabot's landfall.

□ From Baddeck (for those who make the tour counterclockwise) the Cabot Trail swings away from Bras d'Or Lake to St. Anns (and its Gaelic College and Gaelic Mod), then through North River Bridge, Indian Brook, North Shore, Briton Cove, Skir Dhu and Wreck Cove. It climbs majestic Cape Smoky, descends into South Ingonish Harbour, then enters the national park at Ingonish Beach.

The trail leaves the park at South Ingonish, re-enters it near Broad Cove, pushes north to Neil Harbour (below, right) and, after climbing South Mountain, plunges again to South Harbour and the village of Cape North. Here a secondary road leads to Cabot's Landing and Sugar Loaf, and on to Bay St. Lawrence and Capstick, fishing villages on the far north coast of Cape Breton Island. From Cape North the trail turns west up Sunrise Valley, crosses the Aspy River and climbs North Mountain. It descends into Grande Anse Valley and Pleasant Bay on the Gulf of St. Lawrence.

Now the trail unfolds vista after vista of the gulf coast and its pounding surf. After climbing to the summits of Mackenzie and French mountains, it slips down Jumping Brook Valley to the sea again. It clings to the gulf for several miles, past Cap Rouge and Presqu'Ile promontory, then turns inland through a narrow valley to leave the national park at the Chéticamp River. From the town of Chéticamp it goes south through other Acadian communities (Grand Etang, Terre Noire, Belle Cote), then into the Margaree Valley and back to Baddeck.

Cape Dorset N.W.T.
This settlement on the south coast of Baffin Island's Foxe Peninsula is the home of the West Baffin Eskimo Co-operative, which is famous for soapstone carvings and sealskin prints.

Cape North N.S.　　　　　　　9FX/23GV
A plaque at the edge of Aspy Bay marks the site of the western terminus of the first cable between Nova Scotia and Newfoundland. It was laid in 1856 between here and Port aux Basques (now Channel-Port aux Basques) and was used until 1867. In that year the first Atlantic cable, linking Valentia, Ireland, and Heart's Content, Nfld., was extended across Cabot Strait. From Money Point at the north end of Aspy Bay the new circuit was continued by landline to North Sydney and Canso, N.S., in 1891.

Cape Race Nfld.　　　　　　　11DZ
A rich find of Precambrian fossils was made in 1968 near this southeast tip of Newfoundland's Avalon Peninsula. The discoveries included a three-foot-long creature an estimated 600,000,000 years old, unlike anything that survives today.

Strange *living* creatures in Newfoundland waters include the kraken or giant squid. Most of these "devil fish" are 30-40 feet long, with suckers as big as saucers, but some reach more than 100 feet. Still larger are the whales that prey on giant squid and are pursued in turn by whalers out of Williamsport, on Newfoundland's north coast.

Cape St. Mary N.S. *see* Wedgeport

Cape St. Mary's Nfld.　　　　　11CZ
Here at the southwest tip of the Avalon Peninsula are great colonies of murres and kittiwakes. Just offshore on a provincial seabird sanctuary called Bird Rock are huge flocks of gannets.

Cape Spear Nfld.　　　　　　　11DZ
This rocky, windswept headland is the most easterly point in North America, a barren and beautiful place of crying seabirds and silent, stunted trees. It has two lighthouses, one in service, the other (built in 1836) being restored as the focal point of 121-acre Cape Spear National Historic Park.

For most of its active life, the 19-room original was the home of lightkeeper James Cantwell and his descendants. He won his job in 1845 when a ship carrying Prince Henry of the Netherlands to St. John's for a visit encountered dense fog and could not find the harbor. Cantwell, in a six-oared open pilot boat, located the prince's ship and guided it in. His reward was to be appointed Cape Spear lightkeeper for as long as he lived, with the right to hand the appointment on to his children and their children. (Cantwells keep the new light.) A parchment commending Cantwell has been signed by every royal visitor to St. John's.

Cape Tormentine N.B.　　　9DX/23BX
Car ferries run between Borden, P.E.I., and this most easterly point in New Brunswick (*see* Borden, P.E.I.).

Cape Wolfe P.E.I.　　　　　9DX/23AV
Offshore at Howard's Cove is a big rock shaped like a giant's armchair.

Caraquet N.B.　　　　　　　　9DW
Le Village Historique Acadien recreates the life and skills of the fun-loving but determined Acadians, many of whom finally settled in this area after being expelled from Nova Scotia by the British in 1755.

The village reflects the period 1780-1880. Some 40 buildings have been brought to the site and restored with construction techniques of bygone days. There are 10 houses and five farms, as well as a fishing center, general store, tavern, school, chapel, blacksmith shop and a reproduction of a bridge built in 1827. Five miles of dikes, used by Acadians to reclaim marshes, have been restored, along with their *aboiteaux* (hinged wooden sluice gates).

Costumed staff cook meals, tend store, demonstrate wool carding and weaving, and manufacture shingles, soap and candles. In the *Centre d'Accueil* (reception center) are a theater, exhibition hall and cafeteria.

A ritual blessing of the fishing fleet of northeastern New Brunswick, symbolic of Christ's blessing of the fishermen of Galilee, opens the annual eight-day Acadian Festival in August. On succeeding days there are

Bird islands of Newfoundland (this is at Cape St. Mary's) shelter vast colonies of puffins, gulls, gannets, murres and kittiwakes.

Blessing of the fleet at Caraquet in August is part of an annual Acadian festival.

sports events and parades; Acadian songs, dances and poetry fill the nights.

In the Sainte-Anne-du-Bocage part of town is a chapel built in 1771 and now used only on the feast day of Sainte Anne, patron of the Micmac Indians and of fishermen and sailors in this region. The walls can be removed; the benches are under the roof but otherwise in the open grove (*bocage*). Some 500 persons can be seated. In a nearby cemetery is a stone marking the grave of Alexis Landry, who settled here in 1756.

Carberry Man.   6AY/15AX
Wilderness trails blazed by Ernest Thompson Seton have become tourist paths through Spruce Woods Provincial Park. The famous artist-naturalist-writer, who became chief of the Boy Scouts of America, homesteaded here in the 1880s. The sand dunes of the Carberry "desert" were the setting of Seton's *The Trail of the Sandhill Stag* (1899) and parts of *Wild Animals I Have Known* (1898). A memorial to Seton stands in Pine Creek Park east of Carberry.

Ninety-square-mile Spruce Woods Park lies in the deep valley of the Assiniboine River and is the eastern segment of Spruce Woods Provincial Forest.

Carbonear Nfld.   11DZ
A gravestone erected more than 200 years ago tells of Sheila Na Geira, an Irish princess who wed (and reformed) an English pirate and lived much of her long life in this Conception Bay town. As a young woman she was captured by Gilbert Pike when he intercepted a ship in the English Channel. They fell in love, Pike abandoned piracy and they settled in Newfoundland. Sheila Na Geira, "wife of Gilbert Pike and daughter of John Na Geira, King of County Down," says the stone, died in 1753, aged 105.

Carcross Y.T.   1AW
It has called itself "the town that discovered the Klondike"—because George Carmack, Skookum Jim and Tagish Charlie set out from here on the prospecting trip that touched off the Klondike Gold Rush. Carcross is at the north end of Bennett Lake, about 32 miles from the Alaska Highway and 53 miles south of Whitehorse. Seventy miles to the south, by the White Pass and Yukon Route, is Skagway. A golden spike was driven here in 1900 on completion of the rail link between the Yukon and the Alaska panhandle.

In the Carcross cemetery are the graves of Carmack's wife Kate, Tagish Charlie (whose headstone is marked "Dawson Char-

Beached stern-wheeler *Tutshi* and a coach that carried the Royal Mail in gold-rush days are monuments to Carcross' colorful Klondike past.

lie") and Skookum Jim ("James Mason"). All were Tagish Indians, all became wealthy, all lived out their days in Carcross.

Another grave is that of William Carpenter Bompas, an Anglican clergyman who ministered to the people of the north long before the gold rush. He was the first bishop of Athabasca (1874), of Mackenzie River (1884) and of Selkirk (1891).

Grouped near the Carcross railway depot are a White Pass and Yukon stagecoach; *Duchess*, a wood-burning locomotive which once hauled supplies on a 2¼-mile rail line between Taku and Atlin Lake in British Columbia; and the old stern-wheeler *Tutshi*, beached since 1955.

Cardston Alta. 4AZ
Canada's only Mormon temple is an octagonal masterpiece in white granite, built in 1915-23 by Mormons who had come to Alberta from Utah a generation earlier. Cardston was named for Charles Ora Card (a son-in-law of Brigham Young), leader of 40 families who migrated to Canada in 1887. He was the town's first mayor. Card's cabin, built the year of the migration, is a museum.

Mormon temple at Cardston is built to a Maltese cross plan. Some parts are open to the public.

Carhagouha Ont. *see* Lafontaine

Carillon Que. 7EY/19AY
A monument to Adam Dollard des Ormeaux and the 16 other French heroes of the Long Sault stands near the Ottawa River at the reputed site of their battle with hundreds of Indians in May 1660.

CARILLON CANAL The Carillon Canal, built in the early 1960s as part of the 654,500-kilowatt Carillon power project, has a 60-foot lock, the highest conventional lock in Canada. It replaces two canals and seven outmoded locks that required as much as four hours for passage. The new lock, 200 feet by 45, raises boats in 20 minutes and from here to Ottawa, 65 miles upriver, navigation is unimpeded. There are tours of the power plant.

"O CANADA" It was in Carillon that Sir Adolphe Routhier wrote the French words of "O Canada." In nearby Saint-Placide a plaque marks Routhier's birthplace.

OLD CARILLON BARRACKS The original doors, stairs and woodwork of this four-story stone structure, built in 1829 for soldiers guarding the first Carillon Canal, have been preserved. The building is now the museum of the Historical Society of Argenteuil County. Displays include a large collection of Indian arrowheads, articles from the French seigniorial days, and furniture and dishes of the first English settlers. The kitchen (where during the Rebellion of 1837-38 meals were prepared for 108 officers and 108 soldiers) has a huge, open fireplace, a wall oven and French habitant furniture. Other rooms show military weapons and uniforms, native birds (including a specimen of the extinct passenger pigeon) and 19th-century women's clothing. One room is a memorial to Sir John J.C. Abbott, a native of nearby St. Andrews East, who was the first Canadian-born prime minister (1891-92). It contains mementoes of Abbott and a portrait and the books of his cousin, Dr. Maude E. Abbott, another native of St. Andrews East, one of Canada's first women doctors.

Carleton Place Ont. 7EY/18CX
A plaque in Memorial Park honors the World War I airman credited with shooting down Germany's top ace, Manfred von Richthofen —the "Red Baron." Arthur Roy Brown was born in Carleton Place in 1893. Richthofen had destroyed 80 Allied planes when Brown downed him April 21, 1918.

The Seventeen

Seventeen men who died at the Long Sault in 1660 probably saved New France from full-scale Indian invasion. Beneath the heroes' names on a monument at Carillon is this bronze bas-relief of their leader, Adam Dollard des Ormeaux, by Alfred Laliberté. Another Carillon monument to the 17—a group of monoliths in Dollard des Ormeaux Park near the Carillon Canal—is by Jacques Folch-Ribas, Jordi Bonet and Paul Borduas.

Carleton-sur-Mer Que.　　　　9CW
A good road leads from the village to the top of Mont Saint-Joseph and the shrine of Notre-Dame Oratory. The 1,821-foot summit gives an exceptional view of the Gaspé coast and the north shore of New Brunswick across Chaleur Bay.

□ Carleton-sur-Mer has an artist-of-the-sea. Rénald Cullen uses nets, floats, fishbones, feathers and driftwood in his creations.

Carlton Sask.　　　　4DX
The site of Carlton House (later Fort Carlton), one of the great 19th-century fur trade posts, has been made a provincial historic park.

The HBC built Carlton House in 1810. Dangerously near the hunting grounds of three groups of Indians (Cree, Blackfoot, Gros Ventres), it shared a common stockade with a North West Company post. After union of the companies in 1821, the fort was strengthened and became headquarters of the HBC's Northern Council and an important prairie supply depot.

From Fort Carlton in 1885 a force of North West Mounted Police and settlers marched east to Duck Lake and the first armed engagement of the Northwest Rebellion. Seeking to nip the insurrection in the bud, they were decisively defeated by Métis under Gabriel Dumont, and fell back to Carlton. The fort was heavily damaged by fire soon after; buildings that survived were sacked and destroyed by the rebels a few days later.

Carlyle Sask.　　　　4FZ
Moose Mountain Provincial Park, 15 miles north, is a wooded and rolling green gem amid the grass and wheatfields of southeastern Saskatchewan. The 154-square-mile upland and its many lakes (created by retreating Ice Age glaciers) were long a hunting and fishing ground for Cree and Assiniboine

---

Palisaded fort at Carlton is a reconstruction of the famous halfway house on the long trek between the Red River and Edmonton. It has an HBC store, a guardhouse and a museum.

Indians—and the home of the moose that gave the area its name. These animals were all but exterminated by the Indians during a hard winter in the early 1800s.

Carmacks Y.T.　　　　1BW
This coal-mining community, 103 miles north of Whitehorse on the Whitehorse-Dawson Highway, was named for George Carmack, one of the discoverers of Klondike gold. A 720-foot highway bridge crosses the Yukon River here.

Carman Man.　　　　6BY/15BY
The Dufferin Historical Society Museum exhibits mementoes of prairie homestead days. Old cars are displayed at Heaman's Antique Autorama, a mile east.

Carp Ont.　　　　7EY/18CX
Christ Church, about three miles from Carp, is a handsome stone church built in 1838 in early Gothic Revival style.

Castlegar B.C.　　　　2EZ
A communal village in Ootischenia, across the Columbia River, was built in 1971-72 to house museums showing the Doukhobor way of life in this west Kootenay country. It was the B.C. centennial project of Castlegar and neighboring Kinnaird.

The Ootischenia village resembles villages built many years ago in Pass Creek, Raspberry, Shoreacres, Glade, Brilliant and other Doukhobor communities. Each consisted of two two-story communal houses at the ends of a U-shaped courtyard. Kitchen/dining room and common room were on the main floor of the communal houses; families lived in second-floor rooms and in some courtyard buildings. A village was home to 75-100 persons.

The big houses at Ootischenia are being furnished with Doukhobor furniture, clothing, tools and handicrafts. In the courtyard buildings are blacksmith, weaving, dairy and other displays.

CASTLEGAR MUSEUM It has a collection of Chinese pottery, liquor jars and opium pipes

Keenleyside Dam at Castlegar looks in silhouette like some ancient ruin. Originally called the Arrow Dam, it was completed in 1969 and enlarged the Arrow Lakes into a lake extending 145 miles north. A billy, Colt .45, handcuffs and wood and brass telescope are among mining camp relics in the Castlegar Museum.

from early B.C. mining camps, an ornate printing press (1893), a wooden camera with brass parts and an early microscope.

DOUKHOBOR MARKET Borscht and Russian bread and noodles are sold Saturday mornings during the summer at a market in the Ootischenia village.

HUGH KEENLEYSIDE DAM The 170-foot-high dam, five miles upstream on the Columbia, has a navigation lock between the 1,200-foot concrete main section and a 1,600-foot earth-fill section.

PETER VERIGIN'S TOMB In neighboring Brilliant is the tomb of the man who led Doukhobors to British Columbia from Saskatchewan in 1912. It has been bomb-damaged several times, apparently by extremist members of the sect, and now is fenced. Verigin died in a mysterious bomb explosion on a train near Farron, B.C., in 1924.

SUSPENSION BRIDGE A 442-foot suspension bridge across the Kootenay, built by Doukhobors in 1913, links Brilliant and Ootischenia. It now is used by pedestrians.

Caughnawaga Que.   19BY

A Mohawk maiden expected to become the first North American Indian saint is especially revered in this village where she died in 1680. Relics of Kateri Tekakwitha (Lily of the Mohawks) lie in a white marble tomb in the Mission Church of St. Francis Xavier (1717) at the heart of the Caughnawaga Indian Reserve. A statue stands outside Tekakwitha School.

French Jesuits established a refuge here in the late 17th century for Iroquois converts to Christianity. One was Kateri Tekakwitha. The orphaned daughter of a pagan Iroquois father and a Christian Algonkian mother, she lived most of her short life in what now is New York State. Baptized at 19, persecuted for her faith, she fled to Caughnawaga. Her austere and saintly life—she died aged 24—led to her being declared venerable in 1941, with the likelihood that she would eventually be canonized.

□ In the sacristy chapel of the mission

Statue of Tekakwitha outside a Caughnawaga school is by Emile Brunet.

church is an elegant tabernacle believed built in France about 1700. In the adjacent fieldstone presbytery (1717-18) are an Iroquois grammar (1813-53) and French-Iroquois and Iroquois-French dictionaries (c. 1844), all written by hand by the Rev. Joseph Marcoux; a dictionary (c. 1860) in the Seneca dialect, by the Rev. Jacques Bruyas; a genealogy of Caughnawaga Indian families dating back to 1700, written by the Rev. Guillaume Forbes (archbishop of Ottawa, 1928-40), and baptismal, marriage and burial registers since 1735. Also in the presbytery is a gold chalice given to the mission in 1854 by Empress Eugénie. (*See* Sainte-Catherine-d'Alexandrie)

Cavendish P.E.I.   23CW
This is Anne's Avonlea and here are the Babbling Brook, the Lake of Shining Waters, the Haunted Woods and the Lovers' Lane of *Anne of Green Gables.* Green Gables itself is here too; the old house immortalized by author Lucy Maud Montgomery is a museum in Prince Edward Island National Park. Close by, in Cavendish cemetery, is Miss Montgomery's grave.

Her Anne, probably the best-loved character in all Canadian fiction, was really Miss Montgomery—just as Avonlea, where Anne lived, was really Cavendish, where Lucy Maud lived. *Anne of Green Gables* (1908) and *Anne of Avonlea* (1909) are the best known of Miss Montgomery's 23 books (nine Anne books, 12 non-Anne novels, a volume of poetry and a collection of magazine stories). *Anne of Green Gables* has been made into a movie (twice) and a musical.

Cliffs at Cavendish, as well as its beaches and dunes, are part of P.E.I. National Park.

Chaffey's Locks Ont.—An attractive old mill dating from the middle 1800s still stands in this resort community on the Rideau Canal. The mill is a private residence. (7DY / 18CY)

The Green Gables that now is a museum was the home of Lucy Maud's friends David and Margaret MacNeill. In the novels this house became Anne's home. Places such as Anne's Babbling Brook are on or near an 18-hole national park golf course.

□ In Cavendish cemetery are the graves of 21 American sailors who drowned in the "Yankee gale" of 1851, a storm which destroyed 174 New England fishing boats.

Off Cavendish is the graveyard of the sailing ship *Marco Polo,* which sprang a leak and foundered on a sandbar in 1883. Built in Saint John, N.B., she had set a speed record—68 days—on a run from Liverpool, England, to Melbourne, Australia, in 1852.

Cayuga Ont.   7CZ/17BZ
A museum in the Haldimand County courthouse (c.1850) displays settlers' effects, Indian relics and military equipment, all related to the county history. A log cabin is furnished in the style of the 1830s.

The town was named for the Cayugas of the Six Nations. A courthouse plaque commemorates the Haldimand Grant of 1784 that gave the Six Nations the land for six miles on each side of the 165-mile Grand River.

Centreville N.S.   22BY
A self-bailing lifeboat (c.1890) outside the Archelaus Smith Museum is a reminder of the Sons of Temperance crews who fought through crashing surf to rescue shipwreck victims off Cape Sable Island. The museum (1896) was a hall used by the Sons of Temperance and the Knights of Maccabees.

Most Cape Sable Islanders are descendants of Archelaus Smith, who came here from Chatham, Mass., in 1761. The museum named in his honor specializes in fishing gear, items salvaged from wrecked ships, ship models and pioneer artifacts. A half-section of a Cape Island boat (*see* Clark's Harbour) shows its distinctive construction.

Chalk River Ont.   7DX/18AV

A small bush settlement before World War II, Chalk River assumed sudden importance when chosen in 1944 as the site for a plant to produce plutonium from uranium. It has been the headquarters of Canada's nuclear energy development ever since.

The Chalk River Nuclear Laboratories (CRNL), part of the Crown corporation Atomic Energy of Canada Limited, have 2,500 employees. Most live in nearby Deep River. One of five nuclear reactors is the ZEEP (Zero Energy Experimental Pile), which began operating Sept. 5, 1945, the first nuclear reactor in Canada and the first in the world outside the United States.

Public tours begin at an information center (June 1 to Sept. 15). Visitors first see a movie and uranium ore samples and hear Geiger counters reporting radioactivity, then go by bus to one of the research reactors: NRX (National Research Experimental), which began operating in 1947, or NRU (National Research Universal), 1957. NRX and NRU produce radioactive isotopes for medical research and cancer therapy.

Fort Chambly on the Richelieu dates from 1709. The names of heroes of New France are carved in stones around the fort entrance: Champlain, Talon, Chambly, Lévis, Montcalm, Bougainville, Rouville, Beaulac, Contrecoeur . . .

Other facilities, some of which can be visited on longer tours (arranged at least 24 hours in advance), include a tandem accelerator or atom smasher, "caves" for remote-control handling of radioactive materials and computers. (*See* Deep River)

Chambly Que.   7FY/19BY

Castle-like Fort Chambly stands old and proud and tall beside "the river of the Iroquois"—the mighty Richelieu that brought Indian warriors and British and American invaders.

The great square fort, with high curtain walls and five-sided corner bastions, was probably the first historic site preserved by the Canadian government. Funds for its maintenance were provided in 1882. It became a national historic park in 1921.

The first fort was built of wood in 1665 by Capt. Jacques de Chambly of le Régiment de Carignan-Salières. Around it grew the first European settlement on the Richelieu. The wooden fort was replaced in 1709-11 by a massive new fortification whose walls still stand. The French occupied the fort until 1760, the English until 1775, when American troops took it; the following year they evacuated and burned the fort. It was repaired in 1777 and garrisoned until 1851. American soldiers were imprisoned in the fort during the War of 1812. Some Canadian *patriotes* were held here in 1837-38.

Three walls have been rebuilt; the fourth, along the river, has been partially reconstructed. A dungeon has been restored. The remains of two great fireplaces—all that is left of the chapel, hospital and chaplain's house—are along the south wall.

Near the fort are the graves of early French settlers, British and American soldiers and

two children caught outside the fort in an Indian raid in 1747.

□ Old houses here include the St. Hubert house (1760), the Maigneault house, built of four-inch-thick planks mortised to a frame of hewn timber, and the Lareau house (1775). Another is the Salaberry family's manor house. In a park facing the town hall is a statue of Charles-Michel de Salaberry, who commanded the Canadian force that defeated the Americans at Lacolle and Châteauguay in 1813. Salaberry's grave is in Chambly's Roman Catholic cemetery.

□ The Chambly Canal was opened about 1843, enabling Richelieu River traffic to by-pass the rapids between Saint-Jean and Chambly. The first locks are near the fort.

Champlain Que.   19DW
A 10-by-12-inch sanctuary lamp carved in maple and painted white with gilt trim serves as a baptismal font in the Church of Notre-Dame-de-la-Visitation. It was used in an earlier church (1710) which was destroyed when the St. Lawrence River undermined the foundations. In the present church, built in 1879, Mass is said on a consecrated stone given to the parish by Jean-Baptiste de la Croix de Chevrières de Saint-Vallier, second Roman Catholic bishop of Quebec. A plaque in memory of Samuel de Champlain was placed in the church in 1900 by William Wicksteed (who lived in the United States). He was the last seigneur of the old Champlain seigniory.

Champion Alta.—Clinging to the railway lines that crisscross the west, some 4,500 grain elevators give prairie towns and villages their own distinctive skyline. Operated by individuals, dealers and cooperatives, they make use of grain's flow qualities and eliminate the need for sacking. Grain is elevated mechanically, then loaded by chute into boxcars. (4AY)

Channel-Port aux Basques Nfld.   9FW/11AZ
In this southwestern Newfoundland town —linked by car ferry with North Sydney, N.S.—is a monument to 133 persons who died when the ferry *Caribou* was torpedoed by a German submarine in 1942.

To the east is Newfoundland's rugged, sparsely settled south coast, a vast area still not served by roads, where village life has changed little in 100 years. Coastal ships steam from here to Terrenceville (about 250 miles), stopping in narrow bays overshadowed by 1,000-foot cliffs, anchoring off harbors that only small boats can enter.

Chapleau Ont.   7BV
A memorial stone honors Louis Hémon, author of *Maria Chapdelaine,* one of the most widely read books on French Canada. Hémon was killed while walking along railway tracks near here in 1913 and is buried in the Chapleau cemetery. (*See* Péribonka)

□ North America's second largest game sanctuary, the Chapleau Crown Game Preserve, is 2,850 square miles of virgin country with a maze of lakes and rivers. Moose, bear, lynx, beaver, mink, otter and wildfowl live unmolested.

Charlesbourg Que.   20BW
Intendant Jean Talon's design for Bourg-Royal, as Charlesbourg was first known, is still evident after three centuries. Streets radiate from the Trait-Carré (central square) like the spokes of a wheel. Saint-Charles-Borromée Church (1825) is at the Trait-Carré, where Bourg-Royal's first parish church stood. Talon's design for securing the town in case of attack put the church at the center, with wedge-shaped farms extending from it. No farmer had far to go to reach the church in an emergency.

Among the city's old buildings are the two-story, stone l'Heureux house (1684), the

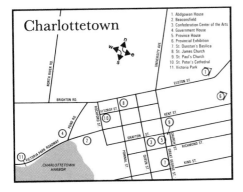

white, wooden Villeneuve house (c.1800) and a mill built by Jesuits about 1750.

Charlo N.B. 9CW

Salmon eggs are hatched and the fish protected to fingerling stage at a federal hatchery on the Charlo River.

Charlottetown P.E.I. 9EX/23CW

Canada's smallest provincial capital and the only city in Prince Edward Island, Charlottetown calls itself the birthplace of Canada, for here in September 1864 the Fathers of Confederation met for the first time.

Three hundred French colonists settled at the harbor entrance in 1720, calling the place Port la Joie. The British took it in 1758 and six years later, across the harbor from Port la Joie, founded Charlottetown.

ABDGOWAN HOUSE (1) This former home of W. H. Pope, provincial secretary at the time of Confederation (and one of its greatest boosters), is owned by the federal government.

BEACONSFIELD (2) A provincial historic site, this mansion erected by a shipbuilder is now

Charlottetown

1. Abdgowan House
2. Beaconsfield
3. Confederation Center of the Arts
4. Government House
5. Province House
6. Provincial Exhibition
7. St. Dunstan's Basilica
8. St. James Church
9. St. Paul's Church
10. St. Peter's Cathedral
11. Victoria Park

Confederation Center of the Arts built in 1964 in the heart of Charlottetown is Canada's national memorial to Confederation. It adjoins historic Province House, in whose Confederation Chamber (above) the first meeting was held to discuss union of England's North American colonies. *Charlottetown Revisited,* a Jean-Paul Lemieux mural nearly 13 feet long, is in the center's art gallery.

---

headquarters of the Prince Edward Island Heritage Foundation.

CONFEDERATION CENTER OF THE ARTS (3) A national memorial to the Fathers of Confederation (*see under* Province House), this complex covers two downtown blocks: a memorial hall, 1,108-seat theater, provincial library, art gallery and museum.

Among the more important pieces in the gallery's permanent collection are *The Local Stars* (an oil painting by Robert Harris), 12 handmade memorial banners (each seven feet by three and commissioned from 12 Canadian artists), *Charlottetown Revisited* (a mural by Jean-Paul Lemieux), *Mother and Child* (soapstone sculpture by Inukpuk) and a cloth tapestry, *Florigorm,* by Heather Maxey. The gallery houses more than 1,500 works from the Robert Harris Memorial Gallery that stood on the site now occupied by the center. Harris painted *The Fathers of Confederation,* destroyed in the Ottawa Parliament Building fire of 1916. He was president of the Royal Canadian Academy for 13 years. His masterpieces, *Harmony* and *A Meeting of the School Trustees,* are in the National Gallery of Canada in Ottawa.

The museum displays contemporary Canadian fine arts. The Charlottetown Festival is held at the center each summer.

CONFEDERATION CHAMBER *see under* Province House

GOVERNMENT HOUSE (4) This imposing white colonial building, home of P.E.I.'s lieutenant governor, was erected in 1834. It overlooks Victoria Park and the harbor.

PROVINCE HOUSE (5) Stone for this three-story, Georgian-style structure, built in 1843-47, was brought from Wallace, N.S., in sailing ships. In a high-ceilinged room now known as the Confederation Chamber, delegates of Britain's North American colonies met in 1864 to discuss union. The chairs they used stand neatly around the long, green-topped table at which they deliberated. A plaque tells that

In the hearts and minds of the delegates who assembled in this room on September 1st 1864 was born the Dominion of Canada. Providence being their Guide, they builded better than they knew.

Among the signatures in a Confederation Chamber guest book is John A. Macdonald's. Revisiting the room in 1890, 10 months before he died, Canada's first prime minister recorded his occupation as "cabinet maker."

Province House also houses the P.E.I. Legislative Assembly. Among plaques on the exterior of the building is one noting that the first submarine cable in North America was laid in 1852 between Carleton Head, P.E.I., and Cape Tormentine, N.B.

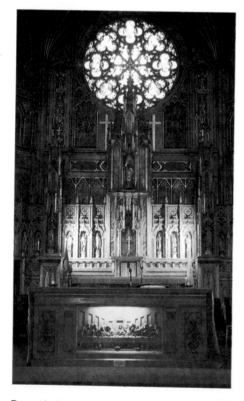

Rose window in St. Dunstan's Basilica in Charlottetown hovers above plaster saints and a three-dimensional wood representation of the Last Supper.

Harness races highlight Charlottetown's Old Home Week and Country Days in August.

PROVINCIAL EXHIBITION (6) Old Home Week and Country Days each August feature one of Canada's best rural fairs, at the Provincial Exhibition Grounds, and harness racing at Charlottetown Driving Park.

ST. DUNSTAN'S BASILICA (7) One of eastern Canada's largest churches, known for its twin Gothic spires, a particularly impressive altar and fine Italian carvings.

ST. JAMES CHURCH (8) A block of granite that rests on a marble slab embedded in the north wall of this Presbyterian kirk was once part of St. Mary's Cathedral on the island of Iona, one of the earliest sites of Christianity in Scotland.

ST. PAUL'S CHURCH (9) The baptismal register of St. Paul's Anglican Church contains the name of Margaret Gordon, sweetheart of Thomas Carlyle and heroine of his masterpiece *Sartor Resartus.*

ST. PETER'S CATHEDRAL (10) Murals in the Anglican cathedral were painted by Robert Harris, famous Canadian portrait painter (*see under* Confederation Center).

VICTORIA PARK (11) Here are the ruins of Fort Edward, built about 1800 as a six-gun battery and one of a series of strongpoints at the entrance to the harbor.

Chasm B.C.   2DY
A canyon here is a mile long and up to 400 feet deep. In it is Chasm Provincial Park.

Châteauguay Que.   7FY/19BY
Southwest of here on Oct. 26, 1813, Col. Charles-Michel de Salaberry's 460 Canadian Voltigeurs defeated a superior force of invading Americans and saved Montreal from attack. A monument stands at the battle site—near Highway 4 between Howick and Ormstown.

The valley of the Châteauguay River, which empties into Lac Saint-Louis opposite Lachine, was the axis of Gen. Wade Hampton's advance on Montreal with 7,500 men. Some 1,600 British and Canadians opposed them but the Battle of Châteauguay was fought chiefly by Salaberry's small force and a 1,500-man American advance party. The American commander was fooled by Salaberry into thinking the Canadian force was stronger. After four hours the advance party fell back. Hampton retreated and the plan to attack Montreal was abandoned.

□ Saint-Joachim Church in neighboring Châteauguay-Centre dates from 1775. The Lang (or old Molson) house in Châteauguay was built by the Hudson's Bay Company. It can be visited.

Château-Richer Que.   9AX/20BW
Some of Quebec's most historic dwellings are near this village, first settled in 1640. They include the Édouard Côté, Cauchon, Louis Simard and Gravel houses, all nearly as old as the settlement itself. A mill here belonged to Bishop Laval, first bishop of New France, who established the parish in 1678 and presumably named it. He often referred in correspondence to the priory of Château-Richer in France. Alongside the highway stand two old ovens—*les fours Turgeon*—in which bread still is baked.

Chatham N.B.   9DX
Cunard family documents and records, including an 1838-41 business ledger, are displayed in the Miramichi Natural History Museum. Joseph Cunard, who later founded the Cunard Line, came here in 1820 from his native Halifax to establish a branch of the family's banking, shipping, iron, lumber and coal business.

Pioneer Days and Old Home Week each August features junior olympics, a chicken barbecue and fireworks.

□ The grave of John Mercer Johnson, a Father of Confederation, is in St. Paul's Anglican Church cemetery 2½ miles west of here.

□ Twelve miles northeast, near Highway 11, is a house built in the 1820s by Alexander McDonald, a Scottish soldier who settled here after serving with MacDonald's Highlanders in the American Revolution. He became a farmer and fisherman, and a colonel in the Northumberland County Militia. His 2½-story, eight-room sandstone house was chosen for restoration as the centerpiece of New Brunswick's first provincial historic park.

Chatham Ont.   7AZ/16BY
Abolitionist John Brown and his followers came here in May 1858 to plan an antislavery government for the United States and some of their meetings were held in what now is First Baptist Church. They adopted a "provisional constitution and ordinance for the people" and chose Brown commander-in-chief. On Oct. 16, 1859, with fewer than two dozen men, he captured a federal arsenal at Harper's Ferry, W. Va., but was taken prisoner in a U.S. Marines counterattack. He was convicted of treason, conspiracy and murder and was hanged.

Chatham and nearby Dresden were among the northern termini of the Underground Railroad. Brown himself escorted 12 Negroes from Missouri to Windsor, Ont., during the winter of 1858-59.

□ Chatham was one of the earliest United Empire Loyalist settlements in southwestern Ontario. The first land grant was made and the first log cabin built in 1798.

□ The Chatham-Kent Museum displays Indian and Kent County pioneer material, war relics, and mementoes of the Rev. Josiah Henson, the "Uncle Tom" made famous by Harriet Beecher Stowe (*see* Dresden). Exhibits include Chatham's first steam fire engine (1870), Indian pottery an estimated 550 years old, an Egyptian mummy, and weapons such as an 1812 signal gun and a gun captured from rebels in 1837. A passenger pigeon and bald eagles are included in a collection of birds, some mounted more than 100 years ago. Another collection is of Australian aboriginal weapons.

Cheapside Ont.   17BZ
A one-room, red brick school built in 1872 and used until 1965 is now the Wilson MacDonald Memorial School Museum. It honors Wilson Pugsley MacDonald, born in Cheapside in 1880 and once a pupil at the school, who became a famous lyric and nature poet of the traditional genre. Among his best works are *A Flagon of Beauty* and *The Song of the Undertow*. The work he considered his greatest is a collection of religious poems, *A Saga*

King Louis' Royal Road to Quebec

Route 2 on the north shore of the St. Lawrence River between Quebec and Montreal was once the Chemin du Roy (the King's road), opened in 1734 during the reign of Louis XV. The 160-mile journey took 4-5 days. Travelers crossed 16 rivers on ferries or rickety bridges and changed horses at 30 relay stations such as Château-Richer and Deschambault (right). There were few inns; villagers put travelers up. Mail delivery along the route was started in 1736. Root cellars are embedded in the bank on the north side of the road at Château-Richer and L'Ange-Gardien.

of Immortality. He also wrote musical comedies and plays. The school's books and equipment reflect the life and education system of the settlers. There is a collection of MacDonald's work. The museum is operated by the Haldimand County Museum Board in Cayuga.

Chebogue N.S.   9CZ/22AY
A life-size marble monument in Town Point Cemetery of a woman resting on sheaves of wheat is a Canadian doctor's memorial to his Scottish wife. Frederick Webster, then a medical student at the University of Edinburgh, met Margaret McNaught while walking in the Scottish countryside. Some say that when she died in Yarmouth, N.S., in 1864, aged 45, Webster had the monument carved as he remembered her from their first meeting. Their descendants tell a less romantic but nonetheless poignant story: about to choose a monument, the grieving Webster spotted a white china match holder on which were carved wheat sheaves and the figure of a girl who resembled his wife. The monument is a reproduction of the carving on the match holder.
  □ From Chebogue Point, south of Chebogue, there is a fine view of the sea and the Tusket Islands. In June and July lupine banks are covered with masses of blue violet (and occasionally pink and white) lupines.

Chemainus B.C.   2BZ/12CX
The MacMillan Bloedel Limited sawmill, one of the world's largest, is the fourth at Chemainus since Thomas Askew built in 1862. Askew's mill produced 730,000 feet of lumber annually; MacMillan Bloedel's capacity is 228,000,000 board feet. Visitors see logs hauled from the water on "jack ladders," cut and planed into lumber, then moved to dockside for shipment.
  □ B.C. Hydro's Georgia Generating Station on Bare Point opposite Chemainus has a unique dock for large oil tankers. Three cantilevered heads, anchored in concrete poured into an almost perpendicular cliff face, jut 50 feet over the water and provide a 250-foot-long face for docking. There was no underwater construction.

Chester N.S.   9DY/22EW
A 20-inch cross in St. Stephen's Anglican Church is made of wood from the keel of *Young Teazer*, an American privateer that preyed on Nova Scotian shipping during the War of 1812. When British ships surrounded the privateer, a British deserter in her crew tossed a torch into gunpowder rather than be captured. The explosion killed him and 27 others. Two were buried in a Chester cemetery. *Young Teazer's* keelson is in 16 feet of water off Gordon's Island.
  Overlooking Mahone Bay, Chester was settled in 1759 by New Englanders, later by Loyalists and Lunenburg Germans. Two 24-pounder cannon from a 20-gun blockhouse built by the first settlers are on the Royal Canadian Legion grounds.

The Sword and Anchor Inn was built in the early 19th century as a private home. Its annex, Sheet Anchor House, dates from about 1783.

Chéticamp N.S.   9FX/23FW
French-Canadian antiques, spool beds, spinning wheels, looms, wooden farm implements and glassware are displayed at the Acadian Museum. There are demonstrations of spinning, carding and weaving. Chéticamp is noted for colorful rugs, handwoven from the wool of local sheep.
  Chéticamp is the western gateway to Cape Breton Highlands National Park. The area has many salmon pools.

St. Peter's Church in the Acadian settlement of Chéticamp was built in 1893 of freestone quarried on Chéticamp Island and hauled by horse and sleigh across the harbor ice.

Chicoutimi Que.   9AW/21CW
The metropolis of the Saguenay and Lac Saint-Jean, Chicoutimi looks back with nostalgia each year at the colorful settlement of "the region" in the mid-1800s. During an eight-day Carnaval-Souvenir (carnival of memories), just before Mardi Gras, the city is filled with the sights and sounds of wood chopping, snowshoe races, tugs-of-war and a torchlight parade. Many of the 35,000 people wear period costumes at home, at work and in the streets during the festivities.
  The Musée du Saguenay features 18th and 19th-century firearms and pioneer furniture.
  Chicoutimi stands on the hilly south shore of the Saguenay at the end of deepwater navigation. At the riverbank is the slope called

Arthur Villeneuve of Chicoutimi was a barber for 34 years before he began to paint. He started on his house and didn't stop until he had run out of walls—inside and out—and ceilings. He switched to canvas and sold his first works for as little as $25. Today Villeneuves fetch thousands of dollars. His multicolored house is open to the public.

Coteau du Portage, where a monument honors pioneers who made the laborious 15-mile trip from the Saguenay to Kénogami Lake. A bridge with a 375-foot swing span connects Chicoutimi with Chicoutimi-Nord.

□ From Chicoutimi there are eight-hour Saguenay cruises to Cap-Trinité and Cap-Eternité and four-hour trips to Sainte-Rose-du-Nord.

□ Chicoutimi-Nord has a magnificent view of the Saguenay River and Chicoutimi from Cap Saint-Joseph, which is topped by a 60-foot steel cross. In Chicoutimi-Nord is a shrine dedicated to Sainte Anne.

Chilliwack B.C. 2CZ/12FX

A gold watch that belonged to a notorious train and stagecoach robber is on display at the Wells Centennial Museum, operated by the Chilliwack Valley Historical Society. A plaque 12 miles east of Kamloops tells how Bill Miner "stole $7,000 in British Columbia's first train holdup, near Mission in 1904. For two years, unsuspected, he lived quietly near Princeton, well-liked by all. In 1906 he stopped the wrong CPR train here and found only $15! After a 50-mile horse chase he was caught and sent to B.C. penitentiary for life, but escaped to the U.S. in 1907." Miner also lived in Chilliwack for short periods between 1903 and 1906.

The museum has many Indian artifacts: carvings believed 2,000 years old, dugout canoes and early examples of Salishan weaving. One Salishan blanket of goat hair was woven in 1830; another is a rare example of twine weave.

□ The Royal Canadian School of Military Engineering has a museum open to the public. It deals with the history of the Royal Canadian Engineers and with the Royal Engineers' exploits in British Columbia, including the building of the Cariboo Road.

CFB Chilliwack's centennial project was a wilderness park (some cedar trees are 12-14 feet in diameter at the base) at the south end of Chilliwack Lake.

□ At nearby Harrison Mills, on many ghost town lists, is the Acton Kilby general store and museum.

□ The annual Vedder River Steelhead Derby is held on Boxing Day. Steelhead are caught also in the Chilliwack and Chehalis rivers. The Vedder, the Harrison and the Fraser are known for spring (king) salmon.

□ Indian Days in June feature war canoe races on Cultus Lake. The event is part of B.C.'s Festival of Sports and the Chilliwack Country Living Festival.

□ East is 80-foot-high Bridal Veil Falls, which starts as a narrow torrent, then spreads into a lacy, shimmering fan across the cliff face.

□ The Chilliwack International Horse Show attracts some 500 entries every May.

□ Most of the hops used in Canadian beer are grown in the Chilliwack area.

□ The Chilliwack Plowing Match held every April is the oldest in western Canada.

Christian Island Ont. 17BV

The remains of the mission of Sainte-Marie II, where Jesuit missionaries and survivors of the Huron nation took refuge after the Iroquois ravaged Huronia, can be seen on this Georgian Bay island. The site is marked by a plaque on a boulder. The Jesuits and Hurons stayed here through the winter of 1649-50, then abandoned the fort and went to the St. Lawrence River valley.

Ojibway women in the island village make handicrafts of porcupine quills, sweet grass and birch bark.

Churchill Man. 5GV

At Canada's northernmost deep-sea port are the partially restored ruins of a great fortress constructed two centuries ago and a space-age range whose rockets probe the shimmering mysteries of Aurora Borealis.

The guns of Fort Prince of Wales still point seaward—guns that were surrendered, without firing a shot, the only time the fort was attacked.

Launchings at the rocket research range average four rockets a week as scientists seek clues to the nature of the northern lights, a phenomenon in the upper atmosphere that is believed to affect weather in the northern hemisphere.

CAPT. JENS MUNCK A cairn marks where the Danish explorer and the crews of his two ships spent the winter of 1620. Of 64 men in the expedition, only Munck and two others survived. They managed to return to Denmark.

ESKIMO MUSEUM The museum, which displays native arts, crafts and artifacts, is near the Roman Catholic mission.

FORT CHURCHILL Six miles southeast is Fort Churchill, once a U.S. Strategic Air Command base, now a public airport.

FORT PRINCE OF WALES This huge stone fortress with walls 30-40 feet thick was finished in 1771 after 40 years of construction. As it was being built lonely men carved their names into a nearby rock. One, clerk of the fort, carved: "Sl. Hearne, July ye 1, 1767." Samuel Hearne won fame later as the first European to see the Arctic Ocean (at the mouth of the Coppermine River) in 1771. In 1775 he became governor of the fort and was in command when a French fleet appeared in the bay in 1782. With a garrison of only 39, Hearne surrendered without firing a shot. The French burned buildings and damaged the walls but most of the fortress

Fort Prince of Wales, North America's most northerly fortress, is a prime tourist attraction at Churchill, Man.

and all its guns survived. It is now part of a 60-acre national historic park.

HARBORS BOARD ELEVATOR During 13 weeks (late July to late October) when Hudson Strait is navigable, Churchill's 5,000,000-bushel elevator and dockside loading facilities are the scene of frantic activity. Ships take up to 25,000,000 bushels of wheat from here annually, lopping two days off the round-trip time between Britain and the St. Lawrence River ports.

HUDSON BAY RAILWAY A CN branch line,

At the end of steel in Churchill, Man., a balloon is readied for launching and a fisherman pursues a beluga whale. The Eskimo Museum's *Dream* (a man's head carried by a bird in flight) was carved by Erkrettok from a whale vertebra.

the HBR runs between Winnipeg and Churchill. Between The Pas and Churchill it crosses 500 miles of rock, tundra and muskeg.

RESEARCH RANGE Southeast of Fort Churchill is the Churchill Research Range of the Space Research Facilities Branch of the National Research Council. Pan American World Airways, under NRC contract, conducts the range operations, which include about 200 rocket and Skyhook balloon launchings each year. The Skyhooks, 100 to 150 feet in diameter, rise as high as 16 miles, then drift 500 miles west to near Uranium City, Sask., where they are recovered by helicopters. Among the rockets are Black Brants produced in Winnipeg.

Churchill P.E.I.
23CW
The Presbyterian church here, originally called the Church of Scotland, is a white frame structure built in 1862.

Churchill Falls Nfld.
10HW
The power of a 245-foot-high cataract in the Labrador wilderness has been harnessed by a complex system of dikes and control dams that made Churchill Falls the western world's largest single-site hydroelectric development. It was the biggest construction project ever undertaken in Canada.

The 2,200-square-mile Smallwood Reservoir, main storehouse for water to power 11 giant turbines, is the third largest man-made body of water in the world and more than a third as great as Lake Ontario. The reservoir was a vast natural basin, larger than Prince Edward Island. Depressions in its rim were plugged with 91 dikes, 30 of which are registered by the International Commission on Large Dams.

The main powerhouse, nearly 1,000 feet long, was hacked out of solid rock almost 1,000 feet underground. Much of Churchill Falls' almost 7,000,000 horsepower is sold to Hydro-Quebec, which shares its power through a grid system with Ontario and parts of the eastern United States.

Church Point N.S.
9CZ/22BX
Twelve trees from a parishioner's woodlot became the pillars that support the soaring arches of St. Mary's Church. Each is 60 feet high and two feet across. St. Mary's, built in 1905, seats 750 and is called the biggest wooden church in North America. Three bronze bells in the 185-foot steeple weigh a total of 3,740 pounds.

Chute-aux-Outardes Que.
9BV
A mile of pipe made from British Columbia pine carries water from a dam on the Rivière aux Outardes here to a generating station which powers a Baie-Comeau paper mill. Hydro-Quebec built two more dams upriver in the late 1960s as part of a plan to harness all of the 300-mile Rivière aux Outardes. Five generating plants (Outardes 3 and 4 and Manic 1, 2 and 5) produce 3,879,810 kilowatts (see Baie-Comeau).

300 Miles to Home

The Clare district of Nova Scotia was settled in 1768 by Acadians who had been expelled by the English 13 years before. The first to return was Joseph Dugas (see Grosses Coques), who walked some 300 miles from New England to Church Point, leading his wife and daughter on a horse. Other Acadians straggled back by canoe or schooner and established the communities now known as Belliveau Cove, Meteghan, Salmon River and Cape St. Mary. These and such places as Comeauville, Saulnierville and St. Bernard make up Nova Scotia's 15-mile-deep "French shore," which extends 40 miles from Weymouth to Beaver River. Most of its nearly 9,000 people are of Acadian descent. An annual Acadian festival alternates between Church Point and Meteghan River.

□ Pointe-aux-Outardes, across the river on the Manicouagan peninsula, has a 104-foot covered bridge.

□ In a chapel at nearby Les Buissons is an altar atop a cord of pulpwood.

Claresholm Alta.
4AZ/13DY
A plaque honors Louise McKinney, the first woman elected to any legislature in the Commonwealth. She went to the Alberta legislature in 1917 as independent member for Claresholm and was narrowly defeated in the 1921 election. Mrs. McKinney was a temperance advocate and when she died in 1931 was Alberta president and world vice-president of the Women's Christian Temperance Union.

□ The Claresholm Museum depicts the life of Alberta homesteaders.

Clark's Harbour N.S.
9DZ/22BY
A fishing village on Cape Sable Island, off the south coast of Nova Scotia, this is the birthplace of the Cape Island boat, famous for its stability and good handling in shallow water and swells. It was developed between 1905 and 1915 by Ephraim Atkinson, a Clark's Harbour boatbuilder whose sons and grandsons produce the boat today. The Cape Island is used mostly for inshore lobster, herring and tuna fishing and is recognized by its high, sharp bow, its wide, flat stern and low freeboard—for easier handling of nets over the side. Atkinson's originals were 20-30 feet long; today's are 36-38 feet and powered by inboard engines.

Clementsport N.S.
9DY/22BW
Built with hewn beams, hand-wrought nails and plaster almost rock-hard from the lime of burned clamshells, Old St. Edward's on the Hill was consecrated in 1797 to serve United Empire Loyalist settlers. The church

is set true east and west and the shadow of the cornice touches a round window at precisely noon. The beams, held in place by wooden pegs, are like the timbers of a ship. Handmade nails and hinges were used in building the box pews (four of which were reserved for blacks).

Two rooms in the church have been set aside as a Loyalist museum. On display are a Communion set, coins, household effects, prayer books, swords, photos, maps and drawings.

Communion silver first used by United Empire Loyalist settlers is displayed at Clementsport.

Clinton B.C. 2DY

The Clinton Ball, a century-old annual event that often lasted a week, is now a two-day affair held in conjunction with May Queen festivities and a rodeo. Townsfolk relive Clinton's colorful beginnings at the junction of the wagon trails—the Cariboo Road and the Cariboo Trail from Lillooet. The Clinton Hotel, a famous stopping place built in 1861, was destroyed by fire in 1958, but some frontier buildings still stand along the main street.

□ In the South Cariboo Historical Society Museum, a former courthouse, are the bones of a prehistoric man, preserved by lime and volcanic ash. Also on display are gold scales from the first general store (1864), a pair of red glass wine decanters from the bar of the Clinton Hotel and an 1858 Seth Thomas fiddle clock, one face telling the hour, another the date and month.

Clive Alta. 4AX/14FY

The Floyd Westling Museum's antiques include a steam engine that is often started to demonstrate how it threshed wheat and pulled stumps.

Cloverdale B.C. 2CZ/12EX

Urban renewal with an Old West touch re-made the main business streets of this southern B.C. community in the early 1970s. Streets are lighted from poles that look like gaslight lamp standards and most stores are decorated in the frontier styles of the 1890s. The renovation was inspired by Cloverdale's annual May rodeo, British Columbia's largest. A major highway was rerouted off the town's main street

and hydro and telephone overhead wires disappeared into underground conduits and back alleys.

□ A rare needlepoint of Charles I saying farewell to his children on the eve of his execution is displayed at the Surrey Centennial Museum. In a "pioneer parlor" are a Chickering and Sons square grand piano (1852) and a single-hand grandfather clock (1762) that still keeps time. Indian artifacts at the museum include arrowheads, rock carving unearthed in the district, beading, basketwork and chisels.

□ In a container embedded in the Peace Arch that straddles the Canadian-U.S. border at Douglas, south of here, are parts of beams from the Pilgrims' ship *Mayflower* and the steamship *Beaver* that the Hudson's Bay Company operated on Canada's west coast in the mid-1800s. On the Canadian side of the arch is inscribed "Brethren dwelling together in unity"; on the U.S. side, "Children of a common mother."

□ South of Cloverdale, in Redwood Park, are more than 115 species of trees, including the giant Sequoia, a tree for which California is famous.

Cluny Alta. 4AY

A metal cross near here that marks the grave of Crowfoot, chief of the Blackfoot, and a federal cairn near Gleichen both describe him as the "father of his people." Only 13 when he took part in his first raid, Crowfoot fought in 19 battles and was wounded six times. But he came to realize the futility of inter-tribal warfare and startled his people by preaching peace. As head chief he signed Treaty Seven near here in 1877.

□ Three miles south of Cluny, at Blackfoot Crossing, is a boulder effigy of Young Medicine Man, a Blood Indian who was killed there in a shoot-out in 1872. Trails of boulders lead from the spread-eagled Young Medicine Man to cairns indicating where he and his North Blackfoot enemy, Walking With A Scalp, stood when they shot at each other. Walking With A Scalp was avenging the death of a North Blackfoot killed in a drunken brawl with Young Medicine Man's band of Bloods.

Steam locomotive takes on water outside a miniature Canadian Pacific station at a museum near Clive. Floyd Westling also demonstrates a hand printing press and his two Model T Fords.

Like the Flash of a Firefly in the Night . . .

Crowfoot, the battle-scarred chief who became a man of peace, was commended by Queen Victoria when he refused to let his Blackfoot join Sitting Bull's Sioux in fighting the white men.

"Tell the Great Mother," he said, "that we have been loyal and that we know she will not let her children starve."

Crowfoot kept the peace when CPR surveyors tried to cross his reserve in 1883. Two years later, despite the urging of his adopted son Poundmaker (*see* Cut Knife), he gave no help to the Métis and Indians in the Northwest Rebellion.

The Rev. Albert Lacombe (*see* St. Albert), whom Crowfoot once rescued from a band of hostile Cree, was with the chief when he died at Blackfoot Crossing, near Calgary, in 1890. He transmitted Crowfoot's last words to the Blackfoot: "A little while and Crowfoot will be gone from among you—whither, he cannot tell. What is life? It is as the flash of a firefly in the night. It is as the breath of a buffalo in the wintertime. It is as the little shadow that runs across the grass and loses itself in the sunset."

Cobalt Ont.   7CW

One dark night in September 1903 (says a local legend) blacksmith Fred LaRose threw a hammer at what he thought was a fox's eyes—and hit the world's richest vein of silver. From a claim that LaRose sold for a mere $30,000 came ore that yielded thousands of ounces of silver to the ton. (As little as 150 ounces a ton is a rich yield.)

One remnant of the boom that followed is a 20,000-ounce (1,250-pound) piece of raw silver. It is part of the Cobalt Northern Ontario Mining Museum's $250,000 display of raw silver, the world's largest.

In one 10-year period metal worth $300,000,000 was produced here. Only the richest ore was mined; valuable tailings were dumped into Cobalt Lake. By 1908, with 50 mines operating, the population was 30,000, but the Depression of the 1930s closed them all. Four were reopened in the 1950s to produce cobalt for the metallurgical, ceramic and aircraft industries.

Visitors see old mine tunnels and learn about mining methods at the museum. It has early mining tools, machinery, books and newspapers dating from 1894. Outside the museum is a silver sidewalk, once lined with blocks of silver. The little not taken by tourists was buried when the sidewalk was paved. The original "silver sidewalk" was a vein of ore four miles out of town, a slab of raw silver 2-5 feet wide and several thousand yards long. The site can be visited.

□ The Cobalt Miners' Festival in early August includes displays of miners' skills, a fiddlers' contest, canoe races and special days for ethnic groups.

□ Two miles southeast a cairn marks the site of William Henry Drummond's house. A doctor who wrote English poetry in French-Canadian dialect, Drummond became famous for *The Habitant* in 1898.

Cobden Ont.   7DX/18BW

A cairn three miles east commemorates the discovery of an astrolabe believed to be the one Champlain lost on his trek up the Ottawa River in 1613. The astrolabe was a forerunner of the sextant. This one, with "Paris, 1603" engraved on it, was found in 1867 on the shore of Green Lake by a farmer who thought it was worthless. But an American visitor paid him $5, had the object appraised, and was told it could have been Champlain's. The astrolabe is in the New York Historical Society Museum in New York City.

□ The Ross Century School Museum, eight miles northeast of Cobden at Foresters Falls, displays school books and furniture from 1867.

Cobourg Ont.   7CY/17EX

Palatial summer homes built in the 1800s adorn the town, a Lake Ontario port and long a popular resort. A house of special interest is the birthplace of silent screen star Marie Dressler. Restored in the style of the 1830s, it is now a tavern and restaurant. A plaque in Miss Dressler's honor is outside St. Peter's Anglican Church.

BELL COLLECTION This museum with an

Turn-of-the-century railway coach is part of the Pioneer and Railway Museum at Cochrane. A courtroom in Cobourg's town hall (1860) is a replica of the Old Bailey in London.

agricultural slant has blacksmith and harness shops (c.1850) and various pioneer tools.

HIGHLAND GAMES Midsummer dancing, piping, drumming, track-and-field events —and a "will ye no come back again?"

JAMES COCKBURN A representative of Upper Canada at the 1864 Quebec Conference, James Cockburn was a Father of Confederation and first Speaker of the House of Commons. A plaque honoring him is in the Cobourg Conservation Area.

VICTORIA COLLEGE Now part of the University of Toronto, Victoria College was founded in Cobourg in 1836. The college building is part of the Ontario Hospital of Cobourg.

WILLIAM WELLER A plaque in the municipal park honors William Weller, Ontario's leading stagecoach proprietor from about 1830 to the mid-1850s. His Royal Mail Line ran from Hamilton to Montreal. In February 1840 he drove from Toronto to Montreal in a record 37 hours and 40 minutes.

Cocagne N.B.   9DX/23AW
After an eight-day stop here, Governor Nicolas Denys wrote 300 years ago, "all my people were so surfeited with game and fish that they wished no more." He gave this land of *cocagne* (plenty) its name. The picturesque village, first settled by Acadians in 1749, is noted for its seafood restaurants.

Cochrane Ont.   7CV/8GZ
The Polar Bear Express, an Ontario Northland Transportation Commission train, winds

from Cochrane through 187 miles of scrub brush and muskeg to Moosonee on James Bay, stopping only at Fraserdale and Otter Rapids. Another train that makes the same run three times a week stops wherever fishermen or hunters flag it. Ontario Northland arranges with Indian guides to take adventuresome passengers the last few miles by canoe to Moose Factory, on an island in the Moose River opposite Moosonee. The island, once a major Hudson's Bay Company post, is the home of a Cree Indian band. On the island is one of Ontario's oldest buildings, a blacksmith shop built in 1740.

□ Northwest of Cochrane is Greenwater Provincial Park, whose 26 vivid green lakes contain some of Ontario's purest water and best trout fishing. As a Provincial Heritage park, it is preserved in a near-natural state. Only four of the lakes are accessible by road. Much of the rest of the 10,000-acre park is accessible by trail.

Cold Lake Alta.   4CW
Indians shun 136-square-mile Cold Lake because of Kinosoo, a monster that lurks in its 370-foot depths. Despite Kinosoo—residents say it's a white, humpbacked creature the size of a whale—Cold Lake is a popular fishing resort. Many trout and no monsters are taken.

CFB Cold Lake, a training base for jet pilots, also houses a satellite tracking base, a part of the North American Air Defense Command.

Coldwater Ont.   7CY/17CV
A cozy log cabin homestead built in 1864 by Archibald Woodrow, a Scottish immigrant settler, is now an arts and crafts and antique shop operated by Coldwater Canadiana, an historical society.

Coldwater was once part of an Ojibway reserve and the Coldwater Memorial Library was built on the site of the first Indian log school. A Coldwater River gristmill built for the Indians in 1833 still operates.

A monument commemorates George Gray,

Down north is up ahead as passengers board the Ontario Northland's Polar Bear Express in Cochrane. Usually a freight and passenger train, the express turns all-passenger for summer excursions to Moosonee on James Bay.

Crowsnest Mountain is a 9,000-foot fortress-like mass of rock west of Coleman, near the eastern entrance to the Crowsnest Pass.

a Coldwater native who was never defeated in 17 years of shot-put competition. He won 188 medals and trophies, all firsts, and held 20 world records in track-and-field events. Gray was born in 1865.

A plaque marks the site of Cowan's Trading Post (1778). Only the chimneys remain.

Coleman Alta.   4AZ/13CZ
Rocks near this Crowsnest Pass mining town are an estimated 100,000,000 years old—older than the Rocky Mountains—and are the only major occurrence of volcanic materials in Alberta. They consist of ash and cinders; some large blocks are like the pumice bombs ejected by some modern volcanoes. Because there is little lava, geologists believe volcanoes here were violent and explosive.

Colinton Alta.   4AW
A clock with 27 wooden gears, a hand-operated flour mill and a sterling silver tea service dating from 1816 are displayed in the Kinnoull Historical Museum. It is in a five-room log cabin built in 1905.

Collingwood Ont.   7BY/17BW
With Nottawasaga Bay at its doorstep and the spectacular Niagara Escarpment as a backdrop, Collingwood is popular with tourists and skiers. The town, incorporated in 1858, was the terminus of the Ontario, Simcoe and Huron Railway, later renamed the Northern Railway of Canada. (The Northern finally became the CNR.)
BLUE MOUNTAIN WINTER PARK Almost 700 acres of ski trails and beautiful scenery, Blue Mountain Winter Park is five miles west. One of five chair lifts operates in summer and in less than 15 minutes riders are carried through a mile of woods to a mountain summit and a panoramic view of Georgian Bay.
COLLINGWOOD MUSEUM A rare Canadian compote in the shape of a sugar shanty is a prized exhibit of the Collingwood Museum, once a railway station. Displays range from ship models and a ship's wheelhouse, re-

flecting the town's marine history, to a pioneer bedroom and a collection of Indian effigy pipes.
COLLINGWOOD SHIPYARDS Collingwood has been a principal Great Lakes shipbuilding center for more than 75 years. Ships are launched sideways instead of stern first.
COUNTRY WOMEN OF THE WORLD A plaque here honors Mrs. Alfred Watt, first president of the international Associated Country Women of the World.
DEVIL'S GLEN Ten miles south is 149-acre Devil's Glen Provincial Park, 1,500 feet up in the Blue Mountains. Devil's Gorge on the Mad River, 250 feet below the park, forms part of a breath-taking view.
EKARENNIONDI A pinnacle of rock five miles west of Collingwood is called Ekarenniondi (where the rock stands out). The Petuns of the Huron nation believed the Head Piercer waited here for Indians bound for the happy hunting grounds so he could remove

Blue Mountain pottery was developed at Collingwood in the late 1940s by Czechoslovak-born Jozo Weider and two fellow immigrants. Visitors see shaping, firing and glazing.

Collingwood/95

their brains and prepare them for the hereafter.

SCENIC CAVES Actually huge fissures in the Niagara Escarpment (2,000 feet above sea level in some places in this area), the Blue Mountain Scenic Caves were formed when the last Ice Age glacier retreated and the earth's crust heaved. The sides of the Preacher's Pulpit cave, if shoved together, would match rock for rock. There are rare ferns in Fern Cavern and ladders descend to a deep cave where ice and snow exist year round. The 14-inch-wide exit from one cave prompted its name—Fat Man's Misery.

Columbia Icefield Alta. *see* Jasper National Park

Colville Lake N.W.T.   3HW
Halfway between Great Bear Lake and the Arctic Ocean, in this remote Indian village, is the most northerly fishing lodge in the western Arctic and a church claimed to be the tallest log structure in the territories. The village grew around an Oblate mission started in 1962 by the Rev. Bernard Brown. In the steeple of Our Lady of the Snows, built of peeled spruce logs, is a bell donated by Iowa Mennonites.

□ Fishermen fly here from Norman Wells for whitefish, northern pike, lake trout and Arctic grayling. Refrigeration is no problem, even when the sun shines 24 hours a day during the Arctic summer: ice houses are set in the tundra's permafrost.

Come By Chance Nfld.   11CY
A huge oil refinery has brought supertankers to this quiet Avalon Peninsula village. They are handled by special port installations and oversize tugboats.

Comiaken B.C.—A missionary priest, the Rev. Peter Rondeault, kept cows and sold butter, using the proceeds to build this "Butter" Church in 1870. It is on a Cowichan Indian reserve near here. (2CZ/12DY).

Comox B.C.   2BY/12BW
"1-Spot," a locomotive brought here in 1909 by the Comox Logging & Railway Company, is on display—along with a colorful Haida totem pole—outside the Courtenay and Dis-

trict Museum. Inside is an impression of a fern in rock found 700 feet down a Cumberland, B.C., coal mine. It is thought to be 70,000,000 years old.

Compton Que.   9AY/20AZ
A house in this Eastern Townships village was the birthplace of Louis St. Laurent, prime minister in 1948-57. Adjoining the house is a general store started by his father in 1879 and operated by other members of the St. Laurent family until the late 1960s. The white frame house and store, with a common veranda, are about 150 years old. Neither is occupied. The house was acquired by a private foundation in the early 1970s with the intention of preserving it as an historic site. St. Laurent's grave is here, in the parish Cemetery of St. Thomas Aquinas.

Coniston Ont. *see* Sudbury

Consort Alta.   4BX
North and east of Consort are Gooseberry Lake Provincial Park and the Neutral Hills —which apparently the Plains Indians kept as a hunting preserve where no fighting or raiding was allowed. Archaeologists have discovered many Indian ceremonial sites.

Contrecoeur Que.   7FX/19CX
The Le Noblet-Duplessis house, among the oldest dwellings in this old village, was built in 1794. It was the home (1811-40) of Joseph Le Noblet-Duplessis. He was the grandfather of Maurice Le Noblet-Duplessis who became premier of Quebec. *Patriote* leaders are said to have met in the house in 1837.

Sainte-Trinité-de-Contrecoeur Church (1864) is on the site of an earlier (1818) parish church. A windmill was built in 1742.

Cookshire Que.   9AY/20BZ
Several interesting 19th-century buildings are still in use in this village that New Hampshire and Vermont settlers founded in the late 1790s. They include the Bailey and Pope houses (early 1800s), the Gothic-style Anglican church (1869) and a grocery store (1851).

Copper Cliff Ont. *see* Sudbury

Copper Mountain B.C.   2DZ
A marker beside the Hope-Princeton highway points to this ghost town and tells of its once-productive life: "From 1920 to 1957, the big Copper Mountain mine shipped 35,000,000 tons of ore containing 600,000,000 pounds of copper to the concentrator at Allenby [about 10 miles north]. The tortuous railroad grade still clings precariously to the wall of the Similkameen River Canyon. . . ." The mine was closed when the known ore body was exhausted.

Corner Brook Nfld.   11BY
Newfoundland's second city (population 30,000) thrives on the market for newsprint.

Humber Valley salmon streams and big game hunting are easily accessible from Corner Brook.

The huge Bowaters Newfoundland Limited mill, one of the world's largest, with a capacity of 410,000 tons a year, ships to countries around the world.

A 10-story Government Center is among the most striking buildings. The nearby Newfoundland government Arts and Culture Center contains a theater, a swimming pool and museum and art exhibition areas. Glynmill Inn, once the community's only hotel, and Corner Brook House, an executive home, were built in the English style in the late 1920s.

□ Parks include Margaret Bowater Park (in the city), the Bowater Park at South Brook (15 miles northeast), Blue Pond and Barachois Pond provincial parks (17 and 36 miles southwest). Marble Mountain is a ski center five miles east of Corner Brook.

Cornwall Ont. 18EX

The headquarters of the St. Lawrence Seaway Authority, Cornwall is the eastern terminus of the old Cornwall Canal and is linked by bridge with Rooseveltown, N.Y. United Empire Loyalists settled here after the American War of Independence and Cornwall became a town in 1834. Within nine years (1843) the canal was completed, bypassing the Long Sault Rapids and enabling lake vessels to reach here. Cotton (1870), paper (1833) and rayon (1923) were successive boosts to Cornwall's economy. (It was in a cotton mill here that Thomas A. Edison, in 1883, installed his first plant for lighting a factory by electricity.) The city now includes Cornwall Island (excluding the St. Regis Reserve) in the St. Lawrence River. Major industries include Domtar Fine Papers, Courtaulds (Canada) Ltd. (rayon) and Canadian Industries Limited (chemicals).

BISHOP STRACHAN CHURCH The Rev. John

Then Leave Them to Cure for a Year

The world's only factory for making wooden lacrosse sticks is on the St. Regis Reserve on Cornwall Island. Indian craftsmen at the Mohawk Lacrosse Stick Company plant fashion as many as 100,000 a year. Lacrosse, one of the roughest of sports, was played by Indian teams of 75 to 200 men long before Europeans arrived in Canada. The crooks of the hickory sticks are bent and wired into shape, then left to cure for a year before the leather webbing is attached. About one-third of the sticks are shipped to the United States. Some go to Britain and Australia.

Molten glass is shaped into exquisite figures at Chalet Artistic Glass Ltd. in Cornwall. There are tours of the plant in summer.

Strachan (later first Anglican bishop of Toronto) was the first rector of Trinity, the Bishop Strachan Memorial Church. It is one of Ontario's oldest Anglican parishes, dating from 1784. Strachan came here in 1803 to head an Anglican mission and soon founded his famous Cornwall Grammar School.

FRENCH WEEK French-Canadian food, music, dancing and joie de vivre: an annual June event built around Saint-Jean-Baptiste Day.

GLENGARRY HOUSE Five miles east a cairn marks the ruins of a stone house built in 1791 by Lt. Col. John Macdonell, who became first Speaker of the Upper Canada Legislative Assembly. The house was destroyed by fire in 1813.

ROBERT H. SAUNDERS-ST. LAWRENCE GENERATING STATION This is the Canadian part of a $600,000,000 power plant built jointly by Canada and the United States when the seaway was created. Together the Canadian powerhouse and the Americans' adjoining Robert Moses Power Dam stretch 3,300 feet across the St. Lawrence. Tours (May to September) take in the Saunders-St. Lawrence control room, a panoramic view from the observation deck and a film about the power development, whose total capacity is 1,824,000 kilowatts. A map shows the river before and after the flooding which created 28-mile-long Lake St. Lawrence and inundated the Long Sault Rapids. In the observation penthouse lobby is an abstract mural 37 feet long, painted by Harold Town on a single piece of canvas.

UNITED COUNTIES MUSEUM The Wood House, a fine stone residence (c.1840), is now the United Counties Museum. Exhibits include general Canadiana, Loyalist and pioneer household articles, furniture, clothing, maps, documents, tools, toys and local pottery. The electrical equipment that Thomas A. Edison installed in the Stormont Cotton Mill is displayed.

Cornwallis N.S.   22BW
Built during World War II (as HMCS *Cornwallis,* the biggest naval training establishment in the Commonwealth), CFB Cornwallis is now a basic training school. Tours can be arranged.

Corran Ban P.E.I.   23CW
Scottish Highlanders who came here about 1772 called their settlement *Corran Ban* (Gaelic for white sickle) because of the froth on the Winter Bay shoreline in the fall.

Corunna Ont.   7AZ/16BX
The Pilot House Museum is the restored center castle of the Great Lakes and coastal oil tanker *Imperial Hamilton*. It includes the master's and officers' quarters, wheelhouse, engine room and bridge—with engine telegraphs, chart table and signal flag locker.

Coteau-du-Lac Que.   7EY/19AY
The ruins of a tiny canal, forerunner of the St. Lawrence Seaway, are the focal point of Fort Coteau-du-Lac, a national historic site. The remains of various buildings and earthworks are also conserved and in an unusual eight-sided blockhouse, a reconstruction of one built in 1812, is an exhibition of artifacts. A model of the fort is displayed in an information center.

The canal was North America's first with locks—its three were later reduced to two—and it was cut through rock in 1779-80.

Boats used Coteau-du-Lac and canals built later at Cascades and Split Rock to avoid rapids on the St. Lawrence River between Lake St. Francis and Lac Saint-Louis. But they were replaced in 1845 by the Beauharnois Canal—which in turn was replaced by the Soulanges Canal in the 1890s. The Soulanges became obsolete with construction of the new Beauharnois Canal and the seaway.

Extensive defenses were built around the Coteau-du-Lac Canal during the War of 1812: a cloverleaf-shaped bastion, other bastions and blockhouses. These and a barracks, bakery, guardhouse, magazine, hospital, cookhouse and officers' quarters eventually fell into ruin and the earthworks were damaged by erosion and excavation. Only a few remains were visible when archaeologists started restoration in 1965.

Courtenay B.C.   2BY/12BW
Vancouver Island's Forbidden Plateau, long avoided by Indians who believed women and children disappeared there without trace, is now thronged by hikers and skiers. It is on the lower slopes of Mount Becher along a 10-mile stretch of the Strait of Georgia, east of Strathcona Provincial Park (*see* Campbell River). The plateau is reached from a lodge 15 miles northwest of Courtenay. About the same distance northeast, on the strait, is Miracle Beach Provincial Park, whose nature house has some 30 natural history exhibits and salt-water aquariums displaying marine life.

A museum run by the Courtenay and District Historical Society features Comox Valley history since 1850. A cairn at nearby Sandwick commemorates the landing of the valley's first settlers in 1862.

Courville Que.   20BW
Maison Montmorency (1786), erected by Gen. Sir Frederick Haldimand when he was governor general, overlooks Montmorency Falls. The house was occupied in 1791-94 by

Octagonal blockhouse at Coteau-du-Lac contains a museum in which are displayed artifacts unearthed during restoration of Fort Coteau-du-Lac. The fort is a national historic site.

the Duke of Kent, father of Queen Victoria, when he commanded the 7th Royal Fusiliers in Quebec. A century later it was enlarged and converted into a hotel. It is now operated in summer by the Quebec Department of Tourism, Game and Fisheries, which acquired it in 1974.

A plaque commemorates a French victory over Wolfe at Courville July 31, 1759.

Cowansville Que.   7FY/19CY
Red brick houses in the part of Cowansville that was the village of Sweetsburg are among Quebec's finest examples of Victorian gingerbread architecture. Cowansville (originally Nelsonville) and Sweetsburg (at first called Churchville) were United Empire Loyalist villages. Together they are a town of about 12,000.

Cowley Alta.   4AZ/13CZ
A steady flow of air from the Rockies ("standing mountain waves") makes excellent soaring conditions here and in other parts of southwestern Alberta. Calgary's Cu Nim Gliding Club often holds competitions here at Easter, the May 24 weekend and Thanksgiving.

□ North of Cowley, at Massacre Butte, a cairn recalls the fate of a wagon train from Minnesota: "In 1867, an immigrant train consisting of about 12 men, women and children was massacred near this hill during the night by a war party of Blood Indians led by Medicine Calf."

Craigellachie B.C.   2EY
The last spike of the Canadian Pacific Railway was driven here Nov. 7, 1885. "A nebulous dream was a reality," says a commemorative plaque, "an iron ribbon crossed Canada from sea to sea. Often following the footsteps of early explorers, nearly 3,000 miles of steel rail pushed across vast prairies, cleft lofty mountain passes, twisted through canyons, and bridged a thousand streams."

The CPR route through Eagle Pass had been discovered 20 years earlier. A sign 20 miles east of Craigellachie records: "In 1865, Walter Moberly, government engineer . . . shot at an eagle's nest and observed the birds fly into a river valley. Following them, he discovered this low pass."

Craigleith Ont.   7BY/17AW
The fossils of creatures extinct for 200,000,000 years abound in 27-acre Craigleith Provincial Park. The story of these trilobites, gastropods, nautiloids and others is told in an Ontario government display.

Craik Sask.   4DY
The Prairie Pioneer Museum is two pioneer buildings in one—a schoolhouse towed here from 25 miles away and a tiny unused local church. Joined in 1972 with the help of a Saskatchewan government grant, they stand alongside the Regina-Saskatoon highway on

land leased from the province for $1. The museum was organized in 1965 to preserve articles used by people who opened up the west. Besides collections of glass, coins and dolls there are such things as a wooden Columbus clock (made in 1892 on the 400th anniversary of Columbus' epic voyage), a pocket "sun watch" (a combination compass and sundial), and a washing machine with a spring-operated handle like a pogo stick.

Cranberry Portage Man.   4FV/5GZ
On the shore of Athapapuskow Lake, Cranberry Portage is the gateway to Grass River Provincial Park, a 565,000-acre wilderness whose chain of 154 lakes flows into Hudson Bay. Two 60-foot suspension bridges across the Grass River were built as a centennial project by militia units from Flin Flon and Pine Falls.

Cranbrook B.C.   2FZ/13AY
The cathedral-like little church on the St. Eugene Reserve was built with cash from an Indian's discovery of a rich lead-silver deposit. A Kootenay named Pierre, in 1893, found a rich galena. outcrop which became the St. Eugene mine near Moyie. The Rev. Nicholas Coccola arranged sale of the claim and with the proceeds built a house for Pierre and a new church.

Trilobite fossils are found at Purcell Basin near Cranbrook. Trilobites were among the first living creatures on earth—about 500,000,000 years ago during the Cambrian period.

Creignish N.S.   9EY/23FX
A magnificent view of St. George's Bay and the Strait of Canso is had from the top of 850-foot Creignish Mountain.

Creston B.C.   2FZ
The distinctive Kootenay canoe once used extensively by Indians here—bow and stern come to a point at or under the waterline—is cited to support the theory that Asians migrated to North America via Siberia and Alaska. The only other place where native people have developed a similar craft is in the Amur River region of southeast Russia.

The "sturgeon-nosed" bark Kootenays were particularly suited to use in marshes. One of the few remaining Kootenays is in the Creston library museum. (The Smithsonian Institution in Washington and the National Museum of Man in Ottawa have one each.) Miniatures made by Mrs. Charlotte Basil of the Lower Kootenay Indian band are sold here, each with a certificate of authenticity.

□ The Creston Valley Wildlife Management Area is 16,000 acres of flat, marshy land and lake on the valley bottom. Thousands of migrating waterfowl, particularly the large white whistling swans, stop spring and fall. Countless other species of birds nest here. The refuge extends from Kootenay Lake to the U.S. border.

□ The Glass House, 25 miles north, is a turreted castle-like structure built of more than 400,000 embalming fluid bottles. The late David Henderson Brown, a funeral director, spent two years collecting the sturdy square-bottomed, stubby-necked bottles. The house he started in 1952—he and his wife lived in it for 16 years—quickly became a tourist attraction and is now run by Brown's son. Each of the bottles is capped, providing the house with excellent insulation.

□ The Butterfly Bonspiel (first weekend in March) got its name when a butterfly lighted on a skip's broom at a natural-ice curling competition one mild winter.

Crestwynd Sask.   4DZ
A roadside plaque near here tells how old women tended fires through a prairie night long ago, enabling a party of Crees to escape from besieging Blackfoot warriors. Only the women were scalped in the Blackfoot attack at dawn. But they still live, legend says, for on windy nights their mocking laughter can be heard from an island in Old Wives' Lake.

Crystal Beach Ont.   17DZ
A plaque marks where a British force set out in small boats to attack two armed U.S. schooners anchored in Lake Erie off American-held Fort Erie in 1814. The British captured the schooners.

Cumberland B.C.   2BY/12BW
The swayback buildings of an almost deserted Chinatown are reminders of Cumberland's days as a booming coal-mining center. So many Chinese were brought in during the 1890s that Cumberland's Chinatown was reputedly bigger than San Francisco's. But since coal mining ended in 1966 the Chinese community has all but disappeared. Cumberland now is a quiet resort village. Old buildings still in use include a frame hospital (1894) and a yellow brick post office (1907).

Cumberland House Sask.   4FW/5GZ
Founded by Samuel Hearne in 1774 as the Hudson's Bay Company's first inland post, Cumberland House is the oldest settlement in Saskatchewan. Its importance as a trading center diminished as overland travel and

communication to the south improved, but the HBC post still exists. The company maintains a muskrat reserve in the Saskatchewan River delta.

In Cumberland House are the remains of the HBC steamer *Northcote,* used against the Métis at Batoche in the Northwest Rebellion in 1885. The Métis tried to stop the *Northcote* by lowering a ferry cable across the South Saskatchewan but succeeded only in knocking off her smokestacks. However, they did delay her long enough to prevent the troops aboard from taking part in the attack at Batoche.

Cupids Nfld. 11DZ
An engraved granite shaft commemorates Sea Forest Plantation, Newfoundland's first official settlement. John Guy led 39 colonists here in 1610; they built a fort and a battery of three guns. But after 18 years of pirate raids and the opposition of English fishermen the colony was disbanded. Some residents of Cupids are descendants of the original settlers.

Cut Knife Sask. 4CX
A gaunt framework of tepee poles marks the lonely grave of Poundmaker, a chief who wanted peace but fought for his people—and was convicted of making war in the Northwest Rebellion of 1885.

He signed Treaty Six for the Crees in 1876, guided the governor-general on a tour of the northwest in 1881, and agitated for better conditions as his people settled on reserves. After the rebellion started, some of Poundmaker's Crees were accused of looting, burning and killing. More than 300 soldiers and policemen, commanded by Col. W.D. Otter, marched on Poundmaker's camp at Cut Knife Hill. Poundmaker, armed only with a whip (to urge his men to protect their women and children), lured Otter into a three-sided trap and Otter withdrew. Poundmaker refused to let his Crees ambush Otter's men on their march east to Battleford. When the rebellion ended he surrendered and was tried for "levying war against Her Majesty."

"I am not guilty," he said. "What I did was for the Great Mother. When my people and the whites met in battle, I saved the Queen's men. I took the firearms from my following and gave them up at Battleford. Had I wanted war, I would not be here but on the prairie. You did not catch me. I gave myself up. You have me because I wanted peace."

Poundmaker served a year in penitentiary. On his release, the hostility of white settlers in Saskatchewan forced him to Alberta, where he died July 4, 1886. His remains were brought to the Poundmaker Reserve near Cut Knife in 1967 and a national historic plaque honoring him was erected on the reserve in 1972.

□ The world's largest tomahawk has a 54-foot, six-ton B.C. fir as a handle and a 2,500-pound fiber glass blade. It was built in Tomahawk Park to publicize Tomahawk Rodeo Days, a celebration in October.

Sunset silhouettes the grave of Poundmaker near Cut Knife. The Cree chief, born near present-day Battleford, Sask., died in 1886 not long after his release from prison.

Cypress Hills (Alta./Sask.) 4CZ
The fascinating, often bizarre Cypress Hills are one of nature's freaks. Surrounded by a gently rolling sea of prairie grass, they form an island capped by rock that a mountain-fed river deposited millions of years ago. The cap resisted erosion and the hills escaped the last grinding glaciation that covered the prairies only 10,000 years ago. The hills, varying from 80 to 100 miles east to west, straddle the Saskatchewan-Alberta border. From 400 feet above sea level in the east they rise to almost 5,000 feet in Alberta.

Cypress Hills natural history is preserved in fossils of sabertooth cats, three-toed horses, tapirs and camels that roamed 30,000,000 years ago. Some pre-Ice Age life has survived, often in mutated form: white ants, horned toads, hognose vipers, kangaroo rats and scorpions, all alien to the Canadian prairie. The usual prairie flowers and grasses grow here; there are also orchids, yucca grass and cactus. Antelope thrive on the rich grass; beaver and a variety of birds live along the creeks and lakes. Saskatchewan and Alberta have established provincial parks in the hills.

Explorers misnamed the area. Confusing the lodgepole pine with jack pine (*cyprès*), Frenchmen called the hills *Montagne du Cyprès.* English explorers compounded the error with a poor translation and the Cypress Hills were named—although there isn't a cypress tree to be found.

□ The Cypress Hills massacre in 1873 speeded up formation of the North West Mounted Police. When a large group of Indians was killed by white American wolf hunters who accused them of horse thieving, indignation ran high in eastern Canada. The NWMP trekked west to clean up the whiskey forts where Indians were fed bad liquor and

Abandoned in 1883, then burned, Fort Walsh in the Cypress Hills was rebuilt in 1944 and now is a national historic park.

cheated of their furs and horses by American traders. (The wolfers fled to Montana and were not punished.)

The NWMP established Fort Walsh (south of what is now Saskatchewan's Cypress Hills

Provincial Park) in 1875. The post was moved to Maple Creek, Sask., in 1883 and Fort Walsh was burned soon after.

Sitting Bull and his Sioux, after defeating the U.S. cavalry in the Battle of the Little Big Horn in Montana, escaped into the Cypress Hills in 1876. For five years a handful of men at the NWMP's Wood Mountain post controlled 3,000 restless Sioux. Some were persuaded to return to the United States under promise of amnesty from Washington. Their defection and the growing destitution of the rest led Sitting Bull to surrender to U.S. authorities at Fort Buford, N. Dak., in 1881.

No NWMP officer was killed by violence until 1879, when Constable Marmaduke Graburn's body was found in a coulee at Horse Camp, near Fort Walsh. An Indian named Star Child was tried two years later but acquitted because of insufficient evidence. A cairn in the Alberta Cypress Hills tells the Graburn story.

Czar Alta.   4BX
The Prairie Panorama Museum has pioneer household items, books, costumes and toys, and displays that illustrate the natural and archaeological history of the prairies.

D

Dalhousie N.B.   9CW
Major displays in the Chaleur Area History Museum deal with pioneer days in northeastern New Brunswick and the growth of fishing, lumbering, shipbuilding, farming and the pulp and paper industry. Pioneer artifacts include a cheese press, boot crimper, yarn measure and Scottish furniture dating from 1790. The museum has an Acadian genealogy from the mid-1600s to 1852 and copies of the logs of British ships in the 1760 Battle of the Restigouche (*see* Restigouche). Another display tells about Dalhousie's first big industry, cooperage, in days when huge amounts of Restigouche salmon were barreled and shipped to Europe in sailing vessels.

Dalhousie, a year-round port at the mouth of the Restigouche River, offers deep-sea fishing and salt-water swimming in sheltered Chaleur Bay. There are tours of the New Brunswick International Paper Company plant.

Dalvay P.E.I. *see* Prince Edward Island National Park

Dartmouth N.S.   9EY/22FW
This "city of lakes"—it has 23—is opposite Halifax on the east side of Halifax harbor. It was founded in 1750, a year after Halifax. The cities are linked by a ferry system started in 1752 and by two modern bridges.
BABES IN THE WOODS (1) A stone in Woodlawn Cemetery marks the grave of Jane and Margaret Meagher, sisters aged six and four

who died of exposure after becoming lost in dense forest here in 1842. Their story was widely told and they became known as "the babes in the woods."

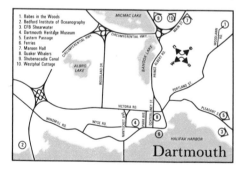

BEDFORD INSTITUTE OF OCEANOGRAPHY (2) Operated by the federal government, this is one of the world's largest centers for exploration of the sea. Its ships search out secrets of currents and tides and seek information on the physical and biological processes of marine environment.
CFB SHEARWATER (3) A jet air base.
DARTMOUTH HERITAGE MUSEUM (4) Main exhibits deal with the Micmac Indians, the founding of Dartmouth, the Shubenacadie Canal, the Halifax-Dartmouth ferries and Joseph Howe, the great Nova Scotian journalist, orator and politician. In the Howe room, a re-creation of his study, are his watch and pipe, a snuffbox made from a ram's

War canoes race on Lake Banook at Dartmouth in a regatta that is part of the city's annual Natal Day celebration in August. Another of Dartmouth's 26 lakes, Micmac Lake, is often the site of water skiing competitions.

head, and books that include Howe's Micmac dictionary (c.1860). A mannequin at a desk has a sculptured head of Howe. Other exhibits in the museum concern Dartmouth and the sea, local aviation history, the 1917 Halifax explosion, and the city's lakes—once the area's main source of ice for summer refrigeration. An art gallery features the work of a Dartmouth painter, George Craig.

EASTERN PASSAGE (5) A Nova Scotian pilot steered the Confederate gunboat *Tallahassee* through this treacherous channel to elude U.S. federal cruisers off the usual harbor entrance during the American Civil War.

FERRIES (6) The oldest salt-water ferry system in Canada is still going strong. It is a good way to see the harbor, naval dockyard and shipping close up.

MAROON HALL (7) High ground east of Lake Loon is the site of Maroon Hall, headquarters for a late 18th-century colony of Maroons from Jamaica. The colony failed and in 1800 most of the Maroons were sent to Sierra Leone. Nothing remains of the building.

QUAKER WHALERS (8) Nantucket Quakers moved here from Massachusetts after the American Civil War. Plaques mark the sites of their meeting house and a whaling company run by Quakers. Several old Quaker homes are still in use.

SHUBENACADIE CANAL (9) This route across Nova Scotia, connecting Halifax harbor with the Bay of Fundy by means of 50 miles of lakes and locks, was started in 1826, abandoned, revived and used during the 1860s. It carried coal, machinery and supplies to the mines of Montague and Waverley and brought quartz, timber, cordwood and bricks from the interior. The remains of some locks survive.

WESTPHAL COTTAGE (10) A plaque marks the birthplace of Philip (1782-1880) and Sir George A. Westphal (1785-1875), brothers who became Royal Navy admirals.

Dauphin Man.   6AX

The music of balalaikas and the beat of wild cossack dances fill this town during the four-day National Ukrainian Festival at the beginning of August. Descendants of Ukrainian settlers (the first came here in 1896) dress in traditional costumes, take part in historical and cultural displays and feast on *pirogi, holupchi* and other Slavic delicacies.

☐ Dauphin lies west of Dauphin Lake, south of Lake Winnipegosis and just north of Riding Mountain National Park. Northwest of Dauphin, in the heart of Duck Mountain Provincial Forest, is 492-square-mile Duck

The Happy Step from Steppe to Prairie

The fifth largest ethnic group in Canada, Ukrainians form 5½ percent of the total population of the prairie provinces. Ukrainian immigration was only a trickle in the 1870s, '80s and early '90s but it became a steady flow in 1896. Most Ukrainians headed for such settlements as Dauphin, where the prairie resembled the steppes of their homeland. Another wave of immigration after 1920 continued into the 1930s. The most recent influx followed World War II, when many Ukrainians fled Russian communism.

Nodding sunflowers, grown for their oil (it is used for shortening), fill a Manitoba plain near Dauphin.

Mountain Provincial Park, with 73 lakes and a major elk herd. Baldy Mountain (2,727 feet), the highest point in Manitoba, is in the park.

□ The McCallum Museum and Trading Post, 4½ miles west, contains pioneer farm implements and vehicles.

Dawson Y.T.   1BV

Battered by fate and slowed by age, Dawson wears the proud marks of its flaming youth as the Yukon's "City of Gold." The 830 permanent residents live nostalgically among the ghosts of more than 25,000 who flocked to Dawson in 1897-1905, on streets where Tex Rickard and Rex Beach strolled (and Glass-Eyed Annie and Overflowing Flora), past silent dance halls and swinging-door saloons and gambling casinos where the motto was "never refuse a drink or kick a dog." Some gold-rush buildings are still in use: Madame Tremblay's emporium of women's wear (now a co-op store), the original post office, the Flora Dora Hotel, Diamond Tooth Gertie's gambling hall (roulette, black jack, can-can girls . . . and bingo). Still other old buildings are part of Klondike Gold Rush International Historic Park (*see below*).

□ Gold was discovered 11 miles southeast of Dawson on Bonanza Creek, a tributary of the Klondike River, in 1896. Word of the strike by George Carmack, Skookum Jim and Tagish Charlie reached the outside world in 1897, touching off the Klondike stampede (*see* Bennett, Carcross, Carmacks). Dawson sprang up at the confluence of the Klondike and Yukon rivers. Between 1896 and 1904, the Klondike creeks gave up more than $100,000,000 in gold. But as the more accessible gold was removed, Dawson's population dwindled. Some gold is still mined and the creeks' total yield has been more than $250,000,000.

BEAR CREEK   On the Klondike Highway, eight miles south of Dawson, Parks Canada is developing an exhibit of placer, hydraulic and dredge mining, including a reconstructed gold room of the sort in which ore was processed and gold was melted into bars.

BONANZA CREEK ROAD   It leads from Dawson to the site of the original Discovery claim

Gold-rush ghosts sometimes seem to clump the wooden sidewalks of old Dawson (opposite). Famous buildings such as the Palace Grand Theater have been restored to former elegance.

Duncan B.C.   2CZ/12DY
The romantic story of logging, British Columbia's mightiest industry, is told with effect at the Cowichan Valley Forest Museum. Three steam engines rumble along 1½ miles of narrow-gauge track through 40 acres of forest, over a 300-foot trestle, past donkey engines, a sawmill, a waterwheel and a cedar log 11 feet in diameter. Along Forester's Walk are 25 species of trees, among them 300-year-old Douglas firs 180 feet high.

The community museum is supported by Duncan, North Cowichan and Lake Cowichan and the British Columbia Forest Service. Among the exhibits are Little Jakey, a steam log-hauler (c.1890), hand-pump cars on 400 and 200 feet of track, a caboose, two gasoline-powered locomotives and a 1918 Maxwell logging truck. In one museum building are hundreds of photographs, pieces of small logging equipment and a slice from the butt of a Douglas fir estimated to date back to 640 A.D.

□ Prime Douglas fir is harvested by four Duncan sawmills, many small mills and independent loggers. Twelve miles southwest, on the southern slope of Waterloo Mountain, a plaque identifies what may be the oldest living tree in Canada—a Douglas fir that was a seedling about 650 A.D. Other trees in the same grove are more than 1,000 years old.

Dundalk Ont.   7BY/17AW
The population of this village is almost doubled—to about 2,000—when amateur square- and step-dance competitions are held each June.

Dundas Ont.   7BZ/17BY
The town hall, designed in a version of Roman classic, is one of Ontario's finest municipal buildings. It was completed in 1849 at a time when the Desjardins Canal brought many ships through the Dundas Marsh from Hamilton and the town promised to become an important industrial and commercial center. With the railroad, growth declined.

□ Costumes, china, glass, archives, military artifacts and pioneer objects are displayed at the Dundas Historical Society Museum.

□ From the highway west of the Dundas Valley is a magnificent view of the valley and town, part of Hamilton and its harbor and Lake Ontario. At the top of the Niagara Escarpment is Webster's Falls Park, where Spencer Creek tumbles 85 feet into a thickly wooded gorge. Stone bridges cross the creek and stairs lead down into the gorge alongside the falls.

□ Much of the Royal Botanical Gardens (*see* Hamilton) is in Dundas.

Dundela Ont.   18DX
A monument and plaque on the McIntosh farm here honor John McIntosh and the famous red apple that bears his name. McIntosh, who migrated from New York in 1796, found and transplanted the original McIntosh Red seedling while clearing his farm in 1811. His son grafted shoots to other trees. Now thousands of McIntosh Red trees, all from the same parent, grow in North America. The original bore fruit until it died in 1906—95 years after McIntosh found it. A stone marks where it stood.

Dunham Que.   7FY/19CZ
Several houses built by Loyalists who came here in 1796 have been preserved.

Dunstaffnage P.E.I.   23CW
A 1938 Packard hearse, a 1916 Buick and a 1931 Ford cabriolet are among the restored automobiles at the Spoke Wheel Car Museum. The Ford was the last sequence of the Model A line. It has a four-cylinder engine, rumble seat, slanted windshield, black fenders and convertible top, beige body and chocolate brown trim.

Dunvegan Alta.   1BZ/2EV
Paintings by an early missionary decorate the chapel of St. Charles Mission near here. The Rev. Emile Grouard built St. Charles, the first Roman Catholic church in northern Alberta, between 1883 and 1885. One painting in the chapel, now a museum, is *The Crucifixion,* a copy on canvas of Father

Duck Lake Jail, from which Almighty Voice escaped, still has rings on the floor to which prisoners were chained. Gabriel Dumont's watch, a gift from the French Canadians of New York City, is in a Duck Lake museum.

St. Charles Mission on the Peace River at Dunvegan, Alta., was the first permanent Roman Catholic church in the vast Peace River district.

Grouard's original, which was done on moosehide. The original was destroyed by fire.

□ Alexander Mackenzie stopped here in 1793 in his search for a route to the Pacific Ocean. A cairn marks where the North West Company built Fort Dunvegan in 1805.

□ A bridge across the Peace River here is the only suspension bridge in Alberta.

Dunvegan Ont.   7EY/18EW

A pot in which Bonnie Prince Charlie and his followers cooked porridge and venison while in hiding in the Hebrides after the Battle of Culloden in 1746 is in a museum here. Before Charles Edward escaped to France his little group included the seven "outlaws of Glenmoriston," among them Donald Chisholm. One of Chisholm's descendants brought the pot to Canada and it was donated to the Glengarry Museum which is located here.

The two-story log building (c. 1830) was a store for 35 years, then (until 1890) the Star Inn. It became a museum in 1961. Also on display are bagpipes believed to have been played in a Highland regiment at the Battle of Waterloo in 1815.

E

Eagle Point B.C.

A bronze pyramid erected in 1904 marks the Canadian-American border. Eagle Point is on the Portland Canal, which separates British Columbia from the southernmost part of the Alaska panhandle.

Ear Falls Ont.   6DX

Examples of transportation used in the development of northwestern Ontario are displayed at the Ear Falls District Museum. Outside are the tugboat *Patricia*, which towed

equipment barges to mines in the Red Lake area 40 miles northwest, and the wreckage of a Junkers 34, an all-metal bush plane; inside are dogsleds used by the Hudson's Bay Company in hauling furs to Winnipeg. Also

Economy N.S.—Tides here are among the highest in the world, sometimes more than 50 feet. Miles of red sand are laid bare at low water. Economy Mountain, 700 feet above Minas Basin, affords spectacular views of the sea and the shoreline. (23BY)

Volcanic residue colors rugged Mount Edziza Provincial Park near Eddontenajon.

exhibited are harnesses, logging equipment and chain and ice saws. Indian pottery and weapons, some 2,000 years old, are displayed.

Ear Falls, on the English River, was an important center in the fur trade and grew during the Red Lake Gold Rush in the late 1920s. The population now is more than 2,000 with workers employed in mining and logging and at an Ontario Hydro generating station.

□ North is Pakwash Lake Provincial Park, its campground a former Ontario highways department camp.

Eastend Sask.   4CZ
The three-foot skull of a prehistoric reptile, the triceratops, is displayed in the natural science museum of the Eastend High School. It was found in one of several bone deposits in this area at the southeast limit of the Cypress Hills.

Nearby at Chimney Coulee are the crumbling remains of cabins where Métis fur traders and buffalo hunters wintered in the mid-1800s.

East Point P.E.I.   9EX/23EW
A white lighthouse marks this eastern extremity of Prince Edward Island.

Eaton Que.   9AY/20BZ
The Compton County Historical Museum is in a former Congregational church built in 1841. It displays a tureen and pitcher brought from Massachusetts in 1794 by Capt. Josiah Sawyer, founder of nearby Sawyerville; a hand gristmill used by Scottish settlers; a three-level wood stove (one stove, two ovens); and a pewter Communion set, 1850 Bible and collection boxes once used in the church.

Eaton town hall (c.1850) was the first high school in this part of the Eastern Townships.

□ A covered bridge on the Eaton River is 112 feet long.

Eddontenajon B.C.   1AX
Mount Edziza Provincial Park and its remarkable examples of volcanic activity are not yet accessible by road but planes and helicopters from here and Dease Lake fly tourists over to see the ruggedly beautiful terrain.

The slopes of the Spectrum Range are vibrant with orange, red and brown stripes and on a north slope there is a startling slash of deep purple. The colors are caused by surface oxidation of volcanic rock. Beyond the Spectrums is a vast barren plateau and north of Raspberry Pass another 6,000-foot plateau with more colored rocks and a scattering of volcanic craters.

Beyond that is 9,143-foot Mount Edziza, with a glacier spilling down its south side, and more volcanic cones. One, the Eve cinder cone, is a remarkable 700-foot-high black cone (1,300 feet in diameter) with a red crater. On its east slope is a dormant volcano that may last have erupted its purple and red lava as recently as 200 years ago.

Farther north is the Stikine River canyon, 500 feet deep in places.

Edgar Ont.   7CY/17BW
An African Episcopal church here was built in 1849 for black settlers who had escaped from slavery in the United States. Outside is a cairn bearing the names of families who worshiped here.

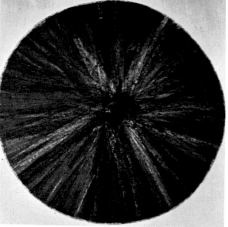

Edmonton Alta.

4AW/14FW

The capital of Alberta, a fast-growing city astride the North Saskatchewan River, prides itself on being the Gateway to the North, the distribution center of Canada's oil industry and an increasingly important industrial center. More and more involved with northern development, and strategically located on the great circle route to the Orient, it also calls itself the Aviation Capital of Canada. Some 10,000 miles of pipelines are linked here. More than 2,250 wells within a 25-mile radius of Edmonton (population 555,000) produce some 10 percent of Canadian oil. This most northerly of Canada's major cities is also a major meat-processing and distribution center. Agriculture still sets the place of the northern Alberta economy.

Edmonton started as a Hudson's Bay Company fur-trading post in 1795. It grew little until 1898 when it became a Klondike gold-rush supply base. In 1905, with a population of 8,350, it was chosen as the capital of the new province.

Rapid growth began in World War II when the Alaska Highway and Canol pipeline were built north and west of here. Discovery of

Easter eggs, embroideries, tapestry and bead-work are displayed in the Ukrainian Women's Association Museum in Edmonton. The Edmonton Art Gallery has a permanent collection with works ranging from A.Y. Jackson's *Three Lone Shacks* to a round enamel on masonite by Arthur McKay. An abstract sculpture (left) at the south end of the site is one of five works by Olle Holmsten on the terraces and facades of the Provincial Museum and Archives of Alberta.

---

oil at nearby Leduc in 1947 launched Edmonton into one of the biggest and longest boom eras any Canadian city has known. (On the derrick from Imperial Oil's Leduc No. 1 well, since moved to Edmonton's southern outskirts, is a sign proclaiming the city the "oil capital of Canada.") A quarter-century after Leduc the Alberta capital had grown into a clean and well-planned big city of high-rise buildings, fine museums, art galleries, live drama and opera troupes and a great university.

ALBERTA TELEPHONE TOWER (1) A museum on the 33rd floor of the provincial government telephone building has displays which range from antique phones housed in a turn-of-the-century drugstore to a World War II naval phone.

CANADA'S AVIATION HALL OF FAME (2) Tells the story of Canadian flying with photos, artifacts and model planes.

CAPITAL CITY RECREATION PARK (3) This 3,000-acre expanse of parkland straddles the North Saskatchewan. There are miles of trails for hiking, snowshoeing, cycling and cross-country skiing, as well as other facilities.

CITADEL THEATER (4) This glass and steel structure, completed in 1976, contains three theaters, the largest seating almost 700.

CITY HALL (5) A handsome building (1954) graced by a modernistic and once controversial "wild goose" fountain, the work of Lionel A. J. Thomas. There is an observation deck.

CIVIC CENTER (6) The city hall, 29-story CN Tower, Edmonton Art Gallery and Centennial Library, all facing Sir Winston Churchill Square.

COMMONWEALTH STADIUM (7) The facilities Edmonton built for 1978's XI Commonwealth Games were designed for continuing use. Among them, the 42,584-seat Commonwealth Stadium is Canada's third largest.

EDMONTON INTERNATIONAL SPEEDWAY (8) A 251-acre complex made up of a drag strip, 2½-mile and 1½-mile road courses and a ⅞-mile oval.

EDMONTON MUNICIPAL AIRPORT (9) Canada's first municipally owned airport, it was Edmonton's base for bush pilots who helped open the North after World War I. Now it boasts the longest runway in Canada (12,000 feet) and hectic daily traffic. There are three other airports in the area: Edmonton International, Villeneuve and one at the CFB base in suburban Namao.

FORT EDMONTON PARK (10) When completed, this 158-acre outdoor museum on the south bank of the North Saskatchewan will reflect most periods of Edmonton's history. It was started in 1969 with construction of a new Fort Edmonton and with workers using the kind of tools employed by Hudson's Bay Company employees when they built the original in 1845. Palisades and bastion en-

Methodist missionary George McDougall built this church in 1872. (It was dedicated two years later.) Now a museum in the heart of Edmonton, it has the first steel plow to break Alberta soil; the first organ, brought west by Red River cart; a candle stand of the Rev. Robert T. Rundle, the first missionary of any denomination to work in the Canadian northwest; and a Cree Bible and hymnbook.

close an Indian trading house, married men's quarters, bachelor clerks' quarters and the chief factor's residence. A windmill like those which operated in the Red River Settlement grinds grain.

An 1885 street has about 30 buildings including replicas of a bakery, drugstore, lumber mill and saloon. A farmers' market sells fresh produce and handicrafts; visitors can ride in horse-drawn wagons or an early steam railway. A reconstruction of Blatchford Airfield, now the municipal airport, is designed to recall bush-pilot days.

HAWRELAK PARK (11) Trout fishing in an artificial lake is reserved for anglers 16 or younger. There is skating in winter.

HIGH LEVEL BRIDGE (12) This Edmonton landmark was built in 1910-13 at a cost of $2,000,000. The top deck of the 2,478-foot span carries trains; motor traffic is on a lower level.

JOHN WALTER HISTORIC SITE (13) Boatbuilder John Walter built this log house in 1874. At various times it was a ferry office, telegraph office and stopping place for goldseekers bound for the Klondike. Also on the site are a log house Walter built in 1886 and a frame house he built in 1899.

JUBILEE AUDITORIUM (14) The Northern Alberta Jubilee Auditorium, with a seating ca-

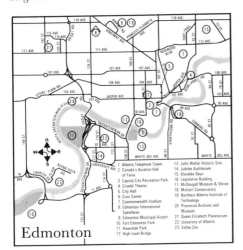

1. Alberta Telephone Tower
2. Canada's Aviation Hall of Fame
3. Capital City Recreation Park
4. Citadel Theater
5. City Hall
6. Civic Center
7. Commonwealth Stadium
8. Edmonton International Speedway
9. Edmonton Municipal Airport
10. Fort Edmonton Park
11. Hawrelak Park
12. High Level Bridge
13. John Walter Historic Site
14. Jubilee Auditorium
15. Klondike Days
16. Legislative Building
17. McDougall Museum & Shrine
18. Muttart Conservatory
19. Northern Alberta Institute of Technology
20. Provincial Archives and Museum
21. Queen Elizabeth Planetarium
22. University of Alberta
23. Valley Zoo

Edmonton

Fair-Haired Pierre Lives as Tête Jaune

Pierre Hatsinaton, a mainly Iroquois guide who had the fair hair of some unidentified white ancestor, was called *Tête Jaune*. The sobriquet lives on: in Yellowhead Pass, in Tête Jaune Cache, B.C. (near where Yellow Head once stored furs), and in the Yellowhead Route, a 1,930-mile highway system. This "main street of the north" goes from Portage la Prairie, Man., to Saskatoon, to Edmonton (where an association promotes the use of the scenic route), to Jasper and on into British Columbia. Just north of Tête Jaune Cache it splits, one fork dropping southwest to Kamloops, the other arcing northwest through Prince George to Prince Rupert on the Pacific coast.

pacity of 2,731, is a twin of an auditorium in Calgary. Both were built in 1955 to commemorate Alberta's 50th anniversary as a province.

KLONDIKE DAYS (15) For 10 days in July Edmonton bounces to a city-wide revival of the excitement of the gold rush of '98. People don Victorian finery, stores acquire false fronts and fancy-lettered signs, pubs and lounges become saloons, and everywhere old songs are sung to the melodies of piano jockeys wearing straw hats. Activities include contests ranging from rock lifting to log chopping, non-stop

Dougall, a Methodist missionary. A peculiarity of its construction is the upright logs in the corners, over the front door and at the windows. Long disused, the building was moved next to McDougall United Church and restored in the 1940s and 1950s. It is now a museum.

A cairn four miles north of Calgary marks where McDougall died during a prairie snowstorm in 1876.

MUTTART CONSERVATORY (18) Four glass-walled pyramids dominate this complex. Plants from tropical, temperate and arid climates are housed in three; the fourth features flowering ornamentals. A mural by Chipewyan artist Alex Janvier encircles the lobby.

NORTHERN ALBERTA INSTITUTE OF TECHNOLOGY (19) Eighteen thousand students and 170 laboratories and shops in 22 acres under one roof.

PROVINCIAL ARCHIVES AND MUSEUM (20) Alberta's 1967 Centennial project was a large building to house both the Archives and Provincial Museum on the 13½-acre grounds of old Government House (once the lieutenant-governor's residence, now a provincial reception center). Parts of the outer walls are faced with Tyndall limestone containing fossils that lived some 445,000,000 years ago in a shallow sea near present-day Tyndall, Man.

The Archives preserve a vast collection of documents, clippings, maps, photos, diaries, newspapers, government records, tape recordings and material on microfilm.

In an orientation gallery of the museum are two larger-than-life sculptures by John B. Weaver: *The Stake* (a pioneer family group) and *The Pronghorns*. An 11-piece bronze frieze

entertainment from a dozen outdoor stages, band parades, flapjack breakfasts and barbecues, and harness racing.

LEGISLATIVE BUILDING (16) Overlooking the North Saskatchewan River, this high-domed building has Quebec, Pennsylvania and Italian marble, much hand-carved oak and solid mahogany doors. Electronic bells with 330 bell tones have been installed in the dome since 1967.

McDOUGALL MUSEUM & SHRINE (17) The first structure outside the walls of Fort Edmonton, it was built in 1872 by the Rev. George Mc-

Refinery Row, east of Edmonton, includes a polyethylene plant, giant storage tanks and pipeline pumping stations.

illustrates the scope of the museum exhibits. There are four main exhibit galleries: Indian, habitat, historical and natural history. Artifacts, models, dioramas, specimens and photographs are used to tell Alberta's story in terms of its paleontology, zoology, geology, Indians, fur traders and pioneers.

A diorama shows five types of dinosaurs and other creatures, trees and plants as they existed near the end of the Age of Reptiles (64,000,000 years ago) in what is now Alberta. In one gallery is the incomplete skeleton of a duck-billed dinosaur found in 1937 near Manyberries, Alta. A fur-trade exhibit includes a model of Fort Edmonton as it was in 1846. Habitat displays include such animals as the pronghorn (*see* Cabri), grizzly bear, moose and white-tailed deer.

Lectures, films and demonstrations are presented in a 400-seat auditorium.

QUEEN ELIZABETH PLANETARIUM (21) Canada's first planetarium was opened in 1960.

UNIVERSITY OF ALBERTA (22) The university, founded in 1908, is on the south bank of the North Saskatchewan. Among its showpieces are a medical sciences complex, the Student Union Building (a black and white structure), and a solar-heated residence.

The geology museum's most prized possessions, in a collection of rocks, minerals and fossils, are the 30-inch head of a flesh-eating dinosaur and a 30-foot wall mount of a duck-billed dinosaur.

The University Art Gallery and Museum has artifacts ranging from Grecian pottery and Roman glass to a Congolese executioner's knife, Eskimo snow goggles made from driftwood, and a 1904 machine for making dental crowns. Indian artifacts include a glass-bead-embroidered buckskin firebag (to carry flint, twigs and sweet grass for smoking meat), and a saddle of carved wood covered with rawhide. The saddle reflects Spanish design and indicates Alberta Indians got the saddle as they did the horse—from the Spanish conquistadores. An archaeological collection includes a clay bowl and lid (3500 B.C.) from Ur and a seventh-century B.C. Corinthian lekane (bowl) of terra-cotta.

VALLEY ZOO (23) Birds and small animals are housed in five acres of fairy-tale settings surrounded by a stockade, entered through a moated castle, linked by a quarter-mile railway.

The zoo specializes in raising young orphan animals and has more than 100 species ranging from camels and seals to sea lions and cougars.

Edmundston N.B. 9BX

Pulp produced here by the Fraser Companies is piped across the Saint John River—the international border—to be made into paper at Fraser's plant in Madawaska, Me. Tours of both plants are available.

The stone and marble Cathedral of the Immaculate Conception is a fine example of rich architectural design. Collège Saint-Louis, an affiliate of the Université de Moncton, overlooks the city.

Edmundston, 90% French-speaking, prides itself on being the capital of the Republic of Madawaska, a mythical border-straddling state with its own flag and coat of arms.

Four miles north of Edmundston is a provincial park, Les Jardins de la République. The Antique Auto Museum in the park displays restored vintage automobiles.

Pre-Christian tau cross (so named from its resemblance to the Greek capital T) is part of the Stations of the Cross by Claude Roussel at Collège Saint-Louis in Edmundston.

Mont Farlagne, three miles west of here, is a ski center. Lac Baker, 25 miles to the west, is five miles long and lined with sandy beaches.

Eganville Ont. 7DX/18BW

The Bonnechère Caves are almost 1,000 feet of twisting passageways in one wall of a Bonnechère River gorge. The caves, six miles east of here, were formed by water erosion in limestone.

Egmont B.C. 2CY/12CW

Salt-water rapids here live and die as regularly as the tides that squeeze back and forth in the Skookumchuck Narrows. The turbulence four times a day is a wild brew of whirlpools and back eddies created as the water fights through the rocky passage. Inland are the Sechelt, Narrows and Salmon inlets; seaward are Jervis Inlet and the Strait of Georgia.

Elbow Sask. 4DY

Lake Diefenbaker, a 140-mile-long reservoir formed by the Gardiner Dam, is 16 miles north. It and the smaller Qu'Appelle Dam, which controls the release of water and is 13 miles southeast of Elbow, are part of the South Saskatchewan River Project. At the

Settler's First Home
A Mini-Palace Soddy

Many of the west's early settlers built their first dwellings from the most abundant building material available, the deep-rooted sod of the seemingly endless prairie. To English homesteaders a soddy was only a rude preliminary to the building of a decent frame house. But settlers from central Europe, accustomed to the use of mud in house building, often turned their sod shacks into mini-palaces with smooth, shiny interiors and cornices adorned with painted figures and flowers. The 20-by-24-foot sod house (right) adjoining the Elbow Museum shows how comfortable the settler could be. The walls are of 30-by-15-inch sods four inches thick; more sod on a framework of logs forms the roof. The furnishings include an organ and a wrought iron stove. The Elbow soddy was built in 1965.

Gardiner Dam is the Coteau Creek hydro-electric station, planned to produce 800,000,000 kilowatt hours of energy a year. Douglas Park, one of four big recreation areas taking shape along the 540-mile shoreline of Lake Diefenbaker, is 12 miles south of Elbow. Danielson and Coldwell parks are near the Gardiner Dam. Saskatchewan Landing Park is 70 miles southwest of Elbow.

In Douglas Park is a small piece of a 400-ton granite rock that could not be saved when Lake Diefenbaker was formed in 1966. The huge boulder, 26 feet by 26 and 14 feet high, was thought to have been moved an esti-

mated 200 miles by Ice Age glaciers. It became a kind of shrine to the Cree Indians (who gave it the name Mistusinne). Archaeologists tried in vain to have it moved to high ground to save it from being flooded. But a piece was salvaged and overlooks the lake that hides the rest of Mistusinne.

Elkhorn Man. 4FY
A 1908 Reo, a 1909 Metz, a 1909 Hupmobile and a 1918 Chevrolet touring—all in running condition—are among the more than 50 antique cars in the Manitoba Automobile Museum.

Elk Island National Park (Alta.) 4AW/14GW
Some 450 buffalo roam the 75 square miles of Elk Island National Park, sharing the rolling hills with moose, mule deer and elk.

Gardiner Dam (top center, beyond the spillway) is three miles long, 210 feet high, one of the world's biggest earth-fill dams. The dam, near Elbow, formed Lake Diefenbaker (top right).

The fenced preserve is covered with poplar, spruce, aspen and birch and dotted with small lakes and sloughs teeming with waterfowl. Started as a game preserve, Elk Island acquired a herd of 40 buffalo in 1907; that was the beginning of the present herd.

At Astotin Lake, the park's largest, is Sandy Beach recreation area, with cabins, trailer and campgrounds, a dance hall, swimming, fishing, boating, golfing and picnicking. A thatched-roof dacha contains the Ukrainian Folk Museum. About 2½ miles east is the Ukrainian Heritage Village—a group of about a dozen pioneer buildings dating from the 1890s.

Elliot Lake Ont.   7BW
Uranium mining and processing are depicted at the Elliot Lake Nuclear and Mining Museum. There are also displays of wildlife and of relics of the lumber industry's early days. Elliot Lake was founded in 1954 when rich uranium strikes were made nearby.

Elmira Ont.   7BY/17AX
A maple syrup festival the first Saturday in April attracts some 30,000 persons to this Waterloo County town. The main street is closed to traffic and becomes a mall where visitors buy bread, pies and cakes and pancakes dripping with fresh maple syrup. There are trips in horse- or tractor-drawn sleighs to sugar bushes in the area.

□ The Elmira Farmers' Market, held in a fairground building every Saturday, has about 60 booths, most operated by Mennonites. Butter, shoofly pie (made chiefly of maple syrup and brown sugar), sauerkraut, cheese and baked goods are sold.

Elmvale Ont.   7CY/17BV
A rustic marker in a field near here describes the Ossossané Bone Pit where every 8-12 years the Indians of Huronia reinterred the bones of relatives in a ceremonial Feast of the Dead. Archaeologists unearthed parts of some 900 skeletons from the communal grave. A sectional model of the burial site is in the Royal Ontario Museum in Toronto.

□ Hendrie Forest, a reforestation project, covers 1,658 acres south of here.

□ Elmvale holds a maple syrup festival every spring.

Elora Ont.   7BY/17AX
The Grand River here flows at the foot of the overhanging limestone walls of Elora Gorge, 75-100 feet deep and riddled with small caves. As it winds 2½ miles through Elora Gorge Conservation Area the river passes The Cascade, a 70-foot waterfall, splits close to where Islet Rock perches in the middle of another waterfall, then passes Hole-in-the-Rock, a cave whose paths lead to the bottom of the gorge, and Hidden Valley, which is accessible on foot. The Grand River Conservation Authority provides swimming, camping and hiking facilities and conservation demonstrations.

□ Pioneer furniture, tools, handicrafts, china and glass are displayed in the Wellington County Historical Museum near Elora.

Emerson Man.   6BZ/15DZ
Western Canada's first jail (c.1879) and customs house (c.1870) are part of the Gateway Stopping Place Museum. It also has a rare Red River cart.

Emerson, on the Red River just north of the U.S. border, was the gateway to the Canadian west in pre-railroad days.

A cairn 1½ miles north marks the site of Fort Dufferin, built by boundary commissioners in 1872. The newly formed North West Mounted Police trekked from Fort Dufferin in 1874.

Empress Alta.   4CY
A dozen refinery towers blaze with light at the gas plant of Pacific Petroleum Ltd., on the prairie 28 miles south of here. Their average height is 75 feet; one tower is 268 feet. In winter, steam rising from the plant gives it the appearance of a ship. The continuously operating plant makes 700,000 gallons of liquefied petroleum products daily.

□ Just across the Saskatchewan border from Empress, where the Red Deer River joins the South Saskatchewan River, is the site of Chesterfield House, a Hudson's Bay Company trading post built in 1800.

Englehart Ont.   7CW
Kap-Kig-Iwan Provincial Park, set in the deep and beautiful gorge of the Blanche River, has five waterfalls, the highest 70 feet.

Englishtown N.S.   9FX/23GW
The grave of Angus McAskill the Cape Breton giant (7 feet 9 inches, more than 400 pounds) is in a cemetery here. Giant McAskill was credited with single-handedly lifting huge logs and pulling heavy wagons. He died at nearby St. Anns (*see entry*) in 1863, aged 38. His boot in the Nova Scotia Museum in Halifax Citadel is 14½ inches long. His oversize chair is in a museum at St. Anns.

□ Cape Breton's first white settlement was here: a cairn marks the site of Sainte-Anne, settled in 1629 by Capt. Charles Daniel. It was renamed Port Dauphin when fortified in 1713, only to decline in importance six years later when Louisbourg was chosen to be the capital of France's Isle Royale (Cape Breton).

Escoumins Que.   9BW/21EX
A cross at Pointe à la Croix is a successor to one erected about 1662 by Indians who had been baptized at Tadoussac. Champlain visited here in 1603 and found signs of a thriving European industry. *C'est le lieu,* he wrote, *où les Basques font la pêche des baleines.* (This is the place where the Basques go whaling.) Evidence that Indians lived here about 600 A.D. has been found at Petit Lac Salé—into which salt water flows through a narrow aperture at high tide.

□ Escoumins was the birthplace of the poet Blanche Lamontagne-Beauregard, author of *Ma Gaspésie* (1928) and other works, and of journalist Robertine Barry (whose pseudonym was Françoise). She founded *Le Journal de Françoise,* a review published in the early 1900s. A framed document in the Hotel Bellevue, once Robertine Barry's home, tells that her father hid four Confederate Army deserters during the American Civil War. They are said to have swum three miles after jumping from ships in which they reached Quebec waters.

□ St. Lawrence River pilots board and disembark from some 4,000 ships a year off Anse aux Basques, two miles west of Escoumins. The pilot station was transferred there from Pointe-au-Père (Father Point) in 1960.

Escuminac N.B.   9DX

Fishing villages line the south shore of Miramichi Bay: Loggieville, Bay du Vin, Hardwicke, Baie-Sainte-Anne and Escuminac. An impressive sculpture by Claude Roussel stands at Escuminac in memory of fishermen lost off these shores.

A lighthouse here dates from 1844.

Espanola Ont.   7BW

A ghost town during the Depression of the 1930s, Espanola revived when a kraft paper mill was established by Kalamazoo Vegetable Parchment in 1945. There are conducted tours in summer.

Esquimalt B.C. *see* Victoria

Esterhazy Sask.   4FY

North America's biggest potash mine produces more than 2,000,000 tons of high-grade ore each year. It is about 10 miles east of here on what may be the world's largest potash deposit.

□ Esterhazy is named for a Hungarian nobleman who settled some of his countrymen here. It has a community museum.

Gravestone at Bienfait, near Estevan: a reminder of tragedy in 1931.

Estevan Sask.   4FZ

On a grave in nearby Bienfait—the common grave of three men accidentally killed by police rifle fire during a coal miners' strike—is a stone that calls the deaths deliberate. "Murdered," says the epitaph that a miners'

Canada geese at Eyebrow don't get caught. Ducks do, in wire traps baited with grain. Scooped out in a net, they are caged, tagged and set free.

union had carved in concrete. "Estevan Sep. 29 1931 by ----" (the word RCMP was removed soon after the stone was raised). The men were killed when several hundred persons marched on police lines in defiance of a town council ban on a public meeting arranged by the Mine Workers of Canada. Five other miners and five bystanders were wounded, 10 policemen injured.

Lignite mining has long been an important industry in the Estevan-Bienfait region. "Mr. Klimax," a dragline with a 35-cubic-yard bucket, is used at a mine that produces lignite for the 582,000-kilowatt Boundary Dam Power Station near here.

Estevan's major industries, in addition to mining, are oil (about 50,000,000 barrels of crude a year from Estevan wells), brick and tile (from extensive clay deposits) and one of western Canada's largest tree nurseries.

A museum in Woodlawn Regional Park, a mile south, is the restored barracks (1886) of the Wood End Depot of the North West Mounted Police. The depot was established in 1873 as a supply center for the British North American Boundary Commission, then served as a NWMP depot.

Eyebrow Sask.   4DY

Under Project Nisk'u (Cree for big goose), a breeding flock of 500 pairs of Canada geese is being built up on the 3,100-acre marsh of Eyebrow Lake, eight miles north of here. By 1985 an estimated 15,000 Nisk'u goslings will have been transplanted to other Saskatchewan lakes. A system of dikes enables motorists to drive through the marsh.

□ Southeast of Eyebrow, at Lake Valley, is a pioneer museum.

□ Many tepee rings in excellent condition are found in the Eyebrow area.

F

Fairfield Village Ont. *see* Thamesville

Fairmont Hot Springs B.C. 2FY/13AX
The temperature of mineral springs at the north end of Columbia Lake, the source of the Columbia River, ranges from 96 to 110 degrees.

Fairvalley Ont. 17BV
A memorial plaque on a concession road in Medonte Township tells of the cost of one man's election campaign in backwoods Ontario in 1841. Elmes Steele, a Royal Navy captain turned farmer, ran for the first parliament of the united province of Upper and Lower Canada. Simcoe County's only polling place, in Barrie, was open for a week during which Steele, like other candidates, held open house. He made it but, says the plaque, "so heavy were his election expenses that he was financially ruined and never ran again." The memorial is near the site of Purbrook, the house Steele built in 1833 and where his son Samuel was born in 1849. Sir Sam Steele (*see* Fort Steele) was a hero of the early North West Mounted Police. A sketch of Purbrook at the memorial was done in 1836 by a daughter of the rector of nearby St. George's Anglican Church.

Falkland B.C. 2EY
In the Valley Museum are an Edison phonograph and cylinder records, early radios, stoves and coffee grinders, and other household furniture and utensils.

Fanshawe Ont. *see* London

Faro Y.T. 1BW
The open-pit Anvil Mine near here is the heart of an ore body expected ultimately to yield lead, zinc and silver worth an estimated $2,000,000,000. The town of Faro sprang from the Yukon wilderness when the mine went into operation in 1969.

Father Point Que. *see* Pointe-au-Père

Fenelon Falls Ont. 7CY/17DV
Maryboro Lodge, built in 1837 by James Wallis, a founder of the village, houses the Fenelon Falls Museum. It displays pioneer objects of the mid-19th century.
 □ One of the Trent waterway's main locks is here, with a lift of 23 feet, 7 inches.

Fergus Ont. 7BY/17AX
This town on the Grand River still has many of the plain, rectangular stone buildings preferred by the Lowland Scots who were its first settlers. Highland games are held in Fergus in August.

Ferguson B.C. 2FY
"The residents of this favored district should be happy," a Ferguson *Eagle* reporter wrote in 1900 when it was a booming mining town. "No banks, lawyers, highway robbers, policemen, sheriff, smallpox or other infectious diseases." Now, like neighboring Trout Lake City and Circle City, Ferguson is a ghost town. Only a few buildings, among them the Lardeau Hotel (once the "best $2-a-day house in the Lardeau district"), live on in the loneliness of their forlorn old age.

Fernie B.C. 2FZ/13BZ
Four miles southeast at what was the settlement of Coal Creek smoke can be seen coming from an underground coal mine. A fire started by a forest fire in 1931 continues to smolder.

Ferryland Nfld.   11DZ

Half-buried cannon on Isle of Bois, at the mouth of the harbor, are remnants of the turbulent past of this quiet fishing village. From Ferryland in the early 17th century the pirate admiral Peter Easton and 1,000 Newfoundland fishermen controlled the western Atlantic. Easton amassed one of the largest fortunes of his day by plundering Spanish treasure fleets. Many of the men in his 40 ships adopted their admiral's surname (as seamen of that era often did) and Easton is a common name in this part of Newfoundland.

A plaque near St. Joseph's High School marks the site of an elegant yellow brick house built in the 1620s by Lord Baltimore (*see* caption below). It was badly damaged when the Dutch sacked Ferryland. Villagers used the site as a quarry and the distinctive yellow bricks disappeared.

Ferryland beat off several sea attacks during the colonial wars and Isle of Bois (then Buoy Island) figured prominently in the town's defenses. There are plaques at the sites of two batteries of naval guns installed in 1743 by Capt. Thomas Smith, governor of Newfoundland. The island was abandoned in 1760 but manned again (and the fortifications enlarged and improved) during the late 1770s and early 1780s. The installations fell into ruin but were repaired and garrisoned in 1812-15.

Family coat of arms of Sir George Calvert, the first Lord Baltimore, is in an old stone church in Ferryland. Calvert received a charter in 1621 to start a colony in Newfoundland. But because of repeated French attacks and the harsh climate, he quit Newfoundland and founded a colony in Maryland in 1634.

Fish Creek Sask.   4DX

Trenches used by Métis sharpshooters in the Northwest Rebellion of 1885 can be traced on a hill here. Led by Gabriel Dumont, the Métis picked off troops led by Maj. Gen. Frederick Middleton as they tried to advance up Tourond's Coulee. Even artillery failed to dislodge the Métis. Before Middleton's reinforcements arrived, the Métis disappeared, ending the Battle of Fish Creek.

Fleming Sask.—The flat prairie, the two rows of poles, the grain elevators at the end of the long, straight road: a photograph of Fleming from 1½ miles west pretty well matches the picture on the reverse of the $1 bill. (4FY)

Five Finger Brook N.B.   9CX

A quaint water-powered gristmill is a favorite of photographers.

Flin Flon Man.   4FV/5GZ

A 20-foot fiber glass statue of Josiah Flintabbatey Flonatin immortalizes a fictional grocer-turned-explorer, hero of a 1905 novel, who gave this mining town its name. In *The Sunless City*, by J.E. Preston-Muddock, Flin Flon explores a bottomless lake, reaches the center of the earth and eventually returns through a hole in the earth's crust. Prospectors found a battered copy of the novel on a portage in 1908. One, Tom Creighton, after falling through lake ice six years later, built a fire which melted snow and revealed mineral-bearing rock. He and his friends decided this was where "old Flin Flon" had found the sunless city. The name stuck. A half-century later Al Capp, creator of the comic strip Li'l Abner, was asked to draw Flin Flon. The statue based on Capp's visualization was unveiled in 1962.

□ More than $1,500,000,000 in gold, silver, copper, cadmium and zinc has been mined here, most by the Hudson Bay Mining and Smelting Co.

□ The 81-mile Canadian Open Gold Rush Canoe Derby is a feature of the Flin Flon Trout Festival in early June. The winning two-man team splits $1,000. Other competitions include flour packing (up to 700 pounds carried by tumpline or headstrap), jigging (dancing), bannock baking, log sawing and fish filleting on Native Day. Manitoba and Saskatchewan girls compete for a mermaid queen title. The main event is a fishing derby in which the winning trout (likely to weigh 40 pounds) and pike (about 25 pounds) fetch $1,000 each.

□ A memorial plaque at the high school in Creighton, adjacent to Flin Flon on the Saskatchewan side of the border, honors Tom Creighton.

□ Flin Flon is the northern end of the Hanson Lake Road which winds 225 miles

Canoe derby teams head down Ross Creek at Flin Flon on the first day of a grueling 81-mile race. Much of Flin Flon is built on the solid rock of the Precambrian shield. Sewer and water pipes are in above-ground wooden conduits that double as sidewalks. Josiah Flintabbatey Flonatin's statue, designed by cartoonist Al Capp, is a Flin Flon landmark.

Birch-bark biting that produces such intricate designs as this may soon be a lost art. Cree Indians of northern Manitoba, near Flin Flon, fold thin bark into a wedge shape, then bite and rub it with the teeth.

through country covered with spruce, poplar and pine and dotted with hundreds of lakes. Mile 0 is at Smeaton, Sask. (*see entry*). Willowvale Wildlife Park has pheasants, peacocks, guinea fowl and other exotic birds.

Foam Lake Sask.   4EX
Pioneer tools, utensils and furniture are displayed at the Foam Lake Pioneer Museum.

Fogo Nfld.   11CX
Funk Island, an outcropping of granite 40 miles from here in the icy Labrador current, is 400 by 800 yards and only 46 feet high at its peak. It is a sanctuary for more than 1,000,000 birds—murres, gannets and, most colorful, puffins.

Forest Ont.   7BY/16CX
One half of the Forest-Lambton Museum, in a house built about 1900, is furnished in pioneer style. In the other half are early telephones, lighting devices and farm equipment and a pioneer schoolroom.

Forestville Que.   9BW/21EW
This town, founded in 1845 as Sault-au-Cochon, was renamed in 1941 in honor of Grant Forrest, onetime manager of a sawmill here. His two-story wooden house, built with enormous pine beams in 1873, is still occupied. It is known as the Price house.

At the Anglo-Canadian Pulp and Paper Mills Ltd. plant here is the world's highest-capacity pulpwood-loading system. It involves opening a power dam gate and using the resulting current to pull logs to a flume entrance. A mile-long, steel-lined wooden flume carries the wood to a loading plant in nine minutes, at an average speed of 600 feet a minute. There a hydraulic cylinder diverts the logs into chutes which slide them onto barges. Tugs push the barges 170 miles

Florenceville N.B.—Fiddleheads, the tender spring shoots of the ostrich ferns that grow in profusion along New Brunswick's rivers, are packed in McCain Foods' Florenceville plant, the only one in North America that freezes these tasty greens. On still nights at harvest time, Indians camped on riverbanks hear the sound of the fast-maturing shoots as they push aside spring flood debris. The fiddlehead has become something of a provincial symbol. The University of New Brunswick's literary publication is *The Fiddlehead*, a radio station boasts that it serves "the fiddlehead country" and fiddlehead-picking excursions have almost become a rite of spring. (9CX)

to Quebec. The lower level dam, the flume and the barge loading can be seen from a public road.

Forillon National Park (Que.)　　9DW/10HZ

Most of a beautiful peninsula at the northeast tip of the Gaspé was set aside in 1970 as 92-square-mile Forillon National Park, a magnificent mix of jagged seaside cliffs and fir-clad highlands. Just outside the park are coastal communities such as Cap-aux-Os, Rivière-au-Renard, Anse-au-Griffon and Cap-des-Rosiers.

The park is in five areas: Le Havre, Cap-Bon-Ami, Grande-Grève, Petit-Gaspé and Penouïl. One of many hiking trails leads from Petit-Gaspé to Cap Gaspé, which is the tip of Presqu'île de Forillon, the narrow extremity of the park. The cape, 200 feet high, drops to a beach accessible only at low tide. The tops of Bonaventure Island and Percé Rock can be seen 18 miles to the south.

Animals abound in the park, and thousands of birds nest in the cliffs. Seals bask on offshore rocks and whales cavort in secluded coves and bays. Plants range from sub-Arctic flora on the top of the cliffs to dune groupings at Penouïl.

There are three campgrounds in the park, which is open year-round. Winter activities include cross-country skiing and snowshoeing.

Forillon derives from *pharillon* (little lighthouse), the name given to a rock that once jutted from the sea at Grande-Grève, three miles from Cap Gaspé. In the early 17th century fires were maintained on it to guide fishermen to good beaches. The rock eventually crumbled into the sea.

Fort Alexander Man.　　6BX/15EW

A cairn marks the site of Fort Maurepas, first built in 1734 by Jean-Baptiste de La Vérendrye, eldest son of explorer Pierre de La Vérendrye. Burned by Indians, it was rebuilt in 1748 by his brother Pierre. Other forts (including Fort Alexander) were built in the area by the North West and Hudson's Bay companies.

Fort Assiniboine Alta.　　4AW

A cairn marks the site of a Hudson's Bay Company fort built in 1823 at the western end of the long portage between the North Saskatchewan River (Fort Edmonton) and the Athabasca River. From Fort Assiniboine the 18th-century water route west led up the Athabasca to Athabasca Pass, through what now is Jasper National Park to Boat Encampment, B.C., and Fort Vancouver (Wash.).

Fort-Chimo Que. *see* Umingmaqautik

Fort Erie Ont.　　7CZ/17DZ

On the Niagara River opposite Buffalo, N.Y., Fort Erie is linked with the big American city by the Peace Bridge opened in 1927 by the Prince of Wales (later Edward VIII). The town was settled by United Empire Loyalists in 1784—some were disbanded soldiers of Butler's Rangers—and was named for a fort built 20 years earlier (*see below*).

Mather Memorial Archway and Park, the gift of American philanthropist Alonzo C.

Man, land and sea in harmony: that is the theme of Forillon National Park, whose chief feature is the rugged Gaspé coastline. Gaspé Bay is sheltered by the Forillon peninsula.

Long shadows of history are cast at Old Fort Erie by a guard in 19th-century uniforms and by a heavy sally port. Restored sections include officers' quarters. Royal Marine buttons were among hundreds unearthed during restoration.

Mather, is at the entrance to the bridge. The Niagara River Parkway extends from here to Niagara-on-the-Lake. Fort Erie also is the terminus of the Queen Elizabeth Way from Toronto. One of Canada's biggest horse-racing tracks is here.

A plaque beside the Niagara River at nearby Frenchman's Creek marks where William Lyon Mackenzie crossed into the United States after his rebels' defeat in December 1837 at Montgomery's Tavern north of York (Toronto).

OLD FORT ERIE This impressive structure, the third fort here, has a dry moat, drawbridge, bastions and guns typical of early 19th-century fortifications. The first (1764) and second forts were destroyed by Niagara River ice and flooding. The third, on higher ground, was captured by an American force in July 1814. The Americans repulsed a British attack in August but destroyed and abandoned the fort a few months later. It was restored in 1939. In the stone barracks buildings are collections of weapons and military equipment, and of uniform buttons and buckles and other relics discovered during the restoration.

Fort Frances Ont. 6DY

The 3½-mile Noden Causeway five miles east of here has a spectacular high-level span to permit the passage of boats 40 feet below in the narrows of Rainy Lake. Fort Frances itself is linked with International Falls, Minn., by a bridge across the Rainy River.

Mainly a pulp and paper town—there are summer tours of the Ontario-Minnesota Paper Company's newsprint plant—Fort Frances is in a prime vacation, fishing and hunting area, much of it as unspoiled as in the days of the voyageurs.

Plaques honor the explorers Jacques de Noyon and Pierre de La Vérendrye. De Noyon discovered Rainy Lake, the Rainy River and Lake of the Woods in 1688; the Kaministiquia canoe route he pioneered became a main link in the route to the west. Fort St. Pierre, a successor to de Noyon's fort on the Rainy River, was built for La Vérendrye in 1731 by Christophe de La Jemerais. It was the first of a chain of posts that La Vérendrye erected (as far west as Fort la Reine near what now is Portage la Prairie, Man.) in his search for the Western Sea.

Another plaque marks the site of the North West Company's Fort Lac la Pluie (Rainy Lake House), constructed about 1770 and abandoned in 1821. A Hudson's Bay Company fort built later about a mile from the Nor'Westers' post was also called Fort Lac la Pluie. It was renamed Fort Frances in 1830 in honor of the wife of the HBC's governor, George Simpson.

□ The Fort Frances museum illustrates the history of northwestern Ontario Indians.

Fort Good Hope N.W.T. 3GW

Amid the log cabins and prefabricated houses of this oldest community on the lower Mackenzie River is the little white Church of Our Lady of Good Hope, started in 1865 by an Oblate lay brother, Patrick Kearney. On

A vision on the Ramparts at Fort Good Hope is depicted in this painting by an Oblate priest.

the interior walls are many paintings, some by the Rev. Bernard Brown. The murals depict biblical scenes, Indian life and tiny details of flowers, fruit and doves.

The first Fort Good Hope (1804) was about 100 miles downstream. The present site, chosen in 1836, is at the north end of a seven-mile-long canyon, the Ramparts. Here the Mackenzie narrows to about 1,500 feet and races between 200-foot-high limestone cliffs.

Fort Langley National Historic Park (B.C.)
see Langley

Fort Macleod Alta.   4AZ/13DZ
A stylized version of the first North West Mounted Police fort stands at the edge of

this southwestern Alberta town. The original fort, built in 1874 after the Mounties' great march west from Manitoba to run out the whiskey traders, was on an island in the Old-man River about a mile east of the present town. It was named for Col. James F. Macleod, NWMP assistant commissioner and commander of the handful of men who spent the first winter of 1874-75 isolated in the land of the Blackfoot. It was here that Macleod met Crowfoot (*see* Cluny), with a cordiality that made the great Blackfoot chief the Mounties' friend for life.

Buildings in the reconstructed fort include a museum with Indian relics, early NWMP weapons and uniforms, and artifacts from the original fort. There are a law office, a blacksmith shop, a chapel and a building in which are displayed pioneer medical and dental equipment. Outside is a cannon found in Fort Whoop-Up (*see* Lethbridge), which the whiskey traders deserted when they learned the Mounties were coming. The museum has wax figures of Mounties and Indians, a stuffed buffalo and a Red River cart.

□ Ten miles west of Fort Macleod is Head-Smashed-In, where Indians lured buffalo over a high cliff. A complex system of drive lines—rows of piled stones to guide the stampeded animals to the cliff edge—starts seven miles from the cliff and covers a 50-square-mile area. At the base of the cliff is a 35-foot layer (about 200 by 800 feet) of bones of buffalo killed from about 3700 B.C. to around 1850.

Fort McMurray Alta.
The Athabasca tar sands, once used only to caulk canoes, are the world's biggest known oil reserve. Oil flushed from tar excavated at the Great Canadian Oil Sands plant 20 miles north of here is piped to Edmonton, then goes by Interprovincial Pipeline to Sarnia, Ont.

At the confluence of the Athabasca and Clearwater rivers, Fort McMurray is the

Mounted patrol at Fort Macleod is dressed in replicas of the uniforms that the North West Mounted Police used in 1878.

Alaska Highway bends and dips, then climbs a mountain near Trutch, about 100 miles south of Fort Nelson.

southern terminus of the vast water transportation system to the Arctic via Great Slave Lake and the Mackenzie River.

The North West Company's Peter Pond, first white man to see the tar sands, established House at the Forks in 1788. The Hudson's Bay Company built Fort McMurray on the same site in 1870.

Fort Nelson B.C.   1BY
The Alaska Highway swings west from here toward the Rocky Mountains and cuts through Stone Mountain and Muncho Lake provincial parks.

A Hudson's Bay Company post built in 1865 is still operated here. A North West Company post established about 1800 was destroyed and some of the inhabitants massacred by Indians in 1813.

Fort Norman N.W.T.   3GW
A bed of low-grade coal near here has been burning for centuries—probably since long before Alexander Mackenzie saw it in 1789. Lightning may have ignited the coal but Indian legend says it happened when a giant's campfire got out of control.

Fort Norman is at the junction of the Great Bear and Mackenzie rivers. The first fort was erected by the North West Company in 1810.

Fort Pitt Sask. *see* Lloydminster

Fort Providence N.W.T.   3HY
The National Historic Sites Service looked for three months for a suitable natural mon-

ument to explorer Alexander Mackenzie —and found it in the bed of the Mackenzie River 30 miles from here: a 25-ton boulder 6½ feet high. It was hoisted from the river, brought here by flatcar and unveiled by Queen Elizabeth in 1970.

Fort Qu'Appelle Sask.   4EY
Southern Saskatchewan's flat prairie is furrowed for 270 miles by the green valley of the Qu'Appelle River. At Fort Qu'Appelle, where the valley is almost two miles wide and 200 feet deep, are Lakes Pasqua, Mission, Katepwa and Echo (all joined by the river) and two provincial parks (Katepwa and Echo Valley).

The legend of Qu'Appelle is told on a marker near Lebret and in a poetic rendering by E. Pauline Johnson (*see* Middleport). It is the story of an Indian who heard his name and cried "Qu'appelle?" (Who calls?) but got no reply. He later came to believe it had been his sweetheart, calling for him just before she died.

The gently contoured valley was a main corridor for settlement of the west. The original Fort Qu'Appelle was a Hudson's Bay Company post erected in 1864 but a Church of England mission had been here since 1854. The cellars of a North West Mounted Police post established in 1877 can be seen on the Fort Qu'Appelle golf course. The fort was the militia base during the Northwest Rebellion of 1885.

ECHO VALLEY PROVINCIAL PARK Six miles west, 1,133 acres.

FISH CULTURE STATION Millions of game fish fry and fingerlings are reared each year for stocking angling waters.

FORT QU'APPELLE MUSEUM A small log and mud building (1864) from the original Fort

Fort Qu'Appelle / 127

Qu'Appelle is part of the museum operated by the Fort Qu'Appelle and Lebret Historical Society. Among the museum's artifacts are Indian beadwork and eagle feather headdresses; a rifle, sword and portmanteau issued to a NWMP man who made the Mounties' historic trek west in 1874; and copies of *The Vidette,* a newspaper first published in Fort Qu'Appelle in 1884.

HANSEN-ROSS POTTERY Craftsmen are seen shaping native clays.

KATEPWA PROVINCIAL PARK Seventeen-acre Katepwa, the smallest provincial park, is nine miles southeast of Fort Qu'Appelle. Other provincial parks in the valley of the Qu'Appelle are Buffalo Pound (*see* Moose Jaw) and Rowan's Ravine (*see* Bulyea).

SIOUX RESERVE An international powwow is held each August. In Fort Qu'Appelle is a Sioux handicraft center.

SUMMER SCHOOL OF THE ARTS Classes in music, drama and dancing are conducted on the grounds of a former sanatorium beside Echo Lake, three miles north of Fort Qu'Appelle. It is run by the Saskatchewan Arts Board.

TREATY MARKER A cairn in the town park marks where Indians surrendered 75,000 square miles of southern Saskatchewan by signing Treaty Four in 1874.

WINTER CARNIVAL A weekend festival in February: hockey, curling, dog racing, a beauty contest.

Fort St. James B.C.   1AY/2CV
Five Hudson's Bay Company buildings dating from 1884-89 and including a warehouse, fish cache and dairy still stand in Fort St. James National Historic Park. Simon Fraser and John Stuart of the North West Company built the first trading post here, in 1806. When the companies amalgamated in 1821 the HBC made Fort St. James its chief post in New Caledonia, a vast area between the Rockies and the Coast Mountains.

A Roman Catholic mission was founded here in 1843 and Lady of Good Hope Church (1870) is still used for services.

A Carrier Indian village—"Carrier" because widows once carried around their dead husbands' ashes—adjoins Fort St. James. In the village is the grave of Kwah, a Carrier chief who saved the life of James Douglas (who became governor of British Columbia) in an Indian uprising. Douglas was an HBC assistant factor at Fort St. James in the late 1820s.

□ There are prehistoric rock paintings just above the high-water mark on the north shore of Stuart Lake, 10 miles west.

Fort St. John B.C.   1BY
The foundations of a fort that Indians burned in 1823 after massacring three Hudson's Bay Company men can be seen about 20 miles southeast of Fort St. John. Just south of the town, Mile 46 of the Alaska Highway, are the log buildings of a later HBC post, a now-disused Roman Catholic chapel (1890)

and a North West Mounted Police barracks and jail.

Alexander Mackenzie traveled up the Peace River here on his epic journey to the Pacific in 1793. Rocky Mountain Fort was built probably in 1797 and later known as Fort St. John; the town claims it is the oldest white settlement in British Columbia.

□ At nearby Taylor the Peace Island Park Museum displays pioneer clothing, furniture, tools, dishes and machinery, a dugout canoe and a birch-bark canoe.

Fort Saskatchewan Alta.   4AW/14FW
A 10-by-6-foot mural in the Fort Saskatchewan Museum tells the town's story from the days of Anthony Henday, the first white man to see this part of Alberta. A Hudson's Bay Company trader-explorer, he traveled 2,000 miles from York Factory on Hudson Bay into Blackfoot country south of here in 1754-55.

The museum has collections of photographs and Indian artifacts. One pioneer artifact is a letter-book (c.1908) in which wet linen and sheets of tin were used for duplicating.

Fort Selkirk Y.T.   1AV
This once-thriving place has become a virtual ghost town, victim of the Alaska Highway and the end of the steamboat era on the Yukon River. Founded in 1848 as a Hudson's Bay Company post, it was destroyed by Indians in 1852. But during the Klondike Gold Rush came some 200 members of the Yukon Field Force, formed to bolster the North West Mounted Police and to help forestall U.S. infringement of Canadian sovereignty in the Yukon. Soon there were cabins, churches and a police barracks.

Some restoration has been done by army cadets and the town is under the protection of the territorial government. Original desks and reading exercises are still in the mission school and many of the buildings are in excellent condition.

Fort Simpson N.W.T.   3GX

The great Liard River fights for survival here after joining the mightier Mackenzie. For some miles downstream from the confluence the broad Mackenzie is often dark and laden with wood that the Liard has carried from the mountains of the Yukon and British Columbia. Gradually the mile-wide Mackenzie swallows all trace of the tributary.

Fort Simpson is on an island with a commanding view of Gros Cap, a 225-foot-high promontory where the rivers meet. The first fort here was the North West Company's Fort of the Forks (1804). The post the Hudson's Bay Company built in 1821 was named for George (later Sir George) Simpson, the HBC governor.

Until 1972 Fort Simpson was the northern terminus of the Mackenzie Highway. A 49-mile extension to Camsell Bend was started that year.

Fort Smith N.W.T.   3HY

The Northern Life Museum, built in 1972, houses a priceless collection of artifacts. There are dinosaur bones and the tusk of a mammoth; early Indian and Eskimo tools and utensils; a kayak·and moosehide and spruce-bark canoes; a printing press that was brought north in 1873; the manuscript of John Tetso's autobiography. *Trapping Is My Life* (1964), and paintings, photographs and other relics of trappers, traders, bush pilots and missionaries.

Displayed outdoors are *Radium King*, the first steel boat built here (in 1937, for the discoverers of the Great Bear Lake radium mines); one of the first tractors used on the 14-mile portage between Fort Smith and Fort Fitzgerald, Alta., and a steam winch from a Hudson's Bay Company shipyard on the Slave River.

□ Fort Smith, less than a mile from the Alberta/Northwest Territories border, is on the Slave River near the Rapids of the Drowned. The portage at the rapids was known at Fort York as early as 1715 but there was no settlement until the HBC established a post in 1874. It was named for Donald A. Smith (later Lord Strathcona), an HBC governor.

The town is the seat of the Roman Catholic bishop of the Mackenzie, whose cathedral (Saint Joseph's) was completed in 1960.

□ Wood Buffalo National Park lies west and south of Fort Smith.

Fort Steele B.C.   2FZ/13AY

An East Kootenay town of the 1890-1905 period was created here in the 1960s. Fort Steele Historic Park is a combination of restored and reconstructed buildings from the gold-rush days of the mid-1860s and new construction of typical turn-of-the-century buildings.

Gold-seekers streamed here in the '60s en route to the rich placer ground on nearby Wild Horse Creek. They came up the Walla Walla and Calispel trails from Washington and the Missoula Trail from Montana and

Wooden waterwheel, 32 feet high, was moved to Fort Steele from a placer mine in Perry Creek, B.C. Mountains tower behind false-front stores and the fort palisade—above which Canadian, B.C. and British flags, on separate poles, look like a single flag. Fort Steele is at an altitude of 2,500 feet, on high benchland overlooking the Kootenay River.

The Legend Called Sam

Samuel Benfield "Sam" Steele was a legend in his own colorful lifetime. As soldier and policeman he turned up at most Canadian trouble spots—and in Canada's wars overseas —for half a century.

As a 17-year-old militiaman, he helped repel Fenians raiding into Upper Canada from the United States. He was given the rank of sergeant major when he joined the fledgling North West Mounted Police in 1873 and was on the great trek of 1874 when the Mounties took the law to the west. He helped police construction of the CPR. In the Northwest Rebellion of 1885 he led the pursuit of the Indian leader, Big Bear. Two years later he built a post at Galbraith's Ferry (later renamed Fort Steele) in British Columbia.

In 1898, sent to police the mountain passes the Klondike gold-seekers used, he became known as the Lion of the Yukon. At the White Pass customs house, where snow seemed to fall endlessly, Mounties suffered great hardships. Steele, racked with bronchitis, heard that the inspector at the customs house was ill. Against doctor's orders he climbed the pass, ordered the inspector off duty and took over.

Steele recruited a cavalry regiment that served with distinction in the South African War. He raised and trained the 2nd Division in Canada in 1915 and led it to Britain. He was made a major general and won a knighthood. He died in England in 1919.

over the long Dewdney Trail (a four-foot-wide mule track) across British Columbia. The population of Galbraith's Ferry, as the town was known then, passed 4,000. Indian trouble brought 75 men of the North West Mounted Police from Fort Macleod, Alta., in 1887 to establish the Mounties' first post in British Columbia. When they left a year later Galbraith's Ferry renamed itself in honor of the Mounties' Maj. (later Maj. Gen.) Sam Steele.

During a silver-lead-zinc boom at nearby Moyie and Kimberley in the 1890s, sternwheelers on the Kootenay River linked Fort Steele with the railway at Jennings, Mont. But Fort Steele began to die when the Canadian Pacific Railway bypassed the town and was routed through Cranbrook, 12 miles southwest. By the end of World War II Fort Steele was almost a ghost town, with a population of fewer than 50 persons.

Fort Steele arrowheads date from 1887 when unrest brought the NWMP to British Columbia.

Its designation as an historic park came in 1961. Among the buildings in the restoration area are NWMP buildings, three churches, a vicarage, schoolhouse, drug and general stores, dentist's and doctor's offices, and harness, blacksmith and barber shops. The ferry office run by John and Robert Galbraith is virtually intact. A customs house was moved here from the U.S. border at Roosville. A reconstruction of an 1897 water tower has an observation lookout.

The Wild Horse Theater presents live Gay Nineties entertainment. There are stagecoach rides and performances by a six-horse hitch from Fort Steele's herd of 12 Clydesdales. A 2.3-mile railway within the park has two steam locomotives: the coal-fired *Dunrobin* built in Glasgow in 1895 and a 1934 shay, a type used on British Columbia logging railways in the 1930s and 1940s.

There is a side trip to Wild Horse Creek and the gold diggings of 1864, and to a picket-fenced cemetery at Fisherville, another relic of the Wild Horse days.

Fortune Nfld.   11CZ
A summer ferry connects this fishing port with the French islands of Saint-Pierre and Miquelon.

Frank Alta.   4AZ/13CZ
A jumble of rocks perhaps 100 feet deep is strewn across a square mile of the valley of the Oldman River in awesome testimony to the Frank slide of April 29, 1903. A massive limestone overhang—3,000 feet wide, 2,100 feet high and 500 feet thick—tore loose and hurtled down the side of Turtle Mountain at 4:10 a.m. In its path was the sleeping coal-

mining town of Frank. After only 100 seconds, 90,000,000 tons of rock lay on the valley floor, some 70 were dead and part of the town had disappeared—a mine plant and railway siding, a bank, shops and some miners' homes. A new Frank was begun 500 yards to the west that same year. A plaque marks the site of the old town; a highway runs through the rock of the slide.

Frankville Ont.   18CY
The Kitley Historical Society Museum is in a log house (1840) furnished as a pioneer dwelling.

□ A plaque honors Louise McKinney, a native of Frankville who was elected to the Alberta legislature in 1917, the first woman in the British Empire to gain a legislature seat (*see* Claresholm).

Fredericton N.B.   9CY
New Brunswick's capital is a city of stately elms, historic buildings and reminders of its famous adopted son, Lord Beaverbrook. It began as the Acadian settlement of Sainte-Anne's Point in 1731. The influence of Loyalists who came later is reflected in its old structures, old tombstones and many plaques and monuments.

A granite boulder in Fredericton's east end is inscribed: "To commemorate the loyalty,

Turtle Mountain slide in 1903 buried the Crowsnest Pass town of Frank, killed 70.

faith, courage, sacrifices and achievements of early settlers who established this City of Fredericton, a grateful posterity has erected this monument." Plaques on the Legislative Building honor prominent New Brunswickers: Sir Howard Douglas, a governor of the province and first chancellor of the University of New Brunswick; Lemuel Allen Wilmot, politician, judge and lieutenant governor; and Charles Fisher, a Father of Confederation. Another Fredericton plaque honors Julia Catherine (Beckwith) Hart whose first novel, *St. Ursula's Convent, or, The Nun of Canada,* was written here when she was 16. Brought out in 1824, it was the first Canadian novel published in Canada.

□ Much of Fredericton bears the stamp of Lord Beaverbrook. Born Max Aitken in Maple, Ont., he came to the province as a child, studied law at UNB for a year, then went into business. He amassed a fortune, entered British politics and then became a newspaper tycoon. New Brunswick, particularly Fredericton, benefited greatly from Beaverbrook's philanthropy. His gifts included a men's residence and gymnasium at UNB, both named for Lady Beaverbrook, and the Bonar Law-Bennett Building which houses the provincial archives. Lady Beaverbrook Rink was a gift to UNB and the city. The Beaverbrook Art Gallery houses one of the world's most important art collections and The Playhouse is the home of Theater New Brunswick, a professional company that tours the province. A plaque on the building commemorates Beaverbrook's long friendship with Sir James Dunn.

A farmers' market on George Street is open Saturdays from 6 a.m to noon. It features an easygoing restaurant with old milk-bottle crate seats.

BEAVERBROOK ART GALLERY (1) There are 34 Krieghoffs and a strong collection of British art, including 47 works by Graham Sutherland, who painted a controversial portrait of Sir Winston Churchill to mark his 80th birthday anniversary. Sutherland's preliminary sketches and studies of Churchill are important Churchilliana. In the Lucile Pillow Room are 130 porcelain pieces represent-

---

Le vieux Saint-Pierre, c'est la vieille France

The sea-battered islands of Saint-Pierre and Miquelon, the last remnant of French empire in North America, are a 20-mile ferry ride from Fortune. Dories upcurved at bow and stern still bob in fog-shrouded harbors where fishermen mend nets, refit boats and sell cod as they have since soon after Jacques Cartier claimed the islands in 1535. Weather-beaten clapboard cottages, shops and sidewalk cafés cluster in the harbors. Steep narrow streets struggle up the hillside above Saint-Pierre, where French gendarmes patrol Place Général de Gaulle and fishermen dance at discotheques, often in rubber boots.

Saint-Pierre's museum displays magnificent figureheads from stranded sailing vessels, and antique documents, stamps and coins. A chart in the Hôtel de France locates 343 of the more than 600 known shipwrecks on the islands' treacherous shoals since 1816. Drifting sand clinging to the wrecks has formed a seven-mile causeway between Miquelon and Langlade.

European-style vaults in Saint-Pierre's cemetery are equipped with portholes for airing and viewing.

A 10-foot sailors' monument recognizes the island's reliance on the sea.

ing the best of English artistry between 1743 and 1840. The gallery building has been called an architectural work of art. The back of the main gallery is a great window looking over the Saint John River.

CHRIST CHURCH CATHEDRAL (2) One of the best examples of decorated Gothic architecture in North America, the Anglican cathedral was built in 1845-53, largely through the efforts of the Rt. Rev. John Medley, first bishop of Fredericton. His memorial tomb, in marble, lies at the end of the north aisle. The nave is a copy of that in St. Mary's Church in Snettisham, Norfolk, England. A gold altar cloth in the cathedral was used at the coronation of William IV of England. Letters patent issued by Queen Victoria in 1845, constituting Fredericton as a city, are in the cathedral archives.

FORT NASHWAAK (3) A cairn marks the approximate site of a fort built at the mouth of the Nashwaak River in 1692 and abandoned six years later.

JONATHAN ODELL HOUSE (4) Jonathan Odell, first provincial secretary and a well-known poet, had this house built in 1785. It is now the residence of the Anglican dean of Fredericton.

LEGISLATIVE BUILDING (5) Flanking the speaker's throne in the Assembly chamber are portraits of George III and Queen Charlotte painted by Sir Joshua Reynolds. A monument on the grounds honors Dr. William Francis Roberts who in 1918 became the first minister of health in the British Empire. In the legislative library are a set of John James Audubon's bird paintings and a set of William Hogarth prints from the original steel engravings. There is also a rare 1783 copy of the Domesday Book, a survey of English property compiled and written (in Latin) at the order of William the Conqueror in 1086. Only one handwritten copy existed until the book was published seven centuries later.

MILITARY COMPOUND (6) The Military Compound opposite Officers Square consists of officers' quarters (1839-69), a guardhouse and barracks. Outside the barracks is a monument to the 500 men of the 104th New Brunswick Regiment who snowshoed from Fredericton to Quebec in 1813. In the officers' quarters is the York-Sunbury Museum. In addition to fine collections of coverlets, furniture and uniforms, it displays a frog that a hotelkeeper in the 1880s is said to have regularly fed whiskey, june bugs and buttermilk. After growing to weigh 42 pounds it was accidentally killed by dynamiting near its pond. The owner had it stuffed.

The compound's guardhouse has been restored to its 1828 appearance, with muskets, uniforms, nominal rolls, leave passes, ration returns and beds. In Officers Square (*see below*), a Changing of the Guard ceremony takes place when possible at 10 a.m. from

Fredericton

1. Beaverbrook Art Gallery
2. Christ Church Cathedral
3. Fort Nashwaak
4. Jonathan Odell House
5. Legislative Building
6. Military Compound
7. Odell Park
8. Officers Square
9. Old Government House
10. Poets' Corner
11. St. Thomas University
12. The Green
13. The Playhouse
14. University of New Brunswick
15. Wilmot United Church

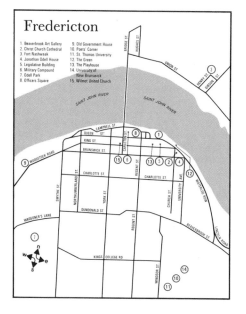

Salvador Dali's canvas, *Santiago el Grande,* 10 feet by 13½ feet high, dominates the central gallery of Fredericton's Beaverbrook Art Gallery. It depicts Saint James being carried to heaven on a horse. The Beaverbrook collection includes 34 works by Cornelius Krieghoff, including *Merrymaking.* A bust of Lord Beaverbrook by Sir Jacob Epstein is in the gallery.

mid-July to late August. The soldiers wear the scarlet tunics, blue trousers and white pith helmets of the Royal Canadian Regiment of the 1900 period, recalling the days when Fredericton was a garrison town.

ODELL PARK (7) There are five miles of walking trails in this 300-acre park named for Jonathan Odell. A year-round recreation center, it boasts a primeval forest area, duck pond, animal sanctuary, and picnic grounds and play equipment for children. There is also skiing, snowshoeing and tobogganing.

OFFICERS SQUARE (8) In this park is a bronze statue of Lord Beaverbrook by the Maltese sculptor Vincent Apap. Beside a pool are two beavers, the first work in stone by Acadian sculptor Claude Roussel, erected by the province to mark Beaverbrook's 80th birthday anniversary May 25, 1959. Nearby is a bronze memorial plaque to John F. Kennedy. He was one of the few U.S. presidents honored by Canadian universities. Lord Beaverbrook, as chancellor of the University of New Brunswick, conferred the honorary degree of doctor of laws on Kennedy in October

1957 when he was a U.S. senator from Massachusetts.

OLD GOVERNMENT HOUSE (9) This old building was once the home of colonial governors, then (until 1892) of provincial lieutenant governors. It is now the provincial headquarters of the RCMP.

POETS' CORNER (10) A memorial on the UNB campus, Poets' Corner of Canada, honors Sir Charles G.D. Roberts, Bliss Carman and Francis Joseph Sherman, all New Brunswickers. Among Sir Charles' works are *The Book of the Native* (1897) and *Songs of the Common Day* (1893). Carman's best are *From the Book of Myths* (1902), *Songs of the Sea Children* (1904) and *Sappho* (1905) and Sherman is known for *Matins* (1896), *In Memorabilia Mortis* (1896) and *A Prelude* (1897).

ST. THOMAS UNIVERSITY (11) This Roman Catholic liberal arts college shares campus library, laboratory and athletic facilities with UNB.

THE GREEN (12) In this park near the Saint John River are a statue of the Scottish poet Robert Burns and a marble fountain donated by Lord Beaverbrook in honor of Sir James Dunn.

THE PLAYHOUSE (13) Donated to the city by Lord Beaverbrook, The Playhouse is a major center of the performing arts in the Maritimes.

UNIVERSITY OF NEW BRUNSWICK (14) With beginnings in 1785, UNB is Canada's oldest provincial institution of higher learning and the second oldest university in the country. Canada's first astronomical observatory (1851) and first engineering school (1854) were here. The arts building is the oldest university building in use in Canada. With campuses here and in Saint John, enrollment is 5,000. The Bonar Law-Bennett Building was Lord Beaverbrook's gift, honoring two natives of New Brunswick—Andrew Bonar Law, the only prime minister of Britain born outside the British Isles, and R.B. Bennett, Canadian prime minister in 1930-35. In the Harriet Irving Library are manuscripts donated by Beaverbrook, among them Bennett's papers and the *Kipling Atlas*, autographed by author Rudyard Kipling—and first editions of Charles Dickens, William Ains-

worth and H.G. Wells. UNB musicians are joined by other professionals from many parts of Canada for a festival of chamber music and jazz during the last week of July.

WILMOT UNITED CHURCH (15) In use since 1852, this wooden church has a high domed roof, a 200-foot steeple, and brilliant stained-glass windows by Alex Colville.

French River Ont.   7CX
A plaque and stone cross at a bridge on the French River commemorate the river as a link in the canoe route between the St. Lawrence and the west. For more than 200 years explorers, missionaries and fur traders traveled the Ottawa and Mattawa rivers to Lake Nipissing, then the French River to Georgian Bay. Etienne Brûlé was probably the first white man to pass this way (in 1611). Later came such men as Champlain, the Jesuit missionaries to Huronia, Radisson and Groseilliers, the La Vérendryes, Alexander Mackenzie, Alexander Henry and David Thompson.

Birch-bark freight canoes with three-ton cargo capacity were paddled by 12 men. A 34-foot canoe, one of the last of its type, is displayed at 'Presqu'île Camp, two miles east of nearby Alban.

Friendly Cove B.C.   2BY
Accessible only by boat or aircraft, this Nootka Sound settlement is a regular stop for the freighter *Uchuck III* which carries cargo

Officers' quarters in the Fredericton Military Compound has stone arches typical of the colonial architecture favored by the Royal Engineers. The York-Sunbury Museum is in the old officers' quarters. The Old Arts Building at the University of New Brunswick (left) dates from the 1820s.

Ikaluit (place of many fish) is a section of the village of Frobisher Bay in the southern part of Baffin Island.

and passengers to isolated communities on Vancouver Island's west coast.

A cairn commemorates the discovery of the sound by Capt. James Cook, whose two ships anchored here for four weeks in 1778. Its plaque tells of the arrival of the Spanish the next year. In 1789 the Spanish occupied Nootka Sound, built a fort and seized some English trading ships, touching off a controversy that almost led to war between Spain and Britain. But Spain was too weak to wage war so relinquished her claim to Nootka Sound.

Frobisher Bay N.W.T.
Carrying on a tradition that pre-dates the arrival of the white man, the 2,500 villagers hold a spring festival, usually in late April. They call it Toonik Time, after the legendary Tooniks, small, hairy men with long arms and close-set eyes, said to have inhabited the north before the Eskimos. Toonik Time today features competition and games from both the native and white worlds, including high-kicking, seal-hunting and seal-skinning, ice-fishing, beard-growing, tea-brewing, and dancing, plus—depending on the weather—dogsledding, snowmobile or motorcycle racing, and cross-country skiing.
☐ Stone, ivory and whalebone carvings produced by Eskimos can be bought at the Ikaluit Cooperative.

Frog Lake Alta. 4BW
In a cemetery two miles west of Frog Lake are the graves of nine men massacred during the Northwest Rebellion of 1885. Cree warriors ransacked the Hudson's Bay Company post, forced a priest to lead a service in the church, stood by mockingly, then slaughtered the nine. Cree chief Big Bear was jailed (although he was not personally involved) and eight Indians were hanged.

Fundy National Park (N.B.) 9DY
Battered by the waves of the Bay of Fundy, the steep sculptured cliffs of Fundy National Park's eight-mile shore are indented with dozens of coves and inlets. The 80-square-mile park rises from the craggy coast to a plateau of rolling maple hills full of tumbling brooks and rivers, placid lakes and flower-filled meadows.

The dense forests shelter moose, white-tailed deer, bear and lynx, and smaller creatures such as flying squirrels and jumping mice. Many of New Brunswick's 300 species of

Massacre victims at Frog Lake lie in graves marked by black, metal crosses.

Sun-dappled water sparkles at low tide off Fundy National Park, which extends for about eight miles along the Bay of Fundy coast.

native birds nest here—among them ravens, double-breasted cormorants, black ducks, olive-sided flycatchers, red-eyed vireos, black and white warblers, hermit thrushes and red-breasted nuthatches. Fishing for speckled and rainbow trout and Atlantic salmon is good.

A nine-hole golf course overlooks the Bay of Fundy. There are chalet cabins, campgrounds, shops, tennis courts, bowling greens, playgrounds, two open-air theaters and a heated salt-water swimming pool.

□ In a spruce grove on a rocky bluff above the Bay of Fundy the New Brunswick School of Arts and Crafts teaches enameling, weaving, wood turning, leatherwork, silk-screen printing, jewelry-making, rug hooking and pottery. Children eight to 13 make baskets,

belts and Indian headdresses in this learn-by-doing school.

□ Kinnie Brook Nature Trail, one of several hiking trails in the park, winds through forest, then along the upper edge of Kinnie Brook Valley. A side trip can be made into the valley to see where Kinnie Brook disappears under glacial till, to reappear 750 feet away. The last Ice Age glaciation, about 10,000 years ago, almost filled the valley with debris. The brook carried some of it downstream but large rocks remain. From a flat-topped cliff in the valley is a view of Hebron Hill (950 feet) east of Alma, part of Owl's Head Cliff on Chignecto Bay, Cape Enragé and, in the distance, the shores of Nova Scotia. Of hundreds of plants along the trail, two of the more interesting are the sundew (a carnivorous plant that catches small insects) and old man's beard, a lichen that festoons the branches of many trees.

G

Gagetown N.B.   9CY

The world-famous Loomcrofters of Gagetown demonstrate weaving in a one-time trading post that is the oldest building (c. 1760) on the Saint John River. The cedar shakes of the small, two-story structure are held together with wooden pegs. It is known as the blockhouse (rifles and ammunition used to be stored in a cellar) and as the Loomcrofters Inn (meals once were served by the weavers).

As many as 35 persons, working in their own homes, produce Loomcrofter tartans, clothing, afghans, draperies and upholstery materials. Tartans designed by the Loomcrofters' Patricia Jenkins include those of the RCAF, the province of New Brunswick and the Highlands of Haliburton (Ont.).

□ The Queens County Museum is in a house whose oldest part dates from 1786. Sir Leonard Tilley, a Father of Confederation, was born here in 1818 and the house is a national historic site. A parlor and parlor bedroom are restored in early Victorian fashion; older parts of the house are in Loyalist style. Off the kitchen is a room that Dr. Frederick Stickles, who built the house, used as an office. A display of equipment that later Gagetown doctors used includes a folding operating table that was moved around the county by buggy, sleigh and train.

□ West of here is CFB Gagetown (*see* Oromocto).

Galt Ont. *see* Cambridge

Gananoque Ont.   7DY/18CZ

An aquamarine water pitcher made in the Mallorytown (Ont.) Glass Works, which operated only from 1825 to 1839, is displayed at the Gananoque Historical Museum. One other Mallorytown pitcher is in the Royal Ontario Museum in Toronto.

Three rooms of the Gananoque museum—bedroom, parlor and kitchen—are furnished in Victorian style. Among the exhibits are a wooden flute (c.1750) and an 1885 gramophone which plays cylinder records ("Edison Gold Moulded Records 'Echo All Over the World'").

□ Gananoque is the chief Canadian entrance to the Thousand Islands, 18 of which

Gabriola Island B.C.—The Malaspina Galleries, on the western shore of the island, are an overhanging rock formation shaped by wind and waves. (2CZ/12DX)

Artist Kenneth Lochhead describes his 72-foot mural at Gander International Airport:

Fruits and grain at the left are symbols of earth's bounty. The first group includes an old man feeding birds, a young man thinking of faraway places, a girl examining a daisy. Next, behind a pair of trumpeter swans, two men "take flight from nature." Boys and girls watch as birds "descend upon the fruits of nature." A man juggling apples represents the coordination of air traffic control and above him is a powerful central figure, the man capable of projecting the flight of aircraft. Unconcerned witnesses beside him provide contrast to the spectacular takeoff of plane-like birds —and "maple leaves forever" are carried far and wide. In a final "tribute to flight" a matron holds the "bluebird of happiness." A family group wonders where the dart came from. Among figures watching at the right is artist Lochhead (behind the tree a boy is descending).

---

form St. Lawrence Islands National Park (*see entry*).

□ A plaque here describes the exploits of "Pirate" Johnson, a Canadian-born renegade who settled in New York and, during the 1837 Rebellion, led armed raids on the Canadian shore and British shipping from his base in the Thousand Islands.

Other plaques honor Col. Joel Stone, a United Empire Loyalist who founded Gananoque in 1789, and commemorate Gananoque's role in maintaining the St. Lawrence supply line in the War of 1812.

Gander Nfld. 11CY
A town of some 8,000 has grown in northeast Newfoundland a few miles from huge Gander International Airport.

The British Air Ministry chose Gander as a transatlantic base in the mid-1930s and the airport went into service in 1938. The RCAF took over in World War II, the Newfoundland government in 1946, and the Canadian government in 1949 when Newfoundland entered Confederation.

In the airport building are *Flight and Its Allegories*, a 72-foot mural by Kenneth Lochhead; an art gallery operated by Memorial University in St. John's; and an aviation museum whose theme is the conquest of the Atlantic.

The museum's prize exhibit is a four-bladed gray wooden propeller from the twin-engine plane that made the first direct nonstop Atlantic flight. Britons John Alcock and Arthur Whitten Brown flew a Vickers Vimy from St. John's, Nfld., to Clifden, Ireland, June 14-15, 1919. The 1,890-mile flight lasted 16 hours and 12 minutes. The museum has models of the Vimy and of Lindbergh's *Spirit of St. Louis*. Other exhibits are of such aircraft as the German *Bremen* and Kingsford-Smith's *Southern Cross*.

Outside the terminal is the Atlantic Ferry Pilot Memorial, a huge cairn surmounted by a Lockheed Hudson bomber in wartime camouflage. It is identical to one that on Nov. 10-11, 1940, made the first transatlantic crossing from Gander, in 11 hours and 12 minutes. That flight was the first of thousands by pilots of the Atlantic Ferry. Captain of the first Hudson and co-founder of the ferry service was Capt. (later Air Vice Marshal) D.C.T. Bennett. A plaque on the cairn bears a quotation from his book *Pathfinder*: "Better be not at all than not be noble."

Christ-Roi Cathedral in Gaspé town is an ultra-modern structure built of wood in 1960.

□ Gander is on the Trans-Canada Highway, in the heart of one of North America's finest hunting and fishing areas. Within 55 miles are three provincial parks and Terra Nova National Park.

Gardenton Man.   6BY/15DZ
The first Orthodox church built in Canada is here on the banks of the Roseau River where Manitoba's first Ukrainian settlement was started in 1896. St. Michael's Ukrainian Orthodox Church was constructed of oak, ash, cedar and tamarack logs and was ready for use in 1899. Until siding and wood shingles were added the next year, the log walls were chinked with swamp moss. On the ornate iconostasis (the partition between sanctuary and nave) are candelabra and lithographed icons bearing the marks of printers in St. Petersburg, Moscow, Kiev and Odessa.

Memorials in the churchyard honor parishioners who died in World War I, the establishment of the church, and Wasyl Zahara, the first settler of the area. Standing apart from the church is a frame belfry built in 1906. It has three bells. Although a new church now serves the community, services are held in St. Michael's twice a year as a reminder of when there was no resident and a priest was sent from Minneapolis at Christmas and Easter to conduct services, solemnize marriages and baptize children.

□ Costumes and rugs made by Gardenton settlers are displayed in a museum run by the Ukrainian Museum and Village Society.

Garson Man.   6BY/15DX
Mottled buff and gray Tyndall limestone, quarried here since 1896, has been used in many important Canadian buildings, among them the Parliament Buildings in Ottawa and the Manitoba Legislative Building in Winnipeg. It is found also in the Hudson's Bay Memorial in Vancouver, the Alberta Provincial Museum and Archives and buildings of the University of Alberta.

The limestone contains fossils of invertebrates that lived in a shallow continental sea an estimated 445,000,000 years ago —250,000,000 years before the first dinosaurs appeared on earth. The mottling is caused by the alteration of parts of the limestone into dolomite. The dolomitized areas may have been the burrows of marine worms.

Gaspé Que.   9DW/10HZ
A 30-foot granite cross erected in 1934 commemorates Jacques Cartier's landing here

Gaspé Rediscovered 400 Years after Cartier

The Gaspé Peninsula remained isolated and relatively unknown for almost 400 years after Jacques Cartier landed in 1534 and claimed the mysterious new land for France. Now a 557-mile highway skirts the Gaspé coast, whose rugged north-shore cliffs and coves give way to gentler bays and beaches on the south. The road links villages previously accessible only by boat or footpath. The Shickshock Mountains in the interior, with the highest peaks in eastern Canada, still largely confine Gaspésians to the coastal settlements. A road from near Anse-Pleureuse to Gaspé goes through Murdochville. Right: Grande-Vallée.

four centuries earlier, on July 24, 1534. He took possession in the name of the King of France and erected a 30-foot wooden cross.

Gaspé, near the eastern extremity of the Gaspé Peninsula, is at the mouth of the York River overlooking Gaspé Bay. The fishing port that grew here was destroyed by Wolfe in 1758. In the late 1700s many United Empire Loyalists settled in the area.

□ A provincial fish hatchery, Canada's oldest (1875), produces 1,000,000 salmon and trout fry annually for Quebec lakes and rivers.

Geneva Park Ont. 17CV

Started in 1909 as a training center for YMCA leaders, Geneva Park has become an important conference center and home of the annual Couchiching Conference sponsored by the Canadian Institute of Public Affairs. The center has two miles of shoreline on a 150-acre Lake Couchiching peninsula.

Gentilly Que. 7FX/19DW

An early 18th-century windmill here is in no way modernized and still grinds flour.

Saint-Edouard-de-Gentilly Church, built of fieldstone in 1848 and classified as an historic building, contains fine oil paintings and goldsmith's work by François Ranvoyzé and Laurent Amyot.

Audiovisual presentations are given at a nuclear generating station owned by Atomic Energy of Canada Limited and operated by Hydro-Quebec.

Georgetown P.E.I. 9EX/23DX

Named for George III in 1765, this seat of King's County has a splendid harbor, a fish processing plant and a shipyard. The courthouse and jail, built of Island sandstone, dates from 1887.

Lower Nelson River power is harnessed by the Kettle Generating Station at Gillam.

Postglacial flooding along the edge of the Precambrian shield formed the archipelago in which Georgian Bay Islands National Park lies. At various places are fine examples of folded and banded rock, much of it pink and pink-and-gray granite, and of glacial boulders.

Depressions in the ground at nearby Brudenell Point—they were once cellars—are all that remains of Jean-Pierre de Roma's dream of a French settlement in Prince Edward Island 2½ centuries ago. De Roma built wharves, bridges, storehouses and dwellings on the point. But some of his people defected, then crops were destroyed by field mice. In 1745, when the settlement was burned by

raiders from New England, de Roma and his family escaped into the forest and reached Quebec.

Four miles west is Brudenell Provincial Resort, two square miles of beach and parkland situated on the Brudenell River. It has a marina, tennis courts, swimming pool, croquet green, an 18-hole championship golf course with nine water holes, and six miles of self-guiding nature trails. Joined to the resort by a rock causeway is an island where Scottish immigrants settled around 1755. In a cemetery on the island is a stone memorial bearing the names of Gordons, Stewarts, MacLarens and other pioneers.

Georgeville Que.   19DY
A cluster of attractive frame houses, some much more than 100 years old, lends charm to this community on the east side of Lake Memphremagog. There is a 92-foot covered bridge at Fitch Bay, five miles southeast.

Georgian Bay Islands National Park (Ont.)
                                              7CX/17BV
Glacier-scraped rock, wind-twisted pine trees and dense, dark woods of maple, beech and oak give a wild beauty to the 50 islands in this park. One island, Flowerpot, 100 miles northwest of the others, is named for its remarkable rock pillars (*see* Tobermory).

Beausoleil Island, which can be reached by boat from Honey Harbour, is 4.2 square miles, more than three times the size of all the other islands combined. Beausoleil, once the home of a band of Chippewas, has facilities for camping, bathing, boating and hiking. Mammals on the island include white-tailed deer, red fox, raccoon, porcupine, skunk, chipmunk, muskrat, mink, beaver, weasel and red and gray squirrel.

Gibsons B.C.   2CZ/12DX
A two-mile tugboat race highlights the three-day Gibsons Sea Cavalcade in August. There are races for water-jet propelled beachcomber boats, sailing and rowing contests and a competition for "sidewinders," iron boom boats used to maneuver logs. Other events include a "war of the hoses" for local firemen, a salmon barbecue, a golf tournament and a parade.

Salmon Rock, one of the province's finest sport fishing areas, is a site of the Sun Fishing Derby in July and of the British Columbia Fish Derby in August.

The Elphinstone Pioneer Museum has Indian and settlers' artifacts, early logging, farming and mining equipment, and collections of shells and Eskimo carvings.

Giffard Que.   20BW
Among interesting old buildings in this Quebec City suburb are the Côté and Parent houses, both more than 200 years old, and the Adélard Roy house. On a boulder near the town hall is a plaque in memory of Robert Giffard (1587-1668), a French physician and surgeon who settled here in 1634.

Gillam Man.   5HW
Kettle Generating Station, first in a series of power developments planned by Manitoba Hydro on the lower Nelson River, will have a total output of 1,224,000 kilowatts. Alternating current produced at Kettle is changed to direct current at the adjacent Radisson Converter Station; then it is transmitted over 565-mile power lines at 900,000 volts, the highest voltage used anywhere. The power is changed back to AC near Winnipeg at a converter station named for the late John Dorsey, a University of Manitoba engineering professor who was an early advocate of DC transmission. It uses only two conductors and is more economical than AC transmission, which needs three.

The hydro development has changed Gillam from a stop on the CN line to Churchill into a modern town of about 2,000.

Gimli Man.   6BY/15DW
The town's first 240 settlers were part of a group of Icelanders who lived for a year at Kinmount, Ont. They migrated to Winnipeg in 1875, then went down the Red River and across Lake Winnipeg in six flat-

Town of the Vikings

A 20-foot fiber glass statue of a bearded Viking warrior stands on the shore of Lake Winnipeg as a symbol of Gimli's settlement by Icelanders a century ago. They gave their new home the Old Norse name for abode of the gods, then set out to build a republic. Soon there were other Icelandic communities on the west side of the lake, among them Arnes, Hecla Island, Hnausa and Arborg. Together they formed self-governing New Iceland during the years 1878-87.

bottomed boats. Gimli now has as many persons of Ukrainian and Polish extraction as of Icelandic descent. But it is still the center of the largest Icelandic community outside Iceland and the town has an *Islendingadagurinn* (Icelandic festival) in midsummer. Descendants of the settlers wear Icelandic dress for two days of parades, singing, dancing, poetry reading and sports events.

□ A T-33 jet training plane, presented to the town by the Canadian Forces when CFB Gimli was closed in 1971, is mounted in a downtown intersection and appears to be flying at rooftop level down Center Street.

□ Much of the Lake Winnipeg commercial fishing industry is based here.

Glace Bay N.S. 9FX/23HW

A colliery under the floor of the Atlantic is the realistic main attraction of the Miners' Museum in this historic coal town. Retired miners guide visitors down a sloping tunnel and through three levels of the Ocean Deeps Colliery, where mining machinery is in place and coal samples can be dug as souvenirs. On the top level, 50 feet below the sea, a flower garden grows in the rock. Ocean Deeps, at one end of the operating Princess Colliery, has never been mined; it was opened as part of the museum in 1967.

Among the exhibits in the museum building on the surface are wrought iron sculptures depicting miners at work, a model of a Sydney and Louisburg Railway coal train, a coal-powered gas street lamp, such mining tools as augers, bores and shovels, and a mine telephone. One display tells of Guglielmo Marconi going into the Caledonia Colliery (now closed) to determine the sort of communication equipment required by miners.

Films on mining are shown in the museum theater.

□ Rich seams of bituminous coal underlie much of the northeastern corner of Cape Breton Island and extend many miles under the sea. Coal was dug at nearby Port Morien as early as 1720 to supply the garrison at Louisbourg. Full-scale production was begun in the 1850s. Soon Glace Bay, Sydney Mines, Dominion, Donkin and New Waterford became synonymous with coal.

□ From Table Head, now part of Glace Bay, Marconi sent the first west-to-east transatlantic wireless message—to Poldhu in Cornwall, England, on Dec 15, 1902. (He had received a message from Poldhu in St. John's, Nfld., the year before.)

Glacier National Park (B.C.) 2EY

The ancient mountains of the Selkirk Range, formed millions of years before the Rockies, cradle more than 100 glaciers in the 521 square miles of this park. Glacier was established in 1886 and for more than 70 years was accessible only by railroad. Now it is traversed by 27 miles of the 92-mile Rogers Pass section of the Trans-Canada Highway.

The Rogers route is one of the world's most beautiful mountain roads. From Golden it moves north through the Columbia River Valley, then follows the Beaver River and enters Rogers Pass in the northeast corner of Glacier Park. It follows the Illecillewaet River out of the park, across 11 miles of provincial land and into Mount Revelstoke National Park (*see entry*).

Trans-Canada Highway (center of picture) is dwarfed by the rugged peaks of Glacier National Park, which saw no automobiles until 1962.

Avalanche Defenses Are Sheds, Big Guns

One of the world's heaviest snowfalls creates not only the great glaciers of Glacier Park but also the need for elaborate defenses against avalanches. Concrete snowsheds cover the Trans-Canada Highway at danger spots in the Rogers Pass and elsewhere and rubble barriers divert and break up dangerous falls of snow, ice and boulders. When scientists observe the buildup of a potential avalanche, an artillery howitzer crew fires shells into the unstable snow. This triggers the avalanche but in controlled conditions.

Glaciers occur in Canada in the Arctic and in the higher mountain ranges. The 110-square-mile Columbia Icefield in Jasper National Park (*see entry*) is the largest in the world outside the Arctic and Antarctic. Glaciers and avalanches form when the rate of snowfall exceeds the rate of melting. The great pressure of the accumulating snow causes downhill movement, either slowly in glaciers, or if the slope is steep, quickly in avalanches.

Rogers Pass, 4,354 feet above sea level, has an average annual snowfall of 342 inches, one of the heaviest in the world. (During the winter of 1953-54 the fall was 680 inches.) This feeds not only glaciers but avalanches too. Elaborate defense and warning systems—and eight concrete snowsheds across the highway—minimize the danger. The CPR's original right-of-way through the pass can be seen at Glacier. One of North America's most dangerous stretches of rail, at the mercy of avalanches, it was superseded in 1916 by the six-mile Connaught Tunnel through Mount MacDonald.

Glacier is one of the most majestic of the national parks. Among the snow-crowned peaks, some more than 11,000 feet, are immense ice fields, richly wooded valleys, canyons and caverns and flower-filled alpine meadows—the whole vast canvas etched with turbulent rivers and tumbling water falls.

The gray head of Mount Sir Donald rises 10,818 feet just east of the park's three campgrounds: Illecillewaet, Loop Creek and Mountain Creek. To the north are Eagle Peak (9,363 feet), Avalanche Peak (9,397) and Mount MacDonald (9,492).

A network of hiking trails radiates from Illecillewaet campground. One affords striking views of Asulkan and Illecillewaet glaciers and surrounding peaks. Another leads to the Cougar Creek valley past the Nakimu Caves, formed by underground erosion. (They are not open to the public.)

Ten square miles of glacier and névé (granular snow) provide superb skiing in the Asulkan Valley.

Glenora Ont. 7DY/18BZ
Near the edge of a cliff 170 feet above the Bay of Quinte is Lake on the Mountain, focal point of a provincial park. The lake appears to have no inlet or outlet and creates the impression that water runs uphill to fill it. But divers discovered that water flows in and out of the lake through underground layers of limestone. In fact it feeds a canal that once powered an old stone gristmill beside the Glenora ferry landing. The mill is on the site of the first gristmill built (c.1790) in Prince Edward County.

Gnadenthal Man. 6BZ/15CZ
Houses with barns attached are characteristic of farms near such Mennonite villages as Chortitz, Rosenort and Gnadenthal. Low German-speaking Mennonites who left Russia in the 1870s to avoid army service settled on both sides of the Red River south of Winnipeg.

Godbout Que. 9CV/10GZ
A mausoleum commemorates Napoléon-Alexandre Comeau, who spent 60 years in this area as naturalist, trapper, game warden and fisheries officer. He died in 1923 aged 75. A plaque on the mausoleum reads: "Humble child of the north, from the book of nature he learned much to the great benefit of his folks and country." Comeau guided naturalists and sportsmen on visits to northeastern Quebec and Labrador. Baie-Comeau is named after him.

Periwinkles (marine snails) are canned in a small plant here.

Goderich Ont. 7BY/16CW
With the largest harbor on the Canadian side of Lake Huron, Goderich has grain elevators of 5,900,000-bushel capacity.

□ In a glass showcase at the north end of the town is a three-by-four-foot piece of

"**The square**" in Goderich is an octagon from which eight streets radiate like spokes of a wheel. Dr. William "Tiger" Dunlop, a physician, writer and soldier, founded Goderich in 1827 and supervised construction according to the "star" design. Plaques honoring him are in Harbour Park and on his tomb just north of town.

Stump puller used by early Ontario farmers is outside a pioneer museum in Goderich.

rock salt. Nearby are salt beds, discovered in 1866, which supply one of the town's primary industries. They underlie much of Huron County.

□ On a pedestal at the airport is a World War II Lancaster bomber, a reminder of the role Goderich played in the British Commonwealth Air Training Plan.

□ The Huron County Pioneer Museum has displays of pioneer village industries, firefighting equipment and home appliances. One shows the development of the washing machine. There are demonstrations of grain cutting, lumbering, flour milling and maple sugar processing.

□ A plaque on Lighthouse Street commemorates the Great Storm of 1913, one of the most disastrous ever to hit the Great Lakes.

□ Four miles north is 555-acre Point Farms Provincial Park on Lake Huron. It is open for pheasant hunting from mid-October to the end of November.

Golden B.C.   2FY
Once there was a St. Peter's Anglican Church 18 miles north of here at Donald. Now it's in Windermere, 80 miles south, minus its original bell and known as St. Peter's the Stolen. The bell is here in Golden, in St. Paul's of the Stolen Bell.

The stealing was in 1897. When the CPR abandoned Donald in favor of Revelstoke, the bishop decided St. Peter's should go there too. But zealous St. Peter's people moving to Windermere dismantled their church and took it with them by rail and Columbia River

barge. En route, in Golden, the bell was pilfered by the equally enterprising Anglicans of Golden.

□ Golden is the eastern terminus of the Rogers Pass section of the Trans-Canada Highway.

Golden Lake Ont.   7DX/18AW
Pioneer and Indian artifacts and exhibits of natural history and mineralogy are displayed in the Golden Lake Algonquin Museum.

Gold River B.C.   2BY
The first all-electric town in Canada, Gold River was built in six months in 1965 to house employees of a pulp mill. It is in the Gold River Valley at the junction of the Gold and Heber rivers, nine miles from the Tahsis Company Ltd. mill. Gold River's electricity, telephone and television cables are underground.

□ *Uchuck III,* a converted World War II minesweeper, runs 35 miles north to Zeballos three times a week, stopping at logging camps and coastal settlements with supplies and passengers. One stop is Friendly Cove (*see entry*), where Capt. James Cook landed in 1778.

Goodsoil Sask.   4CW
An historic plaque tells that the Northwest Rebellion ended here in June 1885 when 13 whites captured at Frog Lake and Fort Pitt (*see* Frog Lake and Lloydminster) were released by Big Bear and his Crees.

□ One entrance to Meadow Lake Provincial Park, 596 square miles of forest, lakes and rivers, is four miles north. A road and trails lead to 18 lakes noted for pike, pickerel and perch. There are many canoe routes.

Gore Bay Ont. *see* Manitoulin Island

Grafton Ont.   7DY/17EW
The Barnum house, just west of here, is one of the finest remaining examples of neo-classic architecture in Ontario. It was built in 1817 by Col. Eliakim Barnum, who had come here from Vermont. Restored to represent the home of a mid-19th-century country gentleman, the house is now a museum. The hand-carved mantel and fireplace are of a design made fashionable by Robert Adam, an 18th-century English architect and designer who led a reaction against the excessively rococo designs of Chippendale. Adam's work was strongly influenced by early Roman design.

Granby Que.   7FY/19CY
Fountains in this industrial city include one that features colored lights at night (on Leclerc Boulevard), another that spouts water from the mouth of a Greek mask (Laval Street) and a first-century Roman fountain that is the showpiece of Pelletier Park. The Roman fountain consists of a sarcophagus (coffin) supported by the capitals (tops) of columns from emperors' palaces. On one side

are carved the sarcophagus' original pagan figures; on the other are figures of the Apostles, added during the Middle Ages. The fountain, once used as an altar in a Roman basilica, was presented to Granby by a group of Italian industrialists. It is one of about a dozen European fountains acquired by the city soon after World War II.

□ In Granby Zoo, one of Canada's largest zoos, are 127 species of animals.

□ The Granby Car Museum has a 1931 Buick limousine used for 10 years by Louis St. Laurent before he became prime minister. Other cars are a 1903 Holsman, 1906 Reo, 1914 McLaughlin, 1918 Ford truck, 1923 Buick convertible, 1929 Pierce Arrow and 1929 Rolls Royce.

□ An annual song festival for French-singing amateurs is organized by Les Loisirs de Granby Inc. Auditions start in June and competition continues through the summer. Eight finalists sing at l'Escale on successive Saturdays during October and November and the festival ends with a gala in December.

□ A baptismal font in St. George's Anglican Church is decorated with a 12th-century sculpture of a bird. The sculpture was presented to the church the year it was built (1908) by the congregation of St. George's in Granby, Nottinghamshire, England.

Roman fountain in Granby's Pelletier Park dates from the first century. Children pet a friendly cheetah in the famous Granby Zoo.

□ Five miles south is Pinery Provincial Park, 5,100 acres of forest and dunes.

Grande Cache Alta.　　1BZ/2EW
This "instant city" was created in 1969 when the mining of coking coal was started here in the foothills of the northern Rockies. By 1972 the population had reached about 4,500. The total output of two underground strip mines is exported to Japan for blast furnaces there.

□ In Willmore Wilderness Provincial Park, south and west of Grande Cache, is 10,165-foot Resthaven Mountain.

Grande Prairie Alta.　　1BZ/2EV
Saskatoon Island Provincial Park, 15 miles west, is one of the few nesting grounds of the trumpeter swan, largest waterfowl bird native to North America. The trumpeter has been saved from the extinction that threatened in the 1930s and numbers about 4,500 today. Some 35 pairs nest in this area.

Seven miles south is 35-acre O'Brien Provincial Park, beside the Wapiti River. In the Kleskun Hills, 15 miles northeast, dinosaur and other fossils have been discovered.

□ Grande Prairie is the business and transportation center of the rich Peace River country, a vast area noted for its wheat. It is between Edmonton and the start of the Alaska Highway at Dawson Creek, B.C.

The Grande Prairie Pioneer Museum's collection of pioneer objects includes a mo-

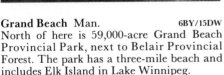

Grand Beach Man.　　6BY/15DW
North of here is 59,000-acre Grand Beach Provincial Park, next to Belair Provincial Forest. The park has a three-mile beach and includes Elk Island in Lake Winnipeg.

Grand Bend Ont.　　7BY/16CW
More than 8,000 items of Canadiana, from threshing machines to early glass and china, are in the five buildings of the Eisenbach Museum. One is furnished as a country store of the 1890s.

Grand Bend is primarily a resort village. Its main street ends at a wide, sand beach near where the Ausable River spills into Lake Huron.

bile dental chair. Among the birds and animals displayed are a trumpeter swan and an albino moose.

Frontier Days and an agricultural exhibition are held in August. Nearby Bezanson and Teepee Creek have annual rodeos.

Grandes-Bergeronnes Que.　　9BW/21EX
At nearby Anse à la Cave are the remains of furnaces built by Basque fishermen to extract oil from sea cows, seven-to-eight-foot mammals that resemble seals and walrus. A plaque on a roadside monument at Bon-Désir Bay points out that Basque fishermen were here in the 16th century (see Escoumins).

□ The Church of Notre-Dame-de-Bon-Désir is named in commemoration of a mission chapel built in 1723.

Grand Falls N.B.   9CX

The Saint John River takes a sudden 80-foot plunge here. A half-mile water-pressure tunnel 27 feet in diameter runs from the falls in the heart of town to a hydroelectric powerhouse in a lower basin.

Pulpit Rock overhangs the narrowest part of the gorge. Nearby are deep holes called the Wells, carved by the river when the falls were farther downstream, and the Coffee Mill whirlpool.

Grand Falls has a 125-foot-wide broadway that was originally a military parade ground. The town is in the heart of New Brunswick potato country and holds a potato festival in early summer.

The CN's Salmon River bridge, 3,918 feet long and 210 feet high, was built in 1910.

Wild and white, the Saint John River roars through a gorge of half-billion-year-old rocks after its 80-foot drop at Grand Falls, N.B.

Grand Falls Nfld.   11CY

Pulp and paper have made Grand Falls the fourth largest urban center in Newfoundland. The town was established in 1909 when the Harmsworth brothers (Lords Northcliffe and Rothermere) started producing newsprint here. The plant, now run by Price (Nfld.) Pulp and Paper Limited, produces 1,000 tons of newsprint a day. Most is shipped from the port of Botwood, 20 miles to the northeast.

□ A monument at Pearson's Point, 10 miles west of Grand Falls, commemorates the opening of the Newfoundland section of the Trans-Canada Highway in 1966.

Grand Forks B.C.   2EZ

Great slag piles mark the site of a copper smelter that was the biggest in the British Empire and from 1900 to 1919 the backbone of Grand Forks' economy. Forestry and farming became the major industries after the smelter was closed. There is some copper mining.

Grand Forks, at the confluence of the Granby and Kettle rivers, is the unofficial capital of the Boundary country, a 130-mile-long chain of valleys along the U.S. border.

The Boundary Museum displays articles as varied as hearse lamps, a Russian samovar and a Doukhobor spinning wheel. (Hundreds of Doukhobor families settled in the Kettle valley in the early 1900s.) Outside exhibits include a stagecoach and an early fire engine—a pumper (c.1897) that once was hooked to the city's mains and kept water flowing while the regular pumps were repaired.

□ East of Grand Forks is Christina Lake, 16 miles long and a mile wide, called the warmest lake in British Columbia.

Grand Manan Island N.B.   9CY

This biggest of the islands at the entrance to the Bay of Fundy is noted for its towering cliffs and picturesque harbors. It's the rugged home of fishermen (lobster, herring, sardine, cod, haddock) and of men who harvest dulse (edible seaweed).

Grand Manan, 55 square miles, lies seven miles off the coast of Maine; the New Brunswick mainland is 18 miles distant. There is a ferry link with the mainland town of Blacks Harbour, N.B.

The island has a typically sub-Arctic bird life and it is a geological curiosity too. On the sheltered east side is an unusual underwater forest of tree stumps. Cliffs on the wilder western shore are as high as 400 feet. Dark Harbour, center of the dulse industry, is the only big break in these precipitous cliffs. At Whale Cove on the northeast coast, seven miles from the main community of Grand Harbour, are seven strata of the earth's crust, known locally as The Seven Days Work (after the story of Creation in Genesis). At Red Point on the southeast shore is a geological contact, where new rock (volcanic) meets old (sedimentary). Other unusual rock formations are Old Bishop, a mass of trap rock at Northern Head, and Hole in the Wall, in the same part of the island. Lighthouses, lobster pounds, herring smokehouses and canneries are among the island's tourist attractions.

On Ross Island, to which visitors can walk at low tide, are the foundations of buildings erected by United Empire Loyalists who settled here in 1784.

Bowdoin College of Brunswick, Me.,

shan, Shansi province. He was buried there. The Chinese have many memorials to Bethune; there is a Bethune Museum and a Bethune Hospital. One of Mao Tse-tung's most widely read essays is entitled *In Memory of Norman Bethune.*

□ Summer band concerts are held on a barge anchored in Gull Lake here.

□ The Scottish-built 1887 paddle-steamer *Segwun*, anchored in Muskoka Bay a half-mile west, is a museum with vintage outboard motors, models of ships that once plied Lake Muskoka, a logging display, pioneer household effects and a picture gallery.

□ Ten miles northwest is Woodwinds Historical Museum. It consists of a log cabin with pioneer furniture, a log church and a modern building with displays of early agriculture, hunting, trapping and steamboating in the Muskoka District.

□ The boat *Lady Muskoka* makes 3½-hour cruises of Lake Muskoka, passing Rankin and Christmas islands, Light House Narrows and Millionaires Row and stopping at Port Carling.

Great Village N.S. 9DY/23BY
In St. James United Church, built by shipwrights in 1884, is the Marine Room, a museum devoted to Great Village's days as a shipbuilding center. There are ships' logs, letters, navigation and account books and models, photographs and paintings of more than 100 ships and captains. One picture is of the *John M. Blaikie*, one of the two four-masted barks built in Canada. She was lost at sea in 1892.

Relics of a different sort are displayed in a one-room museum in the Robert F. Layton general store: "kidney flushers, guaranteed to cure the ills of man," pattern books of the 1920s, school slates and chalk, a cracker barrel, a vinegar barrel with stand and spout, and a variety of hatpins, plumes, silks, harness hardware and lanterns. A clamp on the end of a cord was attached to the hem of a long dress: a tug lifted the skirt clear of mud.

Because most buildings are painted white, Great Village is often called the "village of white."

Greenwood B.C. 2EZ
In the leaded skylight of a former B.C. Supreme Court building, now the Greenwood Museum, is a pattern of dogwood flowers surrounding the Cross of St. George. Windows on the north side of the courthouse show the coats of arms of the seven provinces in Confederation when the building was erected in 1902-3. The museum displays early mining and logging equipment, pioneer clothing and Japanese artifacts. (About 2,500 Japanese Canadians were moved here from the west coast after Canada went to war with Japan in 1941.)

Greenwood N.S. 9DY/22CV
This village was established for families of airmen stationed at CFB Greenwood, a long-range maritime patrol base. Tours of the base are arranged through the public relations officer.

Grimsby Ont. 7CZ/17CY
A farm shop built about 1800 and used by Canadian, British and American blacksmiths during the War of 1812 now houses the Stone Shop Museum. When the building was renovated as a museum, the door of the Marlatt Tavern (1855-73) was incorporated. Exhibits include a chest used by Dr. Cyrus Sumner in the War of 1812 and a document by which he was appointed a surgeon of the militia at $1.50 a day. There are models of a sulky plow and of a temple built in 1888 on a Methodist camp meeting ground at Grimsby Beach; a crazy quilt that was awarded first prize at the Chicago World's Fair in 1893, and a Windsor side chair that belonged to

Most Canadian wine is from grapes grown in the rich soil and temperate climate of the Niagara Peninsula—from roughly Winona east through Grimsby to Vineland and Jordan.

Col. Robert Nelles, one of the first settlers at The Forty, as Grimsby was known. (It is on Forty Mile Creek, so named for its distance from the Niagara River.)

The Manor, built by Nelles in 1798, is a fine example of a colonial home. It is marked with an historic plaque.

St. Andrew's Anglican Church and graveyard are on land donated by Nelles. A log church was built in 1794, the present stone church in 1818-25. Many of the town's founding Loyalists were buried in the graveyard.

□ A plaque near the Lake Ontario shore tells how in 1813 British ships bombarded American troops retiring after their defeat at Stoney Creek. Indians and militiamen joined in the attack, forcing the Americans back to Fort George. The action became known as the Battle of The Forty.

Another plaque commemorates a meeting April 5, 1790, that is believed to have been the first municipal government session in what is now Ontario. It dealt with such matters as the height of fences and the registration of livestock marks.

□ Beamer Memorial Park on the Niagara Escarpment overlooking the town commemorates a pioneer family who operated a mill at Beamer's Falls on Forty Mile Creek. From the Point, adjacent to the park, the Niagara fruit belt can be seen against the deep blue of Lake Ontario.

Grimshaw Alta.   1BZ/3GZ

This is the start of the Mackenzie Route, an exciting system of northern roads through green forests, across spongy muskeg, past duck-filled sloughs and lakes, over and alongside swift rivers. It has opened thousands of square miles of wilderness and when completed will stretch more than 1,300 miles to Tuktoyaktuk on the Arctic Ocean.

The route consists of five main roads: the Mackenzie Highway, from Grimshaw to Camsell Bend, from where it is being pushed north to Inuvik and Tuktoyaktuk; the 215-mile Yellowknife Highway, which connects with the Ingraham Trail at Yellowknife; and the Hay River, Fort Resolution and Fort Smith highways.

The first major side trip for travelers northbound on the Mackenzie Highway is east from Keg River junction, 119 miles north of Grimshaw, to Fort Vermilion. From here a ferry crosses the Peace River to a road that rejoins the Mackenzie Highway at High Level. Near Enterprise, 52 miles north of the Alberta-N.W.T. border, are Alexandra Falls and Louise Falls (*see* Hay River). At Enterprise the Hay River Highway leads to Hay River and Great Slave Lake and joins the Fort Resolution Highway. It in turn is tied to the Fort Smith Highway, which crosses a part of Wood Buffalo National Park.

It is at Enterprise that the Mackenzie Highway starts its wide end run around Great Slave Lake. Fifty-three miles northwest of Enterprise a side road leads to Kakisa Lake and Lady Evelyn Falls (*see* Hay River). Twelve miles farther is the junction with the Yellowknife Highway.

At Dory Point the MV *Johnny Berens*, named for a famous Hudson's Bay Company river pilot, shuttles Yellowknife Highway traffic across the Mackenzie River. (Vehicles use the river ice in winter.) On the north side of the river a side road leads to Fort Providence (*see entry*). Near Rae, 144 miles north of Fort Providence, the highway crosses the North Arm of Great Slave Lake on a high steel bridge, then goes southeast to Yellowknife. From Yellowknife the 40-mile Ingraham Trail goes east across the Yellowknife River to several excellent fishing lakes and Cameron River falls and rapids.

From the Yellowknife Highway junction the Mackenzie Highway follows the Mackenzie River Valley west to Fort Simpson and Camsell Bend, then north across the river just as the Mackenzie turns for the last leg of its long journey to the Arctic Ocean.

Grondines Que.   20AW

Champlain wrote of the noise the water makes among boulders at the edge of the St. Lawrence River here—the low rumble (*grondement*) that gave the village its name. It can be heard for a mile on still nights.

One 17th-century mill here is a river navigation signal station. Another is a restaurant furnished with antiques.

Saint-Charles-des-Grondines Church dates from 1841. The rectory (1844) is classified as an historic monument.

North of Yellowknife near a winter road to Port Radium—a kind of extension of the Mackenzie Route—is Faber Lake, typical of the wild beauty of the Northwest Territories. The Mackenzie Route starts at Grimshaw and thrusts deep into the sparsely settled north.

Mud beaches and hard sand on both coasts yield clams in commercial quantities—and lots more for family digs too.

Gros Morne National Park (Nfld.)   11BX

In this rugged park (established in 1970) are the most spectacular of the Long Range Mountains of Newfoundland's Great Northern Peninsula, including 2,644-foot Gros Morne. The mountains rise dramatically and abruptly from a low coastal plain. Along the rugged 40-mile coast are fine beaches and expanses of shifting dunes. Inland are dense forests, narrow mountain lakes, a tidal inlet and streams noted for trout and salmon. Saltwater fishing is also good in the area. The park has a nature interpretation center, campgrounds and hiking trails.

Grosse Ile Que.   20CW

In this secluded spot lie the mortal remains of 5,424 persons who, fleeing from pestilence and famine in Ireland in the year 1847, found in America but a grave. This is the epitaph on a monument where Canada's first immigrant quarantine station was established in 1832. The 5,424 Irishmen who died in 1847—in crowded immigrant ships or after reaching Grosse Ile—were victims of typhus.

The quarantine station was relocated at Quebec in 1937 and during World War II Grosse Ile was a base for biological warfare experiments.

Grosses Coques N.S.   9DZ/22BW

Big clams from St. Mary's Bay kept the first Acadian settlers alive through a long bitter winter and gave this village its name. The six-to-eight-inch clams harvested here are among the largest on the east coast of North America.

□ The first frame house in Grosses Coques, built by Joseph Dugas, apparently in the late 1700s, is still occupied. A cairn marks the site of the first church here. It was built of logs in 1769.

Guelph Ont.   7BY/17BY

A bylaw requires that all buildings on Wyndham Street, Guelph's 100-foot-wide main thoroughfare, have facades of the local gray limestone that the city's first settlers used. Off one end of Wyndham Street is one of the best-known limestone buildings, the city hall (1). Erected soon after Guelph's incorporation as a town in 1856, it is a fine example of classic architecture, little changed from its original state.

Guelph was settled in 1827 by Scottish and English immigrants brought here by the Canada Company. Its other main settlements were Goderich and Galt (now part of Cambridge), named after the company superintendent, John Galt. The heart of Guelph is St. George's Square, where settlers played cricket in 1831. The radial pattern of the streets, similar to the spokes of a wheel, was designed by Galt.

CIVIC MUSEUM (2) It has a collection of 87 dolls in costumes of many countries, pioneer clothing and furniture and 19th-century sleighs, toys and tools. Typewriters (1895), a piano, a melodeon, a harmonium, a parlor organ and decorative light bulbs were all made in Guelph. A baby seat made of pine,

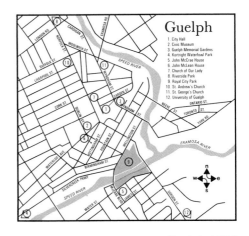

Guelph

1. City Hall
2. Civic Museum
3. Guelph Memorial Gardens
4. Kortright Waterfowl Park
5. John McCrae House
6. John McLean House
7. Church of Our Lady
8. Riverside Park
9. Royal City Park
10. St. Andrew's Church
11. St. George's Church
12. University of Guelph

a forerunner of modern baby exercisers, was once suspended from a door frame.

GUELPH MEMORIAL GARDENS (3) A plaque at this 4,000-seat arena honors Edward Johnson, a Guelph native and world-famous opera singer in the first half of this century. The Gardens are in Johnson's old neighborhood.

KORTRIGHT WATERFOWL PARK (4) More than 300 Giant Canada geese (a subspecies considered nearly extinct a few years ago) thrive here along with other geese, more than 23 species of ducks, mute swans, pheasants, grouse, hawks and owls. The park is operated by the Ontario Waterfowl Research Foundation.

JOHN McCRAE HOUSE (5) The birthplace of Col. John McCrae (1872-1918), author of *In Flanders Fields*, is a national historic site. He wrote the famous poem in 1915:

> *In Flanders fields the poppies blow*
> *Between the crosses, row on row,*
> *That mark our place; and in the sky*
> *The larks, still bravely singing, fly*
> *Scarce heard amid the guns below.*
>
> *We are the Dead. Short days ago*
> *We lived, felt dawn, saw sunset glow,*
> *Loved, and were loved, and now we lie*
> *   In Flanders fields.*
>
> *Take up our quarrel with the foe:*
> *To you from failing hands we throw*
> *The torch; be yours to hold it high.*
> *If ye break faith with us who die*
> *We shall not sleep, though poppies grow*
> *   In Flanders fields.*

In McCrae Memorial Gardens, adjacent to his birthplace, a light burns in memory of McCrae.

Twin Gothic towers of the Church of Our Lady of the Immaculate Conception—"Cologne in miniature"—are a Guelph landmark.

JOHN McLEAN HOUSE (6) John McLean, author of *Notes of a Twenty-five Years' Service in the Hudson's Bay Company*, was the first white man to see Grand Falls (renamed Churchill Falls) on the Hamilton River in Labrador (*see* Churchill Falls).

CHURCH OF OUR LADY (7) The Roman Catholic Church of Our Lady of the Immaculate Conception, styled after the decorated

From Slaughter at Ypres ... an Immortal Poem

A bedroom and combined dining room and kitchen (above) of John McCrae's birthplace in Guelph are furnished as he knew them. Copies of his poems and pencil sketches are displayed. (The date and significance of his "dim old forest" sketch are not known.) McCrae served as a gunner in the South African War and practised medicine in Montreal for 14 years before going overseas as an army medical officer. He reached Flanders in 1915 and, as an artillery brigade surgeon, witnessed the Second Battle of Ypres from his frontline dressing station in a hole in the bank of the Ypres Canal. He wrote *In Flanders Fields* during a lull in the slaughter, between batches of wounded, as the wooden crosses of the newly dead grew to be a great cemetery. The poem first appeared in *Punch* Dec. 8, 1915. McCrae died in 1918 and was buried at Wimereux in northern France.

Gothic cathedral of Cologne in Germany, was started in 1877 and its twin towers were added in 1926. The sweeping interior lines are of wood, granite and marble and much of the inside is painted blue and gold. The most remarkable of many stained-glass windows is the St. Catherine wheel window, more than 18 feet in diameter.

RIVERSIDE PARK (8) A model of the Priory, the first house John Galt built in Guelph in 1827, and a garden in his honor, are here. A floral clock 44 feet across has between 6,000 and 7,000 flowers in 14 varieties. The minute hand is 12 feet, six inches long, the hour hand is three feet shorter. The clock also registers the date in flowers.

ROYAL CITY PARK (9) A plaque tells of Scottish settlers who came here after failure of their colony at La Guayra, Venezuela. Another plaque honors John Galt.

ST. ANDREW'S CHURCH (10) A Presbyterian church built in 1857.

ST. GEORGE'S CHURCH (11) An Anglican church with a 23-bell carillon.

UNIVERSITY OF GUELPH (12) When the university was created in 1964 it incorporated Ontario Agricultural College (1874), largest agricultural college in the Commonwealth; Ontario Veterinary College (1862), oldest veterinary college in North America; Macdonald Institute (now the College of Family and Consumer Studies), a "school for young ladies" started in 1903 and the new Wellington College of Arts and Sciences. There now are 10,500 students in seven colleges on the 1,100-acre campus.

Gull Lake Sask.   4CZ
Twenty miles west, where once the great "76" ranch had its headquarters, is a monument honoring Saskatchewan's ranching industry. The "76," one of the largest spreads in the west in the days of the open range, started in Saskatchewan in 1888 and ran as many as 20,000 head of cattle and 30,000 sheep from the South Saskatchewan River to the U.S. border. The ranch was broken up in 1921.

H

Hacketts Cove N.S.   22EW
A tombstone marks the grave of Jannet McDonald, said to have been a relative of the Flora Macdonald who helped Bonnie Prince Charlie after the Battle of Culloden in Scotland in 1746. The prince took refuge in Skye; Flora disguised him as a maid and he escaped to France. She later married, emigrated to America and lived one winter in Windsor, N.S. (*see entry*). A family legend says Jannet was buried (in 1789) in sheets on which the prince slept during the escape.

Haileybury Ont.   7CW
This resort town on Lake Timiskaming was the home of men who became wealthy almost overnight in the Cobalt silver boom of 1903. They forsook the mining camps and built fine homes on the lakeshore here. Many still exist, having escaped a 1922 fire which destroyed much of the town.

Haines Junction Y.T.   1AW
This town at Mile 1016 of the Alaska Highway lies in the Shakwak Valley within sight of the mighty St. Elias Mountains and some of the highest peaks in North America. It lies just outside Kluane National Park.

Klukshu, an Indian village where salmon trapping is a major occupation, is on the 159-mile Haines Highway that leads south to the Alaska port of Haines. Ferries connect Haines with Prince Rupert, B.C.

Three miles west of Haines Junction is Canada's most northerly experimental farm. East, at Mile 995, a road leads north to Otter Falls, which was shown on the Canadian $5 bill, and to Aishihik Lake, noted for trout. At Champagne (Mile 974) are a 70-year-old trading post and a cemetery containing 20 of the small spirit houses that Tlingit Indians used to build over graves.

An Indian Madonna and Child are over the door of a tiny Quonset mission chapel in Haines Junction. It is called Our Lady of the Way.

Haliburton Ont.   7CY
This village and the thickly wooded Haliburton Highlands were named for Judge Thomas Chandler Haliburton, the Nova Scotian author of the Sam Slick stories (*see* Windsor, N.S.). He was the first chairman of the Canadian Land and Emigration Company which settled the region in the 1860s. A plaque here commemorates that settlement.

The Haliburton Highlands Pioneer Museum includes a pioneer house and a collection of tools and implements used in lumbering, farming and trapping.

Haliburton has an unusual tourist information center: a Grand Trunk Railway steam locomotive and a wooden caboose. Skyline Park is a 350-foot hill with a converted fire tower that provides good views of the highlands.

Halifax N.S.   9EY/22EW/P.156
The storied past of this old city seems as real as the timeless sea at its doorstep.

□ In a Halifax of skyscrapers and expressways are little streets where Cornwallis and Wolfe and Captain Cook walked—and Royal Navy press gangs hunted.

□ A classic round music room and a heart-shaped pool speak of an English prince and his French-Canadian love.

□ Joseph Howe stands in bronze where he won a courtroom battle for freedom of the press in 1835.

□ In a north-end cemetery are long, tragic rows of *Titanic* graves.

□ Two modern bridges leap the great harbor where a munitions ship exploded in 1917 in the biggest non-nuclear blast ever.

□ The ghosts of World War II's vast convoys ride at restless anchor in Bedford Basin. . . .

Overlooking the city and its harbor, among the finest in the world, is Citadel Hill, crowned by a huge, star-shaped, stone fort, successor to the stockade that Governor Edward Cornwallis built when he founded Halifax in 1749.

Halifax is the biggest city in the Atlantic provinces, the capital of Nova Scotia, Canada's third largest general scientific center (next to Ottawa and Toronto) and the financial, educational, medical, cultural and business leader of Atlantic Canada.

The city core is on a peninsula with tidewater on three sides. The outer harbor, 1,600 yards wide and four miles long, has 32 berths on a frontage of 19,000 feet and accommo-

dates the largest vessels. A narrow passage leads to the inner harbor, Bedford Basin. The whole harbor is ice-free and operates year round, with increased winter activity when St. Lawrence ports are closed. More than 3,300 ships turn annually in Halifax.

Throughout the city are reminders of the explosion of Dec. 6, 1917, which killed 1,600 persons, injured several thousand, leveled a square mile of the north end and part of neighboring Dartmouth, and caused an estimated $35,000,000 property damage. The French ship *Mont Blanc*, carrying munitions, caught fire and exploded after colliding with the Norwegian *Imo,* loaded with supplies for Belgian relief. It was the biggest man-made explosion prior to the dropping of the first atomic bomb at Hiroshima in August 1945.

Several buildings are associated with Prince Edward, Duke of Kent, Halifax commander-in-chief from 1794 to 1800. He directed a reconstruction of the Citadel and construction of York Redoubt (*see under*), a Martello tower (*see under* Point Pleasant

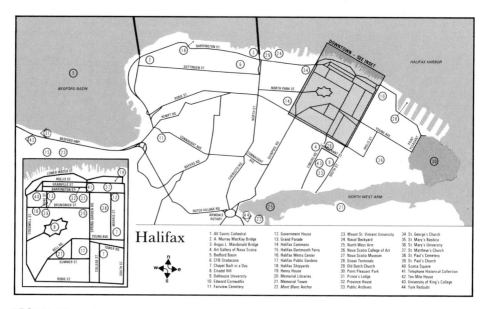

Halifax

n
w + e
s

1. All Saints Cathedral
2. A. Murray MacKay Bridge
3. Angus L. Macdonald Bridge
4. Art Gallery of Nova Scotia
5. Bedford Basin
6. CFB Stadacona
7. Chapel Built in a Day
8. Citadel Hill
9. Dalhousie University
10. Edward Cornwallis
11. Fairview Cemetery

12. Government House
13. Grand Parade
14. Halifax Commons
15. Halifax-Dartmouth Ferry
16. Halifax Metro Center
17. Halifax Public Gardens
18. Halifax Shipyards
19. Henry House
20. Memorial Libraries
21. Memorial Tower
22. *Mont Blanc* Anchor

23. Mount St. Vincent University
24. Naval Dockyard
25. North West Arm
26. Nova Scotia College of Art
27. Nova Scotia Museum
28. Ocean Terminals
29. Old Dutch Church
30. Point Pleasant Park
31. Prince's Lodge
32. Province House
33. Public Archives

34. St. Mary's Basilica
35. St. Mary's University
36. St. Matthew's Church
37. St. Paul's Cemetery
38. St. Paul's Church
39. Scotia Square
40. Telephone Historical Collection
41. Ten Mile House
42. University of King's College
43. York Redoubt

High-rise buildings dominate the Halifax skyline, towering over the gable-roofed old waterfront structures (including the stone Privateer Warehouse) of Historic Properties. Modern warships berth in North America's oldest naval dockyard.

Park), a round church (*see under* St. George's Church) and the Old Town Clock (*see under* Citadel Hill). One of Halifax's great love stories was the prince's romance with Mme Julie de St. Laurent, a commoner he could not wed. He returned to England in 1800 and 18 years later married. A daughter born in 1819 became Queen Victoria.

ADMIRALTY HOUSE *see* CFB Stadacona

ALL SAINTS CATHEDRAL (1) The Cathedral Church of All Saints was built in 1907-10 to commemorate the 200th anniversary of the first Anglican service in Nova Scotia. All wood carvings are in English oak.

A. MURRAY MacKAY BRIDGE (2) This 1,400-foot bridge connects Halifax and Dartmouth at the Narrows, between the outer harbor and Bedford Basin. A. Murray MacKay was chairman of the Halifax-Dartmouth Bridge Commission.

ANGUS L. MACDONALD BRIDGE (3) A 1,447-foot control span makes it one of the longest suspension bridges in the Commonwealth. Angus L. Macdonald was a Nova Scotia premier and wartime federal navy minister.

ARMY MUSEUM *see under* Citadel Hill

ART GALLERY OF NOVA SCOTIA (4) Features temporary and traveling exhibitions and a permanent collection with works by Picasso, Constable, Salvator Rosa, Ernest Lawson and Carol Fraser as well as folk art. A branch, the Centennial Art Gallery, is on Citadel Hill.

BEDFORD BASIN (5) The famous convoy assembly place of the two world wars, the six-square-mile basin is big enough and deep enough to accommodate the combined navies of the world.

CENTENNIAL ART GALLERY *see under* Citadel Hill

CFB STADACONA (6) Here are Admiralty House, once the home of the British commander of the Halifax naval base, and a cut-stone monument commemorating HMS

Shannon's victory over the U.S. frigate *Chesapeake* off Boston in 1813. *Shannon*, based in Halifax, brought her prize here after the battle (in which *Chesapeake*'s captain spoke the words "Don't give up the ship!"—now the motto of the U.S. Navy).

In the base chapel is a Battle of the Atlantic window in memory of Canada's RCN and RCAF (Maritime Command) dead in World War II.

CHAPEL BUILT IN A DAY (7) Two thousand persons built the chapel of Our Lady of Sorrows in Holy Cross Cemetery on Aug. 31, 1843. It has a stained glass window dating from 1661 and wooden carvings from a Flemish church of 1550. The cemetery contains the graves of Sir John Thompson, prime minister in 1892-94, and of two seamen hanged for piracy in 1844.

CITADEL HILL (8) The massive fort on this 225-foot-high oval hill is a national historic park. In it are three museums, one of which contains an art gallery. Also on the hill are the Old Town Clock (1803) and the noon gun. (A gun has been fired at noon every day since the city's founding. Originally it was to draw mariners' attention to the Citadel flagstaff and the dropping of a black ball a few seconds later as a check on ships' timepieces.)

□ The first fort, in 1749, was part of the wooden palisade around Cornwallis' settlement. More substantial wood and earth citadels occupied the site before the present structure was begun in 1828. When completed 30 years later it could accommodate about 500 men and had underground reservoirs that held 200,000 gallons of water in case of siege. But by 1870 it was obsolete. None of the forts ever was attacked. British troops manned the Citadel until 1906, when the Canadian Army took over.

□ The Army Museum occupies five upper and four lower casements in the Citadel redan (bastion). Its collections include military equipment, uniforms and weapons, with emphasis on Canadian and Nova Scotia military history. The many exhibits include a model (14 feet by 10 by 10) of Halifax in 1750 and models of Fortress Louisbourg (1745), Fort Anne at Annapolis Royal (1605) and York Redoubt (1798) (*see under*).

□ General historical exhibits include Nova Scotia furniture, farm implements, musical instruments and crafts.

□ Halifax got its Old Town Clock because of Prince Edward's fixation about punctuality. After leaving here in 1800 he ordered a garrison clock made in London. It arrived in Halifax in 1803, an unusual clock with different peals for the quarter-hour, half-hour and hour. The bell tower is a replica.

DALHOUSIE UNIVERSITY (9) Dalhousie, founded in 1818 (but opened in 1838), is famous for its law and medical schools. Its imposing 15-story Sir Charles Tupper Medical Building housing the faculty of medicine, was Nova Scotia's provincial centennial project in 1967.

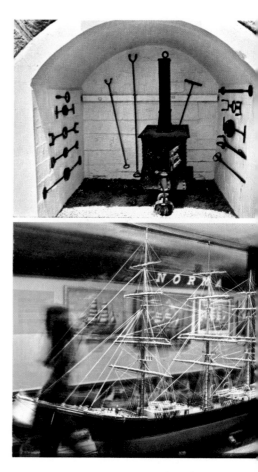

Angus McAskill (*see* Englishtown) was 7 feet, 9 inches, weighed 425 and had an 80-inch waist. This model and one of his size 14½ boots are in the Halifax Citadel museum. Other exhibits include a stove and implements for heating cannonballs. A model of the three-masted *Annie E. Wright*, a 237.9-foot ship built at Harvey, N.B., in 1885, is part of the extensive maritime collection of the Nova Scotia Museum.

In the five-level Dalhousie University Arts Center are a music auditorium, theater, art gallery and the departments of music and theater. Representative of the gallery's permanent collection are works by Bruno Bobak, Guido Molinari, Guy Montpetit and E. Vigée-Lebrun. The gallery has pre-Inca pottery, bird and animal carvings and a collection of classical sculpture reproductions.

EDWARD CORNWALLIS (10) In a small park in front of the Hotel Nova Scotian is a statue of Governor Edward Cornwallis.

GOVERNMENT HOUSE (12) This big stone building (c.1800), closed to the public, is the residence of the lieutenant governor of Nova Scotia.

GRAND PARADE (13) Originally the Halifax garrison parade ground (where the town crier read the news), it contains city hall, the Halifax War Memorial (by Scottish sculptor John Massey Rhind) and a 128-foot flagpole.

HALIFAX COMMONS (14) A park and recreation area north of the Citadel.

HALIFAX-DARTMOUTH FERRY (15) Passengers only, on the ferries of a system that has operated since 1752.

HALIFAX METRO CENTER (16) Largest exhibition center east of Montreal, this glittering downtown complex opened in 1978 and promptly became the city's major showplace. It offers a wide variety of entertainment, and has a coliseum seating nearly 10,000.

HALIFAX PUBLIC GARDENS (17) Set amid a network of lily ponds and flower-bordered walks are an old-fashioned bandstand built to celebrate Queen Victoria's golden jubilee, a fountain commemorating her diamond jubilee and another fountain in memory of Nova Scotians killed in the South African War. There are statues of Ceres, Diana and Flora (goddesses of agriculture, the bath and flowers), the stately descendants of two swans donated by George V and an oak planted by George VI in 1939.

HALIFAX SHIPYARDS (18) Here were repaired more than 7,000 ships damaged in the World War II Battle of the Atlantic.

HENRY HOUSE (19) This national historic site is a restaurant too. It was the home of William Alexander Henry (1816-88), a Father of Confederation and mayor of Halifax.

MEMORIAL LIBRARIES (20) The Halifax Me-

morial Library was erected in memory of
the city's dead in the world wars. The Halifax
North Memorial Library is a monument to
the victims of the 1917 explosion. Outside the
building is a Jordi Bonet sculpture, 15 feet
long and 10 feet high, symbolic of the
catastrophe and the city's subsequent rebirth.
One part of the sculpture uses polished
bronze, strong brass and battered wood to
symbolize the human aspect of the tragedy;
the faint outline of a doll represents the child
victims. An authentic piece of metal from the
ship *Mont Blanc* is incorporated into the base
of the sculpture.

MEMORIAL TOWER (21) The tower in the Din-
gle, popular name for Fleming Park, was
started in 1908 to commemorate the first
elective assembly in Canada (in Halifax,
Oct. 2, 1758). It was completed in 1912. Inside, inset in the walls, are carved tablets
in native stone contributed by Empire countries, the provinces of Canada and Canadian
universities.

MONT BLANC ANCHOR (22) The half-ton shank
of an anchor from the *Mont Blanc* lies where
it landed Dec. 6, 1917, three miles from the
explosion in the Narrows.

MOUNT ST. VINCENT UNIVERSITY (23) An affiliate of Dalhousie University, it is operated
by the Sisters of Charity. It is coeducational.

NAVAL DOCKYARD (24) The oldest naval
dockyard in North America was begun in
1759. A tablet outside CFB Stadacona marks
the site of that first yard. An ornate 34-foot
state barge on display near CFB Maritime
Command headquarters was presented to
Queen Victoria on her golden jubilee in 1887
by the Lords of the Admiralty. Queen Elizabeth presented it to the Nova Scotia Museum
in 1959.

NORTH WEST ARM (25) A 2½-mile-long inlet

Public Gardens, opened in 1867, are a 17-acre
oasis of calm and stubborn nostalgia in the heart
of bustling, modern Halifax.

Numbered graves of 125 persons who died in
the 1912 *Titanic* sinking are in Fairview Cemetery
in Halifax. In the same cemetery are memorials
marking the common grave of unidentified victims
of the Halifax explosion of 1917.

of the sea, sheltered by low hills, it is the
city's main aquatic playground.

NOVA SCOTIA COLLEGE OF ART (26) One of
the founders (1887) of the Nova Scotia College of Art and Design was Anna Leono-
wens—the Anna of *Anna and the King of Siam*
and *The King and I*. She lived here from 1878
to 1897.

NOVA SCOTIA MUSEUM (27) It has two loca-
tions in Halifax and branches in Balmoral,
Barrington, Liverpool, Maitland, Mount Uniacke, Shelburne, Sherbrooke and Windsor.
The theme of the main museum here is Man
and His Environment in Nova Scotia.

OCEAN TERMINALS (28) Alongside deep
water, the Ocean Terminals are big enough
to have berthed the *Queen Mary* and *Queen
Elizabeth* end to end.

OLD DUTCH CHURCH (29) Only 40 feet by
20, it was built in 1756 by German settlers
and was the first Lutheran church in Canada.

POINT PLEASANT PARK (30) One of several
forts in the 186-acre park is the Prince of
Wales Martello Tower (1796), a national his-

toric site. The original for this and similar towers was a fort at Cape Mortella in Corsica, which resisted British attack in 1794. The British built similar forts along the English coast and Prince Edward, when commander-in-chief here, had five erected around Halifax. All had thick walls and tapered slightly toward the top. This one, which was named for the prince's brother, is the only one remaining.

The National Sailors' Memorial in the park honors Canadian Navy and Merchant Service men who lost their lives in the world wars and have no known graves.

Also in the park is a cairn in memory of the freighter *Point Pleasant Park* and nine men who died when she was torpedoed in the South Atlantic in 1945.

A plaque honors Rear Adm. Walter Hose, founder of the Canadian Navy and of the naval reserve.

PRINCE'S LODGE (31) This round, domed building was the music room of Prince Edward's residence (1794-1800). No other buildings of the lodge remain. The rotunda has been restored and designated as an historic site. It is not open to the public; the grounds are.

Prince's Lodge in Halifax overlooks a heart-shaped pool built for Julie de St. Laurent and part of the paths that Prince Edward, Duke of Kent, designed to spell her name.

PROVINCE HOUSE (32) The legislative assembly meets in this fine stone building. Completed in 1818, it is a leading example of Georgian architecture and the oldest legislative building in use in Canada. At the main entrance are two lamps from London's Waterloo Bridge and a brace of cannon used in the duel between HMS *Shannon* and the U.S. frigate *Chesapeake* in 1813 (*see under* CFB Stadacona). In the Red Room is the table at which Cornwallis and his advisers sat—in a ship in the harbor—as they planned the Halifax settlement in 1749. A plaque commemorates the first printing press in British North America (1751), on which Canada's first newspaper, the *Halifax Gazette,* was printed March 23, 1752. Other plaques record that the first legislative assembly in Canada was held in Halifax Oct. 2, 1758, and that the first responsible government sat in Prov-

The Loyalist Bishop

St. Paul's Church, the only building that remains from the founding of Halifax (1749), was the cathedral of Charles Inglis, first Anglican bishop of Nova Scotia. He had been acting rector of Trinity Church in New York and he lives in history not least for having prayed for George III soon after the declaration of Independence in 1776—and with George Washington in a front pew. A rebel general, Inglis wrote later, "left Word that 'General Washington would be at Church, and would be glad if the violent Prayers for the King and Royal Family were omitted.' This Message was brought to me, and as You may suppose I paid no Regard to it."

ince House in 1848, almost two decades before Confederation.

In the Legislative Library, once a courtroom, is a plaster replica of a statue of the great Nova Scotia patriot Joseph Howe, his right arm gesturing in debate. (The bronze original is outside Province House.) As journalist, orator and politician Howe battled for democratic government and a free press. He was a member of the legislature for more than 25 years, premier in 1860-63. He first opposed, then went along with Confederation, winning better terms for Nova Scotia, and became a member of Parliament. Many of Howe's personal effects are in the Heritage Museum in neighboring Dartmouth.

PUBLIC ARCHIVES (33) The Public Archives of Nova Scotia contain a library and a museum in which are historical documents, maps, manuscripts, newspapers, stamps, coins, prints and ship models. Joseph Howe's printing press can be seen.

ST. GEORGE'S CHURCH (34) This round church, built in 1800 under the direction of Prince Edward, is one of the few round Byzantine churches in North America.

ST. MARY'S BASILICA (35) St. Mary's is one of the oldest stone edifices in Canada, with parts dating from 1820, and it has the tallest polished granite spire (189 feet) in the world. It is on the site of Horseman's Fort, the south gate of the early Halifax palisade. There are tablets in memory of the Rev. Pierre

Maillard, a missionary to the Micmac Indians of Nova Scotia, who died in 1762; of the Most Rev. Edmund Burke, first Roman Catholic bishop of Halifax, who planned the basilica and placed the cornerstone; and of Sir John Thompson, a parishioner who became prime minister (1892).

ST. MARY'S UNIVERSITY (36) Established in 1841 and coeducational since 1968, it was one of the oldest English Roman Catholic institutions in Canada. Since 1970 it has been public.

ST. MATTHEW'S CHURCH (37) This United church, built in 1858, is the oldest dissenting (non-Anglican Protestant) congregation in Canada.

ST. PAUL'S CEMETERY (38) Three blocks from St. Paul's Church, it contains the graves of some of the founders of Halifax. Here is the Sebastopol Monument, one of the few Crimean War memorials in North America. On the cemetery gates is inscribed: "Originally this location was outside the south palisade of the town. Scalps from the dead were sometimes taken. Therefore many of the early graves have no markers."

ST. PAUL'S CHURCH (39) Timbers were brought by sea from Boston in 1749 to build this first Protestant church in Canada. It contains a royal pew, hatchments displaying the armorial devices of old families, and scores of memorial tablets. The body of Charles Inglis, first Anglican bishop of Nova Scotia (his jurisdiction extended from Newfoundland to Detroit), is buried under the chancel. The vaults contain the remains of such men as Vice Adm. Sir Philip Durell, commander-in-chief at Halifax in the 1750s and 1760s, and Rear Adm. Leonard W. Murray, Commander-in-Chief Canadian Northwest Atlantic in World War II. A hole blown in a window of the church by the 1917 explosion resembles the profile of a man and has been retained between a double-pane window.

SCOTIA SQUARE (40) A 19-acre renewal project in the heart of Halifax provides a 312-room hotel, 14- and 18-story office buildings, five apartment building, a trade mart and more than 100 stores and boutiques.

TELEPHONE HISTORICAL COLLECTION (41) Instruments include a miniature telephone transmitter constructed in 1936 to enable men trapped in a mine at Moose River Gold Mines, N.S., to communicate with the surface. The collection is at the Maritime Telegraph & Telephone Company Limited.

TEN MILE HOUSE (42) The three-story wooden building in suburban Bedford, 200 years old and once a stagecoach stop, is an art gallery.

UNIVERSITY OF KING'S COLLEGE (43) Established in Windsor, N.S., in 1789, King's is the oldest university in the Commonwealth outside the British Isles. It was moved to Halifax in 1923 and shares a campus with Dalhousie University.

YORK REDOUBT (44) This national historic site has been a fortified battery position since 1793, the seaward extension of the historic Halifax defense complex. The base of a late 18th-century Martello tower and the remains of 19th-century gun emplacements can be seen. None of the redoubt's guns ever was fired in anger, even during World War II when it was a key part of the port's defenses against German submarines.

Hamilton Ont.   7CZ/17BY

This "Pittsburgh of Canada," at the west end of Lake Ontario, is Canada's leading steel maker and the country's third city in industrial production (behind Toronto and Montreal). Its landlocked harbor, with 13 miles of waterfront, is one of the largest on the Great Lakes.

The city is the seat of McMaster University and Mohawk College of Applied Arts and Technology. There are some 70 parks, totaling more than 2,500 acres, in addition to the Royal Botanical Gardens (parts of which are in Burlington and Dundas). The city has three publicly-owned 18-hole golf courses. Dundurn Castle, a restored 19th-century mansion, is a Canadian showplace. Hamilton lies below and on top of the Niagara Escarpment with its creeks and waterfalls and panoramic views.

ART GALLERY OF HAMILTON (1) Ensconced in

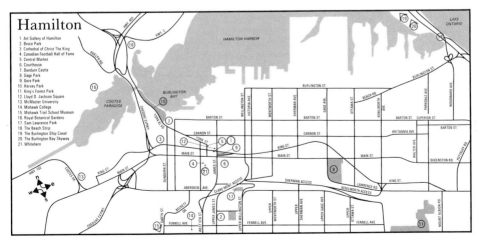

Hamilton

1. Art Gallery of Hamilton
2. Bruce Park
3. Cathedral of Christ The King
4. Canadian Football Hall of Fame
5. Central Market
6. Courthouse
7. Dundurn Castle
8. Gage Park
9. Gore Park
10. Harvey Park
11. King's Forest Park
12. Lloyd D. Jackson Square
13. McMaster University
14. Mohawk College
15. Mohawk Trail School Museum
16. Royal Botanical Gardens
17. Sam Lawrence Park
18. The Beach Strip
19. The Burlington Ship Canal
20. The Burlington Bay Skyway
21. Whitehern

a new gallery are a permanent collection of some 3,500 Canadian, British and American works of art, and the world documentation center for the graphic work of Holland's famous Karel Appel. Canadian artists represented include Cornelius Krieghoff, Alex Colville and Maurice Cullen. Thirty works by William Blair Bruce (1859-1906), a gift of his family and the foundation of the gallery's collection, now have their own display. A plaque commemorating Bruce, who is represented also in the National Gallery in Ottawa, is in Bruce Park (2).

CATHEDRAL OF CHRIST THE KING (3) Completed in 1933, the cathedral was built of Credit Valley limestone from Georgetown, Ont., in 13th-century English Gothic style. It has a 165-foot tower and a 23-bell carillon. The highlight of its simple interior is a ciborium of Italian marble. The 82 stained glass windows are by Franz Mayer.

CANADIAN FOOTBALL HALL OF FAME (4) In the shrine room of the hall of fame are busts of football's builders and great players, a computer that answers questions about Canadian Football League records, and a theater showing Grey Cup and other films. The hall of fame is in City Hall Plaza.

CENTRAL MARKET (5) Founded in 1837, in Market Square, it is one of Canada's biggest farmers' markets.

COURTHOUSE (6) A bronze group outside the Hamilton-Wentworth Regional Courthouse is in memory of the United Empire Loyalists. It depicts a family looking at the land they had drawn by lot.

DUNDURN CASTLE (7) Restoration of this great mansion gave Hamilton a showplace of 19th-century elegance and privilege—and an unusual setting for concerts and puppet shows, opera, drama and ethnic dancing. It

Dundurn Castle in Hamilton epitomizes early Victorian elegance. Master bedroom and drawing room are among 35 rooms in 1850 style.

was built in 1832-34, a grand Regency villa overlooking Burlington Bay (now Hamilton harbor), and was the home of Sir Allan Napier MacNab, a hero of the War of 1812 and the 1837 rebellion, a lawyer, promoter, financier and politician who became prime minister of the United Province of Canada in 1854-56. He was heavily in debt when he died in 1862; the house passed through the hands of several owners and for some 60 years was used as a museum. The city of Hamilton, as a 1967 centennial project, restored and refurnished some 35 rooms and recaptured the splendor of Dundurn's great days in the 1850s.

Wallpaper in the entrance hall, where a portrait of MacNab hangs, reproduces the original and reflects his loyalties in a pattern of English rose, Scottish thistle and French fleur-de-lis. The tiled floor and carpeted, curved staircase are original. In a high-ceilinged drawing room, its mauve walls enliv-

ened by rich scarlet drapes and black walnut paneling, is a collection of period furniture, including a Regency rosewood piano, and a tinted chandelier. The carpet design matches that of the plasterwork of the ceiling.

Sir Allan, Hamilton's first lawyer, practised law from the black walnut library. He entertained in a dining room whose walls are dark green, at a gleaming mahogany Georgian table that seats 20 persons. Above it is a magnificent crystal chandelier (c.1830) with green Wedgwood mounts and some 720 prisms whose sparkle is picked up by a bull's-eye mirror over the fireplace.

The plaster walls of the upstairs hall are painted to resemble sienna marble. There is a fleur-de-lis carpet and a Bishop and Bradley scroll and pillar clock with all wooden works except for brass hands and pendulum.

The master bedroom has windows on three sides. Among the furniture is a three-posted mahogany bed, believed made in Quebec about 1835, and a gout stool. Lady MacNab's boudoir is decorated in its original style and colors.

Three second-story bedrooms have been connected to form a museum. One room contains exhibits pertaining to settlement of the Hamilton area; another depicts the life and times of Sir Allan; the third shows the uses the castle has been put to since his death. One display recalls how, as colonel of the Men of Gore (Township), he helped suppress William Lyon Mackenzie's rebellion at York (Toronto) in 1837.

The castle garden and courtyard are used for summer theater and musical performances. Children's plays are presented at the Cockpit Theater, a restored small pillared building with an octagonal cupola. It is thought to have been used for cockfights in the castle's great days.

Royal Botanical Gardens in and near Hamilton have an arboretum and herbarium, a tea house, a children's garden, lectures and guided tours.

Works by Canadians are prominent in the permanent collection of the Art Gallery of Hamilton. These three (from left) are detail from Alfred Pellan's *Evasion,* Goodridge Roberts' *Reclining Nude No. 2* and William Kurelek's *Nativity Near Stoney Creek.*

Dundurn's Battery Lodge, a gatehouse built on the site of a War of 1812 gun emplacement, is now a military museum with exhibits from Loyalist days to World War II.

GAGE PARK (8) A 72-acre park with rose gardens, band concerts, and a children's museum.

GORE PARK (9) The cenotaph, an illuminated fountain, statues of Queen Victoria and Sir John A. Macdonald and a plaque commemorating the founding of the Cooperative Union of Canada here in 1909.

Raw steel from Dofasco (above) and Stelco in Hamilton makes up about two-thirds of Canadian production. Together these two employ some 25,000 persons. Both steel mills and some of the city's 500 other plants may be toured.

HARVEY PARK (10) A cairn marks the site of fortifications built here on Burlington Heights during the War of 1812. On it is a plaque commemorating Lt. Col. John Harvey, whose victory at Stoney Creek (*see entry*) saved the heights from attack by the Americans.

KING'S FOREST PARK (11) This 750-acre park clings to winding Redhill Creek as part of a green belt with a golf course near the city's eastern limits.

LLOYD D. JACKSON SQUARE (12) Named for a former mayor, it stands opposite city hall and boasts Hamilton Place, a massive concrete-brick-glass mecca for theater, concerts, conventions and other functions. A library and hotel are to be added.

McMASTER UNIVERSITY (13) Founded by Canadian Baptists in Toronto in 1887, McMaster was moved to Hamilton in 1930. It is coeducational and nondenominational. The university is noted for its nuclear reactor—the first privately owned reactor in Canada—and for its coup in acquiring all of the papers of Lord Bertrand Russell, the British philosopher, mathematician and writer. Student enrollment is nearly 14,000.

MOHAWK COLLEGE (14) One of Ontario's largest community colleges, Mohawk has some 4,300 students at its three Hamilton campuses. Other campuses are in Brantford and Stoney Creek.

MOHAWK TRAIL SCHOOL MUSEUM (15) This museum doubles as a teaching aid: school-children are brought here to experience 19th-century classroom conditions. It was a school from 1882 to 1964. When it became a museum the interior was restored to its original appearance.

ROYAL BOTANICAL GARDENS (16) The 2,000 acres include the famous Rock Garden at the northwest tip of Hamilton; the Spring Garden (in Burlington), with June displays of irises, lilies and peonies, and the marsh and game preserve of Cootes Paradise, which lies in Dundas, Hamilton and West Flamborough.

SAM LAWRENCE PARK (17) The park extends for 1,200 feet along the brow of Hamilton Mountain, affording panoramic views of the city and harbor and, to the northeast, the Burlington Bay Skyway and Lake Ontario. In the park, named for a former mayor of Hamilton, are floral displays and a plaque which details the geological history of the Niagara Escarpment, of which the mountain is a part.

THE BEACH STRIP (18) This sandy ridge separates landlocked Hamilton harbor from Lake Ontario. The Burlington ship canal (19) cuts through the strip and above much of it is the Burlington Bay Skyway (20).

WHITEHERN (21) A handsome limestone house surrounded by parking lots, railway tracks and high-rise buildings—where once there were churches and other mansions—has been preserved in the heart of downtown Hamilton. Whitehern, built in the 1840s and for more than a century the home of the McQuesten family, was deeded to the city in 1959 to be preserved as a period piece open to the public.

Hampton N.B.   9DY
The King's County Historical Society Museum contains photographs, documents, early furniture, clothing and pioneer household and farm items. A 147-foot covered bridge near here was built in 1918.

Haney B.C.   2CZ/12EX
The Anglican Church of St. John the Divine is the oldest church in British Columbia. It was built in 1858 at Derby, two miles up the Fraser River, and moved here in 1882.

Hanna Alta.   4BY
The eight buildings of the Hanna Pioneer Museum include an old ranch house and schoolhouse, a pioneer church with home-made pews and altar, a blacksmith shop, a vintage CNR station with track and a handcar, and a reconstruction of Hanna's first telephone office. Displays in the other two buildings include pioneer furniture, restored farm machinery and vintage automobiles, Hanna's first fire bell and fire engine (1913) and a carved wooden model of a steam threshing outfit.

Hanover Ont.   7BY/16DV
Noah Brusso, who as Tommy Burns won the heavyweight boxing championship of the world in 1907, is commemorated by a plaque in this, his birthplace. Brusso (1881-1955) was the only Canadian to hold the title.

□ The Saugeen Valley Conservation Authority has headquarters at a 25-acre wildfowl refuge south of here. The sanctuary attracts migrating ducks and Giant Canada geese. Also close to Hanover are the authority's Durham and Brucedale conservation areas and the Allan Park Trout Pond run by the Ontario Ministry of Natural Resources.

Hantsport N.S. 22EV

Mementoes of an era when Hantsport was one of the world's great shipbuilding towns are displayed in the Marine Memorial Room of the community center. They include a model of a full-rigged sailing ship; framed lists of ships, owners, builders and seamen; ships' wheels, anchors, lights, logs, sextants and chronometers and shipbuilding tools.

Part of the Hantsport Memorial Community Center is a great three-story house built in 1860 by Ezra Churchill, founder of the Churchill shipyards, for his son John.

□ A cairn marks the grave of William Hall, V.C. A Nova Scotian, son of a slave brought from Virginia, he served with the Royal Navy throughout the Crimean War and in a naval brigade at the relief of Lucknow during the Indian Mutiny of 1857. When the others of a gun crew were killed, Hall breached the mutineers' defenses and made possible the relief of the garrison. He was the first black, the first Nova Scotian and the first Canadian sailor to win the Victoria Cross. Hall died in 1904 at nearby Avonport.

Harbour Grace Nfld. 11DZ

One of Newfoundland's oldest and most historic towns, Harbour Grace was settled about 1550 and in 1610 was fortified by the English pirate Peter Easton.

Plaques commemorate the Rev. Lawrence Coughlan, who established North America's first Wesleyan mission here in 1765; and Harbour Grace's key role in transatlantic flying when it had Newfoundland's only runway.

Wiley Post started a round-the-world flight here in 1931, and Amelia Earhart took off in 1932 on a solo flight to Londonderry. Kingsford-Smith and Jimmy Mollison were others who flew from Harbour Grace.

The Conception Bay Museum, a century-old brick and stone customs house on the site of Easton's fort, has an exhibit chronicling the history of early transatlantic flight.

Outside the courthouse, erected in 1831 and believed the oldest such building still in service in Canada, is a plaque in memory of Sir Thomas Roddick, a Harbour Grace native. He was deputy surgeon-general in the expeditionary force that put down the Northwest Rebellion in 1885, president of the British Medical Association, a Canadian MP and dean of medicine at McGill University in Montreal. McGill's Roddick Gates are named for him.

□ The Harbour Grace regatta is held at midsummer.

Hargrave Man. 4FY

Antique guns in the Half-Way House Museum include a matched pair of flintlock pistols (c.1765), a North West Company trade musket, an over-and-under rifle-shotgun (c.1840), a Spencer carbine (1866) and an early Winchester that was used in the Northwest Rebellion of 1885.

Harrison Hot Springs B.C. 2CZ/12FX

This spa at the south end of Harrison Lake has sulphur and potash hot springs that feed

Harrington Harbour Que.—Just north of this Gulf of St. Lawrence fishing community is Tête-à-la-Baleine, seen here in the soft light and shadow of a crisp midwinter day. (11AX)

one indoor and two outdoor pools at the famed Harrison Hotel. The 30-mile-long lake is surrounded by peaks of the Coast range.

Hartland N.B. 9CX

The world's longest covered bridge (picture, p.313) is a 1,282-foot giant whose seven spans leap the broad Saint John River here. It was built in 1896 as a toll bridge. Upstream is the Hugh John Flemming Bridge, erected in 1955 as part of the Trans-Canada Highway.

Hartland stages a potato blossom festival in June. Tours of Humpty Dumpty Foods Ltd., whose main product is potato chips, are available year round on request.

Hauterive Que. 9BV

Founded in 1950, this prosperous town at the mouth of the Manicouagan River rides the crest of prosperity generated by Hydro-Quebec installations on the Manicouagan and the Rivière aux Outardes. It has come to rival its older neighbor, Baie-Comeau, five miles east.

The ruins of the sawmill village of Saint-Eugène-de-Manicouagan, which thrived briefly at the turn of the century, lie southwest of Hauterive.

Havelock Ont. 7DY/17EW

The Trent River Museum just south of here displays settlers' clothing, furniture, utensils and implements. Eleven of the museum's 12 buildings are log structures.

Hay Bay Ont. 18BZ

The oldest Methodist church west of the Maritimes, erected in 1792, abandoned in the 1860s and restored in 1912 at the age of 120, is an imposing monument to the Loyalists who built it and to the great days of Methodism. For many years, until population shifts led to its abandonment, the Hay Bay Church was the center of a Methodism that grew to be the largest Protestant body in Canada and the biggest communion that entered the United Church of Canada in 1925. The old church is used once a year, for a commemorative service the last Sunday in August, but may be visited at other times.

□ A cairn near the church marks the site of a house that Sir John A. Macdonald lived in as a boy.

Hay River N.W.T. 3HY

Three spectacular waterfalls near here are Alexandra and Louise Falls, on the Hay River to the south, and Lady Evelyn Falls, on the Kakisa River to the northwest. Alexandra has a sheer drop of 109 feet. At Louise, less than 1½ miles downstream, the river drops another 46 feet in a series of steps. Below Louise Falls in a gorge 170 feet deep are three miles of rapids. Lady Evelyn Falls drops 48 feet. All three falls are close to the Mackenzie Highway (see Grimshaw).

□ Hay River, with 3,000 population, is one of the territories' biggest communities. It is at the mouth of the Hay River near where the Mackenzie River starts its 1,117-mile journey to the Arctic Ocean. Goods brought here via the Mackenzie Highway and the Great Slave Lake Railway from Roma, Alta., are shipped by barge to settlements along the river. Hay River is also the chief center of the Great Slave Lake fishing industry. The annual catch of whitefish and trout in this fifth largest North American lake exceeds 600,000 pounds.

□ A Hay River secondary school, named for writer-anthropologist Diamond Jenness, has no exterior corners or straight lines, only curves. It is made of metal painted a purple that looks bluish on dull days, warmly red in bright sun. An Indian architect designed the two- and three-story building with a central concourse like an Elizabethan theater. From it radiate blocks of facilities (arts, gymnasium, laboratories, music) separated by transparent walls.

□ The 103-foot riverboat *Norweta* cruises (mid-June to early October) between Fort Providence and Inuvik. Passengers go by bus from here to Fort Providence.

□ A road east from Hay River leads to Fort Smith and Wood Buffalo National Park (*see entries*) and to the lead and zinc mining community of Pine Point and on to Fort Resolution on Great Slave Lake.

Hazelton B.C.

'Ksan is a reproduction of a Gitksan Indian village that stood here—where the Skeena and Bulkley rivers meet—when the first white men reached Hazelton in 1872. The village's six cedar longhouses, its totem poles, fish traps, smokehouses and canoes make it the showplace of a region rich in Indian culture, a heavily forested land the Gitksan considered holy. In such places as Kitwancool, Kitwanga, Kitseguecla, Kisgegas and Kispiox, all within 40 miles of Hazelton, is British Columbia's greatest concentration of standing totem poles.

'Ksan (the Gitksan word for Skeena) is an undertaking of the federal and B.C. governments and the 'Ksan Association. Two longhouses have painted designs over the doorways and most have carved interior poles. In the Stone Age House are some 50 mannequins of Indians making clothes and utensils from cedar bark. The Feast House shows the life of the Gitksan people after traders brought muskets, iron kettles and blankets. The Treasure House is a museum of costumes, handicrafts and carvings. Gitksan crafts are offered for sale in another longhouse. In two others Indian students are taught carving design and experienced carvers can be seen at work.

□ The Hand of History Trail from Hazelton has the snowcapped Rocher Déboulé range as a constant backdrop. It takes in an Indian cemetery (and gravehouses) near here, the Hagwilget Canyon and its 460-foot suspension bridge 240 feet above the Bulkley, and most of the totem pole villages throughout the area.

Totem Pole Creatures Tell Indian Family History

Totem poles for which the Indians of British Columbia are famous probably originated as supports for the roof beams of their houses. The stylized birds and mammals they carved usually told family history. Not until about 1850 did Indians erect poles separate from their dwellings, as in the 'Ksan reproduction (top picture). It is at Hazelton, in the heart of country that Emily Carr portrayed in such paintings as (left) *Totem Poles, Kitseukla* (Vancouver Art Gallery). The poles below are at Alert Bay, Kitwanga (2) and Kispiox.

Heart's Content Nfld.   11DY

North America's first cable relay station, closed in 1965 after 92 years' service, has been reopened as a museum. The first transatlantic cable was landed across Trinity Bay at Bay Bulls Arm (now Sunnyside) in 1858 but it failed after only a few weeks. The cable ship *Great Eastern* landed the first successful cable July 27, 1866, linking Heart's Content with Valentia in Ireland.

In the museum is all of the early equipment used in the Heart's Content station. The oldest section of the building is furnished as it was when erected in 1873. There are demonstrations of how messages were received at that time by reflecting galvanometer. A tiny magnet and small mirror were swung from a silk thread and the mirror reflected a spot of light onto a screen. Every change in the current in the cable deflected the magnet. These movements were too slight to be seen with the naked eye, but the movements of the mirror-reflected speck of light could be seen, enabling the receiving operator to read the sender's dots and dashes. The reader then passed the message to a telegraphist for relay.

   □ Two communities just south of Heart's Content are Heart's Desire and Heart's Delight.

Founder of Hébertville, Abbé Nicolas de Tolentin Hébert, and a pioneer settler were created in bronze in 1926 by French sculptor Guéniot.

Heatherton N.S.—A teapot that Queen Victoria sent to a Nova Scotia sea captain for his "humanity and kindness" to shipwreck victims is displayed at his son's home here. Capt. Angus MacDonald of the brigantine *Trust* stood by in heavy weather for a week to rescue the crew of the British ship *Coronet* after she foundered off Maitland, N.S., in 1881. The teapot, solid silver with an ebony handle, was presented by the governor-general on behalf of the Queen and the British government. Captain MacDonald, who made more than 55 Atlantic crossings, died in 1935 at the age of 100. (9EY/23EY)

Hébertville Que.   9AW/21BX

A monument on the main street honors the town's founder, Abbé Nicolas de Tolentin Hébert. He directed the colonization of this first parish in the Lac Saint-Jean region, starting in 1849. The parish church dates from 1881.

   □ Black granite from the nearby Saint-Gédéon quarries is worked at Hébertville-Station, four miles north of here. At Hébert-

ville-Station the Museum of Quebec Fauna displays some 600 specimens of native birds and animals.

Hecla Man.   6BX

A provincial park being developed in Lake Winnipeg will include Hecla Island and Black, Deer and several smaller islands. A main attraction will be a reconstruction of a fishing village that Icelandic settlers established in 1876 on the east side of Hecla Island.

Hemmingford Que.   7FY/19BZ

At 200-acre Park Safari Africain visitors drive among lions, tigers, baboons, elephants, giraffes, cheetahs, rhinos, zebras and ostriches. There are also wolves, bears, antelopes and wallabies.

Hespeler Ont. *see* Cambridge

Hibbs Cove Nfld.   11DZ

Large, square wooden houses crowd the tiny rock-ringed harbor of Hibbs Cove, the embodiment of the Newfoundland outport. A museum is stocked with the handmade tools and equipment that fishermen once used. In a former one-room school is a gallery that displays work produced in a children's art school.

High Prairie Alta.   1BZ/2FV

A 1½-foot sword and a 3,000-year-old stone adze are among the intriguing objects in the High Prairie and District Museum. The sword, possibly made in the early 1800s, was plowed up about a mile from here in 1923. How it got there is a mystery. The adze, made of metamorphic stone of a type not native to this area, was found near where the sword was unearthed.

High River Alta. 4AY/13DX
At the base of a cliff known as Old Woman's Buffalo Jump, where for 1,500 years Indians stampeded whole herds to the slaughter, is a 20-foot layer of sun-bleached bones. Traces of hunting villages and Indian ritual—cairns, medicine wheels (boulders placed in circles) and ceremonial encampments—have been found throughout the High River area. Joe Clark, made Progressive Conservative leader in 1976, was born here in 1939.
 □ Canada's original Little Britches Rodeo (16 years and under) is held each May.
 □ Replicas of a barber shop and a blacksmith shop are in the Museum of the Highwood, a branch of the Medicine Tree Pow Wow Association. Settlers' and ranchers' tools and effects, prehistoric and historic Indian artifacts are exhibited.
 □ Nearby is the EP Ranch, purchased in 1919 by the Prince of Wales (later King Edward VIII) and now part of the "D" Ranch.

Hillcrest Alta. 4AZ/13CZ
One of Canada's worst mining disasters was a gas and dust explosion that killed 189 men here June 19, 1914. Near the disaster site is their mass grave, unmarked but for a concrete fence.

Hill Island Ont. 18CZ
The view from the Thousand Islands Skydeck, 400 feet above the St. Lawrence River, is 40 miles on a clear day. Three observation levels are reached by elevator: a glassed-in deck, an open-air upper deck and a crowsnest. Hill Island is between spans of the Thousand Islands International Bridge. A plaque commemorates the opening of the bridge by Prime Minister Mackenzie King and President Franklin D. Roosevelt in 1938.

Hinton Alta. 2FW
About 1,000 wild horses roam here in the wooded foothills of the Rockies where once there were great herds of the animals. Relentlessly rounded up, first by cowboys, then by hunters to supply pet food manufacturers, wild horses have all but disappeared from the Canadian west.
 The foothills explode in summer with the colors of the wild rose, tiger lily, red Indian paintbrush, brown-eyed Susan and flowering wild raspberry.

Holland Landing Ont. 7CY/17CW
A 3,575-pound anchor in Anchor Park apparently was meant for a warship being built at Penetanguishene during the War of 1812. It has a 16-foot shank, is 10 feet across between the tips of its flukes, and bears the stamp "Chatham England Navy Yard." It was brought from York (now Toronto) by ox-drawn sleigh and abandoned near here when news of the war's end on Dec. 24, 1814, was received.

Holyrood Nfld. 11DZ
Delightful scenery and excellent fishing make Holyrood a favorite summer resort. Nearby streams yield salmon and trout and Conception Bay is famous for giant bluefin tuna. Close by are jigging grounds where fishermen use squid-jiggers (grouped hooks with radiating points) to hook squid.

Hope B.C. 2DZ/12GX
An 83-mile roller coaster route through magnificent country, the Hope-Princeton Highway was opened in 1949, making the 176,500

Fire simulator at an Alberta Forest Service school at Hinton is used by forestry students from the Northern Alberta Institute of Technology. Colored lights, rotating disks and film create an illusion of fire raging through a forest. There are tours of the school.

acres of Manning Provincial Park accessible to the public. The highway climbs from near sea level at Hope to the 4,436-foot summit of Allison Pass.

At Mile 16 and Mile 22 east of Hope are the remains of the Dewdney Trail that the Royal Engineers hacked out of the wilderness in 1860-61. A favorite spot off the highway is Rhododendron Flats, where a mile-long footpath passes thousands of the pink-mauve flowers. In summer the alpine meadows along the highway erupt in blue lupine, yellow arnica and red Indian paintbrush.

Ten miles east of Hope huge boulders are strewn over a wide area and a plaque at a lookout tells how, in January 1965, an estimated 100,000,000 tons of rock—the side of Johnson Peak—plunged into the valley below, burying the highway to a depth of 260 feet.

□ Animals in Manning Provincial Park range from deer, elk and bear to rabbit-like pika about seven inches long. The 176,500-acre park has many mountains more than 7,000 feet high.

□ Centennial Trail is a hiking route from Simon Fraser University in Vancouver to Manning Park Lodge. It connects with Cathedral Provincial Park 20 miles east.

□ Christ Church (Anglican) in Hope was built in 1859 and is one of British Columbia's oldest churches.

Hopeville Ont.   7BY/17AW

A plaque here honors Agnes Campbell Macphail, first woman member of the House of Commons (1921) and an MP for 19 years. She was a member of the Canadian delegation to the League of Nations in 1929. In 1943-45 and 1948-51 she sat in the Ontario legislature.

Hopewell Cape N.B.   9DY/23AX

The Albert County Museum is in a former county jail, built in 1846 with cut-stone walls 26 inches thick. It has barred windows and a three-inch-thick iron-reinforced wooden door. The museum features models and photographs of ships and plans and tools used in building sailing ships. In other rooms are pioneer candlesticks, whale-oil lamps and chandeliers.

□ A monument in Hopewell Cape Park honors Richard Bedford Bennett, born at his grandfather's home near here, raised at Hopewell Cape and the only New Brunswicker to become prime minister of Canada (1930-35). He settled in England in 1939 and became Viscount Bennett of Mickleham, Calgary and Hopewell.

Horseshoe Bay B.C.   2CZ/12DX

Overlooking Fishermans Cove is a plaque telling of Spanish and British seafarers who charted the Strait of Georgia, one of the most complex waterways in the world. The first was José Maria Narvaez in 1791. In June 1792 Spaniards met with Capt. George Vancouver off Spanish Banks (across Burrard Inlet near where the University of British Columbia is now) and agreed to work together. By 1794 the whole rugged, deeply indented coastline, including the coast of what is now British Columbia, had been effectively mapped.

□ Ferries link Horseshoe Bay with Langdale, near Gibsons, and with Departure Bay, near Nanaimo on Vancouver Island.

Hudson's Hope B.C.   1AY

Behind the W.A.C. Bennett Dam, 1¼ miles long and 600 feet high (one of the world's largest earth-fill dams), is 220-mile-long, 640-square-mile Williston Lake, B.C.'s biggest. The dam, completed in 1967, and the Gordon M. Shrum powerhouse (2,130,000 kilowatts) are on the Peace River 13 miles west of here.

The Rocks near the mouth of the Petitcodiac River at Hopewell Cape were formed by centuries of frost, wind and sea action. At high tide they appear as tree-covered islands; the receding water exposes grotesque "flowerpots."

Hull Que.   7EY/18DW

A city of 110,000 across the Ottawa River from Ottawa, Hull is part of the National Capital Region. It was founded in 1800, 26 years before Ottawa (Bytown) began to develop. The first settler was Philemon Wright, an American who cleared a farm near the 25-foot Chaudière Falls. He is commemorated by a stone column bearing a bronze medallion of his likeness. Since Wright took his first load of lumber to Quebec in 1806, Hull has become one of North America's biggest lumber, pulp and paper centers. It is the

The Cloisters is the most striking of the ruins that Mackenzie King collected at Kingsmere, in the Gatineau Hills northwest of Hull. The highest part is a window from the Ottawa home of Simon-Napoléon Parent, premier of Quebec in 1900-5. Kingsmere is physically part of Gatineau Park (*see* p.265).

home of the E.B. Eddy Company complex, which began as a pine match factory in 1851.

□ The July Raftsmen's Festival, a part of Festival Canada (*see* Ottawa), recalls the heyday of the Ottawa River raftsmen. Events include the Strong Men's Canadian Championship, lumberjack competitions, canoeing, logrolling, tug-of-war and freckle contests, an art exhibit and nightly entertainment.

□ The Ottawa River Museum, in a stone building (c.1830), has exhibits dealing with the history of the Ottawa River forest industry.

□ Saint-Jean-de-Brébeuf Park is named after a Jesuit missionary martyred in 1649 (*see* Midland). A statue in the park honors him.

□ There are tours of the Government Printing Bureau, where Hansard, the record of parliamentary business, is produced.

Humboldt Sask.   4EX

A replica of the Humboldt telegraph station as it was in 1885, an important relay on the Dominion Telegraph line between Fort William and Edmonton, stands in Humboldt Historic Park.

□ Artist Berthold von Imhoff (*see* St. Walburg) decorated the interior of St. Peter's Cathedral at nearby Muenster in 1919, using local persons as models for 102 life-size and bigger-than-life figures of the saints. His work is on 38 canvases and the cathedral walls.

100 Mile House B.C.   2DX

A red stagecoach that jolted passengers along the Cariboo Road in gold-rush days lives in retirement as a tourist attraction in this one-time stopping place, now a village of more than 1,200. It is at the Red Coach Inn, near the 100 Mile Lodge built in 1930 by Lord Martin Cecil. He is the president of Bridge Creek Estate Ltd., a 12,410-acre ranch

that surrounds the community. 100 Mile House came into being in 1862 as a stopping place 100 miles from Lillooet, Mile 0 on the Cariboo Road.

Attractions in the area include 60-foot Canim Falls on the Canim River and Canim and Mahood lakes, the latter in Wells Gray Provincial Park. This 1,302,837 acres of virtual wilderness is reached by road from Mahood Falls or from Clearwater on the Yellowhead South Highway, or by 17 miles of road and trail from Blue River. On its many rivers, which race through broken terrain, are scores of cataracts. The most impressive, Helmcken Falls, is 450 feet.

The Outriders Club sponsors the three-day Little Britches Rodeo here in May. Children and teen-agers compete in bronc riding, calf roping and other events.

Huntsville Ont.   7CX

Madill Church, one of few remaining examples of the squared timber construction of settlement days, is four miles south of here. Built in 1872-73 by Wesleyan Methodists, it now is used only for an annual United Church commemorative service. In Huntsville, clustered around the modern Muskoka Museum, is Muskoka Pioneer Village: five houses, a store and a school restored and furnished with pioneer furniture.

This year-round resort town is a main gateway to the scenic Lake of Bays (106 miles of shoreline) and to Algonquin Provincial Park (*see* Whitney).

A chair lift six miles east of Huntsville gives access to Peninsula Peak and a view of hundreds of square miles of Muskoka lakes and forests. Seven miles northeast is the Dyer Memorial, erected by a Detroit man in memory of his wife. A tower on a flag-stone terrace is surrounded by a 10-acre botanical garden and park overlooking the East River.

Autumn in Muskoka: a warm sun, a nip in the air, a symphony of gold and red and yellow. Huntsville stages a September festival of color.

I

Iberville Que.   7FY/19CY
Opposite city hall is the first monument raised to Sir Wilfrid Laurier. It was unveiled by his widow in 1920.

At nearby Saint-Grégoire, birthplace of Brother André, is a monument celebrating his inspiration to build St. Joseph's Oratory in Montreal.

One of several families that in 1758 were given exclusive right to catch eels in the Richelieu River here still holds the privilege.

The motherhouse of the Marist brothers, a teaching order, is in Iberville.

Iddesleigh Alta.   4BY
Pioneer artifacts in the Rainy Hills Historical Museum include needlework, kitchen utensils and cobbler and blacksmith tools.

Ile aux Coudres Que.   9BX/20DV
Time seems to have stopped on Ile aux Coudres. The three-foot-thick stone walls of its farmhouses, the lazy look of its windmills, the pace and the peace of this little island keep it a living miniature of 18th-century New France.

Seven miles by three, Ile aux Coudres is about a mile from the north shore of the St. Lawrence River and is linked by ferry with Saint-Joseph-de-la-Rive. Jacques Cartier gave the island its name (for its abundance of hazel trees) when he landed Sept. 7, 1535. The first Mass on Canadian soil, celebrated that same day, is commemorated by a granite cross at Saint-Bernard on the north side of the island. Among buildings classified as historic monuments are procession chapels (1836), the Bouchard house (1654) and Desgagnés windmill (c.1770), all at Saint-Louis, and the Leclerc house (1750) at La Baleine. The Leclerc house is open in summer as a museum of antique furniture and wood sculptures.

A small wooden cross near the ferry mooring commemorates a visit to the island by the Rev. Jean-Baptiste La Brosse, a Jesuit missionary, in 1767.

Ile-aux-Noix Que. *see* Saint-Paul-de-l'Ile-aux-Noix

Ile d'Orléans Que.   20CW
So important is Ile d'Orléans as an echo of Quebec rural life in the 1700s that the whole island, 21 miles by five, is designated as an *arrondissement historique.* Ile d'Orléans' centuries of isolation in the St. Lawrence River ended in 1935 when a mile-long bridge linked it with north-shore Montmorency. But the islanders still cling to old ways, proud of churches and houses and farms that have been here for 200-300 years, symbols of French Canada's beginnings.

Cartier called the island Bacchus because of its wild grapes but renamed it after the Duke of Orléans, son of Francis I of France. Roberval landed here in 1542, Champlain in 1608, the year he founded Quebec. It was offered to de Maisonneuve in 1641; he chose the island of Montreal instead. Settlement on Ile d'Orléans started in 1648 and the first chapel was built five years later. By 1712 there were five prosperous parishes (there now are six).

Ile d'Orléans has asphalt and motels and snowmobiles today but some weaving and bread baking are still done in the manner of the settlers—on long, narrow habitant farms, each with its piece of riverfront. The rich soil produces strawberries, potatoes, plums and other fruits and vegetables as it did for the settlers. And nothing diminishes the magnificence of the old churches or the dignity and strength of the Norman-roofed stone houses.

A 42-mile road around the island, if traveled counterclockwise from the bridge, leads to these places in this order:

BEAULIEU Better known by its parish name, Sainte-Pétronille, Beaulieu has a panoramic view of Lauzon, Lévis and the heights of Quebec. Several hundred Huron Indians, refugees from Iroquois attacks at Trois-Rivières, lived here in the 1650s and the first French settlers also chose this western end

Settlers Fought Raiders from Windmill Forts

The windmills of New France (such as this one on Ile aux Coudres) were constructed primarily for grinding the habitant farmers' grain. But the massive stone towers—some were 25-30 feet high—had another important use: they served farm families as forts during Indian raids. The four-foot-thick walls often were built with loopholes through which settlers could fire on attackers. Windmills were not as common as water mills in pioneer Canada. Eventually both were rendered obsolete by the far more efficient steam engine.

New France lives in the solid buildings of Ile d'Orléans. No car approaches Restaurant L'Atre (left) at Sainte-Famille: a horse-drawn calèche brings patrons from the parking lot. The Guimont farm (lower left) is at Saint-François, whose church (below) dates from 1734.

of the island. Wolfe used Beaulieu as a headquarters from which he could watch both channels of the St. Lawrence during part of his 1759 campaign against Quebec.

SAINT-LAURENT A four-story stone water mill built about 1635 is now a restaurant. The Gendreau house dates from before 1759. In a 100-year-old wooden barn is an art center displaying Canadian painting, sculpture, weaving, ceramics, tapestry and copper work. Pleasure craft are built in the Lachance boatyard.

SAINT-JEAN Mauvide-Genest Manor (1734) boasts the scars of cannonballs shot in 1759. It is a private home but may be visited by appointment during the summer. The church (1734) and Dubuc house (c.1750) are of particular interest.

SAINT-FRANCOIS The church (1734) and rectory were requisitioned in 1759 as a hospital for English soldiers. On a pulpit carved by Louis-Xavier Leprohon in 1845 and covered with gold leaf are the figures of Saint Thomas of Aquinas and Saint Paul. Vault and cornice (1832-40) were done by André Paquet, the churchwardens' seat (1840) by Thomas Berlinguet, the baptismal fonts (1854) by Olivier Sanson. The church, the Ecole de Fabrique and the Imbeau and Nadeau houses are classified as historic buildings. Across the river, from north of Saint-François, can be seen Cap-Tourmente, Saint-Joachim, and Sainte-Anne-de-Beaupré and its basilica, all with the Laurentians in the background.

SAINTE-FAMILLE The church (1749) has three bell towers. In five alcoves in the gray stone facade are replicas of gold-painted statues carved in wood about 1748 by François-Noël Levasseur. The originals are in the Provincial Museum in Quebec. The church's interior ornamentation is chiefly by the Baillargés. L'Atre is a farmhouse-restaurant about 300 years old (open only in summer). The convent of the Sisters of the Congregation of Notre-Dame, one of Canada's oldest religious orders, is nearby. A massive stone windmill near Sainte-Famille is the last on the island.

SAINT-PIERRE The church, built in 1717-20 in early Norman style, is a classified historical monument no longer used for services but open to visitors. Altar and sanctuary carvings by Vézina date back to the 1730s. A bell tower was added about 1843 by Thomas Baillargé. A wooden barn, Le Galendor, is a summer theater.

Ile-Perrot Que.   7FY/19BY

At Pointe-du-Moulin, near the eastern end of this island at the confluence of the Ottawa and St. Lawrence rivers, are a stone windmill and a house that date from about 1700. At the northeast corner of the island is the Lotbinière windmill (1778) which once stood

at Vaudreuil. It was dismantled and rebuilt here in the late 1950s.

A sewage treatment plant in the town of Pointe-du-Moulin is covered in white stucco and decorated with a ceramic brick mural by the artist Claude Vermette.

The Church of Sainte-Jeanne-Françoise-de-Chantal, in the town of Notre-Dame-de-l'Ile-Perrot on the island's south shore, dates from 1753. Near it is a chapel built from the stones of Ile-Perrot's original chapel (1740). It serves as a part of the museum at Vaudreuil (*see entry*).

Iles-de-la-Madeleine Que. *see* Magdalen Islands

Ilets-Jérémie Que.   9BW
In the reconstructed chapel (1724) of Ilets-Jérémie Mission is an altar installed by Jesuit missionaries in 1735. A steeple cross forged from iron, the chapel doors and the legs of a Communion table all date from 1767. The chapel is open to summer visitors.

Ilets-Jérémie is named for three rocks (*îlets*) in the bay and for Noël Jérémie de la Montagne, who established a fur-trading post here in 1670. It was operated until settlement started in 1858.

Near the chapel is a small monument commemorating the birth here in 1848 of naturalist Napoléon-Alexandre Comeau (*see* Godbout).

Imperial Sask.   4DY
More than 75 oil paintings by barber Nels Berggren are displayed, along with local antiques and artifacts, in his shop in this south Saskatchewan town.

Indian Head Sask.   4EY
A round, stone horse barn near here is a relic of the Bell Farm and the more than 100 tenant farmers who worked it in the 1880s. It was managed by Maj. W.R. Bell for the Qu'Appelle Valley Farming Company.

In 1887 part of the farm became the first experimental farm in what was then the Northwest Territories. A federal government forestry station established in 1903 has distributed millions of trees to prairie farmers.

Indian Head has an impressive row of grain elevators, symbols of prairie fertility. The Territorial Grain Growers' Association founded here in 1901 was the forerunner of the big Saskatchewan and Alberta farm organizations.

Ingersoll Ont.   7BZ/16DX
The establishment of Canada's first cheese factory (1864) is commemorated by a plaque on the post office building.

South of town a second plaque marks the site of another factory which made a 7,300-pound cheese (3 feet high, 20 feet in circumference) that was shipped to England in 1866 to advertise Oxford County cheese.

lands, Dickinson's Landing and Wales. Ingleside and another new town, Long Sault (*see entry*), are at the ends of the Long Sault Parkway, a six-mile road whose bridges and causeways link eight islands created by the flooding.

Anglican, Presbyterian, Roman Catholic and United churches face Ingleside's church square.

Farran Park here is an 88-acre picnic and recreation area. A few miles west is Nairne Island campground and a wildlife sanctuary and Canada goose compound.

Archers from many parts of North America compete in a two-day bow-and-arrow carp hunt in May.

Ingonish Beach N.S. *see* Cape Breton Highlands National Park

Innisville Ont.   7DY/18CX
Spokeless wagon wheels cut from tree trunks are among 500 pioneer artifacts in the 1863 school that is the Innisville and District Museum. Others are a wooden cheese press, a side saddle, a copper kettle and a mustache cup, all dating from settlement days in the 1820s.

International Peace Garden (Man./N.Dak.)
      6AZ
A 2,433-acre garden dedicated to peace straddles the Canada-U.S. border midway between the Atlantic and Pacific and only 45 miles from the geographic center of North America (at Rugby, N.Dak.). "To God in his glory," reads a tablet on a cairn unveiled at the opening in 1932, "we two nations dedicate this garden and pledge ourselves that as long as men shall live we will not take up arms against one another." The central area consists of pools drained by ornamental spillways and surrounded by formal gardens. On the stone walls of a chapel are engraved the words of great men of peace, among them Lester B. Pearson, Mohandas Gandhi, Bernard Shaw, William Osler, Abraham Lincoln and Dag Hammarskjöld. In a sunken garden which surrounds a cloverleaf pool are more than 2,000 rose bushes. There is a floral clock 18 feet across.

An international music camp started in 1956 is now a complete summer school of fine arts. Almost 3,000 students and a staff of 130 take part. Summer concerts and plays are staged in a 1,000-seat open-air theater.

At an athletic camp run by the Royal Canadian Legion, 50 coaches instruct boys in football and soccer, and boys and girls in track and field, volleyball and horsemanship.

The Canadian part of the peace garden is in Turtle Mountain Provincial Park, 47,000 acres of forested hills and valleys.

Ingersoll town hall (1856) is in an Italian brick style popular in pioneer Ontario. The town, long the center of a thriving dairy farm region, is named for Maj. Thomas Ingersoll, who came here from Massachusetts in 1793. He was the father of Laura Secord.

Ingleside Ont.   7EY/18EX
This town was created in 1957 for residents of places flooded by the St. Lawrence Seaway project: Aultsville, Farran's Point, Wood-

Bell Farm at Indian Head had this combined barn and fort, now used for grain storage.

Inuvik N.W.T.   3GV

Buildings in this town 100 miles north of the Arctic Circle are on pilings embedded in the permafrost that lies under the tundra. Construction directly on the tundra melts the permafrost and makes the ground marshy. In Inuvik, to prevent this, holes were steamed into the permafrost, pilings driven in and the permafrost allowed to refreeze before construction was begun. Sewer and water pipes are in above-ground conduits.

The town came into being in 1954 when the federal government moved western Arctic administrative facilities from Aklavik (*see entry*). Inuvik (Eskimo for the place of man) was the first place north of the Arctic Circle built to provide the normal facilities of a Canadian community.

Located in the Mackenzie River delta, Inuvik is a center for muskrat trapping, one of the principal industries of the area.

Our Lady of Victory Church, shaped like an igloo, is built of sheets of plywood painted white to resemble ice.

□ Canadian and Alaskan curlers come here in March for the International Bonspiel, and in April cross-country skiers from several countries compete in the Top of the World Ski Meet.

□ An Easter Week Muskrat Jamboree features dog-team, snowshoe and snowmobile races, tea-boiling, bannock-making, ice-chopping and muskrat-skinning contests.

The Northern Games in July attract athletes from the Yukon, the Northwest Territories and Alaska for traditional Eskimo and Indian sports, dances and drumming contests.

Invermere B.C.   2FY/13AW

A monument four miles north commemorates Kootenae House, the first trading post on the Columbia River, established in 1807 by David Thompson. From here Thompson explored the Columbia to the Pacific Ocean between present-day Washington and Oregon.

At Canterbury Point, a half-mile from the village center, a plaque on a fire-charred tree stump, once a tall Douglas fir, tells of Thompson's men camping there. When the tree was felled in 1942 a count of the annual growth rings established that it was burned in 1807. Thompson's own descriptions of the bay here offer further proof that the stump marks one of his campsites.

The Windermere District Historical Museum displays musket balls believed left by Thompson's party; the bell of the *Selkirk*, last paddle-wheeler on the Upper Columbia River, and a Jesuit medal dated 1830, thought to have been brought here in 1842 by missionary Jean de Smet.

Iona N.S.   9FY/23GX

The Gaelic culture of Scots who settled in Cape Breton Island in the early 19th century is lovingly preserved here. The village, named after the Hebridean island closely associated with Saint Columba, is in "the highland heart of Nova Scotia." It has a Saint Columba Church and a small pioneer museum, is the home of the Highland Village Pipe Band and stages a summer festival of Scottish music and art. The museum, in which settlers' belongings are labeled in English and Gaelic, is the nucleus of a village that will include replicas of 19th-century Hebridean crofter cottages, early Cape Breton homesteads and displays of Scottish heraldry, dress and crafts.

Iona Ont.   7BZ/16DY

A double-walled earthwork of uncertain age stands south of here in Southwold Township like a monument to its unknown Indian builders. They may have been the Attiwandaronk (Neutral) people who lived in this part of southwestern Ontario before being driven out by the Iroquois about 1650. The earthwork consists of two circular walls, one inside the other, the outer one about 200 yards in diameter. Both walls are five to 10 feet wide and approximately four feet above the 100-foot-wide ditch that separates them.

Iroquois Ont.   7EY/18DY

The Carman house (c.1810), built of stone —and on high ground—was the only Iroquois building that did not have to be moved when the St. Lawrence Seaway was constructed. Iroquois was the largest of several villages relocated: about 1,100 residents and 157 buildings were moved to a site three-quarters of a mile north of the original.

The 1½-story Carman house, now a craft house and museum, contains many original furnishings, a hewn-stone sink and a Dutch oven and hearth.

Straddling the Canadian-U.S. border is a huge international control dam which maintains the river at the best level for seaway navigation.

J

Jacksons Point Ont. *see* Sutton

Jasper National Park (Alta.) 2EX
This is a 4,200-square-mile expanse of scenic beauty—of awesome mountains and sprawling, centuries-old glacier ice, of flower-filled alpine meadows, thundering waterfalls and mirrorlike lakes. Accommodation ranges from wilderness campsites to elegant Jasper Park Lodge in Jasper, a tourist town with a resident population of about 4,000. The park borders Banff National Park to the south, an Alberta provincial park to the north. On Jasper's western flank are B.C.'s Mount Robson and Hamber provincial parks and the vast Columbia Icefield, with 11 peaks more than 11,000 feet high. Activities include golf, tennis, horseback riding, mountain climbing, canoeing, fishing and rafting.

AMETHYST LAKES Good fishing in these Tonquin Valley lakes.

ANGEL GLACIER *see under* Mount Edith Cavell

ATHABASCA FALLS A bridge over Athabasca Falls provides a view of the 75-foot falls, just off the Icefields Parkway.

ATHABASCA GLACIER *see under* Columbia Icefield

COLUMBIA ICEFIELD The greatest accumulation of ice in the Rockies covers 110 square miles and is up to 1,000 feet thick. Three main glaciers feed major river systems: the Athabasca and Mackenzie, which flow to the Arctic Ocean; the Columbia, emptying into the Pacific; and the Saskatchewan, which flows to Hudson Bay. The Icefields Parkway between Banff and Jasper passes the foot of Athabasca Glacier. Snowmobiles take tourists along the main stream of the 4½-mile-long river of ice, which fills the valley and is crossed with deep crevasses. Although the glacier once extended to the road, it has receded at 90 to 100 feet a year, except from 1960 to 1962 when it mysteriously slowed, receding only two feet. To the west is the Icefield Chalet, near the foot of Athabasca Glacier.

COMMITTEE PUNCH BOWL This small lake at the summit of Athabasca Pass was a rendezvous for 19th-century fur brigades.

HENRY HOUSE A cairn near the Old Fort Point bridge marks the site of Henry House, built by William Henry in 1811 for the North West Company.

ICEFIELDS PARKWAY *see* Banff National Park

JASPER HOUSE A cairn near the mouth of the Rocky River commemorates a supply post built by the North West Company in 1813 and run by Jasper Hawes. The town and park are named for him.

JASPER PARK LODGE Luxury accommodation is enjoyed in a superb setting. Behind the main lodge are cottages of from two to 11 rooms. In every direction are magnificent mountains. The lodge has a heated outdoor

Maligne Lake in Jasper National Park is a gem among the glacial lakes of the Canadian Rockies. It is 30 miles southeast of the town of Jasper.

Jasper Park Lodge is famous for bicycle-riding waiters who whisk loaded trays of food from the main building to the cottages. Not far from all this elegance, shy but apparently unafraid, elk cross a Jasper Park stream.

swimming pool beside Lac Beauvert. Food is often delivered to the cottages by waiters on bicycles.

MALIGNE CANYON The Maligne River carved this craggy canyon by erosion and by dissolving the underlying limestone formations. In places the river disappears into a large underground river system. Medicine Lake almost disappears in November and water can be seen going underground in several places and a subterranean waterfall can be heard.

MALIGNE LAKE A glacial lake set against a backdrop of snowcapped peaks.

MARMOT BASIN SKI AREA Good conditions from December until May.

MIETTE HOT SPRINGS The hottest spring water in the Canadians Rockies—129-136 degrees—is piped to a swimming pool and cooled to 99-100 degrees.

MOUNT EDITH CAVELL This majestic peak is named for a British nurse executed by a German firing squad in World War I for sheltering British and French troops in Belgium. Angel Glacier lies in a saddle on the flank of the mountain and a tongue of the glacier licks into the valley. Below is Lake Cavell.

MOUNT ROBSON This highest peak in the Canadian Rockies (12,972 feet) is outside the park but can be seen in all its beauty from Whistlers Mountain, near Jasper.

PUNCH BOWL FALLS At a brook on the road to Miette Hot Springs, falling water has worn smooth, rounded basins at two levels.

SKY TRAM Starting at 4,226 feet on the side of Whistlers Mountain, enclosed cable cars whisk passengers at 1,400 feet a minute to the 7,500-foot level, where there are picnic sites, nature trails, a tearoom and an observation balcony.

SUNWAPTA FALLS A trail leads to a spot downstream on the Sunwapta River for the best view of cataract and canyon. Aeons of erosion by the river have shaped the beautiful gorge.

Icefields Parkway between Banff and Jasper passes within a mile of the Athabasca Glacier, a tongue of the vast Columbia Icefield. Beside the road, in Sunwapta Pass, is the Columbia Icefield Chalet.

Virgin and Child in the Joliette Museum of Art was carved from stone in 14th-century France. Also in the museum are a gilded wooden altar (1830) by François Normand and a statue of Saint Jean-Baptiste. The museum is in the Joliette Seminary.

TONQUIN VALLEY At the base of the Rampart Mountains almost at the timberline.

TOTEM POLE This pole outside the CN station in Jasper was carved by Masset Haida Indians of the Queen Charlotte Islands.

WHISTLERS MOUNTAIN Whistling marmots and squirrels gave this peak its name. Its year-round glacier skiing is accessible by car or sky tram.

Joggins N.S. 9DY/23AY
The fossils of trees that grew 300,000,000 years ago are embedded in 100-foot gray sandstone cliffs along the shore of Chignecto Bay. Flooding partially covered the trees with sediment which, combined with immense pressure, caused trees to become fossilized in an upright position. There are also fossilized plants and evidence of amphibians, reptiles, insects and fish. The cliff face is continually cracked and eroded by 35-to-40-foot tides and winter frost, revealing more of the fossilized trees. The Fossil Shop has an extensive display and Joggins fossils are found in universities and museums.

Johnstown Ont. *see* Prescott

Joliette Que. 7FX/19BX
In the provincial house of the Brothers of Saint-Viateur, built in 1939 to resemble a 13th-century Norman abbey, is a chapel with stained glass windows and sculptures by Marius Plamondon. There are also wood sculptures by local artist Sylvia Daoust. The ceramic altar was crafted by Louis Parent, the artist who made the Stations of the Cross at St. Joseph's Oratory in Montreal.

Designed by the Rev. Pierre Conefroy, Saint-Paul Church was built in 1803-4 and decorated by Jean-Chrysostôme Perrault and Amable Charron.

The Joliette Museum of Art (in the Seminary of Joliette) exhibits European and Canadian paintings, decorative religious art and natural history collections.

In an old tobacco drying shed the Théâtre des Prairies presents two plays every summer.

Jonquière Que. 9AW/21CX
Two boldly designed Jonquière churches are among the Saguenay region's contributions to a revival in Quebec religious architecture during the 1960s.

Saint-Raphaël Church has no side walls: the copper roof sweeps 65 feet up from ground level, not to a conventional peak but to a six-foot strip of solid plastic that runs the length of the building. At one end, following the roof line, yellow-tinted glass two feet wide dips from the peak to frame the altar and sanctuary in what seems like perpetual sunshine. At the other it flows into an all-glass wall.

Notre-Dame-de-Fatima Church is shaped like a tepee split vertically, the two halves slightly offset but joined with modern stained glass windows.

The Saguenay Arts Institute has a collec-

Dramatic church of Notre-Dame-de-Fatima at Jonquière has stained glass windows by artist Jean-Guy Barbeau of Chicoutimi. His brother Jacques, of Quebec, sculpted the wooden crucifix.

Cider press at the Jordan Historical Museum of the Twenty is a pioneer version of the wine presses of ancient Rome. It crushed apples under a beam 27 feet long and 20 inches square. Manipulated by a nine-foot screw carved from black walnut, the beam exerted a force of 18 tons.

tion of works by such artists as Guytay (Guy Tremblay), Gatien Moisan, René Bergeron, Gilles Hébert, Clément Leclerc and John Hugh Barrett.

□ Five miles south is 17-mile-long Kénogami Lake. The Rivière aux Sables and the Chicoutimi River drain it into the Saguenay River, but both rivers have been dammed to maintain Kénogami Lake as a reservoir.

Jordan Ont. 17CY
A museum in this Niagara Peninsula town, the Jordan Historical Museum of the Twenty, consists of the Vintage (c.1840) and Jacob Fry (1815) houses, a schoolhouse and a churchyard whose headstones mark the graves of early Mennonite settlers. The Fry house is a two-story log building sheathed in clapboard. Jacob Fry's son Samuel was a weaver and many of his textiles and patterns are displayed, as well as furniture used by the Fry family. A plaque commemorates Mennonites who settled here in 1799.

Vintage house displays the finer goods of the settlers—a dark blue Mennonite wedding dress (c.1812), glassware and dishes, dower linen and examples of ornate fraktur painting. The handsome stone schoolhouse (1859) contains early farm implements, yokes for oxen, a cobbler's bench and a blacksmith's corner.

□ The pioneer settlement of Glen Elgin near Ball's Falls is now the Ball's Falls Museum. It has a gristmill (1809), two log cabins furnished in the style of the late 1700s and early 1800s, a restored fruit and vegetable drying shed and limekilns in which Niagara Escarpment limestone was heated to produce lime for mortar. The settlement is in the 179-acre Ball's Falls Conservation Area.

Jordan Falls N.S. 9DZ/22CY
An anchor on a cairn of granite beach stones honors Donald McKay, the master builder of clipper ships, born here Sept. 4, 1810. McKay went to New York at 16 and became an apprentice. By 1841 he had his own business and the next year built a ship of his own design, the 380-ton *Courier*. Her speed astonished seamen and he went on to build many more clippers.

The Clipper Man

The long, slender clipper ship, with its rakish bow, three swept-back masts and huge cloud of canvas, was the highest achievement of shipbuilders in the days of sail. Some of the best of the clippers that dominated the seas in the 1850s and '60s were built by Donald McKay, Jordan Falls' most famous son: *Flying Cloud, Sovereign of the Seas, Great Republic* and *Glory of the Seas*. McKay died in Hamilton, Mass., in 1880.

K

Kakabeka Falls Ont. 6EY
A waterfall on the Kaministikwia River, 108 feet high and 326 feet wide, is the centerpiece of 841-acre Kakabeka Falls Provincial Park.

Kamloops B.C. 2DY
The tang of sagebrush clings to the hills around this bustling city of more than 55,000.

The rich mountain meadows have supported cattle and sheep ever since gold petered out in the Cariboo in the 1860s and Kamloops ceased to be a supply point for treasure-hunters.

□ A Hudson's Bay Company trading post, built of logs in 1821 within the palisade of Fort Kamloops, has been dismantled and re-assembled in the Kamloops Museum in the public library. The museum displays Salish-an Indian basketry and carvings, has a furnished Victorian drawing room and sewing room, and exhibits birds, animals, insects and gem stones found near Kamloops. There is medical equipment used in an early Kamloops hospital and, from the Kamloops jail, an invitation to a hanging in 1899.

□ A replica of Fort Kamloops in Riverside Park has a factor's cabin and trading post and displays early stagecoaches and farm machinery. A plaque in the park commemorates Samuel Black, a trader who was murdered here in 1841.

□ Overlooking the city a log and shake building honors James McIntosh, who built Kamloops' first mills and water system.

□ North of Kamloops on the Yellowhead Route a marker honors the Overlanders, would-be miners lured from England by the Overland Transit Company which promised cheap and easy passage to the Cariboo goldfields. More than 150 men, women and children made it through Yellowhead Pass before splitting into two groups. One group headed north on the Fraser River on rafts and made it to what is now Quesnel only to find the gold gone. Thirty-six others struggled down the North Thompson River and, half-starved, reached Fort Kamloops.

□ Kamloops is the southern terminus of the Yellowhead Route section from Tête Jaune Cache.

□ The British Columbia Wildlife Park in Kamloops is one of the few zoos in the world where moose are successfully bred. The 100-acre park has bears, cougars, deer, eagles and other wildlife.

□ A sign 14 miles east of Kamloops tells of steamboats that plied the Thompson River in the 1880s, helping exploration and settlement of the interior. They were vital in building the CPR and were doomed when the railway was completed.

□ Kamloops' tourist attractions include ski resorts and fishing for one of the largest of rainbow trout, the Kamloops trout of Kamloops Lake. Tod Mountain ski resort 25 miles northeast has eight runs through its seven square miles of slopes, from beginners' inclines to five-mile runs for experts. The longest double chair lift in North America takes skiers 9,143 feet to the summit.

□ Five major lakes, dozens of rivers and several waterfalls are in the 1,300,000-acre wilderness of Wells Gray Provincial Park. The park, 100 miles north of Kamloops, is reached by gravel roads running north from the Yellowhead Route near Clearwater, 35 miles north. On the Murtle River are the 300-foot-wide Dawson Falls and, a few miles north, spectacular Helmcken Falls, which explode from a cleft in a cliff and tumble 450 feet into a canyon. Black bears roam throughout the park, grizzlies and mountain goats are common in the northern mountains and moose are found in the southern part of the park.

Kamouraska Que.   9BW
One of several fine old houses here, the 90-foot-long L'Anglais house (1725) has four chimneys.

In the St. Lawrence River opposite Kamouraska is a chain of islands where a great variety of birds nest.

July at Kamloops is Kami-Overlander Days and raft races on the North Thompson River —and hills and meadows alive with Mariposa lily (below) and St. Johnswort, honeysuckle and milkweed (bottom, left to right).

Last of the stern-wheelers on Kootenay Lake, S.S. *Moyie* was retired in 1957.

Kamsack Sask. 4FX

St. Andrew's Anglican Church on the Key Reserve 20 miles northwest of here was built in 1885 by Saulteaux Indians and is one of the oldest churches in the province. It has six pews of hewn boards, a handmade baptismal font, the minister's rough-hewn chair, a huge box stove and mats woven from bulrushes. A large bell in an outside belfry was cast in 1888.

□ Six miles north of Kamsack on the Coté Reserve a marker honors Gabriel Coté, chief of the band when Treaty Four was signed in 1874.

□ The Assiniboine Elbow, about 15 miles north and slightly west of Kamsack, is a pronounced bend in the Assiniboine River. A marker tells of several posts built in the area by the rival Hudson's Bay and North West companies and by independent fur traders. The first was built in 1793 and the last operated until 1912. Farther north was Fort Livingstone, known as Swan River Barracks. Built in 1874 as headquarters of the new North West Mounted Police, the fort was abandoned in 1875 as being too far from the center of the vast area the force was to police. But two years later the first session of the North West Council was held there. Nothing remains of the fort.

□ The aspen-covered hills of Duck Mountain Provincial Park rise gradually to about 700 feet. Island-dotted Madge Lake, the center of park activity, is noted for boating and fishing. Turkey vultures live in the park and occasionally a bald eagle is seen. Moose, white-tailed deer, black bear and beaver are plentiful.

□ Evidence of Doukhobor, Ukrainian and Russian influence is seen in Kamsack and nearby towns and villages. In Kamsack are the onion-shaped domes of Ukrainian Orthodox and Ukrainian Catholic churches and a Russian-style meeting hall. A meeting hall

three miles south is all that remains of the village of Voskrissenie. (*See* Veregin)

Kapuskasing Ont. 6HW

A steam locomotive and two railway coaches house the Kapuskasing Public Museum. In one coach is a model railroad; in the other are furniture and other objects dating back to Kapuskasing's settlement around 1910.

The Spruce Falls Power and Paper Co. was formed by *The New York Times* and the Kimberly-Clark Corporation to produce newsprint. Half of the plant's daily output of 1,000 tons goes to *The Times,* the rest to several other newspapers. Plant tours show how logs are transformed into paper.

Kaslo B.C. 2FZ

S.S. *Moyie,* last of the Kootenay Lake stern-wheelers, is now both a museum and a monument to Kaslo's pioneers. Her wood and steel hull was built in Toronto in 1896 and shipped west in sections; the 162-foot vessel was assembled in Nelson, on the west arm of the lake, in 1898. After almost 60 years of service she was retired in 1957.

Big silver strikes in 1893 made Kaslo a thriving city. It is now a village again, a popular resort and distribution center for the Lardeau Valley.

□ The Duncan Dam between Duncan and Kootenay lakes, 26 miles north, is 130 feet high and 2,600 feet long and one of the Columbia River dams built under the provisions of the 1961 Columbia Treaty between Canada and the United States. To compensate for spawning grounds lost when the dam was built B.C. Hydro constructed a spawning channel southwest of the dam on Meadow Creek. Some 200,000 kokanee (landlocked salmon) spawn in the two-mile-long channel every year.

Keene Ont. 7DY/17EW

A mysterious race of men now known as Point Peninsula Indians raised the burial mounds that are preserved in a provincial park on the shore of Rice Lake, two miles south of Keene. The mounds, believed built about 2,000 years ago, are on a point of land. One, five feet high and 190 feet long, is shaped like a serpent, its head separate from the body. Near the head is a large oval mound; close by are six lesser mounds.

All the mounds contained mass graves, and evidence suggests that the Point Peninsula Indians held periodic burial rituals, transferring bodies to the mounds from temporary resting places. Men, women and children were interred here. Persons of high status apparently were buried in trenches under the mounds. Copper and silver beads, pottery, a pick, bone and stone artifacts from the Serpent Mounds Provincial Park site are in the Royal Ontario Museum in Toronto.

□ It was at Rice Lake in the 1820s and '30s that Methodist missionary James Evans started to develop a syllabic alphabet for Indians and Eskimos (*see* Norway House).

Kejimkujik National Park (N.S.) 9DZ/22CW
The 145-square-mile park was opened in 1969
to preserve some of Nova Scotia's finest inland countryside and to protect Indian pictographs from vandalism. Island-dotted lakes
are surrounded by gently rolling forested
hills. Among 200 varieties of birds are the
great blue heron and loon. Black bear, deer,
red fox, lynx, otter and beaver roam and there
is greater variety of amphibians and reptiles
here (many species of frogs, toads, salaman-
ders, snakes and turtles) than anywhere else
in eastern Canada. In spring the forest is carpeted with trailing arbutus, violets, star-
flowers, trilliums, lady's slipper, orchids,
bunchberries and wild iris. Mounds and
ridges of gravel are evidence of Ice Age glaciers that carved this region. The park entrance is at Maitland Bridge. There are several wilderness hiking trails and canoe routes,
and a large campground.

Indian pictographs scratched on rock long ago
are found in Kejimkujik National Park, especially
at Kejimkujik Lake. Micmacs used hard rock and
beaver teeth (and, later, European tools) to record
battle and hunting scenes and to sketch animals,
fish and canoes. Early settlers sometimes added
their own touches. The date that appears near the
stern of the paddle-wheeler in this Kejimkujik
sketch is 1849.

Kelowna B.C. 2EZ
A third of all apples harvested in Canada
are shipped from this city in the heart of
the Okanagan Valley, a city whose Okanagan
Lake is the reputed home of the monster
Ogopogo, the locale of the Kelowna International Regatta and the site of a 4,620-foot
floating bridge, the only one of its kind in
Canada.
  □ For many years Indians threw live animals into Okanagan Lake to appease a monster they said lived in a cave off Squally
Point. A small stone statue of Ogopogo in
a Kelowna park is all most people see but
there are occasional reports from persons who
claim to have seen the real thing. Ogopogo
is thought to be 35-65 feet long, a fast swimmer with a head shaped like that of a sheep,
goat or horse. It has dark skin and humps
along its back.
  □ The regatta in early August is the city's

biggest annual event. The 150 competitions
and exhibitions include a water ballet,
water-skiing tournaments and hydroplane
races.
  □ The floating bridge, built in 1958, links
Kelowna and Westbank. It floats on 12 concrete pontoons, each held in place by a pair
of 70-ton anchors. The amount of water in
the pontoons is adjusted according to the
lake's water level. One 265-foot metal span
lifts for boat traffic. The bridge made the
ferry *Pendozi* obsolete. It was beached behind
a breakwater and is the home of the Westbank Yacht Club. The ship may be visited.
  □ Interior Salish Indians once made baskets so tightly woven they were used as cooking vessels. Examples are among the Indian
artifacts at Kelowna Centennial Museum.
A diorama shows a Salishan *kekuli*, a partly
underground winter dwelling (*see* Squilax).
The same kind of shelter is built by people
of the Chukchi Peninsula of Siberia. Also
in the museum is a small, squared-log Hudson's Bay Company post built in 1861 by
John McDougall. It was dismantled, reas-
sembled and furnished in 1860s style. The
museum has a 1907 Tudhope-McIntyre
chain-driven car built in Orillia, Ont. Among
stuffed wildlife displayed are a whooping
crane and a huge Kodiak bear.
  □ The first white settlement in the Okanagan was in 1859 at Okanagan Mission, three
miles southeast of Kelowna. The Rev.
Charles Pandosy and others planted fruit
trees and grapevines, the base of today's
Okanagan fruit industry, and their farm and
ranch (their brand was OM for Oblates of
Mary) attracted other settlers. The Pandosy
mission is now a provincial historic site.
Three log buildings have been restored and
three other log structures have been moved
to the site. One, the two-story home of John
McDougall, has furnishings of the 1860s. In
summer, high school students reenact the arrival of Father Pandosy and his companions.

Kelsey Bay B.C. 2BY
The ferry *Queen of Prince Rupert* (picture, p.184)
leaves every other day on a 20-hour, 300-mile
trip through the Inside Passage to Prince Rupert. Protected from the open sea by a series
of islands, the passage is part of a sheltered
waterway stretching from Puget Sound in
Washington to Skagway, Alaska. Between
here and Prince Rupert passengers see spectacular fjords and channels, Pacific fingers
flanked by awesome, mist-shrouded mountains and reaching as far as 80 miles inland.

Kemano B.C. 2BV
Water from a reservoir on the Nechako River
falls 2,600 feet as it hurtles through a 10-
mile-long mountain tunnel to a power plant
in an enormous man-made cave here. In the
cave, created by removing 550,000 cubic
yards of rock from DuBose Mountain, is generated the electricity needed 51 miles away
at the Aluminum Company of Canada
smelter at Kitimat (*see entry*). To transmit

Queen of Prince Rupert (here in the Grenville Channel) sails British Columbia's Inside Passage between Kelsey Bay and Prince Rupert.

electricity across mile-high Kildala Pass, huge aluminum and steel cables are suspended from towers designed to withstand ice, storms and avalanches.

The Kemano River flows into the Gardner Canal, a fjord-like arm of the Pacific Ocean between towering snowcapped peaks.

Kénogami Que.   9AW/21CW
A monument in Price Park honors Sir William Price, who founded the first papermaking company in this region. The Price plants may be toured.

Kenogami Lake Ont.   7CV
The height of land that is the Arctic watershed is crossed by a major highway seven miles north of here. A sign one mile south of where Highway 11 crosses the White Clay River records that the elevation is 1,060 feet above sea level. From there streams flow north toward James Bay or south into the Great Lakes drainage system.

Kenora Ont.   6CY
This mining and pulp and paper town on island-studded Lake of the Woods is also a popular resort and an outfitting center for fishermen and hunters. The lake, called Lac du Bois by Jacques de Noyon in 1688, spills over a waterfall into the Winnipeg River here.

Pierre de La Vérendrye built Fort St. Charles on the northwest angle of the lake in 1732. Four years later his son, Jean-Baptiste, and the Rev. Jean-Pierre Aulneau were killed by Sioux Indians on Massacre Island. The fort was destroyed in another Indian attack in 1763. A concrete replica of the fort is in the chapel of Fort St. Charles, built in 1950 by the Knights of Columbus to honor La Vérendrye and Father Aulneau. A Hudson's Bay Company fort built on the island in 1836 was moved in 1861 to the mainland at Rat Portage (now Kenora).

The Lake of the Woods Museum in Memorial Park displays pioneer relics and an extensive mineralogy collection. A copy of the *London Daily Times* from 1815 contains Wellington's dispatches from Waterloo listing the names of the killed and wounded. A 1798 edition of the *Times Gazette* chronicles Nelson's victory over the French in the Battle of the Nile.

A plaque in the park commemorates the Thistles team that in 1907 won the Stanley Cup for Kenora, the smallest community ever to boast such a victory.

The Rev. Albert Lacombe (*see* St. Albert) is honored by a plaque at Notre-Dame-du-Portage Church (1890). A previous church started by Father Lacombe in 1881 when he was working among Indians and CPR building crews was destroyed by fire.

□ Lake of the Woods has about 14,600 islands. One is Coney Island, with picnic facilities, beach and boardwalk. The cruiser *Argyle II* stops there.

□ At Longbow Corners, 11 miles east, a cairn marks the junction of the Trans-Canada Highway and the Great River Road, a scenic highway from New Orleans, La.

□ The Lake of the Woods sailing regatta is held in early August. Many classes of boats from Canada, the United States and Britain take part in a seven-day race from Kenora, around the lake and back.

Kensington P.E.I. *see* Burlington P.E.I.

cathedral in a new church constructed in 1882.

ST. MARY'S CATHEDRAL (12) This Roman Catholic diocesan church was constructed in 1842-48.

STONE FRIGATE (13) This huge limestone building was erected (to store naval gear) just after the signing of the Rush-Bagot Convention of 1817, limiting naval forces on the Great Lakes. The first cadets to enter the Royal Military College in 1876 used it as a dormitory. It remains part of RMC.

Kingston Mills Ont. 18CZ

A stone and timber blockhouse stands protectively here at the south end of the Rideau Canal, built in 1826-32 because of tension between the United States and British North America.

The only American invaders have been peaceful, in pleasure craft that make the 48-foot climb through four hand-operated locks here on their way up the Cataraqui River from Kingston.

A plaque in a small park commemorates construction of the canal by British Army engineers under Col. John By. It provided a secure route between Montreal and Lake Ontario via the Ottawa River and the canal, bypassing the international section of the St. Lawrence, where military and supply ships were vulnerable to attack by U.S. forces.

Kingsville Ont. 7AZ/16AZ

Daily in the migratory season wild geese and ducks blacken the sky and settle with a thunder of wings on the fields and ponds of the Jack Miner Bird Sanctuary. Rest, food and protection await them in a haven that the great naturalist established two miles north of here in 1904. It is open six days a week from Oct. 1 to April 15.

The Sunday closing respects Miner's religious beliefs, as does the free admission. Long before he died in 1944 he said: "In the name of God, let us have one place on earth where no money changes hands." Miner supported his sanctuary, the model for some 250 like it in the United States, by lecturing throughout North America. It now is run as a perpetual public trust by his sons Manly and Jasper.

The best time for visiting is late afternoons the last 10 days of October and first two weeks of November—and the last 10 days of March and the first 10 of April—when an estimated 40,000 geese and ducks break their migrations at the sanctuary.

At 4 p.m. on open days a tractor is driven among resting birds in back fields to signal feeding time. The birds flock to the sky, whirling and crying, finally landing in front fields to feed on grain as thousands of persons watch. Guides demonstrate banding and feeding and answer questions on wildlife and conservation.

Kirkfield Ont. 7CY/17CV

An ingenious lift lock teeter-totters pleasure boats over this high point on the Trent-Severn Waterway that links Lakes Ontario and Huron. From Kirkfield, 598 feet above Lake Ontario and 268 above Georgian Bay, waters flow both east and west. The hydraulic lock, eight miles east of Lake Simcoe, raises and lowers more than 7,000 boats a season in two lift chambers or pontoons.

Kirkland Lake Ont. 7CV

A bronze bust of Harry Oakes in the Museum of Northern History is a reminder of Kirkland Lake's boom days. Oakes (later Sir Harry Oakes—*see* Niagara Falls) staked a claim in 1912 that became the famous Lake Shore mine, one of 12 producers along Kirkland Lake's Golden Mile. The biggest years were 1927 and 1928. Now, of the gold mines, only the Macassa produces; among the famous mines in Kirkland Lake's past were Wright-Hargreaves, Sylvanite and Teck-Hughes.

The first strike here, six months before Oakes', was by Bill Wright. With his brother-in-law, Ed Hargreaves, he founded Wright-Hargreaves. The lake the town was named for has disappeared, filled with tailings.

Among the museum displays are mining equipment, ore samples, photographs and records of mining history. Indian and pioneer artifacts include a dugout canoe, pottery, arrowheads and knives and various pieces of handmade farming equipment.

Harry Oakes, a leading figure in early Ontario mining history, made one of the great gold discoveries at Kirkland Lake. A museum there displays this bust of Oakes.

Alas, Adolf, Alas!

The community of Swastika had existed in northern Ontario for 14 years before Hitler and his German Nazis adopted the "crooked cross" symbol. (Some say a pro-Nazi British peer with mining claims in Swastika suggested the emblem to Hitler.) During World War II, when Ottawa changed Swastika's post office name to Winston (after Churchill), the Swastika Drug Company rebelled—on its matchboxes. One box is in the Museum of Northern History at Kirkland Lake.

Kispiox B.C. *see* Hazelton

Kitchener Ont. 7BY/17AY

The twin cities of Kitchener and Waterloo (*see entry*) together form one of Canada's leading industrial communities and are the "capital" of Ontario's Mennonite country. Kitchener was founded in 1799 by Swiss-German Mennonite farmers from Pennsylvania. With the arrival of settlers from Germany in 1833 the village was called Berlin. In 1916, at the height of World War I (and anti-German feeling), the name was dropped; Berlin became Kitchener, after Lord Kitchener of Khartoum.

The famous Kitchener Farmers' Market, which downtown redevelopment transferred to a new building in 1973, enlivens Kitchener on Saturday mornings (Wednesdays too in summer). There are arrays of sausages, cheeses, eggs, poultry, fruit, vegetables and flowers, and such Mennonite dishes as shoofly (molasses) pie, *kochkase* (processed curd cheese) and *kimmel kirsche* (pickled cherries). The Kitchener Stock Yards Farmers' Market, just northeast of the city, is held Thursday afternoons.

Kitchener's biggest annual celebration is Oktoberfest, nine days of German food and drink, oompah bands and dancing. There are special events to salute shoemakers, woodworkers, furniture makers and rubber workers —the employees of some of Kitchener's key industries.

A Winterfest in January is highlighted by a Sno-do 100, a 100-mile endurance run for snowmobilers.

JOSEPH SCHNEIDER HOUSE Built in 1820 by Joseph Schneider, a Pennsylvanian who settled here in 1807, the frame structure is Kitchener's oldest house.

KITCHENER WATERLOO ART GALLERY A permanent collection of about 200 works of art includes oil paintings and sketches by Homer Watson, who lived at nearby Doon (*see entry*). Among works on permanent loan from the National Gallery of Canada are *Split Rock Georgian Bay* by Tom Thomson and *Winter Moonlight* by A.Y. Jackson.

ROCKWAY GARDENS Illuminated fountains, flower gardens and rockeries.

WOODSIDE NATIONAL HISTORIC PARK Woodside, a large gray brick house in which Prime Minister Mackenzie King lived as a boy, is set in 11.5 acres of park-like grounds. It was built in 1853 by James Calquhoun and leased by Mackenzie King's father in 1886-93. A group of citizens purchased it in 1943 and undertook to restore it to the condition in which Mackenzie King had known it as a boy. It was deeded to the government of Canada in 1954 and designated as a national historic park. The L-shaped house is a good example of Victorian English country style transplanted to Canada and is in many ways typical of upper-middle-class Ontario homes of that period. It has ornamental gables and bargeboard with an intricate fleur-de-lis pattern. It was heated by stoves—there were no fireplaces—and had no basement, although one has been added and contains displays relating to Mackenzie King's life. One is a document he treasured: a government proclamation putting a price of £1,000 on the head of his grandfather, William Lyon Mackenzie, leader of the 1837 rebellion in Upper Canada.

The rest of the 10-room house is furnished in the cluttered, comfortable fashion of the Victorian era. It has the look of a home, not a museum. Among the highlights are a marble-top table that belonged to William Lyon Mackenzie, a fine old kitchen cookstove, a white timber wolf rug, a Royal Doulton washstand set, a gleaming brass bed and a grand piano that Mackenzie King willed to be returned to Woodside. There are also brass spittoons, scores of doilies, various bric-a-brac and a stereopticon, a picture-viewing device giving a three-dimensional image.

Paper and shoemaker's wax is provided for visitors to make rubbings of a brass plaque of Mackenzie King.

Mennonite farmers go to meeting in horse-drawn buggies as Mennonites have done for centuries. Triangular safety reflectors are a concession to the cars and trucks that also use the back roads of Waterloo County, near Kitchener.

Kitimat B.C.

One of the world's biggest aluminum smelters is here at the head of Douglas Channel. Kitimat was planted in the wilderness in the early 1950s when the Aluminum Company of Canada chose the site because of its deep-sea harbor, the proximity of hydroelectric power at Kemano (*see entry*) and its level land for building.

With the establishment of a Eurocan Pulp and Paper Co. mill in 1968, and the growth of service industries and logging operations, Kitimat's population has climbed to approximately 12,000.

Alcan employs close to 2,400 persons here. The smelter, with an annual capacity of 300,000 tons, is five miles from the city center; a mile farther on is the harbor where bauxite from Jamaica and fluorspar from Newfoundland are unloaded and from which Kitimat aluminum ingots are shipped to dozens of countries. Illustrated lectures, films and bus tours of the smelter and dock areas are provided in summer.

□ Douglas Channel and the Gardner Canal (leading to the Kemano River) are among British Columbia's finest scenic attractions. There is year-round salt-water fishing in the

Tom Thomson's shack, now at Kleinburg, was the great artist's home during his most productive period. Lawren Harris wrote that Thomson felt a studio in a spanking new building in Toronto would be pretentious, so he moved into "a dilapidated old shack on the back of the property. . . . Tom made himself a bunk, shelves, a table, and an easel, and lived in that place as he would a cabin in the north. It became Tom's shack and was his home until he died in 1917." The McMichael Collection at Kleinburg has 63 Thomson works and such other outstanding works as Lionel FitzGerald's *The Little Plant* and F.H. Varley's *Indians Crossing Georgian Bay.*

channel (2-pound cod to 70-pound salmon and 200-pound halibut) and during most seasons there is good fishing in the Kitimat River and its tributaries (salmon, trout and Dolly Varden). Small and big game hunting grounds are close.

□ The Kitimat Museum has art exhibits and natural history displays.

Kitseguecla B.C. *see* Hazelton

Kitwancool B.C. *see* Hazelton

Kitwanga B.C. *see* Hazelton

Kleinburg Ont.   7CY/17CX
The vivid art of the Group of Seven and their leading Canadian contemporaries is exhibited in the 27 gallery rooms of the Mc-

Michael Canadian Collection. It contains 63 oils, watercolors, pen-and-ink and pencil sketches by Tom Thomson (*see* Owen Sound, Whitney), the largest permanent display of his art.

There are works by the Group's founders —A.Y. Jackson, J.E.H. MacDonald, Lawren Harris, Arthur Lismer, F.H. Varley, Franklin Carmichael and Frank H. "Franz" Johnston —and later members A.J. Casson and Edwin Holgate. Also represented are David Milne (*see* Paisley), Emily Carr (*see* Victoria), Clarence A. Gagnon, J.W. Morrice, Yvonne McKague Housser, Lionel FitzGerald, Albert H. Robinson, Randolph Hewton and Thoreau MacDonald. There are also paintings by Sir Frederick Banting, J.W. Beatty, Isabel McLaughlin and Maurice Cullen.

The studio shack in which Thomson painted many of his masterpieces is on the 30-acre grounds of the McMichael collection. So are the graves of Lismer, Varley and Harris, each under a large Algoma boulder. Jackson lived in a studio-apartment above the gallery from 1968 until he died in 1974.

The collection was begun as a hobby by Robert and Signe McMichael in an L-shaped, six-room house they called Tapawingo (an Indian word for place of joy). It was built in 1954 of century-old local stone and century-old timber from pioneer barns and houses. The same materials were used for the five additions to the house since then. In 1965, when the collection had grown to more than 300 works, the McMichaels turned it over to the Province of Ontario. Tapawingo and a surrounding 600 acres became the McMichael Conservation Area, a public institution administered by the provincial government.

There are now more than 800 paintings

largest non-polar glacier systems, dating from the end of the Ice Age, are maintained by moisture-laden air from the Pacific. The Steele Glacier moved downhill 2,300 feet in one month in 1966.

The Alaska Highway runs for 80 miles along the park's northeastern boundary. Part of 184-square-mile Kluane Lake, the Yukon's biggest, borders the park and highway. Near the lake are Soldier's Summit, where the Alaska Highway was formally opened Nov. 20, 1942, and abandoned buildings that are the only remains of Silver City, a trading and RCMP post built about 1903.

Knowlton Que. *see* Lac-Brome

Canada's Matterhorn, 11,870-foot Mount Assiniboine, gives its name to a British Columbia provincial park that can be reached from Kootenay and Banff national parks.

and other works of art, including Indian and Eskimo totems, masks and figures and pioneer artifacts.

Kluane National Park (Y.T.)   1AV
Canada's highest mountains and most spectacular ice fields are in this 8,500-square-mile wilderness park in the southwest corner of the Yukon. It also has some of North America's last unhunted major populations of grizzly bears and of curly-horned Dall sheep. There are moose and caribou, wolves and wolverines, large numbers of golden eagles and ptarmigans.

The St. Elias Mountains, including Mount Logan, at 19,524 feet Canada's highest, run through the park. Mount St. Elias is 18,008 feet and a dozen other peaks are over 15,000 feet. The St. Elias Icefields, one of the world's

Kootenay National Park (B.C.)   2FY/13AV
Rich in scenery and big game, Kootenay is one of Canada's most accessible mountain parks. The 543-square-mile reserve extends for about five miles on each side of a 65-mile stretch of the Banff-Windermere Highway, following the valleys of the Vermilion and Kootenay rivers. This park, on the western slopes of the Rockies along the Continental Divide, adjoins Yoho and Banff national parks to the north and east.

Kootenay is a spectacular area of high glaciers and deep canyons, icy alpine lakes and hot mineral springs. Bear, deer, moose, elk and Rocky Mountain sheep are seen. From Vermilion Pass in the north the highway leads to Marble Canyon, its walls of gray limestone and quartzite shot with layers of white and grayish marble, then on to Paint

Pots Nature Trail, named for ocher beds that Indians used for makeup and to color pots and garments. Farther south the road runs between the Iron Gates, the first of the towering red sandstone cliffs of Sinclair Canyon, and leads to Radium Hot Springs. The odorless, tasteless water of Radium's springs (113 degrees) is cooled and fed to outdoor pools operated by the National Parks Service.

At the confluence of the Vermilion and Simpson rivers is a cairn in tribute to Sir George Simpson, governor of the Hudson's Bay Company territories from 1821 to 1860.

Just inside the park, two miles south of Radium Junction, is a plaque commemorating James Sinclair, an HBC clerk who in 1841 guided 200 Red River settlers through the Rockies to Oregon.

Kouchibouguac National Park (N.B.) 9DX
A 15½-mile sweep of offshore sandbars is a feature of this 93-square-mile park established in 1969 on Kouchibouguac Bay at the north end of Northumberland Strait. There is good swimming in the tidewater lagoons behind the sandbars. Underlying the park's salt marshes and dunes are extensive peat bogs an estimated 10,000 years old. The bogs contain a rich variety of plant life including colorful bog laurel and lambkill, and carnivorous pitcher plants and sundews.

L

Labrieville Que. 9BV
Hydro Quebec's 1,200,000-horsepower plant on the Bersimis River here generates power for Montreal and, by submarine cable across the St. Lawrence River, for the copper mines of Murdochville in the Gaspé. A 7½-mile tunnel 31 feet in diameter feeds water from Lake Cassé to Bersimis 1, a giant generating station carved from solid rock. Bersimis 2, 25 miles downstream, has a 900,000-horsepower capacity.

Lac-Bouchette Que. 9AW/21AX
At the shrine of Our Lady of Lourdes and Saint Anthony here is a grotto similar to the one at Lourdes, France.

Lac-Brome Que. 7FY/19DY
A World War I German Fokker aircraft, its camouflage and fabric skin intact, is displayed in an annex of the Brome County Historical Museum. Pioneer artifacts and archives are in the main museum, a white brick building that was Knowlton Academy, the village's first school, founded in 1854.

Lac du Bonnet Man. *see* West Hawk Lake

Lac-Etchemin Que. 9AX/20CX
An international regatta is held on 3½-mile-long Lake Etchemin in early June.

Lachine Que. *see* Montreal

Lachute Que. 7FX/19AX
The weekly Lachute Commission Sale is not only a livestock auction but a farmers' market and flea market as well. From the backs of trucks and from tents and card tables and cars are sold fresh produce, antique furniture, secondhand clothing, hubcaps, tractor hitches, crutches . . .

□ The shrine of Notre-Dame-de-Lourdes resembles the famous grotto at Lourdes in France.

□ The Lachute Spring Fair, first held in 1825, is an annual June event.

□ The main section of the Jean Marchand Dam, 12 miles northeast, is a 300-foot-long reinforced concrete arch. The dam, on William Creek, has created an 800,000,000-gallon reservoir.

Museum at Lac-Brome is a memorial to the town's founder, Paul Holland Knowlton. The community was called Knowlton from 1851 to 1971.

Lac la Biche Alta.   4BW

Powwows that Cree Indians held at Lac la Biche until the arrival of white settlers are the genesis of the Powwow days staged here in August in conjunction with the Blue Feather Fish Derby. Indians from a vast area used to gather here for dances and games and to ask the Manitou's blessing. Revived in 1964, the four-day celebration features a parade, baseball, dancing, watersport demonstrations and sky-diving exhibitions.

Lac la Hache B.C.   2DX

The 12-mile-long lake from which this community gets its name teems with landlocked kokanee salmon, Arctic char and rainbow trout. Rainbow also thrive in smaller Greeny, Timothy, Rail and Spout lakes. Eight miles north of here, off the Cariboo Highway, is Lac la Hache Provincial Park.

The Cariboo Regatta in late July features hydroplane and other boat races.

Lac-Mégantic Que.   9AY/20CZ

A plaque in city hall notes that U.S. troops under Gen. Benedict Arnold camped here on their way to join Gen. Richard Montgomery's army for an attack on Quebec Dec. 31, 1775. The attack failed.

A dozen plays are presented in August at the Quebec Student Drama Festival.

Lacolle Que.   7FY/19BZ

Across the narrow Lacolle River from this village stands an 1812 fortress with an overhanging casemate. Lacolle was the site of an 1814 battle in which fewer than 400 Voltigeurs, commanded by Col. Charles-Michel de Salaberry, and a few British troops defeated nearly 10 times as many Americans.

La Have N.S.—This is one of the earliest settled places in Canada. De Monts and Champlain were here in 1604 and a cairn marks the site of a fort that Isaac de Razilly, lieutenant general of Acadia, built in 1632. It was captured by the English in 1670, used by pirates and burned by Boston privateers. Today it is a farming and fishing center and, with superb scenery, a favorite of tourists. (9DZ/22DX)

Ladner B.C.   2CZ/12EX

This is the administrative center of the district municipality of Delta, a peninsula bounded by the Fraser River, Boundary Bay and the Strait of Georgia.

Under the Oregon Treaty of 1846 the six-square-mile southern tip of the peninsula, Point Roberts, became a part of the United States. About 80 percent of Point Roberts' permanent residents are Canadians and water service is supplied by Delta.

At English Bluff, overlooking the Strait of Georgia, is a 40-ton Scottish granite obelisk erected in 1861 to mark the 49th parallel, the boundary between the United States and the four western provinces.

Ladysmith B.C.   2BZ/12DX

Early logging equipment is displayed among trees from around the world at the Crown Zellerbach Canada Museum and Arboretum. Trees in the arboretum include Port Orford cedar (California), dawn redwood (central China), yew (England) and Scotch pine (Scandinavia).

Lafontaine Ont.   7CY/17BV

The first Mass in what is now Ontario was celebrated near here Aug. 12, 1615, in the

Huron Indian village of Carhagouha. A 20-foot stone cross erected by the Knights of Columbus marks the site and a memorial service is often held on the Sunday closest to Aug. 12.

Lakefield Ont.   7CY/17EW
At Westove, once the home of writer Catharine Parr Traill (and now privately owned), is a plaque which commemorates this author of books on pioneering in Upper Canada.

Old Christ Church (Anglican) (1853) was built largely through the efforts of Mrs. Traill's brother, Col. Samuel Strickland. He came to Canada in 1825, worked for the Canada Company under John Galt, then farmed in the wilderness near Lakefield. He chronicled his adventures in *Twenty-seven Years in Canada West.*

Mrs. Traill's *Backwoods of Canada* (1836) tells of the hardships she and her husband endured on their Otonabee district farm. In an attempt to counteract land companies' glowing accounts of pioneer life, she wrote *The Canadian Settler's Guide* (1855). Her talent as one of the leading naturalists of her day is reflected in *Canadian Wild Flowers* (1836) and *Studies of Plant Life in Canada* (1885). Her sister, Susanna Moodie, wrote the famous *Roughing It in the Bush.*

Lake Louise Alta. *see* Banff National Park

Lakeside N.B.   9DY
One of New Brunswick's few remaining lychgates is at St. Paul's Anglican Church. It was built in 1828. The coffin was placed under the roofed gate during the first part of a burial service. Inside the present church (1871) is a 15-by-25-foot petit point carpet in a red fleur-de-lis design.

La Malbaie Que.   9BW
Champlain came here in 1608, anchored at high tide, found his ship hard aground by morning, and called the place *malle baye* (bad bay). A century and a half later, two Scottish soldiers who settled in La Malbaie sought to change its name to honor their general, James Murray, successor to Wolfe. They never succeeded—officially. Murray Bay it is to some; to most, though, including the Scots' French-speaking descendants, it remains La Malbaie.

□ A museum honors Laure Conan, Canada's first woman novelist of renown. The writer, whose real name was Félicité Angers, was born in 1845 in La Malbaie, and lived here most of her life. She is best known for *Angéline de Montbrun, La Sève Immortelle* and *L'Oublié,* which in 1903 became the first Canadian book selected for an award by the prestigious Académie française.

The museum displays certain of Laure Conan's personal belongings and such other objects as a rifle once owned by Sitting Bull and a cassock that belonged to Canon Lionel Groulx, an historian who started the Action Catholique movement in 1901 and came to

be known throughout Canada as Quebec's *grand nationaliste.*

□ Saint-Etienne Church is known for stained glass windows by Max Ingrand.

La Mauricie National Park (Que.)   7FX
This heavily wooded, 211-square-mile park in the Saint-Maurice River Valley has campgrounds, beaches and wilderness and wildlife areas. Moose, bear, deer and beaver share the forest with a small pack of wolves. The park, bounded by the Saint-Maurice and Matawin rivers, has 154 lakes, many unnamed. Canoe-camping is a popular activity, giving canoeists an opportunity to reach isolated parts of the park. In autumn the woods are aglow with brilliant colors.

Lang Ont.   17EW
Century Village has 14 restored 19th-century pioneer buildings, including a blacksmith shop, a sawmill, a shingle mill, log houses, a church and a general store.

L'Ange-Gardien Que.   20BW
Part of the La Berge house, a private residence, is thought to date from the 1670s. The walls are three feet thick at the base and average two feet in thickness. The 1½-story fieldstone house is one of several Norman-style houses here.

Langley B.C.   2CZ/12EX
A Hudson's Bay Company fort built in 1840 has been partially restored in Fort Langley National Historic Park. It has a palisade of split red cedar logs, the original store, new bastions, a carpenter shop and a replica of the officers' quarters. A museum in a new building describes life in the Fraser River Valley a century ago. The Langley Centennial Museum outside the walls has Indian and pioneer artifacts.

It was in Fort Langley on Nov. 19, 1858, that James Douglas, an HBC officer, proclaimed the birth of the Crown colony of British Columbia. He was sworn in as its first governor and made Fort Langley the colony's first capital. Since 1958, when restoration began, the B.C. premier and his cabinet have met in the fort each Nov. 19 to commemorate the event.

A cairn in the courtyard of St. George's Anglican Church marks the site of an old HBC cemetery. On the road from Langley to Fort Langley, just past Schloss Klipphaus, a private residence resembling a castle on the Rhine, is a marker noting that the first section of the Collins Overland Telegraph line (*see* Burns Lake) was started here in 1865. A nearby cairn records that HBC Chief Factor James McMillan discovered the mouth of the Fraser in 1824, three years before he established Fort Langley.

□ The British Columbia Farm Machinery Museum displays antique agricultural implements, farm wagons, threshing machines, crude binders and six 15-horsepower Case traction engines dating from 1902.

L'Anse aux Meadows Nfld.   11CW

A Viking settlement was established here, in what may have been the Vinland of the Norse sagas, about the year 1000. In the 1960s, a Norwegian archaeological team found remains of seven buildings including the layout of a 76-by-15-foot "great hall." Near the southeast wall, they turned up a tiny spindle-whorl of carved soapstone, the earliest European household article unearthed in North America. Since then, archaeologists have found a bronze pin, a floorboard from a small boat, a perforated glass bead of a type common in the Norse world of the 11th century, and the remains of a smithy and a sauna. Reproductions of the collected artifacts are displayed in an interpretive center in L'Anse aux Meadows National Historic Park.

Lantz N.S.   9EY/22FV

Ernest Lorenzen, a Lantz potter, has reproduced in ceramic form 130 species of Nova Scotia mushrooms. They are in the Museum of Science in Halifax.

La Pérade Que.   9AX/20AX

The remains of Madeleine de Verchères, one of French Canada's great heroines (*see* Verchères), lie in an unmarked grave here, near a river that teems with tommycod every winter. Madeleine de Verchères married Pierre-Thomas de Lanaudière, seigneur of La Pérade, and when she died in 1747 was buried under the seigniorial pew of the village church. Her remains were moved when the church was demolished about 1775, and have been moved several times since.

□ La Pérade boasts the ruin of the seigniorial manor house built in 1676 and the well-preserved Gouin house (1669), Du Tremblay house (1669), Dorion house (1719) and Baribeau house (1717). Another house was the birthplace of the second bishop of Trois-Rivières, Louis-François Richer-Laflèche. In twin-towered Sainte-Anne-de-la-Pérade Church is a six-foot statue of Sainte Anne, carved from a single piece of wood.

It's tommycod time at La Pérade and the frozen Sainte-Anne River blossoms with the happily tilting cabins of thousands of fishermen. A Mr. Tommycod and a festival queen and princesses preside over the town's two-month annual tommycod festival.

La Pocatière Que.   9BX/20DV

Stations of the Cross in modern Sainte-Anne-de-la-Pocatière Cathedral were carved by Médard Bourgault, the Saint-Jean-Port-Joli sculptor. The cathedral interior is finished in natural wood and has padded armchairs instead of pews. Nearby, at a shrine to Notre-Dame-de-Fatima, is a statue of the Virgin Mary surrounded by child shepherds.

A museum at Collège de Sainte-Anne-de-la-Pocatière has a collection of mounted animals and about 2,000 stuffed birds, including one of the passenger pigeon, which became extinct in 1914. The museum has a three-foot wooden statue of Saint Joseph by François-Noël Levasseur.

□ Two covered bridges of 81 and 132 feet cross the nearby Ouelle River.

La Prairie Que.   7FY/19BY

A cairn here commemorates a 1691 battle in which French settlers repelled an invading force of New Englanders and averted an attack on Montreal. The ruins of a fort erected four years earlier, to protect against Iroquois raids, can be seen in the middle of town.

Is Newfoundland the Vinland of the Sagas?

Norwegian author and explorer Helge Ingstad thinks that these cairns, on an 80-foot-high ridge 300 yards west of Viking site at L'Anse aux Meadows, might have served as a timepiece. Four cairns were found, each about two feet high, but surrounding stones indicated they were once about seven feet high so Ingstad rebuilt them. Viewed from the Norse site, the cairns are silhouetted against the sky. Research left a pattern of shallow diggings approximating the layout of the original Viking buildings but there are no standing ruins. A government guide takes visitors through the site. Ingstad believes northern Newfoundland is the Vinland of the Norse sagas.

La Prairie was one terminus (the other was Saint-Jean) of Canada's first railway. A plaque records that this 16-mile line was built in 1836.

The Church of the Nativity, in Italian baroque style, dates from 1839. The pulpit was carved by Victor Bourgeau.

The St. Lawrence Brick Co. plant, one of the largest brick factories in North America, may be toured.

La Rivière Man. 6AZ/15BZ
The Archibald Historical Museum, in an old barn, contains the household effects of western pioneers and a collection of buggies and early cars and tractors. At the museum is a log cabin in which Nellie L. McClung lived as a pioneer teacher. Built in 1878, it is refurbished according to the description of it in her book *Clearing In The West*.

La Ronge Sask. 4DV
Holy Trinity Anglican Church (1856), 40 miles northeast at Stanley Mission, near a Cree Indian reserve, is the oldest building in Saskatchewan. Mission and reserve adjoin Lac La Ronge Provincial Park, which lies along the north end of 500-square-mile Lac La Ronge.

Larouche Que. 21BW
Saint-Gérard-Majella Church, built in 1960, is distinctively modern in architecture but traditional in form. The gray asphalt shingle roof, sweeping up in two curved planes to its highest point above the altar, is supported by white concrete walls. They describe four quarter-arcs to form the conventional cross-shaped ground plan.

La Sarre Que. 7DV
The Society of History and Archaeology of Abitibi has an exhibition of Stone Age tools in the town hall. La Sarre hosts an industrial and agricultural exhibition in August, a western festival in June and a winter carnival in February.

A covered bridge on the La Sarre River is 236 feet long.

L'Assomption Que. 7FX/19BX
Most of the many old stone houses in L'Assomption are typical early French Canadian, with gabled roofs and chimneys at both ends. None of the houses may be visited but their distinctive exteriors are among the town's main attractions. One of the oldest is the Desmarais house (c.1750).

Latchford Ont. 7CW
At a dam where the Montreal River widens into Bay Lake is the world's largest hydraulic compressed air plant. A pipeline transmits the compressed air to silver mines at Cobalt, 10 miles north.
□ The Latchford House of Memories Museum has domestic furnishings from the turn of the century, geological displays and logging sleighs, hoists, broadaxes and peaveys (spiked poles for handling logs).

La Tuque Que. 7FW
The International Canoe Classic, one of the world's toughest, is a 125-mile race down the Saint-Maurice River on Labor Day weekend. Two-man teams paddle 52 miles from La Tuque to Saint-Roch-de-Mékinac the first day. The 48-mile run to Shawinigan the second day features a 1½-mile portage at Grand'-Mère and a second portage around rapids three miles downstream from Grand'Mère. The 25-mile run the third day is to Trois-Rivières, where there is a sprint for the Arthur Pellerin memorial trophy. The over-all winners get the René Bellemare trophy. In La Tuque the race is preceded by a week-long program that includes the Quebec pistol shooting championship.

Laurentides Que.—The boyhood home of Canada's seventh prime minister, Sir Wilfrid Laurier, is a national historic site. On the main floor are a kitchen (left), dining room, living room and bedroom. Upstairs are a bedroom and spinning and weaving rooms. Laurentides is often called Saint-Lin. (7FX/19BX)

Stations of the Cross at Lebret lead to a hillside chapel that overlooks Mission Lake in Saskatchewan's Qu'Appelle Valley.

□ Two-man teams compete in a 75-mile swimming marathon on Lac Saint-Louis here in July. One man swims, the other walks along the shore until the swimmer tires; then they change places.

□ Two 136-foot covered bridges cross the Bostonnais River northeast of La Tuque.

□ In the Canadian International Paper Company mill here is a 283-inch-wide kraft paper machine, the world's largest. It produces 700 tons a day.

Lauzon Que.   9AX/20BW
On a height behind this city across from Quebec is Fort Lévis I, the object of a major restoration by the federal government. It is the only remaining fort of three built in the area in the 1860s to protect Quebec against possible invasion by the Americans.

□ A statue of Guillaume Couture, the first man to settle on the south shore of the St. Lawrence River here, stands near Saint-Joseph Church. It was unveiled in 1947 on the 300th anniversary of his arrival.

□ The 19th-century church's works of art

International Canoe Classic portage near Saint-Etienne-des-Grès is on the third day of the 125-mile race from La Tuque to Trois-Rivières.

include *L'Assomption*, an oil painting (1818) by Antoine Plamondon. A plaque records that a previous church on the site was used as a British field hospital during the siege of Quebec in 1759 and that the body of Wolfe was kept there until it could be transported to England.

□ Lauzon is an important shipbuilding center. There are tours of Davie Shipbuilding Ltd., one of Canada's largest shipyards.

Lawrencetown N.S.   22CV
Student surveyors are a common sight along highways and railway lines near Lawrencetown: it is the home of the Nova Scotia Land Survey Institute, Canada's only school devoted exclusively to cartography, land surveying and photogrammetry.

Leamington Ont.   7AZ/16BZ
One of the world's largest tomato-processing plants, H.J. Heinz Company of Canada Limited, is in this town on the north shore of Lake Erie. There are tours in summer.

Leaskdale Ont.   17CW
A plaque at the Leaskdale church manse commemorates Lucy Maud Montgomery, author of *Anne of Green Gables*. She lived here in 1911-26 with her husband, the Rev. Ewan MacDonald, a Presbyterian minister, and their three sons. Mrs. MacDonald wrote 11 of her 23 books while in Leaskdale. (*See* Cavendish)

Lebret Sask.   4EY
A life-size statue on the grounds of an Indian industrial school honors the Rev. Joseph Hugonard, the first principal of one of Canada's oldest Indian residential schools. It was

founded in 1884 for the education of Métis settlers and the present buildings date from 1935. On a hill overlooking the village, an illuminated cross stands where a cross was placed in 1865 to mark a mission site.

Leduc Alta. 4AX/14FX

The location of Imperial Leduc No. 1, the well that on Feb. 13, 1947, tapped the 300,000,000-barrel Leduc oil field, is marked by a plaque nine miles northwest of here. Imperial Oil had drilled 133 consecutive dry holes before striking oil at 5,066 feet. The Leduc No. 1 drilling rig now stands at the southern entrance to Edmonton.

Also near Leduc is the site of Atlantic No. 3, a well that went out of control in 1948 and spewed oil for almost six months before catching fire. An estimated 1,250,000 barrels of oil and vast amounts of gas were lost before the fire was extinguished. The fire focused more attention on the Leduc potential than did the initial discovery.

Lennoxville Que. 9AY/20AZ

Bishop's University in this predominantly English-speaking, Loyalist-settled town was established in 1843 by the Rt. Rev. George Jehoshaphat Mountain, Anglican bishop of Quebec. Bishop's College School, a boarding school for boys, was founded in 1836. Its cadet corps, started 25 years later, is one of the oldest in the Commonwealth.

The Massawippi, Coaticook, Au Saumon and Ascot rivers meet here at Petites Fourches (little forks) as they flow into the Saint-François River.

Canadian dramas with top Canadian actors and directors are staged in summer at Festival Lennoxville in the 650-seat Centennial Theater of Bishop's University.

Les Eboulements Que. 9BW

The village gets its name from landslides in 1663 caused by an earthquake said to have been so violent that a mountain on the shore became an island in the St. Lawrence River.

Notre-Dame de L'Assomption Church is on a 1,500-foot hill. In the sacristy are the remains of a fine carved retable (c.1775), a shelf above the altar.

The De Sales Laterrière seigniorial manor (c.1710) is owned by the Brothers of the Sacred Heart. Villagers still bring grain to a water-powered seigniorial mill believed built about 1812. It can be visited.

Lethbridge Alta. 4BZ

One of the world's most spectacular railway bridges and North America's biggest Japanese garden are here, not far from the site of Fort Whoop-Up and the scene of the last great Indian battle on Canadian soil.

Lethbridge (originally Coalbanks) was built on coal in the 1870s. But coal now is secondary to the livestock, grain, vegetables and sugar beets and the oil and gas that spring from the surrounding million acres of irrigated land.

Whiskey forts probably flew a fur-trade flag, not the Stars and Stripes in this painting of Fort Whoop-Up in the RCMP Museum in Regina. A prime buffalo robe sold at Whoop-Up (near present-day Lethbridge) for a drink that was one part alcohol to three parts water, flavored with pepper and colored with tobacco juice.

FORT WHOOP-UP Southwest, at the junction of the St. Mary and Oldman rivers, a cairn marks the site of a fort where traders peddled cheap liquor to the Indians. Whoop-Up and other such forts were put out of business by the North West Mounted Police.

GALT GARDENS Named for Sir Alexander Galt, a Father of Confederation, the gardens were created at the place where in the 1880s bull carts from Montana turned and headed south again.

GENEVIEVE E. YATES MEMORIAL CENTER Dramas, musicals, concerts, operettas and recitals are staged in this 500-seat theater next to city hall.

HIGH-LEVEL BRIDGE Built in 1909, this bridge across the Oldman River is the world's longest (one mile) for its height (314 feet).

INDIAN BATTLE PARK Here, near what is now downtown Lethbridge, some 800 Cree and Assiniboine warriors attacked Blood and Blackfoot camps on the Oldman River in 1870. The South Peigans (Blackfoot allies) were camped on the St. Mary River above Fort Whoop-Up. Expecting an easy victory over the smallpox-ridden Blackfoot, the Crees and Assiniboines were surprised when they met fierce resistance. The next morning the Peigans, armed with repeating rifles, joined in. The Crees were beaten back, then relentlessly pursued, and lost 200 to 300 men. Blackfoot losses were 40 killed and 50 wounded.

A replica of Fort Whoop-Up and a cannon from the fort are in the park.

LETHBRIDGE RESEARCH STATION With 1,100 acres and more than 70 scientists, it is second only to the Central Experimental Farm in Ottawa.

NIKKA YUKO CENTENNIAL GARDEN It was built in Henderson Lake Park as a joint centennial project of Lethbridge and 6,000 Japanese Canadians who were brought here from their Pacific coast homes when Canada de-

clared war on Japan in 1941. Flower-arrangement classes and tea ceremonies are held in a cypress-wood pavilion. There is an *Azumaya*, a shelter where visitors can listen to a stream which has its source nearby. A small island in a pond is shaped like a turtle, the Japanese symbol of longevity.

ST. MARY RIVER DAM This 202-foot-high dam 35 miles southwest of Lethbridge is one of the largest earth-fill dams in Canada. It created a 17-mile-long reservoir that irrigates 300,000 acres of southern Alberta.

SIR ALEXANDER GALT MUSEUM Exhibits depict the human history of southern Alberta and the history of mining in Lethbridge.

WHOOP-UP DAYS Rodeo, horse show, horse racing, midway and grandstand show attract more than 100,000 during the third week of July.

Lévis Que.   9AX/20BW
The Church of Notre-Dame-de-la-Victoire (1850), better known as Notre-Dame-de-Lévis, was designed by Thomas Baillargé in Louis XVI style and decorated by André Paquet. A plaque and two cannon near the church mark where English artillery fired across the St. Lawrence River to bombard Quebec in 1759.

□ A plaque marks the home of Alphonse Desjardins, who developed the idea of caisses populaires (cooperative saving and loan associations) on a parish basis. The caisse populaire he started at his home in 1900 was the first of more than 1,300 in Quebec. The associations have almost 3,000,000 members. A monument with a bust of Desjardins is on the grounds of the Fédération de Québec des Caisses Populaires Desjardins.

Lewisporte Nfld.   11CY
This town on Notre Dame Bay serves both international aviation and faraway lobster lovers. Its storage tanks supply fuel to Gander

Louis Fréchette, the first French-Canadian poet honored by the Académie française, lived in this house in Lévis. Fréchette was a lawyer, journalist and politician, but was most famous as a poet. He won the académie's Prix Montyon for *Poésies Diverses* (1879).

Five-tiered pagoda in Nikka Yuko Garden was built in Japan, dismantled, shipped to Lethbridge for reassembly. A ceremonial bell cast in Japan commemorates Japanese-Canadian amity.

airport, 33 miles southeast, and through Gander each year are shipped some 100,000 pounds of Lewisporte lobsters.

Liard Hot Springs B.C.   1BX
Water with a temperature of 120 degrees flows from springs near Mile 496 of the Alaska Highway.

Lillooet B.C.   2DY
In the early 1860s, Lillooet was a major stopping place on a primitive trail from the Pacific coast to the Cariboo gold fields. In 1861-63 the original Cariboo Wagon Road was pushed north 170 miles from Lillooet to Soda Creek. Stopping places along the way, such as 70 Mile House, 100 Mile House and 150 Mile House, were named for their distances from Lillooet. Eventually, the road bypassed

Newfoundland cod fishery, at such places as Lewisporte (p.201), uses squid (above) as bait.

Lillooet, linking Barkerville and Yale (*see entries*). A cairn of stones from old placer mines marks the original Mile 0.

Lindsay Ont.   7CY/17DW
The Victoria County Historical Society Museum displays pioneer household furnishings, early farm tools and other Canadiana. A plaque on the museum grounds commemorates writer Ernest Thompson Seton (*see* Carberry), who emigrated from England to a farm near Lindsay in 1866.

Sir Sam Hughes, one of the creators of the Canadian Army, also is commemorated. He was a Lindsay newspaper publisher and became minister of militia and defense in 1911.

Lion's Head Ont.   7BX
Limestone caves are among the sights in this Bruce Peninsula village on the shore of Georgian Bay. It is named after a massive rock formation nearby.

L'Islet-sur-Mer Que.   9BX/20DV
This village has produced seafarers for almost three centuries and is known as *la patrie des marins*, the sailors' homeland. A marine museum, in a former convent built in 1878, especially honors Capt. Joseph-Elzéar Bernier, a native son whose seven voyages between 1904 and 1925 established Canada's sovereignty over the Arctic islands. His octant and instruments from his ship *Arctic* are in the museum. So is the template used to cast a plaque that Bernier placed in claiming the islands for Canada.

A monument to Bernier, in a park next to the museum, is an aluminum globe on which his Arctic voyages are indicated.

The museum has ribs from the bow of Jacques Cartier's ship *La Petite Hermine*; a barometer from the brig *Rob Roy*, which sank in 1827 with a loss of 34 lives; and an anchor from the liner *Empress of Ireland*, which sank 10 miles east of Pointe-au-Père (*see entry*) in 1914.

L'Islet Church, dating from 1768, was designated as a Quebec historic monument in 1965. It is rich in art objects, many from two churches (1700 and 1721) that no longer exist. The facade, dominated by twin spires, is adorned by statues of Christ, Saint Jean-Baptiste and Our Lady of Bonsecours, the church patroness, each more than a century old. Over the main altar hangs *L'Annonciation,* a large oil canvas painted in 1776 by the Rev. Jean-Antoine Aide-Créquy. The church has an important collection of wood sculptures, handcrafted gold and silver chalices and liturgical vestments.

Lismore N.S.   9EY/23DY
St. Mary's, the first church to be built in Nova Scotia by Roman Catholic Highland Scots, dates from 1834. A plaque on a cairn in the center of the village commemorates Angus MacDonald, Hugh MacDonald and John MacPherson—"soldiers of Prince Charlie" and veterans of the Battle of Culloden in 1746—who settled near here in 1790-91.

Little Current Ont. *see* Manitoulin Island

Little Salmon Village Y.T.   1BW
Spirit houses mark the graves in a cemetery near this Yukon historic site, once a Kutchin Indian village.

Liverpool N.S.   9DZ/22DX
Settlers from Cape Cod who founded Liverpool in 1759 spent much of the next 50 years protecting homes, fisheries and shipping from French and Spanish raiders and Yankee privateers. They fought for survival, once in their own streets, often on the high seas, through the American Revolution, the Napoleonic wars and the War of 1812, outfitting

their own privateers with Royal Navy cannon. A cairn in Fort Point Park honors Liverpool captains who took wars of retaliation to the New England coast, the Spanish Main and the Caribbean.

□ Simeon Perkins, a shipbuilder, public official and merchant who came from Connecticut in 1762, kept a diary of colonial life which is a valuable historical document. The original is in a Royal Bank vault here; copies are on view at his house, now a museum owned by the Nova Scotia government, and at archives in Halifax and Ottawa. Perkins' house, much as it was when he lived there, contains 18th-century furnishings and books and artifacts of the period.

Barr colonists built this church at Lloydminster. It has been designated as an historic site.

Lloydminster Alta./Sask.　　　4BX
A little log church erected in 1904 by the Barr colonists was used as an auto-wrecking shop and bottle exchange before being rescued and preserved as an historic site. Nearly 2,000 Londoners were recruited by Anglican clergyman Isaac M. Barr ("Canada for the British," was his cry). About 1,000 arrived here in 1903—but without him. Fed up with Barr's incompetence, they dismissed him at Saskatoon and continued under the leadership of the Rev. George Exton Lloyd (later Anglican bishop of Saskatchewan), after whom they named their community Lloydminster.

The Barr Colony Museum, in Weaver Park, contains pioneer furnishings and machinery, the Imhoff Art Gallery and the Fuchs Wildlife Display of more than 1,000 exhibits, representing a lifetime of hunting and taxidermy by Nicholas Fuchs, owner and operator.

A marker one mile north of town indicates the campsite of the first Barr colonists; another commemorates discoveries of commercial gas and oil in 1934-35.

□ Forty miles northeast of Lloydminster is the site of Fort Pitt, a major Hudson's Bay Company post on the North Saskatchewan River from 1829 to 1885. Crees led by Big Bear besieged the post for two days during the Northwest Rebellion of 1885. The defenders were 25 men of the North West Mounted Police led by Inspector Francis Dickens (son of author Charles Dickens). When the Mount-

ies were forced to withdraw to Battleford, some civilians were captured by Big Bear and the fort was sacked. Plaques tell about the fort and, in English, French and Cree, about the life of Big Bear.

□ A thriving oil and agricultural community, Lloydminster straddles the Alberta-Saskatchewan border, with city status in both provinces.

Lloydtown Ont.　　　17BX
A century-old barn has been converted into a bookshop and library with 25,000 volumes, many of them old and valuable Canadiana.

Across the road is a house believed built in the 1820s, shortly after Pennsylvania Quaker Jesse Lloyd built a gristmill and founded Lloydtown. A two-story fieldstone and brick house in which Lloyd lived in the 1830s is still a private residence.

Loch Lomond N.S.　　　9FY/23GX
Scots who settled in lake country here in 1827 named their new home in remembrance of Scotland's famous loch.

Lockeport N.S.　　　9DZ/22CY
The town's first schoolhouse, built around 1845 on the approach to a mile-long sandy beach, has been restored as the Little School Museum. It reproduces classrooms of a century ago and displays such artifacts as a parlor organ, a potbellied stove and a spinning wheel.

Lockport Man.　　　6BY/15DX
The St. Andrew's lock, opened in 1910 and still the only lock in the prairie provinces, bypasses rapids on the Red River about 17

Old St. Andrew's at Lockport has original fixtures, including buffalo-hide-covered kneelers.

miles north of Winnipeg, permitting freight and pleasure navigation to and from Lake Winnipeg.

St. Andrew's Anglican Church, dating from the early 1800s, is the oldest stone church in western Canada continuously used for public worship. The original rectory (1853) houses the William S. Dunlop Museum, with many antiques.

Red River House Museum, a stone house built in 1866 by William Kennedy, a Hudson's Bay Company fur trader and Arctic explorer, evokes 19th-century colonial life in Manitoba.

London Ont. 7BZ/16DX

Lieutenant Governor John Graves Simcoe called it New London—and its river the Thames—and wanted to build the capital of Upper Canada here. Higher powers decided otherwise and in 1793 the capital went to York (Toronto). But the new London grew into a charming, prosperous city where streets named Oxford, Piccadilly and Pall Mall, a Blackfriars Bridge and a section called Chelsea Green recall its affinity with the British capital.

CENTENNIAL MUSEUM (1) A social and cultural center built in 1967-69 in the shape of Canada's centennial symbol.

COURTHOUSE (2) The fortress-like stone structure was built in 1827.

COVENT GARDEN (3) A farmers' market with fresh produce, home baking, flowers, ethnic specialties and handicrafts.

ELDON HOUSE (4) London's oldest remaining residence, this white frame house was built in 1834 by Capt. John Harris, RN, whose descendants gave it to the city. It now is a memorial to 19th-century London, its rooms furnished with Harris family household goods and personal possessions. An English bed in the blue bedroom was made in 1780, the dining room's copper tea urn in 1795. Dining table and chairs are Canadian, and fine examples of Waterford glass adorn a mahogany sideboard. In a room decorated with shields, spears and horns is a walking stick stand made from an elephant's foot.

Middlesex County Courthouse in London is modeled after Malahide Castle in Ireland. Malahide was the birthplace of Col. Thomas Talbot, who supervised early settlement in this area.

FANSHAWE PIONEER VILLAGE (5) The life style of the prerailroad era of the 19th century is reproduced in this crossroads village. Here are the log cabins, barns and general store and the blacksmith, weaver, barber and carriagemaker shops of more than a century ago. There are also an Orange hall and a Presbyterian church. The village is at 640-acre Fanshawe Lake, created by the damming of the Thames River to prevent floods.

HURON COLLEGE (6) Founded in 1863 by Anglican Bishop Benjamin Cronyn, Huron affiliated with the University of Western Ontario in 1881.

LABATT'S PIONEER BREWERY (7) A 19th-century brewery has been restored to its original appearance, with kegs, brew kettle, hop jack and fermenter.

LONDON INTERNATIONAL AIR SHOW (8) For two days each June thousands watch planes and pilots from various countries.

LONDON REGIONAL ART GALLERY (9) By late 1979 this striking new edifice, designed by Raymond Moriyama, takes over the valuable permanent art collection housed in the London Public Library and Art Museum. The collection includes *Niagara Falls from the British Side* (Cornelius Krieghoff), *The Gaol and Courthouse, London* (G. R. Dartnell), *Covent Garden Market, London, Ontario* (Paul Peel) and *L'été* (Jean-Paul Lemieux).

METROPOLITAN UNITED CHURCH (10) A downtown church built in 1854 of red brick.

OKTOBERFEST (11) A German carnival held the first week in October at the Western Fairgrounds: much beer and Bavarian music.

RCR MUSEUM (12) This museum is in Wolseley Barracks, the home of the Royal Canadian Regiment, Canada's oldest regular infantry regiment. It has more than 1,200 items showing the RCR's role in Canadian history from the Northwest Rebellion of 1885 to modern UN peacekeeping.

ST. PAUL'S CATHEDRAL (13) The Anglican cathedral for Huron diocese serves a congregation originally established in 1829. It was built in 1846.

London

1. Centennial Museum
2. Courthouse
3. Covent Garden
4. Eldon House
5. Fanshawe Pioneer Village
6. Huron College
7. Labatt's Pioneer Brewery
8. London International Air Show
9. London Regional Art Gallery
10. Metropolitan United Church
11. Oktoberfest
12. RCR Museum
13. St. Paul's Cathedral
14. St. Peter's Basilica
15. Sir Adam Beck House
16. Sifton Botanical Bog
17. Springbank Park
18. University of Western Ontario
19. Victoria Boat Disaster
20. Western Fair

ST. PETER'S BASILICA (14) Seat of the Roman Catholic diocese of London, the basilica dates from 1881.

SIR ADAM BECK HOUSE (15) A plaque in front of his London residence honors Adam Beck (1857-1925), who pioneered Ontario's hydroelectric power system. He was mayor of London in 1902-04. In Sir Adam Beck Collegiate is Herbert Ariss' mural *The Image of Man through the Ages.*

SIFTON BOTANICAL BOG (16) This is no swamp but a true bog, having existed for 10,000 years. In the center is a floating mat of sphagnum moss which shelters bird, animal and insect life.

SPRINGBANK PARK (17) This 350-acre park on the Thames has a bird sanctuary, flower gardens, a zoo and Storybook Gardens, a child's fairyland of animals and nursery tale characters and scenes.

UNIVERSITY OF WESTERN ONTARIO (18) Academic quality and physical beauty are combined on a 500-acre campus. A plaque on the administration building honors the first chancellor, the Rt. Rev. Isaac Hellmuth, Anglican

Labatt's of London has reconstructed John Labatt's original brewery—from well and pump to delivery yard (left) and cooperage (above).

bishop of Huron in 1872-83. He was primarily responsible for founding the university in 1878.

The university's McIntosh Memorial Art Gallery has about 560 works, most of them by Canadians. Among these are *beach-hcaeb* (Michael Snow), *Jesus in the House of Mary and Martha* (David Milne), untitled sculpture by Walter Redinger, *Museum Ship* (Edward Hughes) and *Eskimo Mother and Child,* sculpture by Osowetok.

The expanding Museum of Indian Archaeology with its collection of prehistoric artifacts is on the campus.

VICTORIA BOAT DISASTER (19) A memorial in McKillop Park to the almost 200 persons who died when the excursion steamer *Victoria* sank in the Thames here in 1881.

WESTERN FAIR (20) Ontario's oldest fall fair, dating from 1868, is held in Queen's Park in September.

North of Lake Superior, a 48-by-60-inch oil painting by Lawren Harris, and William McElcheran's *Peripatetic,* an 18¼-inch-wide bronze, are in London's permanent art collection.

Long River P.E.I.   23BW
Ye Olde Mill Museum, in a building erected in 1820, displays a Scottish wool-carding machine, a weaving loom (c.1820), spinning

wheels, a variety of wagons and sleighs and antique furniture and kitchenware.

Long Sault Ont. 7EY/18EX
The communities of Mille Roches and Moulinette were merged to form Long Sault when the north shore of the St. Lawrence River was flooded because of the seaway project (*see* Ingleside).

Longueuil Que. 19BY
Several French regime houses still stand in this city, founded in 1657 by Charles Le Moyne. The Charles Le Moyne Historical Museum, constructed in 1962, is modeled after a fort that Le Moyne built in 1685 to protect the settlement against Iroquois raids.

Le Moyne's son Pierre (Sieur d'Iberville) discovered the delta of the Mississippi River and founded Louisiana. Another son, Jean-Baptiste (Sieur de Bienville), was twice governor of the French colony. Books, documents, charts, engravings and military equipment in the museum depict the life of the Le Moyne family in the society of New France.

Loretteville Que. 9AX/20BW
The little stone chapel of Notre-Dame-de-Lorette, on the Indian reserve here, was built in 1730 by François Vincent, a Huron apprenticed to sculptor François-Noël Levasseur. In the chapel are a silver sanctuary lamp also dating from 1730 and contemporary Stations of the Cross, 2½ feet high, carved by Médard Bourgault. There is a 3½-foot wooden statue of the Madonna, sculpted by Levasseur.

Loretteville Indians make snowshoes with cowhide and white ash, much as their ancestors did 300 years ago.

L'Orignal Ont. 7EY/18EW
Ontario's oldest remaining courthouse, for many years the judicial and administrative center of the old Ottawa district, is in this town. The central portion, built in Loyalist neo-classic style, was completed in 1825.

A plaque at St. Andrew's United Church (1832) commemorates the founding of an early Presbyterian congregation.

The first seigniory in what is now Ontario was granted here in 1674 but significant development did not start for 100 years.

Lotbinière Que. 9AX/20AW
Saint-Louis de Lotbinière Church, which dates from 1818, was designed by Abbé Jérôme Demers and François Baillargé. Sculptures are by André Paquet.

A plaque on a roadside chapel commemorates Léon Pamphile Lemay, a poet, novelist and jurist born here in 1837.

A water mill dates from about 1720.

Louisbourg N.S. 9FY/23HX
The great French fortress of Louisbourg dominates the foggy eastern tip of Cape Breton Island just as it did in the 18th century. Fortress of Louisbourg National Historic Park, a reconstruction project lasting 20 years and costing more than $25 million, is Canada's most ambitious attempt to recall the past.

Restored to the way it was in 1745 when under siege by New Englanders, Louisbourg portrays both the splendor and squalor of its time. Visitors are immediately challenged—in French—by a sentry in authentically scruffy dress. Then each person receives a written pass stating that he or she has promised to avoid "evil, indolence and blasphemy," and enters into a town that is authentic down to the last detail.

The garrison, at one time about 5,000 and the largest in North America, manned a base that served a huge fishing fleet and the privateers that preyed on New England shipping. The great stone-walled citadel cost so much that Louis XV said he expected to see its towers rising above the Atlantic. Twenty years of construction were barely completed when New England volunteers captured the fortress after a seven-week siege in 1745. It was returned to the French by treaty but was recaptured by the British in 1758. Two years later it was destroyed so it might never again be used against British interests. What had been the biggest French bastion in North America was little more than a grassy quarry near a quiet fishing port until the restoration project began in 1961.

Architects pored over more than 600,000 pages of plans, maps and drawings in order to rebuild the town as accurately as possible. While some 50 buildings have been restored and refurnished, other structures are left as blackened ruins to heighten the impression of a fortress under siege. The tools, materials and methods of 200 years ago were used wherever possible. Exteriors and interiors have been hand finished, timber hewn and squared

by hand, planks hand pegged, and ironwork wrought with old-fashioned techniques.

Old wells were opened and old cellars cleaned so that the original line of streets could be noted. Officers stroll along the cobblestone and soldiers patrol the bastions. Costumed staff launder clothes, bake bread, mold bullets and make rope.

The three-story King's Bastion Barracks, protected by a drawbridge, has been fully restored. This replica of what was the largest building in the New World contains the governor's luxurious 10-room suite, officers' quarters and soldiers' barracks along with a chapel, prison, judicial quarters and artillery school. An itemized list prepared when a French governor's possessions were sold proved invaluable to historians in restoring the governor's quarters.

Most of the other restored buildings reflect Louisbourg's busy commercial life. They include shops, a bakery, laundry, forge, stable, and the Hôtel de la Marine—a waterfront tavern that serves 18th-century meals.

This major archaeological site, upon which nothing of significance had been built since its virtual abandonment in 1760, has turned up more than 2,000,000 artifacts; they now

The Fortress of Louisbourg has risen again out of its misty past. The King's Bastion Barracks, with dry moat and palisade, basks once more in the Cape Breton sun. Staff wear authentic 18th-century garb.

furnish the reconstructed buildings or are exhibited in the King's Bastion Barracks. Crystal and pewter goblets still in usable condition, glazed earthenware dishes, flour barrels, clay pipes, toys and armoire locks are displayed. When original artifacts could not be found, craftsmen used 18th-century methods to produce replicas.

The museum exhibits architects' plans and drawings of both the original and reconstructed forts, newspaper accounts of the two English sieges of Louisbourg and numerous editions of contemporary memoirs and journals. Interpretative galleries offer a comprehensive look behind the scenes at the skills involved in the reconstruction.

Cairns and tablets in the 20-square-mile park locate historical features and sites. One is Kennington Cove, where Wolfe landed to start the siege of 1758.

□ A concrete lighthouse across the harbor was erected in 1923 by the Canadian govern-

From clocks to crystal, all furnishings in reconstructed Louisbourg are authentic. Everything in Governor Du Quesnel's bedroom and such rooms as the officers' mess and the kitchens is either an original or a replica made by 18th-century methods. Much of the Louisbourg reconstruction was done by onetime miners displaced by the decline of the Cape Breton coal industry. Some 160 men learned the skills of 18th-century stone-cutters, stonemasons, carpenters and wrought iron workers.

ment on the ruins of a lighthouse constructed by the French in 1730-34. It burned fish oil and was the first in Canada. A lead plaque, salvaged from the original building, is embedded in the newer structure.

Louiseville Que. 7FX/19CW
This busy industrial town with the hunting and fishing of the Saint-Maurice Valley at its back door has several historic stone houses from the 18th century. One built in 1760 was the home of composer Ernest Gagnon, author of the first important collection of French-Canadian folklore.

In Saint-Antoine Church, which has a marble interior, are seven oil paintings (c.1952) by the Rev. Antonio Cianci, an Italian artist. They represent the seven virtues.

A 115-foot covered bridge spans the Maskinongé River about 10 miles north of here.

Lucerne Que. 18CW
Vintage golf balls, one-piece wooden clubs and the brassies and mashies, spoons and niblicks that were the forerunners of today's numbered woods and irons are displayed at the Canadian Golf Museum here. In a stone house built about 1812, now the clubhouse

of the Kingsway Park Golf and Country Club, the lore of the royal and ancient game is traced by equipment, prints, books and photos of famous golfers. Nineteenth-century clubs include a leather-faced wooden spoon used by Willie Park, winner of the first British Open in 1860. A display shows evolution from the early feather ball to modern high-compression golf balls.

Lunenburg N.S. 9DZ/22DW
Long one of North America's great fishing ports, Lunenburg is renowned also for shipbuilding, and especially as the home of *Bluenose*, winner of four international schooner races. She was launched here in 1921.

On a peninsula with front and back harbors, Lunenburg is an ideal base for fishing the teeming waters of the Banks, where the Labrador current meets the Gulf Stream. Townspeople base their lives mainly on seafaring and fishing, but there is substantial farming too. Local industries produce ship's iron, brasswork, sails, dories and fishing craft, marine engines, canned and smoked fish, kegs and stoves. At Lunenburg Sea Products Ltd. visitors see fish processing from trawler to packaging and freezing.

Lucan Ont.—In a shaded corner of St. Patrick's Cemetery is a stone whose grim repetition of one date is like a bell tolling for all the dead Donnellys. Five were slain Feb. 4, 1880, in the bloody climax to one of Canada's most notorious feuds. It started in Ireland in the 1840s and, feeding on religious hate, festered for 40 years until the night vigilantes massacred James and Johannah, John, Thomas and Bridget Donnelly. All six men charged with the murders were acquitted. The stone was erected in the 1960s. (7BZ/16DX)

First an Indian village, then a 17th-century French fishing post, the site was settled in 1753 by Protestant families mainly from Germany and Switzerland. The site was named as a compliment to George II, Lüneburg having been one of his ancestral dominions. Some of the churches the settlers built, among the oldest in Canada, are still in use.

BLUENOSE MONUMENT *Bluenose* was sold to a West Indian trading company in 1942 and was converted to a motorized freighter. She perished on a reef near Haiti in 1946. An inscription on the monument calls the schooner a symbol of "the transformation of an inland people." Planted here as farmers, the German, French and Swiss immigrants cleared the wilderness, fished first off the coast, then gradually went on to the Banks to vie with the best of deep-sea fishermen. *Bluenose II*, a replica of the original and, like her, built by Smith and Rhuland of Lunenburg, was launched in 1963. Now owned by the province, she may be visited.

EARL BAILLY STUDIO Bailly (1903-77) was a gifted, paralytic artist who painted with a brush held in his teeth. Open to the public.

FISHERMEN'S MEMORIAL ROOM A quiet room in the community center at the exhibition grounds, dedicated to the memory and records of Lunenburg sailors lost at sea. It may be visited.

INTERNATIONAL DORY RACE A highlight of the annual Lunenburg Fair, the race pits local men against rivals from Gloucester, Mass., in a rowing test of skill, timing and strength.

LUNENBURG FAIR (Nova Scotia Fisheries Exhibition and Fishermen's Reunion) Begun in 1916 as a fishermen's picnic, this five-day summer festival has become an international event that attracts more than 50,000

Rugged and seaworthy, dories are 400-pound rowboats pointed at both ends and slope-sided for easy stacking on fishing boat decks. The International Dory Race is a prime attraction of the annual Lunenburg Fair.

Oils and watercolors by Lunenburg artist Joe Purcell (and by his wife and five children) are exhibited in a family gallery. Purcell has had shows in Montreal, New York and London.

persons. There are races for yachts, sailboats and dories. Huge crowds watch contests of fish filleting, scallop shucking, cable splicing and net mending. There are religious ceremonies of thanksgiving and remembrance and a blessing of the fleet.

LUNENBURG FISHERIES MUSEUM Veteran fishermen guide visitors through this museum in an historic ship moored to a Lunenburg quay. *Theresa E. Connor*, last of the Lunenburg dory schooners (built here in 1938), has been converted below decks to house exhibits of the era

of the salt bank fleet and Nova Scotia schoonermen. Also part of the museum are the Prohibition rumrunner *Reo II* and the dragger *Cape North*.

LUNENBURG MONUMENT A plaque describes the sack of Lunenburg on July, 1, 1782, by privateers from Boston, in reprisal for the capture of a Boston ship in 1780. The invaders exacted a ransom of a promissory note for £1,000.

ST. ANDREW'S CHURCH One of Canada's first Presbyterian congregations was founded here in 1753. The present church building was erected in 1828.

ST. JOHN'S CHURCH Founded in 1754, this Anglican church was presented with Communion vessels by George III. A Queen Anne pewter chalice (1754) is on display.

ZION LUTHERAN CHURCH The high church steeple overlooking town and harbor contains the bell that once rang in the chapel of the French fortress at Louisbourg. When the fortress fell to the British in 1758, the bell was taken to Halifax and remained in a warehouse for 18 years. German settlers in Lunenburg, building Zion Evangelical Lutheran Church, heard about the bell and purchased it. It heralded the first Communion service in the church on Aug. 10, 1776.

Bluenose II is a replica of the famous schooner whose likeness is on the Canadian dime. Both ships were built in Lunenburg.

M

Maccan N.S.　　　　　　　　　　　23AY
A surging tidal bore fills two rivers twice daily
as the tide rises and divides in Cumberland
Basin at the top of the Bay of Fundy. Two
walls of water 18 inches high at full tide sweep
up the River Hébert and the Maccan River
at six miles an hour. In 15 minutes both rivers
rise four feet.

Mactaquac N.B.　　　　　　　　　　9CY
New Brunswick calls this Superpark: a year-
round recreation area on the 65-mile-long
head pond formed when the Mactaquac
power development was built on the Saint
John River. Besides well-equipped campgrounds, picnic grounds and playgrounds
there is a lodge with accommodation and
dining rooms. Beaches, marinas, a golf course,
fishing and nature and hiking trails offer summer pleasures. In winter there are some campsites for the hardy, snowmobile trails and
horse-drawn sleighs, cross-country skiing, and
skating, snowshoeing and ice fishing.

The power plant, New Brunswick's largest,
with a projected capacity of 600,000 kilowatts, may be toured in summer. So may an
Atlantic salmon hatchery just below the 133-
foot dam.

Nearby, in Woolastook Wildlife Provincial
Park, are native animals and birds in natural
surroundings.

Madoc Ont.　　　　　　　　　7DY/18AY
A waterpowered sawmill like those that cut
lumber to build pioneer towns a century ago
has been put into running order here. The
mill, built about 1845 by James O'Hara,
operated until 1908. Its waterwheel, muley
saw, saw-frame carriage, steel drive shaft and
wooden connecting rod are fine examples of
carpentry and 19th-century industry.

The Moira River Conservation Authority
has restored the O'Hara mill and its dam and
millpond. The O'Hara house (c.1845) has furnishings and artifacts of the period. There is
a log schoolhouse (c.1861).

Near Madoc is Lester B. Pearson Peace
Park, named after the Canadian prime minister and Nobel Peace Prize winner. The park
has an International Peace Column and a
Peace Pagoda, a gift from peace groups in Japan who had contacts with the park founders,
Roy and Priscilla Cadwell. As a 1967 centennial project, the Cadwells donated 40 acres
of their Madoc-Tweed Art Center property
for a park to promote peace.

Magdalen Islands Que.　　　　　　　9EX
Like Jacques Cartier (who stopped here in
1534), visitors are struck by the lonely beauty
of these islands, the sea-scarred peaks of
mountains now low and remote in the Gulf
of St. Lawrence. Close by magnificent sand
beaches is sandstone so red that it once was
used for making paint. It has been weirdly
sculpted by sea and grinding ice into cliffs,
chasms, pillars and ledges.

There are about a dozen islands. The 13,500
Madelinots are mainly French speaking, descendants of Acadians who fled their Nova
Scotia homes and British authority to settle
here in 1765. They do some farming on the
grassy hills, but most are fishermen, living by
the rhythm of the sea and selling their catch
through cooperatives. Ports and settlements
dot the 60-mile length of the chain. Many
have canneries, smokehouses and freezing
plants. Fish wells keep lobster alive for fresh
shipment. In spring, seals gather on ice floes
a few miles offshore.

The islands are on bird migration flight
paths and have spectacular colonies of herons, cormorants, terns, gulls, gannets, puffins, murres and kittiwakes. "The birds sit
there as thicke as stones lie on a paved street,"
wrote Charles Leigh, an English explorer, in
1597.

Cap-aux-Meules, commercial center of the Magdalen Islands, is linked by ferry with Souris, P.E.I.
The Magdalens are known for fine beaches and
soft red sandstone cliffs.

Magog Que.   7FY/20AZ

Near this resort town at the north end of 30-mile Lake Memphremagog is Mount Orford, at 2,795 feet one of the highest peaks in the Eastern Townships. Mount Orford Provincial Park is a ski center and the home of an annual summer festival of classical music.

The Eastern Townships are the 11 counties that lie between the St. Lawrence lowlands and Quebec's border with Vermont, New Hampshire and Maine. The scenic lakes, rivers, hills and mountains of the 7,500-square-mile region make it a prime year-round resort area. Its ski hills rival those

Jeunesses Musicales du Canada maintains an arts center in Mount Orford Park near Magog. Young musicians practise at huts scattered through the woods.

La Marjolaine, a summer theater 10 miles south at Eastman, features musical comedies in French.

Mahone Bay N.S.   9DZ/22DW

Three old churches stand in a row beside the bay here: St. James' Anglican Church, a sand-colored edifice completed in 1833, and two white structures, St. John's Lutheran (c.1869) and Trinity United (1862). All are frame.

Maitland N.S.   9EY/23BY

The home of W.D. Lawrence, builder of the largest wooden ship ever launched in Canada, is a fine example of the great houses of Nova Scotian shipbuilders and sea captains. Built around 1870, the 2½-story wooden house has a portico reminiscent of a ship's bridge, with double curved stairways leading to the entrance hall. Operated by the Nova Scotia Museum, the house contains most of its original Victorian furniture, tinware and crockery and there are shipbuilding artifacts and pictures of 19th-century ships.

Lawrence's ship, *W.D. Lawrence,* was a 262-foot, 2,459-ton, three-masted vessel launched in 1874. She was later converted into a barge but her ultimate end is not known. A seven-foot half model is in the museum.

In a nearby park is Hayes Cave, containing

of the Laurentians. In Lakes Memphremagog and Massawippi anglers fish for the famous ouananiche (landlocked salmon). The townships were settled first by Loyalists after the American Revolution, then by British immigrants. Now most of the population is French Canadian.

stalactite, stalagmite, dripstone and flowstone formations.

Maitland Ont. 7EY/18DY

At the Blue Church, a wooden building erected in 1845 on the site of two previous chapels, are the graves of many of Ontario's earliest settlers, including Barbara Heck, the founder of Methodism in North America. Born in Ireland, she emigrated to New York in 1760; there she founded a Methodist society and the continent's first Wesleyan church. She came here after the American Revolution, formed Upper Canada's first Methodist society and lived here until her death.

□ A stone house built in 1800 by Dr. Solomon Jones, one of Upper Canada's earliest physicians and a member of the colonial legislature, is two miles east of here.

Barbara Heck, says her gravestone at Maitland, Ont., "put her brave soul against the rugged possibilities of the future and under God brought into existence American and Canadian Methodism."

Malartic Que. 7DW

A museum in this northwestern Quebec gold-mining town has a simulated gold mine on its first floor. Tunnels, shafts and crossbeams are filled with mining equipment. Specimens of gold, asbestos, molybdenite and quartz are displayed on other floors.

Malpeque P.E.I. 9EX/23BW

Strange "clotheslines" seen in Malpeque Bay are nurseries for the famous Malpeque oysters (see Bideford). Young oysters (spat) attach themselves to collectors suspended from wires strung on crossed stakes. The oysters are then transplanted to tidal rivers or bays until they are large enough to harvest.

A tower in Cabot Provincial Park gives a view of Malpeque Harbour. A monument in the park commemorates the barque *Annabella,* wrecked here in 1770 after a voyage from Scotland. Sixty families lost their possessions but found shelter in French homes.

Manitou Beach Sask. 4DX

Little Manitou Lake bordering Manitou Regional Park is famous for its unusual buoyancy. Salt has accumulated for thousands of years in the 12-mile-long lake, which has no outlet and no inflowing streams.

Manitoulin Island Ont. 7BX

Indian influence continues strong on this largest of the world's freshwater islands, once thought to be the home of both the good spirit Gitchi-Manitou and his evil adversary Matchi-Manitou. At many places on the island, 100 miles long by as much as 40 miles wide, Indians make and sell handicrafts close to sites where archaeologists have discovered evidence of human habitation 12,000 years ago. Nearly half of the island's 4,200 Indians (who are some 40 percent of the population) live on land never ceded to the government. These 180 square miles are the largest unceded Indian settlement in North America.

Manitoulin has nearly 1,000 miles of picturesque coastline, most of it facing the open water of Lake Huron and Georgian Bay, the rest along the North Channel that separates the island from the mainland. There are many fine sand beaches and Manitoulin waters are a favorite of sailors. Lake Manitou offers excellent trout fishing, and a one-week bow-and-arrow season for deer complements a one-week gun season.

Manitoulin's towns are Gore Bay and Little Current. Smaller communities include Honora, Manitowaning, Meldrum Bay, Sheguiandah, South Baymouth and Wikwemikong.

GORE BAY The Western Manitoulin Historical Museum is in a former courthouse and jail. Some cells, bars and jail furniture remain. There are relics from an ancient Sheguiandah Indian settlement, old coins and pioneer articles and a collection from a wreck believed that of La Salle's *Griffon,* the first ship to sail the upper Great Lakes. She was lost in a storm in Mississagi Strait at the west end of the island in 1679.

HONORA The Cup and Saucer Lookout, about 500 feet above the surrounding terrain and the highest point on the island, offers a 25-mile view in all directions. It is named for its resemblance, when seen from a distance, to a cup and saucer.

LITTLE CURRENT A plaque at the R.H. Ripley house tells of an attempt to establish a Hudson's Bay Company post here in 1856. It was abandoned due to opposition from Indians and missionaries. Part of the stone base of the Ripley house, built on the site of the post, came from the original fort. Near Little Current are the remains of a Jesuit mission operated in 1648-50 by the Rev. Joseph Poncet, the first known European resident of the island. A September cattle auction here is one of the continent's largest.

MANITOWANING The Assiginack Museum, in a 19th-century stone jail, details the life of Indians and European settlers in the region. It displays early household and agricultural items and a beaded wampum belt worn by Chief Assiginack, an Ottawa Indian who sided with the British during the War of 1812. St. Paul's Anglican Church, a white wooden church completed by Indians in 1849, is the oldest church on Manitoulin.

MELDRUM BAY The Net Shed Museum: tools used by pioneer lumbermen, farmers and fishermen, household furnishings, utensils and costumes.

SHEGUIANDAH The Little Current-Howland Centennial Museum: settlers' furnishings, clothes and records.

SOUTH BAYMOUTH The Little Red Schoolhouse Museum, an original school building, contains early school books, churns, ox yokes, quilts and handwoven rugs.

WIKWEMIKONG Eighteen tribes from six North American Indian nations attend a powwow here each August.

Names and cowboys (and frustration: *just IX more days*) were carved long ago on a jail wall at Gore Bay on Manitoulin Island. The lockup now is part of a museum. A lighthouse at South Baymouth is typical of beacons that dot the island's 1,000-mile coast.

Manitowaning Ont. *see* Manitoulin Island

Maniwaki Que.   7EX
Lumberjack chain saw and axe competitions, a handicrafts exhibition and hockey matches feature a carnival here in January.

Manor Sask.   4FZ
A clutch of buildings eight miles north is the ghost of a colony of English aristocrats who transplanted themselves to the prairie in the late 19th century. At Cannington Manor, established in 1882, English country life was lived to the full, with a hunt club, horse racing, cricket, tennis and billiards. The settle-

ment declined after 1900 when the railway was routed 10 miles south at the present village of Manor.

All Saints, the original Anglican church, has been restored. Constructed of logs, in the shape of a cross, and later sided with timber, it contains pews made with birch from Moose Mountain and silver donated by English relatives of the colonists.

The three-story wooden Hewlett house, once the home of James Humphrys, who designed most Cannington Manor buildings, may be visited. It contains a scale model of the settlement in its heyday, and relics of the period. These include watercolor sketches of the area dating from 1870, and a 1900 billiard table. The sites of demolished buildings are marked by upright plaques.

Near Parkman, 10 miles east of Cannington Manor, is the derelict 26-room stone Beckton Mansion, once the center of many of the settlement's sporting activities.

Manotick Ont.   7EY/18DX
Watson's Mill, a three-story stone gristmill on the Rideau River, dates from 1860. It has been restored and is part of the Dickinson Square Conservation Area.

Maple Ont.   7CY/17CX
The Canada Synod of the Lutheran Church was founded in 1861 at Zion Evangelical Lutheran Church two miles south.

Maple Creek Sask.   4CZ
The Old Timers' Museum collection includes arrowheads, guns, a Red River cart and a hand-operated fire engine (c.1888).
□ When "A" Division of the NWMP was moved here in 1882 (from Fort Walsh—*see* Cypress Hills), a fort was built with salvaged material hauled in wagons along the 35-mile Fort Walsh-Maple Creek Trail. Many NWMP men lie in a police cemetery here. One grave is that of Louis Lavallie, a famous scout and interpreter.
□ In Frontier Village, three miles south, are buildings moved to the site from the surrounding countryside: a frame school (1915), a log church (1894), a ranch office building (c.1900) and a log house (c.1890).

Margaree Forks N.S.   9FX/23FW
The Forks, Thornbush, Hut and Long pools here are among Canada's best salmon grounds. The Salmon Museum at Northeast Margaree contains anglers' and poachers' rods, spears, jig hooks and flambeaux. There is a trout and salmon aquarium.

Maria Que.   9CW
On a Micmac reserve here is a church in the shape of a tepee 65 feet in diameter and 75 feet high. Built with aluminum tiling, the church has a wood-paneled interior.

Markham Ont.   7CY/17CX
A two-story red brick building with a bell tower, built in 1907 as Mount Joy School, is

now Markham Township Museum. Among its exhibits are wooden rakes and shovels dating from 1820, 1850 police handcuffs, early photographs, early 19th-century fat lamps and handmade tools.

Marten River Ont.   7CW
The Northern Ontario Trapper's Museum has a trapper's cabin, a trading post, a miniature trapline, a beaver house and a collection of trapping gear.

Lazy Susan table is in the Old Timers' Museum in Maple Creek.

Huge Sitka spruce, its lower branches thick with mosses, is typical of dense forest growth near Masset. The bluish bush is huckleberry.

Maskinongé Que.   7FX/19CW
The high altar in Saint-Joseph Church was sculpted in wood by Jean Baillargé about 1790. The church for which it was made (1783) was demolished and the present one built in 1892.

Masset B.C.
The rugged mountains and lush forests of the Queen Charlotte Islands are often obscured by low cloud and drizzle, heightening the mystery of a land long haunted by Haida legends.

The Queen Charlotte group of 150 islands is about 180 miles long and 60 miles across at its widest. It is at the brink of the continental shelf. On the west, mountains slope steeply into the sea and level out only near the ocean floor at 10,000 feet. But the bottom of Hecate Strait, which separates the islands from the mainland, is part of the continental shelf and only 50-300 feet down.

The Queen Charlottes were once the exclusive domain of the Haida, the elite of coast Indians, who still represent some 40 percent of the 3,400 population. Haida craftsmen are noted for their carvings in wood and argilite (a black, hardened mud stone). Many old totems are rotting in the rain forests; new ones are sometimes erected, particularly in the Indian village of Haida, near Masset. At the Delkatlah Wildlife Sanctuary in Masset are Canada geese, ducks and swans. Masset, on the north end of Graham Island, is connected by road with Queen Charlotte (known locally as Queen Charlotte City), 70 miles away on Skidegate Inlet. The islands are reached by air and ferry from Vancouver and Prince Rupert. Rivers and lakes in the Queen Charlottes teem with trout (including steelheads) and coho salmon. The sea yields salmon, halibut, octopus, cod and crab. Deer, black bear and elk are common and bald eagles are plentiful.

Massey Ont.　　　　　　　　　　7BW
A scale model of Fort Lacloche, a trading post that stood eight miles southwest of here from 1790 to 1890, is in the Massey Pioneer Museum. There are samples of basketry, quillwork and art from the nearby Spanish River Indian Reserve. Dioramas show lumberjacks at work and the interior of a lumber camp bunkhouse.

Matane Que.　　　　　　　9CW/10GZ
Salmon migrate up a channel through the heart of the city on their way to Matane River spawning grounds. Fishing boats out of Matane harvest cod, halibut and shrimp from the St. Lawrence River.
　□ The Gaspésian Shrimp Festival in late June and early July features exhibitions of native arts and crafts.
　□ Matane Provincial Park in the Shickshock Mountains is a 417-square-mile area covered with black spruce, balsam fir, white birch and occasional maple trees. Mount Logan (3,725 feet) is the highest peak in the park. Caribou, deer and black bear roam and at l'Etang à la Truite there is a large concentration of moose.
　□ There are covered bridges at Saint-René (170 feet) and Saint-Jérôme-de-Matane and Saint-Luc (both 145 feet).

Matheson Ont.　　　　　　7CV/8HZ
A plaque three-quarters of a mile south of Matheson describes "The Great Fire of 1916" that destroyed 500,000 acres of forest and the settlements of Porquis Junction, Iroquois Falls, Kelso, Nushla, Ramore and Matheson. The fire claimed 223 lives.

Mattawa Ont.　　　　　　　　7CX
A cairn at Explorers' Point commemorates the canoe route from Montreal to the Great Lakes (*see* French River). Ontario Hydro's

275,100-horsepower Otto Holden Generating Station is five miles north of Mattawa on the Ottawa River.

Meadow Lake Sask.　　　　　　4CW
A marker and a bronze map at Steele Narrows, 45 miles west of here, commemorate the final battle of the Northwest Rebellion and the last military engagement on Canadian soil. A few dozen scouts led by Maj. Sam Steele of the North West Mounted Police (*see* p.130) fought Big Bear's Cree Indian band there June 3, 1885, withdrew because of a shortage of ammunition and food, and returned two days later to find the Indians had fled. Big Bear soon set his white captives free and surrendered.

Meaford Ont.　　　　　　7BY/17AV
Beautiful Joe, the dog hero of Margaret Marshall Saunders' classic story, is buried in Beautiful Joe Park here. A plaque at the head of the grave tells how the author gained inspiration for *Beautiful Joe* during a visit to Meaford about 1892.
　□ An elaborately carved oak chair at the Meaford Museum was used by Senator Thomas Simpson Sproule when he was speaker of the House of Commons. On his retirement in 1917, after 39 years as an MP, the chair was presented to him according to the custom of the day.

Medicine Hat Alta.　　　　　　4BZ
The three-day Medicine Hat Exhibition and Stampede in July is a major annual event in this city "with all hell for a basement." (Rudyard Kipling so described Medicine Hat on a visit in 1907, because of the immense deposits of natural gas under the city.)
　□ Skeletons of saber-toothed tigers, camels, horses and bison have been unearthed at two nearby sites along the South Saskatchewan River. One is believed 9,000 years old. Arrowheads, pottery, skin scrapers and stone tepee rings have also been found.
　□ The Medicine Hat District Centennial Historical Museum displays dinosaur bones and remains found within a 35-mile radius of Medicine Hat.
　□ Visitors to Medicine Hat watch crafts-

Maxville Ont.—The Glengarry Highland Games, biggest such gathering in North America, are held here in the heart of Glengarry County, first settled by Scottish pioneers some 200 years ago. This is the part of southeastern Ontario in which Ralph Connor (the Rev. Charles William Gordon) set his novels *The Man from Glengarry* and *Glengarry School Days*. The games, in early August, include the North American Pipe Championships. (7EY/18EX)

Cowboy charioteers whoop it up at the Medicine Hat stampede; some chariots are made from oil drums split in halves. Costumed children march in the stampede's colorful parades.

men sculpt and blow glass ornaments at the Altaglass plant, and tour the 16 greenhouses which supply flowers and vegetables as far east as the Great Lakes. One 10½-acre greenhouse is among Canada's largest.

Meductic N.B.   9CY
A cairn marks the site of a chapel built by Malecite Indians in 1717 (*see* Kingsclear).

Melville Sask.   4FY
A 1919 CNR steam engine is on display at McLeod Regional Park.

Merrickville Ont.   7EY/18DX
The Blockhouse Museum, in the largest of four forts constructed in 1826-32 to defend the Rideau Canal, exhibits military, domestic and agricultural artifacts from the 18th and 19th centuries. Built by Col. John By, who gave his name to Bytown (Ottawa), the blockhouse has 3½-foot-thick walls, roof beams held together by wooden pins, huge pillars of solid tree trunks, and rifle slits in the upstairs walls and firing platform floors.

The house in which Colonel By lived while supervising the canal's construction still stands, as do the 1821 house of William Merrick, the Loyalist who founded the town in 1790, and his three sons' houses, all dating from the 1840s. The Merrick family tavern (1830) and sawmill (1848) are also to be seen.

Merritt B.C.   2DY
Douglas Lake Ranch, one of the largest working ranches in the Commonwealth, is 35 miles northeast. It covers 500,000 acres and has 16,000 head of cattle, 250 cowboy horses and 120 cutting horses (trained to separate a particular animal from the herd).

□ A rodeo in Merritt in September features regular rodeo events and wild-cow milking, boys' steer riding and a cutting horse competition.

Meteghan N.S.   9CZ/22BX
One of the oldest Acadian dwellings, a 1½-story wooden house dating from the 1760s, is still in original condition. La Vieille Maison, now a museum, has white woodwork and a blue door surmounted by the Robicheau family coat of arms. The interior, painted in Acadian white, blue and yellow, contains sea chests, rawhide chairs, spinning wheels, wooden and earthenware cooking utensils, churns, butter molds, ironstone china and examples of Acadian crafts.

□ The bishop of Yarmouth blesses the fishing fleet here in early June, in the only such ceremony in Nova Scotia (*see* Caraquet).

Métis-sur-Mer Que.   9CW
The village, one of the most popular summer resorts on the lower St. Lawrence, has four miles of beach. Métis Park at nearby Grand-Métis specializes in alpine flowers and plants.

Mica Creek B.C.   2EX
The world's second highest earth-fill dam is six miles north. Mica Dam, 640 feet high, is the biggest of British Columbia's three Columbia Treaty dams and forms a reservoir 135 miles long. It was completed in 1973.

Middleport Ont.   17BZ
Chiefswood, an early Ontario classic-style house on the Six Nations Reserve, is the restored birthplace of E. Pauline Johnson, whose poems in English won international recognition and established her as a spokeswoman for her people.

The house was built in 1853 by her father, Chief G.H.M. Johnson, a leader of the Six Nations, as a wedding gift for his English bride. One of the few Indian mansions to survive from pre-Confederation days, it has large, high-ceilinged rooms furnished in 1870s

style. Some of Pauline Johnson's possessions are displayed, among them her christening dress, a toy tea set, beads, a writing desk and some of her poetry, written in her hand.

Middleton N.S.   9DY/22CV
Old Holy Trinity Anglican Church, built in 1788 by Loyalist settlers from New England, still has its original straight-backed pews, each with a numbered door. It is no longer in use but may be visited. In new Holy Trinity Church (1893) are objects from the old

church: a Bible and prayer book dating from 1783, a paten and flagon made in 1792 and a bell cast in 1792.

Midland Ont.   7CY/17BV
This is the heart of Huronia where, deep in the 17th-century wilderness, Jesuit missionaries built tiny Sainte-Marie and where five of them suffered savage torture and died the lonely death of martyrs. The palisade and buildings of Sainte-Marie among the Hurons have been reconstructed with painstaking authenticity on the bank of the Wye River, below a hill on which now stands the Martyrs' Shrine.

The Jesuits first came to Huronia, 800 hazardous miles by canoe from Quebec, in 1626. They ministered to the Indians during a period of mounting Iroquois raids that eventually all but destroyed the Huron nation. Among the missionaries were North America's eight martyr saints. Jean de Brébeuf, Charles Garnier, Gabriel Lalemant, Antoine Daniel and Noël Chabanel all died in Huronia. Saints Isaac Jogues, René Goupil and Jean de La Lande were killed in what is now New York State.

Sainte-Marie never fell to the Iroquois. To prevent its capture, the Europeans burned the little settlement in 1649. They and the remnants of the Huron nation went to Christian Island in Georgian Bay. There they founded Sainte-Marie II but, after a long and vicious winter took its toll, the survivors fled to Quebec, leaving Huronia virtually without Hurons.

The achievements of the Jesuits and their helpers and the life-style of the Hurons in the 17th century are seen not only in reconstructed Sainte-Marie and the Martyrs' Shrine but also in a replica of a Huron village and at the Huronia Museum.

Martyrs' Shrine at Midland was built in 1926 close to Sainte-Marie among the Hurons. Near the twin-spired church are a grotto dedicated to Our Lady of Huronia, patroness of Sainte-Marie and the martyred Jesuits, and Stations of the Cross molded in bronze in France.

Hardy Blueberries Thrive Where Soil Is Poor

Canada's most valuable native fruit, the blueberry, produces a multimillion-dollar cash crop. Low-growing species thrive in Quebec, northern Ontario and the Atlantic provinces—in acid soil with a high proportion of sand. Much of this heathland, suitable for few other crops, is Crown land, but blueberries are increasingly being privately cultivated in areas such as Mistassini, the blueberry capital of Quebec, where a blueberry festival is held each August. About one quarter of the nearly 30,000,000 pounds harvested annually in Canada comes from Quebec, where the harvest makes a major contribution to farm incomes. The highbush blueberry, which produces fruits a half inch in diameter but does not survive severe winters, is cultivated in the Fraser Delta of British Columbia and in western Nova Scotia. Blueberries are used in wine, syrup, pies and fresh-fruit desserts.

In Saint-Georges-de-Mingan Chapel, built in 1917-18, is a tabernacle of wood crafted in tepee form by Montagnais Indians and their parish priest.

Minnedosa Man.   6AY
An old-fashioned place with an artificial lake and sandy beaches, Minnedosa has several times been chosen as Manitoba's most beautiful town. The Minnedosa and District Pioneer Home Museum displays artifacts of pioneer life.

Mirabel Que.   19AX
The world's largest airport, Mirabel International, opened in 1975. With facilities spread over 138 square miles west of Montreal, it is designed to serve up to 10 million passengers a year eventually.

Miscouche P.E.I.   9DX/23BW
Wood from dikes built at Grand Pré, N.S., about 1700 and a brick from Jean-Pierre de Roma's 18th-century settlement at Brudenell Point, P.E.I. (*see* Georgetown) are exhibited in the Acadian Museum.

Mission City B.C.   2CZ/12FX
The 168-foot Pfitzer Tower is the dramatic centerpiece of Westminster Abbey, a Benedictine monastery that is a Fraser Valley landmark. The abbey and the adjoining Seminary of Christ the King are on Mount Mary Ann, overlooking the Fraser River.

Two miles of winding (almost zigzag) ditch parallel Weaver Creek here, forming a spawning channel for salmon and other fish and protecting them from flash floods.

Mission Raceways, a quarter-mile drag course, and Derby Downs, site of the Western Canada Soap Box Derby championships, are here. The soapbox derby, run on the July 1

weekend on a quarter-mile, three-lane paved track, attracts more than 60 racers.

Mississauga Ont.   17CY
The Lewis Bradley Pioneer Museum is a restored clapboard farmhouse that was the home of a United Empire Loyalist family who settled here in 1811. The house dates from the 1830s.

Mistassini Que.   9AV/21AV
A monastery built in 1892, when Mistassini was a wilderness, is the center of a huge Trappist farm along the Mistassibi River opposite this town. The monastery has been an abbey since 1935.

Minton Sask.—A giant turtle effigy built of stones on the prairie eight miles west of here, near Big Muddy Lake, may be several centuries old. It is 135 feet from nose to tail. The purpose of "Chief Turtle" is unknown but turtles were sacred to the Saulteaux Indians and symbols of bravery to many tribes because turtles do not often turn from danger. (4EZ)

Monastery N.S. 9EY/23EY

The first Trappist monastery in North America was founded here in 1825 and gave the village its name. The massive group of buildings, most of red brick and some dating from 1892, have since 1938 been St. Augustine's Monastery, the Augustinian order's first in Canada. A dramatic altar backdrop in the modern (1960) chapel tells in oils and stained glass the story of Saint Augustine and saints of the order named after him. Outside, Stations of the Cross lead to the Shrine of Our Lady of Grace and an eight-foot cedar cross with a carved wooden figure of Christ.

Moncton's historic Free Meeting House was built in 1821 and served 11 denominations of Christians and the Hebrew congregation between then and 1963.

Les Hommes d'Action, a seven-foot limestone sculpture by Claude Roussel, and *La Dispersion des Acadiens,* an oil painting by Henri Beau, are in the Université de Moncton collection.

Moncton N.B. 9DY/23AX

This city is the transportation hub of the Maritimes and the biggest rail center east of Montreal. A third of its population is French speaking and it has the only French-language university east of Quebec City.

Among Moncton's parks is Bore View, named after the tidal bore, a small wall of water forced up the Petitcodiac River twice daily by Fundy's tides. It reaches a height of two feet in early spring and fall.

CENTENNIAL PARK (1) Near Jones Lake in the center of the city, the 390-acre park has picnic sites, swimming, tennis, nature trails and playgrounds. Among displays are a 1918 steam locomotive, a Sherman tank and a CF-100 jet aircraft.

CN HUMP YARD (2) Canada's first electronic railcar classification yard may be toured.

FREE MEETING HOUSE (3) The oldest complete building in Moncton, this plain wooden one-story house of worship has no steeple, bell or cornerstone; 56 gravestones dating from 1816 to 1876 are in an adjoining burial ground.

MAGNETIC HILL (4) An optical illusion apparently explains why vehicles seem to roll uphill on a gravel road five miles north of Moncton. A car is driven to the "bottom" of the hill. There the motor is stopped, the gears put in neutral, the brakes released. The car moves backward, coasting "up" the hill. The illusion is so powerful that it is difficult not to believe the car is being pulled by some magnetic force. Opposite the hill is a game farm with animals native to New Brunswick.

MONCTON CIVIC MUSEUM (5) This two-story, white concrete museum, incorporating the neo-classical columns of the old city hall (1916), displays Moncton's past from Micmac Indian days to the present. Exhibits include scale models of ships and trains.

MONCTON COLISEUM (6) The 7,000-seat coli-

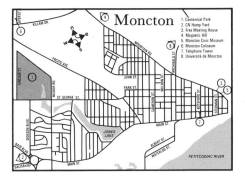

Moncton
1. Centennial Park
2. CN Hump Yard
3. Free Meeting House
4. Magnetic Hill
5. Moncton Civic Museum
6. Moncton Coliseum
7. Telephone Tower
8. Université de Moncton

seum offers sports events and other functions.

TELEPHONE TOWER (7) The 350-foot concrete communications tower was built in 16 record-breaking days of continuous pouring.

UNIVERSITE DE MONCTON (8) The modern campus houses the Centre d'Etudes Acadiennes with its collection of documents, microfilm and maps relating to the history of Acadia. The center's Musée Acadien has looms and spinning wheels, a smithy, paintings, a 1614 French organ and the broken metal key of St. Charles Church in Grand Pré (*see entry*).

The university's Centre de l'éducation physique et des sports is one of the most modern and widely used athletic complexes in Canada.

Montague P.E.I.   9EX/23DX

Among relics of early Prince Edward Island at the Garden of the Gulf Museum are a 1698 Bible, clocks with wooden works and letters written by Lucy Maud Montgomery, author of *Anne of Green Gables*.

□ Four miles south, a small herd of buffalo graze in a 100-acre park.

Montebello Que.—The stone baronial mansion of Louis-Joseph Papineau, leader of the 1837 rebellion in Lower Canada, is on the grounds of the Château Montebello (formerly the famous Seigniory Club). The Papineau house, which dates from 1850, now serves as a clubhouse. (7EX/18EW) (*See* Papineauville)

Mont-Laurier Que.   7EX

La Vérendrye Park, whose southern entrance is 33 miles northwest, is Quebec's largest fishing and game reserve. The 5,257-square-mile park, named after the discoverer of the Rocky Mountains, contains more than 120 species of birds and some 50 of mammals, including moose, bear and deer. Its more than 4,000 lakes teem with northern and walleyed pike and speckled, gray and red trout. A scenic paved highway winds for 110 miles through the park.

□ Two-man canoes are raced between here and Ferme-Neuve, 12 miles up the Lièvre River, during a weekend in late August. The races attract as many as 15,000 persons.

□ A monastery of local pink granite was built in 1952 in traditional French-Canadian style with a round tower and a long row of dormer windows. The nuns (Bénédictines du Précieux-Sang) have a small farm and sell chocolate, caramel, cottage cheese and a goat's milk concentrate they call *vie nouvelle* (new life).

Montmagny Que.   9AX/20CW

A seven-foot granite statue on an eight-foot granite plinth honors Sir Etienne-Paschal Taché, prime minister of the Province of Canada in 1856-57 and 1864-65 and a Father of Confederation. He was born and practised medicine here. The statue was carved by Jean-Julien Bourgault in the style of the miniature wooden figurines done by his Saint-Jean-Port-Joli family.

The two-story wooden Taché house may be visited, as may the restored two-story wooden Manoir Couillard-Dupuis, which has a large stone bread oven (1800) and now serves as a tourist bureau.

The ground floor of a 1634 communal mill, operated by wind or water, is now a museum displaying mill components.

Montmorency Que.   20BW

A spectacular 274-foot cataract named by Champlain, Montmorency Falls is 100 feet higher than Niagara. Spray from the falls in winter builds a cone of ice called the sugarloaf. It is often 60-70 feet high.

Montreal Que.   7FY/19BY/P.229

Close to half the population of Quebec lives in Greater Montreal: two million people on a 32-mile-long island in the St. Lawrence and more than 800,000 in adjacent areas. Montreal is the world's second largest French-speaking city (after Paris) but is known above all for its diversity. One Montrealer in three is non-French and the resulting mélange of Gallic and Anglo-Saxon cultures, the traditions of numerous ethnic groups and the dynamics of North American get-up-and-go contribute to a cosmopolitan atmosphere and a celebrated *joie de vivre*.

□ When Jacques Cartier reached the site in 1535 he found the Indian village of Hochelaga. He named the island's mountain Monreale, after an Italian cardinal; it later

Montreal: sidewalk cafés, brick walls splashed with color, the Olympic Stadium . . . a skyline with a mountain of volcanic origin for a backdrop . . . a haggle of housewives on market day . . . art galleries that are Métro stations . . . bars for all seasons . . . the umbrellas of Place Ville Marie at noontime . . . and, on the grass of wooded Mount Royal, an escape from the big-city din mere minutes below.

became Mount Royal. Hochelaga's estimated population of 3,500 had disappeared by 1611 when Champlain established a trading post on the island. In 1642 de Maisonneuve founded a missionary center which he named Ville-Marie de Montréal. The tiny fortified settlement survived a half-century of Iroquois attacks and became the capital of the fur trade in the 1700s. The settlement fell to a besieging British army in 1760 and 15 years later succumbed again during the American Revolution, this time to the Continental Army. It was held by the Americans for seven months. From 1844 to 1849 Montreal was the capital of Canada.

□ Montreal's international image has soared along with its skyscrapers, Expo 67 and the 1976 Olympic Games. The Canadian Imperial Bank of Commerce Building, Place Ville Marie, Place Victoria, CIL House, the Banque Canadienne Nationale building and Place Desjardins now dwarf the city below. Montreal responded to Expo 67 and the Olympics with triumphant spectacles: new hotels, increased convention and recreation facilities and the ultramodern Métro, a subway with rubber-tired trains and distinctively decorated stations. Orchestras, and singing, dancing and theater groups flourish.

Even as the city grew higher a new world was created underground. Networks of tunnels and subterranean passageways cover some 200 acres. In winter Montrealers seem to hibernate in this underground, retreating from an annual snowfall of more than eight feet. Here they have access to office towers, almost 1,000 shops and boutiques, over a dozen theaters, countless restaurants and bars, hotels and the Métro. One can travel along spacious promenades from Place Ville Marie to Central Station, below the Queen Elizabeth Hotel, and on to Place Bonaventure, several blocks away, without emerging to the surface. Similar shopping areas exist in Place du Canada, Place Victoria, the Alexis Nihon Plaza and Place Desjardins. Even a downtown extension of the Trans-Canada Highway is underground.

Montreal is a transportation hub. Its port, at the head of the St. Lawrence Seaway, is eastern Canada's largest. The harbor, with 134 berths and 52 transit sheds, handles about 3,500 commercial ships a year. Thirty-four miles to the west is ultramodern Mirabel International Airport (see Mirabel). The city is the headquarters of the International Air Transport Association, the International Civil Aviation Organization and Air Canada. The head offices of two of the world's largest railway systems, Canadian National and CP Rail, are here.

Orchestras, singers, ballet and theater troupes perform at the three magnificent halls of Place des Arts. La Poudrière, formerly the powder magazine of a fort on St. Helen's Island, presents works in French and English and occasionally in German and Spanish. Productions are staged in French and English at the Saidye Bronfman Center, Théâtre du

Nouveau Monde, Théâtre du Rideau Vert and an open-air theater in Lafontaine Park.

AUBERGE LE VIEUX SAINT-GABRIEL (1) Part of a two-story dwelling built in 1688 by Etienne Truteau still stands in this quaint restaurant in Old Montreal. The original inn opened beside the house in 1754 and was one of Canada's oldest. A copy of its first liquor permit, issued in 1769 by George III, hangs in the restaurant.

BANK OF MONTREAL MUSEUM (2) It has collections of coins, bills, banking documents and maps of Montreal and a model of Canada's first bank (1817). The museum is in a new edifice beside the bank's main office, an elegant domed building with a classic portico of Corinthian pillars. It dates from 1848.

BONSECOURS MARKET (3) It housed the Parliament of Canada in 1849-52 and was the city hall until 1878, when it was converted to a market. It now contains the city's Housing Department.

CARTIER HOUSE (4) A three-story stone house (1840), once the residence of Sir George Etienne Cartier, a Father of Confederation.

CHATEAU DE RAMEZAY (5) This fine stone house, built in 1705 for Claude de Ramezay, governor of Montréal, was the government seat of French Canada until de Ramezay's death in 1724. It was later used by the East India Company as a fur storehouse. English governors resided here from 1763 until 1775, when it became the headquarters of the American Continental Army during its occupation of Montréal. The château was a courthouse and a university before becoming a museum in 1895.

CHRIST CHURCH CATHEDRAL (6) This Anglican cathedral, an example of pure Gothic, was built in 1859 of gray limestone trimmed with Caen stone. It has a 221-foot spire.

CITE DU HAVRE (7) Here are the International Broadcast Center, the Museum of Contemporary Art, Habitat, Olympic House, and Expo Theater. At the broadcast center visitors watch the taping of CBC television programs. The museum stresses Quebec art since 1940. It includes works by Paul-Emile Borduas, founder of painting's automatiste school, and by Alfred Pellan and Jean-Paul Riopelle. There are displays of sculpture, graphics, photography and audiovisual presentations. Habitat, a 158-dwelling edifice designed by Moshe Safdie, was built in 1967 in a modular architectural style, with self-contained, podlike units forming the whole structure. A museum at Olympic House, the office of the Canadian Olympic Association, has photos, medals and trophies of Canadian athletes. The Expo Theater produces plays in English and French.

CITY HALL (8) The massive, five-story building, completed in 1926, resembles the hôtel de ville in Paris. The ornate example of French Renaissance architecture is surmounted by mansards and a tower. A statue sculpted by Eugène Bénet honors Jean Vauquelin, naval defender of Quebec in 1759.

CONCORDIA UNIVERSITY (9) Formed in 1973 by the merger of Sir George Williams University and Loyola College.

CONGREGATION OF NOTRE-DAME (10) In the Marguerite Bourgeoys Center at this motherhouse are some of the writings of the order's founder and her portrait painted by Pierre Le Ber hours after her death in 1700. A nearby room has a marble chest with her remains.

DOMINION GALLERY (11) Two life-size statues, Henry Moore's *Upright Motive No. 5* and Auguste Rodin's *Jean d'Aire* (one of his six *Burghers of Calais*), stand outside the city's largest private commercial gallery. Inside are more than 400 sculptures and paintings by about 200 Canadians.

DOMINION SQUARE (12) Monuments to Sir Wilfrid Laurier and Sir John A. Macdonald, to Canadian soldiers who died in three wars, and to Queen Victoria and Robert Burns, the Scottish poet.

DOW PLANETARIUM (13) The aluminum dome serves as a screen on which photographs of planets, galaxies, nebulas and about 9,000 stars are projected. Special effects such as meteor showers, comets, clouds, thunderstorms, rainbows and the northern lights can be created.

GRAND SEMINAIRE DE MONTREAL (14) Two stone towers remain from a fort built by the Sulpician fathers in 1694.

HOTEL-DIEU HOSPITAL (15) The archives of this hospital, which has operated continuously on various sites since 1644, contain a bell that was used not only as a call to prayer but also as a warning of Iroquois attack. Several pieces of glazed French earthenware include an inkwell once owned by Jeanne Mance, the hospital founder. A 4½-foot wooden statue of the Virgin and Child was sculpted in 1755 by Paul Jourdain *dit* Labrosse. The Sisters of St. Joseph, the order founded by Jeanne Mance, have a hospital account book from 1696-1756, a list of soldiers treated in 1756-60 and a map dating from 1589.

HURTUBISE HOUSE (16) This gray fieldstone house (1688) now contains two restaurants.

LACHINE HISTORICAL MUSEUM (17) This fieldstone manor is one of Canada's oldest buildings and still has foundations from the original, built about 1670 by Charles Le Moyne (*see* Longueuil). The museum contains a 20-foot model of the *Dorchester* (1836), the first locomotive in Canada, which ran between La Prairie and Saint-Jean.

□ Plaques in Lachine record the massacre of Aug. 4-5, 1689, when Iroquois raiders killed some 200 settlers. Many stone buildings date from the early 1800s and a monument across from city hall honors René-Robert Cavelier de La Salle, who founded Lachine in 1667.

LAFONTAINE PARK (18) The Garden of Wonders children's zoo has more than 550 small animals and birds set in fairy-tale scenes.

De Maisonneuve in Place d'Armes: A pale winter sun highlights Philippe Hébert's statue of the founder of Montreal, seen through the branches of trees across the square.

The 80-acre park has two artificial lagoons (boating in summer, skating in winter) and an open-air theater for puppet shows, folk dancing, concerts and plays.

LE MOYNE HOUSE (19) A plaque marks the site of the Le Moyne house, birthplace of Pierre Le Moyne (*see* Longueuil).

MAIN POST OFFICE (20) A tablet commemorates the establishment, in 1763, of the first organized postal service in Canada.

MAISON DE RADIO-CANADA (21) This CBC radio and television complex has a 23-story tower. Tours include Studio 42, a huge auditorium used for TV variety shows.

MAISONNEUVE PARK (22) An internationally known botanical garden is organized in individual gardens ranging from miniature deserts to lush tropical forests. There are rock, shrub and aquatic gardens and an arboretum with flowers and trees from many parts of the world. The central conservatory has displays of gardens typical of many countries. The park has tennis courts, the Maurice Richard Arena (hockey, skating, circuses) and the Pierre Charbonneau Center (gymnasium and swimming pool).

MAISON SAINT-GABRIEL (23) Rebuilt in 1698 on the original 1668 foundations, the house is among the oldest continuously occupied dwellings in Quebec. Marguerite Bourgeoys moved her congregation of Notre-Dame (Canada's first religious order) to the house in 1699. The house has its 1668 fireplace, 17th- and 18th-century furniture, birch baskets, limestone sinks, molds for pewter dishes, and utensils for making butter and candles. The altar in the chapel dates from 1722.

MAN AND HIS WORLD (24) Successor to Expo 67, this exhibition has national pavilions and others on such themes as humor, the environment, antique cars and weapons—all amid breezy avenues, pretty flower gardens and sloping lawns. La Ronde has a midway, games of chance, puppet shows, bistros and Carrefour International, a cluster of boutiques.

MARIE-MARGUERITE D'YOUVILLE CENTER (25) Opened in 1959, the year of the beatification of Marie-Marguerite d'Youville, the center has an oratory, furnished rooms and an historical museum. The remains of the founder of the Sisters of Charity lie in the wall behind the oratory altar. The museum has some of her belongings, including books, clothing, a clock and knife and fork.

MARY QUEEN OF THE WORLD BASILICA (26) Modeled after St. Peter's in Rome and covering about one half of the area of the Roman basilica, it is 333 feet long and 150 feet wide. Begun in 1870, the basilica took 16 years to complete. Its dome rises 252 feet above the floor and is 75 feet wide. The high altar, modeled after that of St. Peter's, is of marble, ivory and onyx.

McGILL UNIVERSITY (27) This old university (1821) is one of Canada's largest, respected especially for its schools of medicine and engineering. McGill occupies more than 75 acres in the heart of Montreal. Its McCord Muse-

um has artifacts from the city's fur-trading days, Indian and Eskimo art, costumes and crafts, china, silver, dolls and furniture. The costume gallery has Canadian clothes dating from 1770. The museum has the extensive Notman collection of Canadian photographs, taken between 1856 and 1934. A boulder on the campus marks the site of the Indian village of Hochelaga.

McTAVISH HOUSE (28) The 1786 home of Simon McTavish, a fur merchant who became chief of the North West Company.

MEMORIAL TOWER (29) The 154-foot tower on Victoria Pier is a monument to Canadian sailors who died in the world wars.

METRO (30) The Berri-de Montigny station, with tracks on three levels, is the hub of an 18.5-mile subway which has 37 stations and is the nervous system of Montreal's "Underground City." A network of passageways, nearly seven miles long in the downtown area alone, connects the stations with major hotels, shopping centers, banks, theaters, parking areas, two railway stations, restaurants, office buildings, the main intercity bus terminal and the Olympic Park.

MOLSON BREWERY (31) Tours may be taken through the oldest brewery in continuous operation in Canada. It was founded in 1786. The reception room has a gun collection spanning the 16th, 17th and 18th centuries.

MONTREAL MUSEUM OF FINE ARTS (32) The oldest and one of the finest art museums in Canada has 30,000 objects and 2,500 paintings ranging from the Dutch and English masters to contemporary art. Among its most valuable pieces are a 16th-century sculpture of Saint Sebastian by the Gothic German master Tilmann Riemenschneider, Henry Moore's sculpture *Reclining Figure: Internal and External Forms* and Pablo Picasso's oil *La Lampe et les Cerises*. There are European tapestries, Oriental art objects, an unusual collection of ancient Roman and Syrian glassworks, a 5,000-year-old Chinese vase and an Egyptian figure from 2500 B.C. in addition to displays of Eskimo art and culture, Indian handicrafts and early Canadian wood carving and furniture. The white marble museum was built in 1912 in Greek neo-classic style, with four Ionic columns as part of the imposing portico. A recent major renovation added a contemporary annex. There now are 32 galleries, sculpture courts, an auditorium, reference library and a café with summer terrace.

MOUNT ROYAL PARK (33) Wooded slopes, gently undulating lawns and man-made Beaver Lake help make this 530-acre park a favorite year-round retreat and playground. There are calèche rides through the park and cars are permitted only on one major parkway. The Mount Royal Art Center holds exhibitions in an old stone farmhouse. The mountain is of volcanic rock and rises 762 feet above sea level. It affords an unsurpassed view of the city. In winter the terrace of Beaver Lake Pavilion becomes a skating rink and there are ski trails, toboggan hills and horse-drawn sleighs. The park's 100-foot illu-

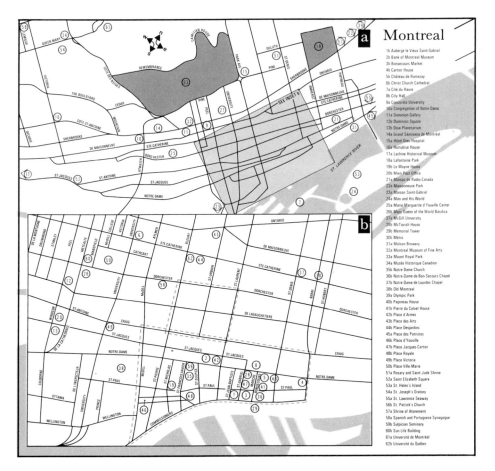

minated cross is a landmark that can be seen for 40 miles. It commemorates a wooden cross planted by de Maisonneuve on the mountain in 1643 after Ville-Marie was spared from a great flood. The park has monuments to Sir George Etienne Cartier and to Simon McTavish.

MUSEE HISTORIQUE CANADIEN (34) The wax museum features a large-scale re-creation of the catacombs of Rome and scenes depicting the torture of Christians, the Roman circus and gladiator combat. Other scenes are from early Canadian history.

NOTRE-DAME CHURCH (35) It accommodates 7,000 worshipers and has one of the world's biggest bells, a 24,780-pound giant called *le gros bourdon*. The church, which resembles Paris' Notre-Dame Cathedral, has 220-foot twin towers completed in 1843, 14 years after the church opened its doors. The exquisite interior was decorated by French-Canadian artists including Ozias Leduc and Victor Bourgeau. Eleven stained-glass windows, nine feet high, depict religious scenes and early Montreal history. Ornate wood and polychromic sculptures include Philippe Hébert's statues of the prophets on the pulpit, a sculpture of the Last Supper on the altar and statues of angels flanking the tabernacle. Notre-Dame Church Museum, located behind the church, has a 39-inch silver Madonna sculpted by

Guillaume Loir and presented by Louis XV.

NOTRE-DAME-DE-BON-SECOURS CHAPEL (36) A 20-foot copper statue of the Virgin Mary faces the harbor from the back of the church, known as the sailors' chapel. The statue, with its crown of stars, has long been a landmark for mariners. A gilded statue of the Virgin, about eight feet high, stands above the main entrance of the church, built in 1773 on the foundations of a 1657 church. Eight model ships hang from the ceiling of the nave. The interior is graced with fine paintings and wall mosaics of Marguerite Bourgeoys, who founded the church in 1657, and of de Maisonneuve. In a basement museum is a collection of dolls in early Montreal settings, depicting the life of Marguerite Bourgeoys, who was beatified in 1950.

NOTRE-DAME-DE-LOURDES CHAPEL (37) The chapel was built in Roman-Byzantine style by the French-Canadian architect, sculptor and painter Napoléon Bourassa. A gilded statue of the Virgin stands atop the stone facade, above a rosette supported by four slender stone columns. The dome, flanked by four cylindrical towers, has small stained glass windows around its base. The rich decor describes biblical themes with elaborate paintings by Bourassa and wooden statues sculpted by Philippe Hébert.

OLD MONTREAL (38) Historic fieldstone dwellings and warehouses hug narrow cobblestone streets in this 95-acre quarter that was the opulent center of the fur trade. Old Montreal was officially declared an historic district in 1963 and a once almost dead area has been nursed back to vibrant life. Scores of buildings have been renovated and occupied. Some have been converted to antique and handicraft shops. Others have become restaurants, museums and art studios. Old Montreal's boundaries are roughly where stood the walls of Montreal in the 1700s.

OLYMPIC PARK (39) When Montreal hosted the 1976 Olympic Games, some 8,500 athletes from 93 countries competed here before 3.2 million spectators and 1.5 billion television viewers awed by the spectacle. This dramatic park was built for the occasion in a welter of construction headaches and ever-inflating costs. Installations included the 60,517-seat Olympic Stadium, a 164- by-82-foot swimming pool, the 7,400-seat Velodrome with a 937-foot wooden bicycle track, and the Olympic Village—four 20-story residential halfpyramids overlooking the whole park. Even so, the Games were so large and varied that

numerous events were staged elsewhere. Today the Village is a commercial housing complex and the park's facilities are used for a wide range of participation and spectator sports. Major league baseball and football are played here by the Expos and the Alouettes. Still missing is a 550-foot tower with a folding roof that will permit the stadium to be used for both indoor and outdoor events. Officials hope to have it in place by the mid-1980s.

PAPINEAU HOUSE (40) Louis-Joseph Papineau, leader of the 1837 rebellion that led to responsible government in a new Canada, was one of seven generations of the Papineau family who lived in this house, built about 1758.

PIERRE DU CALVET HOUSE (41) This was the home of a French Huguenot who served three years in prison for selling supplies to an invading American army in 1775-76. The three-story stone building at 401 Bonsecours Street now is a museum and contains early Canadian furniture, paintings and handicrafts.

PLACE D'ARMES (42) This historic square was the site of the first major skirmish between the Iroquois and the settlers of tiny Ville-Marie. De Maisonneuve, who founded the colo-

Old and new, side by side, lend charm to historic Montreal. Opposite page: Place Jacques Cartier, once a busy marketplace, is a wide boulevard rimmed by restaurants and hotels. At the Rue Notre-Dame end are a monument to Nelson and the French-Renaissance city hall. In the roof of the Sulpician Seminary (1685)—here reflected in the windows of the Banque Canadienne Nationale building—is a clock that dates from 1700, one of the oldest in North America. Dominating the facade of Mary Queen of the World Basilica are 13 bronze statues, the patron saints of parishes that donated to the basilica's construction. The tower of the Maison de Radio-Canada (lower left, opposite) rises not far from the dome of old Bonsecours Market, now housing municipal offices, on cobblestoned Rue Saint-Paul. (In the background is Notre-Dame-de-Bon-Secours, the famous sailors' chapel.) Below: the Royal Bank building, part of Place Ville Marie, is a backdrop for the spire of Christ Church Cathedral. The huge cruciform building is part of the skyline as seen from the fort on St. Helen's Island in the St. Lawrence River. The outside staircases of older parts of Montreal give quick access to upper stories, save space by eliminating inside stairs, and serve as fire escapes. Maison Saint-Gabriel (lower right) is a building almost as old as Montreal itself.

Caen stone reredos behind the altar of Christ Church Cathedral in Montreal was carved by the Warham Guild of London. The figures, from left, represent Saints George, Martin and Lawrence, Christ, Saint John the Baptist and Saints Nicholas and Michael. Below are the Annunciation, the Visit of the Magi, the Baptism of Christ, the Crucifixion, Entombment, Resurrection and Ascension. Below: the enormous apse of the basilica of St. Joseph's Oratory. The 75-foot-high metal grillwork behind the altar was designed by Robert Prévost. Mosaics around the grillwork represent scenes from the life of Saint Joseph.

ny, killed the Indian chief and his men repulsed the invaders. At de Maisonneuve's feet in a monument erected in 1895 are Lambert Closse, de Maisonneuve's lieutenant, and Charles Le Moyne (*see* Longueuil), Jeanne Mance and an unknown Indian. On the south side of the square are Notre-Dame Church and a seminary where Sulpicians have lived since 1685. The Duluth building on the east side has plaques to Daniel Greysolon du Lhut, for whom Duluth in Minnesota is named, and Antoine de la Mothe-Cadillac, founder of Detroit, both of whom were Montreal natives.

PLACE DES ARTS (43) Salle Wilfrid Pelletier, one of three theaters in the seven-acre Place des Arts complex, is one of North America's finest concert halls. It is the home of the Montreal Symphony Orchestra and is used for opera, ballet and folk dancing. None of its 3,000 seats is more than 135 feet from the stage. The other theaters are the 1,300-seat Maisonneuve and the 800-seat Port Royal.

PLACE DESJARDINS (44) Some 15,000 people work in this Montreal's largest commercial complex. Completed in 1975, it has three levels of boutiques, shops, restaurants, towers of 27, 32 and 41 stories with nearly 2 million square feet of office space, and a 616-room hotel.

PLACE DES PATRIOTES (45) A monument honors six men publicly hanged here for their activities in the Rebellion of 1837.

PLACE D'YOUVILLE (46) Youville Stables, a three-story, U-shaped structure built in 1717-44, has been reconstructed to contain boutiques, workshops, a restaurant and offices around an inner court. The building is distinguished by a bull's-eye, the traditional round window of Quebec architecture, under the eaves at each end. Nearby is one of the city's oldest structures, built as a hospital in 1693-94 and later enlarged by Marie-Marguerite d'Youville to accommodate the Sisters of Charity.

PLACE JACQUES-CARTIER (47) A 68½-foot Nelson monument, erected in 1809, is the city's oldest and was the world's first to honor the hero of Trafalgar.

PLACE ROYALE (48) Named by Champlain in 1603 and cleared by him in 1611, this was the first area settled in Montreal. A 40-foot obelisk stands approximately where de Maisonneuve founded Ville-Marie de Montréal in 1642. Place Royale became its first marketplace in 1657.

PLACE VICTORIA (49) A 47-story tower here is one of the Commonwealth's tallest buildings at 624 feet. It contains brokerages and financial offices and the Montreal Stock Exchange. The world's tallest glass sculpture, suspended from the ceiling of the lobby, descends four stories through an elliptical stairway to shopping promenades below. Handblown in Murano, Italy, the colorful sculpture contains 3,000 pieces of cubed and oblong glass and weighs 6,200 pounds.

PLACE VILLE MARIE (50) It groups four large office buildings around a business, commercial and entertainment nucleus. The main structure is the 45-story Royal Bank of Canada complex, the world's largest cruciform building, with some 1,000 offices. The Greenshields, Esso and IBM buildings are also part of the complex.

ROSARY AND SAINT JUDE SHRINE (51) A magnificent 36-foot stained-glass window depicting the Trinity.

SAINT ELIZABETH SQUARE (52) Robert Pelletier's statue of Louis Cyr honors the famous Quebec strong man who once lifted 4,337 pounds on his back and a 553-pound weight with one finger. The 300-pound Cyr, born in 1863 in Napierville, Que., once patrolled a policeman's beat around this square.

ST. HELEN'S ISLAND (53) The Montreal Aquarium has dolphins, sharks, penguins, eels, sea turtles and brilliantly colored coral reef fish. The Montreal Military and Maritime Museum is in the arsenal of a fort built in 1820-24. Students drill in the uniforms of the Fraser Highlanders and the Compagnie Franche de la Marine, a unit founded in 1683 by Cardinal Richelieu. The museum displays uniforms and military equipment dating from 1534; a model of Montreal before 1776; globes (1632-36), one showing New France (with the Great Lakes as one large sea). St. Helen's Island is reached by the 8,670-foot Jacques Cartier Bridge.

ST. JOSEPH'S ORATORY (54) The oratory has evolved from the small chapel of a devoted lay brother to a world-renowned shrine that receives more than 3,000,000 visitors a year. Alfred Bessette joined the Congregation of Holy Cross in 1870, taking the name Brother André. In 1904, on the slope of Mount Royal, he built a small wooden chapel to honor Saint Joseph and began to treat the sick and afflicted, preaching that complete faith and devotion to the saint would relieve their suffering. Many left the oratory feeling cured, discarding wheelchairs, canes, braces and crutches in the shrine's Votive Chapel. When Brother André died in 1937, aged 91, an estimated 1,000,000 persons filed past his coffin.

□ Work on the predominantly Renaissance-style basilica, which can accommodate 15,000 persons and another 1,000 in its Crypt Church, was begun in 1924 and not completed until 1967. The interior has massive stone arches, mosaics around the apse, stained-glass windows, and altar, pulpit and celebrant's seat carved from stone. Oak statues of the 12 Apostles in the transepts were sculpted by Henri Charlier. The oratory's huge octagonal dome, designed by the French master Dom Paul Bellot, is a Montreal landmark. The 56-bell carillon outside is Canada's second largest.

□ The Votive Chapel has a statue of Saint Joseph above 3,500 vigil lights, and a nine-foot marble sculpture of the saint stands over the main altar of the Crypt Church. The Stations of the Cross, set in the oratory gardens, were created from stone by Canadian artist Louis Parent and Ercolo Barbieri, an Italian. The gardens also have a monument to the Resurrection.

Museums in Montreal boast rich collections of art. Examples are Alex Colville's *Church and Horse,* acrylic polymer on untempered masonite, and Picasso's *La Lampe et les Cerises,* an oil, both in the Montreal Museum of Fine Arts. At the Museum of Contemporary Art (right) are such modern Quebec works as Paul-Emile Borduas' *La Femme à la Mandoline,* an oil on canvas. McGill University's McCord Museum is a treasure house of early Canadiana. Its Indian artifacts include an Iroquois False Face mask (crooked nose) and a 66-inch Sioux ceremonial headdress of eagle feathers tipped with peacock.

□ Brother André, whose beatification is being considered in Rome, is remembered throughout the oratory. His original mountainside chapel was restored after being heavily damaged by fire in 1951.

ST. LAWRENCE SEAWAY (55) The observation deck atop the Seaway Authority building at the Saint-Lambert lock overlooks the seaway and the 5,200 ships that pass each year.

ST. PATRICK'S CHURCH (56) Completed March 17, 1847, to serve the Irish community, St. Patrick's is Gothic in style, with some Roman influence. The elaborate interior of the Roman Catholic church is likened to that of St. Mark's Cathedral in Venice. There are

150 oil paintings of the saints in the nave and the 14 paintings at the Stations of the Cross were done by the Italian artist Patriglia. Two paintings (each 31 feet by 14 feet) on the side walls of the sanctuary are the work of Alex Locke. There are memorial plaques to D'Arcy McGee, the Father of Confederation assassinated in 1868 (his pew here bears its original marker), and to poet Emile Nelligan, who was baptized here.

SHRINE OF ATONEMENT (57) A 15-foot gilded bronze statue of the Sacred Heart of Jesus stands about 100 feet high atop one of the shrine's two chapels. Inside is a statue of the Sacred Heart of Montmartre, so named be-

The look of the past is everywhere at Morrisburg—in every mannequin, every costumed model, every reconstruction. Resplendent in scarlet and gold, an officer of wax and wood stands at a frozen alert in the Battle Memorial building of Crysler's Farm Park. The staff of Upper Canada Village, in reconstructed dwellings or on a coach nearing the community, dress as their Loyalist forebears did. All houses have been furnished to mirror the tiniest details of pioneer existence. From hand-forged nails and doorlatches to wallpaper and hand-dipped candles, everything is matched to authentic originals.

impression of the great, deep forest of pioneer days.

□ Adjoining the village is 2,000-acre Crysler's Farm Battlefield Park, commemorating a crucial battle in the War of 1812. Near this site in November 1813, on militia Capt. John Crysler's farm (now flooded by the St. Lawrence Seaway), a force of 800 British and Canadian troops under Lieut.-Col. Joseph Morrison routed some 8,000 invading Americans. The victory stopped an assault that was aimed at Montreal. A 50-foot memorial mound of battlefield soil has been constructed in the park. Atop the mound a 15-foot obelisk remembering those killed in the invasion. An impressive 1,600-foot, tree-lined mall leads to the monument from the park entrance.

The nearby Pioneer Memorial was constructed with bricks from demolished pioneer houses and churches in towns later submerged by the seaway. Gravestones from the cemeteries were built into the walls of the memorial.

A memorial to Loyalists who settled in Upper Canada after the American Revolution has a nine-foot bronze figure of a soldier in tattered uniform, putting his musket behind him and picking up an axe. The walls of a cross-shaped garden are built of bricks, stones and timbers of Loyalist homes and hold headstones from several old Loyalist graveyards.

Mosport Ont. 7CY/17DW
One of the finest Grand Prix racetracks in North America, Mosport is a 2½-mile circuit of varying gradients, curves and straightaways. The Canadian Grand Prix has been held here.

Mount Carmel P.E.I. 9DX/23BW
The log houses, church, barn and smithy of Pioneer Village are a re-creation of a 19th-century Acadian settlement. Each house, two rooms with a sleeping loft, is simply furnished with a washstand, a commode, rough-hewn log bed frames and handmade quilts.

Mount Currie B.C. 2CY
The one-day Mount Currie Rodeo in May features bronco busting and a race of horse-drawn wagons.

Mount Hope Ont. 7CZ/17BY
The childhood home of the Maggie of *When You and I Were Young, Maggie* is three miles west of here. A bronze plaque near the square, stone house commemorates both Maggie Clark and her husband, George Washington Johnson, who wrote the words shortly before their marriage in 1864. He was a schoolteacher and she had been one of his pupils. Published in his volume *Maple Leaves*, the poem was set to music by J.A. Butterfield in 1866. Maggie had died the year before, of tuberculosis, aged 23. Her grave is here.

Mount Pleasant Ont. 7BZ/17BZ
A plaque commemorates two doctors—mother and daughter—who were prominent in the struggle for women's suffrage in the late 19th century. Emily Stowe completed medical studies in New York in 1867 and became a licensed physician in Ontario in 1880. Her daughter, Augusta Stowe-Gullen, born here in 1857, became a doctor in 1883. She was the first woman to both train and practise as a physician in Canada.

□ An octagonal, stone-stucco house built in 1840 is a Mount Pleasant landmark.

Old Slavic lettering of this illuminated Bible in the Basilian Fathers Monastery at Mundare was done in the 15th century. The book is open at the first page of St. Mark's Gospel.

Mount Revelstoke National Park (B.C.) 2EY
Cross-country skiing, snowmobiling and mountain hiking are chief attractions in the rolling alpine terrain of this 100-square-mile park. It is bounded by the Columbia and Illecillewaet rivers and the Clachnacudainn mountain range. A 7½-mile stretch of the Trans-Canada Highway runs through the park. A lookout atop Mount Revelstoke, (6,300 feet) can be reached in summer by car along a winding 16-mile gravel road from the Trans-Canada Highway.

More than 40 miles of trails lead mountain hikers through the flower-strewn meadows and spruce forests of a 6,000-foot plateau surrounded by jagged, 8,000-foot peaks. One trail winds nine miles from the summit lookout to Eva, Millar and Jade lakes, where asters, blue lupines and avalanche lilies abound in summer.

Mount Uniacke N.S. 9DY/22EV
Original furnishings still grace Uniacke House, an elegant colonial mansion built in 1813-15 by Richard John Uniacke, an Irish adventurer who became attorney general of Nova Scotia. The two-story, eight-bedroom white wooden house is one of the finest examples of colonial architecture. It once was at the center of a 5,000-acre estate.

Beneath a wide, two-story portico, the main entrance leads into a spacious hall where family and servants said morning prayers. In the hall are 12 Adam chairs of Honduras mahogany and a chair from the cabin of Adm. Edward Boscawen, who commanded the British fleet at the capture of Louisbourg from the French in 1758.

Mundare Alta. 4BW
In a museum building at the Basilian Fathers Monastery (The Order of St. Basil the Great in Canada) is an unusual collection of East European art, church relics and Ukrainian artifacts. It includes a 12th-century gospel handwritten in Old Slavic, four 14th-century icons, a 15th-century illuminated Bible in Old Slavic, copies of the first printed Latin Bible (1520) and the first printed French Bible (1558), and some of the earliest (1707) printed Old Slavic church music. Also displayed are such varied things as a 17th-century cossack uniform, an Italian violin (1723), a 17th-century altar cloth embroidered in silver, painted Easter eggs and Ukrainian, Chinese and Japanese ceramics—and handcuffs used on the Métis leader Louis Riel (*see* Batoche). The handcuffs were a gift from a priest who had been given them by the son of one of Riel's jailers.

The monastery itself, a two-story brick building finished with a coat of sand and cement, was built in 1923 by monks who came here from Galicia.

The monastery's St. Peter and Paul Church is an octagonal brick structure with a wooden dome, crowned by eight semi-arches and an aluminum cross. It was built in 1968 to replace a traditional onion-domed church. Stained glass windows in the new church depict the life of Christ and the history of Mundare and the Ukrainian people. In a chapel-like nook in the vestibule is an enlarged reproduction of an icon (of the Mother of God) at Pochayev in the western Ukraine. The original icon was investigated by a church commission in 1770 and accredited with 539 miracles. The church has two cornerstones. One contains a stone from the Rock of the Primacy at Tabigha in the Holy Land, where Christ said to Peter, "Feed my lambs, feed my sheep." The other contains a stone from the Ostian Way in Rome, along which Paul was led to martyrdom.

Murdochville Que. 9DW/10HZ
Trucks load ore in 150-foot-high galleries in a copper mine here. It started operations in 1952 and was the first mine in Canada to use the "room and pillar" technique that leaves pillars of rock to support the ceiling.

Murray Bay Que. *see* La Malbaie

N

Nahanni National Park (N.W.T.) 1BX/3GX
The South Nahanni River plunges over a 294-foot cataract and crashes through three immense canyons in this park at the southwest corner of the Northwest Territories. The park, accessible by plane from Fort Simpson and Watson Lake, takes in 1,840 square miles of mountains and rivers once visited only by a few Indians, trappers and prospectors.

A 130-mile boat trip up the South Nahanni from Nahanni Butte, a settlement at the junction of the Nahanni and Liard rivers, ends at majestic Virginia Falls. The first stage is 40 miles through the Splits, a multichanneled section of the Nahanni in a wide valley dominated by Twisted Mountain (4,200 feet), to hot springs that form 98-degree pools of sulphurous water at the mouth of the First Canyon. Leaving 20-mile First Canyon with its towering, cave-dotted, 3,500-foot walls, boats enter Deadmen Valley (often called Headless Valley). This eight-mile stretch was named by a man who found the headless bodies of his two prospector brothers there in 1908.

Twenty-mile Second Canyon, a 2,000-foot-deep channel through the snowcapped Headless Mountains, leads to 15-mile, 2,800-foot-deep Third Canyon, carved by the river through the Funeral Range. The upper end of Third Canyon is guarded by 250-foot Pulpit Rock. It is at The Gate, a narrow hairpin bend with rock walls 1,500 feet high. Twenty-one miles upstream, in a broad low valley, is the junction with the Flat River. After a further 21 miles, Virginia Falls is approached through Hell's Gate, a sharp turn where the river is abruptly blocked by a vertical wall of rock. Virginia Falls is an awesome four acres of vertical water, starting as a single chute, then dividing as it slams into a spruce-capped rock in its 294-foot descent.

Below Hole-in-the-Wall Lake, at the northern edge of the park where the Ragged Mountains rise to 9,000 feet, the 70-degree Rabbitkettle hot springs trickle from the top of a 90-foot snow-white terraced castle of layered calcium carbonate.

The park flora, which includes species of

bulrush and clover found nowhere else in the north, ranges from the flowering aster, goldenrod, wild mint, lady's slipper and orchids at the hot springs, to the sedges and lichens of the alpine tundra. The 79 species of birds and 31 species of mammals found here include golden eagles, Canada geese, owls, loons, many songbirds, moose, wolves, Dall sheep, caribou, deer and bears.

Nanaimo B.C.   2BZ/12CX

The Bastion was built in 1853 as part of a Hudson's Bay Company fort protecting miners brought from England and Scotland to dig coal. The wooden blockhouse, guarded by two original cannon, is a museum with exhibits on three levels, the last reached by ship's ladder.

□ At the Nanaimo Centennial Museum is an 800-square-foot reproduction of a coal mine digging area, showing equipment and methods used from 1853 to 1968; a reproduction of a Victorian living room, an Indian collection, relics from the city's HBC period (1852-62) and an early 19th-century table

Powered bathtubs and other outlandish craft are navigated 34 miles across the Strait of Georgia from Nanaimo to Vancouver in a race each July. Most boats in Nanaimo's busy harbor are conventional fishing and pleasure craft.

from the local Chinese community. The two-story museum is in Piper Park, where there is also an 1870 steam locomotive.

□ Petroglyph Provincial Park, on a hog-back ridge two miles south, is thought to have been the center of a prehistoric cult. Highly stylized rock carvings represent humans, birds, wolves, lizards, sea monsters and supernatural creatures. Parallel straight lines, some as long as 40 feet, are incised in the rock.

Napanee Ont. 7DY/18BZ
A ball of wood fiber paper at the Lennox and Addington Museum was preserved by John Thomson after his first successful attempt to duplicate the wood pulp process he had learned in the United States before settling here. In 1872, on the Napanee River, he built the first mill in Ontario designed to make paper from wood pulp only.

Also in the museum is a British army lieutenant's account of a 1784 trip up the St. Lawrence River from Sillery (near Quebec) with Napanee's first settlers, a group of United Empire Loyalists.

The museum is a many-windowed Georgian mansion built in 1826. It reflects the affluence of its original owner, Allan Macpherson, the town's first industrialist. Furniture includes a Regency couch and a Sheridan love seat, both dating from 1830.

Two blocks away is a privately owned house that was the Red Tavern, built in 1810. The white-columned town hall dates from 1856, the courthouse from 1864. Gibbard's, the oldest furniture factory in Ontario, has operated since 1835.

Napier Ont. 7BZ/16CY
St. Mary's Anglican Church, built about 1842 by retired sailors and soldiers, is believed the oldest church in Middlesex County. The white wooden building has an oak ceiling, box pews of black walnut, a late 19th-century organ and the church's original Bible.

Nappan N.S. 23AX
More than 100 acres of the 600-acre federal experimental farm here were once marshland, flooded regularly by Bay of Fundy tides. But with dikes the land was drained and it now yields excellent forage crops. The gates of aboideaux (tunnels) in the dikes swing freely outward; the pressure of seawater keeps them closed at high tide but at low tide surface water behind the dikes forces the gates open and flows into the sea.

Neepawa Man. 6AY
About 300 painters, sculptors and musicians—most from Canada, a few from the United States—gather here in July for a two-week Holiday Festival of the Arts.

Neguac N.B. 9DX
A painting depicting Christ's baptism by John the Baptist, done by an unknown French painter around 1780, is in the sacristy of the Church of St. Bernard.

Nelson B.C. 2EZ
Square dancing and main street pancake breakfasts are part of Midsummer Bonspiel, a week-long curling event in July which attracts more than 160 rinks.

Nelson's 31 acres of parks include Lakeside Park, where greenhouses produce thousands of plants and flowers, and Sportsman Park, where British Columbia's first hydroelectric plant was built in 1896 at 175-foot Cottonwood Falls.

□ Jagged peaks tower to 9,200 feet above ice cliffs and alpine lakes in nearby Kokanee Glacier Provincial Park. The 65-foot Bonnington Falls and rapids boil on the Kootenay River below some spectacular mountain scenery. Rocks in the area bear Indian paintings of undetermined age and origin.

□ The Kootenay Museum displays Indian flint arrowheads and pioneer furnishings of the late 1800s.

□ The Nelson Highland Games are held for three days in September.

Nephton Ont.—The Peterborough Petroglyphs, discovered near here in the early 1950s, are a rich example of North American prehistoric art. Some 300 figures carved into sloping limestone 100 feet by 180, apparently between 1000 and 1500 A.D., are identifiable as animals, humans, mythical forms and fertility symbols. Ninety-foot High Falls, on Eels Creek, is reached by a three-mile trail from the petroglyphs. (17EV)

Neuville Que. 20BW
A half-domed sanctuary that dates from 1697 is part of Saint-François-de-Sales Church. The sanctuary was started that year by an unknown artist and completed about a century later, perhaps by Jean Baillargé or his son François. When a nave was added in 1845, the walls of the church were rebuilt but the sanctuary was preserved. The church's treasures include a wooden baldachin (altar canopy) dating from 1775, three late-18th-century altars sculpted by François Baillargé, a silver chalice crafted by François Ranvoyzé and 21 Antoine Plamondon paintings.

□ Neuville's old houses include the Denis (c.1780), Darveau (1785), Anger (1797), Soulard (1760-80) and Poitier (1795) houses. None is marked with a plaque or other indication of historical value. All are occupied.

Newburgh Ont.   7DY/18BZ

A plaque commemorates John Thomson, who perfected a process of manufacturing paper from wood pulp (*see* Napanee).

New Carlisle Que.   9DW

Zion United Church (originally Presbyterian) dates from about 1820.

Newcastle N.B.   9DX

A bronze bust of Lord Beaverbrook, who spent his boyhood here, stands in the Square on a seven-foot pedestal containing his ashes. Beaverbrook gave Newcastle a civic center, an arena and a library (in the Old Manse where he grew up). Another gift, Enclosure Park, contains a graveyard; one grave is that of William Davidson, the first English-speaking settler in the Miramichi area.

A tablet at the post office commemorates Peter Mitchell, a Father of Confederation and premier of New Brunswick in 1866-67.

New Denmark N.B.   9CX

Folk dancing and pageants here June 19 commemorate the arrival in 1872 of Danish settlers who founded what now is Canada's largest Danish community. Many of the 1,000 townspeople wear Danish dress and dance such traditional steps as King Gustav's Skoal, The Crested Hen, Norwegian Mountain March and The Finger Polka. Pageants describe the 29 original immigrants' voyage from Copenhagen and the difficulties they faced in carving a settlement from the forest.

A museum on the site of the original clearing has a narrow-waisted brown dress brought from Denmark in 1872, an old wedding dress, boots from an immigrant's army service in Denmark, tax records from the late 1800s and early school books.

New Denver B.C.   2EZ

A steep hiking trail up 7,479-foot Idaho Peak is lined with abandoned tunnels and mine dumps, ghosts of the 1890s when rich silver, lead and zinc deposits first made the Slocan Valley famous. Along the trail is Sandon,

The Immigrants

New Denmark's first 29 immigrants—six couples, 10 children and seven single men—traveled by ship and paddle-wheeler and finally horse and sled, deep into the New Brunswick forest. For them and the Danes who followed, it was a hostile, isolated place. Only the hardiest survived the early years, eking a living from patches of cleared land. Sometimes they buried felled trees in an attempt to gain crop space. Cash was scarce and any small farm surplus was carried nine miles to market in Grand Falls. Gradually dairying became profitable. By 1915 potatoes were a major crop, as they continue to be today.

once a silver boom town. The Idaho Lookout, one of the highest provincial fire towers, provides a vast panorama of lakes, glaciers and peaks.

New Germany N.S.   9DZ/22DW

Hollow metal grave markers in a cemetery at the Anglican Church of St. John in the Wilderness were once used by enterprising parishioners to store home brew liquor for sale after services. Marker plates engraved with the names of the deceased slide back to reveal the hollow enclosures. The frame church was built in 1844 in what was then a wilderness area as an offshoot of St. John Church in Lunenburg. The church has most of its original plain windows, a wooden bishop's chair and a Bible and prayer book dating from 1840.

New Glasgow N.S.   9EY/23DY

Samson, the first locomotive in Canada to run on steel rails, is on display at the Pictou County Historical Museum. It was built in 1838, used wood as fuel and made a six-mile run between Stellarton and Abercrombie.

Acadian step dances and the traditional songs of New Brunswick's colorful lumbermen are highlights of the Miramichi Folk Song Festival at Newcastle in August. Long narrative chants about great feats and lost loves are sung to the foot-tapping music of fiddle, accordion and mouth organ.

New Liskeard Ont. 7CW
The 1,000,000-acre little clay belt is a 35-mile-wide strip of rich farmland between New Liskeard and Englehart, 28 miles west.

□ Forty-foot-high Metawapika Falls is 17 miles southwest of New Liskeard.

New London P.E.I. 9EX/23BW
A green-trimmed white cottage here was the birthplace of Lucy Maud Montgomery (*see* Cavendish), author of *Anne of Green Gables*. In the house, now a provincial historic site, are Miss Montgomery's wedding dress, scrapbooks and a replica of the blue chest she wrote about in *The Story Girl*.

Newmarket Ont. 7CY/17CX
The remains of huge concrete locks, part of a canal that never saw a boat, are like giant steps down the little Holland River two miles north of here. Proponents of the canal, which was to make Newmarket a Great Lakes port, convinced a Liberal government to start it in 1908. In 1911, by which time $500,000 had been spent, a new Conservative government killed the project. More than half a century later the South Lake Simcoe Conservation Authority acquired 100 acres around the locks, used one of the giant structures to dam the Holland River and created a conservation area with a 45-acre reservoir.

□ Just south of Newmarket is a well-preserved Quaker meetinghouse built in 1810. The town was founded in 1800 by Timothy Rogers, who brought in about 40 other Quaker families.

New Mills N.B. 9DW
Huge Atlantic salmon are seen in a rearing pond that was created by building a seawall across a small ocean inlet here.

New Ross N.S. 9DY/22DW
Plows are pulled by oxen and grain is cut by scythe and sickle at a living museum of agriculture, where methods common 100 years ago are used to work the land. Ross Farm Museum of Agriculture dates from 1816, when Capt. William Ross of the Nova Scotia Fencibles undertook to settle 172 discharged soldiers in the area.

On two floors of an 1892 red wooden barn are implements illustrating farm technology from 1600 to 1925. In the collection are plows dating from 1610, reapers, threshing and winnowing machines powered by horse or dog treadmills, hoes, flails for beating grain, winnowing baskets for separating chaff and cant hooks for removing stumps.

Barrels and casks are made and repaired in the cooperage at the farm workshop. There are demonstrations of yoke- and shingle-making and ox-shoeing.

Rosebank, the Ross family home, is a two-story plank-walled frame house built by William Ross in 1817 to replace his first rough log house. It has five fireplaces and hand-fashioned mantels, cupboards, chair rails and baseboards. Exhibits include a piano (c.1820)

that four soldiers carried 15 miles from Chester.

New Waterford N.S. 9FX/23HW
Flat Point Light, three miles west, guides ships into Sydney harbor. The beacon of the 120-foot concrete lighthouse, built in the 1930s, can be seen 75 miles at sea.

New Westminster B.C. 2CZ/12EX
The Irving House Historical Center and the New Westminster Museum offer visitors a look at British Columbia history. Irving House is a two-story, 14-room structure built for pioneer steamboat operator Capt. William Irving in 1862-64. It has its original European wallpaper, Wilton carpets imported from England in the 1860s, period furniture and an autographed engraving of Sir John Franklin, presented by the Arctic explorer's widow in the 1850s. In the New Westminster Museum are about 50 cameras and projectors dating from 1870, a 1929 fire truck and a coach built for Governor General Lord Dufferin's 1876 visit to the Cariboo goldfields.

□ New Westminster, called the Royal City because it was named by Queen Victoria, is the largest freshwater port on Canada's Pacific coast. It was the first city in the province and the provincial capital from 1859 to 1868. The oldest parts of New Westminster were built by the Royal Engineers, including Irving House and the wooden St. Mary's Church (1865) in the Sapperton district. Sapperton was named after the Royal Engineers sappers (privates) whose arrival in 1855 to keep order in the new Crown colony is commemorated by a cairn.

□ John "Gassy Jack" Deighton (*see* page 373), whose saloon was the first building in what is now downtown Vancouver, is buried in the Fraserview Cemetery.

□ A plaque on the courthouse honors Frederick William Howey, celebrated provincial historian; a tablet commemorating Sir Richard McBride, provincial prime minister in 1903-15, is at the public school named after him. A bronze bust of explorer Simon Fraser overlooks the river bearing his name.

□ A May queen is crowned during a four-day fete based on traditional English May festivities. The Hyack Anvil Battery fires a salute on Queen Victoria's birthday anniversary. When the Royal Engineers left in 1863—with their cannon—the annual noisemaking was taken over by the city's first fire brigade, using gunpowder and two anvils to produce the explosion.

□ The Lacrosse Hall of Fame here honors great field and box lacrosse players.

Niagara Falls Ont. 7CZ/17CY
Museums, parks and historic sites here are visited by millions each year but men and their works are dwarfed by the grandeur of one

Mighty Niagara thunders a misty welcome to the dawn. This is the Canadian Horseshoe Falls, 176 feet high and 2,200 feet across.

The Village Blacksmith, with animated men, horses, hammers and bellows, is among the Moïse Potvin miniatures in a museum at Niagara Falls. Other Potvin wood carvings include *New Year's Eve in Canada, Stampede of the Texas Longhorns, A Little Bit of Ireland* and his masterpiece *Home Sweet Home,* depicting the splendor of a Victorian living room.

of the world's great natural wonders. The falls, first described in 1678 by the Rev. Louis Hennépin, a priest who traveled with La Salle, have attracted newlyweds, stunt men and tourists since the early 1800s.

The falls, among the largest in the world, are more remarkable for their width than their height. Canada's deeply curved Horseshoe Falls is 2,200 feet wide, 176 feet high; the straight-crested American Falls is 1,000 and 184 feet. They are separated by Goat Island, an American island that extends to the brink. Below the falls, the Niagara River flows to Lake Ontario through the rapids and whirlpools of the Niagara Gorge, formed by the gradual advance of the falls toward Lake Erie through erosion.

The river provides hydroelectric power for much of Ontario and New York. On the Canadian side a tunnel carries water five miles under the city to power Sir Adam Beck Generating Station No. 2 (*see* Queenston).

Annual festivals in Niagara Falls include a winter carnival (February), a blossom festival (May), a national beauty pageant (July) and elements of the Niagara Grape and Wine Festival (September) (*see* St. Catharines).

CANADA TOWER This 350-foot structure with observation deck was to open in 1979.

DRUMMOND HILL CEMETERY It covers part of the Lundy's Lane battlefield, site of a decisive encounter in the War of 1812. Soldiers from both sides are buried here, as is Laura Secord (*see* Queenston).

HOLY TRINITY CHURCH It was built in 1846 on the site of a wooden church burned in 1839 by supporters of William Lyon Mackenzie, leader of the 1837 rebellion.

HOUDINI MUSEUM Houses most of the famous illusionist's equipment and props.

MAID OF THE MIST Three diesel vessels take sightseers, protected against the spray by rubber coats, to the foot of the falls. The boats are named after a young woman in an Indian legend who went over the falls in a canoe and whose ghost is said to be seen occasionally in the spray.

MARINELAND Trained dolphins and sea lions at a 4,500-seat aqua-theater; bears, buffalo, elk, lynx, llamas and deer in a 75-acre game park.

NAVY ISLAND A plaque opposite this island three miles upstream from the falls commemorates the destruction of the 46-ton American

side-wheeler *Caroline* by Capt. Andrew Drew of the Royal Navy and a group of volunteers. William Lyon Mackenzie's rebels and provisional government, established on the island in 1837, used *Caroline* as a supply vessel. Drew's force crossed the river, cut her loose and set her afire. She ran aground and burned on the brink of the Horseshoe Falls.

NIAGARA FALLS MUSEUM The Daredevil Gallery houses relics and exhibits of persons who have challenged the falls on tightropes and in barrels, boats and rubber balls. Among the most celebrated Niagara daredevils was The Great Blondin (Jean-François Gravelet), a French acrobat, the first to walk a tightrope across the Niagara Gorge, in 1859. He crossed many times, carrying his manager on his shoulders, cooking his dinner, riding a bicycle, and blindfolded.

NIAGARA GLEN Rare plants, ferns, trees and flowers abound in a gorge filled with strangely shaped rocks and potholes formed by a once turbulent river.

NIAGARA PARKS COMMISSION The administration building houses a collection of old prints of the falls. A plaque beside the main entrance honors Sir Casimir Gzowski, first chairman of the commission, who planned the park system.

OAKES GARDEN THEATER Rock gardens, lily ponds, terraces and promenades overlooking the falls are the setting for this amphitheater given to the city by Sir Harry Oakes.

OAK HALL Oak paneling from Cardinal Wolsey's Hampton Court Palace near London, carved teak chairs used at the signing of the treaty which ended the Boxer Rebellion in 1901 and a nine-hole, par-three golf course are among the attractions of the former home of Sir Harry Oakes, the Canadian mining magnate. The 37-room stone mansion overlooks the Dufferin Islands a quarter-mile upstream from the falls. It has 15 bathrooms (with colored fixtures), three wall safes and metal doors.

PANASONIC CENTER The observation deck in the seven-story crown of the 325-foot tower has specially tinted glass and built-in light meters as aids to photography.

QUEEN VICTORIA PARK More than 300,000 yellow daffodils bloom during a blossom festival each spring.

RAINBOW BRIDGE A 55-bell carillon tower at the Canadian end of the bridge offers con-

Black Gold: 90 Years From Oil Springs to Leduc

In only 90 years the Canadian oil industry went from modest beginnings in Ontario to the boom that the great discovery at Leduc *(see entry)* touched off in 1947. A replica at Oil Springs (left) commemorates James Miller Williams' 1857 well, the first of many thousands. (Williams erected the first refinery the same year.) Most wells today are in the west, often pumping black gold from under fields of grain. Canadian production for the entire 1857-1947 period was about 117,000,000 barrels. It was 476,000,000 barrels in 1971 alone.

of the world's great distance runners. He won the 1907 Boston marathon.

Another plaque commemorates Joseph Brant's son John, the first Indian superintendent of the Six Nations and the first Indian elected to the Upper Canada legislative assembly (in 1832).

Many old Iroquois customs are still carried on in longhouses here. In the council house, built in 1864 to replace one built of logs in 1784, are pictures of Longboat, an oil portrait of Joseph Brant, and the Haldimand Grant of 1784, on a 36-by-48-inch piece of deerskin, the document that assigned the Six Nations their reserve.

Oil Springs Ont.   7AZ/16BY
Outside the Oil Museum of Canada near here is a replica of North America's first commercial oil well, which James Miller Williams put into production in 1857. That same year he built the first Canadian oil refinery. In the museum are wooden hand pumps, early power pumps and refinery stills, geological displays and exhibits tracing the history of lighting. (*See* Petrolia)

Oka Que.   7FY/19AY
Seven stone chapels on a mountain here were built in 1740-42 as a Way of the Cross. There is a procession to the three remaining chapels on Holy Cross Day, Sept. 14.
    □ Manoir d'Argenteuil, built about 1720, became a convent in 1864 but is now again a private residence.

Cistercian monastery overlooking Lake of Two Mountains at Oka is famous for Oka cheese. Monks in this huge Trappist institution also market honey, pheasants and Cornish game hens.

    □ Paul Sauvé Provincial Park, on Lake of Two Mountains, is two miles east of Oka.

O'Leary P.E.I.   9DX/23AV
The Prince Edward Island Potato Blossom Festival is held here in July.

Oliphant Ont.   7BX
The picturesque ruins of a stone building on Main Station Island, 2½ miles west of here, are all that remains of a fishing station established in the 1830s.
    □ Oliphant's three-day regatta in August has boat races and distance swimming events.

Champlain monument by Vernon March in Couchiching Beach Park at Orillia is one of the finest bronze works in North America. Figures at the base are of Indians and a fur trader.

Oliver B.C.   2DZ
The rare California bighorn sheep is commoner in British Columbia than in California and nowhere more common than in the Vaseux Lake region north of here. Vaseux Lake, a federal migratory bird sanctuary since 1923, is the winter home of a group of rare trumpeter swans.

□ A threshing machine that dates from the early 1900s and a horsepowered hay baler are among pioneer agricultural machines at the Bluebell Museum.

Orillia Ont.   7CY/17CV
Located at the narrows between Lake Couchiching and Lake Simcoe, this industrial and resort city was the model for Mariposa in Stephen Leacock's *Sunshine Sketches of a Little Town*. The internationally famous professor and humorist had his summer home here. The town still has the tree-shaded streets and old homes Leacock made famous.

CHURCH OF ST. JAMES This Anglican church, built in 1857, has a memorial to William Yellowhead, an Ojibway chief who fought for the British during the War of 1812.

COUCHICHING BEACH PARK A plaque honors Yellowhead, who settled with his tribe in Orillia in 1830 before the pressure of white settlement in the area forced them across Lake Couchiching to Rama in 1838-39. A 15-foot totem pole constructed by the Orillia Artists' Guild stands near the Champlain monument (picture, this page), as does the statue *Somebody's Mother* (Emily Begg), commissioned by her son Ralph and unveiled in 1935.

JAKE GAUDAUR BRIDGE This bridge at the Atherley Narrows is near the site of a log house in which Jake Gaudaur, world champion sculler, was born in 1858.

J.B. TUDHOPE MEMORIAL PARK The 17-acre park is in memory of the man who built the Tudhope-McIntyre horseless carriage.

ORILLIA PUBLIC LIBRARY The library has a bronze bust of Stephen Leacock by Elizabeth Wyn Wood and a large collection of the humorist's works.

STEPHEN LEACOCK MEMORIAL HOME The author's summer home on Lake Couchiching's Brewery Bay has been converted to a museum

Half-Clown, Half-Satirist

"An essentially Canadian humorist, dry and droll, half-clown, half-satirist." So wrote J.B. Priestley of Stephen Leacock, Canada's most famous literary figure and possibly the greatest humorist of his time. He was born in Swanmore, Hampshire, England, in 1869. As professor of political science at McGill University in Montreal, he was a campus character with "his angular overcoat, his missing buttons and his faded hat," but his *Elements of Political Science* (1906) became a standard textbook. He was also an historian and a literary critic. He wrote three volumes of the *Chronicles of Canada* series and a study of *Montreal, Seaport and City*. As a humorist Leacock was prolific: after *Literary Lapses* (1910), his first book of humor, at least one volume a year was written in the cluttered study of the 19-room white stucco summer home he designed and had built at Orillia. He died in Toronto in 1944, having written 61 books and given laughter and insight to millions.

Portrait of a Shirt, a five-by-four-foot oil by Tom Hodgson, is part of the Painters Eleven collection in the Robert McLaughlin Gallery in Oshawa. The 11 were Ontario artists who banded together in the 1950s to show abstract art. Bruce Garner's five-foot bronze *Skipping Girl* is in the McLaughlin Gallery permanent collection.

of Leacock memorabilia. Many of his papers, including the original handwritten manuscript of *Sunshine Sketches of a Little Town* and some of his correspondence with other authors, are displayed.

WINTER CARNIVAL Three days of festivities in February include an ice-fishing derby, car and harness racing on ice, a figure-skating show and hockey, skiing and curling.

Oromocto N.B.   9CY
This town is at the north end of CFB Gagetown, the Commonwealth's third largest mi-

Orsainville Que.—Zebras graze in a shaded corner of the Quebec Zoological Garden. It has some 70 species of mammals, including polar bear, elk and caribou, and 240 species of birds. The DuBerger River, dammed to create pools for sea lions and beaver, flows through lush gardens. (9AX/20BW)

litary camp. It covers 427 square miles and has a 120-mile perimeter.

Oshawa Ont.   7CY/17DX
The Canadian Automotive Museum and the Robert McLaughlin Gallery, named for the head of the pioneer car-building family, testify to Oshawa's role as a major automotive center. More than one-third of the labor force is employed by General Motors of Canada and other thousands work in plants that make parts and accessories. The carriage manufacturing business that Robert McLaughlin moved here from Enniskillen, Ont., in 1876 became the largest in the British Empire. In 1907 his son R.S. McLaughlin founded the McLaughlin Motor Car Company and began assembling some of the earliest Canadian automobiles, including the McLaughlin and McLaughlin Buick. The younger McLaughlin

Spotted Lake, whose waters have one of the world's heaviest concentrations of minerals, is near Osoyoos. For most of the year it is almost solid minerals, concentrated in roughly circular pools, some hot, some cold. Indians used the lake for its healing qualities; it now has a spa.

sold his interests to GM in 1918 but remained president of GM of Canada.

CANADIAN AUTOMOTIVE MUSEUM It traces Canada's contribution to the development of the automobile and describes the 84 makes that have been built in this country.

CANADIAN CABIN MUSEUM This settler's cabin four miles east of Oshawa has been restored and refurnished to the 1830s.

HENRY HOUSE This house in Lakeview Park is a museum of the 1850-80 period, with furnishings, costumes, household and farm implements and tools.

McLAUGHLIN ESTATE The 3¾-acre estate of R.S. McLaughlin has Japanese gardens with orchids, African violets and other exotic flowers and illuminated pools and fountains. It is open to the public.

McLAUGHLIN FARM Robert McLaughlin is honored by a plaque at the farm of his grandson Ewart, 10 miles east of Oshawa.

MEMORIAL PARK The war memorial is built of stones from Westminster Abbey, from all the Allied countries of World War I and from most of the battlefields where Canadians fought in that conflict.

NATIONAL STUD FARM The third largest stud farm in North America has produced several champions, including Northern Dancer, the first Canadian-bred horse to win the Kentucky Derby (in 1964).

ROBINSON HOUSE MUSEUM The house was built in 1846 and has been restored as a museum. One display is of rushlights (rushes saturated in fat), whale, kerosene and oil lamps and early electric light bulbs.

Osoyoos B.C. 2DZ

In semi-desert here are lizards, painted turtles, magpies, canyon wrens and burrowing owls. Cacti and ponderosa pines thrive in a hot, dry climate that helps produce the earliest fruits and vegetables in Canada.

Ottawa Ont. 7EY/18DW

. . . in the judgment of Her Majesty the City of Ottawa combines more advantages than any other place in Canada for the permanent seat of the future government . . . and is selected by Her Majesty accordingly.

Queen Victoria made the choice in 1857, ending the aspirations of Montreal, Quebec, Toronto and Kingston to become the capital of Canada. There was fierce opposition—Ottawa, said author Goldwin Smith, was "a sub-Arctic lumber-village converted . . . into a political cockpit"—but the Parliament Buildings were started in 1859 and Ottawa's status was confirmed by the British North America Act of 1867.

. The first settler had been Nicholas Sparks, who cleared a farm in the early 1800s near where Sparks Street is today. The farm was isolated until 1826 when Col. John By and the Royal Engineers came to build the Rideau Canal. When that job was completed in 1832, a small lumbering town called Bytown began to grow. Its name was changed in 1855: Ottawa seemed a better bet than Bytown in the competition to become the national capital. So it was that Ottawa became the "Westminster of the Wilderness."

□ Today the sober dignity of Victorian buildings is complemented by the soaring beauty of modern architecture and flower-lined parks, drives and squares. Development of the National Capital Region is carefully supervised by the National Capital Commission. It has redesigned the city center and vets all building projects. Among the commission's decisions were to convert the Rideau Canal into an illuminated 4½-mile skating area and to turn Sparks Street into a colorful tree-lined pedestrian mall.

One of the most stirring sights in Canada is the 45-minute Changing of the Guard on Parliament Hill (daily between mid-June and Labor Day). Men of the Governor-General's Foot Guards and the Canadian Grenadier Guards, with two bands, take part.

More than 3,000,000 tulips bloom throughout the city during the Festival of Spring. The festival began when Juliana of the Netherlands presented bulbs in gratitude for the hospitality shown her throughout her stay here during World War II. The stock of bulbs is replenished each year. The Central Canada Exhibition at Lansdowne Park in August features agricultural, industrial and scientific exhibits. Festival Canada offers drama, sports, films, exhibitions and music throughout July, many of the programs taking place in the National Arts Center. February winter sports competitions include a two-day ice-fishing derby. In October there is a winter fair, stressing agriculture.

The Peace Tower rises 301½ feet above Parliament Hill in Ottawa. One room in the East Block (background) is the cabinet chamber, now almost filled by a table that has been added to as the cabinet has grown.

Natural gas bubbling through a continuous flow of water feeds the Centennial Flame on Parliament Hill. This symbol of Confederation burns not far from the National War Memorial in Confederation Square. It is built of Canadian granite, with sculptures by Vernon and Sydney March. There are statues of members of the armed forces, the medical corps and nursing association, and winged figures representing Peace and Freedom.

A beautiful city of history, pageantry, festivals and the arts, Ottawa is also the center of government. Ministries and departments that implement the decisions of Parliament are spread through the city. The embassies and high commissions of more than 50 foreign states are also here.

BIKEWAYS (1) Bicycle riders take over Western Park Driveway and Colonel By Drive Sunday mornings.

BILLINGS ESTATE (2) A Loyalist homestead with some of Ottawa's oldest buildings and a private burial ground is being preserved and restored as a civic museum.

BYTOWN MUSEUM (3) Housed in Ottawa's oldest building, Colonel By's three-story stone commissariat store (1827), the museum features relics and documents relating to the

Coats of arms of the provinces are cut in the Tyndall limestone of Confederation Hall's Gothic Revival arches. The unicorn (top) is at the west side of the main Peace Tower entrance to the Parliament Buildings. Among many other carved figures on Parliament Hill are a monster and an Indian wielding a bow and arrow. Marshall Wood's 10-foot white marble statue of Queen Victoria is in the center of the circular Library of Parliament, under its 132-foot-high ceiling.

construction of the Rideau Canal and the history of Bytown.

CANADIAN FILM INSTITUTE (4) Its three divisions include a National Film Library, National Film Theater with weekly shows, and publications.

CANADIAN WAR MUSEUM (5) Collections of weapons, equipment, badges, insignia, decorations, medals, models and paintings relate to Canada's military history. Exhibits include the fuselage of the aircraft in which Maj. W.G. Barker won the Victoria Cross in 1918; the orders, medals and decorations of Canada's greatest World War I flying ace, Lt. Col. (later Air Marshal) W.A. "Billy" Bishop, V.C.; and a staff car used by Field Marshal Alexander, Supreme Allied Commander in the

Mediterranean in 1944-45 and Canada's first postwar governor-general. A diorama shows the landing of the 3rd Canadian Division in Normandy on D-Day, June 6, 1944.

CARLETON UNIVERSITY (6) About 15,000 full-time and part-time students study at this university on the banks of the Rideau River. Elegant modern buildings, including the soaring 22-story Arts Tower, are fronted by a courtyard with spacious lawns. In the Henry Marshall Tory Science Building are a geological display and an 11-by-168-foot mosaic mural by Gerald Trottier.

CENTRAL EXPERIMENTAL FARM (7) A 1,200-acre farm in the heart of the city is the headquarters of the Department of Agriculture and its research branch, Canada's largest research organization.

CHAMPLAIN BRIDGE (8) The 4,725-foot bridge crosses the Ottawa River to Hull by way of Bate Island, which provides a view of the Remic Rapids.

CHATEAU LAURIER (9) This famous hotel, built of granite and Indiana sandstone, with towers, turrets and steeply pitched copper roofs, was opened in 1912.

CHAUDIERE FALLS (10) The 235-foot Chaudière Union Bridge provides a view of the 25-foot falls, near the site of the first white settlement in the Ottawa area (see Hull).

CONFEDERATION SQUARE PARK (11) Illumination of the trees is controlled by sensitive microphones: the lights brighten as more noise is made by visitors.

D'ARCY McGEE (12) A plaque marks where McGee, a Father of Confederation, was shot outside his boarding house in 1868. The Fenians were blamed for Canada's first political assassination and a young Irishman, Patrick James Whelan, was convicted. He was hanged in Ottawa's last public execution.

EARNSCLIFFE (13) This three-story house (1855), Sir John A. Macdonald's home in 1883-91, is the residence of the United Kingdom high commissioner.

GARDEN OF THE PROVINCES (14) Provincial flags and coats of arms fly from flagpoles; enameled bronze plaques of the provincial flowers are inset in stone balustrades.

GOVERNMENT HOUSE (15) Rideau Hall, the governor-general's residence, is a three-story limestone house built about 1838 and set in 88 acres of grounds.

GOVERNOR-GENERAL'S FOOT GUARDS MUSEUM (16) The regimental colors, medals, badges, trophies, weapons and uniforms, from 1872.

Blossoming tulips turn Ottawa's scenic driveways and footpaths into a Maytime riot of color. With some 3,000,000 blossoms, it is North America's largest tulip display. World War I soldiers silhouetted against the Ottawa sky are part of the National War Memorial in Confederation Square. George VI unveiled the memorial in May 1939.

KITCHISSIPPI LOOKOUT (17) A plaque commemorates the voyageurs who took Col. Garnet Wolseley's forces through the cataracts of the Nile in the 1884 expedition to rescue Gordon of Khartoum. Wolseley had become familiar with the voyageurs' skill while stationed in Canada in 1861-70.

LAURIER HOUSE (18) The three-story stone house is filled with photographs, documents and furniture belonging to the prime ministers who lived there, Sir Wilfrid Laurier and Mackenzie King. A prie-dieu (c.1550) from Mary Queen of Scots' castle and an oak chair said to have been used at the coronation of James I of England were both bought by King in Scotland. There is a portrait of Laurier by Georges Delfosse.

MAJOR'S HILL PARK (19) A gun fired here every noon but Sunday (10 a.m.), in a tradition that goes back to 1869, was made in 1807 and is said to have been used in the Crimean War. Two stones from the Sappers' Bridge that crossed the canal mark the site of Colonel By's house.

MUSEUM OF CANADIAN SCOUTING (20) Exhibits that trace the life of Lord Baden-Powell and the history of scouting include photographs of him as a child, one of his school reports and the illustrated log he kept of his visit to Canada in 1910.

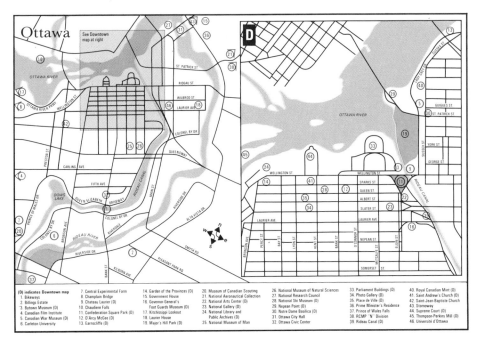

(D) indicates Downtown map	7. Central Experimental Farm	14. Garden of the Provinces (D)
1. Bikeways	8. Champlain Bridge	15. Government House
2. Billings Estate	9. Chateau Laurier (D)	16. Governor-General's
3. Bytown Museum (D)	10. Chaudiere Falls	Foot Guards Museum (D)
4. Canadian Film Institute	11. Confederation Square Park (D)	17. Kitchissippi Lookout
5. Canadian War Museum (D)	12. D'Arcy McGee (D)	18. Laurier House
6. Carleton University	13. Earnscliffe (D)	19. Major's Hill Park (D)

20. Museum of Canadian Scouting	26. National Museum of Natural Sciences	33. Parliament Buildings (D)
21. National Aeronautical Collection	27. National Research Council	34. Photo Gallery (D)
22. National Arts Center (D)	28. National Ski Museum (D)	35. Place de Ville (D)
23. National Gallery (D)	29. Nepean Point (D)	36. Prime Minister's Residence
24. National Library and	30. Notre Dame Basilica (D)	37. Prince of Wales Falls
Public Archives (D)	31. Ottawa City Hall	38. RCMP "N" Division
25. National Museum of Man	32. Ottawa Civic Center	39. Rideau Canal (D)

40. Royal Canadian Mint (D)
41. Saint Andrew's Church (D)
42. Saint Jean-Baptiste Church
43. Stornoway
44. Supreme Court (D)
45. Thompson-Perkins Mill (D)
46. Université d'Ottawa

Frozen Rideau Canal is used by about 500,000 Ottawa skaters every winter. The 4½-mile rink (from the National Arts Center to Carleton University) has 39 access stairways and six activity centers, each with parking, food, skate sharpening.

National Arts Center doors of cast aluminum, by Jordi Bonet, are 22 feet high, each eight feet wide. They are between the lobby and the Salon.

Canada's biggest art collection, in the National Gallery in Ottawa, has works from many countries. Its 6,000 Canadian possessions, dating from the 17th century, include Arthur Lismer's *The Guide's Home, Algonquin* (above) and Paul-Emile Borduas' *Sous le vent de l'île* (below), both oils. *Seated Girl*, a 45-inch-high bronze, is by Italian Giacomo Manzu. Fernand Léger, a French artist, painted *Le Mécanicien* (lower right). The gallery (founded 1880) has some 13,000 works.

NATIONAL AERONAUTICAL COLLECTION (21)
Part of the National Museum of Science and Technology, it illustrates the history of aviation in Canada from early days through bush flying, two world wars and the jet age. Among nearly 100 aircraft is a replica of the *Silver Dart*, which made the first flight in the British Empire, in 1909 (*see* Baddeck).

NATIONAL ARTS CENTER (22) In this complex of interrelated concrete structures on the west bank of the Rideau Canal are the 2,300-seat Opera House, the 900-seat Theater, the hexagonal Studio (with a movable stage) and the Salon, for recitals. Performances range from symphony concerts and opera to avant-garde jazz, from Shakespearean drama to underground films. The Opera House stage is 189 feet by 114, with 77 trapdoors.

NATIONAL GALLERY (23) Canada's most extensive art collection specializes in Canadian works and every major Canadian artist is represented. The gallery has many works by other Canadian artists and commissions and collects works by contemporary painters and sculptors. The foreign art collection includes works by Piero di Cosimo, Canaletto, Rubens, Rembrandt, El Greco, Murillo, Turner, Corot, Dégas, Cézanne and Mondrian.

NATIONAL LIBRARY and PUBLIC ARCHIVES (24)
In one massive building are two vital repositories of the Canadian heritage. The National Library has hundreds of thousands of books. The Public Archives collects significant archival material. Historic documents are stored on more than 100 miles of fireproof, corrosion-resistant shelves.

NATIONAL MUSEUM OF MAN (25) Artifacts,

Mackenzie King's mother is enshrined in the third-floor library of Laurier House in Ottawa. The portrait was painted by J.W.L. Forster in 1905.

films and dioramas illustrate Indian and Eskimo culture, the development of Canada as a nation, and Canadian folk cultures. The Immense Journey, a four-dome multi-media display, illustrates the poetic and mystic vision of man through the ages. A reconstruction of an archaeological dig is among exhibits telling the story of prehistoric man in Canada.

NATIONAL MUSEUM OF NATURAL SCIENCES (26)
Preserved specimens of animals and birds from across Canada are displayed in re-creations of their natural habitats. There are fossils, minerals, plants and exhibits that illustrate the natural forces that shape our world. One hall traces eons of animal evolution.

NATIONAL RESEARCH COUNCIL (27) Wind tunnels for aeronautical research, a ship basin for testing ship designs and an atomic clock are among attractions at the 45-building headquarters of the council, which has facilities across Canada. The council conducts research in natural sciences and engineering, establishes the standards for the measurement of length, mass, heat and time, and maintains the National Science Library.

NATIONAL SKI MUSEUM (28) Skis dating from when Scandinavians introduced skiing to North America include a pair (c.1870) with one ski 10 feet long, the other only five feet. The skier used the short ski, covered with animal skin for traction, to push himself along. On display are skis belonging to Ann Heggtveit, Lucille Wheeler, Betsy Clifford and Cathie Kreiner and the racing numbers worn by Nancy Greene (*see* Rossland).

NEPEAN POINT (29) A lookout with a panoramic view of the Ottawa River.

NOTRE DAME BASILICA (30) Around the Gothic ogival-style choir, above the stalls, are Philippe Hébert statues of patriarchs, prophets,

Royal Canadian Mint in Ottawa produces hundreds of millions of Canadian coins a year—and many millions of coins and blanks for other countries. (Canadian bank notes are printed by private firms in Ottawa.) A few gold coins were struck at a government assay office in New Westminster, B.C., in 1862 but it was the Klondike Gold Rush at the turn of the century that led to establishment (in 1908) of a mint in Ottawa.

evangelists, founders of religious orders and doctors of the Church. The basilica, begun in 1841, has 180-foot twin towers. There is a memorial to Msgr. Joseph-Eugène Guigues, founder of the Université d'Ottawa.

OTTAWA CITY HALL (31) About 40 royal swans and an unusual freestanding stair finished in white marble and aluminum are features of this eight-story building overlooking the 40-foot Rideau Falls.

OTTAWA CIVIC CENTER (32) Part of Lansdowne Park, with its 35,000-seat football stadium and 9,355-seat arena.

PARLIAMENT BUILDINGS (33) Three huge Victorian Gothic buildings dominate Ottawa from Parliament Hill: the Center Block (House of Commons and Senate), the East Block (governor-general's, privy council's and prime minister's offices and cabinet chamber) and the West Block (office space and committee rooms).

□ A white light at the base of the Peace Tower flagpole burns at night and a ring of eight lights at the top is lighted when Parliament is sitting. The top floor has a 53-bell carillon whose heaviest bell, the 22,400-pound tenor, is inscribed in English and French with the words "Glory to God in the highest and on earth peace good will toward men."

□ Below the carillon is the Memorial Chamber, with altars on which rest the four Books of Remembrance, listing the names of Canadians who fell in the South African War, World War I, World War II and the Korean War. The pages are turned so that each name is seen once a year. Carved in sandstone walls that rise 47 feet to a vaulted dome are lines from John McCrae, Rudyard Kipling, Victor Hugo, John Bunyan and the New Testament in keeping with the chamber's spirit. It is paved with stones from the battlefields of France and Belgium.

□ The Peace Tower entrance to the Center Block has a Gothic arch. It leads to Confederation Hall, whose pillars are symbolic of Confederation and the provinces. The ceiling of the House of Commons, the Green Chamber, is of hand-painted Irish linen. The speaker's chair, a replica of the one at Westminster, is made of English oak from Westminster Hall and from Nelson's flagship, *Victory*. In the Commons foyer is a 120-foot-long limestone frieze depicting the history of Canada. The ornate Senate Chamber has murals of World War I battlefields and a ceiling gilded with 24-carat gold leaf. Behind the Center Block is the Library of Parliament, the only part of the original building (completed in 1876) to survive a fire in 1916.

PHOTO GALLERY (34) Exhibits from the Still Photograph Division of the National Film Board are changed every three months.

PLACE DE VILLE (35) This three-tower complex was the first development in Ottawa to top a 150-foot, 15-story maximum. The limit, amended for Place de Ville, was designed to preserve the dominance of the Peace Tower.

PRIME MINISTER'S RESIDENCE (36) The famous 24 Sussex Drive.

PRINCE OF WALES FALLS (37) The Rideau

River cascades about 60 feet in a gorge called Hog's Back.

RCMP "N" DIVISION (38) Visitors see band rehearsals and the training of RCMP horses.

RIDEAU CANAL (39) The canal connects Ottawa and Kingston, following natural waterways and 12 miles of artificial channels. The 125-mile waterway has 49 locks, eight of which, near the Parliament Buildings, are Canada's best examples of flight locks.

ROYAL CANADIAN MINT (40) Visitors see metal being rolled to coin thickness, blanks being annealed and impressions being struck. A small museum has Canadian and foreign coins.

SAINT ANDREW'S CHURCH (41) The pews of this stone church (1872) are arranged in an old Scottish pattern in a semicircle around the pulpit. The lectern, with a Dutch coat of arms, was presented by Princess Juliana. She joined the congregation, the oldest in Ottawa (1828), while living here during World War II.

SAINT-JEAN-BAPTISTE CHURCH (42) This massive stone church, consecrated in 1932, has a 47-bell carillon. In the sanctuary is a wooden statue of Christ carved by Médard Bourgault.

STORNOWAY (43) The traditional residence of the Leader of the Opposition.

SUPREME COURT (44) Tours of this massive stone building include the two Federal Courts, the Supreme Court and the judges' chambers.

THOMPSON-PERKINS MILL (45) The renovated gristmill and sawmill (1842) overlooks a log flume on the Ottawa River.

Airmail pioneer of the 1920s, this single-engine Fairchild is in the National Aeronautical Collection. Foreground: a Bellanca Pacemaker (c. 1935).

UNIVERSITE D'OTTAWA (46) Canada's oldest bilingual university (the original Bytown College was founded in 1848) is also its largest. By the late 1970s enrollment had exceeded 18,000.

Gatineau Park: Playground for the Capital

The rolling Gatineau Hills, once the domain of Algonquin and Iroquois Indians, lie just north of the capital, across the Ottawa River in Quebec. Some of the range is preserved as Gatineau Park, a 137½-square-mile recreation area and bird and game sanctuary administered by the National Capital Commission. The park's southern entrance is five miles north of Ottawa on the Gatineau Parkway, a 22-mile scenic drive from Hull to the Champlain Lookout. The lookout offers a panoramic view of the hills, especially beautiful in autumn when the predominantly deciduous trees of the park are a glorious blaze of reds and yellows. The parkway also gives access to Mackenzie King's summer home and the ruins he collected there (picture, p. 171). Park wildlife includes fox, bear, deer and moose.

Outlook Sask.   4DY
Dozens of 800-year-old elm trees are found in Outlook and District Regional Park on the banks of the South Saskatchewan River.

Owen Sound Ont.   7BY
The Tom Thomson Memorial Gallery and Museum of Fine Art honors the great landscape artist, a native of nearby Claremont. In addition to its Thomson collection, the gallery owns a number of Group of Seven paintings, including A.Y. Jackson's *Quebec Landscape* and *Spring in Bienville,* Frank H. "Franz" Johnston's *Hills, Great Bear Lake,* Lawren Harris' *Islands North of Greenland* and J.E.H. MacDonald's *Moonlight, Algonquin Park.* The gallery also has Robert Kemp's *Just South of Rocklyn,* Susan Ross' *Cree Grandmother* and Osowetok's sculpture *Spirit of the Narwhal.*

Near the gallery is a tablet honoring W.A. "Billy" Bishop, V.C., an Owen Sound native and a leading World War I flying ace. He downed 72 enemy aircraft, 25 of them in one 10-day period. Another plaque honors Thomas William Holmes, V.C., who captured a German pillbox that was delaying the Canadian advance at Passchendaele in 1917.

BRUCE TRAIL The northernmost part of the Bruce Trail (from here to Tobermory) is the most rugged. Towering cliffs drop as much as 300 feet to the rocky shores of Georgian Bay, and deep gorges and secluded caves indent the escarpment.

COUNTY OF GREY AND OWEN SOUND MUSEUM The museum has a half-scale model of an Ojibway Indian encampment. There are settlers' household utensils and tools, clothing, toys and furniture. The pioneer arts of wool spinning, harness-making, birch-bark canoe building and shingle-making are demonstrated.

INGLIS FALLS CONSERVATION AREA There is swimming and fishing in a dammed pond near the brink of 100-foot Inglis Falls.

PROVINCIAL FISH HATCHERY It produces about 1,250,000 fish annually for Ontario waters, including several kinds of salmon and trout.

Oxbow Sask.   4FZ
The Ralph Allen Memorial Museum is dedicated to the memory of the famous author and newspaperman who spent part of his boyhood here. Ralph Allen left Oxbow at 16 to join the Winnipeg *Tribune* in 1930. He was a Toronto *Globe and Mail* correspondent in Europe in World War II, editor of *Maclean's* in the 1950s and managing editor of *The Toronto Star* at his death in 1966. The museum, in a former CPR station, also has CPR artifacts and early oil-drilling equipment.

P

Pacific Rim National Park (B.C.)   2BZ/12BY
The park, between Tofino and Port Renfrew, has three parts: Long Beach and the area behind it; Barkley Sound, including the Broken Group Islands; and the West Coast Trail, a wilderness area between Bamfield and Port Renfrew.

LONG BEACH At low tide on a sunny day the beach is a half-mile deep and postcard perfect. Its mood becomes mysterious in fog or when the sand steams after a rain shower. For beachcombers there is clam digging or searching for shells or for glass fishing floats that wind and current have pushed all the way from Japan. As many as 200 sea lions can be seen sunning themselves on a summer day. At the high-water mark the beach is choked with logs once destined for coastal sawmills but claimed and then rejected by the sea. There are several campsites in the park. Forest trails lead off the beach, which is backed by the 4,000-foot Mackenzie Range. Inland from Long Beach is 33-mile Kennedy Lake, the largest freshwater lake on Vancouver Island.

BARKLEY SOUND Some 200 recorded shipwrecks since 1803 have earned Barkley Sound the title "graveyard of the Pacific." Killer whales are often seen in the sound, particularly around some of the Broken Group Islands where sea lions perch on the rocks. At the south end of the sound is Bamfield, a tiny settlement clinging to the water's edge.

WEST COAST TRAIL The trail snakes from Bamfield to Port Renfrew, 45 miles south. It was established for shipwrecked sailors. They could walk inland, pick up the trail and return to civilization.

Paisley Ont.   7BY
David Milne, one of Canada's most brilliant artists, is honored by a plaque in the Horticultural Society Park. Milne was born near here in 1882 and taught school before studying art. He worked in New York, joined the Canadian Army in 1917 and was appointed a war artist. He lived for much of the 1920s in the United States and then, until his death in 1953, in various places in Ontario.

Thomson, Milne Set Pace in Canadian Art

Tom Thomson and David Milne deeply influenced Canadian painting. In a gallery in Owen Sound, near Thomson's Claremont birthplace, is his *Canoe Lake* (far left), an oil believed painted in 1914. (Thomson was drowned in Canoe Lake in Algonquin Park in 1917.) Milne, born near Paisley, is represented by 424 works in the National Gallery in Ottawa. His watercolor *Mist and Frost Pattern* (left) is in the Kitchener Waterloo Art Gallery. It was done in 1917. Painting was Milne's consuming passion: "I would rather be dead than not paint," he once said.

Pakan Alta. 4BW
The inventiveness of pioneer settlers is seen in many homemade objects in the Fort Victoria Museum here. They include not only tools (rake, hoe, bucksaw), a flour mill, a buckwheat sheller and a spinning wheel but also a violin and a tooth extractor. The museum has a 30-by-60-foot reproduction of Fort Victoria, which the Hudson's Bay Company built here in 1864.

Pakenham Ont. 18CX
A 268-foot bridge over the Mississippi River here, the Pakenham Five Span Stone Bridge,

Long Beach, the jewel of Pacific Rim National Park, is 7½ miles of hard sand, set against a breath-taking backdrop of brooding mountains, dense evergreen forests and craggy headlands. The 48-square-mile park extends for 65 miles along the rugged coast.

has five 40-foot arches. It was built in 1901 at a cost of $16,500.

Papineauville Que. 18EW
This village is named for Louis-Joseph Papineau, the French-Canadian *patriote* leader and chief architect of the Rebellion of 1837. The first mayor was Papineau's grandson Henri Bourassa, founder of the Montreal daily newspaper *Le Devoir*.

A two-story wooden gristmill here, built in 1817, belonged to the Papineau family seigniory, La Petite Nation.

Paris Ont. 7BZ/17AY
The Paris Plains Church (1845) is a rare example of a type of cobblestone construction favored by early settlers. The church was used by Methodists until 1921 and in 1948 was restored as a memorial to local pioneers.

Another early structure is Penmarvian

(formerly The Stone House), built in 1845-48 in Greek Revival style by Hiram "King" Capron, the town's founder. A later owner, John Penman, renamed the house and added towers, bays, verandas and other Victorian flourishes. It is now owned by the Presbyterian Church.

When Capron arrived from Vermont in 1822 this was the Forks of the Grand (the Nith and Grand rivers join here). Due to Capron's efforts gypsum deposits were developed and plaster of Paris made, giving the new town its name.

A plaque in downtown Paris marks the building in which Alexander Graham Bell received the first long distance telephone call in 1876—from Brantford (*see entry*), eight miles away.

Park Corner P.E.I.   23BW
The Story Girl and Silver Bush House gets its name and fame from two novels written by Lucy Maud Montgomery, who lived here with her aunt and uncle after her parents died. It was in this house in 1911 that she married the Rev. Ewan MacDonald, a Presbyterian minister. *The Story Girl* (1911) and *Pat of Silver Bush* (1933) were based on incidents that occurred here. (*See* Cavendish)

Parksville B.C.   2BZ/12CX
A mile-long sand beach on the Strait of Georgia, good salmon and trout fishing and two picturesque waterfalls combine to make Parksville a popular resort. Falls about 10 miles west on the Englishman River drop a total of 120 feet; eight miles farther west is a total drop of 200 feet on the Little Qualicum River. Each site has a provincial park. The one at Little Qualicum Falls runs along the south shore of Cameron Lake to MacMillan Provincial Park (*see* Port Alberni.)

Parrsboro N.S.   9DY/23AY
When the tide ebbs in Minas Basin, an arm of the Bay of Fundy, it drains Parrsboro harbor. Falling as much as 50 feet, it goes out a mile, leaving vessels hard aground. Across Minas Basin is Burntcoat Head (*see* Noel), where the world's highest tides are recorded. Fishermen here string nets on poles in the sand, catching fish at high tide, harvesting them at low tide.

□ There are miles of public beaches here and in several areas amethysts, agates and other semiprecious stones are found. Many are displayed at the Parrsboro Museum, which demonstrates how stones are polished, cut and set. The museum sponsors a four-day Rockhound Round-Up in August. It features Cabachon cutting and polishing, tumbling, faceting and micromounting, and exhibits of Nova Scotia minerals and ores.

□ At East Bay, three miles east, are the 250,000,000-year-old footprints of a small dinosaur and prehistoric lizards, discovered in 1902. Photographs and plaster casts of 108 of the footprints were sent to the National Museum of Natural Sciences. There are also fossilized leaves, fish, lizards and amphibians.

Parry Sound Ont.   7CX
Twelve sets of stairs zigzag up an 80-foot fire tower on a hill here. From the top, 249 feet above Georgian Bay, there is a spectacular view of some of the Thirty Thousand Islands and the rolling forest and lake country inland. Six towers remain of 22 built in the Parry Sound Forest District in the 1920s, before aircraft proved better for fire spotting.

□ A plaque in the Parry Sound marketplace records that all 24 persons aboard the 200-ton side-wheeler *Waubuno* perished when she sank near here in a snowstorm in 1879.

Passburg Alta.   13CZ
The Back to God Chapel, which holds only eight persons, is visited by about 20,000 travelers a year. The Bible Museum behind the chapel has several late-17th-century Bibles.

Peace River Alta.   1BZ/3GZ
Three cellars and parts of two chimneys remain at Fort Fork, from which Alexander Mackenzie left in 1793 on his incredible journey to the Pacific Ocean (*see* Bella Coola).

Pelee Island Ont.   7AZ
This largest of Canada's Lake Erie islands, seven miles by four, is the southernmost part

Peggy's Cove N.S.—One of Canada's most photographed places and a favorite of painters too, Peggy's Cove is famous for its trim houses, its weatherworn wharves and the fishing boats bobbing in its sheltered little harbor. Peggy's is 27 miles from Halifax. (9DZ/22EW)

Everyman's Friend

The tombstone of Henry Fuller "Twelve-Foot" Davis, on a hill overlooking Peace River, records that "he was everyman's friend and never locked his cabin door." A polished wood statue in the town represents Davis as a physical giant. He was really a little man, a Vermonter who went to the Cariboo (*see* Barkerville) in 1861. He discovered two claims that exceeded regulation width, claimed the 12-foot space between them for his own and mined $15,000 in gold. Later, in the Peace River country, he was a trader and explorer whose kindness was legendary. As he lay near death he was asked whether he was afraid. Said Davis: "I never kilt nobody, I never stole from nobody, and I kept open house for travelers all my life. No, I ain't afraid to die."

of Canada—except for tiny Middle Island. Both islands lie south of parts of 27 states of the United States.

Pelee Island has a municipally financed game farm where birds are raised for the four-day Pelee Island Pheasant Shoot in late October and early November.

Pembroke Ont.   7DX/18AW
A stone lifter at the Champlain Trail Museum is made from gun carriages used in the War of 1812. When the 10-foot-high four-wheeled vehicle was positioned over a boulder, logging chains were fastened underneath and the stone was winched up with a fifth wheel. Other mementoes of the days of pioneer settlement and the great Ottawa Valley timber industry include a two-by-three-foot model of a lumber raft, a wooden pulley used to pull logs through rapids, timber stampers which identified the owners of logs, and a steam threshing engine.

□ Pansy Patch Memorial Park, three acres on the mainland and six on an island in the Muskrat River at the center of Pembroke, contains many species of trees. They include black walnut, Carpathian walnut, larch, aspen, butternut and oak.

Penetanguishene Ont.   7CY/17BV
Many residents of bilingual Penetanguishene are descendants of French and English fur traders and pioneers who settled near the Royal Navy and Military Establishments here in the period 1814-56.

The naval base was established in 1814 to protect the British supply route to Michilimackinac on Lake Michigan. Supplies were brought from Kempenfeldt Bay along the 30-mile Penetanguishene Road, built that same year by Dr. William "Tiger" Dunlop (*see* Goderich). In 1817 the base became a harbor for ships disarmed after the War of 1812,

and a busy shipbuilding program was begun. The British Army garrisoned Penetanguishene in 1828 but that post was abandoned in 1856 owing to British preoccupation with the Crimean War.

The one surviving military building, a one-story stone officers' quarters, has been restored as a museum. Reconstructed buildings and installations include officers' quarters, barracks, offices, a guardhouse, a storehouse and a sawpit. On the grounds are the skeleton hulls of two ships. One is unidentified. The other was *Tecumseth*, built in Chippawa in 1815. She so rotted that she sank here about 1835; the hull was raised in 1953.

St. James-on-the-Lines, a garrison church built in 1836-38, is still used. It has wooden pews carved by soldiers and an aisle wide enough for men to march four abreast.

□ The goodwill between English and French here is symbolized by the town's twin statues of angels representing Ontario and Quebec.

□ A bronze plaque at the foot of Main Street honors Sir John Franklin, who assembled his second Arctic expedition here in 1825.

□ The Penetanguishene Museum's artifacts of pioneer and turn-of-the-century history include a one-cylinder 1903 Oldsmobile. The museum is in what was a store (c.1870). Outside is an 1878 locomotive once used in a lumberyard.

Penticton B.C.   2DZ
Thomas Ellis, who arrived here from Ireland in 1866 and planted the first orchard in the Okanagan Valley, is honored by a plaque 4½

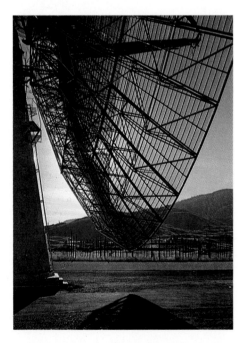

Radio telescope at the Dominion Radio Astrophysical Observatory near Penticton is used by scientists to study distant galaxies, quasars, nebulas and planets by the radio waves they emit.

miles south at Lake Skaha. A scale model of Ellis' homestead and some of his farm equipment are displayed at the Penticton Museum and Archives. The museum exhibits arrowheads, stone and bone tools, baskets and beadwork of the Salish Indians, and has collections of guns.

□ *Sicamous*, the last regular CPR sternwheeler on Okanagan Lake (she was retired in 1951), is moored here.

□ Lions, tigers, giraffes, zebras and camels are among more than 250 animals at the 560-acre Okanagan Game Farm, five miles south of Penticton.

□ Penticton holds a peach festival and the British Columbia Square Dance Jubilee in August.

Percé Que.   9DW
Bonaventure Island, two miles from the beaches of this picturesque resort town, is a famous bird sanctuary. Tens of thousands of gannets make their home on the island's 300-foot-high red cliffs from April to October. Amid the blizzard of scaling and wheeling white gannets are other birds too: murres, kittiwakes, common puffins, gulls and razor-

billed auks. Sight-seeing boats circle the 1,024-acre island.

Nearby is another bird sanctuary, Percé Rock (Pierced Rock), named by Champlain for the soaring natural arch (60 feet high and 100 feet wide) that distinguishes this enormous block of limestone in the Gulf of St. Lawrence. The multicolored strata of the 1,550-foot-long rock contain millions of fossils. Percé Rock is reached on foot at low tide.

Percé, once the largest fishing center in the Gaspé, is now almost dependent on the tourist trade. Behind it are scenic hills and mountains including Mont Joli, Les Trois Soeurs, Pic de l'Aurore (Dawn Peak) and Cap Blanc. Atop 1,050-foot Mont Sainte-Anne is a statue of the saint, the object of local fishermen's devotions on her feast day, July 26. The mountain is a landmark for fishermen at sea.

Near Cap Canon is Logan Memorial Park, where a plaque honors Sir William Logan, founder and first director of Canada's Geological Survey.

Péribonka Que.   9AW/21BW
The Bouchard house where French novelist Louis Hémon lived in 1912 and where he prepared the material for *Maria Chapdelaine* is now the Maria Chapdelaine Museum. One exhibit is a spinning wheel used by Eva Bouchard, on whom Hémon based the character of his heroine. Hémon was born in Brest and came to Canada in 1911. In Péribonka he worked as a farmhand among French settlers whose simple lives and quiet courage formed the basis for *Maria Chapdelaine*.

Perth Ont.   7DY/18CX
Robert Lyon, who "fell in mortal combat" — as is recorded on his gravestone in the Old Burying Ground here—was killed in Canada's

Percé Rock, here like some monster rising from the depths, is an island 288 feet high. Southwest along the Gaspé coast near New Carlisle, fishermen spread cod to dry on wire flakes.

Marathon swimmers pit themselves against chilly Lac Saint-Jean in an annual August race from Péribonka to Roberval *(see entry)*.

last fatal duel, June 13, 1833. Lyon, 20, made an insulting remark about the fiancée of a fellow law student, John Wilson, and Wilson issued a challenge. Wilson, charged with murder, pleaded his own case, contending he had been forced into the duel to preserve his honor. He was acquitted and later became a judge of the Ontario Supreme Court.

□ A rounded block of concrete at the old CPR station represents a 22,000-pound cheese made here and sent as a Canadian contribution to the 1893 Chicago World's Fair. The cheese was six feet high and 28 feet in circumference. The nearby Balderson Cheese factory may be visited.

□ Two three-pounder Belgian cannon that stand in front of the courthouse (1842) date from 1775-76.

□ The John Bowes Museum, in a gristmill which dates from the 1820s, has pioneer artifacts and electrical devices from the pre-1922 period when the mill also produced hydroelectric power for Perth.

□ The Perth Winter Carnival in January has ice fishing and ice sculpturing, dogsled races, sleigh rides and log-sawing and -chopping competitions. A summer festival includes a reenactment of the Wilson-Lyon duel.

□ The Inge-Va house built in 1823 by the Rev. Michael Harris is an excellent example of Colonial Georgian architecture. A blacksmith shop at nearby Fallbrook has been operated since 1888.

□ A plaque at the Royal Canadian Legion honors Herbert Taylor Reade, a Perth native awarded the Victoria Cross during the Indian Mutiny in 1857. Another honors Alexander Morris, a member of Sir John A. Macdonald's cabinet and lieutenant governor of Manitoba.

Other plaques commemorate Perth's founding in 1816, the last fatal duel and Malcolm Cameron, a member of the Baldwin-Lafontaine government in 1848-50.

Petawawa Ont. 7DX/18AV
A plaque commemorates the first military demonstration of aircraft flight in Canada. On Aug. 2, 1909, J.A.D. McCurdy and F.W. "Casey" Baldwin made four successful flights in the *Silver Dart* (*see* Baddeck). The plane was destroyed on its fifth landing. The *Baddeck No. 1* made further flights Aug. 12 and 13.

Peterborough Ont. 7CY/17EW
A mosaic tile map on the floor of the city hall rotunda points out Peterborough's position in the heart of the Kawartha Lakes resort region. This is a rugged countryside with 500 lakes and many drumlins—low hills formed during the Ice Age.

The Ontario Whitewater Slalom Championships (for canoes and kayaks) are held on Labor Day along the 18-mile stretch of the Trent-Severn Waterway between here and Burleigh Falls. In an annual Ice Floe Race in March teams cut floes at Lock 22 of the canal and race them a mile.

COURTHOUSE AND JAIL (1) An impressive neo-classic stone building completed in 1840.

RIVERVIEW PARK AND ZOO (2) A park on the Otonabee River; llamas, monkeys, bison, deer, pheasants and a miniature train.

HUTCHISON HOUSE (3) Peterborough's first stone house, it was built in 1837 by citizens seeking to dissuade their first resident physician, Dr. John Hutchison, from moving to York (Toronto). He lived in the house until his death. In 1845-47 it was the home of Sir Sandford Fleming, who later designed the first Canadian postage stamp, became engineer-in-chief of the CPR and was a leading proponent of international standard time.

LIFT LOCKS (4) The city's hydraulic lift locks, considered a major construction achievement when they were completed in 1904, are like hydraulic elevators with connected presses:

Dueling pistols in the Archibald M. Campbell Memorial Museum in Perth were used in 1833 in Canada's last fatal duel. The principals were law students; the survivor eventually became a judge in the court where he was tried.

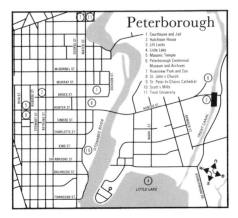

Peterborough

1. Courthouse and Jail
2. Hutchison House
3. Lift Locks
4. Little Lake
5. Masonic Temple
6. Peterborough Centennial Museum and Archives
7. Riverview Park and Zoo
8. St. John's Church
9. St. Peter-In-Chains Cathedral
10. Scott's Mills
11. Trent University

as one lock descends, it forces water into the system which makes the other lock ascend.

LITTLE LAKE (5) This midtown lake, by Beavermead Park, has a fountain with a 250-foot jet. Each summer there are free open air concerts and (in August) an Arts and Water Festival.

MASONIC TEMPLE (6) Part of this Greek Revival stone building dates from 1847.

PETERBOROUGH CENTENNIAL MUSEUM AND ARCHIVES (7) Its features include the Denne collection of a century of tinted photographs, the Peter Robinson Papers on Irish immigration in the 1820s, a display of carriages and dolls (one doll dating from 1800), and fossils from 500 million years ago. There is a working model of the Trent-Severn Waterway, an exhibit about its history, and a pioneer room with garments and artifacts.

ST. JOHN'S CHURCH (8) An Anglican church (1834-36) built in Gothic style with a square tower.

ST. PETER-IN-CHAINS CATHEDRAL (9) The Gothic-style Roman Catholic cathedral, built in 1837-38, has a bell cast in Spain more than 200 years ago.

SCOTT'S MILLS (10) A plaque commemorates Adam Scott, first settler on the site of Peterborough. He built a sawmill and gristmill in 1821.

TRENT UNIVERSITY (11) Trent is set on 1,500 rolling, wooded acres on both sides of the Otonabee River.

Petersfield Man.   6BY/15DW
The Netley Marsh at the south end of Lake Winnipeg, near the mouth of the Red River, is one of the continent's great waterfowl nesting areas.

Petrolia Ont.   7AZ/16BX
Several buildings survive from Petrolia's glory days as the oil capital of Canada in the 1880s and '90s. The town once had hundreds of drilling rigs, 15 refineries, the world's first oil exchange and the headquarters of Imperial Oil. It has not been a major oil town since the turn of the century. (*See* Oil Springs)

□ One gray stucco house was once the Little Red Bank, founded in 1869; one of the country's last private banks, it served Petrolia until 1924. On the second floor of the two-story, white brick town hall (1887) is the 700-seat Victoria Opera House.

Philipsburg Que.   19CZ
The shrine of Notre-Dame-du-Laus, in Saint-Philippe-de-Philipsburg Church, has a

Trent University (top) is on the Otonabee River at Peterborough. Its modern buildings have won national and international awards for architectural excellence. Peterborough boasts the world's highest hydraulic lift locks, part of which is seen (left) from a pedestrian tunnel through the north end of the structure. The twin locks, which raise and lower vessels 65 feet, were completed in 1904 to serve commercial traffic; they now mainly accommodate pleasure craft. There are boat tours of the locks.

45-inch plaster statue of the Virgin and Child copied from a statue in Laus in the Dauphiné region of southeast France. A cloak which once adorned the statue in Laus is in the reliquary of the shrine here.

☐ Philipsburg United Church, the oldest United church in Quebec still in use, dates from 1819. Originally a Methodist church, it was a rallying point for soldiers in the Rebellion of 1837 and during Indian and Fenian raids in 1865-67.

☐ A 48-foot covered bridge over a creek at Saint-Armand-Ouest, about six miles east, is the shortest in Quebec (picture, p. 312).

Phoenix B.C.   2EZ

Once Canada's highest incorporated city (4,500 feet above sea level), Phoenix boomed on copper in the 1890s, grew to have 3,500 people and 28 saloons, sent its sons to war, started to die when the price of copper tumbled, and was deserted by 1920. It now is a ghost town. In a cemetery are the graves of mine-accident victims. On a cenotaph are the names of 15 other men killed in World War I.

Pickering Ont.   7CY/17CX

Displays at Ontario Hydro's nuclear power station here describe in simple terms the conversion of nuclear energy into power and compare the energy capabilities of coal, uranium and hydroelectric, thermal and nuclear power. Visitors use machines that explain nuclear-generated power and employ a Geiger counter to compare different substances as shields against radiation.

Picton Ont.   7DY

The White Chapel, two miles east of Picton, was built in 1809-11 and has been maintained as a place of worship longer than any other Ontario church of Methodist origin. Although regular services ceased in 1820 (when the congregation moved to the site of what now is Picton United Church), Sunday School classes were held in the chapel until the 1920s. A commemorative service is held in June.

☐ Sir John A. Macdonald, Canada's first prime minister, practised law in the Prince Edward County courthouse here. It was built in 1832-34 in Greek Revival style and is one of the oldest remaining structures of its type in Ontario. A plaque at the post office records that Macdonald was secretary of the Prince Edward District School Board.

☐ Old St. Mary Magdalene's Church is a red brick Gothic edifice erected in 1825-27 by the Rev. William Macaulay, a pioneer Anglican priest. In the early 1970s the building was donated to Prince Edward County to be converted into a museum. A second St. Mary Magdalene's, built in 1913, is still in use.

☐ A plaque at Picton United Church, first built in 1820 and rebuilt in 1854 and 1898, marks the site of two important Methodist conferences. One resulted in the separation of the Canadian and American Methodist churches in 1824, the other in the foundation of Toronto's Victoria University in 1831.

☐ A brick farmhouse four miles west of Picton was the West Lake Boarding School, the first Quaker seminary in Canada. Built in the mid-1830s, it is a fine example of Loyalist neo-classic architecture.

☐ The Prince Edward Gold Cup Races for large inboard motorboats are held here in late summer.

Pictou N.S.   9EY/23DY

In the Micmac Museum are objects from two Indian burial mounds uncovered here in 1955: native articles and goods traded to the Indians by the French as early as 1605 and buried before 1672. Copper cooking utensils, axes, knives, spearheads, glass beads and woven grass baskets were found, along with human bones.

☐ The town holds a lobster festival in July, with power and lobster boat races, seafood dinners, a parade and massed pipe bands.

☐ A monument to some 180 colonists who came from Scotland in the barque *Hector* was erected in 1923 on the 150th anniversary of their 1773 arrival here. In 1816 the settlers established Pictou Academy, a widely known educational center still in use. Norway House, now the Maritime Odd Fellows Home, was built in 1813.

Lobster suppers, often outdoors and hopefully under a blue sky and a hot sun, are a summertime tradition down east. Some towns, such as Pictou, have lobster festivals lasting several days.

Pierreville Que.   7FX/19CX

Canada's biggest producer of fire engines, Pierre Thibault 1972 Ltd., manufactures an average of 150 a year. There are tours of the foundry, machine shop, painting and woodworking shops and engineering department.

St. Mary River snakes in from the south (top) to join the Oldman River (foreground) near Lethbridge. The Oldman rises west of Pincher Creek; it and the Bow become the South Saskatchewan.

Pilot Mound Man.   6BZ/15AZ

A plaque records that excavations of an Indian burial mound in 1908 "uncovered evidence of a civilization dating back perhaps 1,000 years." Shell and copper beads and wristbands with rawhide strings were among the objects found. The mound, from which Pilot Mound takes its name, was later used as a gathering place for buffalo hunters and for Indians who staged ceremonial dances.

□ The Pilot Mound Museum has a Wilfrid Laurier chair (c.1895), with a picture of the former prime minister set into the back rest, and a "Little Wanzer" sewing machine, made by the Wanzer Company of Hamilton, Ont. An agent's card reports the machine "was awarded the first and highest prize medal for family sewing machines at the world's fair held in Paris, 1867, competing with 87 other machines." This "latest novelty of the age" was equipped with "tucker, gauge, quilting gauge, hemmer, friller, self-sewer, braid holder, thread, oiler, oilcan (filled with oil), screwdriver, four bobbins, four needles, spool of thread and printed instructions."

Pincher Creek Alta.   4AZ/13CZ

A pygmy medicine mask, a sorcerer's mask and an elephant hide war shield taken during the conquest of the Belgian Congo in the late 1800s are part of a collection in the home of Gaston Rigaux. Other African objects—all collected by Rigaux's father, Ferdinand—include harpoons, knives, axes, baskets and musical instruments. A table and two chairs once owned by an African king (who alone among his people was permitted to own a chair) were carried 1,500 miles along a caravan route to the sea.

The collection also includes antiques that date from the 1500s. There are two Italian paintings, one (1610) on a copper base, the other (1605) on wood, and an Italian cabinet (1515) inlaid with ivory, marble, semiprecious stones and tortoise shell. The furniture includes a Louis XIII writing desk and chairs, William and Mary chairs and a 16th-century Belgian chest.

The Rigaux house is made of logs and fitted with low, heavy-hinged Gothic doors and many-paned windows. It may be visited.

Pine Falls Man.   6BY/15EW

Manitoba Hydro's 82,000-kilowatt Pine Falls generating station and the Abitibi Paper Company mill here may be toured.

Placentia Nfld.   11DZ

Ruins of the fortifications from which the French directed forays against British settlements in Newfoundland in the 1600s stand in 60-acre Castle Hill National Historic Park. The French built Fort Royal in 1692 and made repeated attacks on the British in St. John's and elsewhere until the 1713 Treaty of Utrecht gave the fortress to the British. The British constructed their own fort, Fort Frederick, in the 1720s and in 1762 rebuilt the French bastion, renaming it Castle Graves.

The park's interpretation center tells Placentia's history from the arrival of the first Basque fishermen and contains artifacts, maps and plans of the French and British forts. It looks out on Placentia Bay, where Churchill and Roosevelt met to sign the Atlantic Charter in August 1941.

Below Castle Hill are a number of French and British batteries and a wall of stone rubble which formed a fortification detached from the main defenses. In the inner fort are the remains of guardrooms, barracks, a powder magazine and the foundations of a British blockhouse. The entrance to the fort is the one used almost three centuries ago by the French.

The town has four historic sites. Markers locate the sites of Fort Louis, Fort Frederick, an old Basque fort that stood on a hill overlooking the town and a blockhouse that protected the beach.

Pleasant Bay N.S. *see* Cape Breton Highlands National Park

Plessisville Que.   9AX/20BX
A cooperative of Quebec maple sugar producers here is the world's biggest processor of such maple products as maple sugar, taffy, candy and syrup. A festival is held in Plessisville during the final week of sugaring off in late April. There are art and handicraft exhibits and prizes for recipes using maple syrup.

Point de Bute N.B.   9DY/23AX
Plaques set in a red sandstone arch (the entrance to a cemetery) commemorate Canada's first Methodist church and first Methodist preacher, the Rev. William Black. The stone church built here about 1788 by settlers from Yorkshire, England, was replaced by another in 1822. It in turn was replaced about 1881 by a frame structure, the present Point de Bute United Church.

Pointe-à-la-Croix Que. *see* Restigouche

Pointe-au-Père Que.   9BW
The sole monument in Empress of Ireland Cemetery is a stark reminder of one of the worst sea tragedies ever—the sinking of the *Empress of Ireland* about 10 miles east of here on May 29, 1914, with a loss of 1,015 lives. Fewer than 500 persons survived. The monument bears the names of 20 of the victims. It marks their burial place and that of "sixty-eight others unidentified." Some victims' bodies were buried elsewhere; many were never recovered. The 14,000-ton liner, headed downriver on a voyage from Quebec to Liverpool, sank in 150 feet of water less than 20 minutes after being struck by the Norwegian collier *Storstad*. The collier, although damaged, reached port; all her crew survived.
□ Pointe-au-Père was named after the Rev. Henri Nouvel (Père Nouvel), a Jesuit missionary who came here in 1663. A cairn commemorates the first Mass he celebrated here.
□ In the parish church, a shrine to Saint Anne of Pointe-au-Père, is a five-foot copper statue of Saint Anne, which a sailor brought from Brittany about 1870.

Pointe-au-Pic Que.   9AW
The grave of William Hume Blake, a lawyer who wrote three books on fishing (*Brown*

Castle Hill fortifications, part of a national historic park, overlook the town of Placentia, nestled between its beach and Southeast Arm.

Waters, In a Fishing Country and *A Fisherman's Creed*) is in the yard of the Murray Bay Protestant Church. Blake translated Louis Hémon's *Maria Chapdelaine* (*see* Péribonka). A plaque in the church honors U.S. President William Howard Taft. Many members of the Taft family have summered here.

Pointe-aux-Anglais Que.   9CW/10GZ
Some 120 parishioners each carried 40 stones three miles from a Gulf of St. Lawrence beach to where Saint-Paul-de-Pointe-aux-Anglais Church was erected in 1962. Bas-relief Stations of the Cross by Médard Bourgault are of basswood on walnut backgrounds. Above the altar is an oak crucifix with a five-foot figure of Christ, also sculpted by Bourgault.

Pointe-aux-Anglais got its name from a disaster that may have saved New France 49 years before it finally fell. A mediocre British seadog, Rear Adm. Sir Hovenden Walker, led a 12,000-man force out of Boston July 30, 1711, bent on the conquest of Quebec. Baffled by fogs, currents and poor pilots, hampered by his own ineptitude, Walker mistook his position after rounding the Gaspé and saw eight vessels plunge aground on Quebec's north shore, killing 850 soldiers and sailors and 35 women ancillaries. Only a wind shift saved others. Walker withdrew, and planned to attack French-held Placentia in Newfoundland. But a shortage of supplies changed his mind, and that attack too was abandoned.

Point Edward Ont. *see* Sarnia

Point Michaud N.S.   9FY/23GY
One of Nova Scotia's most beautiful beaches is here, level white sand stretching for two miles along the shore of the Atlantic Ocean.

Point Pelee National Park (Ont.) 7AZ/16BZ
This southernmost tip of the Canadian mainland, at the same latitude as Rome, Ankara

and northern California, has a unique combination of plant and animal life. Many species here are usually associated with more southerly areas. There are white sassafras trees, and such shrubs as hop-tree, spice bush and fragrant sumac, all rarely seen elsewhere in Canada. Many of the trees are covered with vines of wild grape and virginia creeper.

The park occupies the last six miles of an 11-mile-long sandy peninsula, constantly struggling to maintain its triangular form against the buffeting of Lake Erie. The lake not only makes its eternal assault on the land but also moderates the seasonal changes and gives the park one of the longest frost-free growing periods in Canada. Some 2,500 acres of the 3,800-acre park is inland freshwater marsh. Trees near the beaches give way to thick grass; closer to the water small plants struggle to hold to the sand. In all, the park is bordered by 14 miles of sand and pebble beaches which are heavily used during the summer.

Plant growth is rapid until late June and there is a spectacular succession of abundant flowers. Prickly pear cactus produces brilliant yellow flowers during late June and early July. The park's deciduous forest is in near-primeval state; evergreens are almost nonexistent. Instead there is a rich variety of black walnut, sycamore, dogwood, shagbark hickory, butternut, hackberry and red cedar. Point Pelee animals include pond muskrats, mink, brown bats, coyotes, tiny (one-ounce) Baird's white-footed mice, cottontail rabbits and white-tailed deer. Point Pelee has probably more types of turtles than anywhere else in the country.

The park's biggest attraction is its birds. Two major migration flyways intersect here and the spring and fall migrations are spectacular. Each spring and autumn, more than 100 species can be seen in a single day; the dawn chorus is unforgettable. Migrating hawks, eagles, blue jays, blackbirds, ducks, geese, herons and terns all stop here. Of 323 species of birds that have been seen in the park, 90 stay to nest, including the great blue heron, green heron and great horned owl.

Many of the park's flowers, trees, birds, animals and insects are identified in a museum. There is a 1¼-mile nature trail through the forest and a 5,100-foot boardwalk tour of the marshland.

□ A plaque at the park entrance tells that Maj. Gen. Sir Isaac Brock, hero of the Battle of Queenston Heights, landed here four days before his successful attack on Detroit during the War of 1812.

Pont-Rouge Que. 9AX/20BW

The three-story stone Déry Mill was powered by water brought from the Jacques Cartier River through an underground canal nearly 2,000 feet long. The mill, built in 1817 as a gristmill, was converted to a pulp mill in 1883 and to a hydroelectric generating station in 1915. It is no longer used.

The village's first two buildings still stand.

They are the two-story clapboard Déry house (1752) and the Trépanier house (1794).

Poplar Point Man. 6BY/15CX

St. Anne's, an Anglican church built of logs in 1859, is still in use.

Porcupine Ont. *see* Timmins

Porquis Junction Ont. 7CV/8HZ

A plaque commemorates a Porquis Junction man, Sgt. Aubrey Cosens, who was posthumously awarded the Victoria Cross for breaking enemy resistance at the German hamlet of Mooshof on Feb. 26, 1945. With four infantrymen providing covering fire, he killed 20 German paratroopers and captured 20 more. He was killed by a sniper as he went to report to his company commander.

Portage la Prairie Man. 6BY/15BX

Cairns near here mark where a great explorer built a key fort in 1738 and where, 134 years later, a farmer from Scotland turned the sod of the first homestead in western Canada. Fort la Reine was Pierre de La Vérendrye's headquarters as he and his sons made their epic journeys across the prairies and eventually discovered the Rocky Mountains. It was only some six miles away that John Sutherland Sanderson homesteaded in 1872.

□ The main building of six at the Fort la Reine Museum and Pioneer Village, one mile east of the city, has displays of Indian weapons and beadwork and of pioneer-day relics that include a dentist's pedal-operated drill and a tooth extractor with a wooden handle and a reversible claw hook. A two-story log house built in the 1880s contains period furnishings and an 1883 church has original pews, organ and pulpit. A schoolhouse dates

Point Tupper N.S.—Giant supertankers, the largest longer than three football fields end to end, disgorge crude oil at a 2,000-foot-long deepwater terminal dock. A ship can berth, unload and sail within 24 hours. One 2,350,000-barrel cargo satisfies the Gulf Oil refinery here for almost a month. The tankers draw about 80 feet but the water at the dock is more than 100 feet deep. (9FY/23FY)

Pond Inlet N.W.T.—A supply ship picks her way among ice floes as she nears this Eskimo settlement in the north part of Baffin Island. One dry cargo ship and one tanker a year visit the remote community.

from 1881. A replica of Fort la Reine has a stockade with two bastions, a log trading post, a smithy and a stable. On the museum grounds are a York boat and a Red River cart.

□ An island in Crescent Lake, in the heart of the city, is preserved as a bird sanctuary where the nesting habits of the Canada goose may be observed. The lake is used for snowmobile racing during a festival in March.

Port Alberni B.C.   2BZ/12BX
Cathedral Grove in MacMillan Provincial Park, 10 miles east, contains hundreds of giant Douglas firs (150-225 feet high and 4-5 feet in diameter). Some are 600 years old.

□ In Sproat Lake Provincial Park, eight miles northwest, are Indian rock carvings of mythological beasts.

□ A cairn at the MacMillan Bloedel pulp mill commemorates the first paper mill in British Columbia, built here in 1894. Incorporated in the monument are the grinding stones, the only relics of the mill that used rags, rope and ferns to produce 50 tons a day.

□ A Chinook salmon hatchery at Robertson Creek, 14 miles northwest, has facilities for incubating 3,000,000 eggs. A fish ladder helps salmon around the falls in Stamp Falls Provincial Park, nine miles north.

Port-Alfred Que.   9AW/21CX
An inscribed stone marks the spot where in 1838 the schooner *Le Sainte-Marie* disembarked pioneers who were to establish the cradle of civilization in the Kingdom of the Saguenay at Grande-Baie. A stone statue of a settler wielding an axe stands on a 20-foot stone pedestal at Grande-Baie, now within the city limits. This monument commemorates the pioneers and their voyage from La Malbaie.

Port-Alfred is on Ha! Ha! Bay, at the head of deepwater navigation on the Saguenay River. The port handles about 500 freighters annually. Cargoes include bauxite, which is then transported by rail to the aluminum smelters at Arvida (*see entry*), and newsprint. The city's paper mills, which may be visited, produce 800 tons of newsprint daily.

Port aux Basques Nfld. *see* Channel-Port aux Basques

Port au Choix Nfld.   11BX
Skeletons and artifacts of "red paint people" who roamed from Maine to Labrador some 5,000 years ago are displayed at Port au Choix National Historic Park.

Little had been known about the red paint people (of the Maritime Archaic culture) until about 100 skeletons or partial skeletons were discovered here in the late 1960s. At other burial sites nearly everything had disintegrated except the ceremonial red ocher which accompanied each burial.

The burials are estimated to have taken place between 2340 and 1270 B.C. The skeletons have peculiarities typical of Indians, resembling Indian skulls found in the Ottawa Valley, the Laurentians and Maine. The graves were always lined with red ocher and frequently marked or protected by boulders or slabs of rock. They often contained bundles of artifacts for use by the dead in the afterlife. These materials provide rich information on the life of the red paint people.

They lived by hunting and fishing. "Bayonets" and spearheads of slate and bone, lances of whalebone, and daggers of antler, caribou bone and walrus ivory are evidence of land hunting; barbed antler or bone harpoons and whalebone foreshafts show that large marine animals were hunted. Smaller saw-toothed and barbed points may have been used for spearing fish or hunting birds. Awls, gouges, adzes and axes show there was a well-developed wood-carving industry, and fine bone needles in decorated caribou bone cases demonstrate the existence of sewn garments.

□ On nearby Pointe Riche, relics were discovered in the late 1950s of a Dorset Eskimo culture dating from 100 A.D. They include weapons and tools and pits covered with bark and skins to make dwellings.

"Red paint people" who thrived 50 centuries ago were little known until discovery of a burial site at Port au Choix. High, dry beaches along the Gulf of St. Lawrence—they now are covered by a layer of peaty humus after several thousand years of forest growth—provided good drainage and alkalinity. That resulted in the unusual state of preservation of the Port au Choix skeletons.

Port Burwell Ont. 7BZ
The Walking Sandhills, nine miles east, are dunes that rise 300 feet out of Lake Erie and are frequently reshaped by winds.

□ Trinity Anglican Church (1836) is an example of Gothic Revival architecture.

Port Carling Ont. 7CX
One of several thousand "disappearing propeller" boats built here in 1920-30 is on display in the Port Carling Pioneer Museum. In log-strewn waters the propeller of this 14-foot wooden craft could be retracted into a housing by operating a lever. Part of the propeller remained in the water so the boat could proceed at reduced speed. The boats became obsolete with the development of stronger propellers in the 1930s.

Port-Cartier Que. 9CV/10GY
The man-made harbor here, blasted from rock by the Quebec Cartier Mining Company, has a minimum pierside depth of 50 feet at low tide. With an annual turnover of 19,000,000 tons it ranks fourth in Canada (behind Sept-Iles, Vancouver and Montreal). Ships from the Great Lakes bring grain to Port-Cartier's 10,000,000-bushel elevator and return

with iron ore that has been shipped here by rail from Gagnon, Que. Other vessels reload the grain for shipment to many countries.

Port Colborne Ont. 7CZ/17CZ
The biggest lock on the Welland Canal is here at the Lake Erie end: 1,380-foot Lock 8, one of the longest in the world.

□ The International Nickel Company refinery here is the world's biggest.

Port Coquitlam B.C. 2CZ/12EX
One of Canada's finest motor-racing circuits is five miles northwest. Westwood Circuit covers 305 acres, has 1.8 miles of track and stages several of Canada's International Sports Car Conference races each year.

Port Dover Ont. 7BZ/17BZ
A 20-foot stone cross marks where two French priests, François Dollier de Casson and René-François de Bréhant de Galinée, landed in 1669 and claimed the lands around Lake Erie for Louis XIV.

□ Port Dover is the home of a 35-boat fishing fleet. An Ontario Hydro generating station at Nanticoke, eight miles east, will have a 4,000,000-kilowatt capacity when completed.

Port Elgin N.B. 23BX
Nine English soldiers killed in an Indian raid here in 1755 are honored by plaques at St. James Presbyterian Church and in a cairn at a nearby lighthouse. The headstones from the soldiers' graves are also here.

Port Elgin Ont. 7BY
A 600-year-old Indian village being reconstructed here is the only one in North America to be rebuilt on its original site and according to its ancient plot plan. Some 500 Petuns, primitive people whose lives were centered around simple farming and fishing, lived here briefly in the mid-14th century.

Archaeologists from the National Museum of Man and the Royal Ontario Museum rebuilt the village, guided by soil moldings and other marks from wood that rotted away hundreds of years ago. The village, surrounded by a double palisade of stakes, consisted of a dozen communal longhouses.

□ The manufacture of curling brooms is seen during tours of the Stevens Hepner Co.

Port Hammond B.C. 12EX
Siding, shingles and shakes—some 75,000,000 board feet every year—are produced here at the Hammond Division of British Columbia Forest Products, Ltd., the world's largest western red cedar sawmill. It may be toured.

Port Hastings N.S. 9FY/23FY
The 4,500-foot-long Canso Causeway linking mainland Nova Scotia with Cape Breton Island is 218 feet deep, probably the deepest causeway in the world. It is 800 feet wide at its base in the Strait of Canso, 80 feet on the surface, and carries a two-lane highway, a railway track and a pedestrian walkway. Ships

use a navigation lock at the Port Hastings (northern) end. The causeway, opened in 1955, keeps ice from entering the strait from the north and thus creates an ice-free harbor 10 miles long (*see* Point Tupper).

Port Hill P.E.I.   23BW
Green Park Provincial Historic Park tells about wooden shipbuilding through an interpretive center, a section of a shipyard, a half-scale model of a ship's cradle, and the restored mansion of a shipbuilder.

Port Hope Ont.   7CY/17EX
St. Mark's Anglican Church, built of wood in Gothic Revival style in 1822 and still in use, is one of Ontario's oldest churches. In the churchyard is the grave of Vincent Massey, Canada's first native-born governor-general.

The Blue Stone House—coated with blue-tinted plaster because the stone is porous—dates from the 1830s. It is an example of Greek Revival architecture.

Trinity College School, founded in 1865, is on the outskirts of town. It is one of Canada's oldest independent boys' schools.

Port La Tour N.S.   22BY
Traces of two 17th-century forts, among the first built in Nova Scotia, are barely visible here. One, at nearby Baccaro Point, was Fort Saint-Louis, built about 1627 by the French trader Charles de La Tour. The other, on Barrington Bay, was Fort Temple (1658), the first English fort on the coast of Acadia.

Port Moody B.C.   2CZ/12EX
A cairn commemorates the arrival here July 4, 1886, of the first train to reach the Pacific from Montreal. Port Moody was not the CPR's western terminus for long; the line was extended 12½ miles to Vancouver in 1887.

□ Port Moody has one of North America's oldest red cedar lumber mills, a division of Weldwood of Canada Ltd. There are tours.

Port Morien N.S. *see* Glace Bay

Portneuf Que.   9AX/20AW
The Manoir Langlois, built of wood about 1690, and a stone house built about 1725 both have steep roofs with two chimneys at each end and four dormer windows on each side.

Port Perry Ont.   ˙7CY/17DW
Buildings that date from the 1860s—including a house, a school and a Methodist church—house the Scugog Shores Historical Museum. A pair of pattens on display is one of only a few remaining pairs in Ontario. The pattens, forerunners of toe rubbers, resemble wooden sandals mounted on circles of wrought iron to elevate the wearer about two inches above muddy streets.

A plaque at the museum honors Jimmy Frise, one of Canada's leading cartoonists, who attended this school and church. Frise collaborated with Greg Clark on Birdseye Center, a Toronto *Star Weekly* cartoon.

Port Rowan Ont.—The oldest mill in Ontario is a gristmill that John Backhouse built, apparently in 1798, on Dedrich Creek, two miles north of here. It was operated by Backhouse's descendants until 1955, then sold to a conservation authority. The long wooden flume took water from the millpond to the waterwheel. A museum near the mill displays pioneer farm implements. A hiking trail winds through woods with rare tulip, sassafras and shagbark hickory trees. (7BZ)

Port Royal N.S.   22BW
A reconstruction of the first successful white settlement in Canada stands on the site of the Port Royal Habitation that Champlain, de Monts and Poutrincourt established in 1605, and that the English destroyed in 1613 (*see* Annapolis Royal). The buildings of 20½-acre Port Royal National Historic Park are based on drawings of the originals by Champlain. They form a square around a courtyard in the style of a 16th-century French farm and are fortified by a palisade and a cannon platform. They include a governor's residence, a priest's house, a chapel, a guardroom, a kitchen, a bakery, a blacksmith shop, living quarters, an artisans' studio, a community room and a trading room where fur trade business was transacted with the Indians. No nails or spikes join the timbers; they are mortised and tenoned and pinned together. All furnishings are reproductions in the style of the early 1600s.

The oak main gate is dotted with iron studs and has a Judas peephole, a small sliding door that allowed inspection of visitors before letting them in. Above the gate are the coats of arms of France and Navarre.

Port Royal Habitation as Champlain, de Monts and Poutrincourt knew it has been reconstructed on the shore of the Annapolis Basin. Over a gate are the coats of arms of France and Navarre. A well dug where the original was has a shingled roof; ovens and fireplaces are of bricks made from clay dug at the site; fieldstone chimneys, as on the governor's residence (right), are mortared with a mixture of clay, sand and cement. In the building with stairs are storerooms, a trading room and a wine cellar.

Here, in 1606, Champlain instituted North America's first social club, *l'Ordre de Bon-Temps* (the Order of Good Cheer). The 15 members of the order took turns being Grand Master, with responsibility for the menu. Each day's meal began with a procession led by the Grand Master wearing his ceremonial collar and carrying his staff of office and ended with a toast as he passed the insignia to his successor. A typical menu included moose-meat pie, beaver tail, salmon, roast caribou and breast of goose.

Marc Lescarbot, a Paris lawyer, wrote and produced North America's first play here. *Le Théâtre de Neptune* was performed in 1607 to welcome Poutrincourt and Champlain back from an exploration down the coast. The colonists grew the first cereals in Canada, built the first mill (*see* p. 32) and converted the first Indians to Christianity.

Port Severn Ont.   17BV
A lock on the Severn River is the western end of the Trent-Severn Waterway linking Georgian Bay with Lake Ontario at Trenton.

Port Stanley Ont.   7BZ/16DY
Migrating blue jays and hawks, whose flyways pass over Port Stanley, can best be observed from Hawk Cliff, two miles east. As many as 500 blue jays a minute can sometimes be seen flying south between mid-September and mid-October. Hawks, up to 25,000 a day in good weather, fly over between September and Christmas.

□ Port Stanley has Canada's largest ballroom (220 feet by 100).

Port Union Nfld.   11DY
On a hill overlooking the town is a huge monument to a labor leader who in 1914 founded

Port Union as the headquarters of his Fishermen's Protective Union. Sir William Coaker's tomb, in a 1½-acre plot surrounded by a concrete fence, is 60 steps up on a platform with a marble railing. At the head of the tomb is a three-foot-high bust of Sir William, who died in 1938. The fishermen's union organized not only a political party but also trading, light-and-power, publishing, shipping, shipbuilding and cold storage companies. All operated as a fishermen's cooperative. While the union did much to combat merchants' exploitation of fishermen, it never realized Coaker's dream of political and economic control of Newfoundland.

Port Williams N.S.   22DV
The port is famous for tides that rise and fall as much as 40 feet. Ships loading at low tide are high and dry beside the wharf.

One feature of a field day here in August is an ox-pull competition. The best of some 35 teams (of two oxen each) drag loads as heavy as 5½ tons.

Powell River B.C.   2BY/12CW
MacMillan Bloedel's newsprint mill, Canada's largest, with capacity to produce 632,000 tons a year, uses 2,000,000,000 gallons of water a day—enough for a city more than 10 times the size of Toronto. There are tours.

□ Among objects in the Powell River Historical Museum is a 10-inch-long cannon (c.1873) of a type the Hudson's Bay Company sold to Indians for mounting on canoes.

Prescott Ont.   7EY/18DY
A three-story blockhouse built in 1838 has been restored as the main attraction of 12.7-acre Fort Wellington National Historic Park. The fort itself dates from 1812, when pentagonal earthworks, a palisade and a dry ditch were constructed as a defense against expected American raids.

None came. Instead, British and Canadian soldiers from Fort Wellington attacked Ogdensburg, N.Y., in one of the most daring raids of the War of 1812. They drilled daily on the ice of the St. Lawrence River during the winter of 1812-13, each day moving closer to the American shore. So accustomed were the Americans to the sight of enemy soldiers nearby that they were taken by surprise when a force broke drill formation and attacked. It easily captured Ogdensburg.

The fort saw service during the Mackenzie Rebellion of 1837, was a major defensive position during the Fenian Raids of 1866 and was last garrisoned in 1885.

The blockhouse has stone walls four feet thick. The ground floor, consisting of a guardroom, storeroom, armory and powder magazine, serves as a museum. Exhibits include rifles, pistols, swords, cannon, shot, ramrods and historical documents and pictures. A three-foot-wide stone-lined underground tunnel leads to a restored stone caponierre, or listening post, outside the fort.

□ A 66-foot stone tower, built as a windmill

in 1820 and converted to a lighthouse in 1873, is one mile east. It was captured in 1838 by Col. Nils Von Schoultz and Americans sympathetic to William Lyon Mackenzie. They later surrendered and Von Schoultz, despite an able defense by John A. Macdonald, was hanged less than a month after the battle.

□ A cairn four miles east commemorates Fort de Lévis, built on Isle Royale in 1760. It was the scene of the last French stand in Canada.

□ Among Loyalist houses here are the Jones house (1827) and the Peck house, both in American neo-classic style.

□ At Johnstown, two miles east, is the Ogdensburg-Prescott International Bridge, 7,385 feet long and 125 feet high.

Preston Ont. *see* Cambridge

Prince Albert Sask.   4DX
The highlight of a festival here in February is the Saskatchewan Championship Dog Derby, in which contestants drive eight-dog teams 16 miles a day for three days. Other features are a junior dog derby, log-sawing, flour-packing and fiddler contests and snowmobile races. A "king trapper" is chosen for proficiency in log sawing, wood chopping, flour packing and bannock baking. Among his prizes is the flour (as much as 1,000 pounds) that he managed to carry in his special harness in the flour-packing contest.

□ One of the first churches in Saskatchewan (then part of the Northwest Territories) was built by the Rev. James Nisbet when he founded Prince Albert in 1866. The little log Presbyterian church, which also served as a school, is now a museum of local history in Bryant Park.

□ In the cemetery of St. Mary's Church (1874-76) are the graves of men of the North West Mounted Police killed in action during the Northwest Rebellion of 1885. Also here are the graves of three Mounties killed in 1895 and 1897 while trying to capture the fugitive Almighty Voice (*see* Duck Lake).

□ A cairn on the north bank of the Saskatchewan River marks where Peter Pond built a fur-trading post in 1776.

□ In the Lund Wildlife Exhibit are more than 800 specimens of Canadian wildlife.

Prince Albert National Park (Sask.)   4DW
Deep in this 1,496-square-mile park, beside Ajawaan Lake, is the grave of Grey Owl. Nearby is the log cabin in which the famous conservationist lived for the last seven years of his life. Grey Owl, who wore buckskin and braided his long black hair, was thought to be an Indian. After his death in 1938 it was revealed that he was an Englishman, Archibald Stansfeld Belaney, who had come to Canada at age 15. During the 1930s, in books and lectures, he battled against the indiscriminate killing of animals for sport.

□ On rocky islands in Lavallée Lake is one of Canada's biggest colonies of the white pelican. At Waskesiu, the park's only townsite, is

an interpretive center with displays of the park's flora and fauna and geology. Mammals in the park include moose, caribou, elk, black bear, beaver, wolves and coyotes. Birds include hawks, eagles, cormorants, pelicans, kingfishers and loons. There is a herd of about 20 buffalo.

Prince Edward Island National Park
9EX/23CW

Some of Canada's finest beaches are here, backed by sand dunes or red sandstone cliffs. Supervised beaches include Brackley, Cavendish, Rustico (*see entries*), Dalvay and Stanhope. The park, nowhere more than 1½ miles wide, extends for 25 miles along the island's north shore. There are more than 900 species of flowering plants on the island, and more than 200 kinds of birds, including the great blue heron, which nests on Rustico Island.

Prince George B.C.
1AZ/2DW

Plaques commemorate Alexander Mackenzie's passage down the Fraser River en route to the Pacific in 1793 (*see* Bella Coola) and Simon Fraser's establishment of Fort George 14 years later.

The city rebuilt Fraser's North West Company fort on its original site in 1958—in 90-acre Fort George Park. The lone building within the palisade is a museum. Mounted birds and animals reflect the area's natural history; the fronts of pioneer buildings—a hotel, a surveyor's office and a general store—serve as backgrounds for exhibits of pioneer furnishings. Near the fort is a Carrier Indian cemetery in which headstones are engraved in a syllabic system of writing developed for the Indians by the Rev. A.G. Morice.

Canada's national parks offer an endless variety of sights and sounds—from the whisper of trees beside a still lake in Prince Albert Park (above) to the crash of the sea in Prince Edward Island Park, where men gather a seaweed called Irish moss. The more than two dozen parks range from Point Pelee, the southernmost tip of Canada's mainland, to Baffin Island in the Arctic, from Pacific Rim on the rugged west coast of Vancouver Island, to Terra Nova on the Atlantic.

□ The 277-mile Cariboo Highway from Cache Creek joins the John Hart Highway here. The Hart cuts 256 miles northeast to Dawson Creek, terminus of the Alaska Highway.

□ Logging sports, scuba diving and dogsled and car races on the Taber Lake ice are features of the week-long Prince George Winter Carnival in January.

□ Off the John Hart Highway at Summit Lake, 30 miles north of Prince George, a plaque marks the divide from which rivers flow north to the Arctic or south (then east and west) to the Atlantic and Pacific.

Prince Rupert B.C.
2AV

This port some 30 miles south of the Alaska panhandle calls itself the halibut capital of the world: it has an annual average catch of 16,000,000 pounds. From Prince Rupert's ice-free harbor, one of the finest natural harbors in the world, as many as 2,000 fishing vessels sail in search also of herring, salmon, cod and sole. The city has six salmon canneries and five cold storage plants, one with a 13,800,000-pound capacity.

Prairie wheat moves through Prince Rupert and its 2,500,000-bushel elevator. The city is one western terminus of the Yellow-

head Route (*see* p.116). It is the southern terminus of the Alaska ferry system and the northernmost British Columbia Ferries stop; the *Queen of Prince Rupert* (picture, p.184) links Prince Rupert and Kelsey Bay by way of the Inside Passage. There are freighter and plane connections between Prince Rupert and the Queen Charlotte Islands (*see* Masset).

□ One of three large totem poles outside the Museum of Northern British Columbia here is a copy of a Tsimshian wolf totem, a famous Nass River pole. The others are Haida totems from the Queen Charlottes, one an unusual flower totem. The museum collection of Indian art, artifacts and handicrafts includes one of the tallest (26½ inches) argillite poles ever carved. There are spoons of horn, shell and wood, a Chilkat Indian blanket of mountain goat wool, and a medicine man's apron trimmed with puffin beaks and Chinese coins. There are also displays of Eskimo art, Oriental art, African artifacts, trees native to the Skeena area and Samoan handicrafts.

□ Haida and Tsimshian totem poles in the city's several parks are among the west coast's finest examples of totem carving.

□ Butze Rapids, a reversing tidal stream between Wainwright and Morse basins in Prince Rupert harbor, are said to rival the famous reversing falls at Saint John, N.B.

Princeton B.C. 2DZ
Twenty-three pictograph sites along the rugged north side of the Similkameen River are the heaviest known concentration of prehistoric Indian art in British Columbia.

□ Gay Nineties relics in the Princeton and District Pioneer Museum include a four-foot-high, wheel-driven forerunner of the modern

cocktail shaker. It came from a bar in Granite Creek, which once had a population of 10,000 and claimed to be one of the largest cities west of Chicago. It is now a ghost town.

□ The Similkameen Mining Company's copper mine may be toured.

Prince William N.B. 9CY
Kings Landing Historical Settlement is an authentic recapturing of the sights and sounds of the towns that pioneers built along the Saint John River. In one of the biggest and most ambitious such projects in Canada, a whole new community has been created

Indian pictograph near Princeton includes three men in a rough circle. One interpretation is that it represents white men who insulted a girl of the Ashnola tribe. After the murder of an Indian who went to avenge the insult, one white man escaped but three others were slain.

here—in an area whose first settlers were discharged veterans of the King's American Dragoons, after the American Revolution. The settlement has 55 buildings open to the public, including a smithy, two mills, a church, an inn and a village hall. Many buildings come from the head pond area behind the modern dam at Mactaquac (*see entry*), 14 miles downstream.

Among the first buildings at Kings Landing were the Hagerman house, the Stone House and the Joslin farmhouse. The Hagerman house was built in the early 1840s on a Bear Island site flooded by the Mactaquac head pond. It has been restored and refurnished to 1870. The Stone House, built of timber and local stone in 1828, was moved here from five miles upriver. The farmhouse dates from 1800; it stood for more than 160 years at Joslin Creek, three miles west. The Joslin Farm complex at Kings Landing is designed to illustrate the life style of a well-established farm family about 1860. In the Joslin yard is an eight-sided wooden outhouse, an elegant structure 12 feet high with windows and plastered inside walls. It has been called "the Taj Mahal of privies."

Young Canadians in the dress of the pioneers chat alongside a road in the Kings Landing settlement at Prince William.

Pugwash N.S.   9EY/23BX
Bagpipes skirl and Highland dancers whirl at the annual July 1 Gathering of the Clans in Pugwash, a community whose street signs are in English and Gaelic.
□ The most famous of many Pugwash tourist establishments is Pineo Lodge, owned by Pugwash-born financier Cyrus Eaton. He started the famous Pugwash conferences here in 1957. The annual conferences, now held in various countries, have attracted worldwide attention.
□ The Canada Salt Company mine here (1,000 tons daily) can be toured.

Pukaskwa National Park (Ont.)   6GX
This 725-square-mile wilderness area is the largest national park in eastern Canada. The southern boundary is a rugged 50-mile stretch of Lake Superior shoreline. The park can be reached only by boat.

Purdy Ont.   7DX
A plaque four miles northeast honors John Wesley Dafoe, one of Canada's great journalists, who was born in 1866 at nearby Combermere. The famous editor of the Manitoba (now Winnipeg) *Free Press* championed Canada's autonomy within the Commonwealth. He was a founder of the Canadian Institute of International Affairs.

Q

Qualicum Beach B.C.   2BY/12CX
Euclataws Cave (1,740 feet long) and Riverbend Cave (1,259 feet) are the gems of Horne Lake Caves Provincial Park, 18 miles northwest, but few persons see them. Smaller caves had been badly damaged by visitors so after Euclataws and Riverbend were discovered in the 1960s both were gated and the area was designated as a park. Only experienced cavers, or parties guided by such cavers, are allowed to visit the new caves. Horne Lake Main Cave and Lower Cave—the old caves—may be visited by anyone.
□ Ten miles north, on the Big Qualicum River, is a 3,400-foot-long artificial spawning channel in which the salmon egg survival rate is 65-70 percent, compared to a rate of 11-12 percent in natural conditions.

Quebec Que.

9AX/20BW/P.287

The oldest city in Canada, perched on towering Cape Diamond, overlooks the sudden narrowing of the St. Lawrence River that once made it the key to the riches of the New World. During the French regime Quebec was the center of French activity in North America, a city of officials, fur traders, nuns, priests and a bishop whose see stretched to Hudson Bay and the Gulf of Mexico. Now it is the provincial capital, a commercial center, a year-round port and one of the most picturesque cities on the continent.

The narrow, cobbled streets, where ancient gray stone houses huddle next to venerable churches and historic monuments, are best seen on foot or from a calèche. Sous-le-Cap, reputed to be the narrowest street in North America, is about three yards wide.

□ Almost since its founding by Champlain in 1608, Quebec has been divided into Upper Town, the center of administration and defense, and Lower Town, the center of commerce. The two are connected by a funicular whose lower station is Louis Jolliet House (1683), once the home of the first white man to explore the Mississippi.

Although defense works were started in 1608, most existing fortifications in North America's only walled city were constructed (or reconstructed) by the British in 1820-32. The remaining city gates—Saint-Louis, Kent and Saint-Jean—are reconstructions (c.1880); the five original gates were demolished to widen streets.

□ The Seven Years' War had broken out in 1756. At first the French in North America under the Marquis de Montcalm held their own but British naval power wore down French resistance. In 1759 a British army sailed up the St. Lawrence to lay siege to Que-

Plains of Abraham, where French and English armies battled in 1759: the Château Frontenac and the Citadel are in the background in this view.

bec and Gen. James Wolfe attacked in July at Montmorency, five miles northeast. Montcalm's troops stood firm and the British retreated. For six weeks Wolfe pounded Quebec with cannon fire from across the river at Lévis; meanwhile, his troops ravaged the countryside, looting, burning, killing and scalping. On the night of Sept. 12 Wolfe ferried troops across the river to l'Anse au Foulon (Wolfe's Cove). The redcoats scaled the cliff and were in position on the heights by morning, catching the French unprepared. The battle lasted only 10 minutes, the French were defeated and more than 1,200 dead and

Grand Théâtre de Québec, a modern complex close to the heart of old Quebec, is the home of the Quebec Symphony Orchestra, Théâtre du Trident and Club musical de Québec.

La Grande Hermine, in Quebec's Cartier-Brébeuf National Historic Park, is a replica of Jacques Cartier's 78-foot wooden flagship. It was built in 1966 using 16th-century-type tools and methods and was displayed at Expo 67 in Montreal.

---

wounded lay on the Plains of Abraham. Wolfe, hit by a sniper's bullet, died on the battlefield. Montcalm, mortally wounded, died in Quebec the following day. The city capitulated Sept. 18 and remained in British hands despite a French victory nearby at Sainte-Foy the next spring. Governor Vaudreuil surrendered New France Sept. 8, 1760.

The last siege of Quebec was in 1775 during the American Revolution. A two-pronged attack failed and the Americans retreated after the arrival of a British fleet.

□ During subsequent peaceful years the city became an important shipbuilding center; *Royal William*, the first steam-powered ship to cross the Atlantic (in 1833), was built here. Shipbuilding has declined but Quebec is an industrial center producing food, petroleum, paper and rubber products and electrical appliances.

□ The world-famous Quebec Winter Carnival is staged in February. First held in 1894, it was discontinued a few years later but revived in 1955. Streets are lined with ice sculptures and there are parades, balls, the crowning of the carnival queen, snowshoe races, car races on ice and an international peewee hockey tournament. One highlight is a canoe race across ice and open water from Lévis. The celebrations are presided over by Bonhomme Carnaval, a seven-foot snowman.

□ Only 30 miles from the bustle of Quebec is the southern entrance of Laurentides Park, a 4,060-square-mile wilderness with more than 1,500 lakes and some of the oldest mountains in the world.

ANCIENNE-LORETTE (1) One of Quebec's oldest parishes, settled in 1647, Ancienne-Lorette is now a city. Its buildings include the renovated white wooden Boisvin house, dating from the mid-1600s, and a mill built by Jesuits in 1755.

AQUARIUM OF QUEBEC (2) More than 170 species of indigenous and tropical fish, plus marine mammals such as Arctic and Atlantic seals, are to be seen in 48 freshwater and 20 salt-water aquariums; also snakes, crocodiles, lizards, turtles.

ARCHBISHOP'S PALACE (3) This four-story stone building (1844-47) was designed by Thomas Baillargé.

ARTILLERY PARK (4) Among the finest examples of French regime military architecture is the Dauphine Redoubt (begun c.1713), remarkable for its underground vaults and rare crossing arches. Also in Artillery Park are the 500-foot-long New Barracks (1749-54) and the Captain's House (1820), formerly the residence of the garrison commanding officer.

BASILICA OF NOTRE-DAME (5) Restored many times after bombardment and fire, this is the church of the archbishop of Quebec, Canada's oldest parish. It was begun in 1647 on the site of Notre-Dame-de-Recouvrance Church, which Champlain built in 1633. The present facade (1843), which is remarkable for its two unequal towers, was designed by Thomas Baillargé.

CARTIER-BRÉBEUF NATIONAL HISTORIC PARK (6) A replica of *La Grande Hermine*, Cartier's flagship, is the focal point of this 22-acre park. Also in the park is a 25-foot granite cross erected in 1935 on the spot where Cartier raised a cross in 1535. The park is believed the site of a house built in 1626. Jesuit martyr Saint Jean de Brébeuf is commemorated by a 10-foot granite monument (*see* Midland).

CHÂTEAU FRONTENAC (7) The city skyline is

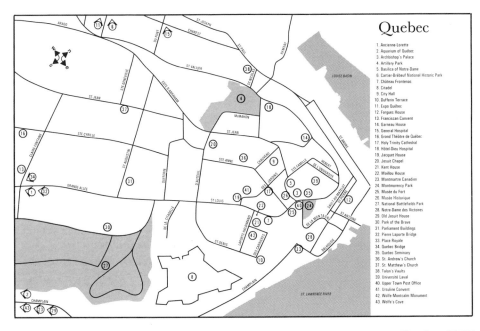

Quebec

1. Ancienne-Lorette
2. Aquarium of Quebec
3. Archbishop's Palace
4. Artillery Park
5. Basilica of Notre-Dame
6. Cartier-Brébeuf National Historic Park
7. Château Frontenac
8. Citadel
9. City Hall
10. Dufferin Terrace
11. Expo Quebec
12. Fargues House
13. Franciscan Convent
14. Garneau House
15. General Hospital
16. Grand Théâtre de Québec
17. Holy Trinity Cathedral
18. Hôtel-Dieu Hospital
19. Jacquet House
20. Jesuit Chapel
21. Kent House
22. Maillou House
23. Montmartre Canadien
24. Montmorency Park
25. Musée du Fort
26. Musée Historique
27. National Battlefields Park
28. Notre-Dame des Victoires
29. Old Jesuit House
30. Park of the Brave
31. Parliament Buildings
32. Pierre Laporte Bridge
33. Place Royale
34. Quebec Bridge
35. Quebec Seminary
36. St. Andrew's Church
37. St. Matthew's Church
38. Talon's Vaults
39. Université Laval
40. Upper Town Post Office
41. Ursuline Convent
42. Wolfe-Montcalm Monument
43. Wolfe's Cove

Wolfe-Montcalm Monument is in the Governors' Garden, flanked by the old houses of Avenue Sainte-Geneviève and Rue Laporte. Nearby is narrow Rue du Trésor, which artists have taken over as their own. In one of Quebec's most venerable buildings, the Jesuit house (c.1700) (opposite page), is a copper weather vane from the Jesuit college closed in 1760. The Quebec Seminary's Procure Wing (immediate right) dates from 1678. Typical of Quebec are its many religious institutions (this nun is one of the Franciscans, famous for needlework), the roofs and chimneys of Place Royale, the sight-seeing calèches waiting in the long shadows of an afternoon in Place d'Armes, where Champlain's soldiers paraded in the early days of New France.

distinguished by the baronial red brick and green copper towers and turrets of the Château, one of Canada's grand hotels, built in 1893-95. Set in the entrance archway in the courtyard is a stone engraved with a Maltese cross. It was carved in 1647 for Governor Charles Huault de Montmagny. Beside the hotel, in Place d'Armes, is the Monument of Faith, commemorating the Recollets, Canada's first missionaries. A figure representing Faith stands 35 feet high atop a finely carved model of a church.

CITADEL (8) This massive gray stone fort stands on the highest point of Cape Diamond, some 350 feet above the St. Lawrence. The cape has been fortified since 1608, when Champlain built earthworks to protect his trading post. Most of the present structure was erected by the British in 1820-32 to defend against possible attack from the United States. The only buildings from the French period are Cape Diamond Redoubt (1693)—the oldest military structure in Quebec—and the

powder magazine (1750), now a museum. The Citadel is a polygon with five bastions, covering 40 acres. It is the home of the Royal 22ᵉ Regiment—the famous Van Doos—and the official summer residence of the governor general. The Van Doos' regimental museum has artifacts and documents relating to the history of the regiment, of Quebec and Canada, the decorations and World War I equipment of Gen. Georges P. Vanier, a Van Doos commanding officer who became governor general, and three Victoria Crosses won by their soldiers. The colorful Changing of the Guard takes place daily in summer.

CITY HALL (9) This five-story stone building (1895) is on the site of a Jesuit college built in 1635 and closed by the British in 1760. Inside is a shield that once decorated one of the city gates.

DUFFERIN TERRACE (10) This wide boardwalk, dotted with Victorian pagodas, stretches from Place d'Armes to the northern tip of the Citadel. There it connects with the Gover-

nors' Promenade, which meanders around the clifftop in front of the Citadel to Battlefields Park. At the north end of the terrace is a marble monument topped by a bronze statue of Champlain. It was sculpted by Paul Chevré in the 1890s. The monument marks the site of Fort Saint-Louis (1620).

EXPO QUÉBEC (11) Agricultural, industrial and craft exhibits at a 10-day show in Exposition Park in September.

FARGUES HOUSE (12) This three-story stone house (1752) is considered Quebec's best surviving example of an 18th-century middle-class home.

FRANCISCAN CONVENT (13) Examples of fine needlework by the nuns are on display.

GARNEAU HOUSE (14) François-Xavier Garneau lived here. His seven-volume *Histoire du Canada* was a reply to Lord Durham's assertion that French Canadians were "a people without history."

GENERAL HOSPITAL (15) Relics in a small museum include furniture, silverware and vestments that belonged to the hospital's founder, Jean de Saint-Vallier, second bishop of Quebec. There is 17th-century pewter used by hospital nuns and 17th-century medical equipment. A Recollet church (1673) is part of the hospital, which was founded in 1692.

GRAND THÉÂTRE DE QUÉBEC (16) Salle Louis-Fréchette, an 1,800-seat auditorium, has a 154-foot stage. Salle Octave-Crémazie, seating 800, accommodates theater-in-the-round, Italian theater and thrust-stage productions.

HOLY TRINITY CATHEDRAL (17) Built to resemble the famous London church, St. Martin-in-the-Fields, Holy Trinity was the first Anglican cathedral outside the British Isles. It was built in 1804 on the site of a Recollet chapel that dated from 1681 and had been used by Anglicans since 1759. It has a Communion service given by George III.

HÔTEL-DIEU HOSPITAL (18) Vaults where nuns and patients hid during the sieges of Quebec reflect the history of this oldest of all North American hospitals. A museum (in a new wing) contains priceless antique furniture, silverware and paintings, and relics (*see under* Jesuit Chapel) of Jesuit missionaries martyred in 1649. A wooden statue of Notre-Dame de Toutes Grâces is venerated by the nuns of the community. It was given as a votive offering in 1738 by a grateful sailor whose ship escaped being wrecked after the crew had committed themselves to the Virgin Mary's care.

Quebec's Citadel is a four-pointed fortress atop Cape Diamond, overlooking the St. Lawrence River to the east. The heart of the city lies just north of the Citadel; to the southwest (foreground, this picture) are the Plains of Abraham. The Royal 22ᵉ Regiment sergeants' mess, with a sweeping, red-carpeted stairway, is in Jebb's Redoubt, once used as a canteen, cookhouse and coal vault.

JACQUET HOUSE (19) This three-story house, typical of the French regime, was built in 1675-76 in a Norman style with a high, pointed red roof. It is a restaurant.

JESUIT CHAPEL (20) A reliquary contains relics of three Canadian martyr saints (*see* Midland): half of Saint Jean de Brébeuf's skull, a piece of Saint Charles Garnier's fibula and part of Saint Gabriel Lalemant's femur.

(Other bones of the three saints are in a museum in Hôtel-Dieu Hospital.)

KENT HOUSE (21) The Duke of Kent, son of George III and father of Queen Victoria, lived here in 1792-94. The four-story stone house, built in 1636, is believed to have been used for the signing of the document which surrendered Quebec to the British in 1759.

MAILLOU HOUSE (22) Antique furniture is housed in this three-story stone house built in 1736 and restored as an historic site in 1959. The vaults were used by the British army paymaster after the fall of Quebec.

MONTMARTRE CANADIEN (23) Overlooking the St. Lawrence River, the national center of the Archconfraternity of Prayer and Penitence of Montmartre includes a modern chapel, auditorium and guest house. On the grounds are a grotto, made of arches in the form of an M in honor of the Virgin Mary, and a small chapel (1926) which is a replica of the Chapel of the Apparitions of the Sacred Heart at Paray-le-Monial in France.

MONTMORENCY PARK (24) A statue of Sir George-Etienne Cartier, a Father of Confederation, stands in the center of this park at the top of Mountain Hill overlooking Lower Town. Also here is a statue of Louis Hébert, Quebec's first colonist, who came to Quebec in 1617.

MUSÉE DU FORT (25) In this small fortress-like building (1965) a 450-square-foot model seems to come alive as light, music, sound effects and narration are used to unfold the story of the six sieges of Quebec.

MUSÉE HISTORIQUE (26) A house built in 1640 contains wax figures in scenes depicting the history of Canada and the United States.

NATIONAL BATTLEFIELDS PARK (27) Granite markers in this 235-acre park trace the course of the most decisive battle in Canadian history, the Battle of the Plains of Abraham. In the Quebec Museum is a rich collection of traditional and modern French-Canadian art: works by Joseph Legaré, Antoine Plamondon, Théophile Hamel, the Baillargés and Levasseurs, François Ranvoyzé, Laurent Amyot, Marc-Aurèle de Foy Suzor-Coté and Alfred Laliberté. The museum has an important collection of antique furniture and houses the provincial archives, with documents dating from the beginning of New France. In the park are a monument to Wolfe, a bust of Sir Georges Garneau, first chairman of the National Battlefields Commission, and an equestrian statue of Joan of Arc. Just outside the park is a statue of Montcalm and an angel, marking the spot where Montcalm was mortally wounded. A Martello tower (c.1804) provides a fine view across the St. Lawrence.

NOTRE-DAME DES VICTOIRES (28) Beautiful wood carvings, paintings by Rubens and Vanloo and an altar carved in the form of a battlemented fortress are among the treasures of this simple little stone church built in 1688 on the site of Champlain's first Habitation. The victories commemorated in the name are those of the French over British Admirals William Phips (1690) and Hovenden Walker

(1711). The church was badly damaged during the bombardment of 1759 and has since been restored several times.

OLD JESUIT HOUSE (29) In front of the present two-story stone house (c.1700) can be seen the foundations of the Jesuit House built in 1637. It was here that "the first Jesuit in North America," the Rev. Enemond Massé, and six of the Canadian martyr saints once lived. Also here are the foundations of Saint-Michel (1644), the first stone church built in Canada, and a vault containing the remains of Father Massé. The Jesuit House has a museum displaying the history of the Jesuits in North America. Exhibits include the weather vane from the Jesuit College (1635), axes forged for the Jesuits in the 17th century, Indian relics, handicrafts, documents and books.

PARK OF THE BRAVE (30) A stone column honors those who fought in the 1760 Battle of Sainte-Foy, at which a French army defeated the British who had captured Quebec the previous fall.

PARLIAMENT BUILDING (31) The elegant Renaissance-style architecture of the seat of the Quebec National Assembly is complemented by statues by French-Canadian sculptors including Philippe Hébert, Alfred Laliberté and Emile Brunet. Persons depicted in statues in niches on the facade include Lord Elgin, Frontenac, de Salaberry, Montcalm, Wolfe, Lévis, Jean Talon, Marquette, Brébeuf, Dorchester and La Vérendrye. The 300-foot-long ivy-covered center block, topped by a 182-foot tower, was completed in 1886. The fresco of Confederation and Canadian historical figures on the ceiling of the National Assembly Chamber was painted in 1921-25 by Charles Huot, who also painted the picture of the first sitting of the Government of Lower Canada (1792) which hangs above the throne.

PIERRE LAPORTE BRIDGE (32) This 3,414-foot bridge to the south shore is seven miles west. The longest suspension bridge in Canada, it was completed in 1970.

PLACE ROYALE (33) Architects and builders are recreating the commercial center of New France and archaeologists are excavating the stone foundations of Champlain's second (1624) Habitation and the remains of a 2,000-year-old Algonkian village beneath. Ravaged by fire in 1682, by war in 1759, by recent neglect, Place Royale will have about 75 restored or rebuilt 17th- and 18th-century buildings. Many will have modern interiors, so it will be both museum and residential area. Among more than 30 already completed is the Hôtel Chevalier (1752), a two-story gray stone house with a painted red roof, now a museum housing relics found in the Place Royale excavations and French-Canadian furniture dating from the 17th century. The two-story Fornel house has stone vaults dating from 1735 and foundations from a house built in 1658. It contains an information exhibit of the history of Place Royale. A bronze bust of Louis XIV, in whose honor the square is named, was presented by the French government in 1928.

QUEBEC BRIDGE (34) When completed in 1917, after a series of misfortunes including the deaths of several Caughnawaga steelworkers when a section collapsed, the bridge was the longest cantilever span in the world (1,800 feet). It is near the Pierre Laporte Bridge.

QUEBEC MUSEUM see under National Battlefields Park

QUEBEC SEMINARY (35) The museum here has an important collection of Canadian and European paintings, including works by Plamondon, Legaré and Suzor-Coté; a silver collection in which the famous Quebec silversmiths Ranvoyzé, Sasseville, Lambert and Varin are represented; a collection of Cypriot ceramics (6000-2000 B.C.); and a collection of Mexican art dating from the 17th and 18th centuries. Also on display are a numismatic collection which includes wampum and playing card money; a collection of Canadian and

Bonhomme Carnaval, a jovial giant snowman, rules over Quebec Winter Carnival festivities. The pièce de résistance is a canoe race across the ice-choked St. Lawrence River.

Coq de clocher in the Quebec Museum
dates from the early 18th century. It is
21 inches high and 24½ inches long.
Daphné ou Nu au Croissant (right) is a
gouache by Jean Dallaire. Below: Marc-
Aurèle Fortin's oil, *A la Baie Saint-Paul*.

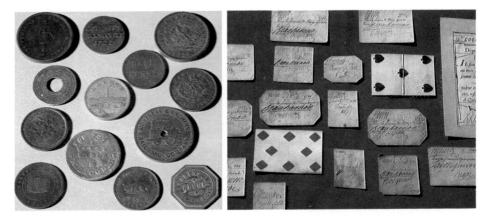

Colonies Françoises coin (center, top) in this collection at the Quebec Seminary museum is dated 1722. Tokens include those of the Montreal & Lachine Railroad Company, the Maison Jacques Cartier in St. Roch, Que., and the Robinson house in Camlachie, Ont. Playing card money was legal tender in New France in 1624-1717 and 1729-59. These cards are signed by the Marquis de Beauharnois, governor in 1726-47.

Vatican stamps, an altar carved by the Levasseur brothers, antique furniture and one of the cannon used by Admiral Phips in his abortive attempt to capture Quebec in 1690. Books and documents include a 15th-century Book of Hours and letters from Louis XIV, Marie-Thérèse, Colbert and Saint François-de-Sales. The seminary was founded in 1663 by Laval, the first bishop of Quebec, to train missionaries and priests. The oldest part of the buildings, dating from 1678, is in the Procure Wing. The third story and attic of this wing were added in 1866 after a fire. The chapel contains a tomb with the bones of Laval.

ST. ANDREW'S CHURCH (36) This Presbyterian church is the home of the oldest congregation of Scottish origin in Canada. Its origins date back to 1759 when the men of the Fraser Highlanders marched through the streets to the skirl of the pipes on their way to services at the old Jesuit College. The church, built in 1810, has a fine hand-carved wooden pulpit, stained-glass windows and a choir loft, formerly the governor's gallery, which is reached by a spiral staircase. Also to be seen are the original organ (1843) and the original baptismal font.

ST. MATTHEW'S CHURCH (37) The ground on which this Anglican church was built in 1872 was a cemetery at the time of the fall of Quebec. Among the graves are those of soldiers in Wolfe's army.

TALON'S VAULTS (38) The vaults of one of the first commercial breweries in Canada were built by Jean Talon in 1668. Now a museum under the present O'Keefe Brewery, the vaults contain 17th-century relics, guns and antique furniture. The original brewery was closed in 1675 and the Intendant's Palace stood here from 1675 to 1775, when it was burned during the American siege.

UNIVERSITÉ LAVAL (39) About 23,000 full-time and 8,000 part-time students attend the oldest French-language university in North America, now located on a 500-acre modern campus at Sainte-Foy. In one contemporary building, flat-roofed but with towers and windows that give it the look of a Gothic cathedral, are the faculty of theology and the university church—which seats 2,000.

UPPER TOWN POST OFFICE (40) Above the post office doorway is the sign of the golden dog, said to have been part of a building on this site made famous in William Kirby's novel *The Golden Dog*. In front of the building is the Laval Monument, a statue honoring the first bishop of Quebec.

URSULINE CONVENT (41) Montcalm's skull is preserved here in the Museum of the Marie de l'Incarnation Center. The museum is on the site of a stone house built in 1644 for Madame de la Peltrie, the convent's first benefactress. The house was demolished in 1836 and a new one designed by François Baillargé was built, using much of the old material. Included in its museum exhibits are one of the oldest. beds in Canada (1686), early musical instruments, a 17th-century kitchen, pharmacy, infirmary and schoolroom. Much of the furniture and many of the books and paintings belonged to Madame de la Peltrie and Mother Marie de l'Incarnation, who was the first mother superior and co-founder of the convent. The chapel (1720) has some of the finest wood carvings in Quebec, including an altarpiece and pulpit by the Levasseur family. Montcalm's tomb is within the walls. A hole blasted by a British shell was used as a grave. A votive lamp has burned since 1717 when it was presented by Madeleine de Repentigny, whose story is told in William Kirby's *The Golden Dog*.

WOLFE-MONTCALM MONUMENT (42) In the Governors' Garden is an obelisk bearing the Latin inscription "Valour gave them a common death, history a common fame, posterity a common monument."

WOLFE'S COVE (43) L'Anse au Foulon, where Wolfe's men landed before the Battle of the Plains of Abraham.

Queen Charlotte Islands *see* Masset

beneath a 184-foot stone monument. The top of the monument, reached by a winding staircase, offers a superb view of the Niagara frontier. Beside Brock's monument is a plaque honoring Sir Roger Hale Sheaffe, Brock's second-in-command, who led his troops to victory after Brock's death.

In Laura Secord's restored 1½-story frame house, now a museum, are a kitchen hutch cupboard containing rare cups without handles, a pendulum chiming clock, a wooden wardrobe displaying period clothes, and a Chippendale strongbox. A collection of lighting devices in use in the early 1800s includes whale oil lamps and rush lights.

□ Also restored as a museum is the two-story stone house in which William Lyon Mackenzie started his newspaper the *Colonial Advocate* in 1824. (Later that year he moved it to York [Toronto], where in 1837 he led the Upper Canada rebellion.) In this museum are desks that belonged to Mackenzie and to William Kirby, author of *The Golden Dog.*

□ The Niagara River is harnessed at the Sir Adam Beck plants here to generate electricity for millions. A tour includes a film and a visit to the Hydro Hall of Memory, where exhibits trace the history of hydroelectric power in Ontario. Outside is a floral clock whose dial is made up of some 25,000 colorful plants.

Queenston Ont.   7CZ/17DY

Maj. Gen. Sir Isaac Brock and Laura Secord, legendary Canadian figures in the War of 1812, are commemorated here. Brock, a general who commanded all the troops in Canada, was killed by a sniper's bullet on Oct. 13, 1812, while leading his men against an American force occupying Queenston Heights. Laura Secord walked nearly 20 miles on June 22 that year to warn of an impending American attack at Beaverdams (*see* Thorold).

Brock is buried in Queenston Heights Park

Across the river the Robert Moses plant provides energy for New York State.

Quesnel B.C.   1AZ/2DW
Cariboo Gold Rush relics in the Quesnel Museum include a gold scale, pan and rockers, a sluice box, shovels and guns. Relics of the Chinese who came as cooks, dishwashers and seekers after gold (and jade and platinum) include an opium bottle, intricate screens, an abacus and a tea jug. Also in the museum are agricultural implements and the daybooks from Cottonwood House, a "mile house" 18 miles east along the road to Barkerville. Parts of the house date from 1865.
□ A wooden waterwheel built in the mid-1800s to remove water from the mines has been reconstructed near the old Fraser River Bridge. Near it is a cairn commemorating the Collins Overland Telegraph (*see* Burns Lake) which was abandoned after reaching this far in 1866.

R

Radium Hot Springs B.C. *see* Kootenay National Park

Ravenswood Ont.   16CX
Spherical rocks resembling huge, old-style kettles are embedded in shale at and below the Lake Huron waterline on the Kettle Point Indian Reserve, three miles northwest.

Rawdon Que.   7FX/19BX
Among the 19th-century buildings in Canadiana Village here are a one-room schoolhouse, a settler's cabin, a blacksmith shop and a general store containing Rawdon's first post office. There are collections of cradles and spinning wheels. A river that flows through Canadiana Village is spanned by a covered bridge that dates from 1888. It was salvaged from a flood at Coaticook, Que.
□ At nearby Darwin Falls is a rock formation in the shape of an Indian's head. A legend says it is the head of a sorcerer who, rejected by a young woman he sought to marry, pushed her into the falls, then was turned to stone.

Raymond Alta.   4AZ
Tradition says that the Raymond Stampede, started in 1902, was the first such show anywhere to be called a stampede. It is held in

Canadiana Village in Rawdon has houses, stores, a school and a church—and, for an extra scoop of nostalgia, this old-time ice cream parlor.

Shell shape of St. Mary's Church in Red Deer places the whole congregation close to the altar. Aisles radiate from the altar like spokes.

July. The word stampede is said to have been suggested by Raymond Knight, for whom the town was named.

Raymore Sask.   4EY
The Raymore Pioneer Museum, in a former church (1911), displays pioneer furniture, utensils and costumes. In Kutawa, 20 miles east, is a telegraph station that dates from 1883. Near it is St. George's Anglican Church, built in 1892 of logs, later stuccoed.

Red Deer Alta.   4AX/14FZ
The city hall, a massive structure of exposed concrete columns and beams, was the winning entry in a Canada-wide design competition in 1961. The building is in a corner of a one-acre formal park.
□ A 1902 Holsman Autobuggy, a 1918 Kissel Kar Speedster and a 1922 Ford Firewagon (a Model T used as a fire engine) are among 21 cars in the C.R. Parker collection here.
□ The Red Deer Highland Games in June are followed by Folk Festival Jamboree Days, with ethnic dancing, food and displays.
□ A native son, architect Douglas Cardinal, designed St. Mary's, a shell-shaped Roman Catholic church with aisles radiating from the altar like wheel spokes.
□ The Gaetz Lakes Bird Sanctuary has walking paths and a variety of wildlife. The lakes, really sloughs, were named for Dr. Leonard Gaetz, minister-turned-homesteader, who donated land for Red Deer's site.

□ Annual events in Red Deer include an exhibition and stampede in July, Oktoberfest, the Snowball Festival in February and the Red Deer Spring Horse Show in May.

Legislative Building in Regina, an adaptation of English Renaissance architecture with elements of Louis XVI, is set off by blue prairie sky and colorful formal gardens.

Red Lake Ont.   6CX

The processing of gold ore into pure gold can be seen at the Campbell and Dickenson mines here. Ore is fed from a mill into a crusher, then through screens, classifiers, agitators, filters, chemical baths and flotation cells. Finally molten gold is poured into molds and allowed to harden.

There have been 15 mines in the Red Lake district (there now are four—Madsen and Robin Red Lake are the others) and more than $360,000,000 in gold has been produced. Gold was discovered in 1897 but there was no rush until 1926, the year after a particularly rich strike. By April 1926 some 1,000 men had filed 3,500 claims. About two miles from Red Lake a plaque commemorates the founding of the Red Lake mining district and the role aircraft played in the region's development. (*See* Sioux Lookout)

Regina Sask.   4EY

This prairie city was originally called Pile of Bones after a mound left by generations of buffalo hunters. Whites called a creek at the site Wascana, from the Indian phrase for the bone heap. The town became the capital of the Northwest Territories in 1882, and its name was changed to Regina in honor of Queen Victoria. It has been the capital of Saskatchewan since 1905.

The city's history is interwoven with that of the Royal Canadian Mounted Police. Force headquarters followed the territorial government here in 1882 and stayed until 1920, when it was transferred to Ottawa. Depot Division here is the RCMP recruit-training establishment.

As its population neared 160,000, Regina finished a dramatic 16-story City Hall in 1976. The city, no longer totally dependent on

NWMP muzzle-loader, one of two that the Mounties took west in 1874, is in the RCMP Museum in Regina. It has this tobacco pouch that belonged to Sitting Bull.

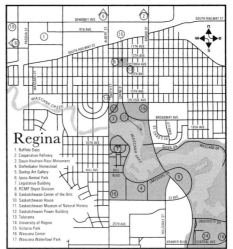

Regina
1. Buffalo Days
2. Cooperative Refinery
3. Davin-Haultain-Ross Monument
4. Diefenbaker Homestead
5. Dunlop Art Gallery
6. Ipsco Animal Park
7. Legislative Building
8. RCMP Depot Division
9. Saskatchewan Center of the Arts
10. Saskatchewan House
11. Saskatchewan Museum of Natural History
12. Saskatchewan Power Building
13. Telorama
14. University of Regina
15. Victoria Park
16. Wascana Center
17. Wascana Waterfowl Park

Diefenbaker Homestead, in which the future prime minister lived as a boy, is in Regina's Wascana Center. The three-room frame house, built in 1906, contains Diefenbaker memorabilia.

wheat, has an economic base broadened by potash mining, oil and other industries. The city's heart is Wascana Center, a 2,300-acre parkland containing the Legislative Building, the University of Regina, a center for the performing arts, a natural history museum, an art gallery and other facilities.

BUFFALO DAYS (1) About 10 days of rodeo, horse racing, barbecues, picnics, band concerts, midway and grandstand entertainment, in conjunction with the Regina Exhibition.

COOPERATIVE REFINERY (2) The world's first cooperative petroleum refinery (1935) is operated by Federated Co-operatives Ltd.

DAVIN-HAULTAIN-ROSS MONUMENT (3) Men who served on the North West Council before Saskatchewan became a province are honored by this monument. Nicholas Flood Davin was the first member of Parliament for West Assiniboia and founder of the *Regina Leader*.

Sir Frederick W.G. Haultain became chief justice of Saskatchewan after serving as territorial premier. James Hamilton Ross, a pioneer rancher, became commissioner of the Yukon Territory in 1901, was elected to Parliament from the Yukon the next year and was named a senator in 1904.

DIEFENBAKER HOMESTEAD (4) The restored boyhood home of John G. Diefenbaker, Canada's 13th prime minister, was moved here from Borden, Sask., in 1967.

DUNLOP ART GALLERY (5) This gallery in the Regina Public Library displays paintings, sculptures and handicrafts by local artists. In a permanent collection are landscapes and war sketches by English-born Inglis Sheldon-Williams, who lived in the Regina area at various times between 1887 and 1922.

Louis Riel's trial for treason in 1885 is reenacted three nights a week from June to August in Regina's Saskatchewan House (10), once the residence of lieutenant-governors. A life-size statue of Riel by John Nugent is in Wascana Center, near the Legislative Building.

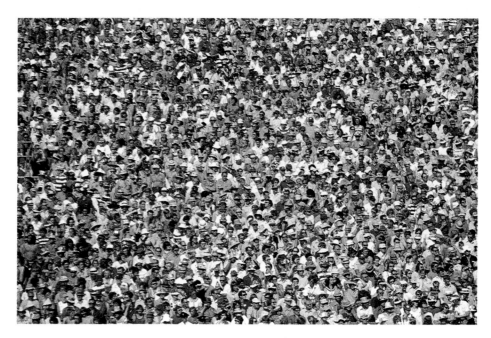

Taylor Field, recently expanded to 30,500 seats, is the home of the Saskatchewan Roughriders and their loyal fans.

IPSCO ANIMAL PARK (6) Buffalo, deer, bears, foxes, Canada geese, in a park run by Interprovincial Steel and Pipe Corp.

LEGISLATIVE BUILDING (7) It was built between 1908 and 1912 of Tyndall (Man.) stone but at least 34 kinds of marble from around the world have been used in its interior. Most impressive are huge, green Cyprus marble columns in the rotunda. In the legislative library is the table at which the Fathers of Confederation sat for the Quebec Conference of 1864. A carving over the building's main entrance depicts Canada as a mother protecting whites and Indians.

RCMP DEPOT DIVISION (8) Some 800 recruits a year are taught law enforcement techniques and are imbued with the traditions of one of the world's most famous police forces. There are barracks, sports facilities and classrooms, the RCMP Centennial Museum and the Little Chapel on the Square.

□ The chapel, built as a mess hall in 1883, was converted 12 years later. Stained-glass windows flanking the chapel altar show RCMP members, one a bugler sounding reveille, the other with head bowed over a rifle in mourning position, butt end up. Commemorative windows on each side of the chapel, depicting the Resurrection and the Nativity, are a World War II memorial. The flags on both sides of the chapel flew over Fort Walsh from 1875 to 1880. A baptismal font is in memory of a Mountie who died of wounds suffered at Cut Knife Hill in the Northwest Rebellion of 1885.

□ The museum provides a chronological record of RCMP history. There is a uniform that belonged to Supt. J. M. Walsh, who nego-

tiated with Sitting Bull in 1877 when the Sioux chief fled north after the Battle of the Little Big Horn. Displays recall such famous cases as the hunt for "the mad trapper of Rat River" (*see* Aklavik). With a model of the RCMP patrol boat *St. Roch* (*see* Vancouver) are souvenirs of her trips through the Northwest Passage. A Louis Riel display includes the crucifix that the Métis leader carried to the scaffold Nov. 16, 1885. It also has three different ropes, all said to have been used to hang Riel.

□ In Barracks Square are a monument commemorating *St. Roch*'s first west-to-east voyage, a tablet honoring Mounties who died in the line of duty (it is flanked by two seven-pounder muzzle-loading rifles that date from 1808) and a monument commemorating the RCMP's 100th anniversary in 1973. Beyond Barracks Square is a cemetery almost as old as the force itself.

SASKATCHEWAN CENTER OF THE ARTS (9) Centennial Theater seats 2,029 persons; Jubilee Theater, 700.

SASKATCHEWAN HOUSE (10) A former viceregal residence, where the treason trial of Louis Riel is reenacted each summer.

SASKATCHEWAN MUSEUM OF NATURAL HISTORY (11) More than 100 mounted birds and animals displayed in dioramas include the whooping crane, blue heron, sage grouse, sandhill crane, caribou, wolf, moose, elk, bison, bobcat and beaver.

SASKATCHEWAN POWER BUILDING (12) An observation deck is on the 13th floor.

TELORAMA (13) A Saskatchewan Government Telephones display describing the development of telephone communication—from Alexander Graham Bell's early equipment to satellite systems and videophones.

UNIVERSITY OF REGINA (14) The Regina campus of the University of Saskatchewan at Saskatoon was established in 1961. In 1974 it became the University of Regina. On campus are the Saskatchewan Archives, with government records, private manuscripts, photographs, maps, pamphlets and newspaper clippings relating to the history of Saskatchewan and the Northwest Territories prior to 1905. In the Norman Mackenzie Art Gallery are permanent collections of English, Dutch, American and Canadian paintings, some Italian Renaissance works, and early Egyptian, Chinese and Greek sculpture.

VICTORIA PARK (15) A monument marks where the inauguration ceremony for the Province of Saskatchewan was held Sept. 4, 1905. There is also a life-size bronze statue of Sir John A. Macdonald.

WASCANA CENTER (16) On the grounds are the Legislative Building, the University of Regina, the Diefenbaker Homestead and the Saskatchewan Center of the Arts. Visitors go by ferry to Willow Island in Wascana Lake, feed ducks and geese at the waterfowl park and hear band concerts. There are swimming, picnicking and barbecuing areas.

WASCANA WATERFOWL PARK (17) A 360-acre marsh and water area in Wascana Center preserves plant and animal life in their natural habitat. Canada Geese, normally migratory, winter here thanks to a feeding program and hot water from a power plant.

Renfrew Ont.   7DX/18BW

Were the name "Champlain" and the date "7 juin 1613"—on a rock at a park eight miles northeast of here—carved by a member of the explorer's party? Champlain did travel up the Ottawa River to nearby Muskrat Lake in 1613 but the authenticity of the carving has not been established.

The 40-acre park—Champlain Storyland —has some 150 fairy-tale characters in 30 settings. There is a wildlife museum with dioramas displaying 150 birds and animals of eastern Canada.

□ In Renfrew's O'Brien Park, on the Bonnechère River, is the McDougall Mill Museum, in a stone gristmill built in 1855.

Rennie Man.   6CY

A goose sanctuary here was started in 1939 when four abandoned goslings were brought to Alfred Hole, a mink rancher and outdoorsman. He nurtured the goslings, built a pond, obtained a gander to mate with the lone female of the brood. She laid four eggs. The resulting goslings joined a flock of geese flying south that fall but returned to the pond in spring. Every year an ever-growing resident flock has returned to the sanctuary and many geese who nest farther north stop here. As many as 800 may be seen in late September and October, including Giant Canada geese, lesser Canada geese, Richardson's geese and lesser snow geese.

In the 3¾-square-mile Alf Hole Sanctuary—which is on the eastern prairie flyway—is an interpretation center with a large window through which visitors may watch feeding

Mystery of the Geese

Tens of thousands of geese fly the skies of Canada each spring and fall in a migration that is one of nature's mysteries. The honking birds travel in great V formations, using long-established flyways with unfailing punctuality and a navigational accuracy as yet unexplained by scientists. Birds on the eastern prairie flyway stop near Rennie, in a corner of Whiteshell Provincial Park. Geese breed there from mid-March to October, then follow their age-old route to winter homes in the central United States.

geese without disturbing them. The center has exhibits of Canada goose subspecies, migratory route maps and an audiovisual slide presentation.

□ The headquarters of Whiteshell Provincial Park (see West Hawk Lake) is at Rennie.

Repentigny Que.   7FY/19BX

The striking contemporary lines of Notre-Dame-des-Champs Church (1963)—by architect Roger D'Astous, who designed the Château Champlain in Montreal—contrast with the simplicity of Repentigny's old (1725) parish church. The first church's main altar was created by Philippe Liébert in 1761. A silver sanctuary lamp is by Laurent Amyot.

□ Jean-Paul Mousseau's three-foot fiber glass sculpture of a beehive stands outside a caisse populaire.

Restigouche Que.   9CW

Relics of the last English-French naval battle in Canada, the 17-day Battle of the Restigouche in July 1760, are displayed here. Part of the hull of the French ship Marquis de Malause was raised from the Restigouche River mud in 1939; it stands in front of the Capuchin monastery of Sainte-Anne-de-Restigouche. Relics at Sainte-Anne-de-Restigouche include cannon, ammunition, ceramics, buttons and a silver shoe buckle.

□ Six ships had sailed from France with munitions, supplies and 400 troops for the relief of besieged Quebec. Two were captured and one wrecked during the Atlantic crossing. At the mouth of the St. Lawrence River the French commander learned from letters in a captured British ship that 12 British vessels had already sailed upriver to Quebec; the mission of the three remaining French ships —the frigate Machault and the merchant ships Marquis de Malause and Bienfaisant—was useless. Anchored in the Restigouche to await instructions from Montreal, they were discovered by five British ships whose cannon outnumbered the French by 265 to 56. Eventually Machault and Bienfaisant ran out of ammunition and were blown up by their captains. Marquis de Malause, unarmed, had taken no part

Up from the river mud, the hull of the merchant ship *Marquis de Malause*, destroyed in 1760, is on display at a monastery in Restigouche.

in the action; she was abandoned and burned to the waterline when accidentally set afire. The British objective of preventing the relief of Quebec was accomplished with the loss of only 12 men.

□ At Cross Point (Pointe-à-la-Croix), one mile northeast, near where the last stages of the naval battle were fought, a bridge crosses Chaleur Bay to Campbellton, N.B.

Revelstoke B.C.   2EY

Canoe races held here Labor Day weekend commemorate explorer David Thompson's voyage to the source of the Columbia River in 1811. Paddlers race their 14-foot canoes 30 miles south to Shelter Bay.

□ Other celebrations here include a snow festival in March and Alpine Days in July.

□ Revelstoke Museum displays a chair that a dentist carried from mine to mine during a gold boom here in the early 1900s—and his brass mold for false teeth. The museum has early mining equipment and CPR artifacts.

Rexton N.B.   9DX

Andrew Bonar Law, a Rexton native who was prime minister of Britain in 1922-23, is commemorated by a plaque on a stone monument here. Bonar Law was the only British prime minister born outside the British Isles.

Richards Landing Ont.   7AW

The ruins of Fort St. Joseph, a strategic British post in the War of 1812, are 22 miles south of here and marked as a national historic site. There are a military cemetery and parts of a blockhouse, a powder magazine and a bakery. A force from Fort St. Joseph captured the American Fort Michilimackinac in 1812.

□ A stone church built in 1900 by people of several faiths is part of the St. Joseph Island Museum five miles south. Other buildings are a barn (1890), a log cabin (1870) and a school (1933).

Richmond Ont.   7EY/18CX

A plaque at St. John's Anglican Church commemorates the founding of the pioneer congregation of St. John's, one of the first in the Ottawa Valley. The first church was built in 1823; the present church dates from 1860.

The annual Richmond Agricultural Fair in September was started about 1830.

On the Columbia River between the Monashee and Selkirk ranges, Revelstoke is at the western end of the Rogers Pass section of the Trans-Canada Highway (*see* Glacier National Park).

Richmond Que.   9AY/20AY
One of the oldest educational institutions in
Quebec's Eastern Townships is a high school
here that was started in 1854—as a college. St.
Francis College was chartered in 1854 and affiliated with Montreal's McGill University.
The original building burned in 1882 and was
replaced two years later by the present one.
It became St. Francis College High School in
1900.
 □ The Richmond County Historical Society Museum in nearby Melbourne, in a house
that dates from 1840, is furnished in late Victorian style.

Richmond Hill Ont.   7CY/17CX
One of the world's largest astronomical telescopes is at the University of Toronto's David
Dunlap Observatory here. The 2½-ton reflecting telescope is aimed through a 15-by-
50-foot opening in the observatory's revolving
dome, which has a 61-foot diameter.
 □ A plaque at St. John's Anglican Church,
two miles north, marks the site of Windham,
a settlement of exiled French Royalists led by
Joseph-Geneviève Comte de Puisaye in 1798.
They proved unsuited to pioneer life and by
1806 Windham was almost deserted. The
count moved to Niagara-on-the-Lake (*see
entry*); his house there is a museum.
 □ In a Lutheran cemetery eight miles north
of Richmond Hill a plaque commemorates
the successful settlement of Germans led by
William von Moll Berczy, who settled first in
New York State, then here.

Ridgeway Ont.   7CZ/17DZ
The scene of the June 1866 Battle of Ridgeway, in which Canadian volunteers repulsed
Fenian raiders from the United States, is
marked by a cairn. A tablet in Ridgeway Memorial United Church honors the Canadians
killed in the battle.

Riding Mountain National Park (Man.) 6AY
This "island" in the prairie is dramatic evidence of Manitoba's geological past. The
2,480-foot-high mountain is part of the Mani-

Clear Lake, nine miles long, is the focal point of
Riding Mountain National Park.

---

toba Escarpment, a jagged, 1,000-mile ridge
that winds across North Dakota, Manitoba
and Saskatchewan, rising as much as 1,600
feet above the countryside. Rivers have cut
the ridge into a series of highlands, of which
Riding Mountain is one. The 1,150-square-
mile park has facilities for camping, picnicking, tennis, golf, boating, horseback riding,
lawn bowling, skiing and snowmobiling.
 An interpretive center in the resort town of
Wasagaming has Indian and pioneer exhibits, displays of prehistoric fossils and the geology of the park, and mounted specimens of
black bear, wolf, coyote and white-tailed
deer. There are heads of bison, wapiti, moose
and caribou. Other animals in the park include the gray (timber) wolf, lynx and beaver.
Beaver, almost extinct when the park was established in 1930, staged a remarkable come-
back, helped by the work of Grey Owl (*see
Prince Albert National Park*). At Beaver
Lodge Lake, northeast of Wasagaming, is a
cabin Grey Owl used. Deep in the park is an
enclosed range where about 40 shaggy buffalo
roam; the herd size is limited to prevent over-
grazing.

Rigaud Que.   7EY/19AY
Inspired by accounts of the Virgin Mary's appearance at Lourdes, a brother at Collège
Bourget placed a statue on a rock shelf on
725-foot Mont Rigaud in 1874. Now thousands of pilgrims worship each year at Rigaud's Shrine of Our Lady of Lourdes.
 □ The Collège Bourget museum has natural history, science and fine arts exhibits.
 □ Old buildings in Rigaud include a stone
water mill (c.1820), the stone Décoste house
(1783) and the wooden Desjardins house
(1809).

Rimbey Alta.   4AX/14EY
A log school built in 1903 and a log church
that dates from 1908 are key attractions at
Pas-Ka-Poo Historical Park.

This old church building, now the Rimouski Regional Museum, dates from 1823. It was a church until 1862, then for 20 years the Collège de Rimouski, later a nuns' motherhouse and a school. Now the art treasures of eastern Quebec are exhibited in its bright, open galleries (right).

Rimouski Que.   9BW
Works by Quebec artists Suzor-Coté, Plamondon, Charles Huot, Duguay and Frédéric Taylor and by the Spaniard José de Ribera and the Dutch artist Joseph Leempoel hang in the Rimouski Regional Museum, once a church. It has Stations of the Cross by Médard Bourgault which once graced a church in Saint-Thomas-de-Cherbourg, Que.
□ The cathedral of Saint-Germain-de-Rimouski dates from 1854.
□ The Rimouski Fall Festival at the end of October features pheasant hunting, smelt fishing, camping, dancing, shooting contests and exhibitions. A five-day farm fair held in August attracts more than 20,000 persons.

Riverhurst Sask.   4DY
A collection in the Fred T. Hill Museum includes Colt handguns (c.1840), a 1906 trade gun and rifles and shotguns from prairie pioneer days. There are Indian tomahawks and spear points and Hudson's Bay Company trade goods, mostly muzzle-loaders.
Across Lake Diefenbaker (traversed here by car ferry) is the Hitchcock Cabin and Museum. The little cabin, built in 1903-4 by Orville Arthur "Jack" Hitchcock, a steam engineer and sometime cowboy, is filled with things made by the ingenious settler.

Rivière-au-Renard Que.   9DW/10HZ
Paintings of the Stations of the Cross by Hungarian artists Edith and Isabelle Piczek adorn Saint-Martin-de-la-Rivière-au-Renard Church. It is in the modern style of Dom Bellot, with walls of pink granite.

Rivière-du-Loup Que.   9BW
A 36-mile stretch of the historic Temiscouata Portage—the part between Saint-Modeste and Cabano, near Lake Témiscouata—is now a scenic hiking route. The great portage, originally an Indian trail, was converted into a road by the Marquis de la Jonquière in 1750. It was a major artery between Quebec and the Maritime provinces until the coming of the railway in the 1860s. A plaque at Cabano commemorates men of the 104th New Brunswick Regiment who used the road in 1813 on a march to Quebec from Fredericton.
□ The Park of the Luminous Cross, with a 75-foot red illuminated cross, overlooks the town center, where there is a 125-foot waterfall on the Rivière du Loup. A plaque downtown marks the site of the house in which the Most Rev. Alexandre-Antonin Taché, bishop of St. Boniface, was born in 1823. Bishop Taché, deeply sympathetic to the Métis, was known as the Apostle of the West.
□ A two-week festival in July has street dances, concerts and sports events. It is climaxed by the crowning of the Queen of the Summer Festival.
□ A ferry crosses the St. Lawrence to Saint-Siméon several times a day from April to January.

Rivière-Ouelle Que.   9BX/20DV
Notre-Dame-de-Liesse Church, built in 1877 on the foundation of a 1792 church torn down after being damaged by earth tremors, has an exquisite wood altar sculpted in France about 1750. Behind the altar is a reredos by Louis Quevillon and an elaborate twin-columned baldachin. A votive painting done by a French officer in 1740 depicts a man's rescue from death by the appearance of the Virgin (Notre Dame de Liesse) on the shore of the St. Lawrence River. There are seven Louis Dulongpré paintings: *L'Assomption, Saint Antoine de Padoue, Saint Bernard* and each of the Evangelists. In the chancel is a chair donated by a Quebec lieutenant governor, Luc Letellier de Saint Just, a Rivière-Ouelle native. The sculpted parts of a second chair (a copy of the first) are by Médard Bourgault. Pine statues of Saint Augustine and Saint Félicité are believed to have been carved in Paris about 1765.
□ A bronze plaque here honors Abbé de Francheville, who in 1690 led 39 parishioners in driving off a detachment from the fleet of

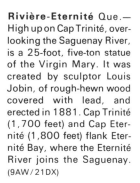

Rivière-Eternité Que.—
High up on Cap Trinité, overlooking the Saguenay River,
is a 25-foot, five-ton statue
of the Virgin Mary. It was
created by sculptor Louis
Jobin, of rough-hewn wood
covered with lead, and
erected in 1881. Cap Trinité
(1,700 feet) and Cap Eternité (1,800 feet) flank Eternité Bay, where the Eternité
River joins the Saguenay.
(9AW/21DX)

Sir William Phips, who was leading a British
expedition against Quebec.

Roberval Que.   9AW/21AW
Swimmers from more than a dozen countries
compete in the Lac Saint-Jean marathon in
August, a 25-mile race from Péribonka to Roberval. The race, first swum in 1955, has become a marathon classic, with prize money
of close to $20,000. It marks the end of Rober-
val's *huitaine de gaieté,* an eight-day festival.

□ Roberval is the first-day stop in the Lac
Saint-Jean bicycle race (*see* Alma).

□ Life-size concrete figures of the eight
North American martyr saints were sculpted
in 1940 for a monument in Saint-Jean-de-
Brébeuf Park.

Roche Percée Sask.   4FZ
Outcroppings of sandstone on the prairie here
have been eroded by wind and rain and mu-
tilated by the knives and axes of autograph-
ers. The arch of the 25-foot-high roche percée
was so damaged by lightning that the rock no
longer seems pierced. Nothing remains of religious symbols that Indians carved centuries
ago—or of any autographs except the most recent.

Rock Island Que.   19DZ
Theatergoers at Rock Island's Haskell Opera
House sit in the United States to watch performances on a stage in Canada. Downstairs
in the Haskell Library adults browse in the
U.S., children on the other side of an invisible
border that runs through the building. In
some houses meals are prepared in Canada
and served in the United States. . . .

Many local buildings were erected before
the international boundary was firmly established here. North of it is Rock Island, south
is Derby Line, Vt.

At Litton Industries, a machine tool factory that straddles the border, strict customs
procedures are followed when materials are
moved from one country to the other inside
the plant. On a footbridge that connects the
two sections is one of the metal boundary
markers that identify the 5,526-mile border
between the two countries.

□ The Barn Museum displays a pioneer system that carried spring water through connected hollow logs. It also has tools—some
are 14 feet long—for hollowing logs. There
are a stagecoach and sleigh (c.1850), a two-
wheeled chaise from the 1790s and a colonist
kitchen with dishes, churns, stoves and looms.

□ The Stanstead Historical Museum, three
miles west in Beebe, has a collection of Canadian military insignia from 1914 on.

Rockton Ont.   17BY
Buildings brought from many parts of southern Ontario make up Westfield Pioneer Village, a re-creation of a mid-19th-century farm

African animals roam the 450-acre African Lion
Safari and Game Park at Rockton. As at some similar parks (*see* Hemmingford, Penticton), visitors
drive among the animals.

settlement. Among them are blacksmith, boot and harness, cabinetmaker and printing shops where craftsmen's tools are on display; a general store (1848) with a potbellied stove, cracker barrel and colorful tea boxes, and a dry-goods store (1850). There are also a drugstore (c.1860), residences with 19th-century furnishings and an 1814 log church from the Six Nations Reserve at Ohsweken (the oldest log church in Ontario). Farm implements are displayed in a museum in a large barn. A railway handcar travels several hundred feet of track between a section toolhouse and an 1896 station, one of the few remaining stations of the Toronto, Hamilton and Buffalo Railway.

Rockwood Ont.   7BY/17BX
Dozens of big potholes, formed by hard granite stones swirling over soft limestone in glacial meltwater, are seen in the 197-acre Rockwood Conservation Area. One, 15 feet wide at the top, is 40 feet deep. Many potholes are at or below the level of the Eramosa River; others are 500 feet away, indicating the one-time size of the stream. Limestone projections as high as 60 feet and three subterranean caves are other features of the conservation area. On the Eramosa are millponds that once powered a woolen mill and a gristmill.
□ The Ontario Electric Railway Historical Association has reconstructed 1¼ miles of the Halton County Radial Railway, on which visitors ride in antique streetcars. The association operates an electric railway museum. Working exhibits include a reversible "stub line" car (1915) with "walk-over" wicker seats, a replica of an 1893 open car with a side running board, a coal-heated wooden streetcar and an early streamlined streetcar that saw service in Toronto from 1938 to 1963.
□ Rockwood Academy, a three-story stone building (1853) now privately owned, is excellently preserved.

Rocky Mountain House Alta.   4AX
Two reconstructed stone chimneys dating from 1866 are the only remains of a series of forts that stood here. The first, established by the North West Company in 1799, was the headquarters of David Thompson. He spent several seasons exploring the Columbia River and its tributaries and reached its mouth in 1811. Exhibits at the fort ruins, a national historic park, deal with the fur trade.

Rocky Point P.E.I.   23CX
Fort Amherst National Historic Park is 223 acres of woods and rolling grassland overlooking Hillsborough Bay and Charlottetown harbor. Only earthworks remain of the fort that the British built soon after the fall of Louisbourg in 1758. Port la Joie, the first white settlement in Prince Edward Island, had been established by the French in 1720. Fort Amherst was abandoned by 1775.
□ A 19-foot Northumberland Strait ice boat is displayed at the park. These wooden boats, with iron runners on both sides of the keel,

were towed across ice and rowed or sailed across water. For most of a century (1827-1917) they were the only winter transportation link between P.E.I. and the mainland.
□ A reconstructed 16th-century Micmac village here portrays Indian life before the coming of white men. In it are birch-bark wigwams, a 200-year old birch-bark canoe, hunting and fishing implements and displays of Indian crafts.

Rogers Pass B.C. *see* Glacier National Park

Rolphton Ont.   7DX/18AV
A nuclear power demonstration plant here, a joint project of Ontario Hydro and Atomic Energy of Canada, was the first in Canada to produce electricity by nuclear fission. It can be seen from a lookout.
□ The 360,000-kilowatt Des Joachims Generating Station is the largest hydroelectric plant on the Ottawa River.

Rose Blanche Nfld.   11AZ
A 28-mile drive from Channel-Port aux Basques to this important fishing settlement is one of the most scenic in all Newfoundland. There are no trees—only peat moss, gushing streams, waterfalls, the rocky landscape and wild seascapes.

Rossland B.C.   2EZ
A museum here provides underground tours of the historic Le Roi gold mine and has a Nancy Greene Wing housing the British Columbia Ski Hall of Fame. Nancy Greene, an Olympic and world champion skier in the 1960s, was born in Rossland.
Displays in the Rossland Historical Museum depict the discovery of gold on Red Mountain and the establishment of such mines as Le Roi, Center Star, War Eagle, Iron Mask, Josie and Nickel Plate—which together produced ore worth $125,000,000 between 1890 and 1929. Outside the museum is a granite

Rose Blanche, a Newfoundland south coast fishing village, may have got its name from the French *roche blanche,* for the white rock of the area.

obelisk in memory of the Rev. Henry "Father Pat" Irwin, a pioneer missionary who was pastor of the famous St. Peter's the Stolen (*see* Golden) and first pastor of St. George's Church, Rossland.

□ Skiing here started in 1900 with the first Dominion championship, won by Olaus Jeldness, whose cups and medals are in the museum. At the Red Mountain Ski Area, three miles north, the average annual snowfall is 12 feet.

Rosthern Sask.   4DX
A plaque identifies the farm where Seager Wheeler grew wheat that won five world championships between 1910 and 1918. Wheeler bred many wheat varieties, including race 10-B of Marquis, which dominated the Canadian prairies for many years.

Rothesay N.B.   9DY
New Brunswick's only independent private school for boys, Rothesay Collegiate School, was founded in 1877. Two buildings date from about 1865. Netherwood School (1891) is the province's only independent private school for girls.

Rougemont Que.   19CY
The Cidrerie du Québec bottles 400,000 gallons of apple cider annually. Visitors see a slide show explaining cider-making, then taste local cheeses and the seven Rougemont varieties of cider.

□ The church of a Cistercian Abbey here has an eight-foot plastic Madonna on a ceramic background and ceramic Stations of the Cross by Guardo, a Quebec artist. In a 120-acre orchard are about 8,000 apple trees.

Round Hill N.S.   22CW
The grave of Col. James Delancey, the "Outlaw of the Bronx" who led pro-British partisans in raids around New York during the

A farmer's day ends under a darkening sky near Rustico, on the red-soil island they call the Garden of the Gulf.

American Revolution, is marked by a white marble stone in a family plot at nearby Tupperville. Delancey settled here after being banished from the United States in 1783.

Routhierville Que.   9CW
A 259-foot covered bridge spans the Matapédia River here.

Rouyn-Noranda Que.   7DV
The Noranda Mines copper smelter here is the world's biggest custom copper smelter, processing ore from elsewhere, and has the world's first continuous smelting process. Its two chimneys, 525 and 422 feet high, dominate these twin cities.

Edmund Horne, who discovered vast ore deposits here in 1911, is commemorated by a six-foot granite monument bearing a copper plaque. Hundreds of millions of dollars worth of copper, zinc and gold were mined before the seams ran out. A museum in a log cabin, once lived in by the first manager, tells the story of the local mines.

□ The Regional Exposition of Western Quebec, featuring exhibits of the forest and paper industry, is held here each August.

Rustico P.E.I.   23CW
A monument to the Rev. Georges-Antoine Belcourt stands between Saint Augustine's Church where he was parish priest from 1859 to 1869 and the Farmers' Bank he founded in 1864. The bank, the smallest ever chartered in Canada, operated on the credit union principle, although credit unions as such were not introduced in Canada until 1900 (*see* Lévis). The two-story brown sandstone bank building (1861-64), now the parish hall, contains a small museum. Exhibits include the bank's

own $5 notes. As a missionary in Manitoba's Red River country and later in North Dakota, Father Belcourt had compiled the first French-Chippewa dictionary. In Rustico he founded a high school, a library and a band and was the owner of Prince Edward Island's first self-propelled vehicle, shipped here from Philadelphia. He first showed off the four-wheeled carriage, powered by a small steam engine, at the church in June 1867.

S

Wild horses of Sable Island may be descended from shipwrecked animals or from horses that New England settlers brought in the early 1700s.

Saanich B.C. *see* Victoria

Sable Island N.S.   9FZ
This shifting strip of sand 190 miles east of Halifax is the notorious "graveyard of the Atlantic" where an estimated 200 ships have been wrecked. The treeless island, 22 miles long and a mile wide, is also the home of some 200 wild horses and a sanctuary for gray and harbor seals. Oil was discovered on Sable Island in the 1960s.

Sabrevois Que.   7FY/19CY
The birthplace of Honoré Mercier, premier of Quebec in 1887-91, is a museum containing 19th-century furniture typical of the Richelieu Valley.

Sackville N.B.   9DY/23AX
A mural and a triptych by realist painter Alex Colville, at one time a Sackville resident, adorn two buildings of Mount Allison University. The 16-by-13½-foot mural *History of Mount Allison* is in Tweedie Hall, in a men's residence. It shows a horse, a Methodist circuit rider and parts of campus buildings and figures, including Charles Allison, the university's founder. The three-paneled *Athletes*, in the university athletic center, shows a pole-vaulter, discus thrower, swimmer and runner. The Owens Art Gallery has three Colville silk-screen prints, 10 prints and a self-portrait in oil by Newfoundland artist Christopher Pratt and a silk-screen print by Kenneth Lochhead. There are also works by the Group of Seven, George Romney's portrait *Mrs. Salisbury and Child*, and pre-1880 English watercolors, etchings and paintings. The gallery has one of Canada's finest collections of graphics.
  □ Canada's first Baptist church, a log structure (long since replaced), was built in 1763 in Middle Sackville, three miles north.
  □ One mile east are the transmitters of Radio Canada International.

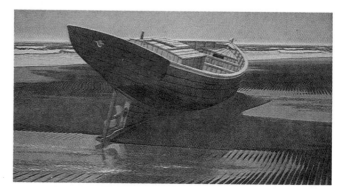

Boat in Sand is a silk-screen print by Newfoundlander Christopher Pratt, done in 1961 when he was a student at Mount Allison University in Sackville. It is in the university's Owens Art Gallery.

of the St. Lawrence. The caribou now are estimated to be 250 strong. The main entrance to the 498-square-mile park is 12 miles south of Sainte-Anne-des-Monts. Mont Jacques-Cartier (4,160 feet), the highest accessible point in eastern Canada, is in the McGerrigle group of the Shickshock range, part of which is within the park boundaries. The higher parts of the park were untouched by the last glaciation so abundant flora survive from the preceding interglacial period: thrift, alpine azalea, alpine campion, Lapland rosebay and bog blueberry are seen on the 12-square-mile treeless plateau which covers the summits of Mont Albert (3,775 and 3,554 feet). The park is one of the few places in Quebec where moose, caribou and deer roam the same territory. A highway through the park crosses the Gaspé Peninsula to New Richmond, 86 miles south on Chaleur Bay.

Sainte-Anne-du-Bocage N.B. *see* Caraquet

St. Anns N.S.   9FX/23GW
Here lived the giant Angus McAskill (*see* Englishtown), who astounded the world with his strength. And here still live the Gaelic tongue, the lore of the clans and the ways of the Scottish pioneers of Cape Breton. The only Gaelic college in North America is in St. Anns, offering summer courses in Highland dancing, arts, crafts and bagpipes and the weaving of tartans.

The Giant McAskill-Highland Pioneers Museum on the college grounds tells of the early settlers and of the mighty McAskill who, after injuring a shoulder while tossing an anchor, returned to St. Anns and operated a mill. The museum displays some of his clothing, his chair and bed. Most townfolk have tales of his strength and appetites, his mallet-sized pipe and his huge wooden bowl for quaffing rum or brandy.

Also at the college is a memorial to the pioneer pastor, the Rev. Norman McLeod, who

Nova Scotia Gaelic Mod, in August, brings thousands of visitors and competitors to St. Anns for a six-day festival of Highland games, piping, song and dance.

eventually led a group of migrants to New Zealand in 1851. Some 870, almost half the village population, emigrated to New Zealand in the 1850s in ships built in St. Anns Harbor.

Eight ceramic murals by Jordi Bonet adorn the rotunda of Curtis Memorial Hospital in St. Anthony. This one depicts a dignified Eskimo couple and a boy. Above the boy is a glazed area that suggests the color of the semiprecious stone labradorite.

St. Anthony Nfld.   11CW
This small town is a beacon of hope for the scattered, isolated people of northern Newfoundland and Labrador. It is the headquarters of the Grenfell Mission, which provides medical and social help along a 1,500-mile coastline that is icebound much of the year. Sir Wilfrid Grenfell, shocked by the poverty and deprivation he had seen as a medical missionary, began the work in 1893 and devoted the rest of his life to it. He died in 1940 at the age of 75; his grave is here.

The International Grenfell Association, formed to carry on his work, has 12 nursing stations, four hospitals, a children's home, a hospital ship, aircraft and air ambulances and handicraft centers. The association's Curtis Memorial Hospital here honors Dr. Charles S. Curtis, another medical missionary who devoted a lifetime to the people.

Saint-Antoine-de-Tilly Que.   20BW
Four paintings brought to Canada by the Rev. Philippe-Jean-Louis Desjardins, a priest fleeing the French Revolution, were acquired by Saint-Antoine-de-Tilly Church in 1817. They are *Le Christ révélant à Saint François d'Assise les statuts de son ordre* (1679), by Frère Luc; *La Visitation* (mid-18th century), by A. Oudry; *Jésus au milieu des Docteurs* (18th century), by Samuel Massé, and *La Sainte Famille* (c.1630), by Aubin Vouet. The church, built in 1788, replaced a church that sheltered 1,200 English soldiers during the siege of Quebec in 1759.

The two-story wood Manoir de Tilly (1786), now a hotel, contains some late-18th-century furnishings. Nearby is a roadside Calvary, a life-size statue of Christ on a 20-foot cross.

Memories Linger Where Great-Grandpa Spooned

At the turn of the century there were thousands. Now Canada has probably fewer than 250 covered bridges. Almost half are in New Brunswick; its 90 include the world's longest (right), the 1,282-foot bridge at Hartland. Most of the rest are in Quebec, among them the province's shortest covered bridge, a 48-footer over a creek at Saint-Armand-Ouest (left, top) in Missisquoi County. It dates from the 1850s. A 105-foot bridge (left) over the Vassan River in Abitibi County was built in the early 1950s—for the same good reasons that applied a century ago in the heyday of covered bridges. The roof shelters the bridge (especially the underpinnings) from the alternate wetness and dryness that injures wood. It also has the reassuring look of a barn, easing farm animals' fears of rushing water. And it's as much a kissin' bridge as the ones great-grandpa favored on those romantic June nights when he went courting.

Saint-Benoît-du-Lac Que.—The tall, square tower of a Dom Bellot-style Benedictine abbey overlooks Lake Memphremagog here. The buildings, of pink granite, are a striking combination of octagonal and square towers, triangular gables and long, thin, pointed windows. (French-born Dom Paul Bellot, who came to Canada in 1937, was one of Quebec's foremost ecclesiastical architects. His most famous work is the dome of St. Joseph's Oratory in Montreal. He collaborated on the design of the abbey here and his grave is in the abbey grounds.) (19DY)

Saint-Armand-Ouest Que.   19CZ
A covered bridge here is only 48 feet long.

St. Bernard N.S.   9CZ/22BW
This village of some 300 population has a great stone church that seats 1,000 persons.

St. Boniface Man. *see* Winnipeg

St. Catharines Ont.   7CZ/17CY
Peach trees, apple orchards, cherry blossoms, vineyards of lush grapes ripening for the wine

vats: it's all here in the Niagara fruit belt, the heart of Canada's greatest grape-growing region.

St. Catharines, settled by United Empire Loyalists in 1792, is a city of more than 100,000, many involved in wine production or the fresh and canned fruit business. The city is important for pulp and paper, auto parts, textiles and electrical equipment and has much to offer the tourist. Attractions include the Welland Canal, parks, scenic drives, festivals, exhibitions and museums.

BROCK UNIVERSITY The university tower, dominating the skyline, offers a panoramic view of the 620-acre campus and the Niagara Escarpment. Opened in 1964, Brock within 10 years had more than 4,500 students seeking degrees in arts and sciences. It was named after Maj. Gen. Sir Isaac Brock, killed in the Battle of Queenston Heights in 1812 (*see* Queenston).

MOUNTAIN MILLS MUSEUM This is a fine old gristmill (1872) at De Cew Falls. A mile east is a plaque marking the foundations of De Cew House, to which Laura Secord made her famous journey (*see* Queenston).

NIAGARA GRAPE FESTIVAL For 10 days in September, during the grape harvest, the city lets go in a carnival that overflows with parades, bands, floats, pretty girls and the music and dancing of the region's many cultures. There are vineyard tours, horse and boat races, hockey games and art exhibitions.

RIDLEY COLLEGE Canada's largest residential private school for boys, this college of venerable buildings and modern appointments is in the manner of English public schools, even to the shaded campus and the cricket pitches.

RODMAN HALL ARTS CENTER The St. Catharines and District Arts Council serves the community with art exhibitions, concerts, lectures in the arts and humanities, and literature and hobby workshops. The hall, an outstanding example of 19th-century architecture, was built by Thomas Rodman Merritt in 1853. Among the center's prized possessions are

Family, a 21-inch sculpture in cement, done by John Ivor Smith in 1961, is in the Rodman Hall Arts Center in St. Catharines.

Royal Canadian Henley Regatta at St. Catharines in July attracts top international oarsmen.

three watercolors by David Milne, two oils by Lawren Harris, a sculpture by John Ivor Smith and a drawing by Sir Jacob Epstein.

ST. CATHARINES HISTORICAL MUSEUM It displays handmade farm tools, butter churns and early Canadian china. A popular item is a pitchfork made in St. Catharines and used in the capture of Rudolf Hess, the German leader who parachuted into Scotland in 1941 on a peace mission. A fire-fighting collection includes an 1873 steam pumper.

ST. CATHARINES KIWANIS HORSE SHOW Canada's largest outdoor horse show, at Garden City Raceway.

WELLAND CANAL A plaque in Centennial Gardens Park describes the building of the first canal from Port Dalhousie (now part of St. Catharines) to Port Robinson in 1824-29, and its completion to Port Colborne on Lake Erie in 1833. (*See* Welland)

Sainte-Catherine-d'Alexandrie Que. 19BY
Near the Church of Sainte-Catherine is the tomb in which the body of Kateri Tekakwitha was placed in 1680. (The remains were later removed to Caughnawaga—*see entry.*) Near the tomb is a three-foot statue of the saintly Mohawk woman.

Saint-Charles Que. 19CX
It was here and at Saint-Denis (*see entry*) that rebellion broke out in Lower Canada on Nov. 23, 1837. Rebels gathered in Saint-Charles, planted a tree of liberty, proclaimed a republic (the Confederation of the Six Counties) and, in an *adresse au peuple canadien*, called for an uprising. Meanwhile, at Saint-Denis, nine miles north, rebels defeated British troops in a six-hour battle. Two days later a second

battle was fought at Saint-Charles. Casualties among rebels and government troops were heavy; 30 rebels were taken prisoner. The victorious military burned the village. A 10-foot stone monument bears the names of the rebel leaders.

Saint-Constant Que. 19BY
A locomotive that was built in 1887 and 73 years later was the last steam engine to haul a CPR train is among the old-timers in the Canadian Railway Museum. No. 29 went into service two years after completion of the CPR transcontinental main line. On Nov. 6, 1960, hauling an excursion train from Montreal to Saint-Lin, Que., it symbolically ended the CPR steam era.

Among 100 pieces of rolling stock in the museum is a 1937 British engine of the type that set a world record of 126 miles an hour for steam locomotives. CN 4110, once (in 1924) the most powerful steam locomotive in the Commonwealth, and the CPR's first Royal Hudson, used for the 1939 royal tour, are here. A British Terrier locomotive dates from 1875, the French *St. Malo* from 1883.

The museum has many Montreal streetcars, including the city's first electric tram (1892) and the Golden Chariot open cars used on scenic tours. There are cabooses, sleepers, tank and freight cars and a school car once used in northern Ontario as a mobile schoolhouse. On the 10-acre museum site are a turntable, a water tank, a roundhouse and a rural station of the 1880s. A replica of the woodburning locomotive *John Molson*, like those used on the earliest lines over a century ago, operates on scheduled days.

Sainte-Croix Que. 9AX/20BW
The Petit Sault River plunges over an 80-foot waterfall before flowing into the St. Lawrence

River. Three miles west of the village is the seigniorial manor of Henri Joly de Lotbinière, built about 1720.

□ Formula, stock and drag cars race at the one-mile Québec-Circuit-Sainte-Croix.

Saint-Denis Que.   7FY/19CX

A larger-than-life statue of a *patriote* in a Saint-Denis park commemorates 12 men killed here Nov. 23, 1837, in one of the first clashes of the Lower Canada rebellion (*see* Saint-Charles). A cairn marks the site of Maison Saint-Germain, a big stone house in which some 300 rebels barricaded themselves against 500 British soldiers sent from Sorel. The rebels, led by Dr. Wolfred Nelson, had fewer than 200 firearms (and only 57 in good working order). During the assault on the house, children with sticks on their shoulders paraded behind a fence to mislead the British as to the number of armed men in the village. The soldiers retreated. Other soldiers set fire to the house nine days later.

□ In Saint-Denis Church (1792) are two altars crafted by Louis Quevillon and a pulpit carved by Urbain Desrochers.

St. Elmo Ont.   18EX

Glengarry Congregationalist Church, built in 1837, is the oldest remaining Congregationalist chapel in Ontario. When membership dwindled around 1912, the little log building was bought by Gordon Presbyterian Church and it has been used since for community and social events.

Saint-Félicien Que.   9AW/21AW

The Zoological Garden of Saint-Félicien is on Ile du Jardin in the Rivière aux Saumons, a tributary of the Chamouchouane River which races through Saint-Félicien with several turbulent rapids and waterfalls. The International Regatta of Lac Saint-Jean, on the Chamouchouane in June, is preceded by a week of sailing, kayak and water-skiing contests, dances and a torchlight boat parade.

□ Saint-Félicien Church, an ornate stone structure that resembles a cathedral, has two

St. François Xavier Man.—A 12-foot statue of a white horse commemorates the Indian legend of the White Horse Plain: a Sioux warrior and his Cree bride, on a white horse, were pursued and killed by her rejected suitor. The horse escaped. For years it was seen roaming the surrounding plain. (15CX)

steeples. It seats nearly 2,000 persons, some in its all-round galleries.

Saint-Féréol-les-Neiges Que.   9AX/20BV

The Rivière Sainte-Anne du Nord descends 410 feet over Les Sept Chutes, a series of waterfalls here. The Jean-Larose River drops 192 feet, also in Saint-Féréol-les-Neiges.

St. George Ont.   7BZ/17BY

The Adelaide Hunter Hoodless Homestead, two miles west, was the birthplace (1857) of the founder of Women's Institutes, which now have nearly 8,000,000 members in 70 countries. The farmhouse, Adelaide Hunter's girlhood home, bears a plaque declaring it a national historic site. It is furnished in the styles of the late 1800s. A half-mile east is a cairn and a plaque honoring Mrs. Hoodless.

Saint-Eustache Que.—The walls of the church here, pocked by cannon shot, bear witness to the bloodiest battle of the Rebellion of 1837. Some 250 *patriotes* led by Jean-Olivier Chénier barricaded themselves in the church. British troops slowly advanced behind heavy cannon and musket fire, broke into the church and set it aflame. Seventy rebels were killed, among them Chénier, whose monument stands at Sacré-Coeur School. (7FY/19AY)

She organized the first Women's Institute at Stoney Creek in 1897, introduced the teaching of domestic science in Ontario schools and was instrumental in starting Macdonald Institute at Guelph.

□ A plaque at the family farm near St. George honors Harry C. Nixon, Ontario's 13th premier, a member of the legislature from 1919 until his death in 1961.

Saint-Georges-Ouest Que.   9AX/20CX
A 15-foot-high bronze statue of Saint George, sculpted in 1912 by Louis Jobin, stands in front of Saint George's Church. It depicts the saint on his horse, slaying a dragon.

□ Two miles north is the Parc des Sept Chutes, named for seven waterfalls that drop 125 feet in a Pozer River gorge.

□ Quebec's longest covered bridge (507 feet) crosses the Chaudière River six miles north in Notre-Dame-des-Pins. The bridge, no longer in use, dates from the early 1900s.

Saint-Grégoire Que.   19DW
The three altars of Saint-Grégoire-le-Grand Church, which date from about 1815, were sculpted by Urbain Desrochers, who also carved the pulpit and part of the reredos. Louis Quevillon sculpted the intricate walls of the sanctuary.

Credence table (c.1813) in Saint-Grégoire-le-Grand Church is believed by Urbain Desrochers.

Saint-Henri Que.   9AX/20BW
Neo-Gothic Saint-Henri-de-Lévis Church has 56 statues of saints and religious personages carved from wood by Louis Jobin and others. Paintings include *La Vision de Saint-Antoine de Padoue* by François-Guy Hallé.

Saint-Hyacinthe Que.   7FY/19CY
Sanair International, 10 miles southeast, has a quarter-mile drag strip, a stock car oval and a twisting, 1.3-mile racetrack. Sanair stages the Grand National drag race for three days in August, the three-day Player's Quebec (part of the Player's Challenge series) in June and the Molson Trans-Am in July.

□ The Church of Notre-Dame-de-la-Présentation-de-Marie in La Présentation, six miles northwest, dates from 1817. The neo-

Casavant organ works, established in Saint-Hyacinthe in 1860, have won international renown. They may be visited.

Gothic chapel of Saint-Hyacinthe Seminary (1927) was modeled after Amiens Cathedral in France.

St. Ignace Ont. *see* Waubaushene

Saint-Irénée Que.   9AW
Here lived Sir Adolphe Routhier, author (in 1880) of the French words of "O Canada." An avenue of poplars near the Routhier house leads to a hospital that was the estate of Sir Rodolphe Forget. A memorial commemorates his role in building a railway between Saint-Joachim and La Malbaie.

Saint-Jean Que.   7FY/19BY
Among the greens and fairways of the Saint-Jean golf course is a cairn commemorating the Battle of Montgomery Creek in 1775. Saint-Jean was attacked by American revolutionaries who came down the Richelieu River from New York. The British garrison put up a stubborn defense but after a 45-day siege the invaders occupied Fort Saint-Jean. They burned it when they left the following year.

Saint-Jean is the home of Canada's first bilingual military college for officer cadets, the Collège militaire royal. Weapons, uniforms, medals and documents in the college museum tell the story of Fort Saint-Jean.

The French built a fort here in 1666 to protect their trading posts and the approaches to Montreal. Rebuilt in 1748 on a site now marked by a plaque on Champlain Street, the fort was burned and abandoned by the French in 1760 after the British conquest. The British rebuilt it then and again after it had been taken and burned during the American Revolution. The present barracks, part of the military college, were built in 1839.

□ A tablet at the CN station commemorates the building of Canada's first railway, the Champlain and St. Lawrence, which was opened July 21, 1836 (*see* La Prairie).

□ Saint-Gérard-Majella Church (1962), with curved brick walls and a roof like a breaking wave, appears both massive and full of motion. It was designed by Guy Desbarats, designer of Place des Arts in Montreal.

□ The Church of Sainte-Marguerite-de-l'Acadie in nearby Lacadie is little changed from when it was built in 1801. The rectory dates from 1823. Both are of fieldstone.

Saint-Jean-Port-Joli Que.   9BX/20DV

An old church here links sculptors who flourished when it was young and modern artists who make Saint-Jean-Port-Joli the wood-carving capital of Quebec. Most of the carving in the church (the building dates from 1779) was done in the late 18th and early 19th centuries by Jean and Pierre Baillargé, Chrysostôme Perrault, Amable Charron and François-Noël Levasseur. But the magnificent pulpit, installed in 1937, is the work of Médard and Jean-Julien Bourgault, founders of the modern revival of wood sculpture.

The tradition they follow goes back to the 1670s when Bishop Laval encouraged the teaching of arts and crafts at a school in Saint-Joachim. A similar school was started on Ile Jésus, near Montreal. For two centuries artists in wood were in demand for decorating churches, public buildings and country homes. Wood carving declined with mass production of furniture and building materials but farmers and seamen kept it alive as a pastime. One seaman, Médard Bourgault, came home to his father's carpenter shop here in 1925 and three years later opened a studio to make a career of wood sculpture. His brothers André and Jean-Julien followed. The Bourgaults were the nucleus of one of the most productive groups of craftsmen in Quebec. Among the fine figures and murals they created are André's *Evangeline,* one of many he did of Longfellow's heroine (it is in André's shop); Médard's *Figure of Christ,* in an Oblate retreat house in Richelieu, and Jean-Julien's *Town Council,* in l'Auberge du Faubourg in Saint-Jean-Port-Joli.

The Bourgaults not only created widely treasured art but also taught scores of village craftsmen. The main tradition is still rustic: a trapper on snowshoes, a logger swinging an axe, an old woman carrying milk pails, the ever-popular habitant. Some of the finest miniature sailboats in the world are made here. There are sculptors of abstract forms, of full-size figures from history and religion, sculptured murals, birds and animals.

About the time the Bourgaults made a profession of their pastime, a Saint-Jean-Port-Joli seaman and lighthouse keeper, Eugène Leclerc, turned full time to carving scale models of sailing ships. His sons Honoré and Lucien learned from him and set up their own studios when he died. Leclerc ships, sold the world over, include large, meticulous models of such vessels as Columbus' *Santa Maria,* the Pilgrims' *Mayflower* and Canada's *Bluenose.*

Other local artists produce copper-enamel art and jewelry, woven fabrics of brilliant

Jean-Julien Bourgault of Saint-Jean-Port-Joli works on a mural depicting a maple syrup harvest scene. The ceiling of the Saint-Jean-Port-Joli Church was carved (c.1800) by Chrysostôme Perrault and Amable Charron.

design, leather and metalwork, marquetry and cabinetwork, mosaics, oil paintings and watercolors. Many Saint-Jean-Port-Joli women have made names in the arts: Marie-Emma Perrault in copper-enamel work and Mme Edmond Chamard, Mme Olivier Bélanger, Gilberte and Hélène Caron in weaving and design.

□ The parish of Saint-Jean-Port-Joli was founded in 1721 but the present stone church was built more than half a century later. It is the burial place of Philippe-Joseph Aubert de Gaspé, born in 1786, author of *Mémoires* and *Les anciens Canadiens,* and last of the seigniorial line of Saint-Jean-Port-Joli.

Saint-Jérôme Que.   7FX/19BX

A bronze statue in Labelle Park honors a man who made a life work of opening the Laurentian wilderness to large-scale settlement. On foot and by canoe in the 1870s and '80s the Most Rev. Antoine Labelle explored the wooded hills, the lakes and rivers, founding 20 parishes long before the Laurentians won fame as Quebec's finest year-round resort area. He saw farms take shape, villages grow and Saint-Jérôme become a distribution center for new settlements and early tourism.

Curé Labelle once told his struggling parishioners: "You who with infinite toil have carved yourselves farms from the wilderness, stay on! Persevere! In another 50 years strangers will flock here, and they will scatter gold by the handful."

Saint-Joachim Que.—About 1780 François Baillargé and his son Thomas started a 40-year work that helped make their parish church here a treasure-house of Quebec art and architecture. Their wood sculptures of the Evangelists (above, Saint Mark and Saint Matthew) and the depth and vitality of their bas-relief panels are precious examples of an old art. The church, completed in 1779, is a showcase for other masters too: the altar of Saint Joachim (above) is by Pierre Emond, the pulpit (1780) by Thomas Berlinguet, church plate by François Ranvoyzé and Laurent Amyot, paintings by Brother Luc.

□ A plaque here honors the Rev. Philippe-René de Portneuf; he and seven parishioners were killed in an attack on British troops in 1759. (20CV)

Saint John N.B.   9DY

A "Loyalist Trail" through downtown Saint John leads past historic public buildings, 18th- and 19th-century houses, stores and churches, a burial ground and the site of the house where renegade American Gen. Benedict Arnold lived in 1787. A 90-minute walk along the trail is a walk into the history of one of North America's oldest cities.

Champlain was here in 1604 and Charles de La Tour established a fortified trading post in 1631. The first permanent English settlement dates from 1762 but Saint John got its main impetus when 4,200 United Empire Loyalists arrived from the United States on May 18, 1783.

Timber, manufacturing and shipbuilding brought fame and fortune to Saint John in the 19th century. By 1901 it was Canada's eighth largest city, about the size of Halifax. But when wooden shipbuilding declined, so did the city, although it remained an important year-round port. New life came to Saint John in the 1960s with huge investments in mining and metals, pulp and paper, sugar and oil refining, a container shipping service and a deepwater terminal for supertankers.

ATLANTIC NATIONAL EXHIBITION (1) Fish, livestock, wildlife and horticultural shows at eastern Canada's largest fair, in late August.

BARBOUR'S GENERAL STORE (2) Tea chests and cracker barrels, hand scales and bolts of cloth . . . clerks and "customers" playing checkers near a potbellied stove . . . all evoke the past. The building dates from 1867.

CARLETON MARTELLO TOWER (3) Dating from the War of 1812, it was manned during the 1866 Fenian scare and two world wars. A national historic site, it affords an impressive view of city and harbor. The circular fort has stone walls more than eight feet thick at the base. There is a lodging floor whose central column—containing more than 75,000 bricks—fans out into an umbrella-arching ceiling.

COUNTY COURTHOUSE (4) An old building (1829) with a self-supporting, three-story spiral stone stairway.

LOYALIST BURIAL GROUND (5) The oldest gravestone is that of Coonradt Hendricks, who died July 13, 1784.

LOYALIST HOUSE (6) In the double parlors are

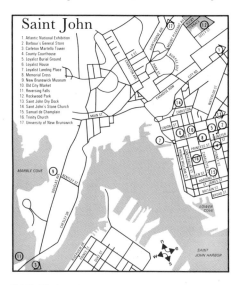

Saint John

1. Atlantic National Exhibition
2. Barbour's General Store
3. Carleton Martello Tower
4. County Courthouse
5. Loyalist Burial Ground
6. Loyalist House
7. Loyalist Landing Place
8. Memorial Cross
9. New Brunswick Museum
10. Old City Market
11. Reversing Falls
12. Rockwood Park
13. Saint John Dry Dock
14. Saint John's Stone Church
15. Samuel de Champlain
16. Trinity Church
17. University of New Brunswick

Old burial ground in downtown Saint John is one focal point of the city's Loyalist Days celebration in July. Children and adults don 18th-century dress and proud tales are told of the Loyalists' arrival in 1783.

Grecian swooning sofas, a piano organ and Duncan Phyfe tables from 1818; in the master bedroom, a canopied bed, mahogany crib and commode chair; in the kitchen, a bake oven and fireplace. The house was finished in 1817 by Daniel David Merritt, a prosperous Loyalist merchant. Lived in by five generations of Merritts, it now is a museum.

LOYALIST LANDING PLACE (7) A boulder memorial marks the landing place of the Loyalists of 1783.

MEMORIAL CROSS (8) Commemorates the founding of the province Aug. 10, 1784.

NEW BRUNSWICK MUSEUM (9) Founded in 1842, it contains a museum of natural and human history, archives, a library and an art gallery. There are extensive collections of flora and fauna, furniture, military uniforms, Loyalist and Indian artifacts, and paintings.

OLD CITY MARKET (10) The block-long structure, built in 1876, survived a fire the next year that destroyed more than half the city.

REVERSING FALLS (11) The mighty Saint John River boils into the sea through a deep, narrow gorge. Twice a day, rising on one of the world's highest tides, the sea throws the river back and sweeps upstream in a fury of foam, rapids and whirlpools.

ROCKWOOD PARK (12) A 2,200-acre park (swimming, boating, fishing, camping, nature trails, children's farm, golf course, zoo).

SAINT JOHN DRY DOCK (13) One of the largest in the world, the main dock is 1,150 feet long and 125 feet wide.

SAINT JOHN'S STONE CHURCH (14) The city's first stone structure was completed in 1825 with stone brought from England as ballast.

SAMUEL DE CHAMPLAIN (15) A monument to the explorer who named the Saint John River on June 24, 1604—after the saint whose feast day it was.

TRINITY CHURCH (16) The royal coat of arms over the great west door was brought here from Boston after the American Revolution. It had decorated the council chamber of the colony of Massachusetts.

UNIVERSITY OF NEW BRUNSWICK (17) The Saint John campus was established in 1964.

St. John's Nfld.   11DZ

Snug in its sheltered harbor, below the majestic rock and old guns of Signal Hill, lies the capital of Newfoundland, once Britain's oldest colony, now the youngest Canadian province. No other city in Canada is quite like St. John's, with its stunning natural setting, its clutter of bright wooden houses clinging to hills behind the waterfront, its managing to suggest that all its stirring history was just the day before yesterday.

The first European visitors to Newfoundland were probably the Vikings (*see* L'Anse aux Meadows). Permanent settlement dates from soon after John Cabot anchored here on St. John's Day in 1497 and claimed the island for England. Within a few years European fishermen were sailing here to harvest the cod of the Grand Banks. (The Portuguese fishing fleet has used St. John's as a supply base continuously since about 1500.) Coastal settlements were established—and often attacked

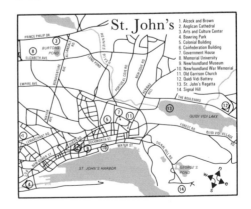

St. John's

1. Alcock and Brown
2. Anglican Cathedral
3. Arts and Culture Center
4. Bowring Park
5. Colonial Building
6. Confederation Building
7. Government House
8. Memorial University
9. Newfoundland Museum
10. Newfoundland War Memorial
11. Old Garrison Church
12. Quidi Vidi Battery
13. St. John's Regatta
14. Signal Hill

Shanawdithit, the last of the Beothucks (*see* p.65), made this caribou-skin coat shortly before her death in 1829. It is displayed at St. John's in the Newfoundland Museum. The Beothuck necklace is made of pieces of bone strung on sinew.

by freebooters and privateers sent out by fishing firms to discourage settlement and destroy one another's bases of operations. In 1583 Sir Humphrey Gilbert landed here and formally claimed the island for Elizabeth I. A Dutch squadron plundered the town in 1665 and French forces from Placentia raided and burned it three times. The British regained possession in 1762.

In World War II the city became a vital link in North Atlantic communications. A main convoy route to Britain was between St. John's and Londonderry, Northern Ireland. In 1949 Newfoundland joined Canada as the 10th province.

The Old Town has changed little since it was rebuilt after a disastrous fire in 1892. A few modern structures have thrust up but most building by government and industry has been in the suburbs. Ships from many nations appear in port, and the shops and bars along Water Street—the oldest street in North America—are alive with foreign tongues.

ALCOCK AND BROWN (1) A plaque on red granite marks where Capt. John Alcock and Lt. Arthur Whitten Brown took off June 14, 1919, on what was the first direct nonstop Atlantic flight (*see* Gander).

ANGLICAN CATHEDRAL (2) This Gothic cathedral designed by Sir Gilbert Scott in the early 19th century was rebuilt after the fire of 1892. A silver Communion service from William IV is in the chapter house.

ARTS AND CULTURE CENTER (3) Newfoundland's main centennial project has a 1,000-seat theater, libraries, archives, three art galleries, an arts and handicrafts teaching area and a maritime museum.

COLONIAL BUILDING (5) A gray limestone building, home of the Newfoundland legislature from 1850 to 1959. It houses the provincial archives.

CONFEDERATION BUILDING (6) This is Newfoundland government headquarters and the meeting place of the legislative assembly. In an 11th-floor observation tower is a museum of Newfoundland naval and military history.

GOVERNMENT HOUSE (7) The Georgian-style stone mansion, the home of Newfoundland governors since it was built in 1830, is the official residence of the lieutenant governor.

MEMORIAL UNIVERSITY (8) Memorial University College, founded in 1925 as a memorial to Newfoundland's World War I dead, became a university in 1949. It moved to a new 120-acre campus in 1961. In the univer-

Queen's Battery, on historic Signal Hill, overlooks the snug harbor of St. John's. The modern city spreads back behind some of North America's oldest streets.

Bowring Park in St. John's has three famous statues: a caribou in memory of the nearly 700 men of the Royal Newfoundland Regiment killed July 1, 1916, in the Battle of the Somme; the Fighting Newfoundlander, and a replica of the Peter Pan statue in London's Kensington Gardens.

sity art gallery is a collection of Canadian paintings that includes *The October Moon, Rivière Beaudette* by Maurice Cullen.

NEWFOUNDLAND MUSEUM (9) It has an important Beothuck Indian collection (*see* p.65) and exhibits dealing with early settlement, sailing, whaling, sealing and cod fishing, pulp and paper, and Newfoundland archaeology and ethnology. There are Eskimo and Nascapi Indian relics, ship models and original plans of the French fort at Placentia (*see entry*).

NEWFOUNDLAND WAR MEMORIAL (10) It is on the King's Beach site where Sir Humphrey Gilbert claimed Newfoundland for England in 1583. The granite structure, almost 25 feet high and flanked by marble steps between Water and Duckworth streets, is topped by a statue of Freedom.

OLD GARRISON CHURCH (11) The Church of St. Thomas (1836) displays the Hanoverian coat of arms and has many memorials from its days as a garrison church.

QUIDI VIDI BATTERY (12) Guns were mounted in 1762 to guard the harbor entrance of Quidi Vidi village, now a part of St. John's. In a small fortification restored to 1812 conditions are displays of relics found on the site.

ST. JOHN'S REGATTA (13) A rowing match is the highlight of what may be North America's oldest annual sporting event, held in August on Quidi Vidi Lake. Six oarsmen in fixed-seat shells 52½ feet long race over a 1.6-mile course. The race is believed to date from the early 19th century.

SIGNAL HILL (14) Sheer rock rises 500 feet from the sea at the narrow harbor entrance. This is Signal Hill, now a 260-acre national historic park studded with the ruins of fortifications that once earned it the name of Fort Impregnable. Here on Dec. 12, 1901, Guglielmo Marconi sent up an aerial on a kite and received the first transatlantic wireless message from Cornwall, England, 1,700 miles

away. A good road to the top leads past Gibbett Hill, used by the British in the mid-18th century to display criminals who had been hanged. St. John's was plundered, captured and recaptured several times before Signal Hill itself was fortified. The Queen's Battery, commanding the entrance to the Narrows, was built in 1763-69; mountings there now probably date from the 1860s. In the Narrows below the Queen's Battery is Chain Rock. As far back as the 1690s, chain and log booms were stretched across the Narrows to keep out enemy ships. Gun batteries have been sited on the rock since 1763. The Cabot Tower was started in 1897 to commemorate the 400th anniversary of Cabot's discovery of Newfoundland and the diamond jubilee of Queen Victoria. It opened on June 20, 1900. Inside are exhibits of early signaling devices and wireless. One section is devoted to the work of Marconi and his assistants.

"I looks towards ye!" That's the toast as a Newfoundlander raises a glass of Screech, the powerful West Indian rum bottled in St. John's. "And I bows accordin'" is the response.

Saint-Joseph-de-Beauce Que.—La Céramique de Beauce, a cooperative, produces 10,000 pieces of pottery a day. The plant and an exhibition hall may be toured. (9AX/20CX)

Saint-Joseph-de-la-Rive Que.   9AX
La Papeterie Saint-Gilles, the only Canadian paper mill specializing in handmade, parchment-like writing paper, is run by a prominent folklorist and author, Msgr. Félix-Antoine Savard. It uses machines only for operations that cannot be done manually. Visitors see rag-fiber pulp combined with pastes and dyes and sifted in a large vat. After sheets are shaped, pressed on blotters and dried on clotheslines, calendering then smooths and presses the white, blue or green paper. By mixing maple leaves, ferns and wild flowers in the pulp, a deluxe parchment is produced. The paper, bearing the effigy of Saint Gilles in its watermark, rivals the chiné papers of Japan, China and France.

□ In Saint-Joseph-de-la-Rive Church are biblical scenes carved in wood by Alphonse Paré. One depicts the Holy Family as left-handed (each holds an object in the left hand); this was Paré's device for ensuring that Saint Joseph would be on the *rive* (shore) side of the church but would not have his back to the altar. Paré's altar sculpture includes fish and four anchors.

□ Saint-Joseph overlooks the main channel of the St. Lawrence River. There is a ferry to Ile aux Coudres.

St. Lawrence Islands National Park (Ont.)
                                        7EY/18CY
A small mainland area, 18 heavily wooded islands and 80 rocky islets between Kingston and Brockville make up this 1,000-acre park. Its scenic beauty and sheltered waters make it a boater's paradise. Some of the islands have docks, campsites, wells and kitchen shelters. The 94-acre mainland area at Mallorytown Landing is accessible by highway. Here are the park headquarters, camping facilities, a visitors' center and a beach. On display is a 54½-foot single-masted vessel raised from nearby Patterson Bay in 1967, thought to be the British gunboat *Radcliffe* which saw service in the War of 1812.

Above Cedar Island stands the limestone Cathcart Tower, built in the 1840s as part of the border defense system. The 36-foot-high tower, manned for a quarter century, was never attacked.

The islands, with such poetic names as Camelot, Mermaid and Endymion, are of Precambrian granite that was rounded and eroded by glaciers about one million years ago. Their rugged beauty is accentuated by the growth of trees to the waterline. Small mammals and a wide variety of amphibians and reptiles are to be found in the oak and hickory forests of the park.

Saint-Léonard N.B.   9CX
The Madawaska Weavers, famous for hand-loomed skirts, scarves, ties and rugs, can be seen at work here.

Saint-Lin-des-Laurentides Que. *see* Laurentides

St. Louis Ont. *see* Victoria Harbour

Saint-Louis-de-Kent N.B.   9DX
A replica of the Grotto of Lourdes overlooks the Kouchibouguacis River here. Built in 1878, it is on the landscaped grounds of the former Saint-Louis-des-Français Church.

Saint-Louis-du-Ha! Ha! Que.   9BW
The Grand-Portage Trail—for hikers, horses and snowmobiles but not cars—winds from here through 60 miles of woods to Rivière-du-Loup.

Sainte-Luce Que.   9BW
A big stone gristmill built in 1848 on the Ruisseau à la Loutre here is one of the oldest in the Gaspé. It contains a provincial tourist office and a collection of 19th-century furniture, farm implements, cooking utensils and other household articles.

Sainte-Luce-sur-Mer Church, designed by François Baillargé and built in 1840, contains a painting by Antoine Plamondon and wood sculptures by André Paquet. One stained glass window depicts Cartier erecting a cross at Gaspé in 1534.

Sainte-Marie (Beauce) Que.   9AX/20CX
The shrine of Sainte-Anne-de-Beauce is between two historic houses. One, built in 1811, was the birthplace of Elzéar-Alexandre Cardinal Taschereau, the first Canadian cardinal. The other was built in the early 1800s by

the cardinal's father, Jean-Thomas Taschereau, a judge.

St. Marys Ont. 7BY/16DX

Many buildings in this attractive town are built of limestone from local quarries. A disused quarry in Centennial Park, now filled with water, is called Ontario's largest outdoor swimming pool (500 yards by 100).

▫ Exhibits at the St. Marys District Museum include a Geneva Bible (1560), a silk-and-wool shawl that belonged to Laura Secord (*see* Queenston) and a 1902 electric car.

▫ A plaque at Anderson, 10 miles northwest, commemorates Arthur Meighen, a native son who became prime minister (1920-21 and 1926). James A. Gardiner, premier of Saskatchewan (1926-29 and 1934-35) and federal agriculture minister (1935-57), is commemorated by a plaque near his birthplace in Usborne Township, about 10 miles west.

▫ Timothy Eaton ran a store here before starting T. Eaton Co. in Toronto in 1869.

Saint-Mathias Que. 19CY

An intricate wooden reredos carved with grape and flower motifs is among the treasures of Saint-Mathias Church. The artist's identity is not known. The church, built in 1784, is surrounded by a five-foot stone wall. When the facade was enlarged in 1815, it was decorated with sculptures by Louis Quevillon.

The 3½-story fieldstone Franchère house, a private residence, dates from 1812.

Saint-Nicolas Que. 20BW

The great white triangular belfry of Saint-Nicolas Church (1962) looks like a billowing sail. It is 76 feet high and only 1½ feet thick. In an oval opening near the top are three bells. A gallery around the outside of the church gives sweeping views of the St. Lawrence.

St. Norbert Man. 6BY/15DY

A cairn in La Barriere Park marks the site of a barricade built by the Métis during the Riel Rebellion of 1870. Emissaries of William McDougall, lieutenant-governor-designate of Manitoba, were turned back at the roadblock as they neared the Red River Settlement (Winnipeg).

Saint-Ours Que. 19CX

The three-story Saint-Ours Manor, now a private residence, was built in 1758. Its stone walls are 3½ feet thick.

Saint-Patrice-de-la-Rivière-du-Loup Que. 9BW

A bronze plaque faces Le Rocher, a villa where Sir John A. Macdonald spent many summers in 1873-90. The federal cabinet met there for 15 days in August 1885 to discuss, among other topics, the Northwest Rebellion and the Canadian Pacific Railway. The villa now is a private residence.

Saint-Patrice Church, built in 1853 and reconstructed in 1893, has 14 wooden statues carved by Louis Jobin.

Saint-Paul-de-l'Ile-aux-Noix Que. 7FY/19CZ

Fort Lennox, one of Canada's finest examples of early-19th-century British military architecture, stands inside earthworks rising from a moat 60 feet wide and 10 feet deep on Ile-aux-Noix in the Richelieu River. The 210-acre island, one mile southeast, is a national historic park, one quarter taken up by the fort. It is reached by ferry from Saint-Paul.

A bridge across the moat leads to the fort

Richelieu River towns such as Saint-Ours (seen from Saint-Roch) are popular summer resorts. A canal here bypasses rapids on the river; beside a modern lock are parts of one built in 1844-49.

Fort Lennox on Ile-aux-Noix, near Saint-Paul, is part of a tradition going back to 1759. The structures standing today were built in 1819-28 when military installations were improved throughout Canada because of the threat of war with the United States.

entrance, a massive stone archway in which the name Lennox is carved. Around a courtyard are a renovated guardhouse (1824), officers' quarters (1826), canteen (1826), barracks (1827-28) and commissariat (1826). All are stone buildings. A magazine (1823) has walls eight feet thick. In the officers' quarters is a museum of military equipment, Indian relics and other objects related to the history of Fort Lennox.

The French fortified the island in 1759. The British took possession the next year and held Ile-aux-Noix until it was captured in 1775 by the Americans as a base for attacks on Montreal and Quebec. It was here that a proclamation urging Canadians to join the American Revolution was issued by Gen. Philip Schuyler. Americans under Gen. Benedict Arnold regrouped here after the retreat from Quebec but a smallpox outbreak forced them to abandon the island in 1776.

The War of 1812 brought more British activity to the island on account of its strategic position only 10 miles from Lake Champlain. Stronger fortifications and a shipyard were built. A brand-new frigate, the 36-gun *Confiance*, sailed from the island in 1814 with shipwrights still working on her; she was captured in the Battle of Plattsburgh.

St. Peters N.S.　　　　　　　　9FY/23FY
A cairn marks the site of a fort and trading post built here in 1650 by Nicolas Denys (*see* Bathurst). Only earth mounds remain. Micmac Indian and pioneer artifacts are displayed in the Nicolas Denys Museum.
　□ The St. Peters Canal, built in 1869, cuts across a half-mile isthmus to connect Bras d'Or Lake (*see* p.40) with the Atlantic. One lock is 300 feet long and 46½ wide. Vessels drawing up to 16 feet use the canal.

St. Raphaels Ont.　　　　　　　　18EX
A cairn commemorates the Most Rev. Alexander Macdonell, first Roman Catholic bishop of Upper Canada. He had organized and been chaplain of the Glengarry Fencibles in Scotland and led members of the disbanded regiment to Canada in 1804. A regiment he formed here, the Glengarry Light Infantry, fought in 14 battles of the War of 1812.
　□ The ruins of St. Raphael's Church, destroyed by fire in 1970, are being preserved by the Ontario Heritage Foundation. The church dated from 1821.
　□ A plaque marks the birthplace of John Sandfield Macdonald, joint prime minister of Canada in 1862-64 and first premier of Ontario in 1867-71.

Saint-Roch-des-Aulnets Que.　　9BX/20DV
A painting of Saint Roch and his dog by the Rev. Jean-Antoine Aide-Créquy and *La Présentation de Jésus au Temple* and *Le Sacré-Coeur* by François Baillargé are in Gothic-style Saint-Roch-des-Aulnets Church (1849). A two-story stone seigniorial manor (1850) is open to the public. Next to the manor is a three-story wooden mill dating from 1722.
　□ The Dupuis Tree Nursery, founded in 1850, was Quebec's first.
　□ The Ouellet family has made spinning wheels here for five generations; current output is 300 a year. A shop where the Dubé brothers carve domestic and wild animals from walnut may be visited.

Saint-Romuald Que.　　　　　　　20BW
Wood sculptures by local artists, including Lauriat Vallière's *Le Père Jean de Brébeuf évangélisant deux jeunes Indiens* and Henri Trudel's *La Table de Communion* decorate Saint-Romuald-d'Etchemin Church (1854). Most of the interior is richly textured and ornamented in a style considered more typical of Europe than of Quebec.

St. Stephen N.B.　　　　　　　　9CY
An international bridge across the St. Croix River links St. Stephen and Calais, Me.,

towns so friendly that they refused to fight when Canada and the United States went to war in 1812. One July 4 during that conflict St. Stephen provided gunpowder for Calais' celebration of U.S. Independence Day. The two communities still celebrate some of each other's national holidays, share the same water supply and answer each other's fire alarms.

Saint-Sulpice Que. 7FX/19BX
The tabernacle of Saint-Sulpice Church, a fieldstone edifice built in 1832, was carved about 1750 by François-Noël and Jean-Baptiste-Antoine Levasseur. Part of the altar is the work of Louis-Amable Quévillon. The church also has six wooden candlesticks, three feet tall, carved by Amable Gauthier, and a baptismal font carved from a tree trunk.

Sunbonnet of the 1870s and fish carved in a walnut sideboard (c. 1850) are among Elgin County Pioneer Museum exhibits at St. Thomas. An English-made pewter Communion service dates from 1566. In the background is an early-19th-century beehouse.

Sainte-Thérèse-de-Blainville Que. *see* Blainville

Saint-Tite Que. 7FX/19DV
About 80,000 persons attend the 10-day Western Festival here in September. There are a rodeo, a parade and industrial exhibits.

St. Thomas Ont. 7BZ/16DY
The Elgin County Pioneer Museum is a two-story white colonial house built in 1848. On

Saint-Sauveur-des-Monts Que. This oldest of the Laurentian ski resorts (it started attracting skiers in 1930) has nearly 30 lifts within two miles of town. North America's second rope tow was erected here in 1934; the first was at Shawbridge, five miles south. Saint-Sauveur nestles below Hills 69 and 70. Close by are the ski areas of Mont Habitant (background, right), La Marquise, Avila, Mont Gabriel and Olympia. Only 45 minutes by autoroute from Montreal, the town sees skiers almost double its 2,500 population every winter weekend. (19AX)

display are fine examples of mid-19th-century joinery, including a four-poster bed made in the late 1840s. There are early ice skates, pioneer kitchen utensils, clothes and tools, and quilts and household linen dating from the mid-1800s. One room contains old medical books, apothecary jars, surgical instruments and an early oxygen machine. In another room are personal effects of Col. Thomas Talbot, founder of the Talbot Settlement and its ruler for nearly 50 years until his death in 1853. The Talbot Road, which passed through St. Thomas, was the best road in Upper Canada in the 1830s and opened up the wilderness to settlers. On the museum grounds is an elegant Gothic-style wooden beehouse (c. 1826). Captured swarms of bees were established in boxes in the house and the honey harvested each fall.

□ The first medical school in Ontario, the Talbot Dispensatory, was founded here in 1824 by Dr. Charles Duncombe and Dr. John Rolph. The site of the school is unknown, but its founding is commemorated by a plaque on Rolph's homestead two miles west.

□ The turreted main building of Alma College, founded in 1881, is a landmark.

□ A plaque and park commemorate Mitchell F. Hepburn, premier of Ontario in 1934-42, who was born here in 1896.

St. Victor Sask.   4DZ
Atop a 60-foot-high sandstone outcrop on the prairie here are some 40 symbols, apparently religious, carved by unknown persons at an undetermined time in the distant past. Among the symbols are hands, a face, footprints and hoof marks. The face is unusual in that the mouth has teeth; most North American petroglyph mouths are toothless. The view from the top of the great outcrop takes in a vast sweep of the prairie.

□ The McGillis Museum is in a settler's house (1889) built of poplar logs and mudded with a mixture of clay and grass. The house has been restored and furnished in turn-of-the-century fashion.

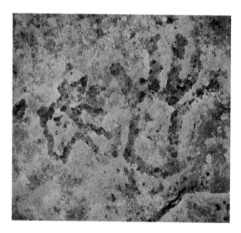

Petroglyphs at St. Victor probably represent a hand and a small human head.

Imhoff gallery at St. Walburg shows works by painter-copyist Berthold von Imhoff.

St. Walburg Sask.   4CW
Some 200 works by Count Berthold von Imhoff, a German-born Renaissance-style painter and copyist who lived here for many years, are displayed at the Imhoff Art Gallery, operated by his son Carl. Among von Imhoff's oils, copied from photographs and other paintings, are portraits of Lincoln, Washington and Queen Mary; Dutch landscapes and Napoleon's retreat from Moscow. Masterpieces copied by von Imhoff and displayed here include da Vinci's *Mona Lisa* and Johann Hofman's *Christ among the Dying* and *Christ and the Rich Man*. Von Imhoff's own *The Crucifixion* is a 13-by-18-foot oil painted in 1929. Two of his murals, depicting scenes in Bavaria, decorate the outside of the gallery.

Von Imhoff was born in Mannheim in 1866. At 16 he won the Berlin Art Academy Medal for his *Glory of the Emperor Frederick* (now in the gallery here). In the early 1900s he decorated some 90 churches in various parts of the United States and Canada. He came here in 1913 and remained until his death in 1939.

Saint-Yvon Que.   9DV/10HZ
On display in a shed in this Gulf of St. Lawrence fishing village are the remains of a torpedo fired by a German submarine Sept. 5, 1942. The torpedo missed its target, a schooner, and exploded on a rock.

Saltspring Island B.C.   2CZ/12DY
The largest of the Gulf Islands in the Strait of Georgia, 70-square-mile Saltspring Island

Salaberry-de-Valleyfield Que.—North America's biggest speedboat regatta is a two-day event held here in July. About 150 boats compete on a 1⅔-mile course laid out in Lake St. Francis. (7FY/19AY)

has forested mountains rising as high as 2,325 feet above its bays and beaches. Ferries connect with Vancouver Island, the other Gulf Islands and the mainland.

Salvage Nfld.   11DY
This village of 350 at the tip of the Eastport Peninsula, the oldest continuously inhabited settlement in Newfoundland, lived in splendid isolation for almost 300 years: until a road was built after World War II its only contact with the outside world was by boat. The floor of a kitchen in the Salvage Fishermen's Museum is covered—in accordance with a custom in early Newfoundland homes—with a ship's canvas sail.

□ For five weeks in early summer the village of Eastport, 10 miles southwest, stages a festival of the arts. There are plays, most by local playwrights and about Newfoundland; handicraft areas on the beach, where macrame, embroidery and leatherwork are taught, and concerts featuring semi-classical works.

□ In Happy Adventure (including Lower and Upper Adventure) fishermen sell live lobsters from a lobster pool. Purchasers use an adjoining kitchen to cook the fresh fare.

Sambro N.S.   9EZ/22EW
Canada's oldest operating lighthouse, dating from 1759, is on rocky Sambro Island, three miles from this mainland village. The light atop the 82-foot tower is 140 feet above sea level and is visible 17 miles out to sea. Originally of stone and concrete, the tower has been covered with wood. A cairn in Sambro tells its history.

Sandon B.C.   2EZ
Restoration of 18 buildings in this virtual ghost town, which boomed on lead and silver in the 1890s, was started in 1973. There is a small museum displaying mining equipment and local mementoes.

Deep in the mountains of southern British Columbia on a flight from Calgary to Vancouver.

Alexander Mackenzie, Canada's second prime minister, whose home was in Sarnia, is honored by two bronze-faced monoliths in the city's Mackenzie Park. They were designed by Walter Yarwood. Chemical Valley at Sarnia has nine petrochemical industries, including Polysar, formerly known as Polymer—it is Canada's largest synthetic rubber plant—and an Imperial Oil refinery that is Canada's biggest. Polysar produces 10 percent of all the synthetic rubber in the world.

Sangudo Alta.   4AW
Lac Ste. Anne Pioneer Museum, a varnished log building in the style of a pioneer house, has turn-of-the-century kitchen utensils, tools, guns, clocks, clothing and photographs. The Lac Ste. Anne Mission founded in 1844 by the Rev. Jean-Baptiste Thibault was Alberta's first Roman Catholic parish. Since 1899 Indians and Métis have made a pilgrimage on July 26, the Feast of Saint Anne.

Sarnia Ont.   7AY/16BX
Chemical Valley, Canada's greatest concentration of petrochemical industries, is just south of here along the St. Clair River. The city itself is at the foot of Lake Huron, where it drains into the St. Clair. A steady parade of freighters sails under the Bluewater International Bridge, a 6,392-foot span that links Canada with Port Huron, Mich. In Point Edward, a village surrounded by Sarnia, is a plaque commemorating La Salle's *Griffon,* the first sailing vessel on the Great Lakes above Niagara.

CANATARA PARK A 262-acre lakefront park with a children's farm, sandy beach, band shell and arboretum.

SARNIA PUBLIC LIBRARY AND ART GALLERY It has oil paintings by Jack Shadbolt, David Milne, Léon Bellefleur, Sir Frederick Banting and the Group of Seven. Major works include Edwin Holgate's *Le Bucheron* (The Lumberjack), Tom Thomson's *Chill November* and

Mother and Child by Florence Wyle and *Laurentian Hills* by Jacques de Tonnancour are in the Sarnia Public Library and Art Gallery.

A.Y. Jackson's *Spring Lower Canada (Maples, Early Spring)*. There are Eskimo carvings and the Holland-Paisley collection of 2,500 photographs, including some of daguerreotypes and oils, depicting Sarnia's history.

ST. CLAIR TUNNEL Built in 1889-91 by the Grand Trunk Railway, the tunnel was the first international submarine railway tunnel in North America. It connects Sarnia and Port Huron under the St. Clair River and is 6,026 feet long.

Saskatoon Sask.   4DX

From sober beginnings in 1883 as a temperance colony—it had only 113 persons two decades later—Saskatoon has become Saskatchewan's second largest city (pop. 134,000). It is the center of Canada's greatest wheatgrowing area and of half the world's potash reserves. Saskatoon is an attractive university city and an important distribution point. It has a 5½-million-bushel grain elevator and one of the west's major meat-packing plants.

Since Saskatoon's development has been largely in the 20th century, it has had town-planning opportunities denied to older cities. Streets are wide and lined with trees; most industries are on the outskirts. Six bridges span the South Saskatchewan River here.

Saskatchimo Exposition, a week-long event in July, is called the biggest pioneer show in North America. There are pageants reenacting Saskatoon history, demonstrations of some steam and gas tractors from the Western Development Museum, displays of horse-drawn carriages and antique automobiles, threshing competitions, harness racing and livestock and agricultural shows.

BARR COLONY CAMPSITE (1) A plaque marks where almost 1,500 colonists led by the Rev. Isaac M. Barr camped for two weeks in April

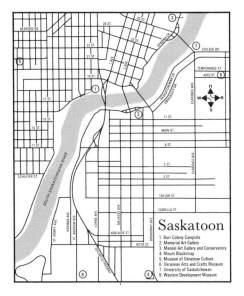

Saskatoon

1. Barr Colony Campsite
2. Memorial Art Gallery
3. Mendel Art Gallery and Conservatory
4. Mount Blackstrap
5. Museum of Ukrainian Culture
6. Ukrainian Arts and Crafts Museum
7. University of Saskatchewan
8. Western Development Museum

1903—while on their way to Lloydminster (*see entry*).

MEMORIAL ART GALLERY (2) Its 50 paintings, all by Canadian artists, include Homer Watson's *A Vista through the Trees*, A. F. Kenderdine's *The Signal* and *Qu'Appelle Valley,* John William Beatty's *The North Country* and Ernest Lindner's *Emma Lake Scene.* The gallery is a memorial to students of Nutana Collegiate Institute killed in World War I.

MENDEL ART GALLERY AND CIVIC CONSERVATORY (3) Flower displays complement works of art in rotating exhibitions and a per-

South Saskatchewan River eases gently through Saskatoon. Here the treeless prairie ends and the parkland of the north country starts.

Girl With Cat is a life-size bronze sculpture by Arthur Price of Ottawa. *North Saskatchewan River Near Borden* is an oil and turpentine painting by Dorothy Knowles of Saskatoon. Both are in Saskatoon's Mendel Gallery.

manent collection that includes works by Canadian artists J. E. H. MacDonald, Lawren Harris, A. Y. Jackson, Arthur Price, Dorothy Knowles, A. F. Kenderdine and Ernest Lindner.

MUSEUM OF UKRAINIAN CULTURE (5) Costumes, tapestries and implements used by Saskatchewan's Ukrainian settlers.

UKRAINIAN MUSEUM OF CANADA (6) Exhibits include a miniature of a Ukrainian house and pottery, costumes, furniture, embroidery and decorated eggs.

UNIVERSITY OF SASKATCHEWAN (7) On campus are the Marquis Hall Art Gallery, an observatory, open to the public, and the restored

stone Victoria School (1887), Saskatoon's first school, containing replicas of original school furniture and equipment.

WESTERN DEVELOPMENT MUSEUM (8) One of Canada's largest collections of agricultural machinery and antique automobiles includes a threshing machine (1910), a 1912 Peerless car, an Abell steam engine (1911) and a Giant Reeves steam engine with a 20-bottom plow.

Sault Ste. Marie Ont. 7AW

The Soo is Canada's second biggest steel producer (after Hamilton) and has one of the busiest canals in the St. Lawrence Seaway system. A lock here and locks on the American side

Village street (c.1910) in the Western Development Museum at Saskatoon represents the kind of community that sprang up throughout Saskatchewan in the early days of the century. The street is the central display in a complex of buildings dedicated to the pioneers who came to settle the prairies. Mount Blackstrap, 25 miles south of Saskatoon, was built for the Canadian Winter Games in 1971. It is 300 feet high and 700 feet at the base. The main run is 1,400 feet.

Ermatinger Old Stone House in Sault Ste. Marie has been residence, hotel, post office, courthouse and apartment building: now it is a museum and a national historic site. The Sault locks are among the busiest on the St. Lawrence Seaway.

of the St. Mary's River, which links Lakes Huron and Superior, handle more than 100,000,000 tons of cargo annually, mostly grain and iron ore. The city is the gateway to the vast Algoma wilderness and North America's last great stand of hardwood. A fine way to visit Algoma is to go by Algoma Central Railway to Agawa (*see entry*).

CANOE LOCK A replica of a lock built in 1799 by the North West Company for its freighter canoes is on the Abitibi Paper Company grounds. The destruction of the original lock by Americans in 1814 is commemorated by a plaque. Nearby is a replica of a Hudson's Bay Company blockhouse built in 1899, now a private residence.

ERMATINGER OLD STONE HOUSE This Georgian-style dwelling was built in 1814-23 by Charles Oakes Ermatinger, a North West Company partner. Restored as a museum and partly furnished in 1800-30 style.

HIAWATHA PARK Crystal Falls drops 100 feet in this 240-acre park.

INTERNATIONAL BRIDGE A two-mile bridge to Sault Ste. Marie, Mich.

ONTARIO AIR SERVICE This is the headquarters of the world's largest fleet of planes (45) for fighting forest fires. Visitors see some of the aircraft and fire-bombing apparatus.

POINT DES CHENES PARK A 73-acre park 18½ miles west, where Lake Superior empties into the St. Mary's River.

POINTE AUX PINS A plaque marks the site of Lake Superior's first shipyard, where in 1735 Louis Denis, Sieur de la Ronde, launched the first decked ship to sail that lake.

SAULT HISTORICAL SOCIETY MUSEUM Military relics and a local history collection.

SAULT LOCKS The four American locks were completed in 1885; the Canadian lock, 900 feet long and 60 feet wide, in 1895. They are the world's busiest.

Savona B.C. 2DY
In Deadman Valley, which starts two miles west of here, are five unusual rock formations called hoodoos, formed by rain and wind erosion. Each 35-40 feet high, they have gravel and clay bases and are a yellow-red color.

Sayward B.C. 2BY
The Link and Pin Logging and Pioneer Museum has British Columbia's only operating steam donkey, used for loading logs onto railway cars. It was the last built before diesel engines were introduced into the industry. The museum, in a log house, has antique kerosene lamps and old logging equipment.

□ A loggers' sports day in July includes a one-mile raft race on the Salmon River.

□ More than 1,000 faces painted on rounds of cedar logs are set against a forest backdrop at the Valley of the Thousand Faces. Painted by artist Hetty Frederickson, who has a studio nearby, the faces depict Indian chiefs, historical and contemporary figures.

Schefferville Que. 10GV
More than 200,000,000 tons of iron ore is estimated to lie within a two-mile radius of this town, which was settled in the early 1950s. There are guided tours of the Iron Ore Company of Canada. Schefferville is the terminus of the 356-mile Quebec North Shore and Labrador Railway from Sept-Iles.

Schumacher Ont. *see* Timmins

Scotchfort P.E.I. 23CW
A marble cross marks the grave of Capt. John MacDonald, who bought land here for Roman Catholic Scots expelled from their Highland homes by a Protestant chieftain. In an old cemetery, originally Acadian, is a granite Celtic cross in memory of the Scots pioneers and their leader, the Rev. James MacDonald, who arrived in 1772.

Scotland Ont. 7BZ/17AZ
A plaque commemorates Dr. Charles Duncombe, who gathered a force here in December

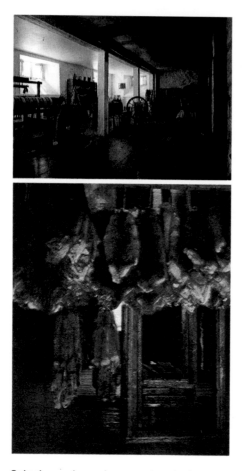

Spinning and weaving were done in these servants' quarters in the Big House at Lower Fort Garry at Selkirk. Furs hang in the fur loft building.

1837 to support rebel William Lyon Mackenzie. The force dispersed when it learned of Mackenzie's defeat at Montgomery's Tavern north of York (Toronto).

Seaforth Ont.   7BY/16DW
A plaque at the Seaforth and District High School honors William "Bible Bill" Aberhart, founder of Social Credit and Alberta premier in 1935-43. Aberhart was born in Hibbert Township and attended the Seaforth school.

Selkirk Man.   6BY/15DX
The romance of the fur trade is recaptured at Lower Fort Garry National Historic Park, a reconstruction of the post that was Hudson's Bay Company headquarters in the mid-1800s. The biggest of 13 buildings is the Big House that was the residence of HBC Governor George Simpson. In a fur loft are traps, axes, bales of wool and whiskey casks and the furs of hundreds of animals. A museum has artifacts of the early HBC and the Selkirk settlers and colorful Indian costumes. In the 11-acre park are Red River carts, York boats and fur presses. Costumed personnel perform the

19th-century tasks of spinning and carding wool and making soap and candles. The names of men of the 2nd Battalion of the Quebec Rifles, part of the force sent to quell the Red River Rebellion in 1870, are carved on the wooden main gates.

□ St. Peter's Dynevor Church (1853) at East Selkirk is on the site of an Anglican mission church built in 1831 for the Saulteaux Indians. The grave of Chief Peguis of the Saulteaux, one of the first western Indian converts to Christianity, is in the churchyard.

□ Selkirk has a one-day Highland gathering and a 2½-day agricultural fair in July.

□ A cruise ship sails from Selkirk down the Red River into Lake Winnipeg and north to Norway House. (*See* Berens River)

Senneville Que. *see* Sainte-Anne-de-Bellevue

Sept-Iles Que.   9CV/10GY
A log fort built in 1661, once owned by explorer Louis Jolliet and burned in 1692 by English troops, has been reconstructed near the Vieux Fort River. It has a 17-foot guard tower, two dwellings, a chapel, powder magazine, store, stable and shed.

□ A small fishing village in 1950, Sept-Iles has boomed into a harbor city of some 31,000 as an outlet for northern iron ore developments.

Seven Sisters Falls Man.   6CY/15EX
Some of the Whiteshell Nuclear Research Establishment, including part of the reactor building and laboratories, is open to visitors. It is nine miles northeast at Pinawa.

□ Manitoba Hydro's Seven Sisters generating station, the largest of six on the Winnipeg River, has a capacity of 150,000 kilowatts.

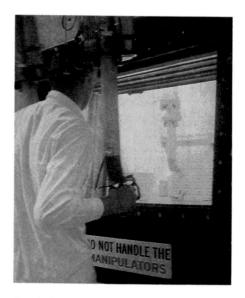

Atomic Energy of Canada scientist near Seven Sisters Falls uses manipulators to examine radioactive experimental fuel.

Vast quantities of iron ore are shipped from the year-round harbor at Sept-Iles. The ore is brought by rail from Schefferville, Wabush and Labrador City.

Shag Harbour N.S.   9CZ/22BY
A magnificent view of islands off the south coast of Nova Scotia is had from Chapel Hill. The lights of five lighthouses are seen.

Shakespeare Ont.   17AY
Fryfogel Inn, 1½ miles east, is an example of Upper Canadian neo-classic architecture. The brick structure was built in 1844-45 by Sebastian Fryfogel, said to have been the first settler in Perth County, to replace his log inn. Once an important stagecoach stop, the inn now is owned by the Perth County Historical Foundation and is open to the public.

Shanty Bay Ont.   17CW
St. Thomas' Anglican Church (1838-39) was built with sun-dried bricks of adobe, a mixture of mud and straw (the mixing perhaps done by the trampling feet of oxen). In the church is a plaque honoring Lucius Richard O'Brien, first president of the Royal Canadian

Academy of Arts, some of whose landscapes hang in the National Gallery in Ottawa. O'Brien was born here in 1832 and is buried in the churchyard.

Sharon Ont.   17CW
The Temple of Peace was built in 1825-31 by a religious sect known as The Children of Peace—or the Davidites, after their leader, David Willson. Founders of the sect were 12

Temple at Sharon has identical sides. The ground floor, 60 feet square, has 24 double windows, each with 72 panes. The second floor is 30 feet square with 12 windows, the top floor 10 feet square with four windows.

families expelled from the Quakers in a dispute over the use of music. The lines of this unique three-story wooden building are symbolic of the sect's beliefs: all sides of the temple are identical (all men are equal before God); each of three roofs has four lamp towers in which candles were burned (the 12 lights represented the Apostles). The temple has been restored as a museum displaying the history of the sect and of York County. One exhibit is a walnut ark, constructed without nails, for the temple Bible. On the museum grounds are Willson's study; a two-story wooden Georgian-style house, once the home of Ebenezer Doan, master builder of the temple; a restored pioneer log cabin; and a driving shed where carriages are displayed.

Shaunavon Sask.   4CZ
Preserved animals and birds, geological specimens and Indian artifacts—including a rare pemmican bag—are displayed at the Grand Coteau Museum.
□ A plaque in Pine Cree Park, 20 miles west, commemorates John Macoun, a botanist who traveled through the Northwest Territories with the Sandford Fleming expedition in 1872. His report on the agricultural possibilities of the area led to rerouting of the CPR through the central prairies.

Shawinigan Que.   7FX/19CW
A lower town promenade provides a spectacular view of thundering 150-foot Shawinigan Falls, highest on the Saint-Maurice River. The falls provide cheap electricity for industry and have been largely responsible for the development of this major industrial city. A Hydro-Quebec plant, which may be visited, has an installed capacity of 313,000 kilowatts. On tours of a Consolidated-Bathurst mill here visitors see the processes by which logs are converted into fine paper.
□ The Shawinigan Cultural Center art gallery has paintings by Léo Ayotte and François Déziel and sculptures by Claude Descoteaux. The Church of Notre-Dame-de-la-Présentation in Shawinigan South has paintings by Osias Leduc.

Shediac N.B.   9DX/23AX
This seaside town famous for lobster stages a five-day festival in mid-July with parades, folk songs and dancing, lobster dinners and sports events. One of New Brunswick's principal resorts, Shediac has several fine beaches, with Atlantic waters reputed to be the warmest north of Virginia. Nearby Parlee Beach Provincial Park has camping facilities.

Sheffield N.B.   9CY
Puritans from New England built New Brunswick's first Protestant church in Maugerville in 1775. Thirteen years later, after a land dispute, they moved the wooden structure here, pushing it five miles along the Saint John River ice. Rebuilt in 1840 with the original lumber, the church is still in use.

Sheguiandah Ont. *see* Manitoulin Island

Shelburne N.S.   9DZ/22CY
The two-story frame Ross-Thomson House, which dates from 1783, the year Shelburne was founded by United Empire Loyalists, is a museum of Loyalist relics. Cape Roseway Light on McNutt's Island in the harbor is one of the oldest lighthouses in Nova Scotia, dating from 1788.

Shelburne Ont.   7BY/17BW
The Dufferin County Historical Museum has a two-story log house furnished to the 1880 period, a log barn, a onetime Orange Hall (1861), a log smithy and a railway flag station (1873).
□ A two-day contest in August attracts about 100 old-time fiddlers.

Sherbrooke N.S.   9EY/22HV
Buildings in the oldest section of town have been restored to the 1860-80 period and the section has been named Sherbrooke Village. Visitors card wool and spin it into yarn, weave on an antique loom, make quilts and hook rugs. Blacksmiths mend tools on a forge and woodworkers make toys and furniture. A waterpowered sawmill is in operation. Eleven restored buildings include a general store,

McDonald Brothers' Sawmill, in Nova Scotia's Sherbrooke Village, is a re-creation of the mill which stood on the same site beside the St. Mary's River for most of the 19th century. Its up-and-down saw is powered by a 12-foot black spruce waterwheel which turns at a maximum of 35 revolutions per minute. The timber trade was Sherbrooke's major industry.

Rural Nova Scotia sometimes still moves at the unhurried pace of the farmer and his horse. Nova Scotians' respect for the past is reflected in a village restoration at Sherbrooke.

post office, courthouse and jail, dwellings, two churches and a school. Meals in a tearoom are served from a menu of about 1880.

□ A plaque on the Sherbrooke courthouse commemorates Fort Sainte Marie, erected in 1655 as a fur-trading post and to protect the French port here. Parts of a dike the French built in the late 1650s—some are three feet high—are discernible near the village.

Sherbrooke Que.   9AY/20AZ
More than 50,000 plants are grown each year for colorful mosaics in this hub of Quebec's

Eastern Townships. Some 15,000 in a garden near the courthouse spell "Dieu et Mon Droit," the motto on Britain's coat of arms; 25,000 form an abstract along King Street, the major thoroughfare. The Magog River tumbles 150 feet through a series of rapids in the city before emptying into the Saint-François River. Sherbrooke, founded by Loyalists in 1796, is Quebec's sixth largest city. Almost 90 percent of its 81,000 people are bilingual French Canadians.

Two pieces of limestone preserved at the Séminaire de Sherbrooke have inscriptions that may have been made by pre-Viking explorers.

BEAUVOIR SHRINE *see under* Sanctuary of the Sacred Heart

Université de Sherbrooke has Hans Schlee's *Conférence* (mollusk-encrusted stone) and Marcelle Ferron's oil painting *Sans Titre*.

EASTERN AGRICULTURAL EXHIBITION The one-week August exhibition has livestock displays, harness racing and a circus.

SAINT-MICHAEL'S BASILICA A Gothic-style Roman Catholic cathedral with interesting stained glass windows and a 20-foot crucifix over the main entrance.

ST. PETER'S CHURCH Built in 1844, St. Peter's is one of the oldest Anglican churches in the Eastern Townships.

SANCTUARY OF THE SACRED HEART This shrine overlooking the Saint-François River at Beauvoir Hill, four miles north, is operated by the Assumptionist Fathers.

UNIVERSITE DE SHERBROOKE This Roman Catholic institution founded in 1954 has eight faculties, a postgraduate school and extensive medical research facilities. An art gallery has paintings and sculptures by Chagall, Picasso and Hans Schlee and by Rita Letendre, Roland Giguère, Alfred Pellan, Norman McLaren and Jean-Paul Riopelle. The medical center has three murals by Charles Suscan. *Medicine through the Ages* (40 feet by 10) is a glazed ceramic work. The others, gray cement drawings, depict religious and nature scenes.

Shilo Man. 6AY

A piece of birch bark on which Louis Riel wrote of "fulfilment of prophecy" is displayed in the Royal Regiment of Canadian Artillery Museum at CFB Shilo. The Métis leader wrote (in English): "I have fulfilment of prophecy—it is necessary to change the language—I must change the language." In a different hand is the notation: "Bark of tree at foot of which two Indians were killed—Battle of Fish Creek, NW, April 24, 1885." The birch bark records that 10 soldiers were killed and 42 wounded; some are named.

The museum has sketches by Col. John McCrae (*see* p. 154) and the plate with which *Punch* printed McCrae's *In Flanders Fields*. It has the gun carriage used to transport the body of Queen Victoria for burial in 1901; Maj. Gen. H.A. Panet's diary of the South African War and a picnic chest that was attached to the running board of his staff car in World War I. A six-pounder brass gun that dates from 1796 was used by Lord Selkirk's settlers on the Red River in 1816.

Shippegan N.B. 9DW

Vast bogs here and on Shippegan Island are among Canada's major sources of peat moss. Most of the local product is shipped to the United States as soil conditioner, stable and poultry litter, insulation and packing material. Shippegan has a fisheries festival in July, with street dancing, tours of fish-packing plants, and deep-sea fishing trips.

Shubenacadie N.S. 9EY/22FV

In an 850-acre wildlife park run by the Nova Scotia Department of Lands and Forests are bear, deer, moose, caribou, wildcats, lynx and porcupines, and owls, peafowl, pheasants, ducks, geese, cranes, turkey and quail.

□ A herd of some 14 plains bison, brought here from Elk Island National Park in Alberta in 1970, can be seen on a nearby farm.

Sicamous B.C. 2EY

Originally a CPR stop on a corner of Shuswap Lake, this town is named after an Indian word meaning "shimmering water." A 91-mile canoe route on the Shuswap River links Sugar and Mara lakes. At Mara Lake are numerous springs of water charged with carbon dioxide.

At several places along the shore of Shuswap and Mara lakes are rock paintings of stick-like animals and birds, human faces and what is thought to be a calendar. Done with raw mercury, fish oil and yellow ocher, they may have been the work of people who came across the Bering Strait.

Silton Sask. 4EY

Last Mountain House, built by the Hudson's Bay Company at nearby Last Mountain Lake in 1869, is a provincial historic site. An interpretive display describes the trade in buffalo meat and hides carried on until the post was closed in 1872.

Silver Islet Ont. *see* Thunder Bay

Simcoe Ont. 7BZ/17BZ

The Eva Brook Donly Museum exhibits oils and watercolors by Mrs. Donly and more than 300 paintings of early Norfolk County life by W. Edgar Cantelon. The museum is in a brick house (c.1836) that was Mrs. Donly's home. There is a display of ironwork dating from the 1820s and '30s—from the pioneer Van Norman forge.

□ A 23-bell carillon at the Norfolk War Memorial honors Norfolk County's dead in the world wars.

□ The Lake George Area is 50 acres of islands, parks and waterways in the heart of Simcoe. Part is a waterfowl sanctuary.

Simoom Sound B.C. 2BX

Kwakiutl carvers are seen as they work and dancers perform at the Na Wa La Gwa Tsi community house near here. The corners of the house are 16-foot totem poles; on its interior are carved a wolf, a bear and a human.

Sioux Lookout Ont. 6DX

Some of Canada's earliest commercial air services and the pioneer bush pilots who flew the aircraft are commemorated by a plaque at nearby Hudson. During the Red Lake Gold Rush more airfreight passed through Hudson than through any other Canadian airport.

Sioux Narrows Ont. 6DY

Among dozens of Indian rock paintings in this region are representations of a canoe and a fort—perhaps a canoe used by Pierre de La Vérendrye and a fort he may have built on Massacre Island (*see* Kenora). On the rectangular fort is a flagpole; from it flies a flag with a suggestion of a pattern.

Most of the Sioux Narrows area paintings, like those elsewhere in Ontario (*see* Agawa, Bon Echo), are near the surface of lakes and rivers. All were done with durable red ocher. Tours of many of the sites start at Sioux Narrows. At Devil's Bay is a stylized thunderbird, a mythological creature usually associated with west coast Indians. At one of seven painting sites on Whitefish Bay is a buffalo, an animal not native to this area. On a channel southeast of the Aulneau Peninsula, is a 15-foot, three-flippered serpent. Fifty feet above the water at Painted Rock Island is a horned sturgeon-serpent with spines along its back. This rock face also has a horned man and weird abstract human figures. At Blindfold Lake is a pig-like creature with a crested back. The drawing is like one in the Lake Baikal region of Siberia.

□ Mink coats are made by the Ojibway Indians of the Whitefish Bay Reserve. Their factory may be toured.

Smeaton Sask. 4EW

Hundreds of lakes and streams once accessible only by aircraft or canoe are now reached by the 225-mile Hanson Lake Road, which pushes through dense coniferous forests and skirts the muskegs of the Precambrian shield. From Smeaton, Mile 0, the road angles north and east to Creighton, Sask., and Flin Flon, Man. It runs for 19 miles through Nipawin Provincial Park. At Mile 97 a gravel highway leads to Lac La Ronge; at Mile 180 a road cuts north to Pelican Narrows.

Smithers B.C. 2BV

Twin waterfalls a quarter-mile apart cascade over the rim of Glacier Gulch, seven miles northwest of here. The falls are on Glacier Creek, which is fed by Kathlyn Glacier, two miles long by 1½ miles wide and some 400 feet deep. Ten miles northeast, on Driftwood Creek, are beds of insect, leaf and fish fossils an estimated 600,000 years old.

Smiths Cove N.S. 22BW

Birch Chapel, built in 1919 with rough-hewn yellow birch logs, stands in a forest clearing here. The interior, which accommodates about 100 persons, has simple pews, altar and altar railing with some birch bark still intact. Anglican services are held in summer.

Smiths Falls Ont. 7EY/18CX

The town is an important lockport on the Rideau Waterway—a system of rivers, lakes and canals connecting the Ottawa River with Lake Ontario. The waterway follows the canal built in 1826-32 under the direction of Col. John By of the Royal Engineers. One of the great engineering feats of its day, it cut through 126 miles of largely wilderness country between Kingston and Bytown (Ottawa), providing a link between Upper and Lower Canada that was relatively safe from enemy attack.

Sombra Ont. 7AZ/16BY

In the Sombra Township Museum, a two-story white frame pioneer dwelling (c.1829), are old glass and silver, walnut cradles, music boxes and pieced quilts, and Indian and military dispiays. A marine room contains photographs of sailing vessels and woodburning freighters that plied the St. Clair River.

Sooke B.C. 2CZ/12DZ

Loggers' competitions on All Sooke Day in July include log rolling, tree chopping, high rigging and axe throwing. Food is prepared at the fairground the way prospectors cooked during the 1864 gold rush at nearby Leech River: beef is roasted in a pit of alder coals and salmon is grilled over open fires.

Sorel Que. 7FX/19CX

On the St. Lawrence River at the mouth of the Richelieu, Sorel is an inland seaport humming with naval construction and related industries. Champlain may have built a blockhouse here; if so, nothing remains of it. Nor

La Maison des Gouverneurs at Sorel, built by Governor-in-Chief Sir Frederick Haldimand in 1781, was for many years a summer residence of the governors-general. It now is a conference and exhibition hall. Marine Industries Ltd. builds about five ships a year, repairs some 25.

Fossil clamshell embedded in an eight-inch rock is from the agate pits east of Souris, Man. Rocks and minerals for collectors and gem cutters are exposed at some 30 sites in Manitoba. A suspension bridge over the Souris River is 582 feet, Canada's longest swinging footbridge.

is there any trace of Fort Richelieu (1642) and its successor (1665), subsequently called Fort Saurel after an officer in le Régiment de Carignan-Salières.

□ Wood sculptures by Augustin Leblanc adorn Saint-Pierre-de-Sorel Church (1826-30). Gothic-style Christ Church (Anglican) was built in 1843.

Souris Man.   6AY
A 582-foot suspension bridge across the Souris River here, the longest swinging footbridge in Canada, was built in 1904. Nearby is Hillcrest Museum, a massive two-story brick structure built as a private home in 1910. In it are furniture and other relics dating from Souris' settlement in the 1880s.

□ The Souris agate pits yield jasper up to the size of a fist, agate pebbles up to four inches across and petrified wood (ruby red to brown and black) in pieces up to 10 pounds.

Souris P.E.I.   9EX/23EW
This easternmost Prince Edward Island town is noted for its deep-sea fishing and lobster industry and for its fine beach on Northumberland Strait. The Black Pond Bird Sanctuary, maintained by the Canadian Wildlife Service, is five miles east of the town. A car ferry (picture, p.211) links Souris with Cap-aux-Meules in the Magdalen Islands.

Southampton Ont.   7BY
Along The Hudson and *Yonkers New York*, early works by David Milne, a Bruce County native (*see* Paisley), are hung in the Bruce County Museum. Milne painted them during the period 1904-13 when he was a student in New York. The museum buildings include a log house (1850) and school (1873) and brick schools that date from 1878 and 1903. Regional history is recounted in displays of pioneer tools, household equipment and furnishings. There are Indian artifacts an estimated 4,500 years old.

□ Southampton has a sand beach nearly a mile long. A mile offshore is Chantry Island, whose lighthouse dates from 1859.

South Bay Ont.   7DY
On a 30-foot limestone tower in Mariners' Memorial Lighthouse Park is the wooden

superstructure of a lighthouse that stood for almost 140 years—from 1828 to 1965—on False Duck Island, 10 miles east of here off Point Traverse. Around the lighthouse are old anchors, one from the French regime; an oak rudder from a schooner sunk in 1861, a schooner mast and other marine relics raised from Lake Ontario.

South Baymouth Ont. *see* Manitoulin Island

South Buxton Ont. *see* North Buxton

South March Ont.   18CW
Hamnet Pinhey is commemorated by a plaque at Horaceville, the 1,000-acre estate he was given in 1820 for fighting Napoleon's blockade of England in 1806-10. An exporter, he used his ships to run the blockade and acted

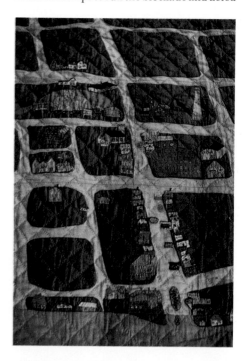

Southampton quilt (54 inches by 70) in the Bruce County Museum represents the town in 1967, down to the hands of the town hall tower clock.

South Lancaster Ont.—A huge cairn on Monument Island in Lake St. Francis was built in 1840-41 by the Highland Militia of Glengarry County. It commemorates Gen. Sir John Colborne, British commander-in-chief in Canada during the Rebellion of 1837-38. The cairn is 52 feet high and 52 feet in diameter at the base. Colborne had commanded the British 52nd Regiment in the Battle of Waterloo in 1815. Monument Island is reached by boat from Lancaster. (19AY)

as King's Messenger, carrying dispatches to British representatives in Europe. Pinhey's stone house (c.1828) is still used as a farmhouse, but Saint Mary's Church, which he completed in 1828, is in ruins.

South Rawdon N.S.   **22EV**
A former Sons of Temperance hall, built in 1867, houses the South Rawdon Museum and its extensive collection of 19th-century rural Nova Scotia artifacts. Rare objects include ice skates (steel blades secured in blocks of wood that were strapped to the skater's boots) and a press for making straw hats.

Sparwood B.C.   **2FZ/13BY**
One of the largest coal-mining operations in the world was started here in 1969, transforming a tiny settlement into a boom town of more than 3,000 persons. Miners and some buildings were brought from the dying coal towns of Natal and Michel in the Crowsnest Pass. The Kaiser Resources complex here includes hydraulic and conventional underground mining and the largest open-pit coking coal mine in Canada.

Spencers Island N.S.   **9DY/23AY**
The brigantine *Mary Celeste*, which figures in one of the great mysteries of the sea, is commemorated by a plaque in this town where she was built in 1861. The mystery started in December 1872 when the 103-foot, two-masted vessel was found under sail—but with no one aboard—in the Atlantic between the Azores and Gibraltar. She had been on a voyage from New York to Genoa. Ten persons, including the captain's two-year-old daughter, had disappeared. So had the ship's boat, sextant, chronometer and navigation book. The brigantine was in good order and had apparently sailed herself unmanned for 378 miles in the 10 days between the last log entry and her discovery. The crew, who from various evidence had left in a hurry (and apparently in the ship's boat), were never found.

Spences Bridge B.C.   **2DY**
The Trans-Canada Highway and the tracks of the CN and CP all squeeze through the narrow Thompson River Valley here.

Springhill N.S.   **9DY/23BY**
The story of this coal-mining town's courage in the face of disaster is told at the Springhill Miners' Museum. Among mining equipment of many kinds—some picks and shovels date from 1885—are rubber air pipes, handsaws, "teapot lights" and breathing apparatus dating from the early 1900s. There are a diary and letters of trapped men, and other relics of Springhill's three worst mine accidents. An explosion in 1891 killed 125 miners; another in 1956 killed 39; a "bump" in 1958 claimed 76 lives. In the 1958 disaster 12 miners were saved after being entombed for six days; seven more were rescued two days later.

At the museum are a washhouse with miners' clothes, hats and boots, and a lamp cabin with a display of miners' lamps from the 1930s to the present. A museum tour includes a 900-foot descent into a mine. On

Main Street a 20-foot monument topped by a statue of a miner commemorates the disasters. A gold medal that the Carnegie Hero Fund Commission awarded to the nearly 400 men who risked their lives to free the miners trapped in 1958 is in the Nova Scotia Museum in Halifax.

Fewer than 150 men now work in two small mines; the large ones have been closed.

Disasters in Springhill have not been limited to the mines. A fire destroyed the heart of the business district the day after Christmas 1957.

Spuzzum B.C.   2DZ/12GW
The Fraser River races at 25 feet a second through a 600-foot-deep canyon at Hells Gate, eight miles north. A rockslide there in 1914 all but blocked the channel, hindering the progress of salmon to their spawning grounds (*see* Squilax) and causing huge losses to the Pacific salmon fishery industry during the next 30 years. Fish ladders built since 1945 bypass the turbulent water, reducing the flow to 1½ feet a second. A trail leads to a suspension bridge from which the fish ladders can be seen.

Squamish B.C.   2CY/12DW
Garibaldi Provincial Park, some 750 square miles of mountains, glaciers, rushing rivers and placid lakes, lies northeast of here. The southern entrance is 13 miles from Squamish. The park has three recreation areas: Black Tusk, Diamond Head and Cheakamus Lake; other regions remain in their natural state.

Near the Black Tusk (7,598 feet), a great block of basalt, are Panorama Ridge (7,400 feet), Helm Glacier and the Garibaldi, Lesser Garibaldi and Barrier lakes. The Barrier, just below Barrier Lake, is a 1,000-foot-high wall formed by the undercutting of a lava flow.

The Diamond Head area includes Diamond Head itself (about 7,000 feet); The Gargoyles, fantastic faces eroded in lava; the Opal Cone, a volcanic mound around which wild flowers grow in profusion, and Mount Garibaldi (8,787 feet). The northern part of the Diamond Head area and all of the Black Tusk area make up the Black Tusk Nature Conservancy Area, totalling 44,000 acres.

A mile below the towering peaks, at an elevation of almost 3,000 feet, is glacier-fed Cheakamus Lake, where there is excellent trout fishing. Wedge Mountain, the park's tallest at 9,484 feet, is in the undeveloped northern part of the park.

Garibaldi Park is forested with fir, hemlock, balsam and red cedar, and alpine flowers bloom in meadows beneath the snow-capped mountains. Wildlife includes grizzly and black bears, mountain goats, deer, wolverines and martens.

□ About a mile southeast of Squamish is the Stawamus Chief, a 2,500-foot mountain resembling the head of an Indian. Two miles south is 650-foot Shannon Falls.

□ Squamish Day, the first Saturday in August, features log-rolling and tree-climbing contests. The village is a lumber center where huge log booms are assembled for towing into Howe Sound.

Squaw Rapids Sask.   4EW
Saskatchewan's first hydroelectric power plant was built here in 1953, backing up the Saskatchewan River to form the Tobin

Lake Reservoir, 45 miles by 10. The plant generates 286,000 kilowatts. There are tours.

Squilax B.C.　　　　　　　　　　　2EY
Every four years, for a three-week period in mid-October, the Adams and Little rivers are in scarlet flood as about 2,000,000 sockeye salmon return here to spawn and die. These salmon have a four-year life cycle. They are hatched here, spend a year in Shuswap Lake and migrate to the Pacific as fingerlings the next spring. In the fourth year they leave the ocean, swim some 17 miles a day up the Fraser and Thompson rivers into Kamloops Lake, and finally through Shuswap Lake to the Adams and the Little. During this 300-mile journey their bodies change from a steely ocean blue to the scarlet of spawning. The salmon run is best seen in the Adams River about five miles north of Squilax. (Some spawning years: 1974, 1978, 1982, 1986.)
　□ In Shuswap Lake Provincial Park, 12 miles north, is a reproduction of a Shuswap Indian *kekuli* (winter dwelling). A *kekuli* was built in a pit two to five feet deep and up to 30 feet in diameter. Logs angled upward were set in the floor of the pit and on them was placed a framework of slim poles, then a layer of grass, brush and bark. On top of all this was put about a foot of earth.

Stanbridge East Que.　　　　　　7FY/19CZ
In a three-story brick gristmill (1830) that now is the Missisquoi County Museum are a 19th-century sugar house, a blacksmith shop and a doctor's office, collections of china and glass, and a parlor, dining room, kitchen and bedroom with period furnishings. On the grounds are a 10-foot replica of the gristmill waterwheel and a plaque to Sir John Johnson, a United Empire Loyalist leader. A two-story brick house (1843) on the main street

Shuswap Lake is where sockeye salmon spend the first year of their lives and through which they return to spawn and die (*see* Squilax).

---

has been restored by the museum as a 19th-century general store with yard goods and penny candy.
　□ At Eccles Hill, seven miles south, is a marker in memory of a woman who was shot and killed in 1866 when mistaken for a Fenian raider. At the Vermont border near Eccles Hill is a monument commemorating a Fenian defeat four years later.
　□ Stanbridge Ridge Stone Chapel, two miles south of here, dates from about 1840.

Stand Off Alta.　　　　　　　　4AZ/13DZ
A cairn on the Blood Reserve here commemorates Red Crow, a warrior, diplomat and ora-

Southern Alberta is still cowboy country—and they start 'em young. One day he'll have his own big herd to battle. The rangeland is Indian country too: Canada's largest reserve is the Blood Reserve near Stand Off.

Mennonite Village Museum at Steinbach salutes pioneer settlers who came from the Ukraine.

---

tor who kept the Bloods out of the Northwest Rebellion and led them in peaceful existence alongside the whites. The reserve, Canada's largest, covers 551 square miles. The Bloods run Kainai Industries, which makes prefabricated houses, but also cling to old customs, such as their two-week summer sun dance ceremonies. Parts of this colorful ritual may be observed with permission from the reserve superintendent.

Stanstead Que.   7FY/19DZ
The Dufferin Heights Pioneer Monument, three miles north, has plaques commemorating the area's first settlers and a relief map showing mountains in Quebec's Eastern Townships and Vermont.

Star Alta.   4BW/14GW
The oldest Ukrainian Catholic parish in Canada is here, dating from 1897. The present church, the third, was built in 1926-27. In it, saved from a fire that destroyed the second church in 1922, are enameled paintings of Christ, the Virgin and the four Evangelists.

Starrs Point N.S.   22DV
Prescott House is a Georgian mansion built in 1799-1802 by Charles Ramage Prescott, a pioneer horticulturist. The 21-room structure has a bell-cast roof, unusual in Nova Scotia, with four dormers and two massive chimneys. The whitewashed brick walls are 13-18 inches thick and the lock on the main door has a 12-inch brass key. The house, now part of the Nova Scotia Museum complex, is open to the public. Among its furnishings are three four-poster beds, a grandfather clock and Coalport china of the early 1800s, an 18th-century maple desk, 12 Regency dining-room chairs and a portrait of Prescott.

Steele Narrows Sask. *see* Meadow Lake

Steinbach Man.   6BY/15DY
Buildings erected in 1874 by the first large group of Mennonites to settle in Manitoba—they came from the Ukraine—have been reconstructed as the Mennonite Village Museum. There are a smithy, cheese factory, sawmill, general store and church-schoolhouse. A wind-driven gristmill is a replica of one used until 1918. There are a thatched-roof log cabin, a barn, stock pens and stake fences. Gardens and fields are worked with steam- and ox-powered equipment. In a modern building are Mennonite documents, books dating from 1588, clothing, dishes and furniture. Also displayed are pioneer tools, Red River carts and Steinbach's first printing press, brought here in 1911. A monument commemorates Johann Bartsch, a leader in the Mennonites' migration from Prussia to Russia in 1788. The early arts of reaping and threshing by hand, spinning and weaving and making butter are demonstrated in September during Pioneer Days at the museum.
  □ A nine-hole fly-in golf course here has a 2,800-foot airstrip open 24 hours a day and lighted at night.

Stellarton N.S.   9EY/23DY
Smoke helmets, hand-mining equipment and lamps dating from the earliest days of Nova Scotia coal mining are displayed in the Stellarton Miners Museum. It also has the 1854 locomotive *Albion* which ran on the General Mining Association line to nearby East River and Abercrombie. In a representation of a coal mine level are loading boxes buried in an explosion in the Foord pit here in 1880 and uncovered some 45 years later. The Foord seam, up to 48 feet wide, was believed the world's thickest. It is no longer mined.

Stoney Creek Ont.   7CZ/17BY
A battle June 6, 1813, in which 700 British regulars routed 2,000 American troops is commemorated in Battlefield Memorial Park. Battlefield House, which was American headquarters, is a museum and on a nearby hill is a 100-foot stone tower called Battlefield Monument. The monument was unveiled in 1913 by Queen Mary—by pushing a button in England.

The battle here changed the course of the War of 1812. If the Americans had won, they likely would have pushed on to cut the highway linking western Ontario with York (Toronto), Kingston and Montreal.

British regulars, with Canadian militiamen, had withdrawn from the Niagara Peninsula and were camped for the night of June 5-6 at Burlington Heights (*see* Hamilton). When a patrol spotted the Americans at Stoney Creek (similar information came from 19-year-old Billy Green, who had slipped through the American lines), an attack was ordered. Lt. Col. John Harvey was in command and Green, armed with a borrowed sword, led the march. The British attack at 3 a.m. overwhelmed the enemy.

In Battlefield House are displays relating to the battle. Furnishings from the period 1790-1860 include a hand-carved oak bedroom suite made for Edward VII when he visited the area in 1860 as Prince of Wales. At Stoney Creek Cemetery is a granite monument honoring Colonel Harvey, Billy Green and Isaac Corman, who learned the American password and passed it to Green.

Festival Theater lights are reflected in Stratford's Avon River. Near the theater is the Rothmans Art Gallery (seen above through a colorful sculpture on the grounds): it has exhibits of contemporary paintings, prints and sculptures. A narrow-gauge locomotive and coach run on a half-mile track at the Minnie Thomson Memorial Museum.

Stratford Ont.   7BY/16DW

About 400,000 persons flock here every summer for the Stratford Shakespearean Festival, one of Canada's premier theater attractions. They see performances not only of works by Shakespeare but also of plays by such authors as Molière, Jonson, Chekhov and Ibsen. The Festival Theater seats 2,258 and no spectator is more than 65 feet from the stage, a modern adaptation of the Elizabethan stage. It has seven acting levels, nine major entrances, a balcony and trapdoors.

The Festival Exhibition, in the Stratford city hall, has displays dealing with the festival themes. At the Rothmans Art Gallery near the Festival Theater are exhibits of contemporary paintings, prints and sculptures.

□ The Minnie Thomson Memorial Museum has a steam calliope built in 1897, 20 antique automobiles (including a rare 1919 Pierce-Arrow five-ton truck) and more than 7,000 pieces of farm machinery.

□ The Brocksden School Museum, 2½ miles east, is in a school building that dates from 1853. It has desks, slates and maps used in 19th-century Ontario rural schools. A collection of books includes a National School textbook (c.1835), one of a series of Irish texts once popular in Ontario.

Strathroy Ont.   7BZ/16CX
A plaque at the Strathroy high school honors Gen. Sir Arthur Currie, commander of the Canadian Corps in World War I.

Strathgartney P.E.I. *see* Bonshaw

Sturgeon Falls Ont.   7CX
The processing of caviar (sturgeon roe) may be seen at the Lake Nipissing Caviar plant.

□ Sturgeon River House Museum, on the site of a Hudson's Bay Company post, has displays related to the fur trade and Indian and pioneer artifacts.

Sudbury Ont.   7BW
The Big Nickel, a 30-foot representation of a five-cent piece, stands in Canadian Centennial Numismatic Park, a symbol of Sudbury's position as the center of the western world's largest nickel-mining and -refining complex. It includes the Ontario divisions of International Nickel and Falconbridge Nickel Mines:

White-hot slag is dumped at an International Nickel Company slag heap in Sudbury. At Numismatic Park you can don a yellow hard hat, stand behind a miner figure and pose with the Big Nickel.

most of their mining and smelting is in the Sudbury Basin. Inco operates the western world's biggest smelting and refining process and has the tallest smokestack (1,250 feet) at Copper Cliff, four miles west.

Slag heaps (gradually diminishing as slag is used in road construction) can be seen from Numismatic Park. An absence of vegetation around former smelters at nearby Coniston, Wahnapitae and Falconbridge is another mark of the mining industry. These areas were stripped of trees, bushes and grass before antipollution controls were applied. Emissions of sulphur dioxide burned trees and combined with rainwater to form sulphuric acid in the soil. The landscape on both sides of the Trans-Canada Highway near Coniston is lunar in appearance with deeply eroded gray clay and blackened rocks stretching for several miles. Denuded areas at Copper Cliff have been replanted with grass and trees.

BELL PARK A plaque details the geological history of the Sudbury Basin, a 35-by-17-mile depression believed formed by the impact of a giant meteor. It contains immense deposits of nickel and 15 other elements found not individually but in combinations with other

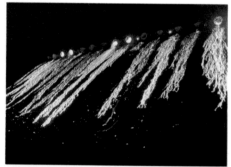

Chief Joseph Brant (*see* Brantford, Burlington) is portrayed in this Frederick Arthur Verner painting in the Museum and Arts Center of Laurentian University at Sudbury.

elements. The park, on the shore of Ramsey Lake—one of four lakes in Sudbury—has a 2,600-seat amphitheater. There are summer concerts and art and handicraft displays.

FALCONBRIDGE NICKEL MINES Visitors see ore hoisted, milled and refined.

INTERNATIONAL NICKEL Tours include open-pit mining operations and the Copper Cliff smelter.

LAURENTIAN LAKE CONSERVATION AREA Lookouts on Ramsey and Laurentian lakes, nature trails through reforested areas, and wildlife that includes muskrat, fox, beaver and great blue heron.

LAURENTIAN UNIVERSITY This bilingual university, composed of Roman Catholic, United Church and Anglican colleges, occupies a scenic 750-acre campus on Lakes Ramsey, Nepahwin and Bethel. Its Museum and Arts Center has rare Eskimo engravings, stone-cut prints and carvings, Canadian paintings (including a number of works on northern Ontario themes) and sculpture. Among major items are Otto Jacobi's *Manitoulin Island*, Frederick Arthur Verner's *Thayendanegea, Mohawk Indian Chief (Chief Joseph Brant)*, Mower Martin's *Valley of the Don from the Iron Bridge (near Toronto)* and Walter Duff's *Algonquin Park*. A Jesuit museum has documents, maps and photographs relating to local and regional history. In a university folklore collection are about 5,000 French songs, some Indian songs and about 150 English songs collected across Canada.

NUMISMATIC PARK The Big Nickel, two feet thick, is made of nickel and stainless steel and mounted on a 12-foot nickel-ore base. A 1965 Canadian penny, built of local copper, is 12 feet in diameter and 1.4 feet thick. Other coins are a 1967 Canadian $20 gold piece and a 1965 American penny, the base of which is a model of Washington's Lincoln Memorial. A flame burns in the center of the black granite base of a 1964 (Kennedy) U.S. half-dollar. Canada's only working model of an underground mine has 500 feet of tunnels showing crosscuts where ore is blasted and collected, cutouts with displays of mining procedures and a room where air is compressed to run the machinery.

Summerside P.E.I.　　　　9DX/23BW

Lobster suppers, sports events and the crowning of Miss Prince Edward Island are features of a mid-July carnival in this seaside resort. The carnival has harness racing and exhibitions of livestock, wildlife and handicrafts.

□ A ceramic centennial fountain in Memorial Square, surrounded by the flags of the

Harness racing is *the* sport in Prince Edward Island. The biggest tracks are at Summerside and Charlottetown.

provinces, was erected in 1964 on the 100th anniversary of the first meeting of the Fathers of Confederation.

□ The Kirk, now a Presbyterian church, was built in 1818 in Bedeque and moved to Summerside in 1899.

□ A week-long carnival in February has ice-sculpture and snowshoeing competitions.

Summerstown Ont.   18EX
A plaque commemorates John A. "Cariboo" Cameron, a Summerstown man who struck it rich in the Cariboo (*see* Barkerville).

Sussex N.B.   9DY
Winston Bronnum's sculptures of some 75 wild animals are displayed in natural settings at 40-acre Animaland. Children climb the larger-than-life sculptures; one, a 25-ton lobster of reinforced concrete, has a slide built into its tail. The park also has live animals and an aquarium with 2,000-2,500 lobsters.

□ A 128-foot covered bridge crosses the Kennebecasis River a mile northeast of Sussex.

Sutton Ont.   7CY/17CW
An 11-room mansion, where in pioneer days a proud Scottish family lived in Old World elegance, is the showpiece of Sibbald Point Provincial Park, four miles east. Eildon Hall was the center of a 500-acre estate that widowed Susan Sibbald ran like an English country manor in the mid-1800s. Tenant farmers tilled the land, peacocks strutted on the well-groomed lawns, servants bustled in the big house. In Eildon Hall, now the Sib-

The grave of Mazo de la Roche, who created the Jalna stories, is in an Anglican churchyard near Sutton.

bald Memorial Museum, are fine examples of Scottish and Canadian furnishings and objects brought from faraway countries by Susan Sibbald's sailor and soldier sons. Ancient Oriental tableware includes a delicate Chinese cloisonné bowl thought to be 1,000 years old; there are Persian swords and a ritualistic dagger from India.

□ A quarter-mile west of Eildon Hall is St. George's Anglican Church, a stone edifice built in 1877 in memory of Susan Sibbald, who had died the year before. It replaced a wooden church erected in 1839. In St. George's is a window designed and made for the first church by the seven daughters of John Graves Simcoe, lieutenant governor of Upper Canada. Another window is a memorial to Mazo de la Roche, author of the Jalna stories. The graves of Miss de la Roche and humorist Stephen Leacock (*see* Orillia) are in the churchyard.

Swan River Man.   4FX
Chuck wagon races, a horse show and a livestock display are featured at the Northwest Roundup and Exhibition in July.

□ The Swan Valley Museum collection includes two fossilized snails an estimated 3,500,000 years old. There are Indian relics, pioneer kitchen utensils and tools and a piano brought here by wagon train in 1896.

Swift Current Sask.   4DY
Saskatchewan's biggest rodeo is staged in July during Swift Current's three-day Frontier Days celebration. There are parades, street dances and a fair.

□ The Swift Current Museum is principally a natural history museum with habitat displays of local wildlife and birds. It also exhibits weapons, pioneer objects and Indian artifacts.

□ At the McIntyre Manufacturing Company is Blowtorch II, a life-sized mechanical horse which rolls on tiny wheels under each hoof. The first Blowtorch was made in 1948 and called the Walking Horse in Ripley's *Believe It or Not.*

Sydney N.S.   9FX/23GX
A Chippendale chair from the wardroom of Nelson's flagship *Victory* is in St. George's Church (1787), one of the oldest Anglican churches in Canada. It is thought that the chair was a gift from Capt. Thomas Hardy, Nelson's second-in-command, who visited here in the early 1800s.

□ St. Patrick's Church, built in 1828 and used as a church until 1950, was restored as a museum in 1966. It has early Sydney artifacts and exhibits of the history of the Cape Breton Colony.

□ More than 1,000,000 tons of steel ingots are produced annually by the Sydney Steel Corporation in the largest self-contained steel plant in North America.

□ A plaque honors Joseph Frederick Wallet DesBarres, founding governor of the Cape Breton Colony in 1785.

T

Tadoussac Que.   9BW/21EX

The fortified house that Pierre Chauvin built in 1600—the first European trading post on the Canadian mainland—has been reconstructed here at the mouth of the Saguenay River. Cartier had landed at Tadoussac in 1535 and Chauvin chose this site for a headquarters after being granted a 10-year monopoly of the fur trade. Of 16 men he left to winter here only three survived. Champlain saw the fort in 1603 and described it as 25 by 20 feet, eight feet high, with a central chimney and surrounded by a palisade and ditch.

The Rev. Jean Dolbeau (*see* Dolbeau), a Recollet, began a mission to the Indians here in 1615. Jesuits took direction of the mission in 1641 and built a brick and stone church. It was replaced in 1747 by a wooden chapel that still stands, the oldest surviving chapel in North America. In its 50-foot tower hangs the bell from the first chapel.

□ A cross beside the Tadoussac Church was erected in 1935 to commemorate Cartier's visit 400 years earlier.

□ A 50-foot lighthouse five miles offshore in the St. Lawrence has a 60,000,000-candlepower xenon light visible for 30 miles.

Tatamagouche N.S.   9EY/23CY

The detailed records of a close vote in an 1867 federal election, without benefit of secret ballot, is displayed at the Sunrise Trail Museum. It is the record of a 211-208 victory for Conservative Charles (later Sir Charles) Tupper over Liberal William Annand in Cumberland riding Sept. 18, 1867. Opposite the name of each elector is the name of the man he voted for. (Tupper was prime minister for two months in 1896.)

The museum exhibits clothing worn by Anna Swan, the 7-foot-11-inch "giantess of Nova Scotia," and her giant husband, Martin Van Buren Bates. Anna Swan was born in nearby New Annan in 1846—she weighed 18 pounds at birth—and was with P.T. Barnum's "Greatest Show on Earth" for some years before her marriage.

□ A globe carved from a pine log in 1820 and used for many years to teach geography is in a private home here. It is about 36 inches in circumference. The continents and lines of longitude and latitude are painted on.

Teeterville Ont.   17AZ

The Windham Township Pioneer Museum, in a log house built in 1849, displays furniture, glass, china, cooking utensils and other relics of township settlers.

L'Enfant Jésus, a small wax figure that Louis XIV gave to the church of the Acadians at Grand Pré, N.S., in 1648, is now in the Indian chapel at Tadoussac. Summer skiers climb 500 steps to the top of a 375-foot sand dune overlooking the St. Lawrence River at Tadoussac.

Down from the clouds, hikers descend toward Trapper Lake, near Telegraph Creek.

Telegraph Creek B.C.   1AX
The Grand Canyon of the Stikine River twists for 60 spectacular miles through the Stikine Plateau east of here. The 335-mile Stikine rises east of Eddontenajon (*see entry*) in the Cassiar and Omineca mountains, crosses the plateau, then cuts through the Coast Mountains to Wrangell, Alaska, and the Pacific Ocean. West of the Stewart-Cassiar Highway, the slopes of the river valley become sheer cliffs of gray, green, pink and purple, 500-600 feet high. The canyon ends about five miles upstream from Telegraph Creek.

    □ Telegraph Creek was named by the Collins Overland Telegraph Company, whose line to Asia was to cross the Stikine here. (*See* Burns Lake)

    □ The log church of the Tahltan Indian Mission, 15 miles upstream from Telegraph Creek, dates from 1901.

Temagami Ont.   7CW
A plaque in Finlayson Point Provincial Park honors Grey Owl (*see* Prince Albert National Park), who lived here in 1906-10. On Bear Island, one of more than 1,200 islands in Lake Temagami, are two buildings of a Hudson's Bay Company post founded in 1870.

Terrace B.C.   2BV
Rare trumpeter swans are sometimes seen southwest of here at Lakelse Lake, not far from the Skoglund hot springs. Kleanza and Lakelse Lake provincial parks, both about 650 acres, are in that area. Kleanza has a scenic gorge 30-40 feet deep.

    The Northern (B.C.) Chamber of Mines

displays some 200 mineral specimens in the Terrace Centennial Library.

Terrace Bay Ont.   6FX
The town is built on sand-and-gravel terraces formed on the shore of Lake Superior by four gigantic ice sheets, the last of which receded 20,000 years ago. Between the terraces are abrupt multicolored escarpments containing amethyst, tyrolite, quartz, opalite and other minerals. This phenomenon can be seen from Centennial Park in the center of town.

    At Aguasabon Gorge, half a mile west, the Aguasabon River makes a right-angled bend, then drops 90 feet and rushes into the narrow rapids below.

Terra Nova National Park (Nfld.)   11DY
Atlantic breakers crash against towering headlands here, and roll up on long, deserted beaches. In early summer the dark blue coastal waters off the 153-square-mile park are dotted with icebergs; schools of cavorting pilot whales and harbor seals are common. Arctic shellfish, rock crabs, green sea urchins, purple starfish, scallops, periwinkles, barnacles, lobsters and mussels abound in the park's bays and inlets. The coastal areas are inhabited by bald eagles, ospreys, gannets, puffins, Arctic terns, dovekies, black-legged kittiwakes, double-crested cormorants and thick-billed murres. Quiet beaches give way to gently rolling hills and dense virgin forests with ponds—where fishermen catch brook trout—streams and bogs, myriad wild flowers and lichens. Observation posts overlook fjords on the rugged shorelines and nature trails lead into the lush vegetation of marshes and forests where moose, black bears and red foxes live. The Trans-Canada Highway runs through the park for 25 miles.

Terrebonne Que.   19BX
Château Masson, an enormous stone mansion built in 1848-54 by the widow of Joseph Masson, a millionaire textile merchant and importer, is the imposing centerpiece of Terrebonne's old quarter. The town itself dates from 1673. The château's first floor serves as a high school; the second is a residence of the Blessed Sacrament Fathers.
 □ A three-story stone bakery on Ile des Moulins in the Mille Iles River dates from the late 1700s. A sawmill, carding mill, flour mill and seigniory office were built in the 1840s.

Teslin Y.T.   1AW
The Nisutlun Bay Bridge, longest water span of the Alaska Highway (1,917 feet), crosses an arm of Teslin Lake here. The highway parallels the 85-mile-long lake for 34 miles.

Tête Jaune Cache B.C.   1AZ/2EW
This town nestled in the Yellowhead Pass is where westbound travelers on the Yellowhead Route (*see* p.116) go west to Prince Rupert or south to Kamloops.

Thamesville Ont.   7AZ/16CY
Fairfield Village Museum, four miles east, traces the history of Moravian missionaries who established a Christian Indian settlement here in 1792. The arts and crafts of Delaware Indian settlers, who came from the United States, are on display. The road by which American troops entered to destroy the village in 1813 has been reconstructed.
 □ Two miles west of Thamesville an inscribed boulder marks where the Shawnee chief Tecumseh was killed in the Battle of the Thames, Oct. 5, 1813.

The Ovens N.S.   22DX
Waves that shatter on rocky bluffs here send up spray like steam from giant ovens. A concrete stairway leads to a lookout near a cave that has been gouged out of the cliffs by the force of the sea. The water compresses a cushion of air in this "blowhole," then "explodes" with a roar as the pressure builds. A small

"**Blowhole**" at The Ovens, where ancient rocks wear the scars of the sea's endless torture.

museum displays relics of a gold rush here in 1861. Old mine workings can be seen.

The Pas Man.   4FW/5GZ
A 150-mile World Championship Dog Derby highlights the four-day Northern Manitoba Trappers' Festival in February. Dogs (a maximum of nine to a team) haul sleds in three 50-mile heats. Other festival competitors test their skills at log throwing, bannock baking, muskrat skinning, tree felling, fiddling, jigging and moose calling.

Opasquia Indian Days at The Pas in August: the color and beat of the old dances, the strength of the flour packers . . . and knife, hatchet and spear throwing and bow-and-arrow contests.

□ In Devon Park is a sundial given to the settlement of The Pas by Sir John Franklin in 1842. Christ Church (Anglican), built in 1896, is adorned with a pulpit, sanctuary chairs, pews and baptismal font carved for an earlier church. All were fashioned in 1848 by a British party that waited out the winter here before setting out to descend the Mackenzie River in a futile search for the Franklin expedition lost in the Arctic.

□ Indian and Eskimo artifacts are displayed in the Sam Waller Little Northern Museum.

Thessalon Ont.   7AW
Aubrey Falls, which drops 174 feet over a series of rapids and cascades on the Mississagi River 65 miles north of here, is within sight of the Chapleau Route, a 145-mile provincial highway from Thessalon to Chapleau.

□ A plaque in Lakeside Park commemorates the capture of two armed American schooners in 1814. Seamen, soldiers and Indians from the British post at Michilimackinac boarded *Tigress* at night in Detour Passage, about 25 miles southwest of Thessalon. Two days later they captured *Scorpion*. (*See* Wasaga Beach.)

Thetford Mines Que.   9AX/20BY
Five open-pit and two underground mines here supply 40 percent of the world's asbestos. The lunar-like mining area may be viewed from four observation posts. A monument at city hall honors Joseph Fecteau, who discovered asbestos in 1876.

Thompson Man.   5GX
Bulldozed out of the bush in 1956, Thompson is now Manitoba's third biggest city, with a population of 18,500. The International Nickel Company here operates the world's second largest fully integrated nickel-producing complex. Tours of above-ground installations are available. Visitors see milling, smelting and refining of ore to 99.9-percent pure nickel. A highlight of Nickel Days in July is the National King Miner contest. Miners from many countries demonstrate their skills in a simulated pit area.

Thorold Ont.   7CZ/17CY
Ships bound through the Welland Canal for Lake Erie reach the base of the Niagara Escarpment here. Then, within a quarter-mile, they are raised 186 feet—139½ feet by three twin flight locks (picture, p. 391) and 46½ feet by a single lock. The twin locks are like a giant double stairway with traffic moving both ways. As three ships are stepped up the escarpment, three others can be simultaneously lowered on the other side of the twin locks. A quarter-mile away the single lock lifts ships the remaining distance to the top of the escarpment. (*See* Welland)

□ A monument commemorates the Battle of Beaver Dams during the War of 1812 and Laura Secord's trek of nearly 20 miles from her home in Queenston (*see entry*) to warn the British here of the approach of an American force. With 50 British regulars and more than 400 Indians, Lt. James Fitzgibbon attacked the Americans in a thick wood. Fearing a massacre, the Americans surrendered.

□ Beaverdams Church (1832) is one of Ontario's oldest Methodist meetinghouses.

Thorsby Alta.   4AX/14EX
Memorials to the Rev. Robert T. Rundle, the first resident missionary in what is now Alberta, stand near the site of an agricultural mission he founded in 1847 at Pigeon Lake, 14 miles south. They are a two-story log and stone retreat house and a large monument. The monument has a stone altar on a 30-foot-square concrete platform. Flanking the altar are two 30-foot-high stylized arms of prestressed concrete. On the arms are 10-foot-high panels with reliefs of symbols of Christianity, Indian culture and agriculture: a cross and a Gothic window, a tepee and arrows, a sower and a reaper. Rundle worked for the Methodist Church in Alberta in 1840-48.

Thunder Bay Ont.   6FY
Formed in 1970 by the amalgamation of Fort William and Port Arthur, this city at the head of navigation on Lake Superior is one of Canada's largest ports. Its main cargoes are Steep Rock iron ore (*see* Atikokan) and prairie

Three Valley Gap B.C.— Buildings in this re-creation of a 19th-century mining town include a three-story 50-room hotel and a saloon with an ornately carved mahogany bar. There are a combination barber shop and dentist's office, a tiny 12-pew wooden church (1886), a trapper's log hut, a log schoolhouse, a blacksmith shop, a jail and a buggy shop. (2EY)

grain. The port's 18 operating elevators have a total capacity of about 86,000,000 bushels; one, the 9,000,000-bushel Saskatchewan Pool Seven, is the largest single-unit grain elevator in the world.

Thunder Bay, the western terminus of the St. Lawrence-Great Lakes Waterway, has a 700-foot drydock, big enough to accommodate any ship on the lakes. The city is the center of Canada's largest pulp-and-paper-producing area.

□ A granite memorial commemorates the first fort here. It was built in 1678 by Daniel Greysolon DuLhut, who gave his name, albeit misspelled, to Duluth, Minn. Some 125 years later the fort became the main post of the North West Company and was named Fort William after William McGillivray, the chief director of the company. Port Arthur had its beginnings in the discovery of minerals in the area in the 1860s. Col. Garnet Wolseley's Red River expedition landed here in 1870 and named it Prince Arthur's Landing after Prince Arthur, later Duke of Connaught. It was named Port Arthur in 1884 and began to develop as a port in 1902 when the Canadian Northern Railway made it its lakehead terminus.

Agricultural exhibits and the Royal Canadian Mounted Police Musical Ride are among the features of the week-long Canadian Lakehead Exhibition and Rendez-Vous Days at the end of June.

BOULEVARD LAKE PARK (1) The 212-foot Black Bay Bridge over the Current River was the first reinforced concrete bridge in Canada. It was built in 1911.

CENTENNIAL BOTANICAL CONSERVATORY (2) Exotic plants in a 5¼-acre garden.

CENTENNIAL PARK (3) A re-creation of a logging camp (c.1910) is the main attraction of this 147-acre park. It has a bunkhouse, cook-

Prairie wheat is loaded at Thunder Bay for shipment to markets in the east and overseas.

ery, stable and blacksmith shop and a sauna such as Finnish loggers used.

CHIPPEWA PARK (4) A 250-acre forest area eight miles south has camping facilities.

FORT WILLIAM (5) A reconstruction of the North West Company post as it was in 1816 includes a naval stores building and a shipbuilding display. There are blacksmith, tinsmith, gunsmith, tailor and cooper workshops, craftsmen's quarters and two canoe sheds. Within a palisade are a hospital, a prison, a gum store (where gum for building canoes was kept), the Great Hall where company partners and traders met annually, and the Cantine Salope eating house.

HILLCREST PARK (6) Sunken gardens and fine views of the waterfront, the bay and the cape called the Sleeping Giant.

INTERNATIONAL FRIENDSHIP GARDEN (7) Polish, Ukrainian, Canadian, Slovakian, German, Italian and Lithuanian gardens are grouped around a lake in this Centennial

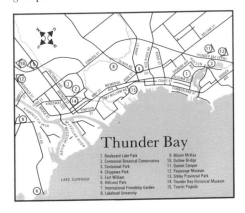

Thunder Bay

1. Boulevard Lake Park
2. Centennial Botanical Conservatory
3. Centennial Park
4. Chippewa Park
5. Fort William
6. Hillcrest Park
7. International Friendship Garden
8. Lakehead University
9. Mount McKay
10. Outlaw Bridge
11. Ouimet Canyon
12. Paipoonge Museum
13. Sibley Provincial Park
14. Thunder Bay Historical Museum
15. Tourist Pagoda

project. Local ethnic groups designed, built and financed them. Finnish and Danish gardens are new additions.

LAKEHEAD UNIVERSITY (8) Northwestern Ontario's only university, founded in 1965, is attended by some 2,900 full-time and 3,600 part-time students.

MOUNT McKAY (9) The 1,600-foot mountain provides a panoramic view of the area. On it is a re-creation (1939), using many of the original stones, of a circular stone sanctuary dedicated to the Sacred Heart. The original was built in 1889 by the Rev. Joseph Hébert.

OUIMET CANYON (10) This impressive, tree-lined gorge, 500 feet across, 300-400 feet deep and half a mile long, is 41 miles east in Ouimet Canyon Provincial Park. Many species of Arctic plants grow on the floor of the canyon, where the temperature is low all year.

OUTLAW BRIDGE (11) A plaque commemorates this bridge, long since dismantled, which was the first to span the Pigeon River to the United States. It was so named because it was built in 1917 without a formal international agreement.

PAIPOONGE MUSEUM (12) Pioneer relics, farm implements and furniture are on display at this museum 10 miles west.

SIBLEY PROVINCIAL PARK (13) This 94-square-mile park occupies most of a 20-mile-long peninsula which rears up into the mighty cape known as the Sleeping Giant. Named for its resemblance to a prone figure, the Sleeping Giant is seven miles long and 1,000 feet high. Also in the park is Silver Islet, a dot of rock some 80 feet in diameter and never more than eight feet above water. It became Canada's first major source of silver. The vertical vein was discovered in 1868 and more than $3,000,000 worth of ore was mined before 1884, when the shaft reached a depth of 1,300 feet and it became impossible to keep the water out.

THUNDER BAY HISTORICAL MUSEUM (14) Indian artifacts, pioneer, marine and military relics, documents, photographs and maps.

TOURIST PAGODA (15) This little Oriental-style structure, dating from 1910, is believed the oldest tourist information center in Canada.

Tidnish N.S.   9DY/23BX
The roadbed and masonry of the Chignecto Ship Railway are intact here at its Northumberland Strait terminus (*see* Amherst).

Timmins Ont.   7CV/8GZ
This city at the center of the Porcupine mining district has fewer than 50,000 persons but its 1,250 square miles is roughly equivalent to the combined areas of Winnipeg, Toronto, Montreal and New York. When Timmins was amalgamated with neighboring townships in 1973, it absorbed Schumacher, Porcupine and South Porcupine.

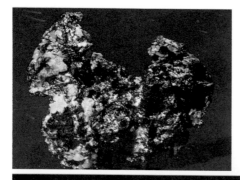

Gold ore specimen approximately three inches by four is displayed by McIntyre Porcupine Mines in Timmins. The McIntyre mill, mine shaft, hoist and boiler house are reflected in Pearl Lake.

Some $1,500,000,000 in gold has been taken from the Porcupine area since the first mine was opened in 1907. There are surface tours during July and August at one of the most famous mines, McIntyre Porcupine.

A copper and zinc strike here in 1964 led to a rush in which some 20,000 claims were staked. Lead and silver also were discovered. The Texasgulf mine soon became the world's biggest producer of zinc and silver in concentrates.

□ The Porcupine Outdoor Museum's relics of early days in the Porcupine include the first recorder's vaults. The H.H. Costain mineral collection in the McIntyre Community Building displays some of the world's finest specimens of rare and semi-rare minerals.

Tintagel B.C.   2CV
The center stone of a cairn here is from a castle in Tintagel, Cornwall, England, where according to legend King Arthur once lived.

Tobermory Ont.   7BX
Four miles out in Georgian Bay is 495-acre Flowerpot Island, part of Georgian Bay Islands National Park (*see entry*). The island is named for two flowerpot-shaped rock formations 50 feet and 35 feet high. Flowers and shrubs grow in crevices in the flowerpots, which have been preserved from further erosion by masonry and waterproof concrete capping. Flowerpot Island lighthouse has been operated since 1873. (A light on Cove Island, four miles west, dates from 1856.)

Fathom Five Provincial Park, Canada's first underwater park, is being developed near here. In its 50 square miles are some 10 wrecks and a variety of rock formations, animal and plant life and fossils.

□ The Peninsula and Saint Edmunds Township Museum here displays pioneer relics and Indian artifacts.

□ A car ferry connects Tobermory with South Baymouth on Manitoulin Island.

Tofield Alta.   4BW/14GW
A reaper (c.1831), handmade tools and furniture, pioneer school registers and a buffalo skull estimated to be 2,000 years old are part of the Tofield Historical Museum collection.

Tofino B.C.   2BY
The Maritime Museum here displays cannonballs, remains of sunken ships, harpoons and sea lion teeth. Five miles north of Tofino, a fishing and resort village and the center of mining and logging operations, are the ruins of Fort Defiance. Robert Gray, a Boston fur trader and master of the ship *Columbia*, built the fort as a winter redoubt in 1791. His crew stripped it before they sailed the next spring. Later, 200 miles south, Gray discovered and named the Columbia River. His ship's logs were accidentally burned and for 174 years the location of Fort Defiance was a mystery. In 1966, using a sketch of the site by the ship's carpenter, Kenneth Gibson of Tofino found the ruins: a few chimney bricks.

Six-foot waves make for fine surfing at Long Beach, near Tofino. With no reef, the surf breaks close to shore. Even in August, the best month, the water is cold enough for wet suits to be worn.

Topsail Nfld.   11DZ
The village affords a fine view of Conception Bay and Bell, Little Bell and Kelly islands.

Toronto Ont.   7CY/17CX/P.355
An explosion of development that started in the early 1960s gave this dynamic capital of Ontario a new face and ranked it among the fastest growing cities in North America. By the late 1970s, with a population heading for 3,000,000, Toronto was vying with Montreal for the title of Canada's most populous urban area. It was already the second largest big city in surface area: its 244 square miles was surpassed only by Winnipeg's 269.

Skyscrapers sprout in all of the metropolitan area—the city of Toronto and the boroughs of Etobicoke, York, North York, East York and Scarborough. Toronto's ultramodern character is seen everywhere, perhaps most of all in the CN Tower, in gleaming bank towers with their business complexes, in the stylistic city hall, the expressways and the rapid-transit system. But vestiges of Toronto's more placid past are seen in sedate buildings such as some in Queen's Park and at the University of Toronto. And in the late 1970s Toronto was the only Canadian city still using some streetcars.

□ John Graves Simcoe, first lieutenant governor of Upper Canada (1791), established the town of York in 1793 and made it the capital, presumably safe from attack. (He added a fort in 1812.) But Americans captured York in 1813 and burned the garrison and public buildings, including the Parliament. The town was rebuilt and, as surrounding farmlands were settled, it prospered. Population was more than 9,000 when York was incorporated as the City of Toronto in 1834.

□ Toronto is an important port and the hub of Canada's densest manufacturing region. The Toronto Stock Exchange, one of the world's busiest exchanges, is the heart of the Bay Street financial district with its many head offices of industries and businesses.

Curved twin towers of Toronto city hall are seen through the glass wall of an office building. It also reflects the 300-foot tower of the old city hall, now a courthouse.

Metropolitan Toronto is served by several major expressways (including a 16-lane section of the Macdonald-Cartier Freeway) and 32 miles of subway. Exhibition Park is the site of the Canadian National Exhibition, the world's biggest annual fair.

ALLAN GARDENS (1) A 13-acre botanical garden stressing tropical and subtropical plants. Has a statue of poet Robert Burns by Scottish sculptor T. W. Stevenson.

ART GALLERY OF ONTARIO (2) Major paintings in Canada's second largest gallery (after the National Gallery in Ottawa) include Tintoretto's *Christ Washing His Disciples' Feet*, Rubens' *The Elevation of the Cross*, Gainsborough's *The Harvest Waggon* and Hals' *Isaak Abrahamsz, Massa*. There are works by Picasso, Renoir, Monet, Delacroix and Dégas. In the Canadian gallery are paintings by Krieghoff, Kane, Borduas, Carr, Colville, Thomson and the Group of Seven. A wing devoted to sculpture has works by Picasso and Henry Moore. Part of the gallery is housed in the Grange, a mansion built in 1817-20. It is furnished as a gentleman's house of 1835.

BLACK CREEK PIONEER VILLAGE (3) Five log farm buildings still stand where they were built by Daniel Stong, a Pennsylvania German colonist; 25 other buildings, including a general store, gristmill and flouring mill, weaver's and shoemaker's shops, were brought from elsewhere. An inn was originally a halfway house at Scarborough. Stong's first house, a three-room dwelling built in 1816, was followed 16 years later by a two-

story, seven-room house of hewn timbers covered with clapboard siding. Burwick House (1844) reflects the more comfortable life of mid-century. Its early Ontario furnishings are complemented by imported rugs and tapestries. In educational programs, students dip candles, churn butter, card wool, spin and hook rugs and bake on a wood stove.

BOROUGH OF YORK MUSEUM (4) Displays of 19th-century tools, fire-fighting equipment from about 1900 and objects from early schoolhouses. Closed in summer.

CN TOWER (5) This communications and observation tower dominates the city skyline and is the world's tallest free-standing structure at more than 1,815 feet. It claims the world's most efficient broadcasting transmission facilities and a 100-mile view.

CANADIAN NATIONAL EXHIBITION (6) The largest annual exhibition in the world, a yearly event since 1879, the CNE runs for three weeks in late summer in Exhibition Park. It has 1½ miles of midway, grandstand shows, sports events, flower shows and an agricultural fair that includes livestock judging, horse jumping and dog shows. There are science, education, industry and fashion exhibits.

CASA LOMA (7) North America's largest castle was built by soldier-industrialist Sir Henry Pellatt in 1911-14. The interior of the 98-room castle is finished in teak, oak, walnut and marble and its conservatory doors are of bronze. The castle, where Sir Henry lived for 12 years, has hidden panels and secret passageways and staircases. Visitors follow an 800-foot tunnel to stables with floors of Spanish tile and stalls of mahogany.

□ The regimental museum of the Queen's Own Rifles of Canada occupies six rooms. It has a diorama portraying the first wave

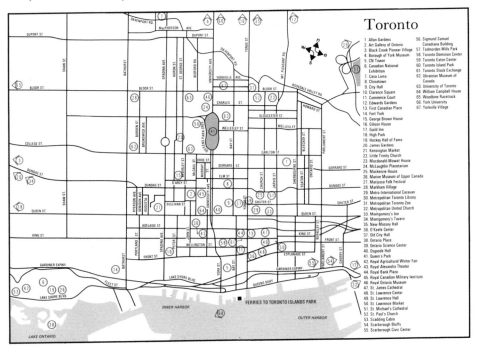

Toronto

1. Allan Gardens
2. Art Gallery of Ontario
3. Black Creek Pioneer Village
4. Borough of York Museum
5. CN Tower
6. Canadian National Exhibition
7. Casa Loma
8. Chinatown
9. City Hall
10. Clarence Square
11. Commerce Court
12. Edwards Gardens
13. First Canadian Place
14. Fort York
15. George Brown House
16. Gibson House
17. Guild Inn
18. High Park
19. Hockey Hall of Fame
20. James Gardens
21. Kensington Market
22. Little Trinity Church
23. Macdonald-Mowat House
24. McLaughlin Planetarium
25. Mackenzie House
26. Marine Museum of Upper Canada
27. Mariposa Folk Festival
28. Markham Village
29. Metro International Caravan
30. Metropolitan Toronto Library
31. Metropolitan Toronto Zoo
32. Metropolitan United Church
33. Montgomery's Inn
34. Montgomery's Tavern
35. New Massey Hall
36. O'Keefe Center
37. Old City Hall
38. Ontario Place
39. Ontario Science Center
40. Osgoode Hall
41. Queen's Park
42. Royal Agricultural Winter Fair
43. Royal Alexandra Theater
44. Royal Bank Plaza
45. Royal Canadian Military Institute
46. Royal Ontario Museum
47. St. James Cathedral
48. St. Lawrence Center
49. St. Lawrence Hall
50. St. Lawrence Market
51. St. Michael's Cathedral
52. St. Paul's Church
53. Scadding Cabin
54. Scarborough Bluffs
55. Scarborough Civic Center
56. Sigmund Samuel Canadiana Building
57. Todmorden Mills Park
58. Toronto-Dominion Center
59. Toronto Eaton Center
60. Toronto Island Park
61. Toronto Stock Exchange
62. Ukrainian Museum of Canada
63. University of Toronto
64. William Campbell House
65. Woodbine Racetrack
66. York University
67. Yorkville Village

Toronto kaleidoscope: a parabolic disc reflects a whisper across a room at the Ontario Science Center . . . the noisy tangle of lights along Yonge Street . . . teeming midway crowds at the Canadian National Exhibition . . . and Emmanuel Hahn's 20-foot statue of Ned Hanlan, world champion sculler in 1878 (at the Marine Museum of Upper Canada). Caribana (below) is a seven-day August festival (music, dancing, handicrafts) organized by Toronto's West Indian community. Toronto is the world's highest elevator ride up the CN Tower . . . the sparkle of the Cinesphere as the sun sets behind Ontario Place . . . the salty pride of *Haida*, Canada's most famous World War II destroyer, now a museum at Ontario Place . . . the fluid beauty of horse and rider at the Royal Agricultural Winter Fair.

Casa Loma by floodlight: visitors climb to the top of the round stone towers and battlements. The highest tower is some 150 feet.

of the regiment landing in Normandy on June 6, 1944, as part of the 3rd Canadian Division.

CHINATOWN (8) Chinese restaurants and Oriental shops that sell carved ivory, jade, silks, linens and bamboo.

CITY HALL (9) The city hall complex (1965) epitomizes the spirit of modern Toronto. Its curved twin towers of 27 and 20 stories partially encircle a three-story, umbrella-shaped podium that contains the city council chambers. Tours of the graceful glass and concrete structures include a 27th-floor observation deck. The Henry Moore sculpture *Archer* is in adjacent Nathan Phillips Square.

CLARENCE SQUARE (10) A plaque honors Alexander Dunn, the first Canadian to win the Victoria Cross (for valor in the charge of the Light Brigade in the Crimea in 1854).

COMMERCE COURT (11) This banking, office and shopping complex consists of three modern buildings of 57, 13 and five stories and a 34-story tower built in 1931. The four surround a tree-lined, one-acre courtyard dominated by an illuminated circular fountain.

EDWARDS GARDENS (12) A hilly, 35-acre park with several gardens and promenades.

FIRST CANADIAN PLACE (13) The 72-story Bank of Montreal Building is covered in white Italian marble.

FORT YORK (14) Scarlet-coated guardsmen parade to the music of fife and drum, fire muskets and a six-pounder cannon and perform sunset retreat. Fort York was heavily damaged in 1813 when its retreating British defenders blew up a gunpowder magazine to prevent its capture. It was rebuilt as married quarters. The story of the American attack in 1813 is told with a relief map and slides in a blockhouse theater; a film depicts daily life at that time. Costumed women bake bread, churn butter, dip candles and card and spin wool. A blacksmith performs on a mobile military forge. A one-day Festival of the Fort in May recreates battle scenes, with cavalry charges. The mace from the first Parliament of Upper Canada, stolen by the Americans in 1813 and returned in 1934, is displayed in one of several museum buildings.

GEORGE BROWN HOUSE (15) A brick house (1877) that was the home of George Brown, a Father of Confederation and founder of the newspaper *The Globe*.

GIBSON HOUSE (16) A red brick Georgian house built in 1849 by David Gibson, one of the rebels of 1837, has been restored to the period.

GUILD INN (17) Historic books and documents, paintings and statues are displayed in the Guild Inn, a guesthouse. The 50-acre wooded estate has a log cabin built in 1790, extensive lawns, gardens, illuminated fountains and a replica of the famous maze at Hampton Court Palace.

HIGH PARK (18) Nature trails wind past rock and sunken gardens, floral displays, a small zoo and Grenadier Pond—where bands play from a barge on summer nights. Much of the park was bequeathed to the city by John Howard, one of Toronto's first surveyors and engineers. His house, Colborne Lodge (1836), is a museum, restored to the 1850s and containing Howard's furniture.

HOCKEY HALL OF FAME (19) Bells used by referees in hockey's pre-whistle days are among the relics displayed here. There are sweaters of all National Hockey League teams, sticks and pucks involved in milestone goals and pictures of all-time greats. The major NHL trophies are here most of the year. In the same building is the Canadian Sports Hall of Fame, where famous performers in other sports are enshrined. The Canadian hall displays a bicycle once ridden by Torchy Peden, skates worn by Barbara Ann Scott and the Queen's Plate trophy.

JAMES GARDENS (20) Flower beds, rock gardens, trees, spring-fed pools and streams.

KENSINGTON MARKET (21) A colorful European-style street market; ethnic restaurants.

LITTLE TRINITY CHURCH (22) Toronto's oldest church, a Gothic-style brick edifice built in 1843.

MACDONALD-MOWAT HOUSE (23) A brick house (1872) that was lived in by Sir John A. Macdonald and by Sir Oliver Mowat, prime minister of Ontario from 1872 to 1896.

McLAUGHLIN PLANETARIUM (24) A pavilion of the Royal Ontario Museum, the planetarium depicts man's knowledge of the universe and has regular programs in its Theater of the Stars.

MACKENZIE HOUSE (25) This two-story stone dwelling was the home of William Lyon Mackenzie, Toronto's first mayor (1835) and leader of the Upper Canada Rebellion in 1837. It was a gift from his supporters in 1859, 10 years after he returned from exile in the United States. In the house are many of his possessions, including his watch, his Bible and some documents. A reconstructed print

Toronto Island Park (top left), accessible only by ferry, is a refreshing change from the pace of downtown. There are 138 acres of lagoons. High Park (top right) is the biggest City of Toronto park (398 acres). Edwards Gardens (above), a beauty spot in Don Mills, is on Wilket Creek, a branch of the Don River. The boutiques of Lothian Mews (below) are in midtown Toronto.

"Interpreters of history" at Black Creek Pioneer Village in Toronto herd animals, pick berries, bake bread and keep shop. Others use pioneer methods to cure meat, forge horseshoes and publish a newspaper. The village is typical of a pre-Confederation rural Ontario community.

shop has Mackenzie's hand-operated flatbed press, on which copies of his newspaper *The Colonial Advocate* are printed.

MARINE MUSEUM OF UPPER CANADA (26) The museum is in the onetime officers' quarters of Stanley Barracks, built in 1841. One room contains memorabilia of Canada's greatest sculler, Edward "Ned" Hanlan, including his practice shell with sliding seat—a device he was the first to use. In other rooms are Indian canoes, Eskimo kayaks, steam whistles and engines, underwater equipment and relics from sunken ships. There are models of the famous schooner *Bluenose* and of *Nancy*, a fur trader converted to a British warship and sunk in the Nottawasaga River by American gunfire in 1814 (*see* Wasaga Beach).

MARIPOSA FOLK FESTIVAL (27) A three-day festival in June: workshops and concerts, ethnic dances, craft displays, children's concerts.

MARKHAM VILLAGE (28) Bric-a-brac, art and antique shops, coffeehouses and outdoor cafés occupy a row of old houses.

MASSEY HALL (29) Built in 1894, Massey Hall is the permanent home of the Toronto Symphony Orchestra. A new Massey Hall is to be opened in 1981, when the existing building will become a general purpose community hall.

METRO INTERNATIONAL CARAVAN (29) This nine-day party is given in June by some 50 ethnic groups in halls, clubs and churches throughout Metropolitan Toronto. Visitors see an English pub and a Greek taberna, hear Mexican mariachis and Russian balalaikas and eat Australian kangaroo tail soup and Bavarian wiener schnitzel. They dance the Israeli hora, the Maori war dance and the Filipino bamboo dance. Handicraft displays range from Lithuanian wood carvings and Dutch wooden shoes to Swiss clocks and Irish linen.

METROPOLITAN TORONTO LIBRARY (31) This striking new (1977) edifice has the most extensive collection of any public library in Canada, including books, films, records, manuscripts, pictures, paintings and reference materials. A feature is the John Ross Robertson collection of historic Canadian pictures and maps.

METROPOLITAN TORONTO ZOO (32) Some 4,000 animals, birds and reptiles live in huge paddocks simulating their natural environments. The zoo, one of the world's five or six largest, groups animals in areas representing the Americas, Africa, Indo-Malaya, Eurasia and Australia. Animals in each area mix with birds, plants, insects and reptiles indigenous to that part of the world. The animals are separated from humans and from animals of other areas by ingenious barriers; many are disguised as natural surroundings and are not seen by the public. Birds fly freely in huge, walk-through enclosures and nocturnal animals live in a dark tunnel. Many visitors see the zoo from a slow, silent train.

METROPOLITAN UNITED CHURCH (33) This former "cathedral of North American Methodism," rebuilt after a fire in 1928, has a 54-bell carillon.

MONTGOMERY'S INN (34) Erected about 1832, the two-story stone inn is an example of Loyalist Georgian architecture..

MONTGOMERY'S TAVERN (35) A plaque marks the site of the inn outside which government loyalists led by Sir Francis Bond Head, and rebels led by William Lyon Mackenzie, clashed on Dec. 7, 1837. The rebels were dispersed and Mackenzie escaped to the United States following a brief battle.

O'KEEFE CENTER (36) Canada's largest concert hall seats 3,200 for plays, concerts, opera and ballet. The graceful limestone, glass and granite center houses the National Ballet of Canada and the Canadian Opera Company. In the lobby is a 100-foot mural, *The Seven Lively Arts*, by York Wilson.

OLD CITY HALL (37) A 300-foot tower with a clock 20 feet in diameter crowns the old city hall, built in 1891-99 of Canadian brownstone and granite. A stained glass window created by Robert McCausland in 1899 and depicting the "union of commerce and industry" is over the main stairway of the Romanesque structure, which now houses provincial courts. A cenotaph outside honors the 8,500 Toronto men who died in the world wars.

ONTARIO PLACE (38) A miniature Venice—waterways and lagoons make up more than half of its 96 acres—Ontario Place is an annual May-to-September exposition on three man-made islands in Lake Ontario. Five interlocked modular pods containing exhibits and restaurants stand above the lake near the Cinesphere, whose curved screen, six stories high and 80 feet wide, is the world's largest. Symphony, country, rock and folk music and opera and ballet are performed at the Forum under a translucent roof. Marching bands, drum and bugle corps, clowns, magicians and Ontario Place's own costumed characters entertain throughout the grounds. A children's village has a rubber forest, a foam swamp, roller slides and a king-of-the-castle climbing and sliding hill. A miniature train weaves

Rerouted expressway (above, through the stocks) skirts Fort York in Toronto. When highway construction threatened in 1958, history-conscious Torontonians battled successfully to save the old fort from destruction. The highway went around; the fort, rebuilt after the War of 1812, stayed put. Eight stone, log and brick buildings that still stand include a spartan barracks, the officers' comfortable dining room (below) and an officer's bedroom complete with four-poster. All eight buildings are original. So is the site: Lake Ontario was mere yards south of the fort wall in 1813; now, on filled land between the fort and the lake are the elevated Gardiner Expressway and several surface streets. The fort is open year-round. A Festival of the Fort is held in May.

Art treasures in Toronto: The Royal Ontario Museum's Chinese collection includes this 50-inch-high glazed earthenware arhat (disciple of Buddha) from the 12th-century Liao dynasty. Among the ROM's Egyptian pieces are a cast of an 18th-dynasty (c.1400 B.C.) temple wall sculpture (right) and a wooden statuette (opposite) believed to date from about 2000 B.C. It is 18 inches high. Masterpieces in the Art Gallery of Ontario include Rembrandt's *Portrait of a Lady with a Lap Dog*. Clarence Gagnon is represented in the Canadian gallery by his *Horse Racing in Winter, Quebec*.

past audiovisual exhibits, reflecting pools, parks, boutiques, restaurants and pubs.

ONTARIO SCIENCE CENTER (39) People are encouraged to pull levers, press buttons and crank handles at the Ontario Science Center. It offers the visitor a chance to take the controls of a spaceship during a simulated space docking or lunar landing, or to pedal a stationary bicycle and generate power to make music or brighten a television screen—on which he sees himself. Youngsters play tic-tac-toe against a computer that never loses. Visitors whispering into eight-foot parabolic sound discs converse across a noisy 150-foot hall. The museum's nearly 600 exhibits allow people to trace cosmic rays on a Geiger counter or watch static electricity stand their hair on end. They can try to crack modern mechanical and electronic locks or test their driving reactions and distance perception.

□ The laboratory in which Frederick Banting and Charles Best discovered insulin is reconstructed and there is a model of the St. Lawrence Seaway Saint-Lambert lock. Lasers, telescopes and antigravity cones are demonstrated. Displays describe the formation of glaciers, boil liquid nitrogen at 400 degrees below zero, chart voice impulses on a television screen and show how exotic musical instruments function. A disorientation room disrupts a visitor's inertial guidance system to demonstrate imbalance.

OSGOODE HALL (40) Erected in 1829-32 by the Law Society of Upper Canada, it is a classic example of early Ontario architecture. The Ontario Supreme Court is here.

QUEEN'S PARK (41) The Ontario Legislative Building is a Romanesque brownstone structure erected in 1886-92. On the lawns are statues of Queen Victoria, Sir John A. Macdonald and John Graves Simcoe.

ROYAL AGRICULTURAL WINTER FAIR (42) A nine-day November fair with livestock, flower, fruit, farm and industrial exhibits and the Royal Horse Show.

ROYAL ALEXANDRA THEATER (43) Restored to its original splendor, the 1,497-seat "Royal Alex" presents plays, opera and ballet. It was the first theater in Canada without vision-obscuring posts.

Queen Elizabeth Park is a Vancouver beauty spot where once there was a rock quarry. In the Bloedel Floral Conservatory, under a plexiglass dome, more than 300 varieties of tropical and desert plants are displayed in a natural setting that includes a choir of exotic songbirds. Point Atkinson lighthouse is at the southern tip of Lighthouse Park. At Kitsilano Beach children clamber over a relic of Canada's greatest railway-building era. Engine 374, festooned with flowers, first steamed into Vancouver on May 23, 1887, hauling the first Montreal-to-Vancouver passenger train. A proud, terse cable was sent to Queen Victoria: "Canada linked."

becoming the first ship to sail the passage in both directions.

MOUNT SEYMOUR PROVINCIAL PARK (22) This alpine wilderness park on the slopes of 4,766-foot Mount Seymour offers skiing from December to May, hiking in summer and autumn. A paved highway winds for eight miles up to the 3,332-foot level.

MUSEUM OF ANTHROPOLOGY (23) This museum was planned to house three major exhibits: the University of British Columbia's 10,000-piece collection of Northwest Coast Indian art, one of the largest in the world; the Walter and Marianne Koerner masterwork collection of classical and tribal art; and a 10,000-piece collection of tribal art from Oceania, Central and South America, Africa, Southeast Asia, the Mediterranean and North America. The museum has some 90,000 items excavated from archaeological sites throughout British Columbia. The museum is sited on cliffs above Tower Beach in an area landscaped to resemble an ancient west coast Indian village on an inlet of the sea. Among the UBC treasures are a Haida whalebone soul boat used by medicine men in treating illness and a collection of massive Indian carvings and totem poles from north coast villages.

NITOBE MEMORIAL GARDEN (24) This Japanese garden on the UBC campus has an artificial "mountain," a waterfall and a lake filled with golden carp and spanned by five bridges. On an island is one of seven lanterns, the Yukimi or snow-scene lantern, so called because its serene beauty is best viewed under a veil of snow. Quiet pathways wind among flowering cherry and maple trees to a Japanese tea garden and teahouse.

OLD HASTINGS MILL STORE MUSEUM (25) The store (1865), in Pioneer Park, is Vancouver's oldest building, one of the few structures not destroyed in an 1886 fire. It houses relics and pictures of the city's early days.

PARK AND TILFORD GARDENS (26) Year-round displays in six gardens—called rhododendron, rose, colonnade, native wood, oriental and flower.

QUEEN ELIZABETH PARK (27) A rock quarry atop Little Mountain has been transformed into two beautiful sunken gardens.

QUEEN ELIZABETH THEATER (28) The 2,800-seat theater is set in a handsome, landscaped plaza. A smaller adjoining theater is the home of the Playhouse Theater Company.

REDWOOD PARK (29) A 59-acre woodland with trees from many parts of the world.

REIFEL BIRD SANCTUARY (30) Some 220 species find haven here on a marshy estuary of Westham Island. The refuge supports Canada's largest wintering waterfowl population and is a resting place for more than 12,000 snow geese flying between Siberia and California. Part of the sanctuary and a nature house are open to visitors.

RICHMOND ART CENTER (31) In this art gallery and history museum in Minoru Park are items of local history and military and aeronautical artifacts. Nearby is the Chapel in the Park, a restored pioneer church built in 1891.

ROBSONSTRASSE (32) Robson Street became Robsonstrasse during the 1950s when German and other European immigrants began to add spice and flavor. Now it has many shops owned by East Indians.

SIMON FRASER UNIVERSITY (33) Built along the forested crest of 1,200-foot Burnaby

Big Raven (opposite), a 34-by-45-inch canvas by Emily Carr, and Théophile Hamel's *The Molson Family* (43 by 33 inches) are in the permanent collection of the Vancouver Art Gallery. Indian objects in the Centennial Museum include a raven rattle carved from wood and a spoon fashioned from the horn of a mountain goat. Both come from the northern B.C. coastal region.

Mountain, the campus is a masterwork of architects Arthur Erickson and Geoffrey Massey. From the spacious, covered central mall, a dramatic flight of stone steps leads to the Academic Quadrangle, set around a large inner courtyard of landscaped lawns and pools—like a modern Parthenon. Designed on a modular basis to permit an eventual expansion to accommodate 11,000 students, the complex is linked by sheltered walkways. Student guides conduct campus tours and the 450-seat theater is open to the public.

SPANISH BANKS (34) Off this long sandy beach on June 22, 1792, Capt. George Vancouver met the captains Galiano and Valdez and accepted Spain's surrender of the northwest coast. "It was dawn for Britain," reads a plaque on the cliffs, "but twilight for Spain."

STANLEY PARK (35) The beauty of the 1,000-acre forest park at Vancouver's doorstep is best explored on foot along its 22 miles of trails. They skirt two lovely lakes, Lost Lagoon and lily-padded Beaver Lake, and giant stands of Douglas fir, hemlock and cedar. A seawall footpath passes Second and Third beaches and Siwash Rock—a young Indian turned to stone, according to the legend told by E. Pauline Johnson. The famous Mohawk poetess (*see* Middleport) so loved the park that she asked that her ashes be buried within sight of Siwash Rock. A rustic memorial fountain marks the spot. A lookout at Prospect Point gives commanding views of the North Shore mountains and the Lions Gate Bridge that spans the harbor entrance. A replica of the fierce dragon figurehead of the liner *Empress of Japan* that plied between the Orient and Vancouver from 1891 to 1922 is on the

seawall path near Brockton Point Lighthouse. Close by is a fine collection of Indian totem poles and one of the Commonwealth's most scenic cricket fields, at Brockton Point.

At Hallelujah Point, named in honor of the Salvation Army, is Vancouver's most famous timepiece, the Nine O'Clock Gun, a cast iron muzzle-loader that has been booming out its time signal each evening since 1894. Also in Stanley Park are Malkin Bowl (open-air concerts and musicals), the Rose Garden, Shakespeare Garden and RCAF Garden of Remembrance, a miniature railway, a zoo and an aquarium (*see below*).

STANLEY PARK ZOO (36) The zoo started modestly in 1888 with a bear cub, the pet of a ranger's wife. Today's modern zoo, adjacent to the Vancouver Aquarium in a landscaped setting of roughly 17 acres, houses some 570 species. Among them are polar bears, otters, monkeys and seals but the show stealers are one of the world's finest collections of king penguins. The zoo has a children's section (goats, rabbits and calves) and a junior zoo (kinkajous, opossums and chinchillas). In a wildlife sanctuary are Arctic wolves and animals found in British Columbia.

STEVESTON (37) A huge salmon processing center, where fresh fish is sold at the wharf, it has a Salmon Queen Carnival each summer.

UNIVERSITY OF BRITISH COLUMBIA (38) Looking out on the mountains and the sea at Point Grey and girded by the wooded Endowment Lands, this 1,000-acre campus is one of the most beautiful in Canada. Its 300 permanent buildings include the UBC Health Sciences Center, one of the most modern teaching and research hospitals anywhere. Many parts of the campus are open to visitors. The gray stone Main Library, containing more than 1,500,000 books, houses the UBC Fine Arts Gallery. At the Geological Sciences Center is the M. Y. Williams Museum of Geology and a mounted skeleton of a dinosaur that once roamed the tropical swamplands of Alberta. Also open are the Frederic Wood Theater, the olympic-size Empire Swimming Pool, the animal barns of the university's farm, the greenhouses and floral displays of the UBC Botanical Gardens, and Totem Park, with Indian displays.

VANCOUVER AQUARIUM (39) Close to 9,000 specimens representing 595 species are housed in three indoor galleries. The B.C. Hall of Fishes takes visitors on a simulated journey from the open Pacific through the Strait of Georgia and into sheltered coastal inlets. There are views of seals, an octopus grotto, colorful sculpins and red rock crabs. In the Rufe Gibbs Hall the journey continues up into the freshwater rivers and lakes for a look at white sturgeon, bass and perch of the warm Okanagan waters, and beautiful pumpkinseed sunfish. Most exotic are the species in the H. R. MacMillan Tropical Gallery, among them sea turtles, clownfish, piranha, lemon sharks, moray eels and Australian lungfish. The whale pool (489,000 gallons), with underwater viewing areas and outdoor terraces, is the home of two killer whales and a Pacific striped dolphin. In other pools live two beluga whales and three rare sea otters, a species hunted almost to extinction during the 19th century.

VANCOUVER ART GALLERY (40) Modern Canadian artists are well represented in a permanent collection that includes works of the Group of Seven—among them Lawren Harris' *North Shore of Lake Superior*—and the major collection of the works of British Columbia artist Emily Carr.

VAN DUSEN BOTANICAL GARDENS (41) Created from 55 rolling acres of a golf course, this beauty spot now has three small lakes, a hedge maze and more than a dozen gardens, among them a Japanese garden, a swamp garden and a garden of fragrance.

WHYTECLIFFE PARK (42) A place to watch the sun set over the Strait of Georgia, the ferries coming in from Vancouver Island and the spectacular sights of Howe Sound.

Vanderhoof B.C.   1AZ/2CW
This town in the Nechako Valley is on a major Canada goose flyway. To the west is Fraser Lake, where Simon Fraser built a North West Company fort in 1806. There is a monument to the great explorer.
□ Sixty miles southwest, behind the 1,500-foot-long Kenney Dam, are the long, narrow "finger" lakes that form the 358-square-mile Kenney Dam Reservoir.

Varennes Que.   19BX
A huge wooden Calvary overlooks the St. Lawrence River here. The figure of Christ is on a cross 80 feet high, those of the two thieves

on crosses about 77 feet high. The Calvary was sculpted in 1776 by Michel Brisset.
□ Varennes' old houses include the Messier house (1712) and the Chaput (1720), Beauchamp (1770) and Beauchemin (1770) houses. All are private residences.
□ The Roman-style Sainte-Anne-de-Varennes Church (c.1885) has a baptismal font resting on lion paws and flanked by scrolls. In the sanctuary are 11 eight-foot statues carved in Norwegian fir by an unknown sculptor in Paris in 1888. They represent the Virgin and Saints Peter, Paul, Anne, Jean-Baptiste, François-Xavier, Thomas Aquinas, Vincent de Paul, Thérèse d'Avila, Joachim and Louis de Gonzague. An 8½-foot Louis Jobin statue of Saint Joseph is in the sacristy.
□ In the center of the village is a procession chapel (1692) dedicated to Saint Anne.

Vaudreuil Que.   7FY/19EY
A stone school built in 1847 houses the Vaudreuil Historical Museum. It has documents, sculpture and paintings dating back to the 1600s and implements, utensils and pine furniture used by early settlers.
□ A tabernacle, candlesticks and an Ecce Homo in Saint-Michel Church (1787) were carved in 1792 by sculptor Philippe Liébert.
□ A plaque in the registry office honors Pierre de Rigaud, marquis de Vaudreuil-Cavagnal, last governor of New France, who surrendered this area to the British in 1760.

Verchères Que.   7FX/19BX
A statue overlooking the St. Lawrence River commemorates Madeleine de Verchères,

Three times life size, this bronze statue of Madeleine de Verchères was sculpted in 1913 by Philippe Hébert. It is at Verchères, the site of the girl's heroic encounter with the Iroquois.

Doukhobor prayerhouse (1917) at Veregin has verandas on four sides. It is still used for Doukhobor services. A small museum contains examples of Doukhobor handicrafts and household articles.

who in 1692, as a 14-year-old, led a defense of her father's seigniorial fort. Her father was in Quebec, her mother in Montreal and the garrison out hunting when Iroquois attacked, killing farmers in the fields. Aided only by her two younger brothers, an old servant, several women and two soldiers, Madeleine stood off the Iroquois for eight days until help arrived.

□ Saint-François-Xavier-de-Verchères Church, built of stone in 1788 and restored after a fire in 1818, has an elaborate reredos with sculpted leaves above a rounded arch. The reredos was carved by Louis Quevillon in 1818-21.

□ A round, stone windmill (c.1700), now without sails but with the original millstones, is one mile northeast. The 26-foot tower has a conical roof typical of mills built in France during that period.

□ A plaque marks the site of a house in which Ludger Duvernay, founder of the Saint-Jean-Baptiste Society (1834), was born in 1799. Verchères was also the birthplace of Calixa Lavallée, who composed the music of "O Canada."

Veregin Sask.   4FX
A Doukhobor prayerhouse here was built in 1917 by Peter Vasilovich Verigin, the legendary Doukhobor leader for whom the town is named. The Doukhobors came here from Russia in 1899. Verigin, who arrived in Canada in 1902, was their theocratic leader from 1886 until his death in a mysterious train explosion in 1924 (*see* Castlegar).

Vernon B.C.   2EY
Exhibits in the Vernon Museum and Archives range from an Indian dugout canoe to a 1908 Metz automobile. There are Salish Indian artifacts, pioneer implements and such turn-of-the-century relics as a livery stable coach and a double cutter. The museum and an art gallery-library are part of the Vernon Civic Center, which includes the city hall, a public safety building and a firehall.

□ Polson Park has a Chinese teahouse, a Japanese garden and a 30-foot floral clock made up of 3,500 plants.

Victoria B.C.   2CZ/12DZ
In the beginning it was a fur-trading post, then a booming gold-rush town. Now it is surely Canada's gentlest city, a civilized place of unhurried streets and enchanting gardens where flowers bloom year-round. "To realize Victoria," wrote Rudyard Kipling, "you must take all that the eye admires in Bournemouth, Torquay, the Isle of Wight, the Happy Valley at Hong Kong, the Doon, Sorrento,

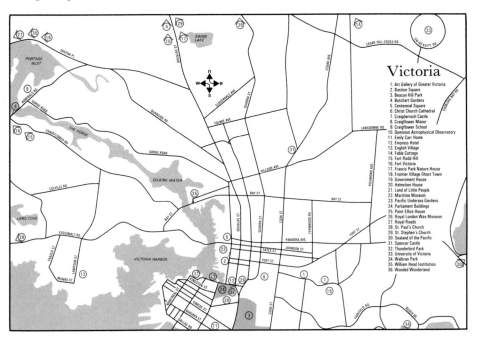

Victoria

1. Art Gallery of Greater Victoria
2. Bastion Square
3. Beacon Hill Park
4. Butchart Gardens
5. Centennial Square
6. Christ Church Cathedral
7. Craigdarroch Castle
8. Craigflower Manor
9. Craigflower School
10. Dominion Astrophysical Observatory
11. Emily Carr Home
12. Empress Hotel
13. English Village
14. Fable Cottage
15. Fort Rodd Hill
16. Francis Park Nature House
17. Frontier Village Ghost Town
18. Government House
19. Government House
20. Helmcken House
21. Land of Little People
22. Maritime Museum
23. Pacific Undersea Gardens
24. Parliament Buildings
25. Point Ellice House
26. Royal London Wax Museum
27. Royal Roads
28. St. Paul's Church
29. St. Stephen's Church
30. Sealand of the Pacific
31. Spencer Castle
32. Thunderbird Park
33. University of Victoria
34. Walbran Park
35. William Head Institution
36. Wooded Wonderland

Malahat Drive on the east coast of Vancouver Island is famous for its scenery (opposite). Victoria's attractions include Hatley Castle (above) at the Royal Roads Military College, totems in Thunderbird Park, beautiful Butchart Gardens and models in the Maritime Museum (below: HMS *Resolution*, in which Capt. James Cook visited Vancouver Island in 1778). Huge Craigdarroch Castle (below, left) houses the Victoria Conservatory of Music. Half-timbered buildings are in English Village.

Camp's Bay, add reminiscences of the Thousand Islands and arrange the whole around the Bay of Naples with some Himalayas for the background."

Victoria, capital of British Columbia, is also Victorian, a bit of England and the Old Empire consciously preserved amid the primitive beauty of Pacific forest, mountain and sea. Some of this is to please the tourists: the double-decker buses and horse-drawn Tally-ho carriages, the fish-and-chip and British souvenir shops. But most of it is natural. The people and city are mainly British by origin; that is reflected in British tweeds and china in the fine shops, white-clad lawn bowlers behind the Crystal Garden, high tea in the Empress Hotel and the crack of cricket bat in Beacon Hill Park.

Victoria is elegant and modern but its past is well honored in its old town reminiscent of gold-rush days, in fine museums, art galleries, pioneer houses and even castles. In Thunderbird Park, near the dignified Parliament Buildings, is a forest of brilliant totem poles that evoke the highly developed and ancient Indian civilizations of the Pacific coast. White men did not appear in this area regularly until the late 18th century.

□ Spain's Juan Perez sailed to Vancouver Island's west coast in 1774. Four years later Capt. James Cook arrived nearby and claimed the island for England, touching off dispute. In 1792 Capt. George Vancouver appeared in HMS *Discovery* for negotiations, and Spain peacefully relinquished her claims in 1795 (*see* Friendly Cove).

Victoria was not settled until 1843. The Hudson's Bay Company needed a new headquarters to replace Fort Vancouver (Wash.), about to be absorbed into the United States with settlement of the Oregon Boundary dispute. HBC factor James Douglas built Fort Victoria across Juan de Fuca Strait, an insular base with a defensible harbor and arable land. This fortified British claims to the whole island; these were recognized in the boundary settlement of 1846. The Crown colony of Vancouver Island was created in 1849.

The 1858 gold rush on the mainland changed Fort Victoria from a frontier fur-trading outpost to a thriving commercial and government center. As the only port in British Columbia, Victoria was the provisioning base for the mining areas and staging point for thousands of gold-hungry prospectors. It was incorporated as a city in 1862. The colonies of Vancouver Island and British Columbia were joined in 1866; two years later Victoria became the capital and remained so when British Columbia joined Confederation in 1871. The city continued to be an administrative center and defense bastion—it was a Royal Navy base from 1865 to 1905—but commercial supremacy passed to Vancouver after completion of the CPR.

Victoria's prime calling now is government service, supplemented by a strong tourist industry and by forest products, fishing, shipbuilding and farming. There is an outer harbor for ocean fishing, liners and coastal shipping, and an inner harbor for ferries, pleasure craft and float planes.

ART GALLERY OF GREATER VICTORIA (1) A noteworthy Oriental collection includes an Arita ware porcelain figure of an actor and a white jade *Pi* (symbol of heaven) from the Ming dynasty. Canadian artists represented include A.Y. Jackson, David Milne, J.L. Shadbolt, Homer Watson and Emily Carr, a native of Victoria. European works include *Mercury Emerging from a Cloud* (bronze statue) by Auguste Rodin, *Twelfth Night* (oil) by Jan Miense Molenaer and *Madonna and Child with Saint John* (tempera) by Pier Fiorentino.

BASTION SQUARE (2) Once a muddy hangout for gold prospectors and drifters, this restored downtown area has such mid-19th-century buildings as the city's first jail and law courts and first house of assembly.

BEACON HILL PARK (3) Here are a Chinese bell cast in 1627 and brought to Victoria by a Royal Navy officer in 1903; a 128-foot totem pole carved by Mungo Martin (*see* Alert Bay) and a plaque marking Mile 0 of the Trans-Canada Highway. A cairn commemorates Marilyn Bell's swimming of 18-mile Juan de Fuca Strait in 1956 and a plaque records that George VI presented colors to the Royal Canadian Navy here in 1939. A small pebblestone bridge commemorates artist-author Emily Carr (*see* under Emily Carr Home) and a monument honors Scottish poet Robert Burns. Another marker is in memory of a five-year-old child, one of several victims of smallpox on a steamship inbound from San Francisco in 1872. The pesthouse was near here on Dallas Road. Swans in 184-acre Beacon Hill Park are descendants of swans brought here in the 1920s from the Royal Swannery at Cookham-on-Thames in England.

BUTCHART GARDENS (4) This giant flower bowl, 50 feet deep, attracts 300,000 persons a year. The gardens, with several distinctive sections, are planned for year-round blooming. The English rose garden is at its best in summer. The Italian garden has sculptured trees, Florentine arches and statuary and a star-shaped lily pond flanked by beds of seasonal flowers. In the Japanese garden are dwarf trees, maples, flowering cherries, rhododendrons, a secluded waterfall, lacquered bridges and lantern-lit summerhouses on stilts. There is a four-acre sunken garden and a fountain fantasy in the Lake garden.

CENTENNIAL SQUARE (5) Redevelopment has revived this area into a handsome square, with an arcade of shops, the renovated 1878 city hall and the McPherson Playhouse, a refurbished 1912 building that is the center of Vancouver Island's regional and professional theater. A fountain, a gift from neighboring communities in 1962, marks the centennial of Victoria as a city.

CHRIST CHURCH CATHEDRAL (6) An Anglican cathedral built in 1926.

CRAIGDARROCH CASTLE (7) Robert Dunsmuir, "coal king of Vancouver Island," built this great mass of stone and stained glass for

Two Crows in Sunset, in the Art Gallery of Greater Victoria, is a 53-by-29-inch hanging scroll (ink and color on silk) by Matsumura Goshun (1752-1811). In the gallery's *Pi*, a Ming dynasty jade carving 7¼ inches in diámeter, a dragon rises to heaven in a waterspout. Below, in the Point Ellice House: a Victorian fan that belonged to Lady Trutch, wife of British Columbia's first lieutenant-governor, and a tazza, a vase made in London in 1823-24. It is 18½ inches high, of gold and silver weighing 356 ounces.

his wife. It was completed only after his death in 1889, and now houses a music conservatory.

CRAIGFLOWER MANOR (8) A Hudson's Bay Company farm here once supplied Fort Victoria with fruit and vegetables, meat and dairy products. Now a museum and a national historic site, the house contains furnishings and possessions of Kenneth McKenzie, the company representative who lived in it.

CRAIGFLOWER SCHOOL (9) The oldest (1855) standing schoolhouse west of the Great Lakes is a museum of pioneer life. It has a schoolroom, farm implements and a stagecoach.

DOMINION ASTROPHYSICAL OBSERVATORY (10) Visitors who tour the observatory peer through the 72-inch telescope, hear talks about astronomy and see photo displays of meteorites, stars and planets.

EMILY CARR HOME (11) Emily Carr was born Dec. 13, 1871, in this two-story frame house and spent part of her childhood here, later describing it in her book *The House of Small.* The house has been restored by the Junior Chamber of Commerce in cooperation with the federal government. Reproductions of Miss Carr's paintings (no originals because of fire risk) hang on the walls and some of her letters and drawings are on display. Emily

Carr created about 1,000 major paintings and drawings. The B.C. government owns 141 and displays some at the provincial museum. Miss Carr lived among B.C. Indians, who called her Klee Wyck (The Laughing One). Her book of that title won a Governor-General's Award in 1941.

EMPRESS HOTEL (12) This imposing pile on the harbor front, in its elaborate lawns and gardens, is an historic site in its own right, as well as a good place to stay. The city's social center, the hotel was opened by the CPR in 1908 and has undergone major renovations since. High tea, with thin sandwiches and small cakes, is served in the lobby each afternoon. But there is also rock music and dancing in the basement discotheque.

ENGLISH VILLAGE (13) Buildings on Chaucer Lane and Lampson Street include replicas of Shakespeare's birthplace and Anne Hathaway's thatched-roof cottage. There are collections of armor, crossbows, flintlocks and 16th- and 17th-century furniture.

FABLE COTTAGE (14) A house with barrel doors, a walk-through fireplace, old guns, castle keys and spinning wheels. Animated dwarfs work and play in Enchanted Forest.

FORT RODD HILL (15) This large fort, which

Family Group, Jack Harman's life-size bronze, is in Colombo Place, part of the Heritage Court complex at the B.C. Parliament Buildings. A three-foot-high head (left) in the provincial museum is from a cedar frontal post on a Haida structure in the Queen Charlotte Islands. A Tsimshian mask carved from birch by Walter Harris of Kispiox has bone teeth; a dentalium shell pierces the nose.

dates from 1895 and was used until 1956, is a national historic park. An exhibition of maps, charts and photographs depicts the evolution of Victoria and Esquimalt coastal defenses from 1878. Nearby Fisgard Lighthouse has been operated since 1860.

FORT VICTORIA (16) A plaque marks the site of the HBC fort (1843) that was the beginning of Victoria. A nearby replica of the fort contains a museum.

FRANCIS PARK NATURE HOUSE (17) A wildlife sanctuary, with nature displays, conducted tours, trail hikes and talks.

FRONTIER VILLAGE GHOST TOWN (18) Twenty-six buildings and scenes, and antiques, wagons, farm implements, machinery, totem poles and a museum of Indian artifacts.

GOVERNMENT HOUSE (19) The residence of the lieutenant governor is set among elegant gardens that are open to the public.

HELMCKEN HOUSE (20) Built in 1852 by J.S. Helmcken, a young physician and pharmacist from London, the house is a provincial museum. Exhibits that include the doctor's medical instruments provide a glimpse of his life as a frontier physician. Helmcken came to Fort Victoria in 1850, at 25, as medical officer for the Hudson's Bay Company. He built his house of logs, squared in the forest and brought to Victoria by water. He served a wide area, mixing remedies at home and sending them by canoe and packhorse to other company forts. Helmcken was the first speaker of the legislative assembly and helped negotiate British Columbia's entry into Confederation in 1871.

LAND OF LITTLE PEOPLE (21) Carved Lilliputian figures; houses, stores, a train, a factory, all to scale.

MARITIME MUSEUM (22) The museum has scale models of an Indian canoe, a Chinese junk and a Viking longboat, navy ships, merchant vessels and fishing, sealing and whaling boats. There are ships' tools, bells, guns and figureheads, naval uniforms, and a cat-o'-nine-tails. A prize exhibit is the 37-foot *Tilikum,* a dugout canoe modified to a three-masted schooner that in 1901-4 Capt. J.C. Voss sailed from Victoria around the Cape of Good Hope to England. The museum also has a model (c.1765) of a 40-gun frigate; a model of the Hudson's Bay Company *Beaver* (1834), the first steamship in the north Pacific, and a model of S.S. *Moyie* (*see* Kaslo).

PACIFIC UNDERSEA GARDENS (23) Sea life seen through windows below the surface of the inner harbor; scuba-diving shows; close-ups of marine creatures, such as wolf eel and octopus, brought to windows by divers.

PARLIAMENT BUILDINGS (24) These imposing buildings house the B.C. government. Nearby is the Heritage Court complex of museums, galleries and archives with their compelling panorama of B.C. life. The main Parliament Building (1898) is of native gray stone roofed with native slates. The steps and landings are of B.C. granite. On top of the great copper-covered dome, 165 feet from the ground, is a statue of Capt. George Vancouver, first circumnavigator of Vancouver Island. On the grounds are a statue of Queen Victoria, the British Columbia cenotaph and an obelisk in memory of James Douglas, the founder of Victoria. In the rotundas are murals and paintings by George Southwell. Across a courtyard from the main building are the provincial museum and archives and the 62-bell Netherlands Centennial Carillon, Canada's biggest. It was a gift to the people of British Columbia in 1967 from Canadians of Dutch origin. A great dugout canoe with eight carved wooden figures of Nootka Indian whalers dominates the first floor of the museum. There are Emily Carr paintings, dioramas of wildlife in natural habitat and fine displays of Indian life and artifacts. A section re-creating the story of British Columbia has an old main street, a sawmill, a mine shaft, a fish-packing house, farm scenes, gold diggings, fur-trade paths and a replica of Captain Cook's HMS *Discovery.*

POINT ELLICE HOUSE (25) A collection of Victorian and Edwardian furnishings in the home (1861) of Peter O'Reilly, one of the founders of British Columbia (first gold commissioner, a county judge, a legislative councillor, a supporter of Confederation).

ROYAL LONDON WAX MUSEUM (26) More than 130 life-size figures include Lincoln, Napoleon, Queen Victoria and members of the present Royal Family.

ROYAL ROADS (27) This military college is renowned for its gardens as well as its production of officers.

ST. PAUL'S CHURCH (28) Here are mementoes of the sea, including a life preserver from HMS *Condor,* a warship that vanished with all hands en route to Hawaii in 1905.

ST. STEPHEN'S CHURCH (29) Oldest church on Vancouver Island (1862).

SEALAND OF THE PACIFIC (30) A glassed-in room provides below-sea-level views of seals, sea lions, eels and sea plumes; there is a killer whale in another pool.

SPENCER CASTLE (31) A Tudor-like mansion built early in this century. A four-story granite turret surrounded by a battlement gives a panoramic view of the ocean, the islands and mountains.

THUNDERBIRD PARK (32) A collection of totem poles shows the styles of the Haida, Kwakiutl, Tsimshian, Bella Coola, Nootka and Coast Salish. The carvings include house-frontal, heraldic, memorial and mortuary poles, houseposts and welcome figures. Here is the house of Mungo Martin, a famous Kwakiutl carver (*see* Alert Bay). Most of the Thunderbird Park poles were carved between 1850 and 1890. As they decay, they are copied, thus preserving traditional designs. The park has dugout canoes made from cedar logs with fire and adze, and a replica of a 19th-century Kwakiutl house.

UNIVERSITY OF VICTORIA (33) The spacious, green campus has Mount Douglas as a scenic backdrop. Formerly Victoria College and affiliated with UBC, it now is an autonomous, coeducational, degree-granting university. Its Maltwood Memorial Museum of Historic Art has an important collection of Oriental pottery. There are Sung and Ming dynasty vases and paintings on silk (among them *Waterlilies, Magpies on a Branch* and *Lady and Stork in Landscape,* all Ming dynasty). There are a Wei third-century unglazed head of a horse and a 16-inch Ming sculpture of the *God of Longevity.*

WALBRAN PARK (34) A granite marker tells of Spanish and English exploration of Juan de Fuca Strait.

WILLIAM HEAD INSTITUTION (35) This rocky thrust into the strait, site of a medium-security penitentiary since 1959, is an historic spot. From 1881 William Head was a quarantine station where immigrants' health was checked. Beneath the choppy waters around the Head lie the hulks of some 35 ships, many driven by storms to founder on the rock-studded coastline. Sunken earth mounds and weathered crosses mark the lonely graves of would-be immigrants.

WOODED WONDERLAND (36) A fairy-tale setting in Beaver Lake Park for displays of storybook characters and scenes.

Victoria Beach N.S.   22BW
A tablet commemorates a pony express that helped speed news from Britain to the United States in 1849, the year after a telegraph line was opened in Saint John, N.B. Dispatches brought to Halifax by Cunard ships were sped 144 miles to Victoria Beach (with fresh horses every 12 miles), then by steamer across the Bay of Fundy to Saint John for relay to New York. The express was suspended at the end of 1849 when Halifax and Saint John were linked by telegraph via Amherst, N.S.

Victoria Harbour Ont.   7CY/17BV
The site of St. Louis, a Huron village and Jesuit mission where Iroquois captured the missionaries Jean de Brébeuf and Gabriel Lalemant, is marked by a cairn two miles south. (*See* Midland)

Victoriaville Que.   9AX/20AY
Sainte-Victoire Church, built of stone in 1897, has an ornate carved wooden interior. The walls and vault are covered with paintings by anonymous artists depicting scenes from the lives of Christ and the Virgin. The vault is supported by sculpted wooden columns.

Victoriaville Hockey Stick Ltd., the world's biggest manufacturer, makes 3,500,000 sticks a year. Seventy percent are sold in Canada. The handles are white ash, the blades maple.

Viking Alta. 4BX

The Ribstones, two quartzite rocks important in Cree Indian hunting rituals, are on high ground nine miles southeast. In each is a half-inch-deep sunk relief of a buffalo backbone and ribs, painstakingly abraded with pebbles and sand an estimated 1,000 years ago. Buffalo used to be sacrificed on the stones to ensure a successful hunt.

□ The Viking Historical Society Museum, a log house built by Scandinavian settlers in 1903, contains pioneer artifacts and a model of a gas well drilled in Viking in 1913.

Ville-Marie Que. 7CW

A three-day canoe race in August covers 122 miles from Ville-Marie to North Bay, Ont. Two-man teams paddle 49 miles the first day, across Lake Témiscamingue to Témiscaming. On the second day they portage several times along a 35-mile stretch of the Ottawa River to Mattawa, Ont. The third day they paddle 38 miles by way of the Mattawa River, Talon Lake and Trout Lake, making 12 portages.

□ Foundations and two chimneys of Fort Témiscamingue, built by the Compagnie du Nord-Ouest in 1720, have been designated as a national historic site. Artifacts uncovered during an archaeological dig were retained for display in a museum to be built on the site. A cairn at a nearby Lake Témiscamingue promontory called La Passe commemorates a French troop that in 1686 marched from Montreal to attack English forts on James Bay. The force of about 100 men was led by the Chevalier de Troyes and the Le Moyne brothers, Pierre and Jacques.

□ Artists display paintings, pottery and copper enamel work at a four-day commercial and industrial exposition in August. Indians exhibit beaded moccasins, necklaces, vests, lamps and toys.

Vimy Ridge Que. 20BY

Visitors to the Asbestos Corporation's Normandie mine and mill here see asbestos taken from the ground, crushed and processed.

Vineland Ont. 7CZ/17CY

The Rittermere Craft Studio has a display of rug hooking and tapestry-making.

Virden Man. 4FY

Discoveries in the 1950s—here and at Daly, 12 miles southwest—have made this Manitoba's chief oil-producing area. A few of 700-odd wells here are within the town. Cairns near Virden mark the sites of the first producing well and of Fort Montagne à Bosse, built by the North West Company in 1790.

□ The Pioneer Home Museum is a house (c.1888) built of Virden brick (from high quality local clay) and restored and refurnished in the styles of the 1880s. Furniture includes a rosewood piano, a rope bed and rocking chair and homemade cabinets stained with a mixture of lampblack and berry juice.

The Ribstones near Viking are rocks at which Indians left beads, tobacco and meat in elaborate hunting rituals. One stone (foreground), about 30 inches by 15, and 20 inches high, represents a cow buffalo. The other, about 50 inches by 35, represents a bull buffalo.

Virginiatown Ont. 7CV

At Kerr-Addison, one of North America's biggest gold mines (more than 800 tons of ore a day), visitors see crushing, screening and extraction of gold. Tours are in July only.

Vittoria Ont. 7BZ/17AZ

On the grounds of red brick Gothic-style Woodhouse United Church (c.1850), two miles south, is a plaque commemorating Egerton Ryerson, who was born near here in 1803. Ryerson, an influential Methodist, writer, publisher and educationist, wrote a report in 1846 on which the educational system of Ontario was based. At Christ Church is a plaque commemorating Vittoria as the capital of the London District in 1815-25. The white frame Anglican church dates from about 1845.

W

Wabush Nfld.   10GX
This town and neighboring Labrador City
were built as the low-grade iron deposits of
the southern Labrador trough were first exploited in the 1960s.

Wainwright Alta.   4BX
A reconstructed post office with furniture and
equipment from the early 1900s, when the
Wainwright district was settled, is part of the
Wainwright Museum.

Wakefield Que.   7EX/18CW
The MacLaren gristmill, a three-story stone
building erected on the Lapêche River in
1835, still operates. On a bank above the mill
is the brick house of David MacLaren, who
bought the mill in 1844 and who also ran
lumbering and brick-making businesses and
a general store here. The mill and house are
owned by the National Capital Commission.
  □ In summer the National Capital Commission runs steam train excursions from Ottawa to Wakefield and return. The engine is
turned around on a hand-pushed turntable.
  □ Canada's 19th prime minister, Lester
Bowles Pearson, is buried in the MacLaren
Cemetery on a hill overlooking the village
and the Gatineau River.
  □ A 288-foot covered bridge crosses the Gatineau River in Wakefield.

Walhachin B.C.   2DY
Shattered irrigation flumes and withered apple trees are remnants of a "garden of Eden"
that weather and war destroyed. The Marquis of Anglesey, persuaded in 1907 that fruit
could be grown on the dry sagebrush tableland above the Thompson River here, had
ditches and flumes built to bring water from
a nearby lake. By 1911 some 3,000 acres had
been irrigated and a prosperous town started
to grow. But three years later, at the outset of
World War I, many of Walhachin's settlers,
retired Imperial Army officers, were recalled

to service. When a torrential rain badly damaged the flumes, there were too few settlers at
home to repair them—and all too few of the
others returned from the battlefields. Walhachin without its men, like the orchards without water, slowly died.

Wallace N.S.   9EY/23CX
Simon Newcomb (1835-1909), a Wallace na-
tive who became a world-famous astronomer,
is honored by a monument near the ruins of
his boyhood home. Newcomb migrated to the
United States at 18. He served at the United
States Naval Observatory in Washington and
over a 20-year period built up the theory and
tables of the planetary system.

Wardner B.C.   2FZ/13AZ
The Kootenay Trout Hatchery, five miles
north, raises some 4,000,000 fish a year. One
aquarium, eight feet long, is a simulated
stream in which is shown the raising of trout
from the collection of roe to the release of fry
and fingerlings.

Warminster Ont.   17CV
Near here is the site of Cahiagué, the principal village of the Huron nation and the biggest Indian community in what now is Canada. Champlain, who wintered at Cahiagué in
1615-16, recorded that it had some 200 longhouses inside a double palisade.

Warsaw Ont.   7CY/17EW
Along cave trails at the Warsaw Caves Conservation Area, about four miles northeast,
are underground streams and fossils of shellfish, plants, snails and a giant dragonfly. One
cave is 285 feet long. Turbulent water formed
the caves perhaps 10,000 years ago.

Wasaga Beach Ont.   17BV
The Museum of the Upper Lakes is on an is-
land formed in the Nottawasaga River by silt
and sand that collected around the hull of a

HMS _Nancy_'s career is
highlighted at the Museum
of the Upper Lakes at Wasaga Beach. Outside (and seen
here between ship models)
is _Nancy_'s hull, recovered
from the Nottawasaga River
in 1927, more than a century after she was sunk. Inside
is a 12-foot model of the
schooner and a replica of
her figurehead (left). In the
museum, which traces 300
years of upper Great Lakes
history, are pilotage, chart-
ing and navigation instruments, including a replica of
a 17th-century astrolabe.
There are cannon, cutlasses
and boarding pikes.

Wasaga Beach / 387

ship sunk in the War of 1812. The schooner *Nancy*, originally a North West Company trader, was fitted out by the Royal Navy as a lightly armed supply vessel. In August 1814 she was sunk by American schooners that included *Scorpion* and *Tigress*—which were captured in revenge by *Nancy*'s crew (*see* Thessalon). The nearby Electronic Theater presents a sound-and-light show, telling the story of *Nancy* and of subsequent naval battles between Canada and the United States.

□ A plaque commemorates the flight of Leonard Reid and James Ayling from Wasaga Beach to Heston, England, in August 1934, the first nonstop flight from the Canadian mainland to Britain.

□ The Ontario Zoological and Botanical Park has more than 1,000 species of animals and birds and more than 2,500 botanical specimens. The 55-acre wooded site has Nile hippopotamuses, jaguars, elephants, water buffalo, cheetahs, rock wallabies and African crowned cranes.

□ Wasaga Beach, nine miles of hard-packed sand on the shore of Georgian Bay, is claimed to be the longest and safest freshwater beach in the world.

Wasdell Falls Ont.   17CV
Ontario Hydro's first generating station (1914) is on the Severn River here. It operated until 1955.

Waterloo Ont.   17AY
Some 40 percent of Waterloo County people are descendants of Mennonite and German

Old ways die hard among descendants of the pioneers who settled near Waterloo, Ont. Traditional Mennonite clothing is common; so are old German markets, food, music, celebrations.

The Swordsman, a 37-by-26-inch banner by Norman Laliberté, is at the University of Waterloo. Wool appliqués are sewn on a wool background.

pioneers who settled here soon after 1800. The communities these German-speaking colonists built include the twin cities of Kitchener (*see entry*) and Waterloo and communities such as New Hamburg, Petersburg, Heidelberg and Conestogo.

LAUREL CREEK CONSERVATION AREA Hiking trails around a dam and reservoir on Laurel Creek.

UNIVERSITY OF WATERLOO On this 1,000-acre campus are colleges affiliated with the

story, wood-framed building became a museum in 1961. One curiosity is an eight-foot wooden figure of Justice that was carved in 1842 and once surmounted the United Counties Courthouse in Brockville.

Wetaskiwin Alta.   4AX/14FX
An Innes car built in Scotland in 1899 (and believed the only one left) is among hundreds of antique cars at the Reynolds Museum. The Innes has a wood frame, tiller steering, wagon wheels and solid rubber tires. A gas economy feature is a compression release enabling the car to run on one cylinder.

The museum has more than 1,000 old cars, trucks, airplanes, tractors, steam engines and carriages. It has a 1917 Curtiss JND4 "Jenny" biplane with wood fuselage and water-cooled engine and a 1916 Renault V8 airplane engine. There are a 1911 Hupp Yeats electric car with solid rubber tires and tiller steering (driven only 394 miles), a 1908 Baker electric with leather fenders, a 1912 Locomobile (manufactured without a windshield), and the only existing Canadian-built Menard automobile (1908).

Weyburn Sask.   4EZ
Ten mosaic panels between the spokes of a brass-rimmed mahogany wagon wheel at city hall depict the history of Weyburn from Indian days. The 2,000-pound wheel is some 13 feet in diameter; the rim is 41½ feet. In the multicolored Italian glass tile of the mosaics are embedded badges of the 152nd Battalion, in which Weyburn men served in World War I, and the South Saskatchewan Regiment, of Dieppe raid and other World War II fame.

□ Indian artifacts at the Soo Line Historical Museum include weapons, pipes, snowshoes, ceremonial costumes of buckskin and blue beading, and coup sticks from which scalps were dangled to recall exploits in battle.

□ The first office (1911) of Dr. William Graham Mainprize, a pioneer physician, is preserved in Dr. Mainprize Regional Park, 35 miles southeast.

Whitby Ont.   7CY/17DX
Ontario Ladies' College, 100 years old in 1974, is in a castle built in 1859-62 by an entrepreneur who dreamed of entertaining royalty. Soon after the dream was realized (Prince Arthur, third son of Queen Victoria, visited Trafalgar Castle in 1869), Nelson G. Reynolds sold the huge structure to the Methodist Church. The college has a stained glass window with the coats of arms of Canada, England, Scotland and Ireland—and of Reynolds' family and his wife's.

□ The Centennial Building, in a former courthouse (1853), is a community center with archives that include letters written by Reynolds in 1853-54.

□ The Whitby Historical Society Museum is in a house built in 1804-5 by Jabez Lynde, a United Empire Loyalist. The two-story building of clapboard and stucco coating was once considered the finest house between

"Grandfather rock" (left) used by an Indian medicine man to invoke the spirits is displayed in the Soo Line Historical Museum at Weyburn. It is nine inches by five. A slightly smaller "effigy head" was used in ritual dances.

York (Toronto) and Kingston. Displays include a coffin (square) grand piano (1868).

□ A onetime Grand Trunk Railway station, built in 1903, houses Whitby Arts Incorporated, where artists exhibit paintings, glassware and pottery. The station was rescued from demolition in 1970.

Whitehorse Y.T.   1AW
This picturesque community lies at a wide bend in the Yukon River, just north of rapids and a canyon that were one of the most hazardous stretches of the Trail of '98. The wild water of Miles Canyon, where gold-seekers risked their lives during the early days of the rush to the Klondike, has been tamed and is one of Whitehorse's tourist attractions. Others are the stern-wheeler *Klondike*, a log "skyscraper" and Sam McGee's cabin (moved here from Lake Laberge, where it had been when Robert Service wrote *The Cremation of Sam McGee*). Still another is the scenic route of the White Pass and Yukon, a railway that links Whitehorse and Skagway, Alaska.

Whitehorse, the Yukon's capital (since 1952) and largest city (15,300), came into being in 1898 as thousands of would-be prospectors climbed the White and Chilkoot passes from Alaska and, just south of here, started a 400-mile journey down the Yukon River to Dawson. Still to be seen are traces of the first settlement, Canyon City, and the route of a tramway built in 1897-98. In horse-drawn carts with metal wheels, miners and their supplies were carried four miles along the log rails of the tramway, bypassing the rapids and the turbulent current of the canyon.

The railway from Skagway was completed in 1900, winding near the original White Pass Trail of the gold-seekers, through some of the Yukon's most awesome terrain. It too bypassed the rapids; now prospectors transferred at Whitehorse from train to stern-wheeler for the rest of the journey to Dawson. The 110-mile White Pass and Yukon Route was the world's first containerized railway (1953) and is still the world's longest commercial narrow-gauge railway.

The first stern-wheeler *Klondike* (1929) was sunk. Another, built in 1937 to carry silver and lead concentrates as well as passengers, later had extra staterooms added. She was

One of the last frontiers, the Yukon is a land of high mountains, big game, swift rivers and the midnight sun. Above: winter on Bennett Lake near Carcross (*see entry*). Beadwork by Loucheux Indians at Old Crow is in the W.D. MacBride Museum in Whitehorse. Outside is a replica of a cart from a Klondike Gold Rush tramway.

beached here in 1955, the last of the Yukon River stern-wheelers.

The building of the Alaska Highway (*see* Dawson Creek) in 1942 brought thousands of men to Whitehorse and confirmed its position as the Yukon's main transportation center. Today's 110-mile gravel road (summer use only) from Whitehorse to Skagway, via Carcross, is part of the Klondike Highway.

□ A tramcar from the log tramway, an early White Pass locomotive and Whitehorse's first telegraph office (1900) are among exhibits at the W.D. MacBride Historical Society Museum. A 2,950-pound copper nugget from the White River country, 200 miles northwest, is the largest ever found in the Yukon.

□ The MV *Schwatka* makes daily cruises through 300-foot-long Miles Canyon from Schwatka Lake, formed by a hydroelectric project that tamed the Whitehorse Rapids in 1958. The Robert Lowe suspension bridge crosses the canyon.

□ A log church built in 1900 served as the cathedral of the Yukon until Christ Church Cathedral was built next door in 1959. The cathedral's altar frontal of beaded caribou hide was made by the people of Old Crow, Y.T. The old log church is a museum of the Yukon's religious history. Among the exhibits is a Communion set that belonged to Bishop William Carpenter Bompas (*see* Carcross) and vestry minutes written by Robert Service. Whitehorse's tallest buildings include a three-story log one erected in 1946.

□ At the Indian Burial Ground many of the graves are covered with small houses believed by the Tlingit Indians to protect the spirits of the dead.

□ At Takhini Hot Springs, 16 miles northwest, 118-degree mineral water is cooled to 96 degrees and fed to a swimming pool.

□ In February the city has a three-day Sourdough Rendezvous attended by Yukoners (sourdoughs) from across the territory. Citizens dress in the colorful costumes of dance-hall girls and Klondike pioneers. There are dogsled races, snowshoe races—one of these is on a three-mile course on the Yukon River—flour-packing and ice-sculpture contests.

□ The Polar Games for children from all parts of the Yukon are held here in winter. Whitehorse is one site of the Arctic Games; others are Yellowknife and Hay River, N.W.T., Anchorage and Fairbanks, Alaska.

White Lake Ont. 7DY/18CX
The Waba Cottage Museum is a reconstruction of the summer home of Archibald McNab, the laird of McNab Township (*see* Arnprior).

Whitewood Sask. 4FY
A lone gabled frame house in St. Hubert, 15 miles south, is the remnant of a village established in the early 1900s by "the French counts of St. Hubert." French noblemen who settled here launched several unsuccessful commercial undertakings and all had left the village (most of them returning to France) by the start of World War I.

Whitney Ont. 7DX
The east gate and headquarters of 2,910-square-mile Algonquin Provincial Park are three miles northwest. Highway 60 runs for 37 miles through the southern part of the park

(to Huntsville, 70 miles west of Whitney) but most of the vast wilderness is accessible only by canoe or on foot. The variety of canoe routes on Algonquin's 2,500 lakes is endless. There are hundreds of portages. In a logging exhibit near the highway are a reconstructed primitive log cabin with no windows or chimney (known as a "camboose" camp), a "saddleback" locomotive, an "alligator" or sidewheeler, and showcases of objects describing 19th-century logging activities in the park, when white pine from here formed a large part of Ontario's lumber production. A 40-foot totem pole on Canoe Lake commemorates artist and woodsman Tom Thomson, who was drowned in the lake in 1917.

Other park features include marked nature trails and conducted hikes. Public wolf howls are held toward the end of August: visitors, sometimes as many as 1,400, are gathered at a spot frequented by wolves. Human howls are often greeted with answering howls from the wolves.

Wiarton Ont. 7BY
Ojibway Indians have turned 560 acres of the Cape Croker Reserve into a park. Visitors camp at the water's edge and on wooded bluffs overlooking Sydney Bay. A 15-mile stretch of the Bruce Trail is in the park.

□ A provincial fish hatchery in Wiarton raises more than 1,200,000 coho salmon and various species of trout a year. Visitors see the roe in incubator trays and young fish up to the fry stage.

Wicklow Ont. 17EX
The oldest Baptist church in Ontario, Wicklow Church is a simple frame building constructed in 1824.

Wilcox Sask. 4EY
The Tower of God, a 55-foot stone structure at Notre Dame College, is emblazoned with symbols and relics of the Christian, Hebrew and Muslim faiths. The tower's Christian wall has a three-by-eight-foot stained glass Window of Christ, donated by the French artist André Rault.

Williamsburg Ont. 7EY/18DX
The house where Dr. W. Mahlon Locke held his internationally known clinic for manipulative surgery still stands here. Locke's treat-

Williams Lake B.C.—This "cowboy capital" of British Columbia, at the heart of the Cariboo (*see* p.44), is the province's biggest cattle-shipping center and the site of a major rodeo. The four-day Williams Lake Stampede in July is the biggest stampede west of Calgary. Most of the bronc busters, steer wrestlers, calf ropers, wild-cow milkers and wild-horse racers are from the ranches of the Cariboo and of the Chilcotin, a vast plateau to the northwest. Some ranches have as many as 8,000 head of cattle. (2DX)

One of Alberta's first Orthodox churches, a log structure built near Chipman by Russian missionaries in 1904, has been restored at the Shandro Museum near Willingdon. The 20-by-25-foot church has an ornate interior with icons, a chandelier and elaborate iconostasis.

ment of arthritis by manipulation of the feet drew patients from many countries in the 1920s and '30s. At one stage he averaged more than 1,000 treatments daily, often receiving patients on his veranda.

Williamstown Ont. 7EY/18EX
The Nor'Westers and Loyalist Museum honors the explorers and other leaders of the North West Company, many of whom lived here and in other parts of Glengarry County. It also pays tribute to the United Empire Loyalists who settled in the area after the American Revolution. The museum is in a red brick Georgian building (1862). Exhibits include a desk that was explorer David Thompson's, a snuffbox that belonged to Simon Fraser (discoverer of the Fraser River), a fur press and furs donated by the Hudson's Bay Company (with which the North West Company was amalgamated in 1821), and a 26-foot birch-bark canoe, made for the museum by Indians in northern Quebec.

Noteworthy houses in and around Williamstown include a red-roofed, white clapboard manor built about 1790 by Sir John Johnson, leader of a group of Loyalists who came here in 1784 from New York's Mohawk Valley. Another is a white frame house built toward the end of the 18th century by the Rev. John Bethune, who founded Upper Canada's first Presbyterian congregation in 1787. It was later (1815-35) the residence of David Thompson. Fraserfield (c.1812), a 23-room stone structure that was one of the finest country houses of its day, was the home of Alexander Fraser, a soldier and legislator. Old St. Andrew's Church (now St. Andrew's United Church) was built in 1812 for the congregation Bethune founded.

The Williamstown Fair, the oldest continuously operated country fair in Canada, is held early in September. It was started about 1810 by Sir John Johnson.

Willingdon Alta. 4BW
The Shandro Historic Village and Pioneer Museum, typical of an early Ukrainian community, is on the farm of Wasyl Zazula, six

Hoodoos of glacial till (intermingled clay, sand, gravel and boulders) tower some 250 feet above Dutch Creek, 15 miles south of Windermere.

Sam Slick: Satire With a Purpose

It was Sam Slick, the fictional Yankee clock peddler created by Thomas Chandler Haliburton, who first said "six of one and half a dozen of the other." Sam was the first to use "stick-in-the-mud" and "upper crust." He first proclaimed that "an ounce of prevention is worth a pound of cure." These and scores of other such phrases were penned by Haliburton at Windsor, N.S., in a house that is now a museum and contains this Sam Slick clock. Haliburton's satire had a serious purpose: he wanted to prod his fellow Nova Scotians into being as industrious and as shrewd as their New England neighbors. "They (Nova Scotians of the 1830s) do nothin' in these parts but eat, drink, smoke, sleep, ride about, lounge at taverns, make speeches at temperance meetin's, and talk about 'House of Assembly,'" said Sam. Nor did he spare the British (although Haliburton eventually moved to England and became a member of Parliament). "Whoever gave them the name of John Bull," Sam once said, "knew what he was about, I tell you; for they are bull-necked, bull-headed folks, I vow. . . ."

miles north. Among the buildings are a one-room schoolhouse, a straw-thatched log house and the dwelling of the first pioneer in the area. There are Ukrainian farm tools and implements, colorful garments and handicrafts.

Willow Bunch Sask.   4EZ
A life-size papier-mâché model of Edouard Beaupré, an eight-foot-three-inch giant born here in 1881, is displayed at the Willow Bunch Museum, along with his clothes, shoes, bed and ring. Beaupré, 14 pounds at birth, grew to 396 pounds with a 58-inch chest, 24-inch neck and size 22 shoes. He joined P.T. Barnum's circus at 17 and died in 1904 from a lung hemorrhage while at the St. Louis (Missouri) Exhibition. The 12-room museum, once a hospital, has an early western kitchen with wood stove, ice cream maker and coffee grinder, an old forge, sewing machine and rope-making machine. An Indian display depicts the story of Sitting Bull, who lived here briefly after the Battle of the Little Big Horn in Montana in 1876.
□ A cairn in 320-acre Jean-Louis Légaré Park, one mile southwest, honors Légaré, a rancher and trader who supplied food to Sitting Bull's Sioux during their years in Canada and in 1881 escorted them back to Montana.

Wilson's Corners Que. *see* Wakefield

Windermere B.C.   2FY/13AW
Outside St. Peter's Anglican Church, often called St. Peter's the Stolen (*see* Golden), is a cairn commemorating the Rev. Henry "Father Pat" Irwin, vicar of the church when it was stolen.

Windsor N.S.   9DY/22EV
The 15-room house in which Judge Thomas Chandler Haliburton wrote the Sam Slick stories is a museum under the jurisdiction of the Nova Scotia Museum. Haliburton built the house in 1834-35, a year before publication of *The Clockmaker*, his first book about the roguish peddler Sam Slick. It and *The Attaché* (1843-44) won Haliburton international acclaim; he went on to build a reputation as the father of Canadian and American humor. The house is furnished to the 1830s and '40s.
□ The Hants County Exhibition, first held in 1765 (and run annually since 1815), is North America's oldest agricultural fair. The September exhibition has horse shows, displays of livestock, fruit, vegetables and local crafts and an ox-pulling event.
□ A blockhouse built by the British in 1750 as part of the defenses of Fort Edward still stands. A cairn marks the site of the fort itself and a section of the moat remains in a park. On the blockhouse is a plaque that records that Flora Macdonald (*see* Hacketts Cove) lived here in 1778-79 when her soldier-husband was stationed at the fort.

Windsor Ont.   7AZ/16AZ
Canada's southernmost city is the nation's fifth biggest industrial producer (after Montreal, Toronto, Hamilton and Vancouver) and, like its neighbor Detroit, a major manufacturer of automobiles. Ford of Canada (1) was established here in 1904, Chrysler (2) in 1925, General Motors (3) in 1928. (All three plants

Windsor
1. Ford of Canada
2. General Motors
3. Chrysler
4. Ambassador Bridge
5. Art Gallery of Windsor
6. Cleary Auditorium
7. Detroit-Windsor Tunnel
8. Dieppe Gardens
9. Great Western Railway
10. Hiram Walker Distillery
11. Hiram Walker Historical Museum
12. Jackson Park
13. Jacques Baby House
14. Jesuit Mission to the Hurons
15. St. Mary's Church
16. Spirit of Windsor
17. The Farm
18. Underground Railroad
19. University of Windsor

Dieppe Gardens, on the Windsor waterfront across from Detroit, commemorate the Dieppe raid of Aug. 19, 1942, in which a local battalion, the Essex Scottish, suffered heavy casualties.

---

may be toured.) Other Windsor industries include textiles, drugs, chemicals, machinery and electronic equipment. Two companies mine vast deposits of salt under the city.

Windsor is Canada's busiest point of entry. Some 10,000,000 persons and 7,500,000 vehicles a year cross into Windsor from Detroit—by the Ambassador Bridge and the tunnel that runs under the Detroit River. An estimated 1,000 Detroiters commute to Windsor, about 4,500 Windsorites to Detroit. From June 24 to July 4 each year the two cities join in an International Freedom Festival.

□ Farmers from Quebec established Ontario's first permanent agricultural settlement here in 1749. The outlines of their long, narrow farms, stretching back from the De-troit River, are seen in aerial photographs. Some streets follow the farm boundaries.

□ Actions in the Windsor area during the War of 1812 included an American invasion in July 1812 and the capture of Detroit by Maj. Gen. Sir Isaac Brock.

AMBASSADOR BRIDGE (4) The world's longest international suspension bridge, with a span of 1,860 feet, was completed in 1929.

ART GALLERY OF WINDSOR (5) The permanent collection, emphasizing Canadian art, includes notable works by Emily Carr, Lawren Harris, A. W. Holdstock, Cornelius Krieghoff, Arthur Lismer, J. E. H. MacDonald, David Milne and Antoine Plamondon. A small collection of works by foreign artists includes *Still Life with Parrot and Monkey* (1677) by Abraham Brueghel. In a collection of Eskimo prints and sculpture are Kenojuak's *Enchanted Owl* and a polar bear by Munamee.

CLEARY AUDITORIUM (6). This multipurpose civic center has an 80-foot-wide stage.

Franco-Ontarian furniture in the Hiram Walker Historical Museum at Windsor includes a rocker (c.1825), probably maple, and an early-19th-century cradle of black walnut (a copy of an 18th-century Quebec style). The rosewood melodeon, made in New York, dates from the 1840s. The ship's anchor outside the museum was taken from the Detroit River north of Amherstburg.

Eastern King, Josef Drenters' wood and metal sculpture, is flanked by Bodo Pfeifer's *Untitled Painting* (acrylic on canvas) (left) and *No. 21,* an oil by Les Levine. Also in the Art Gallery of Windsor is *The Old Pioneer's Companion,* a 16-inch-high bronze by Marc-Aurèle de Foy Suzor-Coté.

DETROIT-WINDSOR TUNNEL (7) The 5,135-foot tunnel, roughly 45 feet below the river, was completed in 1930.

DIEPPE GARDENS (8) A plaque describes the Battle of Windsor, last engagement of the Rebellion of 1837-38. Supporters of William Lyon Mackenzie who crossed from Detroit were defeated by militia under Col. John Prince. He executed five of the invaders.

GREAT WESTERN RAILWAY (9) A plaque commemorates this railway from Niagara Falls to Windsor, completed in 1854.

HIRAM WALKER DISTILLERY (11) Windsor's first industry, a steam flour mill and distillery built by Hiram Walker in 1858, developed into a major supplier of alcoholic beverages. The modern distillery may be visited.

HIRAM WALKER HISTORICAL MUSEUM (11) This two-story, neo-classic-style house, built in 1812, is the oldest brick house west of Niagara. The museum collection features Indian artifacts, firearms, tools, household furniture and equipment and cloth-making devices that include a pioneer loom (1830). A large brass circumferentor (a mid-19th-century surveyor's transit) has a compass demonstrating that Windsor is south of Detroit.

JACKSON PARK (12) More than 400 ornamental lights illuminate colorful sunken flower beds. Mounted on a pedestal in the park is a World War II Lancaster bomber.

JACQUES BABY HOUSE (13) A plaque on this two-story frame house (1808) commemorates Jacques Bâby, inspector general of Upper Canada in 1815-33. He was the brother of François Bâby, whose house is now the Hiram Walker Historical Museum.

JESUIT MISSION TO THE HURONS (14) A plaque tells the story of a mission established at Fort Pontchartrain (Detroit) in 1701 and moved here in 1748. The mission formed the nucleus of the Parish of Assumption, the first in Ontario.

ST. MARY'S CHURCH (15) This Gothic-style Anglican church (1903-4) was designed by American architect Ralph Adams Cram, who also designed the Cathedral of St. John the Divine in New York.

SPIRIT OF WINDSOR (16) A CN locomotive built in 1911 is displayed near modern riverside rail facilities.

THE FARM (17) A children's park with live animals and a mechanical cow.

UNDERGROUND RAILROAD (18) A plaque on Ouellette Avenue commemorates Windsor's role as a major terminus of the escape route used by slaves before the American Civil War.

UNIVERSITY OF WINDSOR (19) Founded in 1857 as Assumption College, it became a university in 1963.

Winnipeg Man.   6BY/15DX

From turbulent beginnings as the Red River Settlement, Winnipeg has become the gateway to the west, the capital of Manitoba and

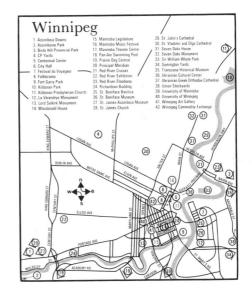

Winnipeg

1. Assiniboia Downs
2. Assiniboine Park
3. Birds Hill Provincial Park
4. CP Yards
5. Centennial Center
6. City Hall
7. Festival du Voyageur
8. Folklorama
9. Fort Garry Park
10. Kildonan Park
11. Kildonan Presbyterian Church
12. La Verendrye Monument
13. Lord Selkirk Monument
14. Macdonald House

15. Manitoba Legislature
16. Manitoba Music Festival
17. Manitoba Theater Center
18. Pan-Am Swimming Pool
19. Prairie Dog Central
20. Principal Meridian
21. Red River Cruises
22. Red River Exhibition
23. Red River Floodway
24. Richardson Building
25. St. Boniface Basilica
26. St. Boniface Museum
27. St. James Assiniboia Museum
28. St. James Church

29. St. John's Cathedral
30. St. Vladimir and Olga Cathedral
31. Seven Oaks House
32. Seven Oaks Monument
33. Sir William Whyte Park
34. Symington Yards
35. Transcona Historical Museum
36. Ukrainian Cultural Center
37. Ukrainian Greek Orthodox Cathedral
38. Union Stockyards
39. University of Manitoba
40. University of Winnipeg
41. Winnipeg Art Gallery
42. Winnipeg Commodity Exchange

Canada's fourth largest city. Amalgamated with 11 suburban municipalities in 1972, it now has a population close to 600,000, better than half Manitoba's total. St. Boniface, now part of Winnipeg, is the largest French-speaking community outside Quebec, the guardian of French culture in the west.

□ When Lord Selkirk founded the Red River Settlement in 1812, on land granted by the Hudson's Bay Company, the rival North West Company feared it would threaten the supply of pemmican for fur-trading posts farther west. In a clash at Seven Oaks in 1816, Nor'Westers murdered about 20 settlers. There was more trouble in 1869 when the Métis, under Louis Riel, rebelled and formed a provisional government (*see* Batoche).

□ With the coming of the CPR in 1881, Winnipeg's location at the junction of the Red and Assiniboine rivers made the city a major railway center. Today the CP yards are the largest privately-owned yards in North America; the CN's computerized Symington Yards are among the most modern in the world.

□ In 1950 a Red River flood forced evacuation of Winnipeg and led to construction of a 29.4-mile floodway.

□ Winnipeg is noted for its beautiful churches and spacious avenues and for the famous intersection of broad, busy Portage Avenue and Main Street. The city has the Commonwealth's largest stockyards and Canada's only commodity futures market.

□ In midsummer a CN train leaves Winnipeg on a 2,230-mile tour of northern Manitoba. Called the Churchill Special, the train weaves around Lake Manitoba to Dauphin and The Pas before crossing 500 miles of tundra and muskeg to Churchill (*see entry*).

□ In January more than 300 snowmobiles leave Winnipeg on a four-day, 500-mile race to St. Paul, Minn. The finish of this St. Paul Winter Carnival International "500" Snowmobile Race, which has stopovers in Crookston, Walker and Alexandria, Minn., opens the St. Paul Winter Carnival.

ASSINIBOIA DOWNS (1) The $35,000 Manitoba Derby for Canadian-bred three-year-olds is run here in September.

ASSINIBOINE PARK (2) This park has a zoo with such exotic animals as the snow leopard, Pere David's deer, hyena, vicuna, common wombat, ruffed lemur and African lion. The North American collection has polar and other bears, bison, moose and elk. There are a tropical house with reptiles, tropical birds and giant tortoises, a children's zoo with domestic and farmyard animals, and an aviary. Assiniboine Park has an English garden, a conservatory and a duck pond.

BIRDS HILL PROVINCIAL PARK (3) The 8,300-acre park, 14 miles northeast, has an 80-acre man-made lake.

CP YARDS (4) They may be seen from the Salter Street and Arlington Street bridges.

CENTENNIAL CENTER (5) It contains the Manitoba Museum of Man and Nature, a large concert hall and a planetarium. There are

Polar bears and bison: the real thing at Winnipeg's Assiniboine Park, life-size bronzes in the lobby of the Manitoba Legislature . . . the pit of the Winnipeg Commodity Exchange, the plaza and planetarium of the Centennial Center, a replica of the Hudson's Bay Company ship *Nonsuch* . . . the domes of the Ukrainian Greek Orthodox Cathedral, the facade of old St. Boniface Basilica incorporated into the rebuilt structure . . . a Chinese dragon dance during Folklorama (an ethnic festival in August) and a youth festival at the Manitoba Theater Center.

replicas of a teepee, a sod hut, a settler's cabin and a Red River cart. The museum has two rare rabbit-skin blankets, a caribou-skin coat, a buffalo robe with painted war scenes, a stained glass window depicting one Métis buffalo hunt and a diorama of another. The concert hall is the home of the Royal Winnipeg Ballet, the Manitoba Opera and the Winnipeg Symphony. The domed planetarium is one of North America's finest.

CITY HALL (6) The council building, connected to the administrative building by an ornamental mall, may be toured.

FESTIVAL DU VOYAGEUR (7) Carnival fun and French-Canadian food, music and dancing enliven St. Boniface during the week-long Festival du Voyageur in February. The pre-Lenten celebrations include a torchlight parade, dogsled and snowshoe races, a fiddling contest, curling, fireworks—and pea soup at all outdoor activities. There are snow and ice sculptures, ice mazes, a toboggan slide and an illuminated ice palace. Traditional French food is served in several auditoriums redecorated as trading posts.

FOLKLORAMA (8) Visitors sample more than 30 ethnic cultures during Folklorama, a one-week August festival. Each group has a pavilion in a church or club where it serves its national dishes, demonstrates ethnic crafts and displays costumes and art works. The festival begins with decorated yachts and cruisers sailing down the Red River to symbolize the arrival of the Red River settlers.

FORT GARRY PARK (9) One gate of the Hudson's Bay Company's Upper Fort Garry (1835) still stands. A tablet commemorates this and other forts at the forks of the Red and Assiniboine rivers: the French Fort Rouge (1738), the North West Company's Fort Gibraltar (1804) and an 1821 HBC fort.

KILDONAN PARK (10) Musicals are performed at Rainbow Stage, a 2,342-seat outdoor theater, in July and August. In the 98-acre park is a monument to Peguis, the Saulteaux chief who aided survivors of the Seven Oaks massacre and signed a treaty with Lord Selkirk in 1817. A two-day Highland dancing competition is held here in June.

KILDONAN PRESBYTERIAN CHURCH (11) Western Canada's first Presbyterian church (1854).

LA VERENDRYE MONUMENT (12) This monu-

The Winnipeg Art Gallery (above) has nine galleries on the third floor, an outdoor sculpture garden on the fourth. The permanent collection includes Anne Kahane's wood polychrome sculpture *Rain*; Esther Warkov's *Night Riders*, acrylic on canvas; and Raoul Dufy's *La Jetée à Trouville*, an oil painting.

---

ment honors Pierre de La Vérendrye. He and his sons were the first white men to reach the junction of the Red and Assiniboine rivers. In 1738 La Vérendrye constructed Fort Rouge, the first building on the site of Winnipeg. Nearby is a plaque marking the formal proclamation of the Red River Settlement on Sept. 4, 1812.

LORD SELKIRK MONUMENT (13) A plaque on a base of native limestone commemorates the founder of the Red River Settlement.

MACDONALD HOUSE (14) A beautiful Victorian house restored to the era of its construction in 1895, it was the home of Sir Hugh John Macdonald, son of Canada's first prime minister and himself the first premier of Manitoba. Known as Dalnavert, it was one of four Winnipeg houses with electricity when Sir Hugh built it. In the front hall is a stained-glass Macdonald coat of arms.

MANITOBA LEGISLATURE (15) Built (1913-19) in classic Greek style, it has marble steps leading from the lobby to the Legislative Chamber's antechamber. Atop the 240-foot dome is the famous *Golden Boy*, a 13½-foot gilded bronze statue of a running youth. Sculpted by Charles Gardet, a Parisian, *Golden Boy* holds a sheaf of wheat representing Manitoba agriculture and a torch representing economic progress and the development of the north. On the legislature grounds are memorials honoring La Vérendrye, Louis Riel, Queen Victoria, Robert Burns, George-Etienne Cartier and the dead of the two world wars.

MANITOBA MUSIC FESTIVAL (16) This two-week March festival draws some 2,600 entries and 27,000 contestants for classical music competitions among choirs, bands, orchestras, ensembles and soloists. The festival has been held since 1919.

MANITOBA THEATER CENTER (17) A main theater has 785 seats (none more than 75 feet from the stage); the 220-seat Warehouse Theater presents experimental plays.

PAN-AM SWIMMING POOL (18) Built for the 1967 Pan-American Games, the 220-by-75-foot pool is open to the public. The Aquatic Hall of Fame and Museum of Canada has pins, medals, badges, literature and statues and one of the world's largest sports stamp collections. The Cutty Sark Club has 26 models of sailing ships.

PRAIRIE DOG CENTRAL (19) This 1900-era train runs Sundays from St. James station on a 25-mile roundtrip.

PRINCIPAL MERIDIAN (20) A cairn marks the point from which all western Canada land surveys were taken. The first survey marker was placed here in 1871.

RED RIVER CRUISES (21) Motor ships and models of old-time paddle-wheelers cruise the Red and Assiniboine rivers.

RED RIVER EXHIBITION (22) This June fair has agricultural, horticultural and commercial exhibits. The American Band Competition features some two dozen concert and marching bands from across North America.

RED RIVER FLOODWAY (23) This channel, constructed to divert the Red River around the city in case of flood, may be seen at close range from Highway 59.

RICHARDSON BUILDING (24) Winnipeg's tallest office building, the 34-story Richardson Building, at Portage and Main, has a 31st-floor observation deck.

ST. BONIFACE BASILICA (25) Destroyed by fire in 1968, this Roman Catholic basilica was rebuilt behind the facade of the old (1908) building. In the yard are the graves of Louis Riel and Marie Anne Gaboury, the first white woman born in western Canada.

ST. BONIFACE MUSEUM (26) Built by the Grey Nuns in 1846, now a museum, it has the coffin which bore Louis Riel's body. Several furnished rooms reflect something of settlement days. The Grey Nuns' home was the first convent, orphanage, hospital and old people's home in western Canada.

ST. JAMES-ASSINIBOIA HISTORICAL MUSEUM (27) Indian artifacts, Eskimo tools and carvings, antique furniture, costumes and guns.

ST. JAMES CHURCH (28) The oldest (1853) log church in western Canada.

ST. JOHN'S CATHEDRAL (29) Sir Sam Steele (*see* p.130) is buried in the cemetery.

ST. VLADIMIR AND OLGA CATHEDRAL (30) A Ukrainian Catholic cathedral with domed towers and colorful adornments typical of Byzantine churches.

SEVEN OAKS HOUSE (31) This two-story house built in 1851-53 by merchant John Inkster has buffalo-hair-bound plaster. It is a museum with the original furnishings.

SEVEN OAKS MONUMENT (32) A stone shaft commemorates the Seven Oaks massacre in 1816.

SIR WILLIAM WHYTE PARK (33) The log Ross House (1852-54) became western Canada's first post office in 1855. It was built by William Ross, son of Alexander Ross, chief trader of the Hudson's Bay Company, who is commemorated by a plaque outside. Furnished to 1855, the house has Ross' postal scales, desk, chairs, an 1850 organ, spinning wheel, letterpress, a cradle and a spool bed of walnut and butternut. A plaque honors the pioneer women of the Red River country.

□ In front of Ross House a cairn marks the site of the Hudson's Bay Company's Fort Douglas, built in 1813 to protect the Red River Settlement.

SYMINGTON YARDS (34) The vast CN marshaling yards, among the most modern in the world, are floodlit and may be seen for miles.

TRANSCONA HISTORICAL MUSEUM (35) Indian artifacts, pottery, chinaware, glassware and other things of regional history.

UKRAINIAN CULTURAL AND EDUCATIONAL CENTER (36) Renovated in 1978, this five-floor building contains a room depicting a middle-class home in a Ukrainian village; it has hand-carved furniture and hand-painted ceramics. Another room, with woven wall coverings and an ornate fireplace, pictures the home of Hutzels, gifted carvers from the Carpathian mountains. The center has a gallery of Ukrainian paintings and handicrafts, and a multi-cultural room with rotating exhibits. There is a museum with silverware dating from 1492, 17th-century church vestments and 16th-century liturgical items. Among 20,000 volumes and manuscripts are a 1658 Gospel and a 1733 church songbook.

UKRAINIAN GREEK ORTHODOX CATHEDRAL (37) It has domes and a rich interior in the Byzantine fashion.

UNION STOCKYARDS (38) These yards, believed the Commonwealth's largest, can handle almost half a million animals annually.

UNIVERSITY OF MANITOBA (39) Western Canada's oldest incorporated university (1877) has four colleges on the main campus (St. John's, University, St. Paul's and St. Andrew's) and one in St. Boniface. An art gallery has contemporary Canadian paintings and prints and a geological museum has 5,000 mineral specimens. There are a zoological museum and a planetarium. The university has about 20,000 full-time students.

UNIVERSITY OF WINNIPEG (40) The institution dates from the 1870s when the Presbyterian Church established Manitoba College and the Methodists founded Wesley College. The two merged in 1926 and were incorporated in 1967.

WINNIPEG ART GALLERY (41) The gallery has paintings and sculptures ranging from 14th- and 15th-century German masters to early and contemporary Canadian artists. It has Henry Moore's bronze sculpture *Reclining Figure*, Marc Chagall's *Flowers, Still Life with Lovers* and Raoul Dufy's *La Jetée à Trouville*. In the Canadian gallery are Frank Lynn's *Dakota Boat*, Frederick Arthur Verner's *Indian Camp—Sunset*, Emily Carr's *Tree Movement*, David

Milne's *Rocks in Spring* and Anne Kahane's polychromatic wood sculpture *Rain*. A large collection of paintings by Lionel FitzGerald includes *Manitoba Landscape* and *Trees in the Park*. There are works by the Group of Seven, Harold Town and Marc-Aurèle de Foy Suzor-Coté. The gallery has Eskimo carvings and porcelain, glass and silver displays.

WINNIPEG COMMODITY EXCHANGE (42) The exchange, which deals in futures of grain, gold and beef, has a visitors' gallery overlooking the sixth-floor trading room.

Witless Bay Nfld.   11DZ
Enormous flocks of seabirds nest on three small islands off the coast here. Murres and three species of gulls are commonest on Green Island, puffins on Great Island, petrels on Gull Island. They are best seen from mid-June through early July.

Wolfville N.S.   9DY/22DV
On a 250-acre campus in the center of town are the 26 major buildings of Acadia University, founded by the Nova Scotia Baptist Education Society in 1838. Some 2,500 students attend classes in the gracious classical buildings, the oldest of which is a women's residence dating from 1879. Theater Arts Festival International is held at Acadia in July.

□ Wolfville United Baptist Church (1912) has the oldest continuing Baptist congregation in Canada, organized in 1763 by the Rev. Ebenezer Moulton. A plaque commemorates Moulton, who arrived from Massachusetts in 1761 and was the first Baptist preacher in Canada.

□ The Wolfville Historical Museum, in an eight-room, two-story frame house built in 1815, contains furnishings from the late 1700s, when the area was resettled by New Englanders following the expulsion of the Acadians in 1755. The museum has a kitchen, drawing room, dining room, playroom, nursery and two bedrooms.

Wolverton Ont.   17AY
A fine brick house built about 1854-55, Wolverton Hall is marked by an historic plaque.

Woodbridge Ont.   7CY/17BX
A country fair here on Thanksgiving weekend dates from 1847.

Wood Buffalo National Park (Alta./N.W.T.)
This is Canada's largest national park. Its 17,300 square miles make it bigger than Denmark, Holland or Switzerland. Much of its dark virgin forests and vast open plains are still unexplored. The park, of which two-thirds is in Alberta, was established in 1922 to protect the 1,500 wood bison in North America's last remaining herd. Some 6,600 plains bison (slightly smaller animals) were shipped from Wainwright, Alta., and, with intermingling of the species, the combined herd now numbers about 12,000. It is North America's largest. Wood Buffalo is also the northern nesting ground of the nearly extinct

Wood Mountain Stampede, first held in 1912, is the oldest continuously operated rodeo in Saskatchewan. The two-day event in July includes a Little Britches Rodeo for children and teen-agers.

whooping crane. (By 1972 only 50 wild birds remained; 21 others were in captivity.) The wild whoopers migrate here in April from nesting grounds on the Gulf of Mexico and stay until October. Among other wildlife in the park are caribou, moose, bear, fox, lynx, mink and ermine. The continent's northernmost colony of pelicans is found here.

Prairie grasses carpet Wood Buffalo's plains. Flowers such as shooting stars, asters and bluebells are found in the lush valleys of the Peace and Slave rivers. Cattails and sedge plants grow in the park's numerous bogs.

About 1,000 sinkholes, where groundwater has dissolved gypsum or limestone and collapsed the upper layers, are found throughout the park. Several depressions are up to 150 feet in diameter and 100 feet deep, some filled with water. Salt plains in the northeast part of the park are flat, open areas with many salty streams and salt springs. Some springs leave deposits: several salt mounds are as much as 70 feet by 50 and 4-5 feet high.

The Caribou and Birch mountains, erosion plateaus on the west and south borders, rise more than 1,500 feet above the surrounding landscape. Along the banks of the Peace River are the Gypsum Cliffs, which show a cross section of the lower layers of the Alberta Plateau. The Little Buffalo Falls drop about 40 feet on the Little Buffalo River near the Alberta-N.W.T. border.

The park has two developed campsites at Pine Lake in the northeastern Alberta corner. The Fort Smith Highway, Wood Buffalo's only major road, cuts southeast from the Fort Resolution Highway and through the park to Fort Smith, N.W.T. It then reenters the park and makes a 185-mile loop south and back to Fort Smith.

Wood Islands P.E.I.   9EY/23DX
Car ferries cross the Northumberland Strait between here and Caribou, N.S., near Pictou.

Wood Mountain Sask.   4DZ
A barracks and mess hall of a North West Mounted Police post from which a handful of Mounties controlled Sitting Bull and his Sioux have been reconstructed in Wood Mountain Historic Park. The Sioux crossed into Saskatchewan after the Battle of the Little Big Horn in Montana in 1876 and remained for five years (*see* Cypress Hills). Exhibits in the reconstructed buildings include a model of the original post, and NWMP and Indian relics that include a saddle that belonged to Sitting Bull. There is a display relating to the life of Jean-Louis Légaré (*see* Willow Bunch).

Woodstock N.B.   9CX
Courtroom, barristers' room and jury room have been preserved in the Old Carleton County Courthouse (1833), an elegant clapboard structure two miles north in Upper Woodstock. The two-story building, seat of New Brunswick's first county council, was also a stagecoach stop and the scene of agricultural fairs, levees and political rallies. It now is a museum operated by the Carleton County Historical Society. One exhibit reflects the careers of Edwin Tappan Adney, a local author, artist, naturalist, authority on heraldic design and expert on North American Indian craftsmanship. A coat of arms created for the courthouse in 1866 is on display, as are documents, paintings, costumes and local handicrafts.

□ A two-story wooden dwelling built in the 1820s by Charles Connell is one of several 19th-century houses in Woodstock. Connell, postmaster general of New Brunswick in 1858-61, is famous for substituting his own likeness for one of Queen Victoria on a new issue of stamps in 1860. In the ensuing protest Connell resigned and the stamp issue was withdrawn.

Woodstock Ont.   7BZ/17AZ
The old town hall, a two-story yellow brick structure built in 1851-52, is a colonial adaptation of the architecture of mid-19th-century British public buildings. It is a national his-

Old town hall in Woodstock, Ont., basically Palladian in design, shows Italianate Revival influence (as in its roundheaded windows and heavy surrounds). In it now is a museum.

Springbank Snow Countess, whose statue is in a downtown park in Woodstock, Ont., set a world record for lifetime butterfat production (9,062 pounds in 1919-36).

toric site and houses the Oxford Museum. The ground-floor council chamber has its original furniture, flags and portraits. A second-floor auditorium has served as lecture hall, opera house and courthouse.

□ The bell tower of St. Paul's Church (1834) is said to have been used as a prison during the Rebellion of 1837. The church has the original box pews. The altar and pulpit were built from the boxes in which the first organ was shipped from England. Vice Adm. Henry

Vansittart, who founded Woodstock in 1834, is buried in the crypt.

□ The Oxford County Courthouse (1890-92) has a three-foot monkey carved in limestone on the facade and four five-inch monkey heads on columns at the front. Monkeys decorated many buildings constructed in the 1890s. A courthouse plaque commemorates Sir Francis Hincks. He introduced the Bank Act of 1871 which laid the foundation of the banking system.

□ A tablet on the grounds of his former residence honors Capt. Andrew Drew, who led the destruction of the American side-wheeler *Caroline* in the Niagara River in 1837 (*see* Niagara Falls).

□ The Chesney Conservation Area is 200 acres of forest and bog 11 miles northeast.

Woody Point Nfld.   11BX
The peaks of some of the most spectacular mountains in eastern North America drop sharply to long narrow fjords along the craggy coast of Bonne Bay near Woody Point. Tiny villages dot the sloping landscape close to the bay.

Wyebridge Ont.   17BV
A plaque marks a former home and studio of Frank H. "Franz" Johnston, an original member of the Group of Seven.

Wyevale Ont.   17BV
One of Ontario's few remaining waterpowered gristmills is on the Wye River here.

YZ

Yale B.C.   2DZ/12GW
The Anglican Church of St. John the Divine, the oldest place of worship in British Columbia on its original site, dates from 1859-60. It was built by miners who flocked here when gold was discovered in 1858 at nearby Hill's Bar. Hill's, the richest of some 25 bars in a 30-mile stretch of the Fraser, yielded gold worth $2,000,000.

From Lytton, 44 miles north, the Fraser races through a deep canyon in which are Hell's Gate (*see* Spuzzum) and a series of fish ladders.

A plaque commemorates Yale's founding in 1848 as a fur-trade post. Seventeen years later it became the terminus of the Cariboo Wagon Road (*see* Lillooet). Later it was important during construction of the CPR.

Yamachiche Que.   19CW
Antoine Gérin-Lajoie, who in 1842 wrote the words of the haunting song *Un Canadien errant*, about the homesick wandering of a *patriote* banished after the Rebellion of 1837, is commemorated by a plaque on the site of his house. An English version, set to the same traditional French melody and called *From His Canadian Home*, was written by John Murray Gibbon in 1927.

Another plaque marks the house of Nérée Beauchemin, a physician and poet (1850-1931) whose writings include *Les Floraisons matutinales* and *Patrie intime.*

Some 1,000 pilgrims gather at Sainte-Anne's Church on the feast of Sainte Anne, July 26. In the stone church (1958) is Alfred Gilles' 18-by-12 foot copper mosaic of the saint's family.

Yarmouth N.S.   9CZ/22BY
A 400-pound stone with inscriptions that some experts believe were carved by Norsemen about 1,000 years ago is displayed at the Yarmouth County Historical Museum. Found here in 1812, the Yarmouth Stone is about three feet long, two feet wide and 18 inches thick. One expert believes the inscription was done by Leif Ericsson. He translates it as "Leif to Eric Raises (This Monument)"—Eric the Red is Leif's father. Another authority feels the characters mean "Harko's Son Addressed the Men." Others theorize that the inscription is of Micmac Indian origin or a result of natural erosion.

□ Two monuments near the harbor recall the days in the mid-1800s when Yarmouth was the major shipbuilding center in Nova Scotia. The Nova Scotia Shipbuilding Memorial is

The Yarmouth light, on Cape Forchu near Yarmouth harbor, can be seen from 30 miles at sea. Champlain named the "forked" cape in 1604. It has had a lighthouse since 1840.

constructed of stones with side panels sculpted by local artist Tom Taylor depicting ships. The Yarmouth County Seamen's Memorial consists of anchors and a cairn at the place where the county's first ship, the schooner *Pompey*, was launched in 1764.

□ The Firefighters' Museum of Nova Scotia has two Hunneman engines made in 1840 and an 1880 Silsby steamer. The museum's 34 engines, from an 1819 truck to aerial pumpers, are Canada's largest such collection.

□ A four-day square dance festival is held here in May.

□ A plaque on Surette's Island marks the grave of Marie Surette, the last of the deported Acadians who returned to Nova Scotia. She was buried in 1862 at 110. (*See* p.91)

Yellowknife N.W.T.   3HY

Situated on the north shore of 11,170-square-mile Great Slave Lake, only 320 miles south of the Arctic Circle, Yellowknife is the capital and largest settlement of the Northwest Territories, with a population of about 10,000. The city dates from the discovery of gold in 1935. New discoveries in 1944 led to the opening of the Giant Yellowknife and Con mines. Surface and underground tours are available at both mines; visitors see molten gold being poured into bricks.

□ PRINCE OF WALES NORTHERN HERITAGE CENTER Opening in 1979, this ambitious establishment is designed to give visitors a grasp of northern heritage, culture and existence and to carry the story to other northern communities through traveling exhibits. Government-run, professionally staffed, it is designed with four main exhibit areas to tell about the geography, resources, history and peoples of the Northwest Territories. The

The Northwest Territories, covering more than a third of Canada (and half as big as the United States), are immense with primeval beauty. The Territories lie mostly in the Precambrian shield and the rugged, rocky terrain is interlaced by mighty rivers (among them the 2,514-mile Mackenzie) and countless lakes. These hunters are on Point Lake, 200 miles northeast of Yellowknife.

program includes educational and extension facilities, and archives and an historical library to aid research. The center is in a park-like setting, with a lake on two sides.

□ A 12-foot granite pylon commemorates the bush pilots of the 1920s and '30s who "penetrated the age-old isolation of remote and virtually uncharted regions, opening the way for present aerial routes. . . ."

□ Annual events include a midnight golf tournament in June, when daylight lasts 24 hours a day, and a Caribou Carnival in March with a three-day, 150-mile "Canadian Championship" dogsled race.

Yoho National Park (B.C.)   2FY/13AV
The Trans-Canada Highway and CP Rail both traverse this 507-square-mile wonderland of spectacular waterfalls, towering peaks and beautiful lakes. Yoho (the word is a Cree exclamation of wonder and astonishment) is on the west slope of the Rockies, adjoining Banff and Kootenay national parks to the east and south, Hamber Provincial Park to the northwest. Yoho's east entrance is near the Kicking Horse Pass; it is the Kicking Horse River that the highway and railway follow across the park. Near Field, which is close to the center of the park, are CP's two Spiral Tunnels; westbound trains descend almost 100 feet in less than a mile.

Yoho's snowcapped peaks (21 are over 10,000 feet) are interlaced with white-water rivers and alpine lakes, among them spectacular deep green Emerald Lake near Field. In the 10-mile-long Yoho River Valley, north of Field, is a mile-long gorge 500 feet deep in places. Into the valley plunge 1,248-foot Takakkaw Falls, fed by Daly Glacier, and 50-foot Laughing Falls, over which hangs an ethereal curtain of mist.

Some 200 miles of trails give access to points of interest in the park. Geological features include a 50-foot-long natural bridge over the Kicking Horse River, and hoodoos, 30-50-foot pillars of glacial till.

Wildlife includes wapiti, bear, moose, deer and Rocky Mountain goats. The valleys are

Ukrainian church fresco in Yorkton appears from the floor, 55 feet below the dome, to have been painted on a flat surface.

clothed with evergreen—lodgepole pine, blue Douglas fir and white spruce—and above the 7,000-foot treeline are colorful alpine flowers and bushes.

York P.E.I.   9EX/23CW
Canadian glassware in a glass museum here ranges from cake plates commemorating Victoria's accession in 1837 to a goblet engraved with beaver and maple leaves and commemorating Saint Jean-Baptiste Day 1880. There are 300 salt cellars, some silver, most glass. The museum is at Jewell's Country Gardens. Also among the flowers are a reconstructed 19th-century one-room frame schoolhouse with original furnishings and relics, and a reconstruction of a 19th-century general store.

York Factory Man.   5HV
A 19th-century fur warehouse is a relic of York Factory's great days as chief North American port and supply depot for the Hudson's Bay Company. It has been classified as a national historic site. Trade goods and supplies for western posts were received here from England and furs were packed here and shipped to London. After 275 years of almost continuous operation, York Factory was closed down in 1957.

Yorkton Sask.   4FY
A fresco on the dome of St. Mary's Ukrainian Catholic Church, depicting the crowning of the Virgin Mary in heaven, is one of the finest religious frescoes in North America. It includes representations of 157 angels and of God as the "Ancient of days." The painting, with a diameter of 62 feet, was done in 1939-41 by Stephen Meush. The main colors are orange, indigo and dull red, choices inspired by Saskatchewan sunsets. The pigments penetrate the plaster to a depth of one-eighth of an inch. The white brick church, built in 1914, has an icon painted in 1964 by Igor Suhacev. He also designed the sanctuary woodwork, including the altar with its 28 figurines representing the saints of the Byzantine Catholic Rite.

□ The Yorkton Branch of the Western Development Museum has a collection of steam and gas tractors, agricultural implements and vintage cars. Rooms furnished in turn-of-the-century styles include an English parlor, a Ukrainian kitchen with a six-foot-high clay oven, a Ukrainian living room displaying decorated Easter eggs and inlaid cedar chests, and an Indian room.

□ Machines are operated at a museum-sponsored Threshermen's Reunion in August. In July are an industrial and agricultural exhibition, held annually since the 1890s, and a rodeo. A film festival is held in October.

Zurich Ont.   7BY/16CW
A festival in late August to publicize Zurich as the center of a white bean-growing area attracts some 20,000 persons. The village, settled by Germans, was named after the Swiss city.

The Buildings of Canada
A guide to pre-20th-century styles in houses, churches and other structures

The architecture of Canadian buildings up to roughly the start of the 20th century followed styles developed largely in France, Britain and the United States. Local adaptations resulted in what can be termed a Canadian architecture. Variations were due in part to restrictions posed by the availability of building skills, materials and technology; they were due also to attempts to relate buildings to their surroundings and to the occupants' functional needs. Stone cottages in rural Ontario and Quebec, prairie grain elevators, small railway stations . . . all reflect indigenous architectural styles. Buildings in which foreign styles and details have been more faithfully copied have a Canadian originality of scale and proportion.

The earliest buildings are of French design, characterized by steeply pitched roofs, broad chimneys and unadorned exterior walls of stone. British and Loyalist settlers introduced the solid Georgian style: simple, rectangular shapes, with symmetrical facades and rectangular window openings. A softening influence appeared about 1810-30: the Neo-classic, developed in Britain under the leadership of the Adam brothers, architects who favored the use of the delicately curved line.

Neo-classic gave way in the early 1830s to Classic Revival—another influence from Britain, where it had developed from a growing interest in the arts of early Greece and Rome. Classic Revival, unlike Neo-classic, emphasized the straight line. The British Regency style, distinguished by tall first-floor windows, wide chimneys and verandas, also appeared in the early 1830s. In the mid-1800s the formality of Classic Revival was gradually replaced by a succession of styles, with much overlapping and borrowing of detail. Gothic Revival, the style in which Britain's Houses of Parliament were designed in 1836, became popular. In the 1860s came Italianate, a style based on the villas of Italy. Second Empire, which followed about 1870, originated in France.

The technological developments of the late 19th century led to varied architectural styles and to a period of eclecticism rather than adaptation. Designs of the late 1880s and 1890s often grafted architectural details of various periods onto buildings of irregular outline. This Queen Anne style persisted, with variations such as the Stick and Chateau styles, until well into the 20th century.

(See glossary, page 421)

409

Dwellings

Canadian houses have varied in size from the one-room cabins of the settlers to large, complicated structures almost like castles. Canadians have dwelt in buildings of sod, of round or squared logs, some willow lathed and plastered. They have built timbered houses, houses of solid brick and of brick veneer, and stone houses of rubble, fieldstone and ashlar. Stone houses predominated in early Quebec; brick became popular in the second half of the 19th centu-

ry, chiefly in Ontario. But due to the geography and the economy of the country, most dwellings have been of wood.

Canadian houses reflect style influences primarily from France, Britain and the United States. Pure examples of any style, however, are comparatively rare. Most houses are highly vernacular, displaying interpretations that were limited (and sometimes inspired) by local resources. Strong regional influence can be seen in the pre-

dominance of certain designs and or construction techniques i various parts of the country.

Of all the styles that influence Canadian architecture, Classi Revival (opposite page) had th greatest impact. To that stylisti pattern we owe medium-pitche gable roofs, front gable plan doors with rectangular transom and sidelights, and all manner o detailed ornamentation such a moldings, columns and pedi mented trim. Classic Reviva

French Regime
(pre-1759)

Houses are 1 or 1½ stories, generally of stone. Steeply pitched gable or hip roofs are finished with either straight or flared eave lines. Chimneys may be centered, or inset from the ends of the roof, or extensions of end walls. Early windows are multipaned casement. A profusion of dormers may be part of the original design but on smaller buildings one or two dormers may be additions.

Triple chimneys, steep gable and bellcast curve at the eaves (top) and multipaned casement windows are typical. Center chimneys (below) also are common.

An early French type has a steep gable roof with no eaves trim. Hip-roof house (below) has slightly flared eaves.

Georgian Tradition
(pre-1820)

Sturdy and secure, usually 2½ stories, these well-proportioned houses follow a tradition started under the Georges who were Britain's kings in the 18th century. Most have medium-pitched gable or hip roofs, with end chimneys usually inset. Balanced facades have 3-5-7 bays and center doors. Openings are rectangular, windows small-paned. The Palladian window is a decorative motif.

A steep hip roof, broad chimneys, and a balanced facade of five bays place this house in the Georgian tradition.

Solid Georgian proportions are combined with a typical hip roof.

The decorative Palladian window over the main door (closeup below) is a dominant feature of many Georgian houses.

Neo-classic
(c.1810-30)

This gracefully proportioned style with its delicate detailing is derived from the work of the Adam brothers in mid-18th-century England. Buildings are rectangular with low-pitched gable roofs or square with hip roofs. There are often four end chimneys. Houses are usually 2-2½ stories, with balanced facades. Semielliptical transoms and sidelights often emphasize center doors.

The low gable, paired chimneys and decorative gable window are characteristic.

The center door has a fan transom and sidelights with a classically detailed pediment and columns.

Small windows of geometric shapes often decorate the ends of Neo-classic houses.

uses are found in greatest prosion in the Maritimes and Onrio and date from the 1830s.
aces of this style are seen in the
est but the older, large houses of
estern Canada tend to follow the
ctates of the Queen Anne Reval style (p.413).

DESCHAMBAULT, QUE.   MOUNT UNIACKE, N.S.

Regency
(c.1810-40)

This style originated during the period 1811-20 when George, Prince of Wales (later George IV), was the British regent. Most Regency-style houses are 1 or 1½ stories with low hip roofs and a villa or cottage appearance. Center door and large first-floor windows with small panes are typical. A Regency house may have a central belvedere; a one-story front gallery is often seen.

Windows, gallery, bell-cast roof of this Quebec vernacular show Regency influence.

More Regency touches: contrasting window sizes, sweeping gallery, tall chimneys.

Gallery, large windows appear also in this low, hip-roof cottage.

Veranda treillage, geometric and finely scaled, belongs to the Regency period.

Classic Revival
(c.1830-60)

The medium-pitched gable roof is common, often with a roof pediment or large center gable. Temple effect is obtained by an open portico across the facade, supported on columns with a heavy entablature, or by flat attached pilasters. Elegant, urbane masonry structures have flat or pedimental hoods over the windows; open porches are supported on fluted columns.

The front gable plan was a Classic Revival design in North America.

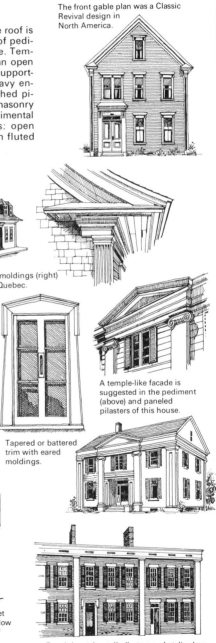

Returned eaves and classical moldings (right) on Classic Revival houses in Quebec.

A bold door surround with heavy entablature is coupled with a front gable plan in this house.

Tapered or battered trim with eared moldings.

A temple-like facade is suggested in the pediment (above) and paneled pilasters of this house.

A classic open porch, parapet gables and contrasting window heads enliven an example of Quebec Classic Revival.

Eared door trim, tall pilasters and stylized entablature decorate this Classic Revival row.

Dwellings

From Gothic Revival to Beaux Arts and Chateau, the styles of the second half of the 19th century followed the sequence found in the influencing countries. Gothic Revival left its mark largely in decorative details, irregular shapes, exaggerated roof pitches and a generally fancy look. Later came the Italianate town houses, solid and square, seeming to emphasize their owners' wealth and importance. (A somewhat restrained Italianate is often seen in the brick farmhouses of Ontario and occasionally in stone in the southern parts of Manitoba and Saskatchewan.)

The Second Empire mansard roof was a practical way to utilize third-floor attic space and was often used to convert a 2½-story gable-roof building to a three-story edifice. The Queen Anne style manifested itself in many forms, most often in Ontario and the west. Characterized by irregular outlines, one- and two-story bay windows and winged brackets, was used in thousands of bri... houses in Ontario cities. Modifi... versions are seen in frame on t... west coast.

Gothic Revival
(c. 1850-70)

These decorative buildings are customarily distinguished by finely scaled gingerbread trim, pointed-arch openings and sharply pitched gables. The decorative detail includes intricate bargeboards and/or veranda treillage and window tracery with the pointed-arch motif. Chimneys are paired, paneled or diagonal and there are finials or drops at the gable peaks and labels over the openings.

Gingerbread trim (detail below), steeply pitched gables and pointed-arch openings (right) mark Gothic Revival.

Elizabethan-Gothic Revival has angular, shaped gables, label window surrounds, Tudor arches on veranda.

Baronial-Gothic Revival is typified by this crenellated tower.

Picturesque and Renaissance Revival
(c. 1850-70, c. 1860-75)

Picturesque houses, often relatively small and reflecting the individual tastes of builders or owners, have decorative elements of Gothic Revival origin: bargeboards, pointed-arch windows, lacy trim on eaves and verandas. Renaissance Revival houses are blocky in mass, with flat, low hip or truncated gable roofs, shaped gables and strong eave lines.

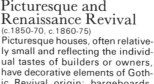

Picturesque, an interpretation of Gothic Revival, utilizes its decorative trim, steeply pitched gables and board and batten siding.

Two elements of Renaissance Revival style are curved Dutch gables and applied pedimental window or door trim.

Italianate
(c. 1850-70)

This strong style was in popular use for town houses about the time of Confederation. Buildings were often square, many with square towers or projecting frontispieces. The towers and main blocks of these houses have low-pitched hip roofs. Under wide eaves are prominent decorative brackets. Other Italianate characteristics are verandas, round-headed windows and belvederes.

Wide, bracketed eaves, round-headed windows and a belvedere are Italianate in style.

Round-headed windows and a projecting frontispiece identify this Italianate.

The style often incorporates a square tower, either central (as here) or asymmetrically located.

This Italianate porch has round-headed openings and strongly modeled detailing.

DON, ONT.   PORT HILL, P.E.I.   SIMCOE, ONT.

Second Empire
(c.1860-80)

The style is distinguished by the mansard roof. Individual houses tend to be square, sometimes with projecting center towers or end pavilions. The upper roof level is sometimes visible but usually very low-pitched. The top of the lower roof slope may be marked by decorative cresting. The frequent use of one- and two-story bay windows tends to make building outlines irregular.

The mansard roof, the distinguishing feature of Second Empire style, here has a concave slope.

The continuous mansard roof of this row of Second Empire town houses is enhanced by an iron cresting.

Bay windows and twin dormers (above) and ornately bracketed eaves (right) make this an eclectic Second Empire house.

Queen Anne Revival
(c.1885-1900)

Large, commodious houses of two or more stories, Queen Anne Revivals have steep hip roofs and tall chimneys. There is often a tower (generally offset) and a broad veranda. The facade may have more than one sheathing or several patterns. Double-hung windows often have one large bottom sash, small panes in the upper sash. The Queen Anne in western Canada is more angular, less voluptuous.

Tower, shaped veranda and irregular massing typify the Queen Anne in eastern Canada.

In western Canada the Queen Anne style is apt to be more contained in plan.

Angularity of decorative features is characteristic of Stick style, a variation of Queen Anne Revival.

Imitation half-timbering is a distinguishing feature of Tudor Revival, another variation of Queen Anne.

Romanesque Revival, Beaux Arts, Chateau
(c.1880-1910)

Romanesque Revival style includes round towers, tall chimneys, steeply pitched roofs, and wide, arched windows and door openings. Undercut decorative stone or terra-cotta trim uses medieval foliate patterns. Beaux Arts uses cold, classic decorative trim (columns, pilasters and capitals). Chateau has steeply pitched hip roofs and multiple tall chimneys.

Undercut trim (stone or terra-cotta) in Romanesque Revival uses medieval foliate patterns for decorative effect.

Wide round-arch openings, circular tower and heavy masonry mark a notable example of Romanesque Revival.

Early 20th-century interpretations of classic motifs define the Beaux Arts.

Irregularity of the roof line, steeply pitched gables and multiple tall chimneys denote Chateau style.

413

Churches

Most early Canadian churches were constructed in Gothic Revival style. Its features, particularly pointed-arch windows, are evident in churches of many denominations and all sizes, from simple log buildings to elaborate stone cathedrals. Exceptions to Gothic Revival include the early Quebec churches with their semicircular-headed windows, and Georgian style churches with similar detailing. A few large churches were designed in Romanesque Revival style. While basic church style is generally derivative, there are small, charming interpretations of Gothic Revival (in wooden churches in the Maritimes) and the "turnip-domed" churches on the prairies. The design of some early churches is severely plain but sometimes an ornately detailed interior contrasts with a simple exterior. Wood carving and plasterwork are often impressive.

ST. ANDREWS, N.B.

French Regime
Steeply pitched roof, flared eaves, rubble masonry, statuary niches in facade.

Georgian Tradition
Symmetrical design, classic proportions, central Palladian window.

Neo-classic
Generally attenuated proportions, pilasters, graceful arcading.

Classic Revival
Temple front, monumental portico.

Gothic Revival
Sharp gables, pointed-arch openings, finials, a rose window.

Gothic Revival
Trefoil lancet window, molded label surround terminating in rosettes.

Picturesque
Slender sham buttresses and delicate spire for a small chapel.

Italianate-Tuscan
A symmetrical main elevation is detailed with flat arcades and coupled with a square bell tower at the side. The style is defined also by semicircular-headed openings.

Ethnic Tradition
"Onion" or "turnip" domes indicate strong ethnic tradition originating in Central and Eastern Europe.

Administrative Buildings

Administrative or "public" buildings in Canada almost invariably display the rather formal approach of the Classic Revival style. This approach is manifested in the recurring use of columns and pediment detailing—a reminder of the temples of Greece and Rome and of the 19th-century movement that dictated the use of a particular style for a particular type of building. A few of Canada's legislative and government buildings did, however, escape this architectural principle. The outstanding example is the Parliament Buildings, which have all the flourish and pointed detail of the Gothic Revival style.

LETHBRIDGE, ALTA.

GREAT VILLAGE, N.S.

Niches, pilasters, pediments and a classical portico—all quietly subdued—identify this building in Neo-classic style.

A bold dome and temple-like portico are Classic Revival hallmarks.

Pointed-arch windows, a central tower and decorative bargeboard on twin gables are Picturesque elements.

This Renaissance Revival post office has segmental dormers, pilasters, balustrade and rusticated first story, as well as a prominent clock tower.

A domed lantern on a flat roof and paired semicircular windows distinguish an Italianate courthouse.

A mansard roof identifies this Second Empire style school.

Round arched windows with bold surrounds light an Italianate drill hall.

Romanesque Revival features include bold towers, rough-faced masonry, terra-cotta panels with medieval designs, and large round arches.

Commercial Buildings

Classic Revival detailing, largely in the form of temple fronts, is used also on commercial buildings, particularly banks. Some major commercial buildings display Renaissance Revival detailing, recalling the style that originated with the great Italian palaces. Commercial buildings of a more modest scale have the segmentally arched windows of post-1870 design, surmounted by a wide and decorative cornice of Italian influence. Most are brick and many once had living quarters on the second and third floors. Signs and advertisements have altered the first-floor levels of so many older commercial buildings that the original fine scale and rhythm of design—and consequently the unity of the streetscape—have been lost.

Modern factories, office buildings, hotels, railway stations, shops (and shopping centers) are a far cry from the examples on these pages. Since the mid-'30s, influenced heavily by new materials and radically new methods of construction, styles in commercial buildings have been markedly changed. Today's styles are generally plainer, seeking to meet the requirements of function, structure and appearance in each unit.

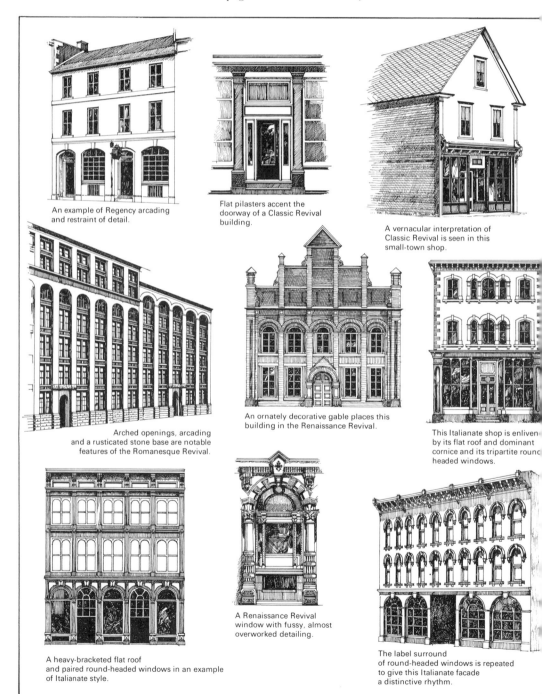

An example of Regency arcading and restraint of detail.

Flat pilasters accent the doorway of a Classic Revival building.

A vernacular interpretation of Classic Revival is seen in this small-town shop.

Arched openings, arcading and a rusticated stone base are notable features of the Romanesque Revival.

An ornately decorative gable places this building in the Renaissance Revival.

This Italianate shop is enlivened by its flat roof and dominant cornice and its tripartite round-headed windows.

A heavy-bracketed flat roof and paired round-headed windows in an example of Italianate style.

A Renaissance Revival window with fussy, almost overworked detailing.

The label surround of round-headed windows is repeated to give this Italianate facade a distinctive rhythm.

WINNIPEG, MAN.

VANCOUVER, B.C.

Bargeboards and center gables decorate
a Picturesque row converted to commercial use.

Renaissance dormers, turrets and a
sharply pitched roof line distinguish
this example of the Chateau style.

A roof line with a multiplicity of
gables tops this Chateau-style railway station.

The boomtown front
on this store
is typical of small
rural commercial
buildings.

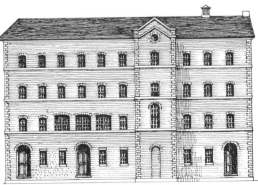

Segmentally headed windows such
as in this distillery were commonly
used in the 1870s.

Miniature kegs in upper-story roundels decorate
this 18th-century brewery.

Barns

The earliest Canadian barns, rude shelters for livestock, were built of logs on newly cleared land. As techniques were improved and imaginations went to work, a wide range of barn designs began to dot the land: square barns, rectangular and polygonal barns, barns that looked like houses (below, bottom left), barns with twin openings, barns with decorative arcades, barns with heavy second-story overhang, massive fortress-like stone barns.

ASHCROFT, B.C.

A hipped gable roof, side windows, dormers and cupola are features of this barn.

Concern for shapes and patterns is seen in the handsome curved doors and windows of a Quebec barn.

Cupolas on barns, some round, some square, others polygonal, provide light and ventilation.

Separate ramps lead to twin openings and a second-story storage area.

A basically circular plan and a series of angular gables: a barn that resembles the Festival Theater in Stratford, Ont.

Second-story overhang continues a tradition common in Europe.

A squared-log storage shed is roofed with thatch.

A parade of arches forms a shaded arcade along one side of a big frame barn.

This slatted wooden barn door resembles medieval prototypes.

The double pitch of the traditional gambrel roof is seen in this prairie barn.

Vertical siding, a hipped gable roof and round-headed windows are all part of this busy facade.

A central cupola tops a polygonal frame barn set on a stone foundation.

Another prairie barn: long and low, built of stone with brick arches over doors and windows.

Vernacular

The vernacular in architectural expression makes use of local forms and materials, clings to familiar forms from old lands and responds to climatic conditions in the new. Canadian vernacular ranges from west coast pagoda roofs to the steep roofs of old Quebec, from mud-walled prairie cottages of relatively recent date to great stone houses built in the days of New France, from prairie grain elevators to Montreal's distinctive outside stairways.

CALIENTO, MAN.

Prairie Vernacular
A grain elevator and adjoining buildings cluster in apparent disorder. A domed wooden church and a thatched-roof, mud-surfaced house continue central European traditions.

West Coast Vernacular
Pagoda-like roof detailing reflects an Oriental flair. The small frame bungalow is typical of British Columbia.

Ontario Vernacular
The beaver in a gable . . . a brick farmhouse with gables and a commodious porch . . . a small, three-bay cottage with hip roof and center gable.

Quebec Vernacular
Stone with two large parapeted gable chimneys: the urbane Quebec town house. Exterior metal stairs, often curved: a Montreal trademark. A steeply pitched hip roof and casement windows: French tradition characteristics.

Maritime Vernacular
Thistles carved in wood as balustrade decoration speak of Scottish heritage. Central upper-story windows that break the eaves line and simple gable roofs with windows tight to the eaves are Maritime types.

Miscellaneous Building Types

Designs of miscellaneous building types often reflect sensitivity that may seem surprising in utilitarian structures. Canadians have built flour mills whose windows would look well in fine town houses, registry offices with attractive arcades, armories like castles. Lighthouses and firehall and water towers have been designed with flair and imagination. The major early styles found in dwellings and churches are seen also in these miscellaneous building types.

ELORA, ONT.

Sawmills such as this, with wooden waterwheels, were once common in many parts of Canada.

Arcade-like openings for windows and a center door were frequently used in small registry offices in the 19th century.

Lighthouses dot the Canadian coastline, one of the longest in the world.

An unusually elaborate municipal water tower has round-arched Italianate decoration.

Sensitive detailing is seen in the segmentally headed windows of this flour mill.

A frame tower for drying hose tops a small-town firehall.

Stylized Baronial Gothic detailing is seen on this turn-of-the-century building.

Martello towers were British copies of a round fort at Cape Mortella in Corsica. The thick walls are tapered slightly.

An interesting carpentry pattern embellishes a fish warehouse.

Crenellated towers in Baronial Gothic style are typical of armories in many cities.

Central Quebec

Sherbrooke, the Chaudière and Quebec

Seaport and provincial capital, Quebec is the commercial and industrial hub of an area whose economy depends mostly on the farms of the St. Lawrence Valley and such primary industry as the rich mines at Thetford Mines and Asbestos. The reasons for the concentration of population in and around Quebec lie in geography and in political and military history.

☐ A condition of the fur-trade monopoly that Champlain sought to activate in 1608 was that a permanent colony be established. He looked for a site on the St. Lawrence River, the main artery of the fur trade, which he had explored in 1603. For the site of his second habitation (he had founded Port Royal in 1605) Champlain chose the Indians' Kebec "where the river narrows." The high cliff of Cape Diamond provided protection against the Iroquois, whom he had alienated by supporting the Hurons; traders could go upriver to the Lachine Rapids to pick up furs from the Indians and return in safety.

The settlement became the center of French activity in North America, dominated by the fur trade, missionary work and the struggle with Britain for control of the continent. Little effort was made to develop the vast territory claimed by France; it remained simply a supplier of raw materials. Compared with the dynamic colonies of New England, New France was sparsely populated and dependent almost entirely on the fur trade. By the time of the British conquest in 1759 the fur trade accounted for 70 percent of New France's economy.

☐ The British maintained the city as capital when the Province of Lower Canada was created in 1791 and again when the Province of Quebec was created by Confed-

Quebec, from a history of Nor

eration in 1867. Mean
first half of the 19th cer
invasion from the Unite
Quebec an important
much the same reasons
chosen the site: its strate

Shipbuilding was a
during the 19th century

Credits are left to right, top to bottom, with additional information as needed. A single credit means all photographs on that page or pages are from the same source.

Endpapers: RV (Apple Trees, Laurentians); 1 deV *Mother and Child* by Isah Seeg, Windsor Art Gallery); 4-5 UK (Morning Dew); 7 Gilles Rivest; 8 deV (Fort Garry, Selkirk); 10 NASA; 14-15 Geological Survey of Canada; 16 PAC; 18 deV PAC; 19 PAC; 20 PAC; 21 FP PAC; 22 PAC CW PAC MS/CW PAC MS/CW; 23 CW; 24 FP (Grand Bay West, Nfld.); 26 RV; 27 deV; 28 PB; 29 PG; 30 deV; 31 NS; 32-33 FP; 34 FP RV; 35 FP deV; 36 PG Alcan; 37 Henry Kalen; 38 Man FP; 39 FP (left), Alexander Graham Bell Museum; 40 FP; 41 PG DB; 42 FP; 43 RV, Louis Hamel 2, Banff Center School of Fine Arts, RV; 45 PB; 46-47 deV, R.E. Merrick/N.S. Museum; 48 deV PB; 49 PG RP; 50 FP; 51 George Hunter; 52 deV BC; 53 RV; 54 Info/Dave Bonner; 56 RV; 57 FP; 58 FP ROM Reader's Digest; 59 PG; 60 FP; 61 deV; 62 deV; 63 FP2 Info/Jarrett; 64 RV; 66 FP3 deV; 67 PB RV; 68-69 RV; 70 RV5 George Hunter; 71 RV; 72 PB; 73 FP; 74 PG; 75 FP; 76 FP NS FP; 78 Georges P. Michaud, PB; 79 RV PG; 80-81 PB4 PG; 82 deV FP; 83 Parks Canada; 84 RV; 85 FP, P.E.I. Department of the Environment and Tourism, Edith Robinson; 86 FP; 87 PG; 88 FP; 89 PG; 90 RV; 92 FP RV; 93 RV; 94 deV; 95 RV deV; 96 PB; 97 FP deV; 98 deV; 99 PG; 100 PB; 101 RV; 102 Saskatchewan Industry Department; 103 Wamboldt-Waterfield, RV2; 104 RV PB; 105 PB; 106 PB; 107 PG; 108 FP deV; 109 FP deV; 110 RV; 111 Henry Kalen, PB; 112 RV FP; 113 BC; 114-115 RV; 116 RV; 117 PG; 118 RV; 120 RV, Gordon Knight; 121 RV; 122 RV deV Man; 123 Mike Haimes, RV2; 124 UK PG; 125 deV; 126 Imperial Oil, RV; 127 PB; 128-129 PB; 130 PAC PB; 131 RV; 132 PG; 133 Harvey Studios, PG2; 134 PG, Publicité Unic Inc.; 135 DB RV; 136 FP; 137 PB; 138-139 Mike Haimes, PG DB; 140 UK RV; 141 Man; 142 PB; 143 deV; 144 deV; 145 Daniel Wiener, DB; 146 PG; 147 FP2, E.N. Wilcox 2, FP2, Mike Haimes; 148 NS; 149 FP; 150 FP; 151 deV; 152 PB; 153 FP; 154 deV; 156 Daniel Wiener; 157 FP; 158-159 FP; 160 FP; 162-163 deV; 164 deV; 165 DB; 167 PB, Jacques Varry, PB4; 168 PG FP; 169 Government of Alberta/Lands & Forests; 170 FP; 171 QueCGTB; 172 PG; 173 PG, Alain Bienvenue, PG; 174-175 FP RV; 177 CGTB; 178 CGTB RV2; 179 PG; 180 Jordan Historical Museum of the Twenty; 181 PB; 182 PB; 183 FP; 184 BC; 185 Albert J. Carter; 186 New Brunswick Tourism; 187 deV; 188 Agnes Etherington Art Center, deV; 189 deV; 190 deV (top) Eddie Duke; 191 deV; 192 deV, McMichael Canadian Collection; Sheman, Laws Ltd.; 193 BC; 194 PB PG; 195 FP; 197 CGTB, John Pope; 198 PG; 199 Saskatchewan Industry Dept., PG; 200 MF; 201 RV PG; 202 BB; 203 RV; 204-205 deV; 206 PG; 207 FP2 CGTB; 208 FP; 209 deV, Horst Ehricht; 210 Sherman Hines, Wamboldt-Waterfield; 211 PG; 212 PG Info/DB; 213 deV; 214 deV, G.J. Harris; 215 PB RV; 216 Ontario Department of Tourism; 217 RV; 218-219 deV; 220 RV; 221 Malak RV; 222 FP; 223 PG; 224 DN2 Malak PG2 DB; 225 ©Derek Caron/The Image Bank of Canada, DN2 ©J.A. Kraulis/The Image Bank of Canada; 227 deV; 230 PG, Barbara Deans, PG3; 231 Barbara Deans (2 left), Claude Lavigne, PG; 232 PG; 234-235 PG; 236 PG; 237 RV, Evergreen Press, UK; 238 deV RV; 239 deV; 240 RV; 241 PAC PB; 242 deV; 243 Ferris Photography; 245 deV; 246 Potvin Museum; 247 deV; 249 Joan Powell; 250 RV deV; 252 deV; 253 deV DN PG; 254 deV; 255 deV, Robert McLaughlin Gallery, PG; 256 Glen Bateman; 257 deV; 258-259 deV; 260 deV; 261 Malak, C.I.P. Studios/James Horvath; 262 NGC; 263 deV NGC; 264-265 deV3, Hans Blohm; 266-267 deV2, J.A. Kraulis; 268 Albert J. Carter; 269 PB; 270 DN PG; 271 PG deV; 272 deV; 273 BB; 274 UK; 275 FP; 276 NS; 277 DB; 278 FP; 279 deV; 280 FP2 NS; 282 PB; 283 Edith Robinson, J. Jackson; 284-285 PG2, Marc Ellefsen; 286 PG; 288 DB PG; 289 PG4 DB2; 290 Que PG; 291 Marc Ellefsen, RV; 292 PG; 293 Malak; 294 deV PB; 295 RV PG; 296-297 RV; 298 RV; 300 PG PB; 301 RV; 302-303 PG3 deV; 304 FP; 305 BB; 306 Fred Bruemmer, FP; 307 Malak, PG2; 308 deV; 309 DB PG; 310 RV; 311 FP CGTB; 312 PG UK DB; 313 New Brunswick Tourism, R.J. Whelan; 314-315 deV2 PG2; 316-317 PG; 318 PG; 319 FP; 320 FP, Phil Smith/Newfoundland Department of Tourism; 321 FP3 Mike Haimes; 322-323 PG; 324 PG; 325 deV; 326 RV; 327 Claude Lavigne, MF; 328 deV, Photo Source/O.J. Dell, Grant Hill 2; 329 DN; 330 RV3 MF: 331 deV, St. Lawrence Seaway Authority; 332 deV; 333 Iron Ore Company, deV; 334 Peter Madely; 335 NS PG2; 337 PG; 338 RV MF deV; 339 deV; 340 UK; 341 PB DN; 342-343 deV; 344-345 deV3, Michael Liu; 346 deV; 347 PG, Marc Ellefsen; 348 UK; 349 FP, Don Rutley 2; 350 PB; 351 deV; 352 Imperial Oil, UK; 353 DN; 354 UK; 356 de V3 Wm. Lowry; 357 deV; 358-359 deV; 360-361 deV; 362 ROM/deV, Art Gallery of Ontario, ROM/deV; 363 Art Gallery of Ontario, ROM/deV; 365 FP; 366 Michel Brière; 367 PG; 368 John C. Loveridge; 369 PG; 370-371 PB; 373 CGTB PB; 374 PB; 375 MF PB2; 376 Jacques Varry; 377 Centennial Museum 2, PB; 378 PG; 379 MF; 380-381 PB5 CGTB PB; 383 PB; 385 PB; 386 PG MF; 387 deV; 388 Maurice Green, deV; 389 RV; 390 PB BB; 391 DN; 392 DB FP; 393 RV; 394 PB; 395 DN PB; 396 RV PB; 397 FP; 398-399 deV; 400 deV3, R.H. Blanchet/CW; 401 deV3, Henry Kalen 2; 402-403 Winnipeg Art Gallery; 405 Sask/Don Varley, deV; 406 deV; 407 BB UK; 408 RV; 411 PG FP; 413 CIHB FP CIHB; 414 CIHB; 415 CIHB FP; 417-420 CIHB; 441 National Air Photo Library (Ottawa Valley); 463-473 PAC; 474-475 Société Historique du Saguenay.

Lithography: Prolith Incorporated
Typesetting: The Graphic Group of Canada Ltd./Compotronic Inc.
Printing: Pierre Des Marais Inc.
Binding: Harpell's Press Co-operative
Paper: Rolland Paper Company Limited

PUBLISHED AND PRINTED IN CANADA